Frommer's®

W9-CNY-062

Provence & the Riviera

7th Edition

by Darwin Porter & Danforth Prince

WILEY

Wiley Publishing, Inc.

Published by:

WILEY PUBLISHING, INC.

111 River St.
Hoboken, NJ 07030-5774

Copyright © 2010 Wiley Publishing, Inc., Hoboken, New Jersey. All rights reserved. No part of this publication may be reproduced, stored in a retrieval system or transmitted in any form or by any means, electronic, mechanical, photocopying, recording, scanning or otherwise, except as permitted under Sections 107 or 108 of the 1976 United States Copyright Act, without either the prior written permission of the Publisher, or authorization through payment of the appropriate per-copy fee to the Copyright Clearance Center, 222 Rosewood Drive, Danvers, MA 01923, 978/750-8400, fax 978/646-8600. Requests to the Publisher for permission should be addressed to the Permissions Department, John Wiley & Sons, Inc., 111 River Street, Hoboken, NJ 07030, 201/748-6011, fax 201/748-6008, or online at http://www.wiley.com/go/permissions.

Wiley and the Wiley Publishing logo are trademarks or registered trademarks of John Wiley & Sons, Inc. and/or its affiliates. Frommer's is a trademark or registered trademark of Arthur Frommer. Used under license. All other trademarks are the property of their respective owners. Wiley Publishing, Inc. is not associated with any product or vendor mentioned in this book.

ISBN: 978-0-470-47065-7

Editor: Christina Summers, with Marc Nadeau
Production Editor: Erin Amick
Cartographer: Guy Ruggiero
Photo Editor: Richard Fox
Production by Wiley Indianapolis Composition Services

Front cover photo: Typical Provençal architecture in Gordes. ©Slow Images/Getty Images
Back cover photo: Sunflowers. ©Steve Vidler/Imagestate RM/Photolibrary

For information on our other products and services or to obtain technical support, please contact our Customer Care Department within the U.S. at 877/762-2974, outside the U.S. at 317/572-3993 or fax 317/572-4002.

Wiley also publishes its books in a variety of electronic formats. Some content that appears in print may not be available in electronic formats.

Manufactured in the United States of America

5 4 3 2 1

CONTENTS

LIST OF MAPS   vi

1 THE BEST OF PROVENCE & THE RIVIERA   1

1 The Best Travel Experiences 1
2 The Best Romantic Getaways.......2
3 The Best Beaches 3
4 The Best Offbeat Experiences 4
5 The Best Small Towns 5
6 The Best Châteaux & Palaces 6
7 The Best Museums.................7

8 The Best Cathedrals & Churches....8
9 The Best Vineyards 9
10 The Best Luxury Hotels............11
11 The Best Hotel Bargains 12
12 The Best Luxury Restaurants.......13
13 The Best Dining Deals.............13
14 The Best Shopping Bets...........14

2 PROVENCE & THE RIVIERA IN DEPTH   15

1 Provence & the Riviera today......15
    Did You Know?......................16
2 Looking Back at Provence &
    the Riviera 17

3 Provence's Art & Architecture......24
4 Provence in Popular Culture.......29
5 Eating & Drinking in Provence.....31

3 PLANNING YOUR TRIP TO PROVENCE & THE RIVIERA   35

1 When to Go......................35
    Provence Calendar of Events........36
2 Entry Requirements..............41
3 Getting There & Getting
    Around 43
4 Money & Costs...................50
    *The Value of the Euro vs. Other
    Popular Currencies*..................50
    What Things Cost in Nice (Euros)....51

    How to Get Your VAT Refund........52
5 Health 52
6 Safety...........................53
7 Specialized Travel Resources 53
8 Sustainable Tourism..............56
9 Special Interest Trips & Escorted
    General-Interest Tours.............56
10 Staying Connected...............59
11 Tips on Accommodations.........61

4 SUGGESTED PROVENCE & THE RIVIERA ITINERARIES 63

1 The Regions in Brief 63
2 Provence in 1 Week 64
3 The Riviera in 2 Weeks. 66
4 Provence & the Riviera
  for Families 71
5 Languedoc-Roussillon &
  the Camargue in 1 Week. 74

5 LANGUEDOC-ROUSSILLON & THE CAMARGUE 76

1 Toulouse. 76
2 Auch. 88
3 Cordes-sur-Ciel. 90
4 Albi 92
  Toulouse-Lautrec: Little Big Man 94
5 Castres. 95
6 Carcassonne 97
7 Perpignan. 102
  Céret: Birthplace of Cubism 103
8 Collioure 107
9 Narbonne. 110
  Liberté, Egalité, Fraternité . . .
  Nudité 112
10 Aigues-Mortes 114
  A Day in the Life of a
  Camargue Cowboy. 117
11 Montpellier 118
  Exploring the Port Town of Séte. . . .123
12 Nîmes. 124

6 PROVENCE 132

1 Orange 132
  Driving Les Routes de
  la Lavande. 136
2 Châteauneuf-du-Pape. 138
3 Avignon 140
4 Uzès 152
5 Arles 155
6 Les Baux 162
  A Drive Through Hell 164
7 St-Rémy-de-Provence. 166
8 Gordes. 172
9 Roussillon & Bonnieux. 175
  The Libertine Trail of the
  Marquis de Sade. 178
10 Apt 181
11 Salon de Provence 184
12 Aix-en-Provence 187
13 Marseille 194
  Exploring the Massif
  des Calanques 197
14 Toulon 209
15 Hyères 212
16 Iles d'Hyères 214
17 Grand Canyon du Verdon 217

7 THE WESTERN RIVIERA: FROM ST-TROPEZ TO CANNES TO CAP D'ANTIBES 221

1 St-Tropez. 221
2 Ste-Maxime. 233
3 Fréjus 237
4 St-Raphaël 239

5 Massif de l'Estérel 243

6 La Napoule-Plage 245

Following La Route Napoleon......247

7 Cannes 248

Seeing Cannes from a Petit Train....249

Ferrying to the Iles de Lérins........252

8 Grasse 266

9 Mougins 268

10 Golfe-Juan & Vallauris 271

11 Juan-les-Pins 274

12 Antibes & Cap d'Antibes......... 277

8 THE EASTERN RIVIERA: FROM BIOT TO MONACO TO MENTON

281

1 Biot 282

2 Tourrettes-sur-Loup 284

3 St-Paul-de-Vence................ 286

4 Vence........................... 290

Exploring the Gorges du Loup......291

5 Cagnes-sur-Mer & Le Haut-de-Cagnes 294

6 Nice 297

7 Villefranche-sur-Mer............. 319

8 St-Jean-Cap-Ferrat 321

9 Beaulieu 324

10 Eze & La Turbie................. 327

11 Peillon 330

12 Monaco.......................... 331

Number, Please: Monaco's Telephone System 334

The Shaky House of Grimaldi 336

13 Roquebrune & Cap-Martin 347

14 Menton......................... 350

9 FAST FACTS

354

1 Fast Facts: The South of France 354

2 Airline, Hotel & Car Rental Websites....................... 358

10 GLOSSARY OF USEFUL TERMS

360

1 Useful French Words & Phrases 360

2 Food, Menu & Cooking Terms ... 362

INDEX

365

LIST OF MAPS

The South of France 37

Provence in 1 Week.............. 65

The Riviera in 2 Weeks........... 67

Provence & the Riviera for
  Families 73

Languedoc-Roussillon &
  the Camargue 77

Toulouse........................ 79

Nîmes 125

Provence........................ 133

Orange 135

Avignon 141

Palais des Papes................ 143

Arles........................... 157

St-Rémy-de-Provence 167

Aix-en-Provence 189

Marseille........................ 195

Toulon.......................... 211

The French Riviera.............. 223

St-Tropez 225

Cannes 250

Nice Attractions................ 299

Nice Accommodations &
  Dining........................ 305

Monaco.......................... 333

ABOUT THE AUTHORS

As a team of veteran travel writers, **Darwin Porter** and **Danforth Prince** have produced numerous titles for Frommer's, including guides to Italy, France, the Caribbean, England, Germany, and Spain. A film critic, newspaper columnist, and radio broadcaster, Porter is also a Hollywood biographer, author of at least four critically acclaimed overviews of little-known aspects of, among others, Humphrey Bogart, Katharine Hepburn, and Howard Hughes. Porter's 2006 biography of Marlon Brando (*Brando Unzipped*) was cited by London's *Sunday Times* as "one of the best show-biz biographies of the year." Prince was formerly employed by the Paris bureau of the *New York Times,* and is today the president of Blood Moon Productions and other media-related firms. Porter and Prince's latest project, *Hollywood Babylon—IT'S BACK!!,* released in 2008, presents a "brainy but prurient" overview of celebrity excess, as filtered through 75 years of Hollywood scandal.

HOW TO CONTACT US

In researching this book, we discovered many wonderful places—hotels, restaurants, shops, and more. We're sure you'll find others. Please tell us about them, so we can share the information with your fellow travelers in upcoming editions. If you were disappointed with a recommendation, we'd love to know that, too. Please write to:

Frommer's Provence & the Riviera, 7th Edition
Wiley Publishing, Inc. • 111 River St. • Hoboken, NJ 07030-5774

AN ADDITIONAL NOTE

Please be advised that travel information is subject to change at any time—and this is especially true of prices. We therefore suggest that you write or call ahead for confirmation when making your travel plans. The authors, editors, and publisher cannot be held responsible for the experiences of readers while traveling. Your safety is important to us, however, so we encourage you to stay alert and be aware of your surroundings. Keep a close eye on cameras, purses, and wallets, all favorite targets of thieves and pickpockets.

FROMMER'S STAR RATINGS, ICONS & ABBREVIATIONS

Every hotel, restaurant, and attraction listing in this guide has been ranked for quality, value, service, amenities, and special features using a **star-rating system.** In country, state, and regional guides, we also rate towns and regions to help you narrow down your choices and budget your time accordingly. Hotels and restaurants are rated on a scale of zero (recommended) to three stars (exceptional). Attractions, shopping, nightlife, towns, and regions are rated according to the following scale: zero stars (recommended), one star (highly recommended), two stars (very highly recommended), and three stars (must-see).

In addition to the star-rating system, we also use **seven feature icons** that point you to the great deals, in-the-know advice, and unique experiences that separate travelers from tourists. Throughout the book, look for:

Finds	Special finds—those places only insiders know about
Fun Facts	Fun facts—details that make travelers more informed and their trips more fun
Kids	Best bets for kids and advice for the whole family
Moments	Special moments—those experiences that memories are made of
Overrated	Places or experiences not worth your time or money
Tips	Insider tips—great ways to save time and money
Value	Great values—where to get the best deals

The following **abbreviations** are used for credit cards:

AE	American Express	**DISC**	Discover	**V**	Visa
DC	Diners Club	**MC**	MasterCard		

TRAVEL RESOURCES AT FROMMERS.COM

Frommer's travel resources don't end with this guide. Frommer's website, **www.frommers. com**, has travel information on more than 4,000 destinations. We update features regularly, giving you access to the most current trip-planning information and the best airfare, lodging, and car-rental bargains. You can also listen to podcasts, connect with other Frommers.com members through our active-reader forums, share your travel photos, read blogs from guide-book editors and fellow travelers, and much more.

The Best of Provence & the Riviera

Provence is one of the world's most evocative regions—both the western area, known simply as Provence, whose landscapes and magical light have seduced innumerable artists, and the eastern coastal area, known as the Riviera, whose beach resorts have seduced innumerable hedonists. Provence and the Riviera are beautiful, and culturally rich, offering everything from amazing art museums to fabulous beaches, white-hot nightlife, and a distinctive cuisine that blends the best of the mountains and the sea.

As you're heading to the south of France to luxuriate in life along the sunny Mediterranean—not to exhaust yourself making difficult decisions—we've searched out the best deals and once-in-a-lifetime experiences for this book. What follows in this chapter is our roster of the best of the best, the kind of discoveries we'd share with our closest friends.

1 THE BEST TRAVEL EXPERIENCES

- **Partying in the Land of Festivals:** Provence is called the Land of Festivals with good reason: It hosts some 500 with an astonishing 4,000 events. The ultimate example is the you-won't-believe-it-until-you've-seen-it Cannes Film Festival in May. July and August are the busiest months, as Aix-en-Provence, Toulon, and Nice host jazz festivals, and Nîmes and Arles stage theater and dance performances. On May 16, St-Tropez's riotous *bravades* honor the saint in theory but are really just an excuse for revelry. Many festivals have deep roots in Provençal folklore, honoring the bounty of earth and sea: the wine harvest in numerous villages, the rice harvest in Languedoc's Camargue, and the apple harvest in Peyruis. See "When to Go" in chapter 3.
- **Absorbing a Unique Lifestyle:** Provence and Languedoc share a uniquely Mediterranean lifestyle. Nothing could be more typical than a game of boules played under shade trees on a hot afternoon in a Provençal village.

This is a region that respects time-honored crafts; Picasso might have arrived here a painter, but he left a potter. And nothing is finer in life than to be invited into a Provençal kitchen—the heart of family life—and smell the aroma of herbs and wines cooking with the catch of the day. To walk in the gardens filled with vegetables, flowers, and fruit trees is reason enough to visit. Attend a harvest, not just of grapes, but perhaps of linden blossoms. See chapters 5 and 6.

- **Dining & Drinking Provence Style:** Many people flock to the south of France specifically to enjoy *cuisine provençale,* a Mediterranean mix of bold flavors with an emphasis on garlic, olive oil, and aromatic local herbs such as thyme and basil. The world's greatest bouillabaisse is made here, particularly in Marseille; Provençal lamb is among the best in France; and the local vegetables (such as asparagus, eggplant, tomatoes, and artichokes) fill the markets of France. Regional wines, though not equaling those of Bordeaux and

Burgundy, are the perfect accompaniment, ranging from the warm, full-bodied Châteauneuf-du-Pape to the rare Bellet, from the hill slopes of Nice.

- **Spending a Day in St-Rémy-de-Provence:** Our favorite town in Provence is St-Rémy. To wander St-Rémy's streets is to recapture Provence's essence, especially its Vieille Ville (Old Town). After exploring its alleys, pause in one of its immaculate leafy squares, then search out an art gallery or two, and reward yourself with a painting and a memory. See "St-Rémy-de-Provence" in chapter 6.

- **Following in the Footsteps of the Great Artists:** Modern art wasn't born in Provence, but artists from all over came here to paint the "glaring festive light." Most of these artists left behind fabulous legacies. Perhaps it all began when Monet arrived with Renoir in 1883. In time, they were followed by a host of others, including Bonnard in St-Tropez. Van Gogh arrived in Arles in 1888, and Gauguin showed up a few months later. Even the fauves sought out this region, notably Matisse, whose masterpiece is his chapel at Vence. Not long afterward, Picasso arrived at Antibes. Deeply jealous of Picasso and Matisse, Chagall moved to Vence and was later infuriated that the street on which he lived was renamed avenue Henri-Matisse. He got over it and lived and painted on the Riviera until he died at 97. See chapters 6, 7, and 8.

- **Sunning & Swimming on the Riviera Beaches:** There are greater beaches but none more fabled, overcrowded though they are. Most of them are sandy, except those stretching from Antibes to the Italian frontier, including the beaches in Nice. These are shingled (covered with gravel or pebbles), but that doesn't stop the world from flocking to them. A beach mattress works just fine on the shingles, and umbrellas are for rent when you want to escape the relentless sun. Along the Riviera, topless sunbathing is de rigueur. Legend says it began with Brigitte Bardot, who pulled off her bra and said, "Let's wake up sleepy St-Trop." Nudist beaches also exist, notably at Cap d'Agde and Port Cros. If you decide not to go topless or bottomless, you can still wear your most daring bikini or thong. See chapters 7 and 8. Also see "The Best Beaches," below.

- **Breaking the Bank at Monte Carlo:** Few other casinos can match the excitement generated at the Monte Carlo Casino. The world's wealthy flocked to Monaco when the casino was opened by Charles Garnier in 1878. But since 1891 much of the nonwealthy world has followed—even those who can't afford losses. During a 3-day gambling spree that year, Charles Deville Wells, an American, turned $400 into $40,000, an astonishing amount back then. His feat was immortalized in the song "The Man Who Broke the Bank at Monte Carlo." Even if you do no more today than play the slot machines, a visit to this casino will be a highlight as you bask amid the extravagant decor and under the gilded rococo ceilings. (Some not as lucky as Wells have leaped to their deaths from the casino windows or the "Suicide Terrace.") See "Monaco" in chapter 8.

2 THE BEST ROMANTIC GETAWAYS

- **Les Baux** (Provence): Les Baux stands in a spectacular position on a promontory of sheer rock ravines. In the distance across the plain, you can view the Val d'Enfer (Valley of Hell). After a turbulent history, the town today is one of the great escapes for savvy French who can gaze from their windows on the thousands of olive trees (many planted by the Greeks) that produce the best oil in France. Posh little Les Baux also has some of the country's grandest inns and finest cuisine. The most notable is **Oustau de Baumanière,** Maussane-les-Alpilles (© **04-90-54-33-07;** www.oustaudebaumaniere. com)—after you and your loved one sample the ravioli with truffles, you'll understand why. See "Les Baux" in chapter 6.

- **Iles d'Hyères** (Provence): If an off-the-record weekend is what you have in mind, there's no better spot than the "Iles d'Or," as they were known during the Renaissance because of the golden glow of the islands' rocks in the sun. This string of enchanting little islands is 39km (24 miles) east-southeast of the port of Toulon. The largest and western-most island is Ile de Porquerolles, thickly covered with heather, eucalyptus, and exotic shrubs. Ile de Port-Cros is hilly and mysterious, with spring-fed lush vegetation. The best spot for a romantic retreat is on this island—**Le Manoir** (© **04-94-05-90-52**), an 18th-century colonial-style mansion set in a park. See "Iles d'Hyères" in chapter 6.

- **Mougins** (Western Riviera): Only 8.1km (5 miles) north of Cannes, the once-fortified town of Mougins is a thousand years old, but never in its history has it been so popular as a place to enjoy the good life. Picasso, who could afford to live anywhere, chose a place nearby, Notre-Dame-de-Vie, to spend his last years. The wonderful old town is known for its cuisine, and Roger Vergé reigns supreme at his elegant **Le**

Moulin de Mougins (© **04-93-75-78-24;** www.moulindemougins.com). However, you can live for less at more secluded and less publicized oases. See "Mougins" in chapter 7.

- **Peillon** (Eastern Riviera): Of all the "perched" villages (*villages perchés*) along the Côte d'Azur, this fortified medieval town on a craggy mountain-top 19km (12 miles) northeast of Nice is our favorite. Peillon is the least spoiled of the perched villages and still guards its medieval look, with covered alleys and extremely narrow streets. Tour buses avoid the place, but artists and writers flock there (we once spotted Françoise Sagan) to escape the mad carnival of the Riviera. For a cozy hide-away with your significant other, try the **Auberge de la Madone** (© **04-93-79-91-17;** www.auberge-madone-peillon. com). Dinner for two on the terrace set among olive trees is the best way to start a romantic evening. See "Peillon" in chapter 8.

- **Roquebrune & Cap-Martin** (Eastern Riviera): Along the Grande Corniche, Roquebrune is one of the most charm-ing of the Côte d'Azur's villages, and its satellite resort of Cap-Martin occupies a lovely wooded peninsula. Between Monaco and Menton, these two have long been romantic retreats. The best choice for hiding away with that certain someone is the **Hôtel Vista Palace,** Grande Corniche (© **04-92-10-40-00;** www.vistapalace.com), a modern lux-ury hotel clinging giddily to a cliff side over Monte Carlo. See "Roquebrune & Cap-Martin" in chapter 8.

3 THE BEST BEACHES

- **La Côte Vermeille** (Languedoc-Rous-sillon): In contrast to the eastern Riviera's pebbly beaches, the Côte Ver-meille is filled with sand stretching

toward Spain's Costa Brava. The best place for fun in the sun is the 11km (7-mile) beach between the resorts of Leucate-Plage and Le Barcarès in the

Pyrénées-Orientales district near Perpignan. The "Vermilion Coast" takes its name from the red-clay soil studded with ubiquitous olive groves. Henri Matisse was so taken with the light on this coast that he chose to make it a subject for many of his paintings. See chapter 5.

- **Ile de Porquerolles** (Provence): This island lies 15 minutes by ferry from the Giens peninsula east of Toulon. One of the Iles d'Hyères, Porquerolles is only 8.1km (5 miles) long and some 2.4km (1½ miles) across and enjoys national park status. Its beaches, along the northern coast facing the mainland, get 275 days of sunshine annually. Several white-sand beaches stretch their way around the island; the best are **Plage d'Argent, Plage de la Courtade,** and **Plage de Notre-Dame.** See "Iles d'Hyères" in chapter 6.

- **Plage de Tahiti** (St-Tropez, Western Riviera): And God created woman and man and all the other critters found on this sizzling sandy beach outside St-Tropez. Tahiti is France's most infamous beach, mainly because of all the topless or nude bathing going on. Ever since the days of Brigitte Bardot, this beach has been a movie star favorite. It's very cruisy and animated, with a French nonchalance about nudity. If you bother to wear a bikini, it should be only the most daring. See "St-Tropez" in chapter 7.

- **Plage Port Grimaud** (St-Tropez, Western Riviera): This long golden-sand beach is set against the backdrop of the urban architect François Spoerry's *cité lacustre,* facing St-Tropez. Spoerry created this 98-hectare (247-acre) marine village inspired by an ancient fishing village. The world has since flocked to Port Grimaud and its beach; homeowner Joan Collins comes here to hide from the paparazzi. Some of the Riviera's most expensive yachts are tied up in the harbor. This beach isn't as decadent as those at St-Trop, but it does pick up the "overflow" on the see-and-be-seen circuit. See "St-Tropez" in chapter 7.

- **Cannes** (Western Riviera): From the Palais des Festivals and west to Mandelieu, the beach at Cannes has real sand, not pebbles as in Nice. This beach resort offers a movable feast-for-the-eyes of high-fashion swimsuits. Ever since the 1920s, the word on the beach here has been: "Menton's dowdy. Monte's brass. Nice is rowdy. Cannes is class!" Along the fabled promenade, La Croisette, the white sands are littered with sun beds and parasols rented at the beach concessions. The beach is actually divided into 32 sections, our favorites being **Plages Gazagnaire, Le Zénith,** and **Waikiki.** Some of the beaches are privately run, but the best public beach is in front of the Palais des Festivals. See "Cannes" in chapter 7.

- **Monte-Carlo Beach** (at the Monaco border, Eastern Riviera): This beach, once frequented by Princess Grace, is actually on French soil. Of all the Riviera's beaches, this is the most fashionable, even though its sands are imported. The property adjoins the ultrachic **Monte-Carlo Beach Hotel,** 22 av. Princesse-Grace (© **04-93-28-66-66**). The great months to be here are July and August, when you never know who's likely to be sharing the sands with you—perhaps Daniel Craig or Claudia Schiffer. See "Monaco" in chapter 8.

4 THE BEST OFFBEAT EXPERIENCES

- **Spending a Night in Aigues-Mortes** (Languedoc-Roussillon): St. Louis sailed

from this port to fight in the Crusades to the east. He died in Tunis in 1270, but his successor, Philip III, held this port, the only stretch of the Mediterranean in French hands at the time. Great walls were built around the town, and ships all the way from Antioch would drop anchor here. But beginning around the mid–14th century, Aigues-Mortes began to live up to its name of "dead waters," as the harbor filled with silt and the waters receded. Today it sits marooned in time and space right in the muck of the advancing Rhône delta. Nothing along the coast is as evocative of the Middle Ages as this town, where you can walk along its walls and slumber in one of the inns. See "Aigues-Mortes" in chapter 5.

- **Checking In & Stripping Down** (Cap d'Agde, Languedoc-Roussillon): Except in foul weather, it's compulsory to walk around nude in the holiday town on the outskirts of Cap d'Agde. Check your apparel at the gate. Along the Languedoc coast, between the Rhône delta and Béziers, Cap d'Agde was constructed like a pastiche of a local fishing village, similar to Port Grimaud near St-Tropez. At its outskirts is a town with supermarkets, nightclubs, a casino, and rooms for 20,000 bodies—nude bodies. See "Liberté, Egalité, Fraternité . . . Nudité" in chapter 5.

- **Exploring Massif des Calanques** (btw. Marseille and Cassis, Provence): At the old fishing port of Cassis, with its white cliffs and beaches that were a favorite of fauve painters, you can rent a boat and explore the Calanques, small fiords along the rugged coast. Covered with gorse and heather, the white cliffs are the backdrop for this adventure. By car from Cassis, you can drive to the creek of Port Miou, with its rock quarries. To reach the Port Pin and En Vau creeks farther west, you must travel on foot (trails are well signposted). You can, however, take a boat excursion from Cassis. If you go on your own (not by boat), take a picnic and spend the day skinny-dipping in these cool crystal waters. See "Exploring the Massif des Calanques" in chapter 6.

5 THE BEST SMALL TOWNS

- **Cordes-sur-Ciel** (Languedoc-Roussillon): Perched like an eagle's nest on a hilltop, Cordes is an arts-and-crafts town, with ancient houses on narrow streets filled with artisans plying their trades. Once fabled in France for the brilliance of its silks, today it's a sleepy town 25km (16 miles) northwest of Albi, the city of Toulouse-Lautrec. Ideally, you should visit Cordes as a side trip from Albi, but you might become enchanted with the place and decide to stay over in this town of a hundred Gothic arches. See "Cordes-sur-Ciel" in chapter 5.

- **Uzès** (Provence): Uzès is a gem, a bit of a time capsule with lofty towers and narrow streets. Racine once lived here and was inspired by the town to write his only comedy, *Les Plaideurs*. André Gide also found a home in this "dream of the Middle Ages." Once Louis XIII called Uzès "the premier duchy of France." You can see why by staying at the stately 18th-century **Château d'Arpaillargues** (© **04-66-22-14-48**; www.chateaudarpaillargues.com). See "Uzès" in chapter 6.

- **Gordes** (Provence): One of the best known of Provence's hill villages, Gordes, east of Avignon, is deservedly called *le plus beau village de France*. Today an escape for in-the-know Parisians, it's a town of silk painters, weavers, and potters. The setting is bucolic, between the Coulon valley and the Vaucluse plateau. Houses built of golden stone rise to the Renaissance château crowning the top. The late artist Victor Vasarély lived here in a fortified château that has been turned into a museum displaying much of his work. See "Gordes" in chapter 6.

- **Roussillon** (Provence): Northeast of Gordes, Roussillon stands on a hilltop in the heart of "ocher country," where the earth is a bright red (*roussillon* means "russet"). This ancient village boasts houses in every shade of burnt orange, dusty pink, and russet red—they take on a particular brilliance at sunset. Roussillon, however, is no longer the sleepy village described in Laurence Wylie's *A Village in the Vaucluse*. Artists, writers, and trendy Parisians have discovered its charms, and today many use it as their second home. See "Roussillon & Bonnieux" in chapter 6.

- **Roquebrune** (Eastern Riviera): This medieval hill village southwest of Menton is the finest along the Côte d'Azur. It has been extensively restored, and not even the souvenir shops can spoil its charm. Steep stairways and alleys lead up to its feudal castle crowning the village. But before heading here, take in rue Moncollet, flanked by houses from the Middle Ages. This castle, dating from the 10th century, is the oldest in France—in fact, it's the only Carolingian castle left standing. See "Roquebrune & Cap-Martin" in chapter 8.

6 THE BEST CHATEAUX & PALACES

- **Château d'If** (off Marseille, Provence): One of France's most notorious fortresses, this was the famous state prison whose mysterious guest was the Man in the Iron Mask. Alexandre Dumas *père's Count of Monte Cristo* made the legend famous around the world. It doesn't really matter that the story was apocryphal: People flock here because they believe it, just as they go to Verona, Italy, to see where Romeo and Juliet lived, loved, and died. The château was built by François I in 1524 as part of the defenses of Marseille. See "Marseille" in chapter 6.

- **Palais des Papes** (Avignon, Provence): This was the seat of Avignon's brief golden age as the capital of Christendom. From 1352 to 1377, seven popes—all French—ruled here, a period dubbed "the Babylonian Captivity." And they lived with pomp and circumstance, knowing "fleshly weaknesses." The Italian poet Petrarch denounced the palace as "the shame of mankind, a sink of vice." Even after Gregory XI was persuaded to return to Rome, some cardinals remained, electing their own pope or "anti-pope," who was finally expelled by force in 1403. See p. 142.

- **Château de la Napoule** (La Napoule, Western Riviera): The Riviera's most eccentric château is also the most fascinating. This great medieval castle was purchased in 1917 by American sculptor Henry Clews, heir to a banking fortune. He lived, worked, and was buried here in 1937. In this castle, Clews created his own grotesque menagerie—scorpions, pelicans, gnomes, monkeys, lizards, whatever came to his tortured mind. His view of feminism? A distorted suffragette depicted in his *Cat Woman*. He likened himself to Don Quixote. See p. 245.

- **Les Grands Appartements du Palais** (Monte Carlo, Monaco, Eastern Riviera): The world has known greater palaces, but this Italianate one on "The Rock" houses the man who presides over the tiny but incredibly rich principality of Monaco, Europe's second-smallest state. In 2005, Prince Rainier III, Europe's longest-reigning monarch, passed away, leaving the throne to

Prince Albert. When the prince is here, a flag flies. You can watch the changing of the guard every day at 11:55am. The throne room is decorated with paintings by Holbein, Bruegel, and others, and in one wing of the palace is a museum devoted to souvenirs of Napoleon. See p. 335.

- **Villa Kérylos** (Beaulieu, Eastern Riviera): This villa is a faithful reconstruction of an ancient Greek palace, built between 1902 and 1908 by the archaeologist Théodore Reinach. Reinach, a bit of an eccentric, lived here for 20 years, preferring to take baths and eat and dress with his male friends (who pretended to be Athenian citizens), while segregating the women to separate suites. Designated a historic monument of France, with its white, yellow, and lavender Italian marble and its ivory and bronze copies of vases and mosaics, Kérylos is a visual knockout. The parties that went on here are legendary. See "Beaulieu" in chapter 8.

7 THE BEST MUSEUMS

- **Musée Toulouse-Lautrec** (Albi, Languedoc-Roussillon): This museum displays the world's greatest collection from this crippled genius, who immortalized cancan dancers, cafe demimonde, and prostitutes. In the brooding 13th-century Palais de la Berbie in the artist's hometown, the "red city" of Albi, this museum takes you into the special but tortured world of Toulouse-Lautrec. Particularly memorable are the posters that marked the beginning of an entirely new art form. When he died, his family donated the works remaining in his studio. See p. 93.

- **Musée Picasso** (Antibes, Western Riviera): After the bleak war years in Paris, Picasso returned to the Mediterranean in 1945. He didn't have a studio, so the curator of this museum offered him space. Picasso labored here for several months—it was one of his most creative periods. At the end of his stay, he astonished the curator by leaving his entire output on permanent loan to the museum, along with some 200 ceramics he produced at Vallauris. This museum reveals Picasso in an exuberant mood, as evoked by his fauns and goats in cubist style, his still lifes of sea urchins, and his masterful *Ulysses et ses Sirènes*. A much-reproduced photograph displayed here shows him holding a sunshade for his lover, Françoise Gilot. See p. 278.

- **Musée National Fernand-Léger** (Biot, Eastern Riviera): Ridiculed as a Tubist, Léger survived many of his most outspoken critics and went on to win great fame. This museum was built by Léger's widow, Nadia, after his death in 1955, and it became one of the first in France dedicated to a single artist. It owns some 300 of Léger's highly original works. You wander into a dazzling array of robotlike figures, girders, machines, cogs, and cubes. The museum allows you to witness how he changed over the years, dabbling first in Impressionism, as shown by his 1905 *Portrait de l'oncle*. Our favorite here—and one of our favorite artworks along the Riviera—is Léger's *Mona Lisa*, contemplating a set of keys and a fish dangling at an angle over her head. See p. 282.

- **Fondation Maeght** (St-Paul-de-Vence, Eastern Riviera): One of Europe's greatest modern art museums, this foundation is remarkable for its setting and its art alike. Built in 1964, the avant-garde building boasts a touch of fantasy, topped by two inverted domes. The colorful canvases radiate with the joy of life. All your favorites are likely to be here: Bonnard, Braque, Soulages, Chagall, Kandinsky, and more. Stunningly designed is a terraced garden that's a setting for Calder murals, Hepworth sculptures, and the fanciful fountains and colorful mosaics of Miró. A courtyard is peopled with Giacometti figures that look like gigantic emaciated chessmen. See p. 287.

- **Musée des Beaux-Arts** (Nice, Eastern Riviera): In the former home of the Ukrainian Princess Kotchubey, the collection comes as an unexpected delight, with not only many Belle Epoque paintings but also modern works, including an impressive number by Sisley, Braque, Degas, and Monet, plus Picasso ceramics. There's whimsy, too, especially in the sugar-sweet canvases by Jules Chéret, who died in Nice in 1932. Well represented also are the Van Loo

family, a clan of Dutch descent whose members worked in Nice. The gallery of sculptors honors Rude, Rodin, and J. B. Carpeaux. See p. 301.

- **Musée Ile-de-France** (St-Jean-Cap-Ferrat, Eastern Riviera): Baronne Ephrussi de Rothschild left a treasure-trove of art and artifacts to the Institut de France on her death in 1934. The Villa Ephrussi, the 1912 palace that contains these pieces, reveals what a woman with unlimited wealth and highly eclectic tastes can collect. It's all here: paintings by Carpaccio and other masters of the Venetian Renaissance; canvases by Sisley, Renoir, and Monet; Ming vases; Dresden porcelain; and more. An eccentric, she named her house after the ocean liner *Ile de France* and insisted that her 35 gardeners dress as sailors. See p. 322.

8 THE BEST CATHEDRALS & CHURCHES

- **Basilique St-Sernin** (Toulouse, Languedoc-Roussillon): Consecrated in 1096, this is the largest and finest Romanesque church extant. It was built to honor the memory of a Gaulish martyr, St. Sernin, and was for a long time a major stop on the pilgrimage route to Santiago de Compostela in Spain. The bell tower is particularly evocative, with five levels of twin brick arches. Unusual for a Romanesque church, St-Sernin has five naves. The crypt, where the saint is buried, is a treasure-trove of ecclesiastical artifacts, some from the days of Charlemagne. See p. 78.

- **Cathédrale St-Jean** (Perpignan, Languedoc-Roussillon): In 1324, Sancho of Aragón began this cathedral, but the consecration didn't come until its completion in 1509. Despite the different builders and architects over the decades, it emerged as one of Languedoc's most evocative cathedrals. The bell tower contains a great bell that dates

from the 1400s. The single nave is typical of church construction in the Middle Ages and is enhanced by the altarpieces of the north chapels and the high altar, the work of the 1400s and the 1500s. See p. 104.

- **Cathédrale St-Just** (Narbonne, Languedoc-Roussillon): Though construction on this cathedral, begun in 1272, was never completed, it's an enduring landmark. Construction had to be halted 82 years later to prevent breaching the city's ancient ramparts to make room for the nave. In High Gothic style, the vaulting in the choir soars to 40m (130 ft.). Battlements and loopholes crown the towering arches of the apse. The cathedral's greatest treasure is the evocative *Tapestry of the Creation,* woven in silk and gold thread. See p. 111.

- **Cathédrale Notre-Dame des Doms** (Avignon, Provence): Next to the Palais des Papes, this was a luminous

Romanesque structure before baroque artists took over. It was partially reconstructed from the 14th through the 17th century. In 1859, it was topped by a tall gilded statue of the Virgin, which earned it harsh criticism from many architectural critics. The cathedral houses the tombs of two popes, John XXII and Benedict XII. You'd think this cathedral would be more impressive because of its role in papal history, but it appears that far more time and money went into the construction of the papal palace. Nevertheless, the cathedral reigned during the heyday of Avignon. See p. 144.

- **Basilique St-Victor** (Marseille, Provence): This is one of France's most ancient churches, first built in the 5th century by St. Cassianus to honor St. Victor, a 3rd-century martyr. The church was destroyed by the Saracens, except for the crypt. In the 11th and 12th centuries, a fortified Gothic church was erected. In the crypt are pagan and early Christian sarcophagi; those depicting the convening of the Apostles and the Companions of St. Maurice are justly renowned. See p. 198.

9 THE BEST VINEYARDS

- **Château de Simone,** 13590 Meyreuil (© **04-42-66-92-58;** www.chateausimone.fr): This well-respected vintner lies less than .5km (⅓ mile) north of Aix-en-Provence. The vineyards surround a small 18th-century palace that might have been transported unchanged from *La Belle du bois dormant.* You can't visit the interior, but you can buy bottles of the recent crops of reds, rosés, and whites for between 26€ and 30€ each. Because production at this vineyard is relatively small, you're limited to purchases of between 3 and 12 bottles, depending on the vintage. Advance notification is important. From Aix, take N7 toward Nice, and then follow the signs to Trois Sautets.

- **Château Virant,** R.D. 10, 13680 Lançon-de-Provence (© **04-90-42-44-47;** www.chateauvirant.com): Set 23km (14 miles) west of Aix-en-Provence and 35km (22 miles) north of Marseille, and named after a nearby rock whose ruined feudal fortress is barely standing, this vineyard produces Appellation d'Origine Contrôlée–designated Côteaux d'Aix-en-Provence, as well as a

translucent brand of olive oil from fruit grown on the property. The English-speaking Cheylan family showcases a labyrinth of cellars dating from 1630 and 1890. Tours and tastings can be arranged. The most expensive bottle here costs 14€. Ask for an explanation of their trademark *vin cuit* (cooked wine) *de Virant,* which is popular around these parts as a beverage at Christmastime. Notification in advance of your visit is wise.

- **Château de Calissanne,** R.D. 10, 13680 Lançon-de-Provence (© **04-90-42-63-03;** www.calissanne.fr): On the premises is a substantial 18th-century white-stone manor house sporting very old terra-cotta tiles and a sense of the ancien régime. Even older is the Gallo-Roman *oppidum Constantine,* a sprawling ruined fortress that you can visit if you obtain a special pass from the sales staff. The white, rosé, and red Côteaux d'Aix-en-Provence and the two grades of olive oil produced by the property are sold in an outbuilding. Wine sells for less than 20€ per bottle. Advance reservations are vital. You'll find this place clearly signposted in Lançon-de-Provence, nearly adjacent to the above-mentioned Château Virant.

- **Château d'Aqueria,** Route de Roquemaure, 30126 Tavel (📞 **04-66-50-04-56;** www.aqueria.com): Wines produced near the Provençal town of Tavel are considered some of the finest rosés in the world, and vintners here are expert at the fermentation of a brand that's sought after by wine lovers from as far away as Paris. An 18th-century château on the premises can be viewed only from the outside, and cellars and wine shops sell bottles of the famous pink wine at prices that rarely exceed 12€ per bottle. To reach it, drive 6km (4 miles) northwest of Avignon along the Route de Bagnols, following the signs to Tavel.

- **Château de Fonscolombe** (📞 **04-42-61-70-01**) and **Château de LaCoste** (📞 **04-42-61-89-98;** www.chateau-de-lacoste.com), 13610 Le Puy Ste-Réparade: These vineyards are adjacent to each other, 20km (13 miles) north of Aix-en-Provence. Fonscolombe has an exterior-only view of an 18th-century manor house, and offers tours of a modern facility of interest to wine-industry professionals. LaCoste is smaller and less state of the art, but it offers an exterior view of a stone-sided villa that was built for a cardinal during the reign of the popes in Avignon. At either of these outfits, you can buy their red, white, and rosé wines, the most expensive of which sells for only 17€. Advance notification is required. From Aix, take the A51 in the direction of Sisteron, exiting at exit 12 toward Le Puy Ste-Réparade.

- **Domaine de Fontavin,** 1468 rte. de la Plaine, 84350 Courthézon (📞 **04-90-70-72-14;** www.fontavin.com): Set 10km (6 miles) north of Carpentras, this is one of the leading producers of the heady, sweet dessert wine Muscat

des Baumes de Venise. As the organization here dates only from 1989, there's nothing particularly noteworthy in terms of architecture on-site. But oenophiles appreciate its proximity to some of the most legendary grapevines in the French-speaking world. Bottles of the sweet elixir are sold at a price that rarely exceeds 16€ each. Follow the N7 from Carpentras in the direction of Orange and Courthézon.

- **Château de Coussin,** 1468 rte. de la Plain, 13530 Trets (📞 **04-90-70-72-14;** www.chateaux-elie-sumeire.fr): This property, 16km (10 miles) east of Aix-en-Provence, is centered on a 16th-century manor whose stone facade bears geometric reliefs associated with Renaissance-era construction in Provence. The vineyards are scattered over three neighboring regions and have been owned by the same family for nearly a century. The château's interior (it contains a vaulted cloister) can be visited only with the hard-to-obtain permission of the owners, but the overview of the winemaking industry as seen within its bottling facility is worth the trip. Bottles sell for a maximum of 36€ each, and in some cases for much less.

- **Château de Grand'Boise,** 13530 Trets (📞 **04-42-29-22-95**): An amiable competitor on property almost immediately adjacent to Château de Coussin, the centerpiece of these vineyards, olive groves, forests, and hunting preserves is a venerable 19th-century château. The organization's cellars, as well as the château itself, can be visited if you phone in advance for an appointment. Bottles of red, white, and rosé sell for less than 14€ each.

- **Château de Capitoul,** Route de Gruissan, 1100 Narbonne (📞 **04-68-49-23-30;** www.chateau-capitoul.com): Set farther to the west than most of the other vineyards mentioned here, Château de Capitoul produces reds ("La Clape des Rocailles"), whites, and rosés that usually sell for 6€ to 10€ per bottle but, in some rare instances, go as high as 38€. Nestled amid its vineyards is a 19th-century manor house that can be visited with special permission granted in advance from the owners. More easily accessible are the cellars, in a nearby annex. Call in advance of your arrival. From Narbonne, drive 5km (3 miles) east, following the D32 (rte. de Gruissan).

10 THE BEST LUXURY HOTELS

- **InterContinental Carlton Cannes** (Western Riviera; ✆ 04-93-06-40-06; www.ichotelsgroup.com): A World War II Allied commander issued orders to bombers to avoid hitting the Carlton "because it's such a good hotel." The 1912 hotel survived the attack and today is at its most frenzied during the annual film festival. Taste and subtlety aren't what the Carlton is about—it's all glitter, glitterati, and glamour, the most splendid of the area's architectural "wedding cakes." The white-turreted doyenne presides over La Croisette like some permanent sand castle. See p. 256.
- **Hôtel du Cap–Eden Roc** (Cap d'Antibes, Western Riviera; ✆ 04-93-61-39-01; www.edenroc-hotel.fr): Looming large in F. Scott Fitzgerald's *Tender Is the Night,* this is the most stylish of the Côte's palaces, standing at the tip of the Cap d'Antibes peninsula in its own manicured garden. The hotel reflects the opulence of a bygone era and has catered to the rich and famous since it opened in 1870. See p. 278.
- **Hôtel Negresco** (Nice, Eastern Riviera; ✆ 04-93-16-64-00; www.hotel-negresco-nice.com): An aging Lillie Langtry sitting alone in the lobby, her once-great beauty camouflaged by a black veil, is but one of the many memories of this nostalgic favorite. Self-made millionaires and wannabes rub shoulders at this 1906 landmark. We could write a book about the Negresco, but here we'll give only two interesting facts: The carpet in the lobby is the largest ever made by the Savonnerie factory (the cost was about one-tenth the cost of the hotel), and the main chandelier was commissioned from Baccarat by Tsar Nicholas II. See p. 304.
- **Grand Hôtel du Cap-Ferrat** (St-Jean-Cap-Ferrat, Eastern Riviera; ✆ 04-93-76-50-50; www.grand-hotel-cap-ferrat.com): The Grand Hôtel, built in 1908, competes with the Hôtel du Cap–Eden Roc as the Riviera's most opulent. Set in a well-manicured garden, it was once a winter haven for royalty. This pocket of posh has it all, including a private beach club with a heated seawater pool and a Michelin-starred restaurant utilizing market-fresh ingredients. See p. 322.
- **Hostellerie du Château de la Chèvre d'Or** (Eze, Eastern Riviera; ✆ 04-92-10-66-66; www.chevredor.com): In striking contrast to the palaces above, this gem lies in a medieval village 396m (1,300 ft.) above sea level. Following in the footsteps of former guests such as Roger Moore and Elizabeth Taylor, you can stay in this artistically converted medieval château. All its elegant rooms open onto vistas of the Mediterranean. Everything here has a refreshingly rustic appeal rather than false glitter. As the paparazzi catch you sipping champagne by the pool, you'll know you've achieved Côte d'Azur chic. See p. 329.
- **Hôtel de Paris** (Monte Carlo, Monaco, Eastern Riviera; ✆ 377-98-06-30-00; www.montecarloresort.com): The

19th-century aristocracy flocked here, and though Onassis, Sinatra, and Churchill long ago checked out, today's movers and shakers still pull up in limousines. This luxury palace houses two Michelin-starred restaurants, the more celebrated of which is Le Louis XV, offering the sublime specialties of Alain Ducasse. Le Grill showcases Ligurian-Niçois cooking, a retractable roof, and a wraparound view of the sea. See p. 340.

11 THE BEST HOTEL BARGAINS

- **La Réserve** (Albi, Languedoc-Roussillon; ☎ 05-63-60-80-80; www.relias chateaux.fr/reservealbi): La Réserve's design approximates a *mas* Provençal, the kind of dignified farmhouse usually surrounded by scrublands, vineyards, olive groves, and cypresses. It's less expensive than many luxurious hideaways along the nearby Côte d'Azur and has the added benefit of lying just outside the center of one of our favorite fortified sites in Europe, the medieval town of Albi. See p. 94.

- **Hôtel Renaissance** (Castres, Languedoc-Roussillon; ☎ 05-63-59-30-42; www.hotel-renaissance.fr): In the quaint town of Castres, with its celebrated Musée Goya, this hotel is a good introduction to the bargains awaiting you in provincial France. Built in the 1600s as a courthouse, it was long ago converted from a dilapidated site into a hotel of discretion and charm—all at an affordable price, even if you opt for a suite. Some rooms have exposed timbers, and you'll sleep in grand but rustic comfort. See p. 96.

- **Hôtel Le Donjon** (Carcassonne, Languedoc-Roussillon; ☎ 04-68-11-23-00; www.hotel-donjon.fr): Built into the solid bulwarks of Carcassonne, one of France's most perfectly preserved medieval towns, is this small-scale hotel whose well-appointed furnishings provide a vivid contrast to the crude stone shell that contains them. A stay here allows you personal contact with a site that provoked bloody battles between medieval armies. See p. 99.

- **Hôtel du Palais** (Montpellier, Languedoc-Roussillon; ☎ 04-67-60-47-38; www.hoteldupalais-montpellier. fr): In the Old Town, in a labyrinth of narrow streets, this hotel dates from the late 18th century but has been successfully modernized to receive guests today at prices within the range of most travelers' budgets. The rooms are cozily arranged, and the hotel has a special French charm. It's one of the most historic hotels in town, and the bedrooms are relatively large, ideal for a short or even a long visit. See p. 121.

- **Hôtel d'Arlatan** (Arles, Provence; ☎ 04-90-93-56-66; www.hotel-arlatan.fr): At reasonable rates, you can stay in one of Provence's most charming cities at the former residence of the *comtes* d'Arlatan de Beaumont, built in the 15th century on the ruins of an old palace. Near the historic place du Forum, this small hotel has been run by the same family since 1920. The rooms are furnished with Provençal antiques, and the antique tapestries are grace notes. See p. 159.

- **Villa La Tour** (Nice, Eastern Riviera; ☎ 04-93-80-08-15; www.villa-la-tour. com) is a former convent from the 18th century which has been converted into an atmospheric little hotel in the center of Nice, a 10-minute walk from the beach. Bedrooms, for the most part, open onto views of the Old Town, a few with balconies. A little roof garden is also open to guests. See p. 312.

12 THE BEST LUXURY RESTAURANTS

- **Le Languedoc** (Carcassonne, Languedoc-Roussillon; ✆ 04-68-25-22-17): Acclaimed chef Didier Faugeras is the creative force behind this century-old dining room that serves some of the finest regional specialties in the area. Its most famous dish is *cassoulet au confit de canard,* a casserole with duck meat cooked in its own fat. See p. 101.

- **Le Jardin des Sens** (Montpellier, Languedoc-Roussillon; ✆ 04-99-58-38-38; www.jardindessens.com): Twins Laurent and Jacques Pourcel have set off a culinary storm in Montpellier. Michelin has bestowed two stars on them, the same rating it gives to Alain Ducasse at his Monaco citadel. Postnouvelle reigns supreme, and both men know how to turn the bounty of Languedoc into meals sublime in flavor and texture. Though inspired by other chefs, they now feel free to let their imaginations roam. The results are often stunning, such as the fricassee of langoustines and lamb sweetbreads. See p. 122.

- **Christian Etienne** (Avignon, Provence; ✆ 04-90-86-16-50; www.christian-etienne.fr): In a house as old as the nearby papal palace, Etienne reigns as Avignon's culinary star. A chef of imagination and discretion, he has a magical hand, reinterpreting and improving French cuisine. He keeps a short menu so that he can give special care and attention to each dish. His menu is often themed—one might be devoted to the tomato. Save room for his chocolate/pine-nut cake, something of a local legend. See p. 148.

- **Oustau de Baumanière** (Les Baux, Provence; ✆ 04-90-54-33-07; www.oustaudebaumaniere.com): This Relais & Châteaux occupies an old Provençal farmhouse. Founded in 1945 by the late Raymond Thuilier, the hotel's restaurant was once touted as France's greatest. It might long ago have lost that lofty position, but it continues to tantalize today's palates. Thuilier's heirs carry on admirably as they reinvent and reinterpret some of the great *provençale* recipes. At the foot of a cliff, you dine in Renaissance charm, enjoying often flawless meals from the bounty of Provence. See p. 164.

- **Le Chantecler** (Nice, Eastern Riviera; ✆ 04-93-16-64-00): The most prestigious restaurant in Nice, and the most intensely cultivated, Chantecler is currently in the hands of Alain Llorca, who's attracting the area's demanding gourmets and gourmands. You dine in a monument to turn-of-the-20th-century extravagance, and the menu is attuned to the seasons and to quality ingredients. A true taste of the country is evident in the fresh asparagus, black truffles, sun-dried tomatoes, and beignets of fresh vegetables—all deftly handled by a chef on the rise. See p. 313.

- **Joël Robuchon Monte-Carlo** (Monte Carlo, Monaco; ✆ 377-93-15-15-15): Critics hail Robuchon as the greatest chef in France. Emerging from retirement, he's become a star-studded culinary attraction in this chic principality, where his take on modern French cuisine is second to none. He seasons his delectable platters with "the perfumes of the Mediterranean." See p. 343.

13 THE BEST DINING DEALS

- **Emile** (Toulouse, Languedoc-Roussillon; ✆ 05-61-21-05-56; www.restaurant-emile.com): On one of the most beautiful old squares of

Toulouse, this restaurant serves one of the finest regional cuisines in the area, all at an affordable price. The cassoulet Toulousain is hailed as the town's best. The flower-filled terrace is a magnet in the summer. See p. 85.

- **Le Bistro Latin** (Aix-en-Provence, Provence; ✆ **04-42-38-22-88**): The economic virtue of this *provençale* restaurant lies in its fixed-price menus, whose composition is something of an art form. The prices are low, the flavors are sensational, and hints of Italian zest pop up frequently in such dishes as risotto with scampi. See p. 194.

- **La Fourchette** (Avignon, Provence; ✆ **04-90-85-20-93**): Creative cooking at modern prices is presented at this authentic bistro in the town center. Long known for its value and good food, the airy dining rooms here tempt you with platter after platter, everything from monkfish stew with endive to fresh sardines flavored with citrus. See p. 149.

14 THE BEST SHOPPING BETS

- **Centre Sant-Vicens** (Perpignan, Languedoc-Roussillon; ✆ **04-68-50-02-18**): This region of France is next door to Catalonia, whose capital is Barcelona. Catalan style, as long ago evoked by Antoni Gaudí, is modern and up-to-date here with forceful geometric patterns in textiles, pottery, and furnishings. See "Perpignan" in chapter 5.

- **Mistral Les Indiens de Nîmes** (Avignon, Provence; ✆ **04-90-86-32-05**): Provence has long been celebrated for its fabrics, and one of the best, most original, and affordable selections is found here. Since the early 1980s, this outlet went into the attic, rediscovering old Provençal fabrics and duplicating them in a wide assortment. Fabric is sold by the meter and can be made into anything from clothing to tableware. See p. 145.

- **Les Olivades Factory Store** (St-Etienne-du-Grès, Provence; ✆ **04-90-49-18-04**): About 12km (7½ miles) north of Arles on the road leading to Tarascon, this store features the region's most fully stocked showroom of art objects and fabrics inspired by the traditions of Provence. You'll find fabrics, dresses, shirts for men and women, table linen, and fabric by the yard. Part of the Olivades chain, this store has the widest selection and the best prices. See p. 158.

- **Santons Fouque** (Aix-en-Provence, Provence; ✆ **04-42-26-33-38;** www.santons-fouque.com): Collectors from all over Europe and North America purchase *santons* (figures of saints) in Provence. You'll find the best ones here, cast in terra cotta, finished by hand, and decorated with an oil-based paint. The figures are from models made in the 1700s. See p. 190.

Provence & the Riviera In Depth

It's been called the world's most exciting stretch of beach and "a sunny place for shady people" by W. Somerset Maugham. Every habitué has a favorite oasis here and will try to convince you of its merits: Some say "Nice is passé." Others maintain that "Cannes is queen." Others shun both in favor of Juan-les-Pins, and still others would winter only at St-Jean-Cap-Ferrat. If you have a large bankroll, you may prefer Cap d'Antibes, but if money is short, you can try the old port of Villefranche.

1 PROVENCE & THE RIVIERA TODAY

Each resort on the Riviera, known as the Côte d'Azur (Azure Coast)—be it Beaulieu by the sea or eagle's-nest Eze—offers its unique flavor and special merits. Glitterati and eccentrics have always been attracted to this narrow strip of fabled real estate, less than 125 miles long, between the Mediterranean and a trio of mountain ranges. The Russians were the most eccentric, fleeing winter's fury for clear skies, blue waters, and orange groves.

A trail of modern artists attracted to the brilliant light and setting of the Côte d'Azur have left a rich heritage: Matisse in his chapel at Vence, Cocteau at Menton and Villefranche, Picasso at Antibes and seemingly everywhere else, Léger at Biot, Renoir at Cagnes, and Bonnard at Le Cannet. The best collection of all is at the Maeght Foundation in St-Paul-de-Vence.

The Riviera's high season used to be winter and spring only. However, with today's changing tastes, July and August have long been the most crowded, and reservations are imperative. The average summer temperature is 75°F; the average winter temperature, 49°F.

The corniches of the Riviera, depicted in countless films, stretch from Nice to Menton. The Alps here drop into the Mediterranean and roads were carved along the way. The lower road, about 20 miles long, is the **Corniche Inférieure.** Along this road are the ports of Villefranche, Cap-Ferrat, Beaulieu, and Cap-Martin. Built between World War I and the beginning of World War II, the **Moyenne Corniche (Middle Road),** 19 miles long, also runs from Nice to Menton, winding spectacularly in and out of tunnels and through mountains. The highlight is at mountaintop Eze. The **Grande Corniche**—the most panoramic—was ordered built by Napoleon in 1806. La Turbie and Le Vistaero are the principal towns along the 20-mile stretch, which reaches more than 1,600 feet high at Col d'Eze.

Provence is more like Italy, its Mediterranean neighbor than the rest of France. It's a land of gnarled, silver-leaf olive trees, cypresses, and umbrella pines, with the occasional almond grove and fields of wild lavender and other *herbes de Provence,* plus countless vineyards. Its curse is the dreaded mistral that blows through the region.

It's amazing how in a relatively short span of time the image of Provence has

Did You Know?

- Two weeks before the Armistice in November 1918, Vita Sackville-West eloped to Monte Carlo with Violet Trefusis. Vita appeared dressed as a soldier named Julian, her hair covered with a khaki bandage.
- Until everybody got rich here, Monaco used to be regarded for generations as a comic opera joke. "Monaco-Gerolstein," Karl Marx called it.
- The most expensive party in the history of St-Tropez cost $1 million in 1988. Prince Léon de Lignac, a Dutchman, transformed a beach here into the Château of Versailles to celebrate his 70th birthday and his 30 years together with a longtime companion known as "Hans."
- Crippled by arthritis, Colette spent spring and summer from 1950 until she died in 1954 at the Hôtel de Paris in Monte Carlo. She called its charm "paperweight."
- In the wake of the 1956 film at St-Tropez, *And God Created Woman* starring Brigitte Bardot, the first topless bathers were arrested. The police didn't know what to do with the women since they'd put Coca-Cola bottle caps over their nipples for modesty.
- The 1956 wedding of Grace Kelly and Prince Rainer attracted 600 guests, including some reporters disguised as cassocked priests and a few jewel thieves who robbed the princess' mother and a bridesmaid and made off with a Rembrandt and a Rubens.
- Scott Fitzgerald warned his editor, Maxwell Perkins, not to mention the Riviera in advertising copy: "Its very mention invokes a feeling of unreality and insubstantiality," he cautioned.
- In 1948 Ambassador Joseph Kennedy's daughter, Kathleen, Lady Harting-ton, died in a chartered plane that was flying off the Riviera with Earl Fitzwilliam.
- On her role as duenna of cultural affairs in Monaco, Princess Caroline has proclaimed, "People do not come to live in Monaco for cultural reasons."
- Lloyd George, in Antibes to celebrate his golden wedding anniversary in 1939, said: "I've never doubted Hitler's greatness and I only wish Britain had a comparable leader."
- When Onassis invited an aging Churchill to go aboard his yacht in Monte Carlo, the Greek ship owner had to hand-feed the World War II leader caviar.

changed. Once northerners characterized the region's peopled as indolent country bumpkins. Now surveys reveal that more French people would rather live and work in Provence than in any other region. Any high-tech industry basing in Provence is virtually guaranteed thousands more applicants than they can accommodate.

Unlike the overbuilt Côte d'Azur, Provence still has vast pockets of rural area, and, yes, old men today still play a leisurely game of boules on a hot afternoon, preferably under shade trees.

Although Provence is hardly the region that Edith Wharton discovered so long ago, it still hasn't been irretrievably spoiled, as many claim. Popularity and overbuilding of the coast and the summer hordes descending on such cities as Avignon have made the province less desirable in parts, especially if you're driving behind miles-long lines of cars in summer heat. The once sweet disposition of its citizens is a bit taxed by the endless tourist pressure. But the vast hilly hinterland of Provence remains relatively intact.

Some of the vast migration to Provence has been good. Many villages in nostalgic decay and depopulation have been rescued by the arrival of craftspeople and artists, including potters and weavers, who have saved buildings from total collapse. Summer residents from Paris and Provence-loving foreigners have poured new energy, vitality, and money into what had been a sleepy backwater of France.

Provence and the Côte d'Azur are more fabled, but Languedoc is another compelling region of France sending out its siren call. Much of the landscape, cuisine, lifestyle, and architecture of Languedoc is similar to its neighbor, Provence. Traditionally, as least since the Middle Ages, the dividing line between Provence and Languedoc has been the mighty Rhône. Even today the river marks the political boundaries between the two regions—that of Provence-Côte d'Azur and that of Languedoc-Roussillon.

Much of Languedoc is so similar that the city of Nîmes appears to be more Provençal in character although officially it is in Languedoc.

Of course, the glory of the ancient province of Languedoc is of another today. It was ruled until the 13th century by the powerful Counts of Toulouse, whose lands swept from the Rhône to the Garonne. Today, the former holdings vastly shrunk, Languedoc-Roussillon consists of only the eastern or *bas* region along the coast, stretching from Carcassonne to Montpellier, taking in the district of Roussillon which is actually the French version of Catalonia, far more linked to Barcelona than to Paris.

For 25 centuries Provence and Bas Languedoc have stood at the crossroads of civilization. They still stand here today, awaiting discovery by a new generation.

2 LOOKING BACK AT PROVENCE & THE RIVIERA

During the Bronze Age, Provence was inhabited by primitive tribes whose art legacy, which began around 6000 B.C. in the form of etched pottery, is described in "Provençal Art." Anthropologists cite the era around 3500 B.C. for the emergence of groupings of humanoids ("Chassey culture") into village life and their cultivation of livestock. By around 700 B.C., traders from Greek-speaking colonies in Greece and around the Aegean established colonies at Antipolis (Antibes), Nikaia (Nice), and Massilia (Marseille). Mediterranean wines, grains, and ceramics were exchanged, it's believed, for pewter and livestock from west–central France.

The Greeks even sailed up the Valley of the Rhône, trading with local Celtic and Ligurian tribes and generally influencing the culture with their more sophisticated ways. To them is credited the introduction of both the grape and the olive, two foodstuffs that would play vital roles in the Provençal economy for millennia to come. The stopping-off point for much of the traffic coming from the Greek-speaking Aegean to Provence was Sicily, sections of which at the time were Greek-speaking strongholds known for their vital commerce and culture.

In 600 B.C., Protis, captain of a group of Greek traders, was the guest of honor at a Provençal celebration held in honor of Gyptis, daughter of a local tribal leader. Swept away by the novelty and charm of her father's guest (and perhaps offered as the pawn in one of the region's many politically motivated marriages), she selected Protis as her future husband. Her dowry included the harborfront of what is now known as Marseille, the gateway through which massive amounts of matériel and ancient warriors and weapons later poured.

Around the same time, waves of migration from the Celtic north added to the non-Mediterranean population of Provence. The Celts allied and intermarried easily with the native Ligurians, and eventually formed a fierce force that to an increasing degree opposed the expansionistic efforts of the Greeks. In 218 B.C., some of the tribes supported Hannibal during his passage across the Alps and his destructive advance upon Rome, an alliance that Rome would severely punish several generations later. As the local forces (Celts and Ligurians, and later, a scattering of Teutonic tribes from the north) faced off against Greek expansionism in the south, tensions grew to the point where the Greeks called on the rapidly emerging power of the Roman Empire to subdue the threat to their colonial power. The resulting genocides and annihilations committed by Rome helped define the future racial and cultural makeup of Provence for the next 2,000 years.

THE ROMANS

In 125 B.C., thrusting northward and flexing his Empire's muscles after some of its spectacular victories over the Carthaginians, Roman general Sextius massacred thousands of Celts and Ligurians on a battlefield at Egremont, a short distance north of Aix-en-Provence. This action was duplicated less than a quarter-century later, in 102 B.C. on an even larger scale, when the Roman general Marius massacred as many as 200,000 Teutonic, Celtic, and Ligurian tribespeople during their attempts at southward incursions. Ever after, partly in remembrance for their fallen comrades, partly because of the need for a cultural buffer between Rome and the savages of Gaul, and partly because of the fertility and desirability of Provence itself, Rome considered the Mediterranean coastline of what is today known as France as one of its most treasured provinces.

The Romans named their new possession *Provincia Transalpina,* a name that was later bastardized into "Provence." They established Narbonne as the region's administrative center, *Gallia Narbonensis.* By 49 B.C., in the ancient world's equivalent of a Nazi *blitzkrieg,* Julius Caesar had conquered all of Gaul, and even invaded England in 55 B.C., an act which suddenly diminished the relative importance of Provence within the much larger context of the Roman Empire. But despite Roman influence throughout the rest of Europe, few other regions received as direct or as concentrated a dose of Romanization as Provence. Evidence of this remains in grandiose construction of amphitheaters, bathhouses, temples, and stadiums at sites that include Arles, Orange, Nîmes, Glanum (near St-Rémy-de-Provence), Fréjus, and Cimiez near Nice. Pont du Gard—an ancient masterpiece of civic engineering and one of the most frequently photographed sites in France—was completed in 19 B.C. Ironically, Marseille, whose pedigree predated that of virtually every other Roman site in Provence, was bypassed during the explosion of Roman building—much to the advantage of other settlements such as Arles—because of its alliance with the losing side in the 49 B.C. civil war between Pompey and Julius Caesar.

Later, as the administration and the scope of the Roman Empire diminished, and the far reaches of the Empire became frayed and tattered at the edges, *Provincia Narbonensis* remained staunchly Roman. Even after the Empire's East-West schism, and long after Paris and the Rhône valley became centerpieces for Frankish resistance against the Roman regime, Provence remained staunchly Roman and a direct beneficiary of trade and attention from whomever happened to rule the Empire at the time.

ROME'S COLLAPSE & THE EARLY MIDDLE AGES

Such scholars as Gore Vidal have claimed that the conversion of Emperor Constantine to Christianity marked the beginning of the end for the military machine that was Rome. Despite Constantine's obsession with territory in the Middle East (especially his namesake city of Constantinople—now Istanbul), he designated Arles as his favorite city in his western empire, and built a palace here. Ironically, faced with the pressures of his position, he rarely visited it. In A.D. 400, the short-lived emperor Honorius launched Arles into a fleeting role as the designated capital of the "Three Gauls," which referred at the time to Britain, Spain, and France. Meanwhile Provence and much of the rest of the Empire seemed to rush headlong toward Christianization. Some of the earliest evidence of the spread of the inflammatory new religion can be viewed in Marseille at the oft-repaired remains of the Abbey of St-Victor, founded in 413.

Regrettably, the pre-eminence of Arles as a centerpiece of Roman culture did not serve it well after the collapse of the Empire. In 471, it was ransacked by the Visigoths, and a few years later, it and many of the other important settlements of Provence were sacked again by other barbarian hordes who were motivated by

greed, expansionism, and an often well-deserved hatred of the Romans. From 600 to 800, the devastations were duplicated by Saracen (Moorish) navies from North Africa, and in rare instances, an occasional Viking raid along the valley of the Rhône.

Ironically, Charles Martel himself, one of the patriarchs of modern France, led his Frankish troops through Provence between 736 and 740 on destructive orgies of appalling brutality. In the aftermath of these recurrent catastrophes, local politics wavered between instability and anarchy as local warlords and feudal barons murdered their opponents, seized power, and were rapidly murdered in turn.

The only exception to the ongoing chaos was the brief ascendency of the Merovingians around A.D. 500. But because their strongholds lay within what is now northeastern France, they didn't focus a lot of creative energy on Provence. Later, Charlemagne passed through Provence en route to Rome in 800, where he was crowned Emperor of the West by the Roman Pope. After Charlemagne's death, when his empire was split among three feuding grandsons, Provence, dominated by the often bizarre preoccupations and conflicting loyalties known as feudalism, was bequeathed to Lothair, the eldest of the three. Lothair placed his own son, Charles, on the throne of Provence, designating it as a kingdom in its own right. By 879, Provence was ruled jointly, somewhat inefficiently, with Burgundy by the medieval ruler Boson, brother-in-law of Charles the Bald.

MEDIEVAL PROVENCE

In 1032, with a capital established at Aix-en-Provence, the eastern half of Provence—the area east of the Rhône—became a member of the Holy Roman Empire, a loose configuration of duchies and kingdoms unified mainly by a shared fear and loathing of the Moors. The area west of the Rhône fell into the orbit of the Counts of Toulouse. Romanesque architecture, poetry, music, and verse flourished for a period of almost 300 years, a cultural high point that today represents a much-studied flowering of the troubadour and the beginnings of literature and popular entertainment as the world knows it today.

By around 1125, most of the power within Provence was controlled by the Counts of Toulouse and the Counts of Barcelona. Except for some political gaffes and a sense of regionalism, it appeared for a time that the Counts of Barcolona and the Counts of Toulouse might, through marriage and treaties against their common enemy, the French, succeed at uniting their neighboring kingdoms. By 1246, control of Provence tipped in favor of the French kings, thanks to a series of politically motivated marriages between the family of St. Louis, the rulers of Barcelona, and royal residents of Provence. Today, the village of Barcelonette (Alpes de Haute-Provence) derives its medieval name from the influence of those counts.

The strategic importance of Provence as a starting point for conquests of other Mediterranean kingdoms was obvious to the Paris-based kings. Construction of one of the most remarkable sites in southern France, the fortified town of Aigues-Mortes, was commissioned by St. Louis as a bulwark against the Moors and other assorted interlopers. In 1248, he, along with a doomed army of soldiers, sailors, and priests, set sail from that city on the Seventh Crusade, only to die en route in Tunis of the plague.

In 1307, in one of the most bizarre political imbroglios of European history, a French-born pope, Clement V, fearful of the instability that prevailed within Rome, decided to move the official seat of the papacy to Avignon. Here, surrounded by an army of courtiers, priests, and soldiers, and purveyors of luxury goods, it remained for 70 years under the protection of the kings of France and counts of Provence. Avignon became a vibrant and prosperous city that resembled a massive construction site throughout the entire process. The papacy was eventually moved back to Rome after violent politicking and even some armed conflicts between the papal factions.

Plagues decimated the population of Provence beginning in 1348, with even more severe outbreaks of the disease beginning in 1375, killing off residents in staggering numbers. At the same time, extortion, plundering, and highway robbery by small-time feudal despots, including the rulers of the much-dreaded Les Baux de Provence (today a noteworthy tourist site), added to a general sense of confusion, unrest, and in many cases, despair.

In 1409, the University of Aix was founded as southern France's answer to the already-thriving University in Paris. In 1434, René of Anjou, former king of Naples, was designated count of an independent Provence, and in his new role fostered economic development and the arts. An event that has been viewed by Provençal nationalists ever since occurred shortly after René's death, when his nephew and heir signed a pact with Paris-based Louis XI, who immediately used it to annex Provence into the orbit of the French monarchs.

CONFLICTS WITH PARIS & WARS OF RELIGION

Perhaps because of its cultural and linguistic differences with northern France, and the deeply inbred and intuitive respect for the pagan religions of ancient Rome, Provence had always been fertile ground for the nurturing of offshoot religions. The Cathar heresy, whose strongholds had thrived most obviously in neighboring Languedoc but whose adherents also lived in Provence, was interpreted as a direct threat to the power of the French monarchs, and was consequently violently obliterated. The rallying cry for French forces during their slaughter of the Cathars—"Kill them all, and God will decide who is guilty . . . "—lives in infamy even today within French classrooms.

In the 1500s, the Reformation changed the social fabric of Europe and the world forever. Influenced by the thriving community of Protestants under John Calvin, whose impenetrable stronghold lay in nearby Geneva, up the Valley of the Rhône, the number of Provence-based Huguenots (Protestants) grew in size and power. One of the most hotheaded of the Provençal sects included the Vaudois, spiritual descendants of the long-since-massacred Cathars. Founded by a wealthy merchant, Valdès or Vaudès, from Lyon in the 1200s, the sect rejected the idea of an ecclesiastical hierarchy, preached the virtues of poverty, and denied the authenticity of the sacraments. All of this was greeted with something akin to horror by the established church. When the Vaudois responded to their persecutors by attacking several Catholic churches in 1545 near their stronghold in the Luberon hills, the armies of Renaissance king François 1er massacred more than 3,000 of them over a 4-day period in April 1545, and sent another 600 into the galleys of the French navy as slaves.

Despite these repressions, Protestantism continued to flourish in the towns of Orange, Uzès, and especially Nîmes. During a 40-year period beginning around 1560, religious battles occurred with almost constant regularity throughout France. Chief of State Richelieu, whose personal obsession involved the unification of all aspects of French society into a form approved by Paris, eventually suppressed or destroyed Huguenot strongholds throughout France. The bloodiest of these suppressions involved the Atlantic coast seaport of La Rochelle, but also affected were the Provençal strongholds at Uzès and Les Baux.

In 1720, a devastating plague was imported through the harbor of Marseille, killing what's conservatively estimated at 100,000 people in the process. Fields lay deserted, and cottage industries were abandoned in the process. Despite that and similar setbacks by the mid-1700s, Provence had become one of the wealthier regions of France. An aesthetic had developed that was distinct to the region, and which is today copied and emulated by decorators throughout the world, as noted in the majestic town houses and *mas* (country estates) that are today prized by real-estate investors.

Some scholars argue that the revolutionary fervor that swept over France in May 1789 was greatly influenced by popular philosophers in Provence. One of the most articulate (and inflammatory) members of Paris's "Etats-Généraux" (the radical committee that helped inaugurate the French Revolution) was the *comte de Mirabeau,* who was elected by the populace of Aix-en-Provence. In 1790 the Revolutionary government carved France and Provence into a labyrinth of political districts *(départements)* that shattered the country's medieval boundaries and political networks. In the process, the once-autonomous region of Provence was subdivided into three and later five subdivisions, an act that greatly hampered the region's national sense of cohesion.

In 1792, a corps of volunteers from Marseille marched through the streets of Paris singing a call to arms that was later renamed "La Marseillaise" from its original title, "Battle Hymn of the Army of the Rhine." A year later, the emerging career of the Corsican general Napoleon Bonaparte received an enormous boost after he masterminded a victory at the siege of Toulon.

THE 19TH CENTURY & THE RISE OF THE BOURGEOISIE

Partly because of its strategic dominance of more than half of France's Mediterranean seaports, Provence gained enormous prosperity during the 19th century. It also increased its prestige as a catalyst for events that changed the course of future events within France. In 1815, Napoleon used a minor seaport near Cannes (Golfe-Juan) as the site of his return to France after his exile on Elba. The enthusiasm his armies received in Provence set a precedent for equivalent welcomes in other non-Provençal towns en route during his march to Paris and his short-lived return to power. The same year, he was defeated by Wellington at the Battle of Waterloo. The route he followed during his march upon Paris—the N85 through Dignes and Sisteron—has been known ever since as the Route Napoleon.

In 1854, fearing the demise of the Provençal language and culture, a group of cultural luminaries founded Félibrige, an organization devoted to the dissemination of the medieval literary forms of Provençal. Five years later, artistic patriarch Frédérick Mistral (d. 1914) published his Provençal poem Mirèio, which was met with widespread approval.

In 1864, a railway line linked Provence with the rest of France, encouraging increased travel and a rapidly spreading reputation of Provence as a site suitable for charming long- or short-term sojourns.

The opening of the Suez Canal in 1869, and the expansion of French influence into Morocco, Algeria, Tunisia, and to some degree, Egypt, thrust the ports of Provence into worldwide prominence and helped develop Marseille into one of the greatest seaports in the world.

Part of the development of Nice and the Riviera into international resorts was the result of the unemployment caused by the phylloxera epidemic in Provençal vineyards and the collapse of the silkworm industry. Tourism was a logical answer to the economic deprivations of pestilence and economic dislocations of the Industrial Age. In 1822 the expatriate British colony in Nice helped finance its namesake promenade. In 1830 Lord Brougham bought an estate in Cannes and promoted it to other international gadflies as a suitably hedonistic place to escape from the fog, the cold, and the Victorian repressions of England. In 1860 the region around Nice, whose administration by the House of Savoy represented an anachronistic holdover from the feudal age, was fully integrated into France. A few years later, the ruler of one of the least prosperous territories of western Europe, Monaco, built the most opulent casino in the world. Thanks to the approval and patronage granted to the site by the wealthy and titled aristocrats of the Belle Epoque, profits came pouring in.

THE 20TH CENTURY

No one denies the agony of World War I, but fortunately for Provence, the most bloodshed and the most destruction occurred in other areas of France, particularly the northeast and east. During World War II, both Provence and neighboring Languedoc were integrated into territory controlled by France's collaborationist Vichy government. In 1940, after Nazi-dominated North Africa fell to Allied forces, the Nazis retracted their pledge not to occupy the zones controlled by Vichy and moved into Provence with heavy artillery. In 1942, when the Nazis moved to confiscate the warships of the French navy, French saboteurs sank most of their Mediterranean fleet in the harbor at Toulon. Many martyrs were created by the conflicts all around them, most notably Jean Moulin, who has several streets and roads named after him within many towns throughout Provence.

On August 15, 1944, Allied forces landed on the Provençal coast between St-Raphaël and St-Tropez as part of a successful attempt to regain control of Europe from Nazi domination. All of Provence was liberated within 14 days of the landing, with some of the most dramatic of liberation scenes occurring in the center of Marseille, a site that was freed over a 6-day period between August 22 and 28.

POSTWAR PROVENCE

Few other regions of the world have zoomed into the international consciousness the way Provence has since 1945. In 1947, Cannes initiated its role as film capital of Europe with its first-ever film festival, an event that would later grow to almost mythic proportions. Beginning around 1950, both farming and industry were modernized to keep pace with technological developments in the rest of Europe. Tourism, which had been a recurrent theme in the region since the 19th-century days of the English expatriates in Nice, took a giant leap forward.

Beginning in the early 1950s, celebrity-watching seemed to go hand-in-hand with voyeurism and exhibitionism, as the Riviera's topless beaches caused a stir as far away as Chicago, and as stars such as Brigette Bardot *(And God Created Woman)* elevated St-Tropez to its continuing role as sybaritic capital of the most sybaritic country in Europe.

In 1953, Socialist politician Gaston Defferre, a pivotal figure in the region's politics, was elected Mayor of Marseille, a post he held for the next 33 years. His ardent appeals for semi-autonomy of Provence finally came to fruition in 1981, 2 years before his death, with the approval, under Mitterrand, of a limited form of self-government. To Defferre's chagrin, the culmination of his life's work—a degree of self-governing autonomy for Provence—helped usher in right-wing opponents to a political landscape that had been dominated by Leftist politics since before the turn of the 20th century.

In 1962 the collapse of the French government in Algeria led to a flood of newly impoverished, newly homeless French citizens who arrived by the thousands in Provence. Mainlanders called them *pied-noirs* (blackfeet). Many opted to relocate here, where their noteworthy business acumen helped revitalize the local economy.

Transit between Provence, Paris, and the rest of world was greatly facilitated in 1970 with the opening of the A6-A7 high-speed autoroute between the French capital and Marseille. Between 1970 and 1977, the year the Marseille subway was inaugurated, at least two major national parks (*Parc Naturel Régional de Camargue* and *Parc Naturel Régional de Lubéron*) were created for the preservation of Provence's native ecology. In 1981, the high-speed *Trains à Grande Vitesse (TGV)* was inaugurated between Paris and Marseille, with other branch lines opened in following years to other parts of France's Mediterranean coast. Transit time by train between Paris and Cannes was reduced to less than 4 hours.

Around 1985 Provence emerged as the national stronghold for anti-immigrant sentiments, perhaps in reaction to the thousands of non-French newcomers, legal and illegal, who have flooded into Provence from North and Central Africa. Voters in Provence supported Jean-Marie Le Pen's anti-immigration platform, Le Front National, or FN, giving a wider approval (23% of the popular vote in the 1992 elections) than they had to the region's traditional vote-getter, the Socialist party. Since then, Provence's regional assembly, though dominated by the center-right, has been forced to rely on support from the FN to avoid being overwhelmed by other voting blocs that include potent alliances from the Socialist, Communist, and "green" party representatives.

In 1993, the European Cup Football (soccer) match was won for the first time in history by a France-based team, the Olympique de Marseille.

PROVENCE TODAY

Late in 1995, the creation of a Euro-Mediterranean free-trade zone by the year 2010 was announced in Barcelona. A vast financial aid program, which was funded through the European Union by loans, was also announced. This vast amount of money, a total of $14 billion, helped Marseille and other ports of Provence just when it seemed that decay was inevitable. Marseille is the largest port on the Mediterranean, with nearly 100 million tons handled annually.

In the past few decades, tourism has become the chief industry of Provence, especially the Riviera resorts. After years of giving Marseille a wide berth because of perceived dangers such as crime, the cruise ships have returned.

Even so, Provence and the Riviera are suffering along with the rest of the world because of the falloff in the global economy. The full, devastating impact won't be thoroughly assessed until the end of 2009 or 2010, but it does not bode well for the region. Locals are hoping for an upturn in business as 2010 deepens.

3 PROVENCE'S ART & ARCHITECTURE

The masonry—usually limestone—buildings that rise from the region's olive groves and pine forests often stir deeply buried reminders of the Ligurians, Celts, ancient Greeks and Romans, and the millions of unnamed merchants and pilgrims who lived, suffered, and died on Provence's sunbaked and windy terrain.

The sense of timelessness that permeates Provençal architecture has derived from ancient origins. Although Paleolithic remains and artifacts have been found in Provence, there's a lot less prehistoric art here than there is in such neighboring sites as Lascaux in the Dordogne. Despite that, excavations that include Terra Amata, just above the old port in Nice, have unearthed remnants of circular huts, each with a central fire pit, that were sited adjacent to what was at the time a freshwater spring. Tombs from the late Paleolithic age (30,000 years ago) have revealed skeletons covered in sea shells strung together into necklaces.

Around 6000 B.C., during the Neolithic era, sheep and other livestock began to be domesticated, and circular huts *(bories)* were erected from flat stones laid on top of each other without mortar. None of the *bories* from that era survive, although many sociologists believe that the later development of rural farmhouses *(mas)* in Provence was affected by them. From around the same time, a series of dolmens or mysterious standing stones and a scattered handful of rock carvings were poised on their ends and raised into vertical positions, for reasons that no one has ever really understood since.

Beginning in the 4th century B.C., for a period of around 400 years, Celtic tribes migrated into Provence, bringing with them an ease for carving rock with iron tools. Their greatest surviving tangible legacy includes a network of fortified *oppidi* (fortresses on hilltops). The trading links that mariners from the Greek-speaking eastern Mediterranean developed around 600 B.C. was with this new breed of Celts, who had by that time intermarried with the local Ligurians. The ports established by the Greeks (Antibes, St-Tropez, La Ciotat, Nice, and Hyères) soon adopted many of the aesthetic preconceptions of the Greek world, although on a scale that wasn't as impressive as the monuments erected later by the Romans. Very little of the Greek era survives in Provence today.

Because of its status as a bastion of ancient Roman culture, and a richly accessorized buffer zone between Italy and the savages of Gaul, Provence was lavished by the ancient Romans with one of the ancient world's most comprehensive assortment of public buildings. Examples include the arenas at Nîmes and Arles; aqueducts, such as the Pont du Gard, that are some of the finest examples of civil engineering anywhere in the ancient world; and triumphal arches at St-Rémy-de-Provence, La Turbie (La Trophée des Alpes), and Orange. Remains of ruined villas can still be seen at Vaison-la-Romaine.

Maison Carré in the center of Nîmes is the most oft-copied monument, after the Parthenon in Athens and the Pantheon in Rome, in the ancient world. The lessons derived from the Romans include the experienced use of the arch, the barrel vault, a technique that involved masonry where individual stones were so carefully cut that the use of mortar was unnecessary, and a primitive form of concrete. These technical accomplishments combined in a scale that's majestic even by today's standards, affected later Provençal and Western architecture in ways that cannot be overemphasized. Since Provence, because of its proximity to Rome, was Christianized before virtually any of the other regions of Gaul, Provence is honored with one of the oldest Christian basilicas in France, the Basilica of St-Victor in Marseille. Inaugurated in the 400s, and enlarged and modified many times since, it's unique in France for its venerable age and its associations with the early Christian church.

After the Roman collapse, when Provence was torn between a rapidly changing parade of feudal anarchies in the Dark Ages, very little of enduring value was built, with the exception of a handful of octagonal baptisteries. Combining aspects of classical Roman design with Frankish motifs from northeastern France, they can be seen in Fréjus, Aix-en-Provence, and the hamlet of Venasque. Other than these, few buildings of any kind remain in Provence from the 300-year Merovingian dynasty from the fifth to the 8 centuries.

Beginning around 1100, however, a revitalized interest in building, usually by monks from various religious orders, began to enrich the architectural landscapes of Provence. Consistent with the explosion of Romanesque architecture in neighboring Italy, floor plans of churches were usually laid out in a form that duplicated a cross, with soaring pillars and barrel vaulting, small, somewhat severe-looking windows, and facades (especially western facades) that were allegorically sculpted with scenes of redemption, salvation, punishment for sins, or whatever. The best examples of Provençal Romanesque can be visited at Aix-en-Provence the Church of St-Sauveur; Arles, the Church of St. Trophime; and at the village churches of St-Rémy and Montmajour.

Beginning around 1250, as Provence was pulled more tightly into the cultural orbit of the rest of France, it began to depend more on artistic and architectural inspiration from such areas as Normandy, especially the newfangled design that had been developed there, the Gothic. Its larger window openings and more elaborate decoration derived from a more sophisticated use of pointed arches, ribbed vaulting, and—as a means of counterbalancing the outward thrust of heavy roofs that rested on sometimes alarmingly delicate pillars—flying buttresses. The sense of verticality that was the result of this was in direct contrast to the more horizontal and more rounded lines of the Romanesque.

Provençal Gothic is most obvious in the newer part of Avignon's Papal Palace, the Basilica at St-Maximin, the cathedral at Béziers, and the cloisters at Fréjus. Flamboyant Gothic, the final, most ornate, and, according to some critics, most decadent phase of the movement can best be viewed in the Church of St. Siffrein in the village of Carpentras and in the facade of the church of St-Sauveur in Aix-en-Provence.

For all the emphasis on ecclesiastical architecture, what might be the most memorable aspect of architecture in Provence involves the fortified towns and villages that dot the region's landscapes. Testimonials to their residents' dogged determination to survive in the face of repeated sieges and attacks, they're often perched atop jagged hills or cliffs, meticulously crafted from chiseled blocks of stone, and are usually punctuated with crenelated battlements and/or a moat. Many have openings through which boiling oil or molten lead could be poured on attackers. The designs of many of them, including Les Baux de Provence, Sisteron, and Tarascon, emerged spontaneously, after buckets of perspiration and decades of brutish labor were expended. A handful of others, including the rigidly symmetrical, intricately preplanned quadrangle of Aigues-Mortes, were commissioned (in this case, by Saint Louis himself) and elaborately designed before the first stone was laid. Carcasonne, a fortified site in neighboring Languedoc built more or less in the same era, is less rigidly symmetrical than Aigues-Mortes but more impregnable.

So great was the fear of attack from heretics, Saracens, Christian groups with differing theologies, or a secular enemy that many Provençal churches incorporated fortifications into their designs. In the event of attack, the church could provide physical as well as spiritual shelter from enemies, a fact that early medieval prelates used as a means of eliciting cheap or free labor from the corps of faithful that built them. Examples include the village church in Les Saintes-Maries, and in neighboring Languedoc, the red-brick Cathédrale Ste-Cécile in Albi.

The development of large-scale cannon in the 1400s made many of the above-mentioned fortifications obsolete, but by that time, defensive warfare had evolved so drastically that the fortress-style churches and towns of Provence were left intact, partly because they served a useful function, partly because they evoked the preoccupations and obsessions of earlier centuries.

In terms of painting and architecture, the Renaissance had more of an effect within nearby Italy than it did within Provence although it left two distinct legacies in Nice and Avignon. In Nice, beginning in the late 1400s, a school of design spearheaded by Louis Bréa produced a wide assortment of painted altarpieces. Because of the way they proliferate throughout the region around Nice, most notably within the village church at Lucéram, they were the most fashionable accessories in and around Nice at the time.

During the same era, an equivalent school of painting flourished in Avignon partly a result of the need to adorn the network of churches built a century earlier during the "Babylonian exile" of the papacy in Avignon. The leading artist of the era was Enguerrand Charenton (also known as "Quarton"). Completed in Avignon, and later moved to Villeneuve, his "Coronation of the Virgin" is the best known painting from that era. A worthy colleague was Nicolas Froment, appointed painter to the court of King René. His most famous painting is "The Burning Bush," which still adorns the interior of the cathedral at Aix. Charenton and Froment are today cited as the founders of the Avignon school of painting, which survived until the 1800s. Members of the school during the 1600s included Nicolas Mignard and members of the Parrocel family, whose works can be seen in museums and churches throughout Provence.

Beginning around 1650, artists began to abandon a reliance on purely religious subjects, opting instead for depictions of themes from antiquity or in some cases, everyday secular subjects. The works of Pierre Puget, a native-born Marseillais who is credited as the greatest sculptor ever produced by Provence, evokes the exalted drama of Bernini. His works are within museums throughout France, especially Paris, Toulon, and Marseille, plus Italy. A Dutch-born family of artists, the Van Loos, painted from bases in Aix and Nice during the 17th century, with some of their best works displayed today in the Musée Cheret at Nice. Despite the fact that he more or less abandoned Provence at an early age for richer and more sophisticated climes near the French court in Paris, Jean-Honoré Fragonard (1732–1806) was born in Grasse. Few other artists ever captured the frivolity and luxury of life during the ancien régime as effectively as he did. Regrettably, very few of his works are exhibited publicly within Provence.

Neoclassicism made much more of an impact in nearby Italy than it did within Provence, but 17th- and 18th-century examples of the style's appeal can be seen in the many private mansions that dot the urban centers of Montpellier, Aix-en-Provence, and Avignon.

During the 1800s, the nature of wealth as produced by the increasing industrialization of Europe, and the way it was displayed, very frequently took the form of elaborate architectural showcases. Public buildings and private villas, commissioned by the wintering wealthy, were erected in styles that ranged from classical revival to mock-feudal to what might be the most unusual of all, neo-Byzantine.

A Provençal example of the latter includes the New Cathedral and the church of Notre-Dame de La Garde, both in Marseille. The casino and the Hôtel de Paris in Monte Carlo were lavished with gilded stucco and ornamentation equivalent to some of the most lavish monuments in Paris. Charles Garnier himself, quintessential designer of the French Belle Epoque, designed some aspects of the building boom in Monte Carlo. A few years later, the Hôtel Négresco in Nice captured the essence of the Gilded Age with elaborate Beaux-Arts ornamentation. Later, around 1910, lavish and ostentatious construction continued in the form of the Hotel Carlton at Cannes.

At the same time that the great fortunes of Europe were changing the face of the Riviera with their upscale architecture, a core of devoted painters and aesthetes were influencing the way the world interpreted light and color. Under the streaming sunlight of Provence, they evolved their theories of luminosity and color.

Paul Cézanne (1839–1906) was born in Aix, and spent large parts of his career depicting the terra-cotta roofs and verdant cypresses of Provence. One of his oft-repeated subjects was the Mont-St-Victoire. Vincent van Gogh (1853–90) lived in Arles for many years, depicting starry heavens and fiercely vibrant landscapes before spending his final years in a mental hospital near St-Rémy. Ironically, there is very little work attributed to either Cézanne or van Gogh that's exhibited for public view in any of the museums of Provence.

By around 1900, Paul Signac (1863–1935), a neo-Impressionist, retreated to the hamlet of St-Tropez, and established a mania for "Le Trop" that has existed ever since, attracting both Matisse and Bonnard for contemplative "paint-fests" within the region. Auguste Renoir (1841–1919) spent his final years near Cagnes-sur-Mer, painting and sculpting devotedly despite bouts of agonizing arthritis.

Matisse (b. 1869) lived at Cimiez, near Nice, and at Vence beginning in 1917, remaining here until his death in 1954. Picasso (1881–1973) came to Antibes in 1945, pouring out paintings during two of the most prolific and pivotal years of his many-faceted career. Later, he would be instrumental in reviving the pottery traditions of a town whose output of ceramics is among the most prolific in France, Vallauris.

Marc Chagall (1887–1985), master of the dreamlike power of artistic free association, moved to the Riviera and promptly created his world-acclaimed "Biblical Message," now displayed in his namesake museum in Nice. Major-leaguers who were to follow their fellow artists' footsteps to Provence included Dufy, Braque, Vlaminck, Léger (who has a namesake museum in Biot), and Vaserély, whose works are exhibited in Gordes and Aix. Even Jean Cocteau (1889–1963), known for his frivolity in his earlier years, reached a more intense level of spirituality during his final years in Provence, as proven by frescoes he crafted on the walls of the Chapelle St-Pierre in Villefranche.

No review of Provençal art and architecture would be complete without mention of the utilitarian rural architecture that is tenaciously associated with the primal appeal of the region itself. Farmhouses *(mas)* built as late as 1910 in many regions were directly influenced by the Middle Ages and their obsession with fortification and an ecological sensitivity to the rigors of the local climate. Thick masonry walls, undersized windows, and solid and stocky doors were all crafted from locally derived lumber, clay, mud, soil, and stone.

North-facing walls were often designed with curved sides and without windows as a means of deflecting the harsh winds of

the mistral, and roofs were pitched at low angles to reduce the possibility of tiles breaking loose from their fasteners and sliding off. Hinged shutters could be opened or closed as protection against heat, wind, and sun; chimneys were deliberately low and squat, never rising high enough to risk being demolished during windstorms. Evergreen cypress trees were usually planted as windbreaks on a farmhouse's north side; and deciduous broadleaved trees such as sycamores provided midsummer shade to the south, but let in the warming sunshine in winter.

The construction techniques for walls, made of coarsely chiseled stone and sometimes sheathed with stucco or plaster, was roughly equivalent to what had been developed 2,000 years previously by the Romans. Virtually every farmhouse and outbuilding in Provence was capped with rounded terra-cotta roof tiles *(tuiles romaines)* that derived both their name and their inspiration from equivalent materials used during the Roman conquest.

Today, the boxy-looking old farmhouses, along with the olives, vines, and cypresses that traditionally surround them, are prized as valuable expressions of vernacular architecture, and fetch awesome sums, especially when they're sited in ways that afford at least some privacy. Of the thousands of technically sophisticated buildings erected in Provence since the end of World War II, an enormous percentage of them were designed along lines inspired by the timeless allure of the Provençal *mas.*

Since World War II, a building boom has transformed many of the suburbs of such cities as Aix-en-Provence, Avignon, and Arles into urbanized landscapes with their attendant banality. Traffic congestion, especially noticeable during July and August, has diminished lots of the charm of roadside neighborhoods. As the need for holiday villas and housing for service personnel has risen, vast blocks of apartment houses, some stylish, some altogether ordinary, have been erected in more or less appealing ways. Many have at least tried to emulate the age-old Provençal farmhouse *(mas)* design described earlier.

A handful, however, including Le Corbusier's 1952 design for a massive apartment block in Marseille (*l'Unité d'Habitation* in Marseille), and J. L. Sert's design for the Fondation Maeght Museum of Modern Art (at St-Paul-de-Vence), are cited for their intelligent application of age-old vernacular styles in bold new ways.

4 PROVENCE IN POPULAR CULTURE

BOOKS

Peter Mayle's best-selling *A Year in Provence* is almost required reading for anyone contemplating a sojourn into Provence. He captures the delight and frustration of the region, with visits to its markets, vineyards, goat races, and mushroom hunts. From the grocers to the butcher, he paints colorful portraits of his neighbors.

Two Towns in Provence, by M.F.K. Fisher, is by the author who practically invented food-based literary books. This memoir tells of the years she spent in France in the two towns of Aix-en-Provence and Marseille. Francophiles heading for Provence, foodies, and lovers of crystalline prose will delight in taking a journey with Ms. Fisher.

Vincent van Gogh—Letters from Provence, by Martin Baily, tells of the artist's last 2 years of life. They were spent in Provence during his most creative period. Van Gogh's letters, a testimony of his struggle to survive and work here, are illustrated with his paintings, drawings, and facsimile letters.

A Pig in Provence: Good Food and Simple Pleasures in the South of France, by Georgeanne Brennan, tells the story of how this cooking teacher and food author fell in love with Provence. A talented storyteller, she writes mainly about food but infuses her prose with the joy of living.

We've Always Had Paris . . . and Provence is by the acclaimed Patricia Wells, who was in the vanguard of the 1970s foodie movement. The book is filled with memorable scenes from her life in France, including her sojourns in Provence. Author Wells and her husband, Walter, achieved what many dream about but few actually do. They bought and restored an 18th-century farmhouse with a vineyard in Provence.

Patricia Wells is also the author of *The Provence Cookbook.* She is the leading voice in France for American home cooks. For this volume, she toured little villages in Provence, picking up culinary tips from restaurateurs, farmers, winemakers, and others. The author also includes plenty of travel information, with tips on the region's many markets and shops. And, incidentally, the recipes are delectable. Her recipe for baked arugula omelet must surely be the world's best.

FILMS

The classic golden oldie film that showcases a lush Riviera setting is *To Catch a Thief* (1955), directed by Alfred Hitchcock. Starring with Cary Grant, Grace Kelly made the film in the months before she became the Princess of Monaco. The photography of the French Riviera is spectacular. Sadly, Princess Grace, on September 14, 1982, was killed in an automobile accident on the very same road as the film's famous chase scene and not far from where she had a cinematic picnic with Grant.

Based on Peter Mayle's best-selling book, the film *A Year in Provence* (1993), directed by David Tucker, consists of four consecutive 90-minute films, two on each DVD. Four seasons in Provence are explored in the movie. This film is quite wonderful, especially for those who have a dream about life in the south of France.

On a very different note, *La Cage aux Folles* (1978) is about two gay men living in St-Tropez whose lives are turned upside down when the son of one of the men announces he is getting married. His future in-laws are on their way. Since its release, the film has become a cult classic. Ugo Tognazzi, a brilliant Italian actor, plays Renato, with Michel Serrault as his nervous, overwrought drag queen "wife."

Manon des sources (1986), a French film with English subtitles, captures a slice of Provençal life. It is a sequel to *Jean de Florette.* The star is Yves Montand. *Manon des sources* is French cinema at its best. Emmanuelle Beart is cast as the beautiful young shepherdess who lives in the idyllic countryside of Provence. She is determined to take revenge upon the men responsible for the death of her father in the first film. There are many scenes of the bucolic countryside and of local customs, including a procession whose participants sing in the Provençal language.

Fanny is a drama/romance based on a Broadway play and directed by Joshua Logan. Released in 1961, it had an all-star cast of French actors, including Leslie Caron (never more enchanting), and such veterans as Charles Boyer and Maurice Chevalier. Much of the action takes place in Marseille, where 19-year-old Marius (Horst Buchholz) wants to take to sea to escape his rut. But he's got a problem. Before he's to leave on a 5-year voyage,

Fanny, a lovely girl, reveals she's in love with him.

Of much recent vintage, *A Good Year* (2006), based on a Peter Mayle novel, starred Russell Crowe, Marion Cotillard, and Albert Finney. It tells the story of a British investment broker who inherits his uncle's château and vineyard in Provence. He discovers a new laid-back lifestyle as he tries to renovate the estate to be sold. Every scene was shot within 8 minutes of the home in Provence where director/producer Ridley Scott lives.

MUSIC

Music written about Provence includes Darius Milhaud's *Suite Provençale;* the opera *Mireille* by Charles Gounod after Frédéric Mistral's poem *Mireio;* George Bizet's *L'Arlésienne;* and the saxophone concerto *Tableaux de Provence* composed by Paule Maurice.

For your listening pleasure before you actually set foot in the region, we suggest a CD, *Provence: A Romantic Journey,* by Roberto Occhipinti, Yuri Sazonoff, Charles T. Cozens, Sergi Skripka, and the Mosfilm Symphony Orchestra.

Ray Smith, also on CD, presents *Tableaux de Provence: The classical saxophones and woodwinds* of Ray Smith. Smith has been called "one of the world's outstanding woodwind artists."

A rare work of enchantment is *Renaissance en Provence—Traditional Music of South of France* by Terra Nova Consort, also available on a CD. Founded in 1988, the Terra Nova group explores ethnic influences in early music. The singers have met wildly appreciative acclaim from audiences around the world. In their CD, the artists emphasize the close cultural and linguistic ties between Provence and Spain. They combine passionate, gritty vocals with early guitars, viols, reeds, and percussion.

THE BOUNTY OF PROVENCE

Because much of the allure of *provençale* cuisine derives from its raw ingredients, menus are likely to state the source of what you're about to consume. To see this wealth firsthand, head for any of the open-air markets where vast amounts of meat, cheese, produce, wine, and herbs are sold from simple kiosks.

BREAD Almost as varied as the cheeses are the shapes and ingredients of the bread. You can buy it as long, thin *ficelles,* marvelously crusty, and as *gibassiers,* baked with a dollop of olive oil for flavor. Choose from *pain d'olives,* with the flesh of the olive in the dough; *pain de raisins,* flavored with dried raisins; *pain à l'anis,* aniseed bread; and earthy *pain au levain,* sourdough bread. In Aix, you'll find a regional recipe for *pain d'Aix,* a double-mounded staple that resembles women's breasts. The most democratic of *provençale* breads is *pain d'égalité,* developed in response to an edict during the Revolution declaring that only one kind of bread could be consumed in an egalitarian society. Today this is something akin to generic supermarket bread, but it's still occasionally available in Provençal markets. Beware of Provençal witches, who, according to legend, will come to dance on any loaf of bread that's turned upside down.

CHEESE In the south of France you could spend hours choosing among the varieties of *chèvre* alone. A Provençal folk saying likens goats to "the poor man's cow," but over the centuries, goat-milk cheese has attained gourmet status. Looking for something esoteric? Ask for a rare *tomme de Camargue,* a firm but creamy cheese that combines milk from both goats and sheep and whose disclike surface is embedded with sprigs of rosemary. There's also *Banon vrai,* a goat-milk cheese made in the hamlet of Banon in northern Provence. During its fermentation, it's marinated in *eau-de-vie,* aged in clay pots on dried chestnut leaves, and wrapped with raffia string. Equally delicious is *lou pevre,* a goat cheese whose pungency is enhanced by a black-pepper coating.

FRUITS & VEGETABLES Strawberries from the village of Carpentras or the district of Bouches-du-Rhône have a special cachet. Melons, especially ogen melons from the town of Cavaillon, were so famous that in 1864, civic leaders opted to present a dozen perfect melons each year to the French novelist Alexandre Dumas *père* as a sign of their ongoing respect. He later wrote that he hoped that the readers of Cavaillon would always find his books as charming as he found their melons. Apricots are delicious anywhere, but if they're from the slopes of the Roussillon, your menu will usually let you know. *Mousserons,* one of many varieties of wild mushrooms you'll see in local markets, evoke *frissons* among gastronomes when they're from the Ardèche, west of the Rhône.

PASTRIES & SWEETS As far as pastries go, southern France is expert at turning out *calissons,* rectangular sweets concocted from almond paste; they invariably taste best when baked in Aix-en-Provence. More recipes exist for *nougat,* honey-sweetened chewy candy flavored with either almonds or pistachios, than anyone could possibly document, although nougat from the industrial-looking town of Montelimar seems to have a slight edge. A variety of almond-and-honey cookies, *croque moines* (crusty monks), were named for the monks who baked them. *Une* *galette provençale,* a tartlet filled with pralines, almond cream, and grated orange zest, is a perennial childhood favorite in Arles and St-Rémy.

THE PROVENÇALE MENU

BULL Throughout the south, but especially in the flat wetlands and bull-raising terrain of the Camargue, look for *gardiane de taureau.* Concocted from tough and somewhat fibrous bull flesh and flavored with olives and red wine, it's invariably served with *riz de Camargue*—rice from the lowlands of the delta of the Rhône.

CASSOULET & BOUILLABAISSE What dish should you especially look for in the southwest? The magic word is cassoulet, not to be confused with a *cassolette,* a fancy word for a small stewpot and whatever ingredients someone might be tempted to throw into it. *Cassoulet* is to Toulouse what bouillabaisse is to Marseille, a succulent mixture of slow-cooked white beans flavored with an herbed combination of roasted lamb, mutton, goose, sausages, duck, and various forms of pork.

Bouillabaisse is Provence's most famous dish. It's hard to imagine that this was once a rough-and-tumble recipe favored by local fisher folk, a way of using the least desirable portion of their catch. Traditionally, it combines a trio of fish: rascasse, grondin, and congre (the spiny red hogfish, gurnet, and conger eel). The original recipe from Marseillaise kitchens actually called for a dozen kinds of fish, including fielan, rouquier, and sard. Increasingly, mussels or, to make it elegant, spiny lobsters are added. The kettle of fish is cooked rapidly in bouillon and flavored with olive oil and various seasonings (bay leaf, saffron, onion, and fennel). A paste of Spanish peppers, called a rouille, sharpens the sauce, giving it an extra reddish color.

GAME If you're planning a trip to the deep south in autumn, you'll discover many game dishes on the menu. These include *perdreau* (partridge), *sanglier* (wild boar), *chevreuil* (venison), *faison* (pheasant), and *lièvre* (wild hare). Often the meat will be marinated in herbs and wine, roasted, and served with vibrant red wine from the Rhône Valley.

GOOSE & DUCK Southwestern France is the world's headquarters of dishes brimming with fattened goose and duck. The appreciation of foie gras has been elevated to something approaching a cult, and many dishes gain a noteworthy unctuousness when fried in *graisse d'oie* (goose fat). Thighs of both species are cooked in large quantities of their own fat to create tender *confits,* and the breast of ducks *(magrets)* are often grilled over charcoal or oak fires. Pâtés made from the byproducts of duck, and sometimes studded with truffles, figure high on most people's favorite appetizer list. Goose, at least in Gascony, might be flambéed in Armagnac, and then slowly braised with wine and vegetables for the classic *daube d'oie.*

HEARTY STEWS A specialty remembered (sometimes fondly, sometimes not) from many Provençaux childhoods is *pieds et paquets,* a combination of mutton or lamb tripe and lambs' feet cooked with cured, unsmoked pork, garlic, wine, and tomatoes. This classic is much appreciated by adventurous gastronomes. An equally prized variation is a *gratin de pieds de porc aux truffes* (gratin of pigs' feet with truffles). *Civet de lapin* is wild rabbit stewed with herbs and red wine, with rabbit blood added to the stew at the last minute as a thickener. *Daube de boeuf à la provençale* is an unusual combination of stewed beef marinated in garlic purée with red wine. *Bourride,* a succulent fish stew, is Languedoc's answer to the bouillabaisse of Provence. *Baudroie* is a simple but flavorful mix of monkfish, thin-sliced potatoes, garlic, onions, herbs, and an unexpected ingredient—the zest of navel oranges.

The Pleasure of Pastis

The proper start to a *provençale* meal is a glass or two of the unpretentious local aperitif, *pastis,* a translucent yellow liqueur that becomes cloudy when you add water or ice. Although it's usually associated with truck drivers and dockyard laborers in Marseille, you might really appreciate it once you develop a taste for it. It's scented with anise, fennel, mint, and licorice, but in the case of France's most popular brand name Ricard or its sweeter rival, Pernod, it contains some additional secret ingredients.

VEGETARIAN DISHES Provence has a delightful emphasis on vegetarian dishes, which seem to have a transcendent earthiness from deep within the soil. Examples are succulent grilled eggplant with basil-tomato sauce, and grilled vegetables garnished with zucchini flowers (stuffed with a purée of zucchini and herbs, coated with batter, and deep-fried). No one denies the international appeal of room-temperature ratatouille, the soothing combination of eggplant, onions, peppers, and herbs slowly stewed in olive oil.

The perfect accompaniment for any of these dishes is aioli, the garlic-laced mayonnaise that's the appropriate foil for fish, grilled vegetables, and plain or toasted bread. Incidentally, aioli can also refer to an entire meal composed of poached salt cod, boiled vegetables, and (in some cases) roasted snails; the garlic mayonnaise binds the disparate ingredients together.

Also look for specialties such as *pissaladière,* a doughy form of onion pizza; *mesclun,* assorted wild greens that make divine salads; and *pistou,* a rich basil-infused soup similar to minestrone.

LES VINS DE PROVENCE

For winemaking purposes, Provence is defined as the area between Cannes, not far from the Italian border, and the eastern banks of the Rhône. Although Avignon, Châteauneuf-du-Pape, and Orange are historically and culturally a part of Provence, their wines fall into a distinctly separate district, the Côtes-du-Rhône, which begins at Avignon and extends about 225km (140 miles) northward up the valley of the Rhône to just south of Lyon, near Côte Rotie. Wine produced west of the Rhône, within an area that extends about 64km (40 miles) north of the Mediterranean coast all the way to the Spanish border, belongs to a still different variety, Languedoc-Roussillon.

Most of the wines from these three districts are red and tend to be strong, solid, and flavorful, usually with a potent level of alcohol (a byproduct of the high sugar content of the grape varieties that thrive in the heat and constant sunlight).

The threat of inadequate rainfall in a region known for its droughts keeps local vintners perennially insecure. Consequently, vintners have traditionally relied on a complicated blending of grapes. Since the phylloxera epidemic of the late 19th century, these grape blends have included varietals from Italy and Spain. The result, according to many connoisseurs enamored with the more aristocratic vintages of Burgundy and Bordeaux, is an occasional inconsistency in the way the wines might age.

In 1923, a distinguished Provençal landowner, Baron Le Roy de Boiseaumarie, inaugurated a series of quality controls from his lands near Châteauneuf-du-Pape. His efforts were instrumental in imposing standards on vintners and helped launch what later evolved into the national Appellations d'Origine Contrôllées (A.O.C.).

Despite the appeal of southern French wines as an accompaniment for strongly flavored foods such as anchovies, sardines, and bouillabaisse, the region has a lower percentage of wines that oenophiles call "great" than do more temperate regions. So pride is taken by vintners with lands in designated A.O.C. districts, and massive investments in recent years have helped elevate many of the region's vintages to international repute. Although it's no guarantee of quality, looking for A.O.C. labels is a beginning point for newcomers who want to distinguish prestigious vintages from ordinary *vin de table*. Many A.O.C. designations are relatively new—upstarts compared to the more venerable designations in Burgundy and Bordeaux. Côtes du Provence, producer of more than 100 million bottles annually, was designated A.O.C. as recently as 1977.

The two best Provençal whites are produced near Aix, most notably the delicate Cassis and the more forthright Palette. Bellet, a relatively small winegrowing district above Nice, produces fashionable reds, whites, and rosés.

Particularly strong reds are Gigondas and Vacqueras, whose alcohol content sometimes exceeds 13%. Names to look for are Côtes de Provence (Pierrefeu and Château Minuty are two important producers) from the dry hills north of Toulon, Côtes du Rhône Villages, Côtes du Vivarais, and Châteauneuf-du-Pape, the only wine in the world that's allowed to bear the crest of the long-ago popes of Avignon. Because of the vagaries of rainfall and the growing season, any bottle of this last wine might be composed of more than a dozen grapes from around the district. A memorable sweet wine from the Côtes du Rhône, favored by pastry chefs as a foil for their concoctions, is Baumes de Venise.

The two most famous rosés of the south are Tavel and Bandol, a worthy producer of which is Château Simone. A recent contender rapidly growing in repute is Listel, a cloudy rosé produced on the sun-baked plains of the Camargue.

The vineyards of Languedoc-Roussillon represent more than a third of France's total acreage devoted to grapes. The fields around Nîmes, Béziers, and Narbonne produce rivers of ordinary table wine, which, thanks to newfangled methods of cultivation and harvesting, have of late been more favorably regarded by wine scholars. Aristocratic vintages from Languedoc include unusual sweet wines such as Banyuls and Muscat de Rivesaltes and the reds from towns on the eastern foothills of the Pyrenees, Côtes de Roussillon.

A cost-effective means of trying ordinary table wines is bringing your own container (usually a plastic jug sold on the premises or in hardware stores) to a large-scale producer. At bargain-basement prices, they'll use a gas pump–inspired nozzle to pump wine from enormous vats directly into your container. In a restaurant, such a vintage would be sold in a glass carafe or ceramic *pichet* at a low price. If you're driving through the vineyards and see one of the many signs announcing *vente au détail*, it means that you'll be able to buy estate-bottled wine by the bottle, invariably at lower prices than in retail wine shop.

Planning Your Trip to Provence & the Riviera

We've compiled everything you need to know about the practical details of planning your trip: what documents you'll need, how to use the euro, how to find the best airfare, when to go, and more.

1 WHEN TO GO

WEATHER

In terms of weather, the most idyllic months for visiting the south of France are May and June. Though the sun is intense, it's not uncomfortable. Coastal waters have warmed up by then, so swimming is possible, and all the resorts have come alive after a winter slumber but aren't yet overrun. The flowers and herbs in the countryside are at their peak, and driving conditions are ideal. In June, it remains light until around 10:30pm.

The most overcrowded times—also the hottest, in more ways than one—are July and August, when seemingly half of Paris shows up in the briefest of bikinis. Reservations are difficult to get, discos are blasting, and space is tight on the popular beaches. The worst traffic jams on the coast occur all the way from St-Tropez to Menton.

Aside from May and June, our favorite time is September and even early October, when the sun is still hot and the great hordes have headed back north.

In November, the weather is often pleasant, especially at midday, though some of the restaurants and inns you'll want to visit might take a sudden vacation: It's the month that many chefs and hoteliers elect

to go on their own vacations after a summer of hard work.

Winter hasn't been the fashionable season since the 1930s. In the early days of tourism, when Queen Victoria came to visit, all the fashionable people showed up in winter, deserting the Côte by April. Today it's the reverse. However, winter on the Riviera is being rediscovered, and many visitors (particularly retired people or those with leisure time) elect to visit then. If you don't mind the absence of sunbathing and beach life, this could be a good time to show up. However, some resorts, like St-Tropez, become ghost towns when the cold weather comes, though Cannes, Nice, Monaco, and Menton remain active year-round.

The Mediterranean coast has the driest climate in France. Most rain falls in spring and autumn. Summers are comfortably dry—beneficial to humans but deadly to vegetation, which (unless it's irrigated) often dries and burns up in the parched months.

Provence dreads *le mistral* (a cold, violent wind from the French and Swiss Alps that roars south down the Rhône Valley). It most often blows in winter, sometimes for a few days, but sometimes for up to 2 weeks.

Marseille	Jan	Feb	Mar	Apr	May	June	July	Aug	Sept	Oct	Nov	Dec
Temp. (°F)	44	46	50	55	62	70	75	74	69	60	51	46
Temp. (°C)	6.7	7.8	10	13	17	21	24	23	21	16	11	7.8
Rainfall (in.)	1.9	1.6	1.8	1.8	1.8	1.0	0.6	1.0	2.5	3.7	3.0	2.3
Rainfall (cm)	4.8	4.1	4.6	4.6	4.6	2.5	1.5	2.5	6.4	9.4	7.6	5.8

Nice	Jan	Feb	Mar	Apr	May	June	July	Aug	Sept	Oct	Nov	Dec
Temp. (°F)	48	49	52	55	62	68	74	74	70	62	54	50
Temp. (°C)	8.9	9.4	11	13	17	20	23	23	21	17	12	10
Rainfall (in.)	3.0	2.9	2.9	2.5	1.9	1.5	0.7	1.2	2.6	4.4	4.6	3.5
Rainfall (cm)	7.6	7.4	7.4	6.4	4.8	3.8	1.8	3	6.6	11.2	11.7	8.9

PROVENCE CALENDAR OF EVENTS

For an exhaustive list of events beyond those listed here, check http://events.frommers.com, where you'll find a searchable, up-to-the-minute roster of what's happening in cities all over the world.

JANUARY

Monte Carlo Motor Rally. The world's most venerable car race. For more information, call ✆ **377-92-16-61-16.** Usually late January.

FEBRUARY

Fête de la Chandeleur (Candlemas), Basilique St-Victor, Marseille. A celebration in honor of the arrival in Marseille of the three Marys. A procession brings the Black Virgin up from the crypt of the abbey. For more information, call ✆ **04-91-13-89-00.** Early February.

Carnival of Nice. Float processions, parades, confetti battles, boat races, street music and food, masked balls, and fireworks are part of this ancient celebration. The climax follows a 114-year-old tradition in which King Carnival is burned in effigy, an event preceded by Les Batailles des Fleurs (Battles of the Flowers), during which members of opposing teams pelt one another with flowers. Come armed with a hotel reservation. For information or reservations, contact the **Nice Convention and Visitors Bureau** at

✆ **08-92-70-74-07** (www.nicetourism.com). Mid-February to early March.

MARCH

Procession des Pénitents (Procession of the Penitents). These marches are conducted in both **Arles** (✆ 04-90-18-41-20) and **Collioure** (✆ 04-68-82-15-47). Good Friday.

Procession du Christ Mort (Procession of the Dead Christ). On the French Riviera, one of the most fascinating religious processions is in **Roquebrune-Cap-Martin;** ✆ **04-93-35-62-87.** Good Friday.

Féria Pascale (Easter Bullfighting Festival), Arles. This is a major bullfighting event that includes not only appearances by the greatest matadors, but also *abrivados* and *bodegas* (wine stalls). For more information, call ✆ 04-90-18-41-20 (www.tourisme.ville-arles.fr). Easter.

MAY

La Fête des Gardians (Camargue Cowboys' Festival), Arles. This event features a procession of Camargue cowboys through the streets of town. Activities feature various games involving

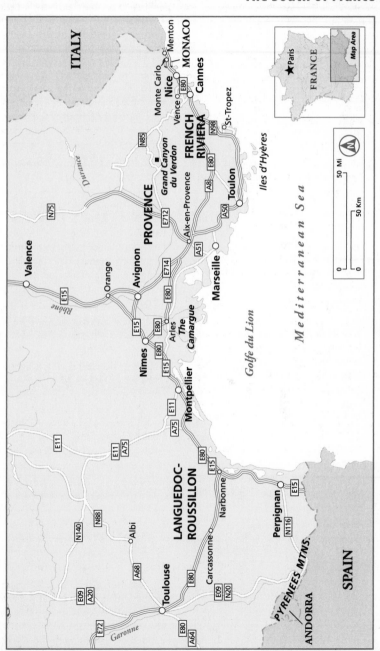

bulls, including Courses Camarguaises, in which competitors have to snatch a rosette from between the horns of a bull. For information, call ℂ **04-90-18-41-20.** May.

Cannes Film Festival. Movie madness transforms this city into the kingdom of the media deal, with daily melodramas acted out in cafes, on sidewalks, and in hotel lobbies. It's great for voyeurs. Reserve early and make a deposit. Getting a table on the Carlton terrace is even more difficult than procuring a room. Admission to some of the prestigious films is by invitation only. There are box-office tickets for the less important films, which play 24 hours. For information, contact the Association Française du Festival International du Film, 3 rue Amélie, 75007 Paris (ℂ **01-53-59-61-00;** www.festival-cannes.org). Mid-May.

Festival des Musiques d'Aujourd'hui, Marseille. This festival presents the works of young French and European composers in music and dance. For more information, call **Experimental Music Groups of Marseille** at ℂ **04-96-20-60-10** (www.gmem.org). Mid-May.

Monaco Grand Prix de Formule. Hundreds of cars race through the narrow streets and winding roads in a surreal blend of high-tech machinery and medieval architecture. For more information, call ℂ **377-93-15-26-00** (www.acm.mc). Late May.

Fête de la Transhumance (Move to Summer Grazing), St-Rémy. This event celebrates the now-abandoned custom of shepherds presenting their flocks to the public before moving them to higher ground for summer. In this mock event, the flocks move off as if really going up to the mountains. For more information, call ℂ **04-90-92-05-22.** May to June.

Le Pélerinage des Gitans (Gypsies' Pilgrimage), Stes-Maries-de-la-Mer. This festival is in memory of the two Marys for whom the town is named (Mary, the mother of James the lesser, and Mary Salome, the mother of James the greater and John). A model boat containing statues of the saints and a statue of St. Sarah, patron saint of Gypsies, is taken to the seashore and blessed by the bishop. For more information, call ℂ **04-90-97-82-55** (www.saintes maries.com). Last week of May.

JUNE

Festival de la St-Eloi, Maussane-les-Alpilles. For this festival, wagons are decorated and raced in the Carreto Ramado, followed by Mass, a procession in traditional dress, and a benediction. Special events are held and local produce and handicrafts are sold. For more information, call ℂ **04-90-54-52-04** (www.maussane.com). Mid-June.

Festival Aix en Musique, Aix-en-Provence. Concerts of classical music and choral singing are held in historic buildings, such as the Théâtre de l'Archevêché and the Hôtel Maynier d'Oppède. For more information, call ℂ **04-42-17-34-34** (www.festival-aix.com). Late June to late July.

Festival d'Expression Provençale, Abbaye St-Michel de Frigolet, Tarascon. At this festival, homage is paid to the region's language with works by Provençal writers that are acted in French and Provençal. For more information, call ℂ **04-90-91-03-52.** Late June to early July.

Fête de la Tarasque, Tarascon. The town relives St. Martha's victory over the dragon known as the Tarasque, which was believed to live in the Rhône in the 1st century. Celebrations include a procession of horsemen, an archery competition, historical events, a medieval tournament, a Tarasque procession, Novilladas (young bullfighters), and an orchestral concert with fireworks. For more information, call ✆ 04-90-91-03-52 (www.tarascon.org). Late June.

Feu de la St-Jean (St. John's Fire), Fontvieille. This event features folk troupes and Camargue cowboys who gather in front of the Château de Montauban. For more information, call ✆ 04-90-54-67-49. Late June.

Reconstitution Historique, Salon-de-Provence. This pageant held in honor of Nostradamus includes a cast of 700 in historical costume and is followed by a *son et lumière* at the Château d'Empéri. For more information, call ✆ 04-90-56-27-60. Late June to early July.

Festival de Marseille Méditerranée. This festival features concerts and recitals of music and song from the entire Mediterranean region. Theater and dance are also presented, along with special exhibitions in the city's main museums. For more information, call ✆ 04-91-13-89-00 or 91-99-00-20. Late June to late July.

La Fête des Pêcheurs (Fishermen's Festival), Cassis. The local "Prud'hommes" (members of the elected industrial tribunal) walk in procession wearing traditional dress, and a Mass is held in honor of St. Peter, followed by a benediction. For more information, call ✆ 08-92-25-98-92. Late June.

JULY

St-Guilhem Music Season, St-Guilhem le Désert, Languedoc. This festival of baroque organ and choral music is held in a medieval monastery. For information, call ✆ 04-67-57-44-33 (www.saint-guilhem-le-desert.com). Month of July.

Les Chorégies d'Orange, Orange. One of southern France's most important lyric festivals presents oratorios and choral works by master performers whose voices are amplified by the ancient acoustics of France's best-preserved Roman amphitheater. For more information, call ✆ 04-90-34-24-24 (www.choregies.asso.fr). Early July to early August.

Bastille Day. Celebrating the birth of modern-day France, the festivities in the south reach their peak in Nice with street fairs, pageants, fireworks, and feasts. The day begins with a parade down the promenade des Anglais and ends with fireworks in the Vieille Ville. No matter where you are, by the end of the day you'll hear Piaf warbling "La Foule" (The Crowd), the song that celebrated her passion for the stranger she met and later lost in a crowd on Bastille Day. Similar celebrations also take place in Cannes, Arles, Aix, Marseille, and Avignon. July 14.

Nuit Taurine (Nocturnal Bull Festival), St-Rémy-de-Provence. At this festival, the focus is on the age-old allure of bulls and their primeval appeal to roaring crowds. *Abrivados* involve bulls in the town square as "chaperoned" by trained herders on horseback; *encierros* highlight a Pamplona-style stampeding of bulls through the streets. Music from local guitarists and flaming torches add drama. For more information, call ✆ 04-90-92-05-22. Mid-July.

Nice Jazz Festival. This is the biggest, flashiest, and most prestigious jazz festival in Europe, with world-class entertainers. Concerts begin in early afternoon and go on until late at night (sometimes all night in the clubs) on the Arènes de Cimiez, a picturesque hill above the city. Reserve hotel rooms way in advance. For information, contact the Grand Parade du Jazz, c/o the tourist office of Nice (✆ 08-92-70-74-07; www.nicejazzfestival.fr). Mid-July.

Festival d'Avignon. One of France's most prestigious theater events, this world-class festival has a reputation for exposing new talent to critical acclaim. The focus is usually on avant-garde works in theater, dance, and music by groups from around the world. Make hotel reservations early. For information, call ☎ **04-90-27-66-50** (www. festival-avignon.com). Last 3 weeks of July.

Fête de la St-Eloi (Feast of St. Eloi), Gémenos. Some hundred draft horses draw a procession of traditional flower-decked wagons. Folk troupes also perform. For more information, call ☎ **04-42-32-18-44.** Late July.

AUGUST

Fêtes Daudet (Daudet Festival), Font-vieille. At this festival, Mass said in Provençal is held on the avenue of pine trees. There's folk dancing outside Daudet's mill and a torchlight procession through the streets of town to the mill. For more information, call ☎ **04-90-54-67-49** (www.fontvieille-provence. com). Mid-August.

Féria de St-Rémy, St-Rémy-de-Provence. This event features a 4-day celebration of bulls with *abrivado* and *encierro* (see the Nuit Taurine entry, above), branding, and Portuguese bull fighting (matadors on horseback). For more information, call ☎ **04-90-92-05-22.** Mid-August.

SEPTEMBER

Féria des Prémices du Riz (Rice Harvest Festival), Arles. Bullfights are held in the amphitheater with leading matadors, and a procession of floats makes its way along boulevard des Lices; there are also traditional events with cowboys and women in regional costume. For more information, call ☎ **04-90-18-41-20.** Early September.

Fête des Olives, Mouriès. A Mass is held in honor of the green olive. There's a procession of groups in traditional costume, an olive tasting, and sales of regional produce. For more information, call ☎ **04-90-47-56-58** (www. mouries.com). Mid-September.

OCTOBER

Perpignan Jazz Festival. Musicians from everywhere jam in what many visitors consider Languedoc's most appealing season. For more information, call ☎ **04-68-51-13-14** (www. jazzebre.com). Late September to late October.

NOVEMBER

Marché aux Santons, Tarascon. Craftspersons from throughout Provence congregate in this medieval village to sell their *santons* (carved representations of saints). For more information, call ☎ **04-90-91-03-52.** Four days in late November. This event is supplemented, sometimes with the same sellers, who move to the **Foire aux Santons** in Marseille, held between late November and Christmas. For more information, call ☎ **04-91-13-89-00.**

DECEMBER

Fête des Bergers (Shepherds Festival), Istres. This festival features a procession of herds on their way to winter pastures. There are cowboys, a Carreto Ramado, a blessing of the horses, an all-night Provençal party with shepherds and Provençal storytellers, and folk troupes. For more information, call ☎ **04-42-55-50-00.** First weekend in December.

Foire de Noël, Mougins. Hundreds of merchants, selling all manner of Christmas ornaments and gifts, descend on Mougins in Provence, to herald in the Christmas spirit. For more information, call ☎ **04-93-75-87-67.** Mid- to late December.

Midnight Mass, Fontvieille. A traditional midnight Mass, including the *pastrage* ceremony, the presentation of a newborn lamb. A procession of folk troupes, Camargue cowboys, and women in traditional costume go from Daudet's mill to the church, followed by the presentation of the lamb. For more information, call © 04-90-54-67-49 (www.fontvieille-provence.com). December 24.

Noël Provençal, Eglise St-Vincent, Les Baux. The procession of shepherds is followed by a traditional midnight Mass, including the *pastrage* ceremony, traditional songs, and performance of a nativity play. For more information, call © 04-90-54-34-39. December 24.

Fête de St-Sylvestre (New Year's Eve), nationwide. Along the Riviera, it's most boisterously celebrated in Nice's Vieille Ville around place Garibaldi. At midnight, the city explodes. Strangers kiss strangers, and place Masséna and the promenade des Anglais become virtual pedestrian malls. December 31.

2 ENTRY REQUIREMENTS

PASSPORTS

All travelers entering France are required to carry a passport. Visas are not required for U.S., Canadian, U.K., Australian, and New Zealand citizens.

For information on how to get a passport, see "Passports" in the "Fast Facts: The South of France" section on p. 356—the websites listed provide downloadable passport applications as well as the current fees for processing passport applications. For an up-to-date, country-by-country listing of passport requirements around the world, go to the "Foreign Entry Requirement" Web page of the U.S. State Department at **http://travel.state.gov**.

To prevent international child abduction, E.U. governments have initiated procedures at entry and exit points. These often (but not always) include requiring documentary evidence of relationship and permission for the child's travel from the parent or legal guardian not present. Having such documentation on hand, even if not required, facilitates entries and exits. Any questions parents or guardians might have can be answered by calling the **National Passport Information Center** at © 877/487-2778 Monday to Friday 8am to 8pm Eastern Standard Time.

CUSTOMS
What You Can Bring into France

Customs restrictions for visitors entering France differ for citizens of European Union (E.U.) and non-E.U. countries. Non-E.U. nationals can bring in duty-free either 200 cigarettes, 100 cigarillos, 50 cigars, or 250 grams of smoking tobacco. This amount is doubled if you live outside Europe. You can also bring in 2 liters of wine and 1 liter of alcohol over 22%, and 2 liters of wine 22% or under. In addition, you can bring in 60cc of perfume and a quarter liter of eau de toilette. Visitors ages 15 and over can bring in other goods totaling 175€; for those under 15, the limit is 90€. Customs officials tend to be lenient about general merchandise as the limits are very low. Citizens of E.U. countries can bring in any amount of goods as long as the goods are intended for their personal use and not for resale.

What You Can Take Home from France

U.S. CITIZENS Returning U.S. citizens who have been away for 48 hours or more are allowed to bring back, once every 30 days, $800 worth of merchandise duty-free. You're charged a flat rate of duty on the next $1,000 worth of purchases, and any dollar amount beyond that is subject to duty at whatever rates apply. On mailed gifts, the duty-free limit is $200. Have your receipts or purchases handy to expedite the declaration process. *Note:* If you owe duty, you are required to pay on your arrival in the United States, using cash, personal check, government or traveler's check, or money order; some locations also accept Visa or MasterCard.

To avoid having to pay duty on foreign-made personal items you owned before your trip, bring along a bill of sale, insurance policy, jeweler's appraisal, or receipt of purchase. Or you can register items that can be readily identified by a permanently affixed serial number or marking—think laptop computers, cameras, and MP3 players—with Customs before you leave. Take the items to the nearest Customs office, or register them with Customs at the airport from which you're departing. You'll receive, at no cost, a Certificate of Registration, which allows duty-free entry for the life of the item.

You cannot bring fresh foodstuffs into the U.S.; canned foods are allowed. For specifics on what you can bring back and the corresponding fees, download the invaluable free pamphlet *Know Before You Go* online at **www.cbp.gov**. (Click on "Travel," and then click on "Know Before You Go.") Or, contact the **U.S. Customs & Border Protection (CBP),** 1300 Pennsylvania Ave. NW, Washington, DC 20229 (© **877/287-8667**), and request the pamphlet.

CANADIAN CITIZENS Canada allows its citizens a C$750 exemption, and you're allowed to bring back duty-free one carton of cigarettes, one can of tobacco, 40 imperial ounces of liquor, and 50 cigars. In addition, you're allowed to mail gifts to Canada from abroad valued at less than C$60 a day, provided they're unsolicited and don't contain alcohol or tobacco (write on the package UNSOLICITED GIFT, UNDER C$60 VALUE). All valuables, including serial numbers of valuables you already own, such as expensive foreign cameras, should be declared on the Y-38 form before departure from Canada. *Note:* The C$750 exemption can be used only once a year and only after an absence of 7 days.

For a clear summary of Canadian rules, write for the booklet *I Declare,* issued by the **Canada Border Services Agency** (© **800/461-9999** in Canada, or 204/983-3500; www.cbsa-asfc.gc.ca).

U.K. CITIZENS Citizens of the U.K. returning from an E.U. country such as France go through a Customs exit (called the "Blue Exit") especially for E.U. travelers. In essence, there is no limit on what you can bring back from an E.U. country, as long as the items are for personal use (this includes gifts) and you have already paid the duty and tax. However, Customs law sets out guidance levels. If you bring in more than these levels, you may be asked to prove that the goods are for your own use. Guidance levels on goods bought in the E.U. for your own use are 3,200 cigarettes, 200 cigars, 400 cigarillos, 3 kilograms of smoking tobacco, 10 liters of spirits, 90 liters of wine, 20 liters of fortified wine (such as port or sherry), and 110 liters of beer.

For information, contact **HM Revenue & Customs** at © **0845/010-9000** (from outside the U.K., 02920/501-261), or consult their website at www.hmrc.gov.uk.

AUSTRALIAN CITIZENS The duty-free allowance in Australia is A$900 or, for those under 18, A$450. Citizens can bring in 250 cigarettes or 250 grams of loose tobacco, and 2.25 liters of alcohol. If you're returning with valuables you already

Tips **Border Crossings to Monaco**

Tiny Monaco (2 sq. km/³/₄ sq. mile) is an independent nation, but document requirements for travel to Monaco are the same as those for France, and there are virtually no border patrols or passport formalities. For information, contact the **Monaco Government Tourist Office,** 565 Fifth Ave., 23rd Floor, New York, NY 10017 (© **800/753-9696** or 212/286-3330; fax 212/286-9890; www.visitmonaco. com); or at the Chambers, Chelsea Harbour, London SW10 OXF (© **020/7491-4264**).

own, such as foreign-made cameras, you should file form B263.

A helpful brochure available from Australian consulates or Customs offices is *Know Before You Go.* For more information, call the **Australian Customs Service** at © **1300/363-263,** or log on to www.customs.gov.au.

NEW ZEALAND CITIZENS The duty-free allowance for New Zealand is NZ$700. Citizens 18 and over can bring in 200 cigarettes, 50 cigars, or 250 grams of tobacco (or a mixture of all three if their combined weight doesn't exceed 250g), plus 4.5 liters of wine and beer, or 1.125 liters of liquor. New Zealand currency does not carry import or export restrictions. Fill

out a certificate of export, listing the valuables you are taking out of the country; that way, you can bring them back without paying duty.

Most questions are answered in a free pamphlet available at New Zealand consulates and Customs offices: *New Zealand Customs Guide for Travellers, Notice no. 4.* For more information, contact **New Zealand Customs Service,** the Customhouse, 17–21 Whitmore St., Box 2218, Wellington (© **04/473-6099** or 0800/428-786; www.customs.govt.nz).

MEDICAL REQUIREMENTS

For information on medical requirements and recommendations, see "Health," p. 52.

3 GETTING THERE & GETTING AROUND

FROM NORTH AMERICA
By Plane
THE MAJOR U.S. CARRIERS All major airlines fly to Paris from the U.S. cities listed below. Once you fly into Orly or Charles de Gaulle, you must take **Air France** (© **800/237-2747;** www.air france.com), to reach your destination in Languedoc, Provence, or the Riviera. From Orly and Charles de Gaulle, there are 20 flights per day to Marseille and to Nice, 16 to Toulouse, and 4 from Monday to Friday and 2 Saturday and Sunday to Avignon.

American Airlines (© **800/433-7300;** www.aa.com) offers daily flights to Paris from Dallas–Fort Worth, Chicago, Miami, Boston, and New York. **Delta Airlines** (© **800/241-4141;** www.delta.com) flies nonstop to Paris from Atlanta, Cincinnati, and New York. All these flights depart late enough in the day to permit transfers from much of Delta's vast North American network. Note that Delta is the only American airline offering nonstop service from New York to Nice.

Continental Airlines (© 800/231-0856; www.continental.com) flies daily nonstop to Paris from Newark and four to seven times a week, depending on the season, from Houston. **US Airways** (© 800/428-4322; www.usairways.com) offers daily nonstop service from Philadelphia to Paris.

THE FRENCH NATIONAL CARRIER

Air France (© 800/237-2747; www.airfrance.com) was formed from a merger combining three of France's largest airlines. The airline offers a daily nonstop flight between New York and Nice and also offers regular flights between Paris and such North American cities as Newark; Washington, D.C.; Miami; Atlanta; Boston; Cincinnati; Chicago; New York; Houston; San Francisco; Los Angeles; Montreal; Toronto; and Mexico City.

THE MAJOR CANADIAN CARRIER

Canadians usually choose the **Air Canada** (© 888/247-2262 in the U.S. and Canada; www.aircanada.com) flights to Paris from Toronto and Montreal that depart every evening. Two of Air Canada's flights from Toronto are shared with Air France and feature Air France aircraft.

FROM PARIS
By Car

For more information on getting to each city and town in this book from within France, see the "Getting There" section of the town of interest.

By Plane

From Paris, if you're heading for the French Riviera, your connecting flight will probably land you in Nice's international airport, Aéroport Nice–Côte d'Azur. There are also airports at Avignon, Marseille, Montpellier, Nîmes, and Toulouse.

By Train

The world's fastest trains link some 50 French cities, allowing you to get from Paris to just about anywhere else in the country in hours. With 39,000km (24,233 miles) of track and about 3,000 stations, **SNCF** (French National Railroads; www.voyages-sncf.com) is fabled for its on-time performance. You can travel in first or second class by day and in couchette by night. Many trains have dining facilities.

INFORMATION If you plan to travel a lot on European railroads, get the latest copy of the *European Rail Timetable*. This 500-plus-page book documents all of Europe's main passenger rail services with detail and accuracy. It's available online at www.raileurope.com.

In the United States: For more information and to purchase rail passes before you leave, contact **Rail Europe** (© 877/272-RAIL [7255]; www.raileurope.com).

In Canada: Call Rail Europe at © 800/361-RAIL [7255].

In London: SNCF has offices at Rail Europe, 179 Piccadilly, London W1V 0BA (© 0870/584-8848).

In Paris: For information or reservations, go online (www.voyages-sncf.fr) or call © 36-35. You can also go to any local travel agency. A simpler way to buy tickets is to use the *billetterie* (ticket machine) in every train station. If you know your PIN, you can use a credit card to buy your ticket.

FRANCE RAIL PASSES Working cooperatively with SNCF, Air Inter Europe, and Avis, Rail Europe offers three flexible rail passes that can reduce travel costs considerably.

The **France Railpass** www.railfrance.com provides unlimited rail transport in France for any 3 days within 1 month, at $293 in first class and $250 in second. You can purchase up to 6 more days for an extra $45 per person per day. Children 4 to 11 travel for half-price.

The **France Rail 'n' Drive Pass,** available only in North America, combines good value on both rail travel and Avis car rentals, and is best used by arriving at a

Tips   Have a Seat

Remember that a train ticket does not guarantee you a seat; it merely gets you from one place to another. On crowded trains and during busy times, you'll have to make a **seat reservation** (and pay for the privilege) if you want to be sure of sitting somewhere other than on top of your luggage. Seat reservations cost 10€ per person.

major rail depot and then striking out to explore the countryside by car. It includes the France Railpass (see above) and use of a rental car. You have 1 month to complete your travel on this pass that grants 2 days of unlimited train travel and 2 days of car rental with unlimited mileage in France. Prices for an economy car begin at $350.

The best deal if you're traveling in France with a friend—or even three or four friends—is the **France Saverpass,** granting 3 days of unlimited travel in a 1-month period. The cost is $249 per person first class or $215 second class. For travelers age 60 and over there is the **France Senior Pass,** which allows 3 days of unlimited first-class travel within 1 month for $268. Up to 6 more additional days may be purchased at $40 per day. There's also a **France Youthpass** for travelers 25 or under, granting 3 days of unlimited train travel within a month. The cost is $217 in first class or $186 in second class.

EURAILPASS   The Eurailpass permits unlimited first-class rail travel in any country in western Europe except the British Isles (good in Ireland). Passes are available for purchase online (www.eurail.com) and at various offices/agents around the world. Travel agents and railway agents in such cities as New York, Montreal, and Los Angeles sell Eurailpasses. You can purchase them at the North American offices of CIT Travel Service, the French National Railroads, the German Federal Railroads, and the Swiss Federal Railways.

It is strongly recommended that you purchase passes before you leave home as not all offers are available in Europe; also, passes purchased in Europe will cost about 20% more. Numerous options are available for travel in France.

The **Eurail Global Pass** allows you unlimited travel in 18 Eurail-affiliated countries. You can travel on any of the days within the validity period, which is available for 15 days, 21 days, 1 month, 2 months, 3 months, and some other possibilities as well. Prices for first-class adult travel are $700 for 15 days, $907 for 21 days, $1,127 for 1 month, $1,590 for 2 months, and $1,962 for 3 months. Children 4 to 11 pay half-fare; those 3 and under travel for free.

A **Eurail Global Pass Saver,** also valid for first-class travel in 18 countries, offers a special deal for two or more people traveling together. This pass costs $539 for 5 days, $770 for 21 days, $956 for 1 month, $1,351 for 2 months, and $1,673 for 3 months.

A **Eurail Global Youth Pass** for those 12 to 25 allows second-class travel in 18 countries. This pass costs $455 for 15 days, $588 for 21 days, $733 for 1 month, $1,034 for 2 months, and $1,278 for 3 months.

Eurail Selectpass: The pass offers unlimited travel on the national rail networks of any three, four, or five bordering countries out of the 22 Eurail nations linked by train or ship. Two or more passengers can travel together for big discounts, getting 5, 6, 8, 10, or 15 days of rail travel within any 2-month period on the national rail networks of any three, four, or five adjoining Eurail countries linked by train or ship. A sample fare: For 5 days in 2 months you pay $425 for three countries.

FROM ELSEWHERE IN EUROPE
By Ferry from England

Ferries and hydrofoils operate day and night in all seasons, with the exception of last-minute cancellations during storms. Many crossings coincide with the arrival and departure of trains (especially those btw. London and Paris). Trains let you off a short walk from the piers. Most ferries carry cars, trucks, and freight, but some hydrofoils take passengers only. The major routes include at least 12 trips a day between Dover or Folkestone and Calais or Boulogne.

Hovercraft and hydrofoils make the trip from Dover to Calais, the shortest distance across the Channel, in just 40 minutes during good weather, while the ferries might take several hours, depending on the weather and tides. If you're bringing a car, it's important to make reservations because space below deck is usually crowded. Timetables can vary depending on weather conditions and many other factors.

The leading operator of ferries across the channel is **P&O Ferries** (© 0870/598-0333; www.poferries.com). It operates car and passenger ferries between Portsmouth, England, and Cherbourg, France (three departures a day; 4¼ hr. each way during daylight hours, 7 hr. each way at night); between Portsmouth and Le Havre, France (three a day; 5½ hr. each way). Most popular is the route between Dover, England, and Calais, France (25 sailings a day; 75 min. each way), costing £25 one-way; children 4 and younger go free.

If you plan to transport a rental car between England and France, check with the company about license and insurance requirements and drop-off charges. Many forbid transport of their vehicles over the water between England and France. A better idea is to ask about a car exchange program (Hertz's is called "Le Swap"), in which you drop off a right-drive car and pick up a left-drive vehicle at Calais.

By Plane

From London, **Air France** (© 0870/142-4343; www.airfrance.com) and **British Airways** (© 0844/493-0787; www.british airways.com) fly frequently to Paris, with a trip time of 1 hour. These airlines operate up to 17 flights daily from Heathrow. Many commercial travelers also use flights originating from the London City Airport in the Docklands. A ballpark figure for rates is London to Paris £29 one-way.

Direct flights to Paris also exist from other U.K. cities such as Manchester, Edinburgh, and Southampton. Contact Air France, British Airways, or **British Midland** (© 0870/607-0555; www.fly bmi.com). Daily papers often carry ads for cheap flights. The highly recommended **Trailfinders** (© 0845/058-5858; www. trailfinders.com) sells discounted fares.

You can reach Paris from any major European capital. Your best bet is to fly on the national carrier, Air France, with more connections into Paris from European capitals than any other airline. From Dublin, try **Aer Lingus** (© 800/IRISH-AIR [47474-247]; www.aerlingus.com), with the most flights to Paris from Ireland. From Amsterdam, the convenient choice is **NWA/KLM** (© 800/225-2525; www. klm.com).

If you don't want to go to Paris before flying to the south of France, you'll find a number of British flights going directly to the Nice–Côte d'Azur Airport, the Marseille-Provence Airport, and the Toulouse Airport. Daily flights are offered by British

Airways, Air France, **British Midland** (www.flybmi.com), and **easyJet** (www.easyjet.com).

By Train

From the U.K., most passengers arrive in Paris before going the rest of the way by train to Provence.

The south of France is connected to both Spain and Italy by rail. Travel time by train to Montpellier from Barcelona, Spain is 4½ hours; from Milan, Italy, to Nice is about 5 hours. Check the timetables on the **SNCF** website www.voyages-sncf.com, and the websites of the national railways of Spain (www.renfe.es) and Italy (www.ferroviedellostato.it).

GETTING AROUND

The most charming Provençal villages and best country hotels always seem to lie away from the main cities and train stations. Renting a car is usually the best way to travel once you get to the south of France, especially if you plan to explore in depth and not stick to the standard route along the coast.

The south of France also has one of the most reliable bus and rail transportation systems in Europe. Trains connect all the major cities and towns, such as Nice and Avignon. Where the train leaves off, you can most often rely on local bus service.

By Bus

While the trains are faster and more efficient if you are traveling between major cities, both the towns and villages of Languedoc and Provence, including the French Riviera, are linked by frequent bus service. You can use the network of buses that link the villages and hamlets with each other and the major cities to get off the beaten path.

Plan to take advantage of the bus services from Monday to Saturday when they run frequently; very few buses run on Sunday.

Sodetrav (© 08-25-00-06-50 or 04-94-12-55-12; www.sodetrav.fr) has some of the best bus routes, and is especially strong in the western Riviera, taking in stopovers at such destinations as St-Raphaël, St-Tropez, Arles, Grasse, Avignon, Marseille, Nîmes, and Hyeres. One of its most popular routes is the run between Toulon and St-Tropez, with 20 buses daily.

Contact information for buses to specific towns can be found in the "Getting There" section of each individual town and city.

By Car

Driving time in Europe is largely a matter of conjecture, urgency, and how much sightseeing you do along the way. The driving time from Marseille to Paris is a matter of national pride, and tall tales abound about how rapidly the French can do it. With the accelerator pressed to the floor, you might conceivably make it in 7 hours, but we always make a 2-day journey of it.

CAR RENTALS To rent a car, you'll need to present a passport, a driver's license, and a credit card. You'll also have to meet the minimum-age requirement of the company. (For the least expensive cars, this is 21 at Hertz, 23 at Avis, and 25 at Budget. More expensive cars might require that you be at least 25.) It usually isn't obligatory within France, but certain companies have at times asked for the presentation of an international driver's license, even though this is becoming increasingly superfluous in western Europe.

Note: The best deal is usually a weekly rental with unlimited mileage. All car-rental bills in France are subject to a 19.6% government tax. The rental company won't usually mind if you drive your car into, say, Germany, Switzerland, Italy, or Spain.

Unless it's factored into the rental agreement, an optional **collision-damage waiver (CDW)** carries an extra charge of 13€ to 21€ per day for the least expensive car. Buying this usually eliminates all but 250€ of your responsibility in the event of accidental damage to the car. Because most newcomers aren't familiar with local driving customs and conditions, we recommend you buy the CDW, though you should check with your credit card company first to see if it will cover this automatically when you rent with its card. (It might cover damage but not liability, so make sure you understand this clearly.) At some companies, the CDW won't protect you against theft, so if this is the case, ask about buying extra theft protection. This cost is 10€ extra per day.

Automatic transmission is considered a luxury in Europe, so if you want it, you'll have to pay dearly.

For rentals of more than 7 days, in most cases cars can be picked up in one French city and dropped off in another, but there are additional charges. Still, Budget's rates are among the most competitive, and its cars are well maintained. **Budget** (www. budget.com) has numerous locations in southern France, including those in **Avignon** at the airport ⓒ 04-90-87-17-75; in **Marseille** at the airport ⓒ 04-42-14-24-55, at 40 bd. De Plombières (ⓒ 04-91-64-40-03); in **Nice** at the airport (ⓒ 04-9 3-21-36-50); and in **Toulouse** at the airport (ⓒ 05-61-71-85-80).

Hertz (www.hertz.com) is also well represented, with offices in **Avignon** at the airport (ⓒ 04-90-84-19-50) and at the train station (ⓒ 04-32-74-62-80); in **Marseille** at the airport (ⓒ 08-25-09-13-13) and at 15 bd. Maurice-Bourdet (ⓒ 04-91-14-04-24); in **Montpellier** at the airport (ⓒ 04-67-20-04-64); in **Nice** at the airport (ⓒ 08-25-34-23-43); in **Toulouse** at the airport (ⓒ 05-61-71-27-09) and at the rail station (ⓒ 05-62-73-39-47).

When making inquiries, be sure to ask about promotional discounts.

Avis (www.avis.com) has offices in **Avignon** at the airport (ⓒ 04-90-87-17-75) and at the railway station (ⓒ 04-90-27-96-10); in **Marseille** at the airport (ⓒ 04-42-14-21-67) and at 267 bd. National (ⓒ 04-91-50-70-11); in **Montpellier** at the airport (ⓒ 04-67-20-14-95) and at the Railway Station (ⓒ 04-67-92-92-00); in **Nice** at the airport (ⓒ 04-93-21-36-33) and at place Massena, 2 av. des Phocéens (ⓒ 04-93-80-63-52); and in **Toulouse** at the airport (ⓒ 05-34-60-46-50) and at the train station (ⓒ 05-61-62-50-40).

National (www.nationalcar.com) is represented in France by Europcar, with locations in **Avignon** at the train station (ⓒ 04-90-27-30-07); in **Marseille** at the airport (ⓒ 04-42-14-24-90) and at the St-Charles train station, 96 bd. Rabatau (ⓒ 04-91-83-05-05); in **Montpellier** at the airport (ⓒ 04-67-15-13-47); in **Nice** at the airport (ⓒ 04-93-21-80-90); and in **Toulouse** at the airport (ⓒ 05-61-30-00-01). You can rent a car on the spot at any of these offices, but lower rates are available by making advance reservations from North America.

Two United States–based agencies that don't have France offices but act as booking agents for France-based agencies are **Kemwel Drive Group** (ⓒ **877/820-0668** or 207/842-2285; www.kemwel.com) and **Auto Europe** (ⓒ **888/223-5555;** www. autoeurope.com). These can make bookings in the United States only, so call before your trip.

GASOLINE Known in France as *essence,* gas is expensive for those accustomed to North American prices. All but the least expensive cars usually require an octane rating that the French classify as *essence super,* the most expensive variety. Depending on your car, you'll need either leaded *(avec plomb)* or unleaded *(sans plomb).*

Beware the mixture of gasoline and oil called *mélange* or *gasoil* sold in some rural communities; this mixture is for very old two-cycle engines.

Note: Sometimes you can drive for miles in rural France without encountering a gas station, so don't let your tank get dangerously low.

DRIVING RULES Everyone in the car, in both the front and the back seats, must wear seat belts. Children 11 and under must ride in the back seat. Drivers are supposed to yield to the car on their right, except where signs indicate otherwise, as at traffic circles.

If you violate the speed limit, expect a big fine. Those limits are about 130kmph (81 mph) on expressways, about 100kmph (62 mph) on major national highways, and 90kmph (56 mph) on country roads. In towns, don't exceed 60kmph (37 mph).

MAPS For France as a whole, most motorists opt for Michelin map 989. For regions, Michelin publishes a series of yellow maps that are quite good. Big travel-book stores in North America carry these maps, and they're commonly available in France (at lower prices). In this age of congested traffic, one useful feature of the Michelin map is its designations of alternative *routes de dégagement,* which let you skirt big cities and avoid traffic-clogged highways. They also highlight routes in green, which are recommended for tourists.

Another recommended option is *Frommer's Road Atlas Europe.*

BREAKDOWNS/ASSISTANCE A breakdown is called *une panne* in France. Call the police at © **17** anywhere in France to be put in touch with the nearest garage. If the breakdown occurs on an expressway, find the nearest roadside emergency phone box, pick up the phone, and put a call through. You'll be connected to the nearest breakdown service facility.

By Plane

Regrettably, there are few competitors in the world of domestic air travel within France. **Air France** (© **800/237-2747;** www.airfrance.com) serves about eight cities in France. Airfares tend to be much higher than for comparable distances in the United States, and discounts are few. Air travel time from Paris to most anywhere in France is about an hour.

By Train

Rail services between the large cities of Languedoc-Roussillon and Provence and the French Riviera are excellent. If you don't have a car, you can tour all the major hot spots by train. Of course, with a car you can also explore the hidden villages, such as the little Riviera hill towns, but for short visits with only major stopovers on your itinerary, such as Nice and Avignon, the train should suffice. Service is fast and frequent.

The major train hub for Languedoc is the city of Toulouse, which has frequent service from Paris and Lyon. Toulouse is also linked to Marseille by 11 trains every day. Montpellier is another major transportation hub for the Languedoc-Roussillon area. Eleven high-speed TGVs arrive daily from Paris, taking just 3½ hours. Montpellier also has good rail connections to Avignon. The ancient city of Nîmes, one of the most visited in the area, also is a major rail terminus, a stop on the rail link between Bordeaux and Marseille.

Marseille, the largest city in the south of France, has rail connections with all major towns on the Riviera as well as with the rest of France. Seventeen high-speed TGVs arrive from Paris daily (trip time: 3 hr. 15 min.).

The major rail transportation hub along the French Riviera is Nice, although Cannes also enjoys good train connections. Nice and Monaco are linked by frequent service, and in summer about eight trains per day connect Nice with the rapid TGV train from Paris to Marseille. In winter, the schedule is curtailed depending on demand.

The most visited Riviera destination in the east, Monaco also has excellent rail links along the Riviera.

The website for the national rail service is **www.voyages-sncf.com**. Otherwise, call ✆ **36-35,** or **08-92-35-35-35** when outside France.

4 MONEY & COSTS

France, and especially the Riviera, is one of the world's most expensive destinations. But, to compensate, it often offers top-value food and lodging. Part of the problem is the value-added tax (VAT—called TVA in France), which tacks between 6% and 33% onto everything.

It's best to exchange currency or traveler's checks at a bank, not a currency exchange desk, hotel, or shop.

CURRENCY

The **euro,** the single European currency, became the official currency of France and 11 other participating countries on January 1, 1999. The old currency, the French franc, disappeared into history on March 1, 2002, replaced by the euro, whose official abbreviation is EUR. Exchange rates of participating countries are locked into a common currency fluctuating against the dollar.

The Value of the Euro vs. Other Popular Currencies

The Euro
The euro is the official currency of France.
The Euro and the U.S. Dollar: At the time of this writing, 1€ was worth approximately US$1.30. Inversely stated, US$1 was worth approximately 76 eurocents.
The Euro and the British Pound: At the time of this writing 1€ was worth approximately 90 pence. Inversely stated, £1 was worth approximately 1.11€.
The Euro and the Canadian Dollar: At the time of this writing, 1€ was worth approximately C$1.60. Inversely stated, C$1 was worth approximately 63 eurocents.
The Euro and the Australian Dollar: At the time of this writing, 1€ was worth approximately Aus$1.90. Inversely stated, Aus$1 equaled approximately 52 eurocents.
The Euro and the New Zealand Dollar: At the time of this writing, 1€ was worth approximately NZ$2.50. Inversely stated, NZ$1 equaled approximately 39 eurocents.

Euro	US$	UK£	C$	Aus$	NZ$
1	1.30	0.90	1.60	1.90	2.50

What Things Cost in Nice (Euros)

Taxi from airport to center of town	30.00–40.00
Bus ride within the center	1.00
Double room at Hotel Negresco (very expensive)	285.00
Double room at Hotel Hi (expensive)	239.00
Double room at Hotel Busby (moderate)	130.00
Double room at Flots d'Azur (inexpensive)	55.00
Lunch for one, no wine, at Restaurant Boccaccio (moderate)	40.00
Lunch for one, no wine, at Au Petit Gari (inexpensive)	13.00
Dinner for one, no wine, at Le Chantecler (very expensive)	90.00
Dinner for one, no wine, at Don Camillo (expensive)	60.00
Dinner for one, no wine, at L'Ane Rouge (moderate)	38.00
Dinner for one, no wine, at Café de Turin (inexpensive)	24.00
Glass of wine in a cafe	4.00
Glass of soda in a cafe	3.40
Cup of espresso	3.00
Admission to Museum Matisse	Free
Movie ticket	12.00
Opéra de Nice	8.00–120.00

Frommer's lists exact prices in the local currency. The currency conversions quoted above were correct at press time. However, rates fluctuate, so before departing consult a currency exchange website such as **www.oanda.com/convert/classic** to check up-to-the-minute rates.

ATMS

The easiest and best way to get cash away from home is from an ATM (automated teller machine), sometimes referred to as a "cash machine" or a "cashpoint." The **Cirrus** (© **800/424-7787;** www.mastercard.com) and **PLUS** (© **800/843-7587;** www.visa.com) networks span the globe. Go to your bank card's website to find ATM locations at your destination. Be sure you know your personal identification number (PIN) and your daily withdrawal limit before you depart. *Note:* Many banks impose a fee every time you use a card at another bank's ATM, and

that fee can be higher for international transactions (up to $5 or more) than for domestic ones (where they're rarely more than $2). In addition, the bank from which you withdraw cash may charge its own fee. For international withdrawal fees, ask your bank.

Note: Banks that are members of the **Global ATM Alliance** charge no transaction fees for cash withdrawals at other Alliance member ATMs; these include Bank of America, Scotiabank (Canada, Caribbean, and Mexico), Barclays (U.K. and parts of Africa), and Deutsche Bank (Germany, Poland, Spain, and Italy), and BNP Paribas (France).

CREDIT CARDS

Credit cards are another safe way to carry money and they generally offer relatively good exchange rates. You can withdraw cash advances from your credit cards at banks or ATMs but high fees make credit

> ## Tips How to Get Your VAT Refund
>
> French sales tax, or **VAT (value-added tax),** is now a hefty 19.6%, but you can get most of that back if you spend 175€ or more at any participating retailer. The name of the refund is *détaxe,* meaning exactly what it says. You never really get the full 19.6% back, but you can come close.
>
> After you spend the required minimum amount, ask for your détaxe papers; fill out the forms before you arrive at the airport and allow at least half an hour for standing in line. All refunds are processed at the final point of departure from the E.U., so if you're going to another E.U. country, apply for the refund there.
>
> If you're considering a major purchase, especially one that falls between 175€ and 304€, ask the store policy before you get too involved—or be willing to waive your right to the refund.

card cash advances a pricey way to get cash. Keep in mind that you'll pay interest from the moment of your withdrawal, even if you pay your monthly bills on time. Also, note that many banks now assess a 1% to 3% "transaction fee" on **all** charges you incur abroad (whether you're using the local currency or your native currency).

5 HEALTH

STAYING HEALTHY
In general, France is viewed as a "safe" destination. You don't need to get shots, most food is safe, and the water is potable. It is easy to get a prescription filled in French towns and cities; Provence and the Riviera have some of the best medical facilities in Europe, and finding an English-speaking doctor is generally no problem in most of the top resorts of the Riviera or major cities in Provence such as Avignon.

If you get sick, consider asking your hotel concierge to recommend a local doctor—even his or her own. Also try the emergency room at a local hospital; many have walk-in clinics for emergency cases that are not life-threatening. You might not get immediate attention, but you won't pay the high price of an emergency room visit.

Contact the **International Association for Medical Assistance to Travelers** (**IAMAT;** © **716/754-4883** or, in Canada, 416/652-0137; www.iamat.org) for tips on travel and health concerns in the countries you're visiting, and for lists of local, English-speaking doctors. The United States **Centers for Disease Control and Prevention** (© **800/232-4636;** www.cdc.gov) provides up-to-date information on health hazards by region or country and offers tips on food safety. **Travel Health Online** (www.tripprep.com), sponsored by a consortium of travel medicine practitioners, may also offer helpful advice on traveling abroad. You can find listings of reliable medical clinics overseas at the **International Society of Travel Medicine** (www.istm.org).

The following government websites offer up-to-date health-related travel advice:

- **Australia:** www.smartraveller.gov.au
- **Canada:** www.hc-sc.gc.ca
- **U.K.:** www.nathnac.org
- **U.S.:** www.cdc.gov/travel

What to Do if You Get Sick Away from Home

For travel abroad, you may have to pay all medical costs upfront and be reimbursed later. Medicare and Medicaid do not provide coverage for medical costs outside the U.S. Before leaving home, find out what medical services your health insurance covers. To protect yourself, consider buying medical travel insurance (see "Insurance" in chapter 9).

U.K. nationals will need a **European Health Insurance Card (EHIC; ℂ 0845/** 605-0707; www.ehic.org.uk) to receive free or reduced-costs health benefits during a visit to a European Economic Area (EEA) country (European Union countries plus Iceland, Liechtenstein, and Norway) or Switzerland.

We list **hospitals** and **emergency numbers** in chapter 9.

If you suffer from a chronic illness, consult your doctor before your departure. Pack **prescription medications** in your carry-on luggage and carry them in their original containers, with pharmacy labels—otherwise they won't make it through airport security. Carry the generic name of prescription medicines, in case a local pharmacist is unfamiliar with the brand name.

6 SAFETY

Criminals frequent tourist attractions such as museums, monuments, restaurants, hotels, beaches, trains, train stations, airports, and subways. Americans in Provence and Monaco should be particularly alert to pickpockets in train stations and on public transportation. Purse snatching and pickpocketing occur throughout the south of France. Passports should be carried on the body when necessary, and over-the-shoulder bags should not be used.

Crimes involving vehicles with nonlocal license plates are common. Thefts from cars stopped at red lights are also common, particularly in the Nice-Antibes-Cannes area and in Marseille. Car doors should be kept locked at all times while traveling to prevent incidents of "snatch and grab" thefts. In this type of scenario, the thief is usually a passenger on a motorcycle. Similar incidents have also occurred at tollbooths and rest areas. Special caution is advised when entering and exiting the car because that offers opportunity for purse-snatchings. There have also been a number of thefts at Nice Airport, particularly at car-rental parking lots where bags have been snatched as drivers have been loading luggage into rental cars.

Break-ins of parked cars are also frequent. Locking valuables in the trunk is not a safeguard. Valuables should not be left unattended in a car.

The loss or theft of a passport should be reported immediately to local police and your nearest embassy or consulate, where you can obtain information about passport replacement.

7 SPECIALIZED TRAVEL RESOURCES

GAY & LESBIAN TRAVELERS

France is one of the world's most tolerant countries toward gays and lesbians, and no special laws discriminate against them. "The Gay Riviera" boasts a large gay population, with dozens of gay clubs and restaurants.

3

Gay Provence, 42 rue du Coq, Marseille (© 04-91-84-08-96; www.gay-provence.org), is operated by a group of gays and lesbians, each native to Provence, who offer tours to American and European gays and lesbians. Various activities can be preplanned or customized according to interests, and tours range from 1 day to 1 week. Participants are welcomed into the private homes of gay or gay-friendly locals—perhaps a cheese brunch at a goat farm or an evening in a private 18th-century castle. Attractions include such outdoor excursions as hiking, biking, or horseback riding, or cultural activities such as Mediterranean cooking lessons or meetings with artists and artisans.

The **International Gay & Lesbian Travel Association (IGLTA;** © **800/448-8550** or 954/776-2626; www.iglta.org) is the trade association for the gay and lesbian travel industry, and offers an online directory of gay- and lesbian-friendly travel businesses.

Many agencies offer tours and travel itineraries specifically for gay and lesbian travelers. **Above and Beyond Tours** (© **800/397-2681;** www.abovebeyond tours.com) are gay Australian tour specialists. **Now, Voyager** (© **800/255-6951;** www.nowvoyager.com) is a well-known San Francisco–based gay-owned and operated travel service. **Olivia Cruises & Resorts** (© **800/631-6277;** www.olivia. com) charters entire resorts and ships for exclusive lesbian vacations and offers smaller group experiences for both gay and lesbian travelers.

Gay.com Travel (© **415/644-8044;** www.gay.com/travel or www.outandabout. com), is an excellent online successor to the popular *Out & About* print magazine. It provides regularly updated information about gay-owned, gay-oriented, and gay-friendly lodging, dining, sightseeing, nightlife, and shopping establishments in every important destination worldwide. British travelers should click on the "Travel" link at **www.gay.com** for advice and gay-friendly trip ideas.

The Canadian website **GayTraveler** (**gaytraveler.ca**) offers ideas and advice for gay travel all over the world.

The following travel guides are available at many bookstores, or you can order them from any online bookseller: *Spartacus International Gay Guide, 35th Edition* (Bruno Gmünder Verlag; www. spartacusworld.com/gayguide) and *Odysseus: The International Gay Travel Planner, 17th Edition* (www.odyusa. com); and the *Damron* guides (www. damron.com), with separate, annual books for gay men and lesbians.

TRAVELERS WITH DISABILITIES

Facilities for travelers with disabilities are above average in France, and nearly all modern hotels in the south of France now provide rooms designed for persons with disabilities. However, older hotels (unless they've been renovated) might not have elevators, special toilet facilities, or ramps for wheelchair access. Always ask before making a reservation.

The new high-speed **TGV trains** are wheelchair accessible; older trains have special compartments for wheelchair boarding. Guide dogs ride free. Be aware that some older stations don't have escalators or elevators.

Association des Paralysés de France, 17 bd. Auguste-Blanqui, 75013 Paris (© **01-40-78-69-66;** www.apf.asso.fr), is a privately funded organization that provides wheelchair-bound individuals with documentation, moral support, and travel ideas. In addition to the central Paris office, it maintains an office in each of the 90 *départements* of France and can help you find accessible hotels, transportation, sightseeing, house rentals, and (in some cases) companionship for paralyzed or partially paralyzed travelers. It's not, however, a travel agency.

Organizations that offer a vast range of resources and assistance to travelers with disabilities include **MossRehab** (𝄐 800/CALL-MOSS [2255-6677]; www.mossresourcenet.org); the **American Foundation for the Blind** (AFB; 𝄐 800/232-5463 or 212/502-7600; www.afb.org); and **SATH** (Society for Accessible Travel & Hospitality; 𝄐 212/447-7284; www.sath.org). **AirAmbulanceCard.com** is now partnered with SATH and allows you to preselect top-notch hospitals in case of an emergency.

Access-Able Travel Source (𝄐 303/232-2979; www.access-able.com) offers a comprehensive database on travel agents from around the world with experience in accessible travel; destination-specific access information; and links to such resources as service animals, equipment rentals, and access guides.

Many travel agencies offer customized tours and itineraries for travelers with disabilities. Among them are **Flying Wheels Travel** (𝄐 507/451-5005; www.flyingwheelstravel.com); and **Accessible Journeys** (𝄐 800/846-4537 or 610/521-0339; www.disabilitytravel.com).

Flying with Disability (www.flying-with-disability.org) is a comprehensive information source on airplane travel. **Avis Rent a Car** (𝄐 888/879-4273) has an "Avis Access" program that offers services for customers with special travel needs. These include specially outfitted vehicles with swivel seats, spinner knobs, and hand controls; mobility scooter rentals; and accessible bus service. Be sure to reserve well in advance.

Also check out the quarterly magazine *Emerging Horizons* (www.emerginghorizons.com), available by subscription ($16.95 per year in the U.S.; $21.95 outside the U.S.).

The "Accessible Travel" link at **Mobility-Advisor.com** (www.mobility-advisor.com) offers a variety of travel resources to persons with disabilities.

British travelers should contact **Holiday Care** (𝄐 0845-124-9971 in the U.K. only; www.holidaycare.org.uk) to access a wide range of travel information and resources for travelers with disabilities and for seniors.

MULTICULTURAL TRAVELERS

Since the days of the celebrated chanteuse Josephine Baker and, later, the author James Baldwin, France has welcomed African-American travelers. That welcome continues today. A good book on the subject is Tyler Stovall's *Paris Noir.* Another worthwhile resource is the website www.cafedelasoul.com.

Regrettably, anti-Semitism has been on the rise in Europe, especially in France, which has registered a significant increase in incidents against Jews. French Jews (not visitors from abroad) have suffered assaults and attacks against synagogues, cemeteries, schools, and other Jewish property. Officials say they believe that attacks in France are linked to the worsening of the Israeli-Palestinian conflict. Some sources—none official—recommend that travelers conceal Star of David jewelry and other such items to ensure personal safety while traveling in France.

Officially, the government of France welcomes Jewish visitors and promises a vigorous defense of their safety and concerns. The French Government Tourist Office website (www.franceguide.com) has a *FranceGuide for the Jewish Traveler* in the "Publications" section with more information.

SENIOR TRAVELERS

Many discounts are available for seniors—men and women of the "third age," as the French say.

At any rail station in France, seniors 60 and over (with proof of age) can get **A La Carte Senior.** The pass costs 53€ and is good for a 50% discount on unlimited rail travel throughout the year. The *carte* also offers reduced prices on some regional bus lines and half-price admission at state-owned museums. There are some restrictions—for example, you can't use it between 3pm Sunday and noon Monday or from noon Friday to noon Saturday.

Air France offers seniors a 10% reduction on its regular nonexcursion tariffs on travel within France. Some restrictions apply. Discounts of around 10% are offered to passengers 62 and over on selected Air France international flights. Be sure to ask for the discount when booking.

Members of **AARP** (© **888/687-2277;** www.aarp.org) get discounts on hotels, airfares, and car rentals. AARP offers members a wide range of benefits, including *AARP The Magazine* and a monthly newsletter. Anyone over 50 can join.

Many reliable agencies and organizations target the 50-plus market. **Elderhostel** (© **800/454-5768;** www.elderhostel.org) arranges study programs for those 55 and over (and a spouse or companion of any age). Most courses last 5 to 7 days in the United States and 2 to 4 weeks abroad, and many include airfare, accommodations in university dormitories or modest inns, meals, and tuition. **ElderTreks** (© **800/741-7956;** www.eldertreks.com) offers small-group tours to off-the-beaten-path or adventure travel locations, restricted to travelers 50 and older.

Recommended publications offering travel resources and discounts for seniors include the quarterly magazine *Travel 50 & Beyond* (www.travel50andbeyond.com) and the paperback *Unbelievably Good Deals and Great Adventures That You Absolutely Can't Get Unless You're Over 50 2005–2006, 16th Edition* (McGraw-Hill), by Joann Rattner Heilman.

8 SUSTAINABLE TOURISM

For information on low-impact activities such as hiking, boating, and biking, see "Special Interest Trips," later in this chapter. **Earthwatch** is an international organization that engages in field research to promote a sustainable environment. Some of their programs feature Provence. The group sets up biking tours through the most scenic parts of Provence, going through meadows, woods, hills, and vineyards, especially those rich in bird life or animal life.

For information about how to participate, you can contact **Earthwatch Institute** at 3 Clock Tower Place, Ste. 100, Box 75 Maynard, MA 01754 (© **800/776-0188;** www.earthwatch.org).

Much of Provence, especially the Riviera, is horribly overbuilt. But if it's a natural setting and wildlife you seek, there are places that offer an escape, especially **Montagne du Lubéron,** a mountain chain reaching a peak of 1,125m (3,690 ft.). If you'd like to explore these unspoiled spaces with tiny villages, you can anchor in at **Bonnieux** (p. 177) or **Roussillon** (p. 175).

9 SPECIAL INTEREST TRIPS & ESCORTED GENERAL-INTEREST TOURS

SPECIAL INTEREST TRIPS

Before the advent of the railways, many of the crops, building supplies, raw materials, and other products that sustained France were barged through a series of rivers, canals, and estuaries. Many of these are still graced with their old-fashioned locks and pumps, allowing shallow-draft barges easy passage through idyllic countryside.

Le Boat, 980 Awald Rd., Annapolis, MD 21403 (© **800/992-0291** or 410/972-3008; www.leboat.com), focuses on regions of France not covered by many other barge operators. The company's trio of barges are luxury craft of a size and shape that fit through the relatively narrow canals and locks of the Camargue, Languedoc, and Provence. Each 6-night tour accommodates no more than 10 passengers in five cabins outfitted with mahogany and brass, plus meals prepared by a *cordon bleu* chef. Prices depend on many factors and are highly variable, but call for information.

ACADEMIC & LANGUAGE TRIPS

A clearinghouse for information on French-language schools is **Lingua Service Worldwide,** 42 Artillery Rd., Woodbury, CT 06798 (© **800/394-5327** or 203/263/6294; www.linguaserviceworldwide.com). Its programs cover Antibes, Aix-en-Provence, Avignon, Cannes, Juan-les-Pins, Montpellier, and Nice. Courses can be long- or short-term, the latter with 20 **language lessons** per week. They range from $708 to $1,890 for 2 weeks, depending on the city, the school, and the accommodations.

ADVENTURE & WELLNESS TRIPS

BICYCLING   A well-recommended company since 1979 is the California-based **Backroads,** 801 Cedar St., Berkeley, CA 94710 (© **800/462-2848** or 510/527-1555; www.backroads.com). Its well-organized tours of Provence last between 6 and 8 days and include stays in everything from Relais & Châteaux hotels to campgrounds where staff members prepare meals featuring local cuisine. All tours include an accompanying vehicle that provides liquid refreshments and assists in the event of breakdowns. A 6-day tour

starts at $2,798 and an 8-day tour starts at $4,798 per person.

Euro-Bike & Walking Tours, P.O. Box 990, DeKalb, IL 60115 (© **800/321-6060** or 815/758-8851; www.eurobike.com), offers 11-day tours in Provence ($3,250–$4,340 per person), and 7-day tours of Provence ($2,295–$3,395 per person). All are escorted and include room, breakfast, and dinner.

If you're interested in bicycling through selected regions of the south of France, the local tourist offices of each of the towns covered in this guide are, to an increasing degree, able to provide addresses, maps, and contacts for whatever a cyclist might need. In many cases, bikes can be rented within railway stations of any given town. For general advice on biking in France, contact the **Fédération Française du Cyclotourisme,** 12 rue Louis Bertrand, 94207 Paris (© **01-56-20-88-88;** www.ffct.org).

FISHING   The Mediterranean provides a variety of fish and fishing methods. You can line fish from the rocks along the coast or from small boats known as *pointu.* Local fishermen often take visitors along when fishing in the sea for tuna. The rivers provide sea trout, speckled trout, and silver eel, and the sandy shores of the Camargue offer the *tellina,* or sunset shell, which are small shellfish. For more information on regulations and access to fishing areas, contact the Comité Régional PACA de la Fédération Française des Pècheurs en Mer (© **05-59-31-00-73;** www.ffpm-national.com).

GOLF   The area around Bouches-du-Rhône has many fine golf courses, with seven 18-hole courses, five 9-hole courses, and several practice courses in the Provence area. One excellent 18-hole course is **Golf de Marseille la Salette,** impasse des Vaudrans, 13011 Marseille (© **04-91-27-12-16;** www.opengolfclub.com). One of the finest courses is **Golf de Valcros,** La

Londe-Les Maures, 37km (23 miles) east of Toulouse off N98. Call © **04-94-66-81-02** for more information.

Golf International, Inc., 14 E. 38th St., New York, NY 10016 (© **800/833-1389** or 212/986-9176; www.golf international.com), offers the Golfing Epicurean package: a weeklong trip based in the historic hilltop village of Mougins, a 10-minute drive from Cannes. Mougins is the golfing capital of southern France and provides a wealth of fine dining opportunities. As part of this package, you spend 6 nights at the luxurious Les Mas Candille, a 200-year-old converted farmhouse in the village. The price includes golf on four of the area's best courses: Royal Mougins, Cannes-Mougins, Valbonne, and Cannes-Mandelieu. Also included is a car rental with collision-damage waiver insurance and unlimited mileage. The cost is $2,885 to $3,485. Call the number above to request a copy of Golf International's *Complete Golfing Vacation Guide.*

For more information on the options available, contact the **Fédération Française de Golf,** 68 rue Anatole, 92300 Levallois-Perret (© **01-41-49-77-00;** www.ffg.org).

HIKING The Bouches-du-Rhône area is a walker's heaven, whether you enjoy a stroll or a strenuous long-distance hike or even mountain climbing. Walking challenges include the wetlands of the Camargue, the semiarid desert of La Crau, and the mountainous hills to the wild rocky inlets of Les Calanques. Long-distance hiking paths, **Sentiers de Grande Randonnée** (GRs), join the area's major places of interest. GR6 starts in Tarascon, runs along the foot of the Lubéron Hills, and crosses the Alpilles Hills. GR9 goes down the Lubéron, passes Mont Ste-Victoire, and ends in Ste-Baume. GR98 is an alternative path linking Ste-Baume with Les Calanques and ends in Marseille. GR51 links Marseille and Arles via La Crau. GR99A links GR9 to the highlands of the Var *département.*

Spring and autumn are the best for hiking; many of the paths are closed in summer because of forest fires. Be sure to check with the *département* before you begin your walk. For information, call © 02-38-58-49-64; or **Comité Départmental Mont-Alp-Escalade (Bouches-du-Rhône Mountaineering & Climbing Committee),** Daniel Gorgeon, 5 impasse du Figuier, 13114 Puyloubier (© **04-42-66-35-05**).

Adventure Center, 1311 63rd St., Ste. 200, Emeryville, CA 94608 (© **800/228-8747** or 510/654-1879; www.adventure center.com), sponsors 8-day hiking/camping trips in Provence, beginning and ending in Nice. The cost of an outing, exclusive of airfare and other travel-related expenses, is $1,300 per person, 160€ of which is a local fee added in France. Included are 4 nights of campground accommodations. Eight evening meals are provided; the other seven lunches are usually purchased in Provençal restaurants along the way. Campers are also expected to purchase three lunches. The company offers 12 trips per year, and though dates might vary, these include departures from May to September.

HORSEBACK RIDING One of the best ways to see the wildlife, salt swamps, and marshlands of the Camargue or the wooded hills around Alpilles, Ste-Baume, and Mont Ste-Victoire is on horseback. For more information, contact **Manade Saliérène,** 13123 Arles (© **04-66-87-45-57;** www.manadesalierene.com) or the **Association Camarguaise de Tourisme Equestre (Camargue Equestrian Tourism Association),** Centre de Ginès-Pont de Gau, 13460 Stes-Maries-de-la-Mer (© **04-90-97-86-32;** www.parc-camargue.fr).

A clearinghouse for at least eight French stables is **Equitours** (The Soul of Provence), P.O. Box 807, Dubois, WY 82513 (© **800/545-0019** or 307/455-3363; www.ridingtours.com). It can arrange 8-day cross-country treks through Provence and the Camargue regions, with prices starting from $2,215 per person.

FOOD & WINE TRIPS

The **French Kitchen,** 5 Ledgewood Way, no. 6, Peabody, MA 01960 (© **800/852-2625;** www.thefrenchkitchen.com), presents **culinary vacations** where you stay in an 18th-century farmhouse (also the school) between Bordeaux and Toulouse. The price of a 6-day/5-night tour is 3,450€ per person, including lodging, cooking classes, most meals, touring, and local transportation. In addition, four people can charter a 26m (85-ft.) barge for a week of cooking, dining, and touring.

ESCORTED GENERAL-INTEREST TOURS

Escorted tours are structured group tours, with a group leader. The price usually includes everything from airfare to hotels, meals, tours, admission costs, and local transportation.

Despite the fact that escorted tours require big deposits and predetermine hotels, restaurants, and itineraries, many people derive security and peace of mind from the structure they offer. Escorted tours—whether they're navigated by bus, motorcoach, train, or boat—let travelers sit back and enjoy the trip without having to drive or worry about details. They take you to the maximum number of sights in the minimum amount of time with the least amount of hassle. They're particularly convenient for people with limited mobility and they can be a great way to make new friends.

On the downside, you'll have little opportunity for serendipitous interactions with locals. The tours can be jampacked with activities, leaving little room for individual sightseeing, whim, or adventure—plus they often focus on the heavily touristed sites, so you miss out on many a lesser-known gem.

BOOKING AN ESCORTED TOUR The two largest tour operators conducting escorted tours of France and Europe are **Globus + Cosmos Tours** (© 866/755-8581; www.globusandcosmos.com) and **Trafalgar** (© 866/854-0103; www.trafalgartours.com). Both companies have first-class tours that run about $300 a day and budget tours for about $100 a day. The differences are mainly in hotel location and the number of activities. There's little difference in the companies' services, so choose your tour based on the itinerary and preferred date of departure. Brochures are available at travel agencies, and all tours must be booked through travel agents.

Tauck World Discovery (© 800/788-7885; www.tauck.com) provides first-class, escorted coach grand tours of France as well as 1-week general tours of regions within France. Its 14-day tour of France covering the Normandy landing beaches, the Bayeux Tapestry, and Mont-St-Michel costs $4,990 per person, double occupancy (land only), while a 13-day trip beginning in Nice and ending in Paris costs $3,350 per person.

10 STAYING CONNECTED

TELEPHONES

To call France:

1. Dial the international access code: 011 from the U.S. and Canada; 00 from the U.K., Ireland, or New Zealand; or 0011 from Australia.

2. Dial the country code 33.

3. Dial the city code and then the number. Most of the numbers in this guide are prefaced with the city code of 04, which must be dialed.

For information on calling Monaco, see p. 334.

To make international calls: To make international calls from France, first dial 00 and then the country code (U.S. or Canada 1, U.K. 44, Ireland 353, Australia 61, New Zealand 64). Next you dial the area code and number. For example, if you wanted to call the British Embassy in Washington, D.C., you would dial 00-1-202/588-7800.

For directory and operator assistance: Dial 12 for assistance in French; in English, dial 0-800/364-775. For international inquiries, dial 08-36-59-32-12. This will link you with a bilingual (French and English) phone operator. You are allowed to request only two numbers for which you pay a service charge of 3€. However, if you wish to use an operator to call your home country, you dial the toll-free number of ✆ **08-00-99-00** plus the following 10 digits of your country code: 08-00-99-00-11 for the U.S. and Canada, and 08-00-99-00-44 for the U.K., or 08-00-99-00-61 for Australia. Other access numbers for long-distance operators include AT&T Direct (✆ **08-00-99-00-11** or 800/222-0300 for information) and MCI WorldPhone (✆ **08-00-99-00-19** or 800/444-4444 for information).

Toll-free numbers: For France, numbers beginning with 08 and followed by 00 are toll-free. But be careful. Numbers that begin with 08 followed by 36 carry a .35€ surcharge per minute.

CELLPHONES

The three letters that define much of the world's wireless capabilities are **GSM** (Global System for Mobile Communications), a big, seamless network that makes for easy cross-border cellphone use throughout Europe and dozens of other countries worldwide. In the U.S., T-Mobile, AT&T Wireless, and Cingular use this quasi-universal system; in Canada, Microcell and some Rogers customers are GSM, and all Europeans and most Australians use GSM. GSM phones function with a removable plastic SIM card, encoded with your phone number and account information. If your cellphone is on a GSM system, and you have a world-capable multiband phone such as many Sony Ericsson, Motorola, or Samsung models, you can make and receive calls across much of the globe. Just call your wireless operator and ask for "international roaming" to be activated on your account. Unfortunately, per-minute charges can be high—usually $1 to $1.50 in western Europe and up to $5 in places like Russia and Indonesia.

For many, **renting** a phone is a good idea. While you can rent a phone from any number of overseas sites, including kiosks at airports and at car-rental agencies, we suggest renting the phone before you leave home. North Americans can rent one before leaving home from **InTouch USA** (✆ **800/872-7626;** www.intouchglobal. com) or **RoadPost** (✆ **888/290-1616** or 905/272-5665; www.roadpost.com). InTouch will also, for free, advise you on whether your existing phone will work overseas.

Buying a phone can be economically attractive, as many nations have cheap prepaid phone systems. Once you arrive at your destination, stop by a local cellphone shop and get the cheapest package; you'll probably pay less than $100 for a phone and a starter calling card. Local calls may be as low as 10¢ per minute, and in many countries incoming calls are free.

INTERNET/E-MAIL

More and more hotels, resorts, airports, cafes, and retailers are going **Wi-Fi** (wireless fidelity), becoming "hotspots" that offer free high-speed Wi-Fi access or charge a small fee for usage. Most laptops sold today have built-in wireless capability. To find public Wi-Fi hotspots at your destination, go to **www.jiwire.com**; its Hotspot Finder holds the world's largest directory of public wireless hotspots.

The French government rates hotels on a one- to four-star system. One-star hotels are budget accommodations, two-star lodgings are quality tourist hotels, three stars go to first-class hotels, and four stars are reserved for deluxe accommodations. In some of the lower categories, the rooms might not have private bathrooms; instead, many have what the French call a *cabinet de toilette* (hot and cold running water and maybe a bidet). In such hotels, bathrooms are down the hall. Not all private bathrooms have a tub/shower combination; ask in advance if it matters to you. Nearly all hotels in France have central heating, but, in some cases, you might wish the owners would turn it up a little on a cold night.

RELAIS & CHÂTEAUX

Known worldwide, this organization of deluxe and first-class hostelries began in France for visitors seeking the ultimate in hotel living and dining in a traditional atmosphere. Relais & Châteaux establishments (there are about 150 in France) are former castles, abbeys, manor houses, and town houses converted into hostelries or inns and elegant hotels. All have a limited number of rooms, so reservations are imperative. Sometimes these owner-run establishments have pools and tennis courts. The Relais part of the organization refers to inns called *relais,* meaning "post house." These tend to be less luxurious than the châteaux but are often charming. Top-quality restaurants are *relais gourmands.* Throughout this guide, we've listed our favorite Relais & Châteaux, but there are many more.

For a catalog of member establishments, send 10€ to **Relais & Châteaux,** 11 E. 44th St., Ste. 707, New York, NY 10017, or download it free of charge on their website. For information and reservations, call ⓒ **800/735-2478,** or check out the website www.relaischateaux.com.

BED-AND-BREAKFASTS

Called *gîtes-chambres d'hôte* in France, these might be one or several bedrooms on a farm or in a village home. Many offer one main meal of the day as well (lunch or dinner).

At least 6,000 of these are listed with **La Maison des Gîtes de France et du Tourisme Vert,** 59 rue St-Lazare, 75439 Paris (ⓒ **01-49-70-75-75;** www.gites-de-france. fr). Sometimes these B&Bs aren't as simple as you might think: Instead of a bare-bones farm room, you might be in a mansion in the French countryside.

In the United States, a good source for this type of accommodations is the **French Experience,** 370 Lexington Ave., Room 511, New York, NY 10017 (ⓒ **800/283-7262** or 212/986-3800; www.french experience.com), which also rents furnished houses for as short a period as 1 week.

The best stateside agency is **Provence West,** P.O. Box 3146, Evergreen, CO 80439 (ⓒ **303/674-3726;** www.provence west.com). They have connections with some 120 of the best accommodations in the region. A 14-page booklet that describes the *gîte* experience is provided upon booking, with valuable tips including how to secure inexpensive car rentals. Another source is **France: Homestyle** (ⓒ 206/325-0132; www.francehome style.com), run by Claudette Hunt. These lodgings are a bit fancier than a typical bare-bones *gîte.* Her repertoire in Provence includes more than 300 properties.

CONDOS, VILLAS, HOUSES & APARTMENTS

If you can stay for at least a week and don't mind doing your own cooking and cleaning, you might want to rent long-term accommodations. The local French Tourist Board might help you obtain a list of agencies that offer this type of rental (which is popular at ski resorts). In France, one of the best groups of estate agents is the **Fédération Nationale des Agents Immobiliers,** 106 rue de l'Université, 75007 Paris (© **01-47-05-44-36;** www.fnpc.fr).

In the United States, **At Home Abroad, Inc.,** 163 Third Ave., Box 319, New York, NY 10003 (© **212/421-9165;** www.at homeabroadinc.com), specializes in villas on the French Riviera and in the Dordogne as well as places in the Provençal hill towns. Rentals are usually for 2 weeks. You'll receive photographs of the properties and a newsletter.

Barclay International Group, 3 School St., Glen Cove, NY 11542 (© **800/845-6636** or 516/364-0064; www.barclayweb.com), can give you access to about 3,000 apartments and villas throughout Languedoc, Provence, and the Riviera, ranging from modest modern units to those among the most stylish. Units rent from 1 night up to 6 months; all have color TVs and kitchenettes, and many have concierge staffs and lobby-level security. Incremental discounts are granted for a stay of 1 week or 3 weeks. Rentals must be prepaid in U.S. dollars or by a major U.S. credit or charge card.

HOTEL ASSOCIATIONS

For budget travelers wanting to trim costs might want to check out the **Mercure** chain, an organization of simple but clean and modern hotels offering attractive values throughout France. Even at the peak of the tourist season, a room at a Mercure in Provence rents for around $125 to $185 per night. For more information on Mercure hotels and a copy of a 100-page directory, call **ACCOR** at © **800/MERCURE [637-2873]** in the United States (www. accor.com).

Formule 1 hotels are bare-bones and basic though clean and safe, offering rooms for up to three at around $35 per night. Built from prefabricated units, these air-conditioned, soundproof hotels are shipped to a site and assembled. (Formule 1, a member of the French hotel giant Accor, also owns the Motel 6 chain in the U.S., to which Formule 1 bears a resemblance.)

Although you can make a reservation at any member of the Accor group through the RESINTER number (© **914/472-0370** in the U.S.), the chain finds that the low cost of Formule 1 makes it unprofitable and impractical to pre-reserve (from the U.S.) rooms in the Formule chain. So, you'll have to reserve your Formule 1 room on arrival in France. Be warned that Formule 1 properties have almost none of the Gallic charm for which some country inns are famous, but you can save money by planning your itinerary at Formule 1 properties. For a directory, contact **Formule 1/ETAP Hotels,** 6–8 rue du Bois Bernard, 91021 Evry CEDEX (© **01-69-36-75-00;** www.hotelformule1.com).

Other worthwhile economy bets, sometimes with a bit more charm, are the hotels and restaurants belonging to the **Fédération Nationale des Logis de France,** 83 av. d'Italie, 75013 Paris (© **01-45-84-83-84;** www.logis-de-france.fr). This is a marketing association of 3,828 hotels, usually simple country inns especially convenient for motorists, most rated one or two stars. The association publishes an annual directory. Copies are available for $25 from the **French Government Tourist Office,** 444 Madison Ave., 16th Floor, New York, NY 10022 (© **514/288-1904**).

At the most inexpensive end, **Hostelling International USA,** 8401 Colesville Rd., Silver Springs, MD 20910 (© **301/495-1240;** www.hiayh.org), offers a directory of low-cost accommodations and hostels around the country.

Suggested Provence & the Riviera Itineraries

If you have unlimited time, one of Europe's greatest pleasures is getting "lost" in Provence and the Riviera, wandering about at random, making new discoveries every day off the beaten path, finding charming towns you may never find on a typical itinerary.

But few of us have a generous amount of time. Vacations are getting shorter, and a "lean-and-mean" schedule is called for if you want to experience the best of any area in a short amount of time.

The south of France ranks with Germany in offering Europe's fastest and best-maintained superhighways, which help cut down on travel times. But part of the fun is to wander the secondary roads that

take you into the hill towns overlooking the Riviera.

Provence also has one of the fastest and most efficient public transportation systems in the world, especially the links along the national train system. For example, you can travel by rail from Paris to Nice in just 6½ hours—or fly much quicker, of course.

The itineraries that follow take you to such major attractions as the museums and beaches of Nice but also direct you to quaint hill towns such as St-Paul-de-Vence. The pace may be a bit brisk for some visitors, so skip a town or sight occasionally to enjoy some downtime—after all, you're on vacation.

1 THE REGIONS IN BRIEF

LANGUEDOC-ROUSSILLON Languedoc might be a less popular destination than Provence, but it's compelling all the same and is also less frenetic and more affordable. Much of its landscape, cuisine, and lifestyle is similar to that of neighboring Provence. **Roussillon** is the rock-strewn arid French answer to ancient Catalonia, just across the Spanish border, linked more to Barcelona than to Paris. The **Camargue** is the name given to the steaming marshy delta formed by two arms of the Rhône River. Rich in bird life, it's famous for its flat expanses of tough grasses and for such fortified medieval sites as **Aigues-Mortes.** Also appealing are **Toulouse,** the bustling pink capital of Languedoc; and the "red city" of **Albi,** birthplace of Toulouse-Lautrec. **Carcassonne,** a marvelously preserved walled city with fortifications begun around A.D. 500, is the region's highlight.

PROVENCE This legendary region flanks the Alps and the Italian border along its eastern end and incorporates a host of sites that have long been frequented by the rich and reclusive. It's a land of gnarled olive trees, cypresses, umbrella pines, almond groves, lavender fields, and countless vineyards. The western section is more like Italy, its Mediterranean neighbor, than like France. Premier destinations are **Aix-en-Provence,** associated with Cézanne; **Arles,** "the soul of Provence," captured so brilliantly by van Gogh; **Avignon,** once the capital of Christendom during the 14th century; and **Marseille,** a port city established by the ancient Phoenicians (in some ways more North African than

French). Special Provence gems are the small villages, such as **Les Baux, Gordes,** and **St-Rémy-de-Provence,** birthplace of Nostradamus.

THE COTE D'AZUR (FRENCH RIVIERA) The chain of glittering coastal towns along Provence's southern edge is known as the Azure Coast. Long a playground of the rich and famous, the Riviera has become hideously overbuilt and spoiled by tourism. Even so, the names of its resorts still ring with excitement and evoke glamour: **Cannes, St-Tropez, Cap d'Antibes, St-Jean-Cap-Ferrat.** July and August are the most crowded times, but spring and fall can be a delight. **Nice** is the most affordable base for exploring the area. The principality of **Monaco,** the fabled centerpiece of the Côte d'Azur, occupies less than a square mile. Don't expect sandy beaches—most are rocky. Topless bathing is common, especially in St-Tropez. Glitterati and eccentrics have always been attracted to this narrow strip of real estate, but so have dozens of artists and their patrons, who have left behind a landscape of world-class galleries and art museums.

2 PROVENCE IN 1 WEEK

The very title of this tour is a misnomer. You cannot see all of Provence in 1 week, merely a few of the highlights. But you can have a memorable vacation in Provence in 1 week if you budget your time carefully.

One week provides just enough time, although barely, to introduce yourself to the attractions of **Avignon** and its papal palace, with extra days spent in such towns as **Arles** to see its famous Roman monuments, and at **Les Baux,** the most dramatically situated town in Provence.

Still, in only a week, visits are also possible at **St-Rémy-de-Provence,** former retreat of Vincent van Gogh, and **Aix-en-Provence,** with its many memories and associations with Cézanne. Finally, you can cap the visit with a stopover in **Marseille,** the largest and most vital city in Provence.

Days ❶ & ❷: Avignon ★★★, Gateway to Provence

At the Gare de Lyon in Paris, you can hop aboard a TGV that will put you in Avignon in just 2 hours and 38 minutes. You can arrive in town for a late lunch.

In the capital of Provence, spend a leisurely afternoon wandering and getting to know the lay of the land in the Old Town. Perhaps you'll buy some colorful Provençal fabrics and see one of the sights, such as the **pont St-Bénézet** (also known as the Bridge of Avignon; p. 144). Before 6pm, duck into the **Cathédrale Notre-Dame des Doms** (p. 144) to see the Gothic tombs of the apostate popes. Order pre-dinner drinks at **Le Grand Café** (p. 150), our favorite

watering hole in Avignon, before enjoying a meal of typical *provençale* specialties that night. Plan to stay here for 2 nights.

The morning of **Day 2,** spend 2 hours touring the **Palais des Papes** (p. 142), which in the 14th century was the capital of Christendom, when the popes lived here during the so-called "Babylonian Captivity."

Before lunch, take a walk through **Quartier de La Balance** (p. 144), where local Gypsies lived in the 19th century. After a *provençale* lunch, try to catch some of the minor sights in the afternoon, notably **La Fondation Angladon-Dubrujeaud** (p. 144), with its splendid art collections, or the **Musée Calvet** (p. 144), with its collection of

ancient silver displayed in an 18th-century town house. If you can make it here before 6pm, you can also see the **Musée Lapidaire** (p. 145), with some of the most intriguing Gallo-Roman sculptures in Provence.

Day ❸: Arles ★★★, the Soul of Provence

On **Day 3,** in a rented car, leave Avignon and drive for 89km (55 miles) to Arles on the Rhône River. Plan to overnight here. You should arrive in time for a long walk through its Old Town that so enchanted van Gogh. Head for a cafe on **place du Forum,** site of the former Café de Nuit, immortalized in a van Gogh painting.

After lunch in a local restaurant, visit the town's two major sights. These include **Musée de l'Arles et de la Provence Antiques** (p. 156), with one of the world's best collections of Roman and Christian sarcophagi, and the **Théâtre Antique/ Amphithéâtre (Les Arènes;** p. 157), the ruins of a Roman theater begun by Augustus in the 1st century. If you have time before its 7pm summer closing, also visit **Les Alyscamps** (p. 156), one of the world's most famous necropolises. This is a burial ground of legend and lore, and was even mentioned in Dante's *Inferno.*

Day ❹: Les Baux ★★★, Nesting Place for Eagles

Leave Arles on **Day 4,** driving 19km (12 miles) to the mysterious little town of Les Baux in the southern Alpilles. It's known for its shadowy rock formations. After checking into a hotel, spend the day exploring the medieval village and its evocative ruins. If time remains, drive through the jagged and bleak **Val d'Enfer** (Valley of Hell; p. 164), stopping en route at the **Cathédrale d'Images** (p. 164).

Day ❺: St-Rémy-de-Provence

From Les Baux on **Day 5,** drive 25km (16 miles) northeast to the little city of St.-Rémy-de-Provence, the former home of the famous French astrologer Nostradamus. This town of considerable charm—our favorite in Provence—was also a favorite retreat of van Gogh, who painted several notable works here, including *Cypresses.* Spend 2 hours before lunch exploring its Old Town.

In the afternoon, you can also visit the town's major attractions, including the **Glanum** (p. 168), with its ancient ruins; the **Musée Archéologique** (p. 182), with its Roman artifacts; and **Monastère de St-Paul-de-Mausolée** (p. 168), a 12th-century asylum made famous by van Gogh's paintings. Overnight in St-Rémy.

Day ❻: Aix-en-Provence

On the morning of **Day 6,** leave St-Rémy and continue southeast 75km (47 miles) to this university city. As you approach Aix, you may recognize some of the landscapes

from the paintings of Cézanne. After checking into a hotel, head immediately to **cours Mirabeau** (p. 188), the most beautiful main street in Europe. Have lunch in one of the sidewalk cafes lining the street. After lunch, visit the main attractions, including the **Atelier de Cézanne** (p. 188), the studio of the painter who founded cubism. Other attractions worth a look include **Cathédrale St-Sauveur** (p. 188) and the **Musée des Tapisseries** (p. 188) in a former archbishop's palace.

Day ❼: Marseille ★★★, Capital of Provence

For your final day in Provence, head to bustling Marseille, the second-largest city in France. It's a 31km (19-mile) drive south of Aix-en-Provence. After checking into a hotel, preferably one along the waterfront, spend 2 hours wandering the **Vieux Port** (p. 197), or Old Port, ducking in and out of its narrow streets. After lunch, enjoy your coffee at **La Canebière,** the main street of town (World War II GIs pronounced it "can of beer").

In the afternoon take a boat to the **Château d'If** (p. 199), an island that Alexandre Dumas used as a setting for his novel, *The Count of Monte Cristo.* If you return to Marseille in time, visit its **Musée Granet** (p. 188) and the **Basilique St-Victor** (p. 198), exploring its early medieval crypt. You must arrive, however, by 7pm. Overnight in Marseille, one of France's great transportation hubs, with numerous rail and plane connections.

3 THE RIVIERA IN 2 WEEKS

With 2 weeks to explore the Riviera, you aren't as rushed as you might have been with only a week for Provence. With more breathing time, you can traverse the Côte d'Azur beginning in the west at **St-Tropez,** hitting the high spots as you eventually make your way to **Menton** in the east on the border with Italy. Highlights include not only St-Tropez, but the chic resort of **Cannes,** bustling **Nice** (the capital of the Riviera), and even elegant **Monaco.**

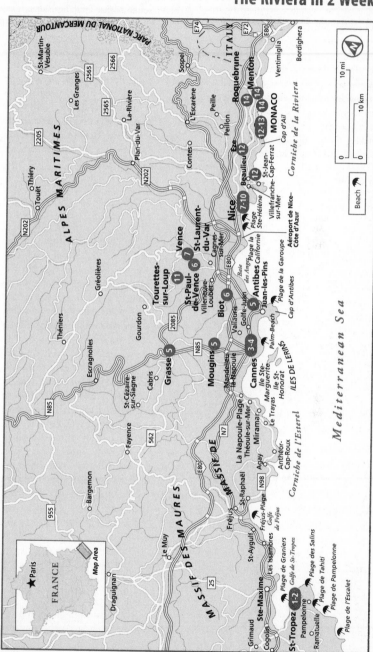

PARC NATIONAL DU MERCANTOUR

ITALY

ALPES MARITIMES

MASSIF DE L'ESTEREL

MASSIF DES MAURES

Mediterranean Sea

Corniche de la Riviera

Corniche de l'Esterel

FRANCE
★ Paris
Map Area

Beach ⛱

0   10 mi
0   10 km

St-Martin-Vésubie · Les Granges · Sospel · Menton 14 · Roquebrune 14 · Ventimiglia · Bordighera · L'Escarène · Peille · Peillon · MONACO 12-13 · Cap d'Ail · Èze 12 · Beaulieu 12 · St-Jean-Cap-Ferrat · Villefranche-sur-Mer · Plage Ste-Hélène · Nice 7-10 · Aéroport de Nice-Côte d'Azur · Contes · Plan-du-Var · La-Rivière · Thiéry · Touët · Théniers · Gréolières · Gourdon · Escragnolles · St-Cézaire-sur-Siagne · Cabris · Grasse 5 · Fayence · Bargemon · Le Muy · Draguignan · St-Aygulf · Fréjus · Fréjus-Plage · Golfe de Fréjus · St-Raphaël · Agay · Anthéor-Cap-Roux · Le Trayas · Miramar · Théoule-sur-Mer · La Napoule-Plage · Mandelieu-la-Napoule · Mougins 5 · Vallauris · Biot 6 · Villeneuve-Loubet · St-Laurent-du-Var · Cagnes-sur-Mer · Vence 7 · St-Paul-de-Vence 6 · Tourettes-sur-Loup 11 · Antibes 5 · Juan-les-Pins · Plage la Californie · Cap d'Antibes · Plage de la Garoupe · Golfe-Juan · Baie des Anges · Cannes 3-4 · Palm-Beach · Ile Ste-Marguerite · Ile St-Honorat · ÎLES DE LÉRINS · Ste-Maxime · Grimaud · Cogolin · St-Tropez 1-2 · Golfe de St-Tropez · Plage de Graniers · Pampelonne · Plage des Salins · Plage de Tahiti · Ramatuelle · Plage de Pampelonne · Plage de l'Escalet

You can take in the best of the beaches, but you may want to save some time to explore a few of the world's best galleries and museums of contemporary art. The Riviera has both in abundance.

Days ❶ & ❷: St-Tropez ★★, Gateway to the Riviera

Following in the footsteps of blonde goddess, actress Brigitte Bardot, you can arrive at the nearest rail station in St-Raphaël, making the rest of the journey to **St-Tropez** by boat or bus. For details, see p. 222.

St-Tropez is all about beaches, the best of which include the Plage de la Bouillabaisse or Plage des Graniers. Following a day at the beach, drop into **Le Café de Paris** (p. 345) for a pre-dinner drink and a look at the locals, the most colorful set of characters on the Riviera. Enjoy a long, lingering dinner and take a stroll along the harborfront at night, inspecting the fleet of yachts from all over the world.

On **Day 2,** before heading for another day at the beach—perhaps a different one this time—inspect the **Musée de l'Annonciade** (p. 225), the first of the modern art collections that opened on the Riviera in 1955. Do some boutique hopping before your descent on Plage de Tahiti, a favorite of exhibitionists. If you dare, wear next to nothing. Head to the harborfront in the center of town for your final night in St-Tropez.

Days ❸ & ❹: Cannes ★★★

On **Day 3,** drive east 86km (53 miles) along the coast to the Riviera's most fabled resort, chic, sophisticated Cannes, site of the famous International Film Festival. After checking into your hotel, take a long walk along the **promenade de la Croisette** (p. 249) to see what the excitement is all about. Find a waterfront restaurant for lunch and then head for the beach—the best one is **Plage de la Croisette,** extending between Vieux Port (Old Port) and Port Canto.

On the morning of **Day 4,** take a ferryboat trip to Ile Ste-Marguerite (p. 252), the most famous of the Lérins Islands, where the mysterious "Man in the Iron Mask" was held prisoner. You can spend all morning exploring the island and have lunch here. You can also visit the second major island, **Ile St-Honorat** (p. 253), with its Abbaye de St-Honorat, or else return to Cannes for another afternoon at the beach. If you're a gambler, you can patronize one of the resort's glittering casinos.

Day ❺: Grasse ★★, Mougins ★ & Antibes ★★

Leaving Cannes by rented car on the morning of **Day 5,** drive north 14km (9 miles) along N85 to Grasse, reached in only 20 minutes. This is the perfume capital of France, and you can visit its factories, or *parfumerie* in French. The best are **Fragonard** (p. 267) and **Molinard** (p. 267). Instead of lunching in Grasse, head back 8km (5 miles) on the road to Cannes but stopping off in the village of **Mougins,** which was a favorite spot for Picasso. The main reason for coming here is to order lunch, as Mougins has some of the best restaurants on the Riviera. Our recommendations begin on p. 270.

Heading back to the coast, follow the route into Antibes where you can spend the night. Picasso also lived here, as evidenced by the array of paintings he left to the **Musée Picasso** (p. 278), one of the greatest collections of his work.

After seeing the museum, drive along the chic **Cap d'Antibes** (p. 277) to see how the very rich live and have done so ever since F. Scott Fitzgerald dramatized the resort strip in his novel, *Tender Is the Night.* Overnight in Antibes and promenade along its port at night, finding a typical seafood bistro.

Day ⑥: Biot ★ & St-Paul-de-Vence ★★

Leaving Antibes in the morning, drive north 12km (7½ miles) to the town of Biot, which is celebrated for its beautiful pottery (our shopping recommendations begin on p. 283). While here, you can also visit the **Musée National Fernand-Léger** (p. 282), with the greatest collection of Léger's work in the world.

After a lunch in town, head northeast 10km (6 miles) for a night in the most famous hill town along the Riviera: **St-Paul-de-Vence.** After checking into your hotel, visit the **Fondation Maeght** (p. 287), the most famous—and the best—gallery of modern art on the Riviera, and actually one of Europe's finest such museums. Spend the late afternoon or early evening wandering the town's cobblestone streets.

Days ⑦ & ⑧: Vence ★ & Nice ★★★

On the morning of **Day 7,** drive 6km (4 miles) over to the neighboring hill town of Vence to see **Chapelle du Rosaire** (p. 292), the chapel that Henri Matisse designed and decorated between 1947 and 1951. He viewed it as his masterpiece. After an hour's visit, drive southeast 40km (25 miles) to Nice for a 3-night visit, part of which will be devoted to excursions.

After checking into a hotel, stroll through **Vieille Ville** (p. 300), the Old Town beginning at the foot of "the Rock." Enjoy a snack of *socca,* a round crepe made with chickpea flour that's sold steaming hot by street vendors.

Then head for the **promenade des Anglais** (p. 300), the wide boulevard along the waterfront. You can spend at least an hour strolling, perhaps stopping at one of the grand cafes bordering the water for a Niçoise lunch. In the afternoon, head for one of the beaches. Back in the Old Town for dinner, visit a typical bistro.

On **Day 8,** try to hit some of the major sights just beyond Nice. These include the two most important museums: **Musée d'Art Moderne et d'Art Contemporain** (p. 301), one of the best modern art museums in the region, and the **Musée des Beaux-Arts** (p. 188), the latter devoted to the masters of the Second Empire and the Belle Epoque era. For the remainder of the afternoon, head for the satellite village of **Cimiez** and try to visit the **Musée Matisse** (p. 302), seeing works by the master himself. Return to Nice for the night, taking in an opera, some casino play, or live music at one of Vieille Ville's many bars.

Day ⑨: Grande Corniche ★★★ & Moyenne Corniche ★★

On **Day 9,** while still based in Nice, head out for the grandest drive in the south of France, the **Grande Corniche** built by Napoleon in 1806. The trip of 32km (20 miles) takes about 3 hours of straight driving, although many motorists stop for a series of grand views, stretching the trip out to at least 5 hours.

From Nice, head east along avenue des Diables-Bleus. From points along the way, you can look down 450m (1,400 ft.) to Monaco. Highlights along the drive are panoramic views at **Vistaëro**—it's signposted—which lies 300m (1,000 ft.) above the sea. Another grand view can be seen at Eze Belvedere. The highest point along the Grande Corniche is **Trophée des Alps** (p. 328), a rock formation at 450m (1,500 ft.).

You can have lunch in **Menton** before returning to Nice along the **Moyenne Corniche** or Middle Corniche, stretching 31km (19 miles). This superhighway, built "between the wars," also runs from Nice to Menton and goes in and out of tunnels cut through mountains. Panoramic views, including some of Monaco, are possible to enjoy at many points along this grand highway. Return to Nice for the night.

Day ⑩: Villefranche-sur-Mer ★ & St-Jean-Cap-Ferrat ★

To save money because of its affordable hotels, you can still use Nice as your home base as you set out to see such highlights along the Riviera as Villefranche and St-Jean-Cap-Ferrat on **Day 10.** You can arrive at **Villefranche** after a 6km (4-mile) drive east of Nice. Walk its vaulted **rue Obscure** (p. 320) and visit its 14th-century Romanesque **Chapelle St-Pierre** (p. 320) with frescoes painted by Jean Cocteau.

By late morning after an hour or two in Villefranche, you can drive over to posh **St-Jean-Cap-Ferrat,** a 15km (9-mile) promontory that lies 10km (6 miles) east of Nice.

Here you will find one of the Côte d'Azur's most legendary villas, today the home of the art-stuffed **Musée Ile-de-France** (p. 322). Budget 2 hours for a visit and get in some beach time, perhaps at **Plage de Paloma,** before returning to Nice for the night.

Day ⑪: Exploring the Gorges du Loup

Again, with Nice as your hotel base, set out on **Day 11** to see some of the most dramatic scenery in the mountains above the Côte d'Azur by visiting **Gorges du Loup** (p. 291). You can take a 13km (8-mile) drive filled with dramatic scenery such as waterfalls, rock spurs, and decaying castles.

For lunch, aim for the town of **Tourrettes-sur-Loup** (coverage begins on p. 284), which lies 29km (18 miles) west of Nice. You can spend the afternoon here wandering its ancient streets and exploring more crafts studios than in any other town its size in Provence. The best of these are showcased along the **Grand'Rue.** Return to Nice in the afternoon, hopefully in time for the beach. Overnight in Nice before checking out the following day to head east.

Days ⑫ & ⑬: Beaulieu ★, Eze & Monaco ★★★

Leave Nice on **Day 12,** heading east along the Lower Corniche or Corniche Inférieure. First stop: the posh resort of **Beaulieu** at a distance of only 10km (6 miles) east of Nice (p. 297). The town opens onto the tranquil Baie des Fourmis, and you can walk its Boulevard Alsace-Lorraine lined with gardens. The seafront promenade is another idyllic place to stroll. The highlight of your visit will be **Villa Kérylos** (p. 324), a replica of an ancient Greek residence filled with art.

After a visit, continue along the coast to the village of **Eze,** lying 11km (7 miles) northeast of Nice. Here you can have lunch and explore the medieval core of this old town, which is filled with shops, artisan studios, and art galleries. Visit the **Jardin d'Eze** (p. 328), which features cacti and offers panoramic views of the eastern Riviera.

After a visit, continue east to the principality of **Monaco,** for a stopover of 2 nights. The location is 18km (11 miles) east of Nice. After checking into a hotel, head for **Le Café de Paris** (p. 345), the heart of local life. Perhaps you'll have dinner here.

On **Day 13,** set out to explore the attractions of this principality, perhaps witnessing the changing of the guard and visiting **Les Grands Appartements du Palais,** where Prince Albert rules the Monégasques. Allow 45 minutes or so to see **Jardin Exotique** (p. 335), filled with exotic plants. The other most visited attraction is the **Musée Océanographique de Monaco** (p. 338) whose name says it all. If time remains, take in **Prince Rainier III's Collection des Voitures Anciennes** (old automobiles; p. 335). Spend yet another night in the principality, walking its seafront promenades before dinner.

Day ⓮: Roquebrune ★★, Cap-Martin ★★ & Menton ★★

On **Day 14,** your final day on the Riviera, continue along the Lower Corniche until you come to the twin attractions of **Roquebrune** and **Cap-Martin.** Roquebrune is a hill village that you can explore in 1½ hours. Stroll its covered streets, which are filled with crafts studios, art galleries, and souvenir shops. The most evocative street is **rue Moncollet** (p. 348), dating from the 10th century. Head for a stopover at Cap-Martin, which lies 2km

(1½ miles) west of Roquebrune. After lunch, take one of the great walks along the Riviera, a 3-hour trek along a coastal path, **Sentier Touristique** (p. 349).

After that, make your way to **Menton** for the night, a distance of 8km (5 miles) east of Monaco. After checking into a hotel, wander its old fishing town, selecting a local bistro.

The following morning, drive back to Nice (26km/16 miles), the transportation hub of the Riviera.

4 PROVENCE & THE RIVIERA FOR FAMILIES

Provence and the Riviera offer many attractions that kids enjoy. Perhaps your main concern with having children along is pacing yourself with museum time. Our suggestion is to spend 2 days in Provence, exploring the two towns with the most appeal to families, **Avignon** and **Les Beaux,** before tackling the three big resorts of the Riviera: **St-Tropez, Cannes,** and **Nice.** Because its hotels are the most affordable on the Riviera, you can spend 3 nights in Nice, using the resort as a base for exploring the two hilltowns, **St-Paul-de-Vence** and **Vence,** with a final day reserved for **Monaco.**

Day ❶: Avignon ★★★, Gateway to Provence

The TGV (high-speed train) from Paris delivers you to the ancient papal city of Avignon in just 2 hours and 38 minutes. If you leave Paris early enough in the morning, you'll have a full day of sightseeing. First, head for the **pont St-Bénézet** (p. 144), the ancient bridge of Avignon, which inspired the nursery-room ditty, *"Sur le pont d'Avignon, l'on y danse, l'on y danse."* After a visit, take your family for a stroll through the Old Town of Avignon, followed by a 2-hour visit to the **Palais des Papes** (p. 142), the papal residence during the so-called period of "Babylonian Captivity," when a pope ruled in Avignon, as well as a rival pope in Rome.

After a lunch in the Old Town, take the kids to the **Musée Requien** (p. 145) for a visit to its herbarium with some 200,000

specimens gathered by botanists from around the globe. Spend the rest of the afternoon wandering around the village of **Villeneuve-lèz-Avignon** (p. 140) across the Rhône.

Day ❷: Les Baux

On **Day 2,** in a rented car from Avignon, drive southwest to Les Baux where you can check into a hotel for the night. This bare rock spur, with ravines on each side, is fascinating to explore. You can wander at leisure, visiting the ruins of a fortified castle, even exploring the "ghost village" (often called "the dead village"). After lunch you can drive into the surrounding area, exploring the gorge **Val d'Enfer** or "Valley of Hell" (p. 164). Plan a stop at the **Cathédrale d'Images** (p. 164), which always fascinates kids. Return to Les Baux for the evening.

4

Day ❸: St-Tropez ★★★, Gateway to the Riviera

From Les Baux drive southeast to the chic resort of **St-Tropez.** Although the world image of St-Tropez is that of a decadent adult retreat, many French parents with children also vacation here. After checking into a hotel, head for the beach. The best sandy strips for families are those near town, including **Plage de la Bouillabaisse** and **Plage des Graniers.** You needn't return to town until later as you can enjoy lunch on the beach. After midafternoon, you can head back to the resort for a stroll along the yacht-clogged harbor and the waterfront. Overnight here.

Day ❹: Cannes

After driving east from St-Tropez to Cannes on **Day 4,** check into a hotel and go for a stroll along the **promenade de la Croisette,** bordering the harbor. This is one of the grandest walks on the Riviera. After lunch, take one of the ferryboats leaving from the harbor for an afternoon visit to **Ile Ste-Marguerite** (p. 252), where the famous prisoner in the iron mask was held. You can return to Cannes for some beach life at the **Plage de la Croisette** before heading back to your hotel and making dinner plans.

Day ❺: Nice ★★★, Capital of the Riviera

On **Day 5,** drive east from Cannes to this larger city, which has more of interest than any other town on the Riviera. It also makes the best place for exploring the hilltowns or the resorts to its immediate east, including Monaco. After checking into a hotel for 3 nights, take the kids on the **Train Touristique de Nice,** which will get them acquainted with the town. After a ride, take a long stroll along the **promenade des Anglais** (p. 300), the wide boulevard bordering the water, before heading into **Vieille Ville** (p. 300), or Old Town, for a lengthy stroll and a lunch at a typical Niçoise tavern. In the afternoon most kids will go along with you to visit Nice's two most important

museums: **Musée d'Art Moderne et d'Art Contemporain** (p. 301) and the **Musée des Beaux-Arts** (p. 188). If they absolutely refuse, then head for the beach.

Day ❻: St-Paul-de-Vence ★★ & Vence ★

While still based in Nice, on **Day 6,** head for the Riviera's most beautiful hilltown, **St-Paul-de-Vence,** 31km (19 miles) to the north. Kids will delight in spending the morning walking the streets of this historic hilltown, especially **rue Grande** (p. 287). After lunch, head to **Fondation Maeght** (p. 287). Even if your child isn't an art lover, this museum is so daringly avant-garde that there will be something of intrigue here.

In the afternoon, drive to Vence to visit the **Chapelle du Rosaire** (p. 292), the chapel that Henri Matisse viewed as his masterpiece. Spend the remaining part of the afternoon exploring the old streets of Vence before returning to Nice.

Day ❼: The Principality of Monaco ★★★

While still based in Nice, on **Day 7,** your final day for the Riviera, head east for a distance of only 18km (11 miles). The tiny little country of Monaco was largely put on the map when Grace Kelly married Prince Rainier and went to live in this fairy-tale kingdom by the sea. Kids delight in watching the **changing of the guard** at **Les Grands Appartements du Palais** (p. 335), where Prince Albert lives. After a visit, take them for a walk through the **Jardin Exotique** (p. 335), known for its cacti collection, before ordering lunch, perhaps at the **Le Café de Paris** (p. 345).

After lunch, you will still have time to visit the fascinating **Musée Océanographique de Monaco** (p. 338), filled with exotic creatures of the sea, as well as the **Collection des Voitures Anciennes** (p. 335, an antique-car collection).

Return to Nice for the night. Because it's the transportation hub of the Riviera, it will be relatively easy from here to get to where you are going next.

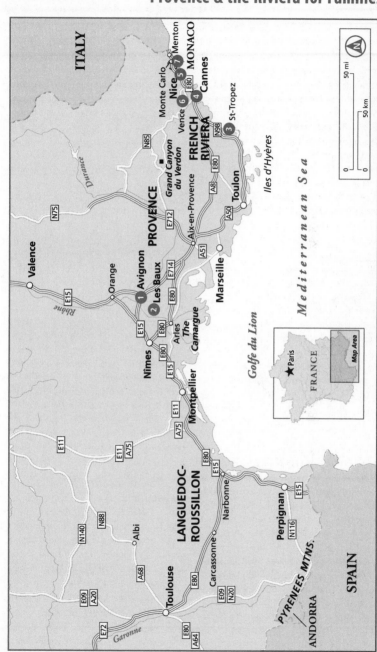

5 LANGUEDOC-ROUSSILLON & THE CAMARGUE IN 1 WEEK

The history-rich regions of **Languedoc, Roussillon,** and the **Camargue** comprise some of the most fascinating terrain in all of France. This region has not only world-class tourist meccas, including the walled city of **Carcassonne** and the ancient capital of **Toulouse,** but also the ancient university city of **Montpellier,** the capital of Mediterranean Languedoc, and the Roman city of **Nîmes,** with one of the best-preserved Roman amphitheaters in the world. Moving with a certain speed, you can take in the chief glories of these provinces in a week, with time enough to dip into the "cowboy country" of France, the Camargue.

Day ❶: Toulouse ★★★, Gateway to Languedoc

The fourth-largest city in France and the old capital of Languedoc, the cosmopolitan city of Toulouse can be reached by air, although most visitors from Paris take the high-speed TGV train, which arrives in Toulouse after only 5 hours.

After checking into a hotel for the night, you can spend 1½ hours exploring the **Basilique St-Sernin** (p. 78), the largest and best Romanesque church extant in Europe. Before lunch, you can also take in the **Cathédrale St-Etienne** (p. 80), Toulouse's other major ecclesiastical monument. After a lunch of some of the specialties of Southwest France, visit the best museum of Toulouse in the afternoon: **Musée des Augustins** (p. 80), a former monastery that today is the repository of splendid art, including some of the best works of old masters long associated with the southwest, including the incomparable Toulouse-Lautrec and Ingres. Allow at least 1½ hours for a visit. Another attraction you might fit into a comfortable afternoon is the **Eglise des Jacobins** (p. 81), a restored convent. Wind down at the end of the day by heading for **place Wilson,** a fabulous 19th-century square known for its fashionable cafes.

Day ❷: Albi, City of Toulouse-Lautrec

In a rented car from Toulouse on **Day 2,** head 76km (47 miles) to the "red city" of Albi on the banks of the River Tarn to see the world's greatest collection of the paintings of hometown boy Toulouse-Lautrec. After checking into a hotel, visit the **Musée Toulouse-Lautrec** (p. 93), allowing 1½ to 2 hours for a visit. Before lunch, you can also visit the town's towering monument, **Cathédrale Ste-Cécile** (p. 93), a cathedral from the 13th century that is fortified with ramparts and parapets. In the afternoon, you can visit the family seat of Toulouse-Lautrec, the **Château de Bosc** (p. 94) in Camjac, 46km (29 miles) from Toulouse. Getting there and back, as well as visiting the château, will eat up the rest of your afternoon. Overnight in Albi.

Day ❸: Carcassonne ★★★, the Walled City

You can leave Albi early in the morning of **Day 3,** making the 105km (65-mile) drive south to Carcassonne, the most heavily visited city in the southwest of France. It is the picture postcard of the Middle Ages. After checking into a hotel, set out to explore the walled city, walking its ramparts. This will occupy the rest of your morning and part of your afternoon. After lunch, you can visit the **Basilique**

St-Nazaire (p. 98) and **Château Comtal** (p. 98). Overnight in Carcassonne.

Day ❹: Narbonne ★ & Perpignan ★★

On **Day 4,** a busy two-city tour, you can drive 96km (60 miles) east of Carcassonne to medieval Narbonne, whose port rivaled Marseille in the days of the Romans. You can arrive early enough in the morning for a walk around its Old Town and a visit to its major monument, **Cathédrale St-Just** (p. 111). Before lunch you can also spend an hour wandering the **Palais des Archevêques.** Of the three museums in this complex, the one that merits attention is the **Musée Archéologique** (p. 182).

After lunch in Narbonne, continue to the ancient Catalonian city of Perpignan, 64km (40 miles) south of Narbonne. Check into a hotel here for the night. Walk around its historic core and visit **Castillet/Musée des Arts et Traditions Populaires Catalans** (p. 103) and the **Cathédrale St-Jean** (p. 104) from the late Middle Ages.

Day ❺: Montpellier ★★, Capital of Mediterranean Languedoc

On **Day 5,** you'll need to backtrack from Perpignan to Narbonne, taking the E15 and bypassing Narbonne to arrive in the ancient university city of Montpellier, 96km (60 miles) east of Narbonne. Check into a hotel for the night.

In what remains of the morning, wander through the **Jardin des Plantes** (p. 119) and pay a visit to the **Cathédrale St-Pierre** (p. 119), spending 1½ to 2 hours taking in one of France's greatest provincial art galleries. Allow time for a long stroll along the 17th-century **promenade de Peyrou,** one of the great terraced parks of southwest France, opening onto the Mediterranean. If time remains, stroll **place de la Comédie,** where you'll find some 120 boutiques selling unusual merchandise.

Day ❻: Nîmes ★★★ & Its Roman Monuments

On **Day 6,** from Montpellier drive 88km (55 miles) northeast to the ancient city of Nîmes, where you can check into a hotel for the night. Set out for a busy day of sightseeing, heading first for **Maison Carrée** (p. 126), one of the world's greatest Roman temples. You can also go to the **Amphithéâtre Romain** (p. 126), taking in the Roman amphitheater before lunch in a typical Nîmes restaurant.

In the afternoon, visit the **Carrée d'Art/ Musée d'Art Contemporain** (p. 126); walk through the beautiful gardens, **Jardin de la Fontaine** (p. 127), taking in views of its Roman ruins. Try also to visit the city's largest museum, **Musée des Beaux-Arts** (p. 188), with its mammoth collection of French painting and sculpture from the 17th century to modern times.

Day ❼: Arles ★★★ & the Camargue

On your final day, **Day 7,** set out in the morning to drive 32km (20 miles) southwest of Nîmes for a morning visit to Arles. Worthy of the trip are **Les Alyscamps** (p. 156), one of the world's most famous necropolises; and **Théâtre Antique/ Amphithéâtre** (p. 157), a Roman theater founded by Augustus in the 1st century and an ancient amphitheater. Have lunch in Arles.

In the afternoon, continue south to the Camargue, heading for the capital of the Camargue, **Aigues-Mortes,** a distance of 48km (30 miles) southwest of Nîmes. Called "the city of dead waters," Aigues-Mortes is France's most preserved walled town and makes a good hotel base for the night. Spend what remains of the afternoon exploring its ancient streets and touring its **ramparts** (p. 115). In the morning, journey to Marseille (139km/86 miles), where you can make rail or plane connections to anywhere in Europe.

Languedoc-Roussillon & the Camargue

Languedoc, one of southern France's great old provinces, is a loosely defined area encompassing such cities as Nîmes, Toulouse, and Carcassonne. It's one of France's leading wine-producing areas and is fabled for its art treasures.

The coast of Languedoc—from Montpellier to the Spanish frontier—might be called France's "second Mediterranean," with first place naturally going to the Côte d'Azur. A land of ancient cities and a generous sea, it's less spoiled than the Côte d'Azur. An almost-continuous strip of sand stretches west from the Rhône and curves snakelike toward the Pyrenees. Back in the days of de Gaulle, the government began an ambitious project to develop the Languedoc-Roussillon coastline that has since become a booming success, as the miles of sun-baking bodies in July and August testify.

Ancient **Roussillon** is a small region of greater Languedoc, forming the Pyrénées-Orientales *département*. It includes the towns of Perpignan and Collioure within its borders. This is the French Catalonia, inspired more by Barcelona in neighboring Spain than by remote Paris. Over its long and colorful history, it has known many rulers. Legally part of the French kingdom until 1258, it was surrendered to James I of Aragón, and until 1344 it was part of the ephemeral kingdom of Majorca, with Perpignan as the capital. By 1463, Roussillon was annexed to France again. Then Ferdinand of Aragón won it back, but by 1659 France had it once again. In spite of some local sentiment for reunion with the Catalans of Spain, France still firmly controls the land.

The **Camargue** encompasses a marshy delta between two arms of the Rhône. Arles serves as the area's northern border, and the village Sète functions as a gateway to the region. South of Arles is cattle country, and here strong wild black bulls are bred for the arenas of Arles and Nîmes. Cattle are herded by *gardiens*, French cowboys, who wear wide-brimmed black hats and ride graceful white horses, said to have been brought here by the Saracens. The whitewashed houses of the Camargue, plaited-straw roofs, pink flamingos that inhabit the muddy marshes, vast plains, endless stretches of sandbars—all this qualifies as "exotic" France.

1 TOULOUSE ★★★

705km (438 miles) SW of Paris; 245km (152 miles) SE of Bordeaux; 97km (60 miles) W of Carcassonne

As the old capital of Languedoc and France's fourth-largest city, Toulouse (known as *la ville en rose*, or the city in pink) is the major city of the southwest, and the gateway to the Pyrenees mountain range. It is an ancient city with a stormy history: Once it was the capital of the Visigoths and later the center of the *comtes de Toulouse* (counts of Toulouse). The city has 20 historic pipe organs, more than any other city in France, and hosts an annual international organ festival.

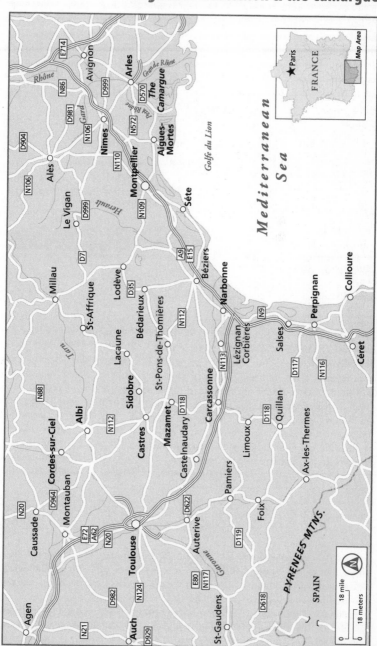

Complementing this distinguished history, Toulouse is also a city of the future and the high-tech center of the aerospace industry in France. It is home to two huge aircraft makers—Airbus and Aérospatiale—and the National Center for Space Research has been headquartered here for more than 3 decades. The first regularly scheduled airline flights from France took off from the local airport in the 1920s. Today long-range passenger planes of the Airbus consortium, the most important rivals in the world to Boeing, are assembled in a gargantuan hangar in the suburb of Colombiers. In 1997, Toulouse launched an air and space museum (see below for **La Cité de l'Espace**). The extraordinarily high population of students also contributes to the pulse of the city.

ESSENTIALS

GETTING THERE   The Toulouse-Blagnac international **airport** lies in the city's northwestern suburbs, 11km (6¾ miles) from the center. For flight information, call © **08-25-38-00-00. Air France** (© **08-20-80-28-02;** www.airfrance.com) has about 25 flights a day from Paris and flies to Toulouse from London twice a day.

Some four high-speed TGV **trains** per day arrive from Paris (trip time: 6 hr.; one-way fare: 85€), 14 from Bordeaux (trip time: 2–3 hr.; one-way fare: 32€), and 8 from Marseille (trip time: 4½ hr.; one-way fare: 52€). For information, call © **36-35,** or visit **www.voyages-sncf.com**.

The **bus station** is located at 68–70 bd. Pierre Sèmard. For information on bus routes, call © **05-61-61-67-67.**

The **drive** from Paris takes 6 to 7 hours. Take A10 south to Bordeaux, connecting to A62 to Toulouse. The Canal du Midi links many of the region's cities with Toulouse by waterway.

VISITOR INFORMATION   The **Office de Tourisme** is in the Donjon du Capitole in the Square de Gaulle (© **05-61-11-02-22;** fax 05-61-23-74-97; www.ot-toulouse.fr).

GETTING AROUND   Toulouse has the most efficient public transportation system of any city in southwestern France. The heart of the city, the historic core of most interest to visitors, is served by a modern and efficient Métro (subway) system administered by TISSEO Réseau urbain, 49 rue de Gironis (© **05-61-41-70-70;** www.tisseo-urbain.fr). The service operates daily from 5am to midnight (until 1am Fri–Sat), and tickets and maps are available at ticket booths. The average Métro fare is 1.40€ per ticket. The most useful stops, which are within walking distance of all the main attractions, are **Capitole, Jean Jaurès,** and **Esquirole.**

THE TOP ATTRACTIONS

Basilique St-Sernin ★★★   Consecrated in 1096, this is the largest and finest Romanesque church in Europe. One of its most outstanding features is the Porte Miègeville, opening onto the south aisle and decorated with 12th-century sculptures. The door into the south transept is the Porte des Comtes; its capitals depict the story of Lazarus. Nearby are the tombs of the *comtes de Toulouse.* Entering by the main west door, you can see the double side aisles that give the church five naves, an unusual feature in Romanesque architecture. An upper cloister forms a passageway around the interior. Look for the Romanesque capitals surmounting the columns.

In the axis of the basilica, in the ambulatory, 11th-century bas-reliefs depict *Christ in His Majesty.* The ambulatory leads to the crypt (ask the custodian for permission to enter), which contains the relics of 128 saints, plus a thorn said to be from the Crown of

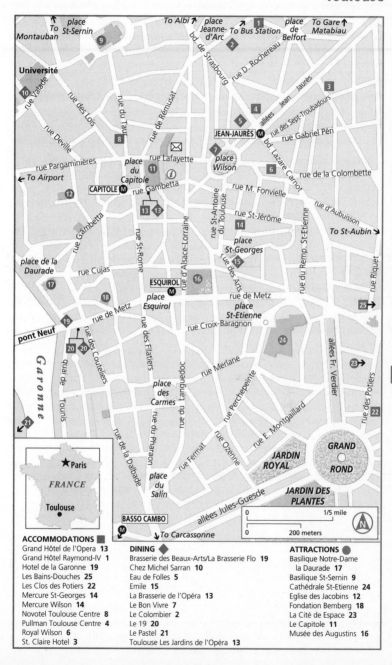

ACCOMMODATIONS ■
Grand Hôtel de l'Opera **13**
Grand Hôtel Raymond-IV **1**
Hotel de la Garonne **19**
Les Bains-Douches **25**
Les Clos des Potiers **22**
Mercure St-Georges **14**
Mercure Wilson **14**
Novotel Toulouse Centre **8**
Pullman Toulouse Centre **4**
Royal Wilson **6**
St. Claire Hotel **3**

DINING ◆
Brasserie des Beaux-Arts/La Brasserie Flo **19**
Chez Michel Sarran **10**
Eau de Folles **5**
Emile **15**
La Brasserie de l'Opéra **13**
Le Bon Vivre **7**
Le Colombier **2**
Le 19 **20**
Le Pastel **21**
Toulouse Les Jardins de l'Opéra **13**

ATTRACTIONS ●
Basilique Notre-Dame
la Daurade **17**
Basilique St-Sernin **9**
Cathédrale St-Etienne **24**
Eglise des Jacobins **12**
Fondation Bemberg **18**
La Cité de Espace **23**
Le Capitole **11**
Musée des Augustins **16**

Thorns. The old baroque retables (altarpieces) and shrine in the ambulatory have been reset; the relics here are those of the apostles and the first bishops of Toulouse.

Place St-Sernin. ✆ **05-61-21-70-18.** Free admission to church; combined admission to the crypt and ambulatory 2€. Church summer daily 8:30am–6:15pm; off season daily 8:30–11:45am and 2–5:45pm; no sightseeing during Sun morning Masses. Crypt and ambulatory summer daily 8:30am–5:45pm; off season Mon–Sat 10–11:30am, daily 2:30–5pm.

Cathédrale St-Etienne ★
Because it took so long to build (it was designed and constructed in the 11th–17th c.), some critics scorn this cathedral for its mishmash of styles. The rectangular bell tower is from the 16th century. A Gothic choir has been added to its unique ogival nave.

Place St-Etienne, at the eastern end of rue de Metz. ✆ **05-61-52-03-82.** Mon–Sat 8am–7pm; Sun 9am–7pm.

Fondation Bemberg
Opened in 1995, this quickly became one of the city's most important museums. Housed in the magnificent Hôtel Assézat (built in 1555), the museum offers an overview of 5 centuries of European art, with world-class paintings from the Renaissance to the late 19th century. The nucleus of the collection represents the lifelong work of German-French collector extraordinaire Georges Bemberg, who donated 331 works. The largest bequest was 28 paintings by Pierre Bonnard, including his *Moulin Rouge.* Bemberg also donated works by Pissarro, Matisse *(Vue d'Antibes),* and Monet, plus the fauves. The foundation also owns Canaletto's much-reproduced *Vue de Mestre.* The mansion houses the **Académie des Jeux-Floraux,** which since 1323 has presented literary awards in the form of wrought-metal flowers to poets.

Place d'Assézat, rue de Metz. ✆ **05-61-12-06-89.** www.fondation-bemberg.fr. Admission 4.60€ adults, 3€ students and children 8–18, free for children 7 and under. Tues–Wed and Fri–Sun 10am–12:30pm and 1:30–6pm; Thurs 10am–9pm.

La Cité de l'Espace ★ Kids
This is the place to go to learn about space exploration. Some half a million visitors a year come here to experience what it's like to program the launch of a satellite or how to maneuver one in space. You learn, for example, how easy it is to lose a satellite by putting on a burst of speed at the wrong point during a launch. Life-size structural models abound, including a model of an astronaut riding an exercise bike in zero gravity. On the grounds you can walk through a replica of Russia's Mir space station. The place is both a teaching tool and a lot of fun to visit. The top floor focuses on exploration of the universe, with close-ups from flybys of the moons of Jupiter.

Av. Jean Gonord. ✆ **08-20-37-72-23.** www.cite-espace.com. Admission 22€ adults, 13€ ages 5–15, free for children 4 and under; family tickets (2 adults, 2 children) 102€. July–Aug daily 9:30am–7pm; Sept–June Tues–Sun 9:30am–5pm (until 6pm Sat–Sun). Closed Jan. Bus: 37 (Sat–Sun only). Follow N126 from the center of town to the E. Peripheral route and take exit 17.

Musée des Augustins ★★
The museum was established in this convent in 1793, shortly after the French Revolution, when revolutionary acts closed the institution—then one of the city's most important monasteries—and adapted it for public use. In addition to the fabulous paintings, a stroll through allows you to view a 14th-century monastery in all of its mystical splendor. This museum's 14th-century cloisters contain the world's largest and most valuable collection of Romanesque capitals. The sculptures and carvings are magnificent, as well as the fine examples of early Christian sarcophagi. On the upper floors is a large painting collection, with works by Toulouse-Lautrec, Gérard, Delacroix, and Ingres. The museum also contains several portraits by Antoine Rivalz, a local artist and major talent.

21 rue de Metz. ✆ **05-61-22-21-82.** www.augustins.org. Admission 3€, free for children 11 and under. Wed 10am–9pm; Thurs–Mon 10am–6pm. Closed Jan 1, May 1, and Dec 25.

The Gothic brick **Eglise des Jacobins** ★★, parvis des Jacobins (✆ **05-61-22-21-92**), in Old Toulouse, is west of place du Capitole along rue Lakanal. The church and the restored convent, daring in its architecture and use of "palm tree"-shaped vaults, form the largest extant monastery complex in France. It's open daily 9am to 7pm. Admission to most of the complex is free, but a visit to the cloisters costs 3€ free for ages 17 and under.

Small, charming, and dating mostly from the 18th century, the **Notre-Dame La Daurade,** 1 place de la Daurade (✆ **05-61-21-38-32**), gets its name from the gilding that covers its partially baroque exterior. Its prize possession is a statue of the Black Virgin, about 1m (3¼ ft.) tall, to which some locals attribute quasi-mystical powers. The one you'll see today was crafted in 1807 as a replacement for a much older statue that was burned during the French Revolution. Admission is free, and the Basilique Notre-Dame is open daily 8:30am to 6:30pm.

In civic architecture, **Le Capitole** ★, place du Capitole (✆ **05-61-22-34-12**), is an outstanding achievement and one of the most potent symbols of Toulouse. Built in a baroque style in 1753, it houses the **Hôtel de Ville** (city hall) as well as the **Théâtre National du Capitole** (✆ **05-61-63-13-13**), which presents concerts, ballets, and operas. Renovated in 1996, it's outfitted in an Italian-inspired 18th-century style with shades of scarlet and gold. Admission, which usually includes a view of the theater, is free. The Capitole complex is open Monday to Saturday 9am to 5pm, and until 7pm during holidays.

After sightseeing, head for **place Wilson,** a showcase 19th-century square (actually an oval) lined with fashionable cafes.

SHOPPING

Head for **rue d'Alsace-Lorraine,** which is rich in clothing and housewares, or the well-stocked shopping mall, the **Centre Commercial St-Georges,** rue du Rempart St-Etienne. For upscale boutiques, stroll down **rue Croix-Baragnon, rue des Arts,** and **rue St-Antoine du T.** The pearly gates of antiques heaven are on **rue Fermat.** More down-market antiques spread out each Sunday from 6am to 1pm during the weekly **flea market** adjacent to the Basilique St-Sernin. In addition to that, in the same spot, a *brocante* sale takes place on the first weekend (Fri–Sun) of each month from 8am to 1pm.

Violets grow in abundance in meadows on the outskirts of Toulouse. Two shops that sell everything imaginable connected with violets include **Violettes & Pastels,** 10 rue St-Pantaléon (✆ **05-61-22-14-22;** www.violettesetpastels.com), and **Péniche Maison de la Violette,** 4 bd. Bonrepos (✆ **05-61-99-01-30;** www.lamaisondelaviolette.fr). Inventories include violet-scented perfume, and clothing—especially scarves—patterned with the dainty purple flower.

WHERE TO STAY
Expensive

Grand Hôtel de l'Opéra ★★★   This is the most elegant oasis in Toulouse, and the owners have won several prestigious awards for transforming this 17th-century convent into a sophisticated hotel. The public rooms contain early-19th-century antiques and Napoleonic-inspired tenting over the bars. Some of the spacious and stylish guest rooms have urn-shaped balustrades overlooking formal squares, and all have high ceilings and modern amenities. The beds are elegantly fitted in tasteful fabrics, with soft pillows, most richly refurbished in the early millennium. The hotel restaurants, **Toulouse-Les Jardins**

de l'Opéra (p. 85) and **La Brasserie de l'Opéra** (p. 86), are two classic venues for French cuisine.

1 place du Capitole, 31000 Toulouse. ✆ **05-61-21-82-66.** Fax 05-61-23-41-04. www.grand-hotel-opera. com. 57 units. 185€–330€ double; 390€–484€ suite. AE, DC, MC, V. Parking 14€. Métro: Capitole. **Amenities:** Restaurant; brasserie; room service; sauna and steam room. *In room:* A/C, TV, hair dryer, minibar, Wi-Fi (free).

Pullman Toulouse Centre ★★ (Kids)

Business travelers deem this hotel, built in 1989, as the best in town (though we prefer the Grand Hôtel de l'Opéra as the most tranquil retreat). Adjacent to place Wilson, this Pullman employs a charming bilingual staff and offers suites big enough to fit an entire family or serve as an office away from the office. The rooms are furnished in chain format.

84 allée Jean-Jaurès, 31000 Toulouse. ✆ **05-61-10-23-10.** Fax 05-61-10-23-20. www.pullmanhotels.com. 119 units. 1300€–350€ double; 145€–400€ suite. AE, DC, MC, V. Parking 17€. Métro: Jean-Jaurès. **Amenities:** Restaurant; bar; babysitting; health club; room service. *In room:* A/C, TV, hair dryer, Internet (free), minibar.

Moderate

Grand Hôtel Raymond-IV

On a quiet street close to the town center and the train station, this 19th-century red-brick building contains pleasant rooms with bland but comfortable furniture and restful beds. All of the individually decorated accommodations are different—some small, others rather grand—with a vaguely Art Deco motif. Breakfast is the only meal available, but the English-speaking staff can direct you to nearby restaurants.

16 rue Raymond-IV, 31000 Toulouse. ✆ **05-61-62-89-41.** Fax 05-61-62-38-01. www.grandhotel raymond4.com. 38 units. 90€–180€ double; 135€–200€ triple. AE, MC, V. Parking 10€. Métro: Jean-Jaurès or Capitole. **Amenities:** Bar; room service. *In room:* A/C, TV, hair dryer, minibar, Wi-Fi (free).

Hôtel de la Garonne ★★ (Finds)

One of the most delightful hotels of Toulouse—certainly the most tranquil—is this little charmer connected with **Le 19** (p. 84), a well-recommended restaurant. Midsize bedrooms are snug and cozy and outfitted in a dignified style, often incorporating tones of deep red and beige. Each comes with a well-equipped private bathroom. If you stay here, you get not only one of the finest rooms in Toulouse, but you can also enjoy one of the best meals in town. The restaurant itself lies directly opposite the hotel in a 16th-century building with a vaulted ceiling of red brick. You get elegance, charm, an affordable price, and a retreat right in the heart of the city.

22 Descente de la Halle aux Poissons, 31000 Toulouse. ✆ **05-34-31-94-80.** Fax 05-34-31-94-81. www. hotelgaronne.com. 14 units. 210€–290€ double; 310€ suite. Rates include breakfast Sat–Sun. AE, DC, MC, V. Parking 15€. Métro: Esquirol. **Amenities:** Restaurant; bar; room service. *In room:* A/C, TV, Internet (free).

Les Bains-Douches ★

This is the best boutique hotel in Toulouse, boasting an elegant cocktail lounge. Located in the historic district of Toulouse, the hotel is installed in an Art Deco style building and has been completely modernized. Its midsize bedrooms have bright colors, first-class fabrics and furnishings, and offer real comfort. A special feature is the hotel's charming patio.

4 & 4 bis, rue du Pont Guilheméry, 31000 Toulouse. ✆ **05-62-72-52-52.** Fax 05-34-42-09-98. www.hotel-bainsdouches.com. 22 units. 140€–210€ double; 280€–330€ suite. MC, V. Parking 12€. **Amenities:** Bar. *In room:* A/C, TV, Internet (free), minibar.

Mercure St-Georges

Just a few paces from the Mercure Wilson (see below; the two share staff and management), this seven-story hotel is the less historic twin of the older and cozier-looking hotel. Decor here is rigidly standardized—bedrooms are identical, though comfortably modern, with small, well-maintained bathrooms. Business travelers are the primary clientele at this location.

Rue St.-Jérome (place Occitaine), 31000 Toulouse. ℂ **05-62-27-79-79.** Fax 05-62-27-79-00. www.mercure.com. 148 units. 110€–170€ double; 210€–280€ suite. AE, DC, MC, V. Parking 17€. Métro: Capitole. **Amenities:** Bar; room service. *In room:* TV, hair dryer, minibar, Wi-Fi (10€).

Mercure Wilson ★ This is the more appealing of the two Mercure hotels that stand almost adjacent to each other in the heart of Toulouse's historic central zone. Built around 1850, this hotel is constructed of the distinctive pink-toned bricks cherished by local preservationists. Mercure has radically upgraded the hotel's interior, transforming it into one of the most up-to-date middle-bracket places in town. Most bedrooms are a comfortable size, and in spite of their chain format, furnishings are agreeable.

7 rue Labéda, 31000 Toulouse. ℂ **05-34-45-40-60.** Fax 05-34-45-40-61. www.mercure.com. 95 units. 125€–195€ double; 225€ family room for 2 adults and up to 2 children. AE, DC, MC, V. Parking 11€. Métro: Capitole. **Amenities:** Restaurant; bar; babysitting. *In room:* A/C, TV, hair dryer, minibar, Wi-Fi (10€ per 12 hr.).

Novotel Toulouse Centre Set in the most verdant part of Toulouse's center, this modern and efficient hotel is a few paces from the city's Japanese gardens, a 5-minute walk from the Matabiau train station, and less than a kilometer (½ mile) from the nerve center of the old city, place St-Sernin. All rooms have a single bed (which can be converted into a couch), a double bed, a long writing desk, and a roomy, fully equipped bathroom. In spite of the chain-style format, this is one of the best Novotel hotels, with larger than usual bedrooms.

5 place Alfonse-Jourdain, 31000 Toulouse. ℂ **05-61-21-74-74.** Fax 05-61-22-81-22. www.novotel.com. 70€–195€ double; 165€–250€ suite. AE, DC, MC, V. Parking 9€. Bus: 1 or 2. **Amenities:** Restaurant; bar; pool (outdoor); room service. *In room:* A/C, TV, hair dryer, Wi-Fi (free in executive rooms, 10€ per 12 hr. in other units).

Inexpensive

Le Clos des Potiers ★ (Value) This *hotel particulier* is installed in a restored mansion dating from the 1850s and standing in the center of Toulouse. It lies near St. Etienne Cathedral and the concert hall. Bedrooms are spacious and tranquil, furnished in a traditional style with elegant bathrooms. In its price range, it's one of the best deals in town.

12 rue des Poitiers, 31000 Toulouse. ℂ **05-61-47-15-15.** Fax 05-61-47-65-75. www.hotel-closdespoitiers. com. 11 units. 100€–125€ double; 150€–220€ suite. MC, V. Parking 10€. **Amenities:** Breakfast room. *In room:* TV, hair dryer, minibar, Wi-Fi (free).

Royal Wilson Set behind a rather formal stone facade, this historic building operates a government-rated two-star hotel in the heart of Toulouse's historic core, a 5-minute walk southwest of place Wilson. Inside, rooms radiate off a glassed-over interior courtyard that contains the touches of wrought-iron filigree that you come to expect in Spain. Bedrooms have high ceilings and, despite the prevalence of angular, not-particularly-distinctive furniture, still retain the relatively large proportions of the building's role as a well-heeled private home. The Royal has no restaurant or bar on-site, but options abound in the surrounding neighborhood. Staff here isn't as helpful or well-informed as that within the nearby competitor, the St-Claire Hotel (see below), but it's nonetheless a worthy and cost-effective choice.

6 rue Labéda, 31000 Toulouse. ℂ **05-61-12-41-41.** Fax 05-61-12-41-53. www.royal-wilson.com. 24 units. 51€–68€ double; 73€–88€ "family room" for 2 adults and up to 2 children. AE, MC, V. Parking 9€. Métro: Place Jean-Jaurès or Capitole. **Amenities:** Wi-Fi (free). *In room:* A/C (in most), TV, hair dryer.

LANGUEDOC-ROUSSILLON & THE CAMARGUE

5

TOULOUSE

St. Claire Hotel   Set in the heart of Toulouse's historic core, this is a well-recommended, government-rated, two-star hotel with few frills but a good location and a solid and comfortable presence. The hotel occupies a narrow, five-story town house whose foundations go back to the 15th century. The owners have brought in a simple collection of furniture, most of it painted in tones of cream and white, and positioned it according to the Chinese principles of feng shui. While you won't find a restaurant on-site, many bars and dining outlets are just a short walk away. The staff is well prepared to offer advice about attractions and diversions within the neighborhood.

29 place Nicolas Bachelier, 31000 Toulouse. ✆ **05-34-40-58-88.** Fax 05-61-57-85-89. www.stclairehotel. fr. 16 units. 82€–138€ double. AE, MC, V. Parking 7€. Métro: Place Jean-Jaurés. **Amenities:** Room service. *In room:* A/C, TV, fax, hair dryer, Wi-Fi (free).

WHERE TO DINE
Expensive

Chez Michel Sarran ★★★ MODERN FRENCH   At the most stylish restaurant in Toulouse you can enjoy the cuisine of master chef Michel Sarran. Sarran's wife, Françoise, oversees the three red, green, or violet dining rooms, on separate floors of a building near the Novotel Centre. The creative dishes have attracted diners as diverse as the prime minister of France and showbiz types such as Sophie Marceau and Gilbert Becaud. Start with a warm soup of foie gras and oysters, or perhaps a cup of organic yogurt studded with black truffles from the Périgord. Move on to a succulent version of poached sea bass served with a creamy polenta and lobster sauce; or perhaps a portion of roasted wild black boar from the underpopulated Bigorre region of France, served in a stewpot with thyme and wine-roasted potatoes. Dessert may include ravioli stuffed with creamed oranges and served with an aspic of sweet white Gaillac wine.

21 bd. Armand Duportal. ✆ **05-61-12-32-32.** www.michel-sarran.com. Reservations recommended. Main courses 36€–68€; fixed-price lunch 48€–125€; fixed-price dinner 98€–125€. AE, DC, MC, V. Mon–Fri noon–2pm and 8–9:45pm (closed Wed for lunch). Closed Aug and 1 week around Christmas. Métro: Capitole.

Le 19 ★ MODERN FRENCH   One of the city's finest restaurants is this high-profile, cellar restaurant affiliated with the **Hôtel de la Garonne** (p. 82). It's 19 steps down from the street, in the high-ceilinged cellar of a medieval building once used for the storage of fish and salt. Inside, wood panels and carpeting stand in contrast with its terra-cotta bricks. The delicate, creative menu changes with the seasons. Among delectable dishes are a terrine of deliberately undercooked foie gras, served with figs; cream of watercress soup with warm oysters; magret of duckling served with ginger and crushed apples; roasted shoulder of rabbit served in a stewpot, with polenta and baby vegetables; filet of baked red snapper with spider-crab sauce; and filet of curried duck breast with Asian-style vegetables. To end your meal, try a stir-fry of mandarin oranges flavored with balsamic vinegar, or saffron-flavored sabayon with ice cream made from unpasteurized milk.

19 descente de la Halle aux Poissons. ✆ **05-34-31-94-84.** www.restaurantle19.com. Reservations recommended. Main courses 20€–27€; fixed-price meals 19€–40€. AE, DC, MC, V. Tues–Fri noon–2pm; Mon–Sat 8–10:30pm. Métro: Esquirol.

Le Pastel ★★ FRENCH   One of the best restaurants in the area occupies a stone-sided manor house built around 1850. It lies 7 minutes southwest of the center by car, but within the city limits. Today it's the domain of Paris-trained chef and entrepreneur Gérard Garrigues. The setting is as restful as the cuisine is superb: Terraces ringed with flowers near an outdoor pergola and dining rooms accented with paintings by local artists contribute to the placidity. The menu changes every week. During our visit, it featured scallops "jubilatoire," roasted at very high temperatures with beef marrow, garlic, and balsamic vinegar; deliberately undercooked foie gras with a confit of quince and cornmeal brioche; roebuck with wine sauce and old-fashioned vegetables; and steak of sea bass with hearts of artichoke and truffled vinegar. Wine choices are as sophisticated as anything you'll find in Toulouse.

237 rte. de St-Simon. (C) **05-62-87-84-30.** Reservations required. Main courses 26€–43€; fixed-price lunch 29€–40€; fixed-price dinner 48€–98€. AE, DC, MC, V. Tues–Sat noon–2pm and 8–9:30pm. Métro: Basso–Cambo.

Toulouse-Les Jardins de l'Opéra ★★★ FRENCH   The entrance to the city's best restaurant is in the 18th-century Florentine courtyard of the **Grand Hôtel de l'Opéra** (p. 81). The dining area is a series of salons, several of which face a winter garden and a reflecting pool. A long-standing staple, praised by gastronomes, is ravioli stuffed with foie gras of duckling and served with essence of truffles. Equally appealing are carpaccio of lobster served with foie gras; tartare of sturgeon, mushrooms, and oysters; sautéed pikeperch with a gratinated crust of shredded coconut, vanilla-flavored citrus sauce, and a chiffonade of fruits, vegetables, and truffles; and spicy breast of pigeon with a "surprise" preparation of the bird's organs decorated with rosettes of zucchini. One of the most appealing desserts is figs poached in red Banyuls wine, stuffed with homemade vanilla ice cream.

In the Grand Hôtel de l'Opéra (p. 81), 1 place du Capitole. (C) **05-61-23-07-76.** www.lesjardinsdelopera. com. Reservations required. All main courses 42€; fixed-price lunch 29€–44€; fixed-price dinner 74€–110€. AE, DC, MC, V. Tues–Sat noon–2pm and 8–10pm. Closed Jan 1–17 and July 28–Aug 29. Métro: Capitole.

Moderate

Brasserie les Beaux-Arts/La Brasserie Flo TRADITIONAL FRENCH   This early-1900s brasserie has an authentic Art Nouveau interior that's been enhanced because of its connection with the Jean Bucher chain (the most successful director of Art Nouveau French brasseries in the world, some of which are classified as national historic monuments). The carefully restored decor features walnut paneling and mirrors. The cuisine emphasizes well-prepared seafood and all the typical local dishes, including cassoulet, magret of duckling, lightly smoked salmon with lentils and mussels, and confit of duckling. Try foie gras or country-style sauerkraut, accompanied by the house Riesling, served in an earthenware pitcher. During warm weather, eat on the terrace. The staff is likely to be hysterical and less than suave during peak times.

In the Hôtel des Beaux-Arts, 1 quai de la Daurade. (C) **05-61-21-12-12.** www.flobrasseries.com. Reservations recommended. Main courses 12€–19€; fixed-price menu 23€–32€. AE, DC, MC, V. Daily noon–3pm and 7:30pm–1am. Métro: Esquirol.

Emile ★ (Finds TOULOUSIAN   In an old-fashioned house on one of Toulouse's most beautiful squares, this restaurant offers the specialties of chef Christophe Fasan. In winter, meals are served upstairs overlooking the square; in summer, seating moves to the street-level dining room and flower-filled terrace. Menu choices include cassoulet Toulousian (cooked in goose fat), magret of duckling in traditional style, a medley of Catalonian fish, and a very fresh *parillade* (mixed grill) of fish with a pungently aromatic cold sauce of sweet peppers and olive oil. The wine list is filled with intriguing surprises.

13 place St-Georges. (C) **05-61-21-05-56.** www.restaurant-emile.com. Reservations recommended. Main courses 19€–35€; fixed-price lunch 20€–30€; fixed-price dinner 36€–55€. AE, DC, MC, V. Oct to mid-May Tues–Sat noon–1:45pm and 7–9:45pm; mid-May to Sept Tues–Sat noon–1:45pm, Mon–Sat 7–10:30pm. Closed Dec 23–Jan 8. Métro: Capitole or Esquirol.

La Brasserie de l'Opéra FRENCH La Brasserie, in the most prestigious hotel in the city, evokes memories of the old Brasserie Lipp in Paris. It is warmly decorated with cove moldings, burnished hardwood, shimmering glass, and cut flowers. Fresh shellfish is featured, while other specialties include braised red snapper, duck stew, "butterfly oysters," and an array of *plats du jour* based on traditional brasserie cuisine. Seasonal ingredients are used "with respect," in the words of one food critic.

In the Grand Hôtel de l'Opéra (p. 81), 1 place du Capitole. ✆ **05-61-21-37-03.** www.brasserieopera.com. Reservations recommended. Main courses 14€–35€; fixed-price lunch 14€–25€; fixed-price dinner 18€–25€. AE, DC, MC, V. Daily noon–2:30pm and 7:30pm–midnight. Métro: Capitole.

Le Colombier ★ TOULOUSIAN Don't tell your cardiologist and slip away to this bastion of regional cookery. Alain Lacoste arguably serves the best cassoulet in Toulouse, and also lures with his foie gras, white beans in pork fat, red sausage, white sausage, and, of course, goose confit. His duck foie gras comes with figs and, of all things, gingerbread. Calves' sweetbreads are delectable with morels, and scallops are served in the *provençale* style. Nearly all locals order the cassoulet; it's slow cooked to perfection. The restaurant itself is a simple stone and brick dining room. All of this fat can be cut with the acidity of strawberry soup with lime sorbet. If not that, then opt for the apple tart.

14 rue Bayard. ✆ **05-61-62-40-05.** www.restaurant-lecolombier.com. Reservations recommended. Main courses 18€–26€; fixed-price menus 21€–49€. MC, V. Mon–Fri noon–2pm and 7:15–10pm; Sat 7:15–10:30pm.

Inexpensive

Eau de Folles TRADITIONAL FRENCH Low prices and the variety of the menu keep patrons coming back to this place. In a room filled with mirrors, you can choose from 10 starters, 10 main courses, and 10 desserts on the fixed-price menu. Choices vary according to the inspiration of the chef and the availability of fresh ingredients. A typical meal may include a marinade of fish, followed by strips of duck meat with green-pepper sauce, and a homemade pastry such as a tarte Tatin. Everything is very simple and served in a cramped but convivial setting.

14 allée du President Roosevelt. ✆ **05-61-23-45-50.** www.eau-de-folles.com. Reservations recommended. Fixed-price lunch 18€; fixed-price dinner 28€. MC, V. Mon–Sat noon–3pm and 7–11pm. Métro: Wilson.

Le Bon Vivre ★ SOUTHWESTERN FRENCH One of downtown Toulouse's most appealing cost-conscious bistros occupies the street level of a historic 18th-century mansion immediately adjacent to the Hôtel de Ville (town hall). Established in 2004, the bistro is ringed by the pink-colored bricks of antique Toulouse, and set beneath a vaulted ceiling. Menu items feature contemporary twists of time-tested French specialties, many of them heralded by workaday diners who appreciate the attractive ratios of value-to-quality. The best examples include an unusual version of macaroni studded with flap mushrooms, truffles, and foie gras; and a version of cassoulet (the specialty of France's southwest) that's made with both duck and pork. An appropriate starter is a braised slice of foie gras with peaches and grapes.

15 bis place Wilson. ✆ **05-61-23-07-17.** www.lebonvivre.com. Reservations recommended. Main courses 17€–28€; fixed-price lunch 26€–38€. AE, DC, MC, V. Daily 11:30am–3pm and 7–11:30pm.

WHERE TO STAY NEARBY

La Flanerie Within a large garden that slopes down to the edge of the Garonne, about 8km (5 miles) south of Toulouse, stands this dignified-looking manor house, originally built in 1799 for a local landowner. Part of its allure derives from the early 1970s, when it was the site of a hotel favored by French celebrities and international rock stars, whose names fill the guest book that the Irish-born owners, the Moloney family, have presented since their acquisition of the place late in 2004. You might be happiest interpreting La Flanerie as an informal bed-and-breakfast, where the rooms just happen to be country-elegant and the welcome particularly warm. A free-standing garage for each of the 12 bedrooms is an unexpected quirk, deriving from one of the auto-obsessed former owners. Accommodations are stylish and midsize.

7 chemin des Etroits, 31320 Vieille-Toulouse. ⓒ 05-61-73-39-12. Fax 05-61-73-18-56. www.hotel laflanerie.com. 12 units. 86€–110€ double. AE, MC, V. Free parking. Bus: R. Take D4 south of Toulouse for 8km (5 miles). **Amenities:** Bar; pool (outdoor). *In room:* A/C, TV, hair dryer, minibar, Wi-Fi (free).

TOULOUSE AFTER DARK

Toulouse's theater, dance, and opera are often on a par with the Paris scene. Pick up a copy of the free monthly magazine *Toulouse Culture* from the Office de Tourisme for the latest happenings.

The city's most notable theaters are the **Théâtre du Capitole,** place du Capitole (ⓒ 05-61-63-13-13; www.theatre-du-capitole.org), which specializes in operas, operettas, and works from the classical French repertoire; the **Théâtre de la Digue,** 3 rue de la Digue (ⓒ 05-61-42-97-79; www.ladigue.org), for ballets and works by local theater companies; and the **Halle aux Grains,** place Dupuy (ⓒ 05-61-63-13-13), the home of the Orchestre du Capitole and a venue for classical concerts. The **Théâtre Garonne,** 1 av. du Château d'Eau (ⓒ 05-62-48-56-56; www.theatregaronne.com), stages everything from works by Molière to current dramas. Another important venue is the **Théâtre Zenith,** 11 av. Raymond-Badiou (ⓒ 05-62-74-49-49), with its large stage and seating capacity. It usually schedules rock concerts, variety acts, and musical comedies from other European cities. A smaller competitor, with a roughly equivalent mix of music and theater, is the **Théâtre de la Cité,** 1 rue Pierre Baudis (ⓒ 05-34-45-05-00; www.tnt-cite.com).

The liveliest squares to wander after dark are **place du Capitole, place St-Georges, place St-Pierre,** and **place Wilson.**

For bars and pubs, **La Tantina de Bourgos,** 27 rue de la Garonette (ⓒ 05-61-55-59-29), has a Latin flair that's popular with students, and the rowdier **Chez Tonton,** 16 place St-Pierre (ⓒ 05-61-21-89-54), has an *après-match* atmosphere, complete with the winning teams boozing it up. A popular bar that schedules both live and recorded music is **Monsieur Carnaval,** 34 rue Bayard (ⓒ 05-61-99-14-56), where there's lots of rocking and rolling *a la française* for the under-35 crowd.

The town's trendiest and most widely sought-after disco for the under-35 set is **Le Purple,** 2 rue Castellane (ⓒ 05-62-73-04-67). Set close to the Sofitel, this disco has the longest lines and elicits the highest level of passion within the city's A-list wannabes. The busiest English-style pub in town, woodsy and Celtic-looking, and often very crowded with the city's English-speaking community, is **Le Frog & Le Roast Beef,** 14 rue de l'Industrie (ⓒ 05-61-99-28-57). Behind a simple, discreetly marked green door is **La Pelouse interdite,** 72 av. des Etats-Unis (ⓒ 05-61-47-30-40; www.pelouseinterdite. net), a charming restaurant and bar with a garden. And if you have a car and don't mind driving about 20 minutes out of town (follow the signs pointing to Albi), a hip and sought-after rendezvous point is **Le Lounge 233,** 233 rte. d'Albi (ⓒ 05-61-48-60-60), where a fussy and complicated list of cocktails, something many young French clubbers are just getting used to, are available for around 12€ each. A somewhat less cutting-edge, but very popular, disco is **Cockpit,** 1 rue du Puits-Vert (© **05-61-21-87-53**), near Le Capitol and the nocturnally animated place Wilson. It's been around longer than Le Purple, and is less modish, but still has a strong appeal to danceaholics. As any good disco, Le Capitol incorporates a mixed crowd of males, females, gay people (who in recent years seem, at least here, to be increasing in their visibility), straight people, and in-betweens.

Mostly heterosexuals migrate to **Disco Le Maximo,** 3 rue Gabrielle-Peri (© **05-61-62-08-07**), which starts hopping Tuesday to Saturday after 11pm, and serves a distinctly French-inspired list of tapas (foie gras on toast, perhaps). For a beer-soaked and raucous time, try the vaguely Iberian-looking establishment, **Bar La Bodega,** 2-3 rue Gabriel-Peri (© **05-61-63-03-63**). It's particularly interesting in the wake of one of the region's football (soccer) games, especially if the home team has won.

The oldest and most deeply entrenched gay bar in Toulouse is **Shanghai Express,** 12 rue de la Pomme (© **05-61-23-37-80**), a men's dance domain playing the latest in techno; farther inside, it gives way to a darker and, at its best, sexy cruise-bar environment with lots of men on the prowl. Entrance is free and it's open every night.

2 AUCH ★

726km (451 miles) SW of Paris; 203km (126 miles) SE of Bordeaux; 64km (40 miles) W of Toulouse

The lively market town of Auch is on the west bank of the Gers in the heart of the ancient Duchy of Gascony, of which it was once the capital.

ESSENTIALS

GETTING THERE   Five to 10 SNCF **trains** or **buses** per day run between Toulouse and Auch (trip time: 1½ hr.); 6 to 13 SNCF buses (© **05-62-05-73-76**) arrive in Auch daily from Agen (trip time: 1½ hr.). The one-way train fare from Toulouse is 14€. For train info, call © **36-35,** or go to **www.voyages-sncf.com.** If you're **driving** to Auch, take N124 west from Toulouse.

VISITOR INFORMATION   The **Office de Tourisme** is at 1 rue Dessoles, at place de la Cathédrale (© **05-62-05-22-89;** www.auch-tourisme.com).

EXPLORING THE TOWN

The town is divided into an upper and a lower quarter, connected by several flights of steps. In the old part of town in the upper quarter, the narrow streets, called *pousterles,* center on **place Salinis,** where you can get a good view of the Pyrenees. Branching off from here, the **Escalier Monumental** leads down to the Le Gers River and the lower quarter of town, a descent of 232 steps.

North of the square is the **Cathédrale Ste-Marie** ★★, place de la Cathédrale (© **05-62-63-28-50**). Built from the 15th to the 17th centuries, this is one of the handsomest Gothic churches in the south of France. It has 113 Renaissance **choir stalls** ★★★ made of carved oak. The impressive stained-glass windows crafted by Arnaud de Moles in the 16th century are also from the Renaissance. Charging no admission, the cathedral is open April to September daily 8:30am to noon and 2 to 6pm; October to March daily 9:30am to noon and 2 to 5pm.

Next to the cathedral stands an 18th-century **archbishop's palace** with a 14th-century bell tower, the **Tour d'Armagnac,** which was once a prison. Both are closed to the public.

For shops and boutiques, walk down **rue Dessoles, rue de Pouille,** and **avenue de l'Alsace,** for everything from confectionery shops to clothing stores. For a town of its relatively small size, Auch produces more wines, fine Armagnacs, foie gras, cheese, cured ham, and a greater number of regional delicacies than a casual visitor might have expected. They'll virtually leap out of store windows as you promenade down the commercial streets of downtown (the rue Dessoles is reserved only for pedestrian traffic, and is especially dense with food outlets). Two of the busiest and most respected outlets for regional foodstuffs, liqueurs (especially Armagnacs), and wines are **La Cave Gourmande,** 15 rue Dessoles (© **05-62-61-81-33;** www.lacavegourmande.com); and **La Cave d'Artagnan,** 3 rue de la République (© **05-62-60-23-80**).

WHERE TO STAY

Hôtel de France (Restaurant Jardin des Saveurs) ★   No longer a mandatory stop in southern France for serious foodies, the hotel is now a solid and reliable choice, even if its Michelin stars are long lost. It was built around the much-modernized 16th-century core of an old inn. The rooms are comfortable, conservative, and furnished with traditional but somewhat nondescript pieces. Some are a bit dowdy. The cuisine somewhat slavishly follows many of the culinary trends established by the since-retired founder, André Daguin, but with less panache. Today, with kitchens directed by Roland Garreau, the cuisine is "innovative within traditional boundaries." Lovers of foie gras look forward to something approaching an inundation of the velvety substance at this restaurant that lies smack in the heart of foie-gras production country. Start off, for example, with a platter featuring four different preparations of the stuff (each with different herbs, spices, and flavorings), or perhaps some marinated Scottish salmon; follow with a main course with an entire lobe (meaning a big portion) of foie gras prepared, house-style, with Provençal herbs and wine. If you're not in the mood for so much foie gras, consider a truffled platter of crayfish instead. Set-price menus for both lunch and dinner are priced from 25€ to 56€, main courses 20€ to 29€. The restaurant is open daily noon to 2pm and Monday to Saturday 7:30 to 9:45pm. During July and August, its also open on Sunday night.

Place de la Libération, 32003 Auch. © **05-62-61-71-84.** Fax 05-62-61-71-81. www.hoteldefrance-auch. com. 29 units. 70€–120€ double; 150€–220€ suite. AE, DC, MC, V. Parking 12€. **Amenities:** Restaurant; bar. *In room:* A/C, TV, minibar.

WHERE TO DINE

Most people still head for the **Hôtel de France** (see above), if only for the memories.

Le Daroles TRADITIONAL FRENCH   Despite its much, much lower prices, this Parisian-style brasserie attracts many of the former clients of the Hôtel de France. Within an old-fashioned setting that includes mirrors, polished copper, mahogany paneling, and leather banquettes, you can enjoy a bustling, no-nonsense cuisine. Examples include strips of duckling with seasonal berries, scallops with herb and wine sauce, sauerkraut, foie gras, and pepper steak.

Place de la Libération. © **05-62-05-00-51.** www.restaurant-le-daroles.com. Main courses 12€–19€; fixed-price lunch or dinner 12€–33€. DC, MC, V. Daily noon–2:30pm and 7:30–10:30pm.

3 CORDES-SUR-CIEL ★★

678km (421 miles) SW of Paris; 25km (16 miles) NW of Albi

This site is remarkable—it's like an eagle's nest on a hilltop, above the Cérou valley. In days gone by, many celebrities, such as Jean-Paul Sartre and Albert Camus, considered this town a favorite hideaway.

The name Cordes is derived from the textile and leather industries that thrived here during the 13th and 14th centuries. As artisans working with linen and leather prospered, the town also became known throughout France for its brilliantly colored silks. In the 16th century, however, plagues and religious wars reduced the city to a minor role. A brief renaissance occurred in the 19th century, when automatic weaving machines were introduced.

Today Cordes is an arts-and-crafts city, and many of the ancient houses on the narrow streets contain artisans plying their skills—blacksmiths, enamelers, graphic artists, weavers, engravers, sculptors, and painters.

ESSENTIALS

GETTING THERE   If you're coming by **train,** get off in Cordes-Vindrac and walk, rent a bicycle, or take a taxi the remaining 3km (1¾ miles) west of Cordes. For train information, call ℂ **36-35,** or **08-92-35-35-35.** For a **minibus,** call Taxi Barrois (ℂ **05-63-56-14-80**). The one-way fare is 4.15€ Monday to Saturday, rising to 6.65€ after 7pm and on Sunday. There's no bus service. If you're **driving,** take N88 northwest from Toulouse to Gaillac, turning north on D922 into Cordes-sur-Ciel. *Note:* You must park outside the city, and then walk through an arch leading to the Old Town.

VISITOR INFORMATION   The **Office de Tourisme** is in the Maison Fonpeyrouse, Grand-Rue Raymond VII (ℂ **05-63-56-00-15;** fax 05-63-56-19-52; www.cordes-sur-ciel.org).

EXPLORING THE TOWN

Often called "the city of a hundred Gothic arches," Cordes contains numerous **maisons Gothiques ★★**, old houses built of pink sandstone. Many of the doors and windows are fashioned of pointed (broken) arches that still retain their 13th- and 14th-century grace. Some of the best preserved line **Grand'Rue,** also called **"rue Droite."**

Musée d'Art et d'Histoire le Portail-Peint (Musée Charles-Portal), Grand'Rue (ℂ **04-85-91-16-82**), is named after the archivist of the Tarn region who was also an avid historian of Cordes. The museum is in a medieval house, the foundations of which date from the Gallo-Roman era. It contains everyday artifacts of the textile industry of long ago, farming measures, samples of local embroidery, a reconstructed peasant home interior, and other medieval memorabilia. The museum is open Wednesday to Monday 2 to 6pm. Admission is 2.30€ adults, 1.10€ students and ages 12 to 25, free for children 11 and under.

Maison du Grand-Fauconnier (House of the Falcon Master), Grand'Rue, is named for the falcons carved into the stonework of the wall. A grandly proportioned staircase in the building leads to the **Musée d'Art Moderne et Contemporain** (ℂ **05-63-56-14-79;** www.cordessurciel.eu). Yves Brayer moved to Cordes in 1940 and became one of its most ardent civic boosters. After watching Cordes fall gradually into decay, he renewed interest in its restoration. The museum is open Wednesday to Monday: June to September 11am to 12:30pm and 2 to 7pm; November to March 2 to 5pm; April to May and in October 11am to 12:30am and 2 to 6:30pm; closed January. Admission costs 3.50€ adults, 2€ students, and free for children 11 and under.

Eglise St-Michel, Grand'Rue, dates from the 13th century, but many alterations have been made since. From the top of the tower you can view the surrounding area. Much of the lateral design of the side chapels was likely influenced by the cathedral at Albi. Before being shipped here, the organ (dating from 1830) was in Notre-Dame de Paris. The church can be visited only as part of guided visits arranged through the tourist office. With many exceptions, they're usually organized every day from 10:30am to 12:30pm and 3 to 6:30pm. Admission is free.

WHERE TO STAY & DINE

Bistrot Tonin'ty (Value) FRENCH   This is the least expensive, and the least fussy, of the several restaurants in Cordes that are owned and operated by Yves Thuriès, a celebrity chef whose recipes have been publicized, and praised, throughout France. (The most upscale of the restaurants in the group is Maison du Grand Ecuyer; see below.) During pleasant weather, you'll dine on aluminum furniture beneath a gnarled 300-year-old wisteria vine whose blue-violet blossoms perfume the courtyard every spring. Otherwise, the mostly scarlet-toned dining room features massive ceiling beams and smallish tables with immaculate napery. Cuisine focuses on the time-tested, the flavorful, and the traditional and includes cassoulet, a croustade of magret of duckling layered with apples; foie gras redolent with spices; roasted salmon in the style of the chef; and a tempting array of sophisticated salads. Prices here are kept deliberately low, with all but a few of the main courses priced 14€ each.

The restaurant is the centerpiece of L'Hostellerie du Vieux Cordes; see the review below for more details.

Rue St-Michel, 81170 Cordes. (© **05-63-53-79-20.** www.thuries.fr. Reservations recommended. Main courses 14€; fixed-price menu (5 courses) 45€). AE, DC, MC, V. May–Oct daily noon–2:30pm and 7:30–9:30pm; Nov–Mar Tues–Sat 7:30–9:30pm, Wed–Sun noon–2:30pm. Closed first 2 weeks of Jan.

Hostellerie du Parc (Value) TRADITIONAL FRENCH   This inn originated in the 18th century as a landowner's home. Today, in a verdant park, the stone house holds this charming getaway *restaurant avec chambres.* It serves generous meals in a garden or a paneled dining room. Specialties include homemade foie gras, duckling, *poularde* (chicken) *occitaine,* rabbit with cabbage leaves, ballotine of duck with foie gras, and confit of roasted rabbit with pink garlic from the nearby town of Lautrec.

The hotel offers 13 comfortable and well-furnished rooms; a double costs 60€ to 100€.

Les Cabannes, 81170 Cordes. (© **05-63-56-02-59.** Fax 05-63-56-18-03. www.hostellerie-du-parc.com. Reservations recommended. Main courses 14€–25€; fixed-price menu 28€–65€. AE, DC, MC, V. June–Oct daily noon–2pm and 7–10pm; off season Tues–Fri noon–2pm, Fri–Sat 7–10pm. Closed 3 weeks in Jan. From the town center, take rte. de St-Antonin (D600) for about 1km (²⁄₃ mile) west.

L'Hostellerie du Vieux Cordes   This stylish and sophisticated inn is set midway along the length of the walled-in medieval city, within what was originally built in the 1200s as the monastery associated with the Eglise St-Michel, which sits immediately next door. Its centerpiece is its restaurant, a glamorous yet intimate affair (see Bistrot Tonin'ty, above). Public areas, including the scarlet-colored dining room, are more richly furnished than the bedrooms, which are outfitted with ceiling beams and massive wooden furniture that includes, in most cases, a bulky armoire. None of the rooms are air-conditioned, but thanks to windows whose views sometimes sweep out over the valley, and ceiling fans, they sit on the receiving end of welcome breezes. Each is accessed via a winding stone staircase that passes such atmosphere-inducing accessories as full suits of armor.

Rue St-Michel, 81170 Cordes. ✆ **05-63-53-79-20.** Fax 05-63-56-02-47. www.thuries.fr. 18 units. 49€–95€ double; 155€ suite. AE, MC, V. Free parking. Closed Jan. **Amenities:** Restaurant; bar; babysitting; Wi-Fi (free). *In room:* TV, hair dryer.

Maison du Grand Ecuyer ★★★ MODERN FRENCH   The medieval monument that contains this restaurant (the 15th-c. hunting lodge of Raymond VII, *comte de Toulouse*) is a national historic treasure. Despite its glamour and undeniable charm, the restaurant remains intimate and unstuffy, although guests in recent years have included King Juan Carlos of Spain, the Emperor of Japan, and even Queen Elizabeth. Chef Yves Thuriès's platters have made his dining room an almost mandatory stop for the rich and famous. Specialties include three confits of lobster, red mullet salad with fondue of vegetables, confit of pigeon with olive oil and rosemary, and noisette of lamb in chicory sauce. The dessert selection is nearly overwhelming.

The hotel has 12 rooms and one suite, all with antiques and modern comforts. Doubles cost 100€ to 160€; the suite is 255€. The most popular room, honoring former guest Albert Camus, has a four-poster bed and a fireplace. During its annual closing, nearby **L'Hostellerie du Vieux Cordes,** 21 rue St-Michel (see above; ✆ **05-63-53-79-20**), also under the management of Thuriès, is an alternative.

Grand-Rue Raymond VIII, Haute de la Cite, 81170 Cordes. ✆ **05-63-53-79-50.** Fax 05-63-53-79-51. www. thuries.fr. Reservations required. Main courses 22€–36€; fixed-price menu 32€–93€. AE, DC, MC, V. July–Aug Fri–Sun noon–1:30pm, daily 7–9:30pm; mid-Mar to June and Sept to mid-Oct Tues–Sun 7–9:30pm. Closed early Nov to mid-Mar.

4 ALBI

697km (433 miles) SW of Paris; 76km (47 miles) NE of Toulouse

The "red city" of Albi straddles both banks of the Tarn River. The cathedral and the bridges spanning the river are made of brick, as are most of the town's buildings, earning Albi its title—in the rosy glow of a setting sun, Albi often looks as if it were in flames, a spectacular sight.

The fortified cathedral that broods over the medieval center is a reminder of the bloody struggle between the Roman Catholic Church and the Cathars, a religious group the Church considered heretical. They were also called Albigenses after the town, which was an important center of their movement. The town is also the birthplace of Toulouse-Lautrec and contains an important museum of his works.

ESSENTIALS

GETTING THERE   Fifteen **trains** per day link Toulouse with Albi (trip time: 1 hr.); the one-way fare is 12€. A night train also runs between Paris and Albi. For rail information, call ✆ **36-35,** or visit **www.voyages-sncf.com.** The **bus** station is located on place Jean-Jaurès (✆ **05-63-54-58-61**). Buses from Toulouse cost 12€ for a one-way ticket. Travel time is 1½ hours.

If you're **driving** from Toulouse, take N88 northeast.

VISITOR INFORMATION   The **Office de Tourisme** is in the Palais de la Berbie, place Ste-Cécile (✆ **05-63-49-48-80;** fax 05-63-49-48-98; www.albi-tourisme.fr).

SEEING THE SIGHTS

Cathédrale Ste-Cécile ★★★   Fortified with ramparts and parapets and containing frescoes and paintings, this 13th-century cathedral was built by a local lord-bishop after a religious struggle with the *comte de Toulouse* (the crusade against the Cathars). Note the exceptional 16th-century rood screen with a unique suit of polychromatic statues from the Old and New Testaments. Free classical concerts take place in July and August on Wednesday at 5pm and Sunday at 4pm.

Near place du Vigan, in the medieval center of town. ✆ **05-63-43-23-43.** Cathédrale: Free admission. Treasury: 2€ adults, free for children 13 and under. June–Sept daily 9am–6:30pm; Oct–May daily 9am–noon and 2–6:30pm.

Musée de Lapérouse   Set on the opposite bank of the Tarn from the bulk of Albi's medieval core (take the Pont-Vieux to reach it), within what was originally built in the 18th century as a pasta factory, this museum honors the achievements of Albi's native son, Jean-François de la Pérouse. Commissioned as an explorer by Louis XVI in the late 1600s, he mapped and charted the coastlines of Alaska, California, and China, bringing the French up to speed with England in its rush for colonies outside Europe. The museum contains maps, charts, navigational instructions, and memorabilia that illustrate the progress and achievements of not only the explorer himself, but also France's self-image during a period of some of its greatest glory.

Square Botany Bay. ✆ **05-63-46-01-87.** Admission 3€ adults, 2€ students and ages 18–25, free for children 17 and under. Mar–June and Sept–Oct Tues–Sun 9am–noon and 2–6pm; July–Aug Mon–Fri 9am–noon and 2–6pm, Sat–Sun 10am–noon and 2–7pm; Nov–Feb Tues–Sun 10am–noon and 2–5pm.

Musée Toulouse-Lautrec ★★   The Palais de la Berbie (Archbishop's Palace) is a fortified structure dating from the 13th century. This museum contains the world's most important collection of the artist's paintings, more than 600 in all. His family bequeathed the works remaining in his studio. The museum also owns paintings by Degas, Bonnard, Matisse, Utrillo, and Rouault. Three additional rooms, each of them a brick-lined refuge within the premises of a neighboring historic building, house some of Toulouse-Lautrec's earliest works, formulated during his earliest creative years.

Opposite the north side of the cathedral. ✆ **05-63-49-48-78.** www.musee-toulouse-lautrec.com. Admission 5€ adults, 2.50€ students, free for children 13 and under. July–Aug daily 9am–6pm; June and Sept daily 9am–noon and 2–6pm; Apr–May daily 10am–noon and 2–6pm; Mar and Oct Wed–Mon 10am–noon and 2–5:30pm; Nov–Feb Wed–Mon 10am–noon and 2–5pm. Closed Jan 1, May 1, Nov 1, and Dec 25.

WHERE TO STAY

Hostellerie St-Antoine ★★   Some historians say this is one of the oldest continuously operated hotels in France. Originally a monastery, then a medieval hospital, the property became an inn in 1734 (when the present building was constructed). The same family has owned it for five generations; today the father-son team of Jacques and Jean-François Rieux are the managers. Jacques's mother drew inspiration from Toulouse-Lautrec when designing the hotel as her grandfather was a friend of the painter and was given a few of his paintings, sketches, and prints (several are in the lounge, which opens onto a rear garden). The rooms have been delightfully decorated, with a sophisticated use of color, reproductions, and occasional antiques. Even if you're not staying, visit the dining room. The Rieux culinary tradition is revealed in their traditional yet creative cuisine.

17 rue St-Antoine, 81000 Albi. ✆ **05-63-54-04-04.** Fax 05-63-47-10-47. www.saint-antoine-albi.com. 44 units. 100€–185€ double; 185€–225€ suite. AE, DC, MC, V. Parking 6.50€. **Amenities:** Restaurant (open only to groups); bar; babysitting; room service. *In room:* A/C, TV, hair dryer, minibar, Wi-Fi (free).

Toulouse-Lautrec: Little Big Man

Although he spent most of his life in Paris, Toulouse-Lautrec is closely connected with Albi. He was born in Albi in the **Hôtel Bosc;** it's still a private home and cannot be toured, but a commemorative plaque hangs on the wall of the building at 14 rue Toulouse-Lautrec, in the historic town core.

You can visit the family's **Château de Bosc,** Camjac, 12800 Naucelle (© 05-65-69-20-83; www.toulouselautreclebosc.com), 47km (29 miles) from Toulouse. It was built in 1180 and renovated in the 1400s. The present owner, Mademoiselle de Céleran, and her team welcome visitors interested in Toulouse-Lautrec, but it's best to call ahead as you can only visit on a guided tour. It is usually open daily from 9am to 7pm. Admission is 5€ for adults, 3€ for children 8 to 12, and free for children 7 and under.

Hôtel Chiffre (Value) This hotel in the city center was built as a lodging for passengers on the mail coaches that hauled letters and people across France. The renovated building retains the original porch that sheltered carriages from the rain and sun. The rooms are artfully cozy, with upholstered walls in floral patterns; some have views of the inner courtyard. The hotel restaurant is popular among locals because of its good-value fixed-price menus. The menu, priced at 20€ to 27€ per person, consists of choices that were compiled after Toulouse-Lautrec's death by his friends. They remembered the way he'd often prepare the dishes himself during his dinner parties. Some of his favorite dishes included radishes stuffed with braised foie gras, suprême of *sandre* (fish), and duckling roasted with garlic.

50 rue Séré-de-Rivières, 81000 Albi. © **05-63-48-58-48.** Fax 05-63-38-11-15. www.hotelchiffre.com. 39 units. 88€–109€ double; 200€ suite. AE, MC, V. Parking 9€. **Amenities:** Restaurant; bar; room service. *In room:* A/C, TV, hair dryer, Wi-Fi (free).

Hôtel La Régence-George V This hotel offers a dignified kind of charm and a spartan, pleasingly old-fashioned setting at fair and reasonable prices. It was built around 1900 and is about a half-kilometer (¼ mile) from the town center. Bedrooms have high ceilings and are generally spacious; bathrooms are small and simply decorated. Breakfast is the only meal served.

29 av. Maréchal-Joffre, 81000 Albi. © **05-63-54-24-16.** Fax 05-63-49-90-78. www.laregence-georgev.fr. 24 units. 50€–55€ double; 55€–60€ triple. AE, MC, V. Parking 5€. *In room:* TV, Wi-Fi (2€).

La Réserve ★★★ This country-club villa in a 1.6-hectare (4-acre) park on the northern outskirts of Albi is managed by the Rieux family, who also run the Hostellerie St-Antoine. A Relais & Châteaux member, La Réserve is a Mediterranean-style villa with a pool and a fine garden. The rooms, well furnished and color coordinated, contain imaginative decorations (but avoid the rooms over the kitchen, which are noisy at mealtimes). The upper-story rooms have sun terraces and French doors.

Rte. de Cordes à Fonvialane, 81000 Albi. © **05-63-60-80-80.** Fax 05-63-47-63-60. www.relaischateaux.fr/reservealbi. 23 units. 158€–398€ double; 398€–498€ suite. AE, DC, MC, V. Closed Nov–Apr. From the center of town, follow signs to Carmaux-Rodez until you cross the Tarn; then follow signs to Cordes. The hotel is adjacent to the main road leading to Cordes, 2km (1¼ miles) from Albi. **Amenities:** Restaurant; bar; babysitting; pool (outdoor). *In room:* A/C, TV, hair dryer, minibar, Wi-Fi (free).

The restaurant at **La Réserve** (see above) is also a wonderful choice.

Jardin des Quatre Saisons ★★ MODERN FRENCH   The best food in Albi is served by Georges Muriel Bermond, who believes that menus, like life, should change with the seasons—which explains the restaurant's name. The service is always competent and polite in his two simple dining rooms. Fine-tuned menu items include delicious fricassee of snails garnished with strips of the famous hams produced in the nearby hamlet of Lacaune, and ravioli stuffed with pulverized shrimp and served with truffled cream sauce. Most delectable of all—an excuse for returning—is *pot-au-feu* of the sea, with three or four species of fish garnished with crayfish-cream sauce. The wine list is the finest in Albi.

19 bd. de Strasbourg. ✆ **05-63-60-77-76.** www.lejardindes4saisons.chez-alice.fr. Reservations recommended. Fixed-price menu 24€–35€. AE, DC, MC, V. Tues–Sun noon–2:30pm; Tues–Sat 7:30–10pm.

Le Lautrec TRADITIONAL FRENCH   Part of its charm derives from its associations with Toulouse-Lautrec—the restaurant lies across the street from his birthplace and is decorated with paintings by local artists. Also appealing is the rich patina of its interior brickwork. The skillfully prepared food includes a salad of fried scallops with rose oil and essence of shrimp; sweetbreads with morels; and roasted rack of lamb marinated in a brewed infusion of Provençal thyme. Hearty regional dishes—beloved by local diners— are a cassoulet of codfish, savory sweetbreads (an acquired taste for some), duckling *en confit,* and rabbit stew.

15 rue Toulouse-Lautrec. ✆ **05-63-54-86-55.** www.restaurant-le-lautrec.com. Reservations recommended. Main courses 18€–38€; fixed-price lunch Tues–Fri 15€–20€; other fixed-price meals 18€–50€. AE, MC, V. Tues–Sun noon–2pm; Tues–Sat 7–9:30pm. Closed Wed night Nov–Mar.

5 CASTRES ★

727km (452 miles) SW of Paris; 42km (26 miles) S of Albi

Built on the bank of the Agout River, Castres is the point of origin for trips to the Sidobre, the mountains of Lacaune, and the Black Mountains. Today the wool industry, whose origins go back to the 14th century, has made Castres one of France's two most important wool-producing areas. The town was formerly a Roman military installation. A Benedictine monastery was founded here in the 9th century, and the town fell under the *comtes d'Albi i*n the 10th century. With its acquisition of a number of 1st-century relics of St. Vincent, and its role as a stopover for pilgrimages to the tomb of St. James in Spain, Castres also held some religious significance. During the 16th-century Wars of Religion, the Protestant town was invaded by religious fanatics, who stole relics from the basilica and dumped them into the river.

ESSENTIALS

GETTING THERE   From Toulouse, seven **trains** make the trip per day (trip time: 1 hr., 15 min.); the one-way fare from Toulouse is 13€. For information, call ✆ **36-35,** or visit **www.voyages-sncf.com.** The Castres **bus** station is at place Soult. Call ✆ **05-63-35-37-31** for information on schedules and fares. Seven buses a day run between Toulouse and Castres, costing 11€ one-way; trip time is 1 hour. Buses to and from Albi depart and arrive every hour, Monday to Saturday, for 5.50€ for a single trip.

   If you're **driving,** Castres is on N126 east of Toulouse and N112 south of Albi.

VISITOR INFORMATION   The **Office de Tourisme** is at 3 place de la République (𝄐 **05-63-62-63-62;** fax 05-63-62-63-60; www.ville-castres.fr).

THE TOP ATTRACTIONS

Eglise St-Benoît   The most prominent church is an outstanding example of French baroque architecture. The architect Caillau began construction in 1677 on the site of a 9th-century Benedictine abbey, but the structure was never completed according to its original plans. Gabriel Briard executed the painting above the altar in the 18th century.

Place du 8-Mai-1945. 𝄐 **05-63-59-05-19.** Free admission. Mon–Sat 9am–noon and 2–6pm; Sun 8:30am– noon. Closed to casual visitors Sun Oct–May, except for religious services.

Le Centre National et Musée Jean-Jaurès   This museum is dedicated to the workers' movements of the late 19th and early 20th centuries. Its collection contains printed material from the various Socialist movements in France during that period, as well as paintings, sculptures, films, and slides. See, in particular, an issue of *L'Aurore* containing Zola's famous *"J'accuse"* article about the Dreyfus case.

2 place Pélisson. 𝄐 **05-63-62-41-83.** Admission 1.50€ adults, .75€ students and children 13 and under. Apr–Sept daily 10am–noon and 2–6pm; Oct–Mar Tues–Sun 10am–noon and 2–5pm.

Musée Goya ★   The museum is in the town hall, an archbishop's palace designed by Mansart in 1669. Some of the spacious public rooms have ceilings supported by a frieze of the archbishop's coats of arms. The collection includes 16th-century tapestries and the works of Spanish painters from the 15th to the 20th centuries. Most notable are the paintings of Francisco Goya y Lucientes, all donated to the town in 1894 by Pierre Briguiboul, son of the Castres-born artist Marcel Briguiboul. *Les Caprices* is a study of figures created in 1799 after the illness that left Goya deaf. Filling much of an entire room, the work consists of symbolic images of demons and monsters, a satire of Spanish society.

In the Jardin de l'Evêché. 𝄐 **05-63-71-59-30.** Admission 2.30€ adults, 1.15€ students, free for children 17 and under. July–Aug daily 10am–6pm; otherwise, daily 9am–noon and 2–6pm.

WHERE TO STAY

Hôtel de l'Europe ★ **(Finds)**   This hotel exudes charm, especially in the bedrooms capped with ceiling beams, where the pinkish-gray masonry from the building's original 18th-century construction still remains. Each room has a view over the oldest part of the historic town, and some rooms feature canopy-draped beds. A number of the bathrooms are quite luxurious and all have the most up-to-date plumbing.

5 rue Victor-Hugo, 81100 Castres. 𝄐 **05-63-59-00-33.** Fax 05-63-59-21-38. 38 units. 65€ double. AE, DC, MC, V. Parking 6€. **Amenities:** Restaurant; bar. *In room:* TV, hair dryer, minibar, Wi-Fi (free on first 3 floors, 4.50€ per hour on 3rd floor).

Hôtel Renaissance ★   The Renaissance is the best hotel in Castres. It was built in the 17th century as a courthouse and had become a colorful but run-down hotel when it was restored in 1993. Today you'll see a dignified building with *colombages*-style half-timbering and a mixture of stone blocks and bricks. Some of the comfortable rooms, each renovated around 2001, have exposed timbers; some are in the style of Napoleon III; some are 18th-century Asiatic; others are country-comfortable with safari-themed fabrics; and still others have hunting themes. Each unit contains a midsize bathroom.

17 rue Victor-Hugo, 81100 Castres. 𝄐 **05-63-59-30-42.** Fax 05-63-72-11-57. www.hotel-renaissance.fr. 20 units. 65€ double; 92€ suite. AE, DC, MC, V. Parking 5€. **Amenities:** Restaurant; bar; room service; rooms for those w/limited mobility; smoke-free rooms. *In room:* A/C, TV, Wi-Fi, minibar, hair dryer.

In addition to those below, another worthy choice is **Le Victoria,** 24 place du 8-Mai-1945 (✆ **05-63-59-14-68;** www.le-victoria-restaurant.com), where meals cost 13€ to 45€. Their superb French cuisine utilizes regional products whenever available.

Brasserie de l'Europe ⓥ**alue** FRENCH/PROVENÇALE   This modern brasserie is a good bet for solid cuisine. The rustic decor features English-inspired furnishings with lots of wood paneling. The expanded menu includes a selection of regional platters as well as pizzas. For example, local sausages served with purée of apples and cheese from the foothills of the Pyrenees; blanquettes of veal; cassoulets; and caramelized pork filets with Provençal herbs. The service is polite, but pressed for time. Many visitors find it especially suitable for a simple noontime meal.

1 place Jean-Jaurès. ✆ **05-63-59-01-44.** Reservations recommended. Main courses 8€–18€; fixed-price lunch 11€–21€; fixed-price dinner 19€. MC, V. Mon–Sat noon–2:30pm and 7–10:30pm.

La Mandragore ★ LANGUEDOCIENNE   On an easily overlooked narrow street, this restaurant, named for a legendary plant with magic powers, occupies a section of one of the wings of the medieval château-fort of Castres. The decor is simple, with stone walls and tones of autumn colors. The regional cuisine is among the best in town, and is served with a smile. Among the best dishes are ravioli stuffed with braised snails and flavored with basil, rack of suckling veal with exotic mushrooms, and magret of duckling with natural Canadian maple syrup. The owners are French citizens who lived in Montreal for 15 years and worked at a famous restaurant there.

1 rue Malpas. ✆ 05-63-59-51-27. Reservations recommended. Main courses 16€–22€; fixed-price menu 13€ at lunch, 15€–24€ at dinner. DC, MC, V. Tues–Sat noon–2pm and 7–10pm. Closed 2 weeks in Sept and 2 weeks in Mar.

6 CARCASSONNE ★★★

797km (495 miles) SW of Paris; 92km (57 miles) SE of Toulouse; 105km (65 miles) S of Albi

Evoking bold knights, fair damsels, and troubadours, the greatest fortress city of Europe rises against a background of the snowcapped Pyrenees. Floodlit at night, it captures a fairy-tale magic, but back in its heyday in the Middle Ages it was the target of assault by battering rams, grapnels, a mobile tower (inspired by the Trojan horse), catapults, flaming arrows, and the mangonel.

Today, the city is overrun with hordes of visitors and tacky gift shops. The elusive charm of Carcassonne comes out in the evening, when day-trippers depart and floodlights bathe the ancient monuments.

ESSENTIALS

GETTING THERE   Carcassonne is a major stop for **trains** between Toulouse and destinations south and east. Five trains per day arrive from Toulouse (trip time: 1 hr.; one-way fare: 15€), nine per day from Montpellier (trip time: 1½ hr.; 23€ one-way), and three trains per day from Marseilles (trip time: 4 hr.; 43€ one-way). For rail information, call ✆ **36-35,** or visit **www.voyages-sncf.com. Bus** service to Carcassonne consists mainly of local buses taking children to school. You'll want to either take a train or drive yourself. If you're **driving,** Carcassonne is on A61 south of Toulouse.

VISITOR INFORMATION   The **Office de Tourisme** has locations at 28 rue de Verdun (© **04-68-10-24-30;** fax 04-68-10-24-38; www.carcassonne-tourisme.com) and in the medieval town at Porte Narbonnaise (© **04-68-10-24-36**).

SPECIAL EVENTS   The town's nightlife sparkles during its summer festivals. During the **Festival de Carcassonne** (www.festivaldecarcassonne.com) in July, concerts, modern and classical dance, operas, and theater fill the city. Tickets run 25€ to 65€ and can be purchased by calling © **04-68-11-59-15** or 04-68-77-74-31. On July 14, **Bastille Day,** one of the best fireworks spectacles in France lights up the skies at 10:30pm. Over 6 weeks in July and August, the merriment and raucousness of the Middle Ages overtake the city during the **Spectacles Medievaux,** in the form of jousts, parades, food fairs, and street festivals. For information, contact the **Office de Tourisme** (© **04-68-10-24-30**).

EXPLORING LA CITE

Carcassonne consists of two towns: the **Bastide St-Louis** (also known as the Ville Basse or Lower City) and the medieval **Cité.** The former has little of interest, but the latter is among the major attractions in France. The fortifications consist of the inner and outer walls, a double line of ramparts. The Visigoths built the inner rampart in the 5th century. Clovis, king of the Franks, attacked it in 506 but failed to breach the fortifications. The Saracens overcame the city in 728, but Pepin the Short (father of Charlemagne) drove them out in 752.

The epic medieval poems *Chansons de Geste* tell the tale of the origin of the town's name. During a siege by Charlemagne, the populace of the city was starving and near surrender until a local noblewoman, Dame Carcas, reputedly gathered up the last of their grain, fed it to a sow, then tossed the pig over the ramparts. The pig burst, scattering the grain. Dame Carcas then ordered the trumpets sounded for a parley and cried, *"Carcas te sonne!"* ("Carcas is calling you!"). The Franks concluded that Carcassonne must have unlimited food supplies and ended their siege.

Carcassonne's walls were further fortified by the *vicomtes de Trencavel* in the 12th century and by Louis IX and Philip the Bold during the following century. By the mid–17th century the city had lost its position as a strategic frontier, and the ramparts were left to decay. In the 19th century, the builders of the Lower Town began to remove the stone for use in new construction. But interest in the Middle Ages revived, and the government ordered Viollet-le-Duc (who restored Notre-Dame in Paris) to repair and, where necessary, rebuild the walls. Reconstruction continued until very recently. A small population lives inside the walls.

In the highest elevation of the Cité, at the uppermost terminus of rue Principale (rue Cros Mayrevielle), you'll find the **Château Comtal,** place du Château (© **04-68-11-70-70**), a restored 12th-century fortress that's open April to September daily 10am to 6:30pm, October to March daily 9:30am to 5pm. Entrance includes an obligatory 40-minute guided tour, in French and broken English. It's also the only way to climb onto the city's inner ramparts. The cost is 7.50€ for adults, 4.80€ for students and ages 18 to 25, and free for children 17 and under. The tour includes access to expositions that display the archaeological remnants discovered on-site, plus an explanation of the 19th-century restorations.

Another important monument in the fortifications is the **Basilique St-Nazaire** ★, La Cité (© **04-68-25-27-65**), dating from the 11th to the 14th centuries and containing some beautiful stained-glass windows and a pair of rose medallions. The nave is in the Romanesque style, and the choir and transept are Gothic. The 16th-century organ is one

of the oldest in southwestern France. The 1266 tomb of Bishop Radulphe is well-preserved. **99**
The cathedral is open in July and August daily 9am to 6pm, September to June daily 9am
to noon and 1 to 5pm. Mass is celebrated on Sunday at 11am. Admission is free.

SHOPPING

Carcassonne has two distinct shopping areas. In the modern lower city, the major streets
for shopping, particularly for clothing, are **rue Clemenceau** and **rue de Verdun.** In the
walled medieval city, the streets are chock-full of tiny stores and boutiques; most sell gift
items such as antiques and local arts and crafts.

Stores worth visiting, all in the Cité, include **Comptoir des Vins,** 3 rue du Comte
Roge (© **04-68-26-44-76**), where you'll find a wide selection of regional wines ranging
from simple table wines to those awarded the distinction of Appellation d'Origine Contrôlée. Some antiques stores of merit are **Mme Faye-Nunez,** 4 place du Château
(© **04-68-47-09-45**), for antique furniture; **Antiquités Safi,** 26 rue Trivalle (© **04-68-
25-60-51**), for paintings and art objects; and **Dominique Sarraute,** 15 porte d'Aude
(© **04-68-47-10-06**), for antique firearms.

WHERE TO STAY
In the Cité

Hôtel de la Cité ★★★   Originally a palace for whatever bishop happened to be in
power at the time, this has been the most desirable hotel in town since 1909. It's within
the walls of the city, adjoining the cathedral. The Orient-Express Hotel group acquired
the hotel in the '90s and fluffed it up to the tune of millions. You enter via a long Gothic
corridor-gallery leading to the lounge. Many rooms open onto the ramparts and a garden, and feature antiques or reproductions. A few accommodations contain wooden
headboards and four-poster beds. The ideal unit is no. 308, which opens onto the most
panoramic view of the city. Modern equipment has been discreetly installed throughout,
including bathrooms of generous size. The hotel is renowned for its restaurant, **La Barbacane** (p. 101).

Place de l'Eglise, 11000 Carcassonne. © **04-68-71-98-71.** Fax 04-68-71-50-15. www.hoteldelacite.com.
61 units. 310€–565€ double; 465€–1,400€ suite. AE, DC, MC, V. Parking 21€. Closed late Nov to late Dec
and Feb to early Mar. **Amenities:** 3 restaurants; bar; babysitting; pool (outdoor); room service. *In room:*
A/C, TV, hair dryer, Wi-Fi (free).

Hôtel Le Donjon ★   An abbey in the 12th century, this building at the edge of a
stone square lies in the town center. It was converted into a charming hotel in 1983 after
major repairs to the masonry and roof. Most rooms were renovated, or at least repainted,
in the late 1990s. The rooms contain no-frills furniture and acceptably comfortable mattresses. Bathrooms are just large enough. The owners are proud of the massive stone
staircase that twists around itself. Make reservations at least a couple of months ahead if
you plan to stay here during summer.

2 rue du Comte-Roger, 11000 Carcassonne. © **04-68-11-23-00.** Fax 04-68-25-06-60. www.hotel-donjon.
fr. 62 units. 105€–158€ double; 150€–390€ suite. AE, DC, MC, V. Parking 8€. **Amenities:** Restaurant; bar;
room service; 2 tennis courts (lit). *In room:* A/C, TV, hair dryer, minibar, Wi-Fi (free).

La Bastide St-Louis

Hôtel du Soleil le Terminus   Originally built in 1913, this hotel was the headquarters of the local Nazi regiments during World War II. Reopening in late April 2005 after a
change in ownership, the hotel was transformed from a grand but rather dowdy family-
owned monument into a streamlined and glossy-looking member of a big-time nationwide

LANGUEDOC-ROUSSILLON & THE CAMARGUE

5

CARCASSONNE

chain. Bedrooms are high-ceilinged and each of a different shape, layout, and size; some are quite spacious, others a bit cramped. Touches of old-fashioned charm remain, thanks to the presence in many of the rooms of Belle Epoque pieces originally brought into the hotel during the late 1920s. The hotel lies in the heart of *La Ville Basse*, adjacent to the railway station and the Canal du Midi, about 3.2km (2 miles) from the medieval Cité.

2 av. Du Maréchal-Joffre, 11001 Carcassonne. ✆ **04-68-25-25-00.** Fax 04-68-72-53-09. www.hotels-du-soleil.com. 100 units. 54€–78€ double; 64€–95€ suite. Rates include breakfast. MC, V. Parking 10€. Bus: 4. **Amenities:** Restaurant; bar; pool (indoor); spa; access to tennis court; Wi-Fi (5€ per hr.). *In room:* A/C, TV, hair dryer, minibar.

Hôtel Montségur ★ (Value) This stately town house with a mansard roof and dormers was built in 1887. Trees and a high wrought-iron fence screen the front garden from the street. Didier and Isabelle Faugeras have furnished the hotel with antiques, lending it a residential feel. Guest rooms vary in size, from small to spacious, and all have small tiled bathrooms. A continental breakfast is available on-site, but for dinner you may wish to visit their highly recommended restaurant across the street, **Le Languedoc** (p. 101), where Didier is the chef.

27 allée d'Iéna, 11000 Carcassonne. ✆ **04-68-25-31-41.** Fax 04-68-47-13-22. www.hotelmontsegur.com. 21 units. 82€–108€ double. AE, DC, MC, V. Free parking. **Amenities:** Restaurant; bar; room service. *In room:* A/C, TV, hair dryer, Wi-Fi (free).

Trois Couronnes ★★ Reliable and dependable, though not exciting, this serviceable favorite is the best choice in Ville-Basse. It lies south of the landmark Square Gambetta, immediately west of the bridge, pont Vieux. Built in 1992, the rooms open onto views of the Aude River and the ramparts of the old city. A government-rated three-star hotel, "Three Crowns" has some of the best facilities in town, including an indoor pool. The rooms are functionally comfortable with tasteful furnishings. Service is top rate, and maintenance is good. A good regional cuisine is served in the on-site restaurant Le Richepin.

2 rue des Trois Couronnes, 11000 Carcassonne. ✆ **04-68-25-36-10.** Fax 04-68-25-92-92. www.hotel-destroiscouronnes.com. 68 units. 83€–120€ double. AE, DC, MC, V. Parking 9€. **Amenities:** Restaurant; bar; exercise room w/sauna; pool (indoor); room service. *In room:* A/C, TV, hair dryer, minibar, Wi-Fi (free).

Where to Stay Nearby

Domaine d'Auriac ★★★ Carcassonne's premier address for both food and lodging is this moss-covered 19th-century manor house located about 2.5km (1½ miles) west of the Cité. It was built around 1880 as a cube-shape building, with three stone-sided annexes (site of many of the bedrooms) on the ruins of a medieval monastery. Each bedroom has a photo-magazine aura, with lots of flowered fabrics, a range of decorative styles, and, in many cases, massive and sometimes sculpted ceiling beams. Bernard and Anne-Marie Rigaudis are the experienced owners, assisted by their grown children, Marie-Hélène and Pierre. Part of the allure of this Relais & Châteaux member is in the well-crafted and well-conceived meals served beside the pool on flowering terraces. Fixed-price menus, priced from 70€ to 150€, change several times each season but always demonstrate a sophisticated twist, making local recipes more glamorous and interesting. Sweeping panoramas over the surrounding countryside are found at the hotel's golf course.

Rte. St-Hilaire, 11009 Carcassonne. ✆ **04-68-25-72-22.** Fax 04-68-47-35-54. www.domaine-d-auriac. com. 24 units. 150€–390€ double; 400€–450€ suite. AE, DC, MC, V. Free parking. Closed Jan 3–Feb 7, Nov 7–14. Take D104 W 2.5km (1½ miles) from Carcassonne. **Amenities:** 2 restaurants; bar; babysitting; golf course; pool (outdoor); room service; tennis court (lit). *In room:* A/C, TV, hair dryer, minibar, Wi-Fi (4.50€ per 1 hr.).

Au Jardin de la Tour INTERNATIONAL   This restaurant and its verdant garden introduce greenery and charm into the city's medieval core. Rustic finds from local antiques fairs decorate the early-19th-century building. You can order from a large selection of salads, beef filet with morels, sushi, cassoulet, terrines of foie gras, and grilled fish. The consistently good cooking relies on fresh ingredients deftly handled by a talented kitchen staff.

11 rue Porte-d'Aude. (𝓒) **04-68-25-71-24.** Reservations recommended in summer. Main courses 15€–25€; fixed-price menu 30€. MC, V. Tues–Sat noon–2pm and 7:30–10pm. Closed Nov 1–Dec 15.

La Barbacane ★ FRENCH   Named after its medieval neighborhood, this restaurant enjoys equal billing with its celebrated hotel. The soothing dining room, with green walls and lots of paneling, features the cuisine of noted chef Jérome Ryon and pastry chef Régis Chanel. The menu is based on seasonal ingredients, with just enough zest. Examples are green ravioli perfumed with *seiche* (a species of octopus) and its own ink, crisp-fried cod with black olives, saltwater crayfish with strips of Bayonne ham, Breton lobster with artichoke hearts and caviar, and organically fed free-range guinea fowl rubbed with vanilla and stuffed with truffles. A star dessert is chestnut parfait with malt-flavored cream sauce and date-flavored ice cream.

In the Hôtel de la Cité (p. 99), place de l'Eglise. (𝓒) **04-68-71-98-71.** Reservations recommended. Main courses 34€–80€; fixed-price menu 75€–160€. AE, DC, MC, V. Daily 7:30–10pm. Closed Dec–Mar.

Le Languedoc ★★ TRADITIONAL FRENCH   Acclaimed chef Didier Faugeras is the creative force behind the inspired cuisine here. The high-ceilinged century-old dining room is filled with antiques, and a brick fireplace contributes to the warm atmosphere. The specialty is *cassoulet au confit de canard* (the famous stew made with duck cooked in its own fat). It has been celebrated here since the early 1960s. A smooth dessert is flambéed crepes Languedoc. In summer you can dine on a patio or in the air-conditioned restaurant. Faugeras and his wife, Isabelle, own the worthy Hôtel Montségur, across the street (p. 100).

32 allée d'Iéna. (𝓒) **04-68-25-22-17.** Reservations recommended. Main courses 18€–28€; fixed-price menu 25€–48€. AE, DC, MC, V. July–Aug Tues–Sun noon–1:30pm and Tues–Sat 7:30–9:30pm. Sept–June open for dinner only. Closed Dec 20–Jan 20.

Where to Dine Nearby

Château St-Martin ★ FRENCH   One of Languedoc's most successful chefs operates out of this 16th-century château at Montredon, 4km (2½ miles) northeast of Carcassonne. Ringed by a wooded park, the restaurant serves the superb cuisine of co-owners Jean-Claude and Jacqueline Rodriguez. Dine inside or on the terrace. Recommended dishes are fish (according to the daily catch) with fondue of baby vegetables, sea bass with scallop mousseline, sole in tarragon, and *confit de canard carcassonnaise* (duck meat cooked in its own fat and kept in earthenware pots). Two other specialties are cassoulet languedocienne (made with pork, mutton, and goose or duck) and *boullinade nouvelloise* (made with an assortment of seafood that includes scallops, sole, and turbot). On the premises are 15 simple, but comfortable, hotel rooms; doubles rent for 80€ to 100€. The hotel is closed November 15 to March 11. Call (𝓒) **04-68-47-44-41** for information on rooms.

Montredon, 11090 Carcassonne. (𝓒) **04-68-71-09-53.** Fax 04-68-25-46-55. www.chateausaintmartin.net. Reservations required. Main courses 17€–25€; fixed-price menu 31€–55€. AE, DC, MC, V. Thurs–Tues noon–1:30pm and 7:30–9:30pm (closed Sun night). From La Cité, follow signs pointing to Stade Albert Domec 4km (2¹⁄₂ miles) northeast.

Nightlife centers on **rue Omer-Sarraut** in La Bastide and **place Marcou** in La Cité. **La Bulle,** 115 rue Barbacane (© **04-68-72-47-70**), explodes with techno and rock dance tunes for an under-30 crowd that keeps the place hopping until 5am Wednesday to Sunday. The cover charge begins at 10€ per person. Another enduringly popular disco, 4km (2½ miles) southwest of town, is **Le Black Bottom,** route de Limoux (© **04-68-47-37-11**), which plays every conceivable kind of dance music Thursday to Sunday beginning at 11pm. Entrance costs 10€ only on Saturday.

7 PERPIGNAN ★★

904km (562 miles) SW of Paris; 369km (229 miles) NW of Marseille; 64km (40 miles) S of Narbonne

At Perpignan you might think you've crossed the border into Spain, for it was once Catalonia's second city after Barcelona. Even earlier it was the capital of the kingdom of Majorca. But when the Roussillon—the French part of Catalonia—was finally partitioned off, Perpignan became permanently French by the Treaty of the Pyrenees in 1659. However, Catalan is still spoken here, especially among the country people.

Legend has it that Perpignan derives its name from Père Pinya, a plowman who followed the Tèt River down the Pyrenees mountains to the site of the town today, where he cultivated the fertile soil while the river kept its promise to water the fields.

Today Perpignan is content to rest on its former glory. Its 120,000 residents enjoy the closeness of the Côte Catalane (the coastline of Catalonia, in neighboring Spain) and the mountains to the north. The pace is relaxed: You'll have time to smell the flowers that grow here in great abundance.

As one of the sunniest places in France, during summer afternoons in July and August, it's a cauldron. That's when many locals catch a ride 9.5km (6 miles) to the beach resort of Canet. Take bus no. 1 from the center of Perpignan costing 2€, running every 15 minutes in summer. A young scene brings energy to Perpignan, especially along the Basse River, site of impromptu nighttime concerts, beer drinking, and tapas devouring, a tradition adopted from nearby Barcelona.

ESSENTIALS

GETTING THERE   Four **trains** per day arrive from Paris from both the Gare St. Lazare and the Gare de Nord (trip time: 6–10 hr.) after stopping at Montpellier; the one-way fare is 91€. Three conventional trains arrive from Marseille via Narbonne (trip time: 4½ hr.; one-way fare: 40€). For rail information and schedules, call © **36-35,** or visit **www. voyages-sncf.com**. Perpignan is well connected to Collioure by **bus.** Five buses run between the two cities Monday to Friday, four on Saturday, and one on Sunday. Buses depart from 17 av. Général Leclerc (© **04-68-35-29-02**), in Perpignan. The fare is 6.60€.

If you're **driving** from the French Riviera, drive west along A9 to Perpignan.

VISITOR INFORMATION   The **Office Municipal du Tourisme** is in the Palais des Congrès, place Armand-Lanoux (© **04-68-66-30-30;** fax 04-68-66-30-26; www. perpignantourisme.com).

SPECIAL EVENTS   In the heat of July during a 4-week cultural binge, **Les Estivales** (© **04-68-35-01-77;** www.estivales.com) causes the city to explode with music, expositions, and theater. Our favorite time to visit this area is during the **grape harvest** in

Finds   **Céret: Birthplace of Cubism**

Driving 31km (19 miles) southwest of Perpignan, you reach this enchanting little town, long an artists' mecca. A group of avant-garde artists was drawn here when the Catalonian sculptor Manolo (1873–1945) let fellow artists in on a secret: **Céret** is a little gem. In time, Picasso and Braque arrived, making Céret the capital of cubism.

In the center of town, you can visit **Musée d'Art Moderne** ★★, 8 bd. Maréchal-Joffre (© **04-68-87-27-76;** www.musee-ceret.com), with one of the finest collections of art in the southwest. The museum is dedicated to the painters who have lived in and around Céret, if only briefly. Of course, most visitors come here to see works by Picasso, which include paintings, sculptures, and sketches. Also displayed are works by Chagall, Braque, Matisse, Maillol, and Miró, plus four paintings by Pierre Brune, founder of the museum. On the second floor, space is devoted to floating exhibits by contemporary French artists from mid-July to mid-September; museum hours are daily from 10am to 7pm. From mid-September to June hours are Wednesday to Monday 10am to 6pm. Admission is 8€ for adults, 6€ for students, and free for ages 12 and under.

Information about the town is found at the **Office de Tourisme,** 1 av. Clemenceau (© **04-68-87-00-53;** www.ot-ceret.fr). Transports Vaills (© **04-68-87-10-70**) runs one bus per hour (trip time: 45 min.) from Perpignan to Céret during the day; one-way fare costs 4.40€.

September. If you visit then, you may want to drive through vineyards of the Rivesaltes district bordering the city to the west and north. Temperatures have usually dropped by then.

Perpignan is host to one of the most widely discussed celebrations of photojournalism in the industry, the **Festival International du Photojournalisme** (© **04-68-62-38-00;** www.visapourlimage.com). Established in the late 1980s, it's also called **Le Visa pour l'Image.** From September 2 to September 17, at least 10 sites of historic (usually medieval) interest are devoted to photojournalistic expositions from around the world. Entrance to the shows is free, and an international committee awards prizes.

SEEING THE SIGHTS

A 3-hour guided **walking tour** is a good way to see the attractions in the town's historic core. Some tour leaders even lace their commentary with English. Tours begin at 3pm daily from mid-June to mid-September, and for 2 weeks around Christmas. The rest of the year, they start at 2:30pm on Wednesday and Saturday only. They depart from in front of the tourist office and cost 5€ per person. For more details, contact the tourist office (see above).

Castillet/Musée des Arts et Traditions Populaires Catalans ★   The Castillet is one of the chief sights of Perpignan. The machicolated and crenelated redbrick building from the 14th century is both a gateway and fortress. It houses the museum, also known as La Casa Païral, which contains exhibitions of Catalan regional artifacts and folkloric items, including typical dress. Part of the charm of the Castillet derives from its bulky-looking tower, which you can climb for a good view of the town.

Place de Verdun. ℂ **04-68-35-42-05.** Admission 4€ adults, 2€ students and children 17 and under. May–Sept Wed–Mon 10am–6:30pm; Oct–Apr Wed–Mon 11am–5:30pm.

Cathédrale St-Jean ★   The cathedral dates from the 14th and 15th centuries and has an admirable nave and interesting 17th-century retables (altarpieces). Leaving through the south door, you'll find on the left a chapel with the *Devost-Christ (Devout Christ)*, a magnificent woodcarving depicting Jesus contorted with pain and suffering, his head, crowned with thorns, drooping on his chest. Sightseeing visits are discouraged during Sunday Mass. On Good Friday, the statue is promenaded through the streets of the town center.

Place Gambetta/rue de l'Horloge. ℂ **04-68-51-33-72.** Free admission. Daily 7:30am–7pm. Closes 5:30pm Dec–Feb.

Palais des Rois de Majorque (Palace of the Kings of Majorca) ★   At the top of the town, the Spanish citadel encloses the Palace of the Kings of Majorca. The government has restored this structure, built in the 13th and 14th centuries, around a court encircled by arcades. You can see the old throne room, with its large fireplaces, and a square tower with a double gallery and a fine view of the Pyrenees. A free guided tour, in French only, departs four times a day if demand warrants it.

Rue des Archers. ℂ **04-68-34-48-29.** Admission 4€ adults, 2€ students, free for children 11 and under. June–Sept daily 10am–6pm; Oct–May daily 9am–5pm.

A Major Historic Site Nearby

Château de Salses ★   This important historic site is in the hamlet of Salses, 25km (15 miles) north of the city center. Since the days of the Romans, this fort has guarded the main road linking Spain and France. Ferdinand of Aragón erected a fort here in 1497 to protect the northern frontier of his kingdom. Even today, Salses marks the language-barrier point between Catalonia in Spain and Languedoc in France. This Spanish-style fort, designed by Ferdinand himself, is a curious example of an Iberian structure in France. In the 17th century, it was modified by the French military engineer Vauban to look more like a château. After many changes of ownership, Salses fell to the forces of Louis XIII in September 1642, and its Spanish garrison left forever. Less than 2 decades later, Roussillon was incorporated into France. A small-scale gift shop dispensing film and cold drinks is on the premises.

Salses, 16km (10 miles) north of the center of Perpignan. ℂ **04-68-38-60-13.** Admission 6.50€ adults, 4.50€ ages 17–25, free for children 16 and under. Oct–May daily 10am–12:15pm and 2–5pm; June–Sept daily 9:30am–7pm. From Perpignan, follow signs to Narbonne and RN9.

SHOPPING

With its inviting storefronts and pedestrian streets, Perpignan is a good town for shopping. Catalan is the style indigenous to the area, and it's reflected in textiles and pottery in strong geometric patterns and sturdily structured furniture. For one of the best selections of Catalan pottery, furniture, and carpets, and even a small inventory of antiques, visit the **Centre Sant-Vicens** ★, rue Sant-Vicens (ℂ **04-68-50-02-18**), site of about a dozen independent merchants. You'll find it 4km (2½ miles) south of the town center, following the signs pointing to Enne and Collioures. In the town center, **La Maison Quinta,** 3 rue des Grand-des-Fabriques (ℂ **04-68-34-41-62;** www.maison-quinta. com), sells Catalan-inspired items for home decorating.

Hôtel de la Loge   This beguiling little place dates from the 16th century but has been renovated into a modern hotel. It's located right in the heart of town, near the Castillet and Loge de Mer, the town hall, from which it takes its name. The cozy rooms are attractively furnished, with a sense of warmth and hospitality. The tiled bathrooms are small but offer adequate shelf space. The staff can arrange scuba diving lessons and sailing.

1 rue des Fabriques d'en-Nabot, 66000 Perpignan. ☏ **04-68-34-41-02.** Fax 04-68-34-25-13. www. hoteldelaloge.fr. 22 units. 48€–68€ double; 69€–75€ triple. AE, DC, MC, V. **Amenities:** Bar. *In room:* A/C, TV, hair dryer, minibar, Wi-Fi (free).

La Villa Duflot ★★★   This is the area's greatest hotel, yet its prices are reasonable for the luxury it offers. Tranquillity, style, and refinement reign supreme. Located in a suburb 4km (2½ miles) from Perpignan, La Villa Duflot is a Mediterranean-style dwelling surrounded by a park of pine, palm, and eucalyptus. You can sunbathe in the gardens surrounding the pool and order drinks from the outside bar. The good-size guest rooms surround a patio planted with century-old olive trees. All are spacious and soundproof, with marble bathrooms and Art Deco interiors. The restaurant (p. 106) is reason enough to stay.

Rond-Point Albert Donnezan, 66000 Perpignan. ☏ **04-68-56-67-67.** Fax 04-68-56-54-05. www.villa-duflot.com. 24 units. 120€–200€ double. Half-board 108€–200€ per person double occupancy. AE, DC, MC, V. From the center of Perpignan, follow signs to Perthus–Le Belou and A9, and travel 3km (1¾ miles) south. Just before you reach A9, you'll see the hotel. **Amenities:** Restaurant; 2 bars; babysitting; pool (outdoor); room service. *In room:* A/C, TV, hair dryer, minibar, Wi-Fi (free).

Park Hotel ★   This four-story hotel facing the Jardins de la Ville offers well-furnished, soundproof rooms. Although the Park is solid and reliable, it is the town's second choice, having none of the glamour of Villa Duflot (see above). Midsize to spacious bedrooms are comfortably furnished with taste but not much flair; each comes with an average-size bathroom.

The restaurant, Le Chapon Fin, serves up first-class Mediterranean cuisine. The food, made from prime regional produce, is some of the finest in the area. Post-nouvelle choices include roast sea scallops flavored with succulent sea urchin velouté (white sauce thickened with white roux), various lobster dishes, and penne with truffles. As an accompaniment, try one of the local wines—perhaps a Collioure or Côtes du Roussillon. The hotel also houses Le Bistrot du Park, a less expensive eatery specializing in seafood.

18 bd. Jean-Bourrat, 66000 Perpignan. ☏ **04-68-35-14-14.** Fax 04-68-35-48-18. www.parkhotel-fr.com. 69 units. 80€–108€ double; 130€–280€ suite. AE, DC, MC, V. Parking 10€. **Amenities:** 2 restaurants; 2 bars; babysitting; pool (outdoor); room service. *In room:* A/C, TV, hair dryer, minibar, Wi-Fi (free).

WHERE TO DINE

L'Assiette Catalane (Value) FRENCH/SPANISH/CATALAN   Known to virtually every resident of Perpignan for its well-prepared cuisine, this restaurant resembles something you'd expect across the Pyrenees in Spain. Hand-painted ceramic plates, rugby and flamenco posters, and antique farm implements cover the thick stone walls. Even the long, lively bar is inlaid with Iberian mosaics, and copies of works by Dalí and Picasso seem to stare back at you as you dine. Menu items include four kinds of *parrilladas* (mixed grills)—one of the most appealing consists entirely of fish served on a hot slab of iron brought directly to your table. Zarzuelas, paella, and tapas, prepared in the Spanish style, are served as an appetizer. Chicken with crayfish is another regional specialty. It seems appropriate to follow up with a portion of flan.

9 rue de la République. ⓒ **04-68-34-77-62.** www.assiettecatalane.com. Reservations recommended. Main courses 12€–18€; fixed-price lunch 8€–16€; fixed-price dinner 16€–27€. MC, V. Mon–Sat noon–2pm; Wed–Mon 7–11pm.

La Villa Duflot ★ FRENCH   Slightly removed from the city center, this *restaurant avec chambres* (see "Where to Stay," above) is the most tranquil oasis in the area. Owner André Duflot employs top-notch chefs who turn out dish after dish with remarkable skill and professionalism. Try, for example, a salad of warm squid, a platter of fresh anchovies marinated in vinegar, excellent foie gras of duckling, or lasagna of foie gras with asparagus points. A wonderful dessert is chocolate cake with saffron-flavored cream sauce. On the premises is an American-style bar.

In La Villa Duflot (p. 105), Rond-Point Albert Donnezan, 66000 Perpignan. ⓒ **04-68-56-67-67.** Fax 04-68-56-54-05. Reservations required. Main courses 19€–25€; Sat–Sun fixed-price menu 31€. AE, DC, MC, V. Daily noon–2pm and 8–11pm. From the center of Perpignan, follow signs to Perthus–Le Belou and A9, and travel 3km (1³/₄ miles) south. Just before you reach A9, you'll see the hotel.

Le Clos des Lys ★ (Value) FRENCH   This restaurant, in a stately building sitting apart from its neighbors, has an outdoor terrace overlooking a copse of cypresses and bubbling fountains. It's supervised by Jean-Claude Vila and Frank Sequret, respected chefs who have been finalists in several culinary competitions. The fixed-price menus vary widely in selection and cost. Dishes may include goat cheese in puff pastry, garnished with sesame seeds and a reduction of Banyuls dessert wine; terrine of three kinds of liver accompanied with a salad of wild greens and walnuts; foie gras of duck with passion fruit and mango chutney sauce; filets of sea wolf fried with sesame seeds and served with eggplant mousse and tomato-flavored risotto; and tournedos of beef with a layer of foie gras, creamed morels, and soufflé potatoes. The restaurant incorporates a thriving catering business that books conventions and weddings.

660 chemin de la Fauceille. ⓒ **04-68-56-79-00.** www.closdeslys.com. Reservations recommended. Fixed-price lunch 20€–79€; fixed-price dinner 30€–79€. AE, DC, MC, V. Tues–Sun noon–2pm; Tues and Thurs–Sat 7–9:30pm. Closed 3 weeks in Feb. From the center of Perpignan, drive 2.5km (1¹/₂ miles) west, following the rte. d'Espagne.

PERPIGNAN AFTER DARK

Perpignan shows its Spanish and Catalan side at night, when a round of tapas and late-night promenades are among the activities. The streets radiating from **place de la Loge** offer a higher concentration of bars and clubs than any other part of town.

An evening on the town involves a drink and a chat in one of the *bars de nuit,* followed by a visit to a disco. Perhaps you will start your night at **Le Habana Bodegita-Club,** 5 rue Grande-des-Fabriques (ⓒ **04-68-34-11-00**), where salsa and merengue play and sunset-colored cocktails flow. Brews with an Irish accent are the attraction at **Le O'Shannon Bar,** 3 rue de l'Incendie (ⓒ **04-68-35-12-48**), where a small community of Irish expats (and Celtic wannabes) wax nostalgic.

Discos in Perpignan open around 11pm. **Le Napoli,** 3 rue place de Catalogne (ⓒ **04-68-51-25-02**), a modern, mirror-sheathed space, may remind you of an airport waiting area without the chairs. (You'll have to stand up and mingle or dance, because there's almost nowhere to sit.) Another option is the **Uba-Club,** 5 bd. Mercader (ⓒ **04-68-34-06-70**), which has a smallish dance floor and, thankfully, sofas and chairs.

During summer, the beachfront strip at the nearby resort of **Canet-Plage,** 12km (7½ miles) east of Perpignan's historic core, abounds with seasonal bars and dance clubs that come and go with the tourist tides.

929km (577 miles) SW of Paris; 27km (17 miles) SE of Perpignan

You might recognize this port and its sailboats from the fauve paintings of Lhote and Derain. It's said to resemble St-Tropez before it was spoiled. In the past, it attracted Matisse, Picasso, and Dalí. Collioure is the most authentic and alluring port of Roussillon, a gem with a vivid Spanish/Catalan image and flavor. Some visitors believe it's the most charming village on the Côte Vermeille. The town's sloping, narrow streets, charming semifortified church, antique lighthouse, and eerily introverted culture make it worth an afternoon stopover. This is the ideal small-town antidote to the condo-choked Riviera.

ESSENTIALS

GETTING THERE Collioure has frequent **train** and bus service, especially from Perpignan (trip time: 20 min.). Sixteen trains a day make the trip, costing a mere 4.90€. For train information and schedules, call *(**36-35,** or visit **www.voyages-sncf.com**. **Bus** service takes a bit longer, and costs more. For more information on getting to Collioure by bus from Perpignan, see p. 102. Many visitors **drive** along the coastal road (RN114) leading to the Spanish border.

VISITOR INFORMATION The **Office de Tourisme** is on place du 18-Juin (*(**04-68-82-15-47;** fax 04-68-82-46-29; www.collioure.com).

SPECIAL EVENTS The annual **Salon des Antiquaires** takes place on a 3-day weekend around November 1. Antiques dealers from throughout southern France set up shop for wholesalers and retailers. For more information, contact the tourist office.

EXPLORING THE TOWN

The two curving ports sit on either side of the heavy masonry of the 13th-century **Château Royal,** place de 8-Mai-1945 (*(**04-68-82-06-43**). It's of interest in its own right for its medieval fortifications and overall bulk, but between the months of May and September, it's also the home to a changing series of special (temporary) exhibitions, each of which comes and goes at regular intervals. Entrance fees are 4€ for adults, 2€ for students and children ages 12 to 18, and free for children 11 and under. From June to September, the château is open daily 10am to 6pm, October to May, daily 9am to 5pm.

Also try to visit the **Musée Jean-Peské,** route de Port-Vendres (*(**04-68-82-10-19**), home to a collection of works by artists who painted here. It's open in July and August daily 10am to noon and 2 to 6pm, September to June Wednesday to Monday 10am to noon and 2 to 6pm. Admission is 2€ for adults, 1.50€ for children 12 to 16 and students, and free for children 11 and under.

WHERE TO STAY

Casa Païral ★ This pleasant family-operated hotel is in a 150-year-old house a very short walk from the port and beach. In the guest rooms, charming old antiques blend with more modern pieces. The best doubles have *petit salons* and small balconies. Breakfast is the only meal served, but the many restaurants nearby guarantee you won't go hungry. On sunny days, guests can take a dip in the pool shaded by century-old trees.

Impasse des Palmiers, 66190 Collioure. *(**04-68-82-05-81.** Fax 04-68-82-52-10. www.hotel-casa-pairal. com. 27 units. 89€–180€ double; 178€–225€ suite. AE, DC, MC, V. Parking 14€. Closed Nov–Mar. **Amenities:** Pool (outdoor); room service. *In room:* A/C, TV, hair dryer, minibar, Wi-Fi (free).

Hôtel Princes de Catalogne   This is a relatively modern hotel of little architectural interest, but it is positioned in the town center and has a hardworking and cooperative staff. Bedrooms are a bit more spacious than you might have expected and contain simple, angular furniture with touches of traditional Provençal upholsteries, writing tables, and comfortable beds. The tidy bathrooms are tiled and small.

Rue des Palmiers, 66190 Collioure. ✆ **04-68-98-30-00.** Fax 04-68-98-30-31. www.hotel-princes catalogne.com. 36 units. 55€–70€ double; 106€–117€ suite. AE, MC, V. Free parking. **Amenities:** Bar; room service. *In room:* A/C, TV, minibar, hair dryer.

Le Bon Port   Built during the 1940s, this stucco-sided hotel perches beside the port, across the water from the town center, which lies within a 5-minute walk. It offers comfortable, appealingly simple bedrooms with summery furniture, tile floors, and flowered upholsteries. Accommodations are scattered among three separate buildings, the smallest of which is a two-unit cabana set beside the swimming pool. Staff is soft-spoken and charming, and knows what's going on in Collioure.

12 rte. de Port-Vendres, 66190 Collioure. ✆ **04-68-82-06-08.** Fax 04-68-82-54-97. www.bon-port.com. 22 units. 98€–102€ double; 118€–130€ triple; 145€–175€ studio. MC, V. **Amenities:** Bar; babysitting; Internet (free); pool (outdoor). *In room:* TV.

Les Caranques (Value)   Constructed around the core of a private villa built after World War II and enlarged twice since then, this comfortably furnished hotel is one of the best bargains in town. The rooms are a bit small but neatly maintained. On the perimeter of Collioure, away from the crush (and the charm) of the center, the hotel features a terrace view of the old port. The terrace also stretches from the hotel to the sea, where guests can swim directly from the rocks.

Rte. de Port-Vendres, 66190 Collioure. ✆ **04-68-82-06-68.** Fax 04-68-82-00-92. www.les-caranques.com. 22 units. 47€–80€ double. AE, MC, V. Free parking. Closed Oct 15–Mar 31. **Amenities:** Room service. *In room:* Minibar.

Les Templiers ★ (Finds)   The most charming and atmospheric hotel in the town center maintains its headquarters about 15m (50 ft.) inland from the port, in a *fin de siècle* house whose ground floor is devoted to a recommended bar and restaurant (p. 109). Part of the charm of the place derives from the clusters of mature local men playing cards (and, in some cases, according to the staff, "cheating") in the bar and conversing in Catalan. The hotel consists of four separate buildings, each within a short walk from one another. The most comfortable and lavishly decorated of the four is the hotel's headquarters and site of registration for the annexes, which do not employ receptionists or check-in staffs of their own. In the main building, expect at least 2,000 paintings—so many that most of the wall surfaces are completely covered with them—and a bar that's artfully sculpted to resemble a boat, complete with a sculpture at one end of a mermaid comforting (or seducing) a much smaller depiction of a sailor. Bedrooms in the main building have polychrome (that is, painted) Catalan-style furniture and views of the town's château and, in some cases, the sea; those in the annexes have a traditional but less-lavish decor and less-inspiring views.

12 Quai de l'Amirauté, 66190 Collioure. ✆ **04-68-98-31-10.** Fax 04-68-98-01-24. www.hotel-templiers. com. 55 units. 50€–130€ double. AE, DC, MC, V. Closed Jan to mid-Feb. **Amenities:** Restaurant; bar; room service. *In room:* A/C, TV, Wi-Fi (5€ per hr.).

Relais des Trois Mas et Restaurant La Balette ★★   This is the town's premier hotel and the restaurant of choice; the hotel was established more than 20 years ago by connecting a trio of older Provençal farmhouses. The decor of its beautiful rooms honors the famous artists who once lived in Collioure. The rooms, which have spacious bathrooms with Jacuzzis, open onto views of the water. Even if you aren't a guest, you may want to take a meal in the dining room to take in its harbor vista, and the work of Jose Vidal, the best chef in town. His cooking is inventive—often simple but always refined. Fixed-price menus cost 37€ to 85€ and are served Wednesday to Sunday at lunch and dinner.

Rte. de Port-Vendres, 66190 Collioure. (℮ **04-68-82-05-07.** Fax 04-68-82-38-08. www.relaisdes3mas.com. 23 units. 100€–290€ double; 190€–460€ suite. Half-board 73€ per person. AE, MC, V. Free parking. Closed Dec–Feb. **Amenities:** Restaurant; babysitting; pool (indoor); room service; sauna; Wi-Fi (free). *In room:* A/C, TV, hair dryer, minibar.

WHERE TO DINE

Note that the **Restaurant La Balette** (see above) is the best dining room in town.

Le Puits CATALAN   Named after its kitchen's now-sealed-off well *(le puits)* that used to provide water for houses nearby, this is a small-scale and charming restaurant that makes special efforts in its preparation of time-honored Catalan specialties. The dining room is accented with exposed beams and soft tones of red and orange, with an additional dozen seats lined up beside the all-pedestrian street in front. The family that owns this place is especially proud of the dining room's critically acclaimed fresco that was painted in 1950 by a local (and at press time, still living) artist named Bernardi (first name unused and mostly unknown). The fresco depicts the grape harvest and fishers of Collioure, and is often cited as a good early example of the artist's work. Come here for, among other dishes, calamari stew prepared with local Banyuls wine; stuffed mussels; grilled pork jowls *(les galtes)* prepared either with local Banyuls wine or with herbs; and tuna steak in Catalan (tomatoes, onions, and peppers) sauce.

2 rue Arago. (℮ **04-68-82-06-24.** Reservations recommended. Main courses 17€–29€; fixed-price menus 17€–35€. MC, V. Daily 11:30am–3pm and 6:30–10:30pm. Closed Thurs Oct–May.

Les Templiers CATALAN   The charm of Les Templiers derives from the bar, where every inch of the wall is covered with paintings, and from a well-established role as the town's most popular card-playing venue for retired Catalan-speaking local gents. After an aperitif in the bar, you'll be prepared for a meal in the dining room, where stone vaults, more paintings, and the possibility of sitting at a table on the pavement in front add to the allure. The menu is entirely based on old-fashioned Catalan traditions. An excellent starter is a platter of grilled anchovies drizzled with olive oil and sprinkled with parsley and other herbs. Other options include a platter of fried fish incorporating whatever was hauled in from the Mediterranean that day, a savory bouillabaisse, fresh codfish served with a "caviar" of mashed eggplant, shoulder of Pyrenean lamb with a spicy onion jam, and seafood paella. Dessert might include a time-tested crème Catalane or an unusual form of ice cream: flavored with steamed and pulverized fennel served with spice bread and saffron sauce.

In Les Templiers Hotel (p. 108), 12 Quai de l'Amirauté, 66190 Collioure. (℮ **04-68-98-31-10.** Reservations recommended in midsummer. Main courses 19€–31€; fixed-price menu 22€. AE, DC, MC, V. Thurs–Mon 12:30–2pm and 7:30–10pm. Closed Jan to mid-Feb.

Le Trémail CATALAN/SEAFOOD   Set on a narrow, cobble-covered alleyway in the oldest part of Collioure, this is a rustic and authentically Catalan restaurant. It functioned for many generations as the family home of the owner, Jean-Paul Fabre. "Le trémail" is local dialect for the small nets used to catch fish in rocky shallow waters. Surrounded by stone walls, hand-painted Spanish tiles, and dangling fishnets, less than

18m (60 ft.) from the edge of the sea, the specialty here is grilled fish *(à la plancha),* invariably served with olive oil and herb-enriched vinaigrette. Examples include marinated anchovies with braised onions and peppers, and a succulent version of the day's catch. A limited number of "noble fish"—sole and turbot—might be on hand, along with a limited roster of meat. Particularly succulent are *rondelles* of calamari with red wine. For dessert, try the *crème Catalán* or a homemade pastry.

1 rue Arago. (© **04-68-82-16-10.** Reservations recommended. Main courses 13€–28€; set menu 16€–35€. AE, DC, MC, V. Daily noon–3pm and 7–10pm (until 11pm June–Oct).

Neptune ★★★ FRENCH/CATALAN   This is the best restaurant in Collioure, but much to the credit of its owners and staff, it's easygoing and remarkably unpretentious. You'll find it on the southeastern edge of town in a salmon-toned Provençal *mas* (farmhouse). For many years the establishment has been the domain of the talented, hardworking Mourlane family. Top-quality ingredients and respect and care in handling go into every item on the menu. Our favorite starter is a platter of local anchovies marinated in herbs; you may opt for a salad of fresh wild greens garnished with chunks of lobster. Main courses change with the seasons but have included grilled Mediterranean sea wolf with oyster-flavored butter sauce; several versions of lobster; or rack of suckling lamb from the nearby salt marshes, served in orange sauce or an herb-flavored pastry crust. Equally appealing are lightly braised scallops in delicate butter, herb, and garlic sauce, and simple but succulent sole meunière.

9 rte. de Porte-Vendres. (© **04-68-82-02-27.** Reservations recommended. Main courses 23€–56€; fixed-price menus 32€–70€. AE, MC, V. Wed–Mon noon–2pm and 7:30–9pm.

9 NARBONNE ★

845km (525 miles) SW of Paris; 61km (38 miles) E of Carcassonne; 93km (58 miles) S of Montpellier

Medieval Narbonne was a port to rival Marseille in Roman days, with its "galleys laden with riches." It was the first town outside Italy to be colonized by the Romans, but the Mediterranean, now 8km (5 miles) away, left it high and dry. It's an intriguing place, steeped in antiquity.

After Lyon, Narbonne was the largest town in Gaul. Even today, one can see evidence of the town's former wealth. Too far from the sea to be a beach town, it attracts history buffs to its memories of a glorious past. Some 50,000 Narbonnais live in what is really a sleepy backwater. However, many locals are trying to make a go with their vineyards. Caves are open to visitors in the surrounding area (the tourist office will advise). If you want to go to the beach, you'll have to head to the nearby sands at the village of **Gruisson** and the beach (Gruisson-Plage) that adjoins it, or to the suburb of **St-Pierre la Mer** and its adjoining beach (Narbonne-Plage). Both lie 14km (9 miles) south of Narbonne. Buses from the town center are frequent and marked with their respective destinations.

ESSENTIALS
GETTING THERE   Narbonne has rail, bus, and highway connections with other cities on the Mediterranean coast and with Toulouse, although rail travel is the most popular way to get here. Fourteen **trains** per day arrive from Perpignan (trip time: 50 min.), 13 per day from Toulouse (trip time: 1½ hr.), and 12 per day from Montpellier (trip time: 1 hr.). Most rail passengers arriving from Paris take the TGV directly to Narbonne (trip

time: 4 hr.). The one-way fare from Paris starts from 85€, from Montpellier, 14€ to 18€.
For rail information, call ✆ **36-35,** or visit **www.voyages-sncf.com**. **Bus** service is
minimal and geared toward resident travelers. If you're **driving,** Narbonne is at the junction of A61 and A9, easily accessible from either Toulouse or the Riviera.

VISITOR INFORMATION The **Office de Tourisme** is on place Roger-Salengro
(✆ **04-68-65-15-60;** fax 04-68-65-59-12; www.mairie-narbonne.fr).

EXPLORING THE TOWN
The Central Complex
The town's sights are concentrated in the medieval Vieille Ville (Old City), a massive
central labyrinth of religious and civic buildings. A combination ticket (5.20€ adults,
3.70€ students and children 17 and under) admits you to all of the attractions listed
below. If you don't visit the palace, you can pay for those attractions separately.

Most visitors buy a *pass-billet,* or *billet global,* valid for 3 days allowing entrance to four
of the town's museums (including the Musée Lapidaire), plus the *donjon,* and the *trésor*
of the cathedral. Tickets are 7.50€ for adults and 5.50€ for children 5 and up. Entrance
to any of the four museums is free for children 4 and under.

The neo-Gothic **Hôtel de Ville** (town hall) in the complex was reconstructed by
Viollet-le-Duc, the 19th-century architect who refurbished Notre-Dame in Paris
between 1845 and 1850.

Cathédrale St-Just ★★ The cathedral's construction began in 1272, but it was
never finished. Only the transept and a choir were completed. The choir is 39m (130 ft.)
high, built in the bold Gothic style of northern France. At each end of the transept are
58m (194-ft.) towers from 1480. The cathedral also holds an impressive collection of
Flemish tapestries and is connected to the archbishop's palace by 14th- and 15th-century
cloisters.

Place de l'Hôtel-de-Ville (enter on rue Gauthier). ✆ **04-68-32-09-52.** Free admission. June–Sept daily
10am–7pm; Oct–May daily 9am–noon and 2–6pm.

Donjon Gilles-Aycelin A watchtower and prison in the late 13th century, it has a
lofty observation platform with a view of the cathedral, the surrounding plain, and the
Pyrenees. If you happen to visit between mid-June and mid-September, you might want
to participate in one of the occasional hikes up the steep steps of the watchtower.

Place de l'Hôtel-de-Ville. ✆ **04-68-90-30-30.** Admission 2.20€. Daily 10am–noon and 2–5pm.

Palais des Archevêques (Archbishop's Palace, or Vieux-Palais) The palace
was conceived as part fortress, part pleasure residence. It has three military-style towers
from the 13th and 14th centuries. The Old Palace on the right dates from the 12th
century, and the so-called "New Palace" on the left dates from the 14th. It's said that the
old, arthritic, and sometimes very overweight archbishops used to be hauled up the
interior's monumental Louis XIII–style stairs on mules.

Today the once-private apartments of the former bishops contain three museums. The
Musée Archéologique ★ contains prehistoric artifacts, Bronze Age tools, 14th-century
frescoes, and Greco-Roman amphorae. Several of the sarcophagi date from the 3rd century, and some of the mosaics are of pagan origin. The **Musée d'Art et d'Histoire de
Narbonne** is located three floors above street level in the archbishop's once-private apartments (the rooms where Louis XII resided during his siege of Perpignan). Their coffered
ceilings are enhanced with panels depicting the nine Muses. A Roman mosaic floor and

5

(Finds) **Liberté, Egalité, Fraternité . . . Nudité**

The municipality known as **Agde,** 40km (25 miles) northeast of Narbonne and 50km (31 miles) southwest of Montpellier, operates like every other *commune* in France, with one startling exception: its flourishing nudist colony. In the 1970s, the community's founder/matriarch, Mademoiselle Geneviève Oltha, had the idea of promoting a simple pine grove beside the sea as a place for an escape from the stresses of urban life. Within less than 25 years, the site burgeoned into the largest nudist colony in Europe, with a roster of about 100 midwinter residents and a midsummer population usually approaching 30,000.

Don't expect everyone in Agde to be nude, since the town's four major subdivisions (Cité d'Agde, Cap d'Agde, Grau d'Agde, and La Tamarissière) offer options for the clothed as well. However, in the clearly signposted and, for the most part, fenced-in **Quartier Naturiste Cap d'Agde** ★ (© **04-67-26-00-26;** www.agdenaturisme.com), nudity is required on the beaches and encouraged elsewhere. Stores, restaurants, and shops (most selling everything except—you guessed it—clothing) are part of the setup. Those who arrive on foot at the compound's gate pay 5€ for entrance; motorists with as many passengers as can be crammed into their cars pay 10€. The **Agde Office de Tourisme,** Espace Molière, Centre Ville (© **04-67-94-29-68**), or its satellite branch, the **Office Municipal de Tourism,** Cap d'Agde, Les Plages (© **04-67-01-04-04**), long ago became accustomed to answering questions for the clothed, the unclothed, and the clothing indecisive.

Conveniently close to but not within the nudist zone are two museums. The **Musée Agathois,** rue de la Fraternité (© **04-67-94-82-51**), is noted for the homage it pays to (clothed) cultural models of the city's 19th-century fishing tradition and the region's handicrafts. The **Musée l'Ephébe,** Mas de la Clape, Cap d'Agde (© **04-67-94-69-60**), showcases the artifacts dredged up by marine explorations of the nearby sea bottom. Its star exhibit and namesake is the nearly life-size **l'Ephébe,** a graceful-looking Greek statue from the 6th century B.C. Admission to each museum costs 4.50€. Both museums are open June to September daily 9am to 7:30pm and October to May Wednesday to Monday 9am to noon and 2 to 6pm.

17th-century portraits are on display, as well as a collection of antique porcelain, enamels, and a portrait bust of Louis XIV. In the **Horreum Romain** is a labyrinth of underground passageways, similar to catacombs but without burial functions, dug by the Gallo-Romans and their successors for storage of food and supplies during times of siege.

Place de l'Hôtel-de-Ville. © **04-68-90-30-66** or 04-68-90-30-66. *Billet global* or 5.20€. Apr–Sept daily 10am–12:15pm and 2–6pm; Oct–Mar Tues–Sun 10am–noon and 2–5pm.

More Sights

Basilique St-Paul-Serge This early Gothic church was built on the site of a 4th-century necropolis. It has an elegant choir with fine Renaissance woodcarvings and ancient Christian sarcophagi. The chancel, from 1229, is admirable. The north door leads to the Paleo-Christian Cemetery, part of an early Christian burial ground.

Rue de l'Hôtel-Dieu. (**Ⓒ 04-68-32-68-98.** Free admission. Daily 9am–7pm; Oct–Mar daily 9am–noon, Mon–Sat 2–6pm.

Musée Lapidaire   Located in the 13th-century Notre-Dame de Lamourguier, this museum contains an important collection of Roman artifacts—broken sculptures and Latin inscriptions—as well as relics of medieval buildings. While it has no major exhibits, it does offer a vast array of classical busts, Roman lintels, and ancient sarcophagi that will satisfy all but the most feverish archaeologist. It takes less than an hour to see it all. You can enter with your general admission ticket to the museums of the archbishop's palace.

Place Lamourguier. (**Ⓒ 04-68-65-53-58.** *Billet global* or 3.70€ adults and students, free for children 9 and under. Oct–Mar Tues–Sun 10am–noon and 2–5pm; Apr–Sept daily 9:30am–12:15pm and 2–6pm.

WHERE TO STAY

Hôtel du Languedoc   Although it competes with a cookie-cutter chain hotel in town, the Novotel, and a motel on the outskirts, the Languedoc remains the traditional favorite because of its old-fashioned ambience and nostalgic feel. It bravely keeps up with the times, however, and has a welcoming atmosphere, thanks to a very helpful staff. It offers well-equipped rooms with acceptably comfortable mattresses. As is typical of an old hotel of this era, rooms come in various shapes and sizes.

Even if you're not a hotel guest, consider a visit to its well-respected restaurant, which features an array of regionally inspired dishes. Try such specialties as grilled salmon served with anchovy butter or tender lamb with broad beans. Fresh oysters are often on the menu. Also on-site is the town's best wine bar, Le Bacchus, offering selections by the glass and specializing in the many esoteric vintages grown nearby.

22 bd. Gambetta, 11100 Narbonne. (**Ⓒ 04-68-65-14-74.** Fax 04-68-65-81-48. www.hoteldulanguedoc. com. 40 units. 58€–75€ double; 90€ suite. AE, DC, MC, V. Parking 8€. **Amenities:** Bar/creperie. *In room:* TV, hair dryer, Wi-Fi (in some; free).

La Résidence ★   Our favorite hotel in Narbonne is near the Cathédrale St-Just. The 19th-century La Résidence, converted from a stately villa, is comfortable and decorated with antiques. The rooms are midsize to spacious, tastefully furnished, and very well maintained. The hotel doesn't have a restaurant but offers breakfast and a gracious welcome.

6 rue du 1er-Mai, 11100 Narbonne. (**Ⓒ 04-68-32-19-41.** Fax 04-68-65-51-82. www.hotelresidence.fr. 26 units. 76€–100€ double. AE, DC, MC, V. Parking 7.50€. Closed Jan 20–Feb 20. **Amenities:** Internet in lobby (free). *In room:* A/C, TV, hair dryer, minibar, Wi-Fi (free).

WHERE TO DINE

La Table St-Crescent ★★★ FRENCH/LANGUEDOCIENNE   This is one of the region's best-respected restaurants. It's just east of town, beside the road leading to Perpignan, in a complex of wine-tasting boutiques established by a local syndicate of growers. The foundations date, it's said, from the 8th century, when the building functioned as an oratory (small chapel) and prayer site. Today it's outfitted with modern furniture that's little more than a foil for the cuisine. The chef delivers refined, brilliantly realized dishes, with sublime sauces and sophisticated herbs and seasonings. The menu changes four times a year based on the availability of seasonal ingredients and the inspiration of the owners. Main courses can include sea bass marinated with olives, beef filet with foie gras and truffles, and lobster ravioli with oil of pistou. Especially succulent are roasted scallops floating on cream of celery soup, filet of red snapper with shellfish and almonds, ravioli stuffed with cheese-laced potatoes, and suprême of duckling with braised cabbage. Wine steward Sabrine Giraud (the chef's wife) and her assistant, Barbara, will help you select the perfect accompaniment.

In the Palais des Vins, 68 av. Général Leclerc, rte. de Perpignan. ✆ **04-68-41-37-37.** www.la-table-saint-crescent.com. Reservations recommended. Main courses 26€–41€; fixed-price lunch Tues–Fri 23€; fixed-price dinner and Sun lunch 40€–79€. AE, DC, MC, V. Tues–Fri and Sun noon–1:30pm; Tues–Sat 8–9:30pm.

Restaurant L'Ecrevisse D'Alsace FRENCH Across from the train station, D'Alsace is Narbonne's most reliable restaurant. The comfortable dining room is done in the English style, with wood paneling and a glass-enclosed patio. In spite of the restaurant's name, the cuisine isn't from Alsace-Lorraine, but is typical of southwestern France, with a focus on seafood. The Sinfreus, who own the place, offer a fry of red mullet, a savory kettle of bourride, and magret of duck with flap mushrooms. Especially delectable is this restaurant's specialty: sea wolf or other whole fish baked in a salt crust, a method that produces a delightfully pungent and flaky dish.

1 av. Pierre-Sémard. ✆ **04-68-65-10-24.** www.restaurant-narbonne.com. Reservations recommended. Main courses 15€–40€. AE, DC, MC, V. Thurs–Sat and Mon–Tues noon–1:45pm and 7–9:30pm. Closed first week of Feb, last week of July, and first 2 weeks of Aug.

NARBONNE AFTER DARK

The city has some routine dance clubs—nothing special. Check out the action, if any, at **Dancing GM Palace,** Centre Commercial Forum Sud, Route de Perpignan (✆ **04-68-41-59-71**), open Friday to Saturday 10pm to 5am and Sunday 3 to 8pm.

10 AIGUES-MORTES ★★

750km (466 miles) SW of Paris; 63km (39 miles) NE of Sète; 40km (25 miles) E of Nîmes; 48km (30 miles) SW of Arles

South of Nîmes, you can explore much of the Camargue by car, mainly on the roads of the **Parc Regional de Carmargue.** The most rewarding target is Aigues-Mortes, the city of the "dead waters." It is France's most perfectly preserved walled town. In the middle of dismal swamps and melancholy lagoons, Aigues-Mortes stands on four navigable canals. Although it is now 6km (4 miles) from the sea, it was once a thriving port. Louis IX and his crusaders set forth from here on the Ninth Crusade.

ESSENTIALS

GETTING THERE Five **trains** and four **buses** per day connect Aigues-Mortes and Nîmes. Trip time is about an hour. For information and train schedules, call ✆ **36-35,** or visit **www.voyages-sncf.com.** For bus information, call **Autocars Telleschi/Cartreize** at ✆ **04-42-28-40-22.** The town does not have a bus station, only a bus stop. If you're **driving** to Aigues-Mortes, take D979 south from Gallargues, or A9 from Montpellier or Nîmes.

VISITOR INFORMATION The **Office de Tourisme** is at place St. Louis (✆ **04-66-53-73-00;** fax 04-66-53-65-94; www.ot-aiguesmortes.fr).

EXPLORING THE TOWN

The main allure in Aigues-Mortes is the city itself. A sense of medievalism still permeates virtually every building, every rampart, and every cobbled street, and the town is still enclosed by **ramparts** ★★ that were constructed between 1272 and 1300. The **Tour de Constance** ★★ (© **04-66-53-61-55**), which looks out on the marshes, is a model castle of the Middle Ages. At the top, which you can reach by elevator, a panoramic view unfolds. Admission is 6.50€ for adults, 4.50€ for ages 18 to 25, and free for children 17 and under. The monument is open May to August daily 10am to 7pm, September to April daily 10am to 5pm.

The city's religious centerpiece is the **Eglise Notre-Dame des Sablons,** rue Jean-Jaurès (no phone). Constructed of wood in 1183, it was rebuilt in stone in 1246 in the ogival style. Its modern stained-glass windows were installed in 1980 as replacements for the badly damaged originals. The church is open May to September daily from 8:30am to 6pm, October to April 10am to 5pm.

WHERE TO STAY

Note that the **Restaurant Les Arcades** (p. 116) also rents rooms.

Hostellerie des Remparts   Opened about 300 years ago, this weather-worn inn lies at the foot of the Tour de Constance, adjacent to the medieval fortifications. Popular and often fully booked (especially in summer), it evokes the defensive atmosphere of the Middle Ages, albeit with charm and a sense of nostalgia. Narrow stone staircases lead to the small, simply furnished rooms. The living here is rather plain and basic. Each well-maintained unit has a small bathroom, but 12 have a tub and shower, while the rest have just showers. Breakfast is the only meal served.

6 place Anatole-France, 30220 Aigues-Mortes. © **04-66-53-82-77.** Fax 04-66-53-73-77. 12 units. 75€–110€ double. AE, MC, V. **Amenities:** Restaurant; bar; room service. *In room:* A/C, TV.

Hôtel Les Templiers ★   The leading inn in town is a gem of peace and tranquillity. Protected by the ramparts built by St-Louis, king of France, this 17th-century residence has small- to medium-size rooms decorated in Provençal style, with just enough decorative objects to lend a homelike aura. You can relax in the courtyard, where you can also enjoy breakfast. The establishment contains two restaurants, each featuring a competent and traditional, if not terribly experimental, menu: The less formal option is open for both lunch and dinner Wednesday to Monday; the somewhat more formal restaurant is open only for dinner, Thursday to Sunday or Tuesday to Sunday in July and August.

23 rue de la République, 30220 Aigues-Mortes. © **04-66-53-66-56.** Fax 04-66-53-69-61. www.hotel templiers.fr. 14 units. 125€–190€ double. MC, V. **Amenities:** 2 restaurants; bar; pool (outdoor); room service. *In room:* A/C, TV, hair dryer, Wi-Fi (free).

Hôtel St-Louis   Though not grand in any way or as fine as Hôtel Les Templiers, this inn near place St-Louis offers small but comfortably furnished bedrooms, each with a tiled and compact bathroom.

Many locals come here to enjoy the regional meals served in the hotel's restaurant, L'Archére, your best bet for steak and fresh fish. The region, of course, is known for its beef, and this dining room (open to nonresidents) serves some of the most tender and juicy steaks in the area. It also has a good bounty of seafood brought in daily from the nearby coast. Chefs are skilled in the kitchen, turning out an array of the local favorites along with homemade desserts prepared fresh every day.

10 rue de l'Amiral-Courbet, 30220 Aigues-Mortes. © **04-66-53-72-68.** Fax 04-66-53-75-92. www.lesaint louis.fr. 22 units. 79€–102€ double. AE, MC, V. Parking 12€. Closed Jan to mid-Mar. **Amenities:** Restaurant; bar; room service. *In room:* A/C, TV, minibar.

Restaurant Les Arcades ★★ TRADITIONAL FRENCH   No contest: This is the area's finest dining choice. This restaurant has several formal sections with beamed ceilings or stone vaults. Almost as old as the nearby fortifications, Les Arcades is especially charming on sultry days, when the thick masonry keeps the interior cool. The good, reasonably priced food is likely to include warm oysters, fish soup, fried stuffed zucchini flowers, grilled beefsteak from the Camargue, roasted monkfish in red-wine sauce, and grilled duckling. A typical local dish is minced bull steak from the local salt marshes, served with regional herb sauce.

The owner also rents nine large, comfortable rooms with air-conditioning and TVs. The double rate of 101€ to 108€ includes breakfast.

23 bd. Gambetta, 30220 Aigues-Mortes. (℃ **04-66-53-81-13.** www.les-arcades.fr. Reservations recommended. Main courses 20€–30€; fixed-price lunch 22€; fixed-price dinner 32€–42€; children's menu 13€. AE, DC, MC, V. Wed and Fri–Sun noon–2pm; Tues–Sun 7:30–10pm; daily July–Aug. Closed 3 weeks in Mar and 2 weeks in Oct.

A SIDE TRIP FROM AIGUES-MORTES

Les Gardiens of the Camargue ★

Steamy, sweaty, and as flat as the plains of Nebraska, the marshy delta of the Rhône has been called a less fertile version of the Nile delta. The waterlogged flatlands encompassing the Grand and Petit Rhône were scorned by conventional farmers throughout the centuries because of their high salt content and root-rotting murk.

However, the area was considered a fit grazing ground for the local black-pelted longhorn cattle, so a breed of cowpokes and cowboys evolved on these surreal flatlands, whose traditions remind one of Dodge City combined with primal hints of ancient Celtic lore. These French cowboys, caretakers of the cattle that survive amid the flamingos, ticks, hawks, snakes, and mosquitoes of the hot, salty wetlands, are known and loved by schoolchildren as *les gardiens.*

The tradition of *les gardiens* originated in the 1600s, when local monasteries began to disintegrate and large tracts of cheap land were bought by private owners. Wearing their

---

The Legacy of Roman Blood & Gore

Bullfighting is alive and well in the Camargue. Bullfighters usually come in from Spain, but these high-energy odes to testosterone aren't completely *espagnol.* Sometimes the bull is killed and sometimes it will mangle a local youth during a bullring celebration. Most *gardiens* (French cowboys) are too shrewd to participate in a head-on confrontation with a bull, though one or two are likely to be on horseback in or near the ring during the contest.

Although some minor bullfights occur in July and August in small arenas in the Camargue, the best ones are staged in Arles at the **Amphitheater (Les Arènes;** p. 237). Tickets range in price from 16€ to 94€. In modern times, the most avid aficionado of the bullfights in Arles was Picasso, who, in gratitude for the blood and gore, donated 70 of his drawings to the city of Arles. The corridas staged here Easter through September have been called "as bloody as anything presented to the Romans."

Moments — A Day in the Life of a Camargue Cowboy

The Camargue, where the cowboys of France ride the range, is an alluvial plain inhabited by wild horses, fighting black bulls, roaming Gypsies, pink flamingos, lagoons, salt marshes, wetlands, and gluttonous mosquitoes. Explore the rugged terrain by boat, bike, horse, or jeep.

With the most fragile ecosystem in France, the Camargue has been a national park since 1970. It's known for its small white horses, whose ancestors were brought here by the Arabs long ago. The horses roam wild in the national park, guarded by cowboys, or *gardiens*, who wear large felt hats and carry long three-pronged sticks to prod the cattle. The cowboys live in thatched huts called *cabanes*. No more evocative sight can be had in the Camargue than that of the proud snow-white horses running at liberty through the marshlands, with hoofs so tough that they don't need shoes. It is said that their long manes and busy tails evolved over the centuries to slap those pesky mosquitoes.

Flora and fauna abound where the delta of the Rhône River empties into the Mediterranean. The bird life is the most luxuriant in Europe. The area, which resembles the Florida Everglades, is known for its colonies of pink flamingos *(flamants roses)*. They share living quarters with some 400 other bird species, including ibises, egrets, kingfishers, owls, wild ducks, swans, and ferocious birds of prey. The best place to see flamingo colonies is around Ginès, a hamlet on N570, 5km (3 miles) north of Camargue's capital, Stes-Maries-de-la-Mer.

Exploring the Camargue is best undertaken on the back of a *camarguais* horse. The steeds can take you into the interior, which you couldn't see otherwise, fording waters to places where the black bulls graze and wild birds nest. You'll find two to three dozen stables (depending on the time of year) along the highway from Arles to Stes-Maries. Virtually all of them charge the same daily rate, 80€ or 17€ per hour, including a picnic lunch. The rides are aimed at the neophyte, not the champion equestrian. They're so easy that they're recommended even for those who have never been on a horse before.

traditional garb of leather pants and wide-rimmed black hats, the *gardiens* present a fascinating picture as they ride through the marshlands on their sturdy horses. Their terrain isn't the romantic wide, open space of America's West, but consists instead of monotonous stretches whose highest point might be a mound of debris left from a medieval salt flat. The *gardiens* tend not to be overly communicative to outsiders; in speaking to one another, they use a clipped, telegraphic form of Provençal whose syntax would make members of the Académie Française shudder. Once the *gardiens* lived in distinctive, single-story *cabanes* with thatched roofs and without windows; bulls' horns were positioned above each building's entrance to drive away evil spirits. But today motor homes and caravans are beginning to appear in the area.

An ally in the business of tending cattle is the strong, heavy-tailed Camargue horse, probably a descendant of Arabian stallions brought here by Moorish invaders after the collapse of the Roman Empire. Brown or black at birth, these horses develop a white coat, usually after their fourth year. Traditionally, they were left to fend for themselves during the stifling summers and bone-chilling winters without sheltered stables.

Today, in the world of modern tourism, the *gardiens* have become living symbols of an antique tradition that hasn't changed much—the cattle still run semiwild, identified by the brand of their *manadier,* or owner. However, today you can expect to see fewer *gardiens* than in the past. They seem willing to participate in tourism only up to a point. Reminders of their traditions are seen in the felt-sided cowboy hats as well as commemorative saddles and boots whose style resembles that of cowherds on the faraway plains of Spain.

The best center for exploring the Camargue is Stes-Maries-de-la-Mer, which lies 19km (12 miles) east of Aigues-Mortes, but is best reached from Arles, a distance of only 15km (9 miles) to the north. Five **buses** a day leave from Arles to Stes-Maries-de-la-Mer, but only one on Sunday. The bus ride from Arles takes less than an hour, costing 5.20€ one-way. For information in Arles, call **Autocars Telleschi/Catreize** (© **04-42-28-40-22**). Stes-Maries-de-la-Mer does not have a bus station: You are let off at place Mireille. At this point, you can rent a bike for further exploration at **Le Vélo Santois,** 19 rue de la République (© **04-90-97-74-56**), costing 15€ per day. Your passport or ID is taken as a deposit. The cash-only outfitter is open daily in July and August from 9am to 7pm, off season daily 9am to noon and 2 to 7pm. It is closed in December.

11 MONTPELLIER ★★

758km (471 miles) SW of Paris; 161km (100 miles) NW of Marseille; 50km (31 miles) SW of Nîmes

The capital of Mediterranean (or Lower) Languedoc, the ancient university city of Montpellier is renowned for its medical school, founded in the 13th century. Nostradamus qualified as a doctor here, and Rabelais studied at the school. Petrarch came to Montpellier in 1317 and stayed for 7 years.

Today Montpellier is a bustling metropolis with a population of 380,000, one of southern France's fastest-growing cities, thanks to an influx of new immigrants. Although some suburbs are dreary, the city has a handsome core, with tree-flanked promenades, broad avenues, and historic monuments. Students make up a quarter of the population, giving the city a lively feel. In recent years, many high-tech corporations, including IBM, have opened offices in Montpellier.

ESSENTIALS

GETTING THERE   Some 12 **trains** per day arrive from Avignon (trip time: 1 hr.), 12 from Marseille (trip time: 1¾ hr.), every 2 hours from Toulouse (trip time: 2 hr.), and 17 per day from Perpignan (trip time: 1½ hr.). Trains arriving hourly from Paris's Gare de Lyon take 8 to 10 hours, depending on the train, and usually require a change of equipment in Lyon. One TGV train arrives daily from Paris, taking less than 3½ hours. The one-way fare starts from 77€. For rail information, call © **36-35,** or visit **www.voyages-sncf.com.**

The Montpellier **bus station** is located at 20 rue du Grand St-Jean (© **04-67-92-01-43**). Two buses a day run between Nîmes and Montpellier, Monday to Saturday only, for 8.50€. The trip takes 1¾ hours.

If you're **driving,** Montpellier lies off A9.

signy (𝄐 **04-67-60-60-60;** fax 04-67-60-60-61; www.ot-montpellier.fr).

SPECIAL EVENTS From June 24 to July 7, classical and modern dancers leap into town for the **Festival International Montpellier Danse.** Tickets for performances cost 6€ to 30€ and can be purchased through the box office, **Montpellierdanse,** 18 rue Ste-Ursule (𝄐 **08-00-60-07-40** or 04-67-60-83-60; www.montpellierdanse.com). From July 12 to July 29, the **Festival de Radio France et de Montpellier** presents orchestral music, jazz, and opera. Tickets run 6€ to 50€; call 𝄐 **04-67-02-02-01** or contact the **Cité des Congrès Le Corum,** esplanade Charles de Gaulle (𝄐 **04-67-61-67-61;** www. festivalradiofrancemontpellier.com).

EXPLORING THE TOWN

Called the Oxford of France because of its academic community, Montpellier is a city of young people, as you'll notice if you sit at one of the cafes on the **place de la Comédie,** with its 18th-century Fountain of the Three Graces. It's the living room of Montpellier, the ideal place to chat, people-watch, or cruise.

Paul Valéry met André Gide in the **Jardin des Plantes,** Boulevard Henri IV (𝄐 **04-67-63-43-22;** www.jardindesplantes.univ-montp1.fr), and you might begin here, as it's the oldest such garden in France. It's reached from boulevard Henri-IV. This botanical garden, filled with exotic plants and a handful of greenhouses, was opened in 1593. Admission is free. It's open April to September, Tuesday to Sunday from noon to 8pm, and October to March, Tuesday to Sunday from noon to 6pm.

The town's greatest attraction is **Musée Fabre** ★★, 2 rue Montpellieret (𝄐 **04-67-14-83-00**), one of France's great provincial art galleries, which occupies the former Hôtel Massilian, where Molière once played for a season. The collection originated when Napoleon sent Montpellier an exhibition of the Royal Academy in 1803. François Fabre, a Montpellier painter, contributed its most important works in 1825. After Fabre's death, other paintings from his collection were donated to the gallery. Several were his own creations, but the more significant works were ones he had acquired—including Poussin's *Venus and Adonis,* plus Italian paintings like *The Mystical Marriage of Saint Catherine.* The museum continued to grow through other donations, notably in 1836 with a collection of Rubens, Gérard Dou, and Téniers. Admission is 6€ for adults and 4€ for students and youths ages 7 to 20, free for children 6 and under. Open Tuesday to Friday and Sunday 10am to 6pm; Wednesday 1 to 9pm; and Saturday 11am to 6pm.

Nearby is the town's spiritual centerpiece, the **Cathédrale St-Pierre,** on place St-Pierre (𝄐 **04-67-66-04-12**), founded in 1364. This is hardly one of the grand cathedrals of France, and it suffered badly in centuries of religious wars and revolutions. For a long time after 1795, it wasn't a cathedral at all, but was occupied by a medical school. Today the cathedral lacks pretension; its greatest architectural achievement is its unusual canopied porch, supported by two conical turrets. The best artworks inside are 17th-century canvasses in the transepts—notably the work of a Huguenot, Montpellier-born Sébastien Bourdon, who painted himself among the "heathen" in *The Fall of Simon Magnus.* Also moving is Jean Troy's *Healing of the Paralytic.* The church can be visited daily from 9am to noon and 2 to 7pm.

Before leaving town, take a leisurely stroll along the 17th-century **promenade du Peyrou** ★★, a terraced park with views of the Cévennes and the Mediterranean. This is a broad esplanade constructed at the loftiest point of Montpellier. Opposite the entrance is an Arc de Triomphe, erected in 1691 to celebrate the victories of Louis XIV. In the center of the promenade is an equestrian statue of Louis XIV and, at the end, the **Château d'Eau,** a pavilion with Corinthian columns that serves as a monument to 18th-century classicism. Water is brought here by a conduit, nearly 14km (8¾ miles) long, and an aqueduct.

SHOPPING

Stroll down **place de la Comédie,** with its ultramodern Polygone shopping center, site of more than 120 independent boutiques, and **rue Jean-Moulin.** For traditional regional delicacies, visit **Au Gourmets,** 2 rue Clos-René (© **04-67-58-57-04**), or visit **Pâtissier Schoeller,** 121 av. de l'Odàve (© **04-67-75-71-55**), for a plentiful supply of Ecusson de Montpellier (a chocolate praline with Grand Marnier wrapped in chocolate).

WHERE TO STAY

Note that **Le Jardin des Sens** (p. 122) also rents rooms.

In Montpellier
Expensive
Holiday Inn Métropole ★   In the heart of Montpellier, this 1898 monument adjacent to the town's railway station stands behind an entrance with a soaring portal set into a dignified stone facade. It has undergone a radical renovation that retained the charming interior garden and the original detailing. The well-furnished, contemporary-looking bedrooms range in size from medium to spacious and are fitted with fine linens; the marble-sheathed bathrooms are roomy.

3 rue Clos-Rene, 34000 Montpellier. © **04-67-12-32-32.** Fax 04-67-92-13-02. www.holiday-inn.com. 80 units. 110€–215€ double. AE, DC, MC, V. Parking 12€. **Amenities:** Restaurant; bar; exercise room; pool (outdoors); room service. *In room:* A/C, TV, fridge, hair dryer, Wi-Fi (11€).

Pullman Montpellier ★   In the heart of Montpellier, this angular, modern, glass-sheathed hotel is the city's top hotel for comfort and first-class amenities. In summer, it does quite a trade with visitors. A particularly appealing feature is the pool, which, along with a bar and breakfast room, occupies most of the top floor. The rooms are chain format but first-class. This is a winning choice, with the most efficient staff in the city, and its bar is one of the coziest hideaways in town.

1 rue des Pertuisanes, 3400 Montpellier. © **04-67-99-72-72.** Fax 04-67-65-17-50. www.pullmanhotels. com. 89 units. 220€–240€ double; 480€ suite. AE, DC, MC, V. Parking 3€–10€. **Amenities:** Restaurant; bar; exercise room; Jacuzzi; room service. *In room:* A/C, TV, hair dryer, Wi-Fi (10€).

Moderate
Best Western Hôtel Le Guilhem ★ (Finds)   Two 16th-century houses make up this oasis on a back street. In its transformation to a hotel, the connected buildings gained all the modern conveniences, including an elevator. Each room is furnished and decorated in individual style, with more than a hint of Laura Ashley design in the striped wallpaper and flowery spreads. Although the accommodations are small, they are tastefully furnished and comfortable. The day begins with a breakfast of freshly baked *pain au chocolat* and croissants served on a terrace overlooking the garden and the cathedral. The location is in the Old Town, an ideal base from which to explore the sights.

18 rue Jean-Jacques-Rousseau, 34000 Montpellier. © **800/528-1234** or 04-67-52-90-90. Fax 04-67-60-67-67. www.leguilhem.com. 36 units. 87€–249€ double; 150€–249€ junior suite. AE, DC, MC, V. Parking 8€ in nearby garage. **Amenities:** Room service. *In room:* A/C, TV, hair dryer, minibar, Wi-Fi (free).

If bending an elbow while holding a glass of wine is, in your opinion, a sport, consider a wine-lover's tour of one of the architectural oddities of Montpellier's wine district. Take a half-day exploration of the cellars and vineyards of the 18th-century **Château de Flaugergues,** in the hamlet of Flaugergues (𝄞 **04-99-52-66-37;** www.flaugergues.com). Positioned within a 10-minute drive east of Montpellier, on the road leading to the seacoast, it accepts visitors who appreciate the nuances of the region's rough-and-ready reds, rosés, and whites. Appointments should be made in advance for visits that are usually scheduled any afternoon between 2:30 and 6:30pm. The castle's elaborate architecture is viewed by locals as one of the local *folies* (follies) of the region.

Hôtel du Palais ★ (Value) This hotel in the heart of a neighborhood loaded with antiques dealers is one of the best bargains in town. Built in the late 18th century, Hôtel du Palais is in the center of Montpellier, amid a labyrinth of narrow streets and monumental plazas and parks. Much of the decor dates from around 1983, when the hotel was richly restored in a style that uses lots of fabrics, big curtains, and faux marble finishes on the walls of public areas. Subsequent renovations have kept the property up to date. The guest rooms are relatively large and appealing, thanks to thoughtful placement of antique reproductions and good maintenance. Breakfast is the only meal served.

3 rue du Palais, 34000 Montpellier. 𝄞 **04-67-60-47-38.** Fax 04-67-60-40-23. 26 units. 69€–92€ double. MC, V. Parking 8€. **Amenities:** Room service. *In room:* A/C, TV, hair dryer, minibar, Wi-Fi (free).

Hôtel du Parc ★ (Finds) One of the town's more charming moderately priced hostelries, this cozy hotel lies in the heart of the city near the Palais des Congrès. It was a Languedocian residence in the 18th century, but has since been turned into a hotel with a lot of grace notes and French Provincial charm. Rooms have been carefully decorated and are accompanied by streamlined bathrooms. A garden and flowering terrace are available for breakfast outside. Numerous restaurants surround the hotel.

8 rue Achille-Bégé, 34090 Montpellier. 𝄞 **04-67-41-16-49.** Fax 04-67-54-10-05. www.hotelduparc-montpellier.com. 19 units. 50€–83€ double; 192€ triple. AE, MC, V. Free parking. **Amenities:** Breakfast room; room service. *In room:* A/C, TV, hair dryer, minibar, Wi-Fi (free).

La Maison Blanche ★★ Few other hotels in the south of France work so hard to emulate the gingerbread and French Creole ambience of New Orleans. Parts of the interior, especially the dining room, may remind you of Louis XIII's France more than Louisiana, but overall the setting, in a verdant park a 10-minute drive northeast of Montpellier's center, is both charming and unusual. Suites are stylishly furnished with plenty of wood paneling, and guest rooms are outfitted with oak. Bathrooms are midsize to roomy.

1796 av. de la Pompignane, 34000 Montpellier. 𝄞 **04-99-58-20-70.** Fax 04-67-79-53-39. www.hotel-maison-blanche.com. 35 units. 76€–104€ double; 145€–160€ suite. AE, DC, MC, V. Free parking. Take bd. d'Antigone east until you reach the intersection with av. de la Pompignane and head north until you see the hotel on your right (trip time: 5 min.). **Amenities:** Restaurant; bar; pool (outdoor); room service. *In room:* A/C, TV, hair dryer, minibar (in some), Wi-Fi (free).

Hôtel Ulysse ★ ⓥvalue One of the city's better bargains, Ulysse delivers a lot of bang for your euro. The owners have worked hard to make the simple hotel as stylish as possible. Each room is uniquely decorated. The furnishings are in an original wrought-iron design, functional but with flair. The comfortable rooms have fully equipped bathrooms. The hotel lies within a 15-minute walk south of Montpellier's center, close to the edge of the sea.

338 av. de St-Maur, 34000 Montpellier. ⓒ **04-67-02-02-30.** Fax 04-67-02-16-50. www.hotel-ulysee.fr. 24 units. 60€–70€ double. AE, DC, MC, V. Parking 5€. Tram: 1 (Le Mosson line). Bus: 8. From bd. d'Antigone, go north on av. Jean-Mermoz to rue de la Pépinière; continue right and make a left at the 1st intersection, which leads to av. de St-Maur. **Amenities:** Room service. *In room:* TV, hair dryer, minibar, Wi-Fi (free).

Les Arceaux It's basic but still most acceptable, and the price is right. A hotel has stood at this prime location, right off the promenade du Peyrou, since the late 1800s. The smallish rooms are simply but pleasantly furnished, each in a different color, and each with a compact bathroom. The on-site bar, which opens into a summer garden, serves simple platters. What you get is a "bar-bistro platter" as this is not a full-fledged restaurant. A terrace adjoins the hotel.

33–35 bd. des Arceaux, 34000 Montpellier. ⓒ **04-67-92-03-03.** Fax 04-67-92-05-09. www.hoteldes arceaux.com. 18 units. 63€–100€ double. AE, MC, V. Parking 6€ in nearby lot. **Amenities:** Bar; room service; smoke-free rooms. *In room:* A/C (in some), TV, minibar, Wi-Fi (free).

Where to Stay Near Montpellier

Demeure des Brousses ★★ ⓕinds This 18th-century country house stands in a large, impressive park about a 10-minute drive from the heart of Montpellier. The house was built by Monsieur and Madame Brousse, who made their fortune as *Epiciers,* or spice merchants. A tranquil choice, it has been skillfully converted for guests. Rooms range from medium-size to spacious, each individually decorated with 19th-century style. Public rooms are decorated like those of a gracious French country house, including loads of antiques, making this an intimate retreat.

Rte. de Vauguières, 34000 Montpellier. ⓒ **04-67-65-77-66.** Fax 04-67-22-22-17. www.demeure-des-brousses.com. 17 units. 94€–175€ double. AE, DC, MC, V. Free parking. Take D-172E 3km (2 miles) east of the town center. **Amenities:** Restaurant; bar; bikes; room service. *In room:* A/C, TV, hair dryer, Wi-Fi (free).

WHERE TO DINE

Expensive

Le Jardin des Sens ★★★ FRENCH This is one of the great restaurants of southern France, with three Michelin stars. The chefs, twins Laurent and Jacques Pourcel, have taken Montpellier by storm, and their cuisine could involve almost anything, depending on where their imaginations roam. The rich bounty of Languedoc goes through a process designed to enhance its natural flavor. A starter may be ravioli stuffed with foie gras of duckling and flap mushrooms, floating in chicken bouillon fortified with truffles, broad beans, and crispy potatoes. Main courses of note are shelled lobster, pressed flat and served with duck meat and vanilla oil; filet of dorado grilled with sesame and served with a marmalade of tomatoes, olives, and caramelized balsamic vinegar; and filet of pigeon stuffed with pistachios. A dessert specialty is gratin of limes with slices of pineapple *en confit.*

Le Jardin des Sens also rents 13 guest rooms, plus two suites, each designed in cutting-edge style by Bruno Borrione, a colleague of Philippe Starck. A double is 170€ to 235€, a suite 310€ to 410€.

Finds **Exploring the Port Town of Séte**

Séte, reached after a 34km (21-mile) drive southwest of Montpellier, is the largest fishing port on the Mediterranean and was once the principal link to France's colonies in North Africa. Even today a car-ferry transports passengers to and from the coasts of North Africa. You can almost picture Marlene Dietrich leaving the port bound for Morocco in a 1930s movie.

In an architectural blend of Art Deco and Second Empire, Séte was built on a limestone rock on the slopes of Mont Saint-Clair and is connected to the mainland by two sand pits. This city of canals sprawls across two islands and a network of estuaries connected and crisscrossed by bridges. These canals evoke comparison with Venice.

If you're staying over, your best bet is **Le Grand Hôtel,** 17 quai Maréchal de Lattre de Tassigny (© **04-67-74-71-77;** fax 04-67-74-29-27; www.legrand hotelsete.com), at the center of the port, near the intersection of the two canals. Try for a front bedroom with its view of the moored boats. The limestone facade of the hotel is accented with elaborate corbels and bas-reliefs, some of which are designed like the prows of boats. The hotel's Beaux Arts charm and grandeur dates from the 1880s, with potted palms, a skylit atrium, and wicker armchairs. The bedrooms are generally roomy, well furnished, and modernized. Rooms are air-conditioned, containing minibars, TVs, and Wi-Fi. Doubles rent for 75€ to 135€.

At the same address is the restaurant **Le Quai 17** (© **04-67-74-71-77**), which takes up two impressive ground-floor rooms of the hotel and is under separate management. The chef specializes in fresh and flavorful seafood. The restaurant is open for lunch Monday to Friday from noon to 2pm, and dinner Monday to Saturday from 7:30 to 10pm. Full meals range in price from 19€ to 47€; reservations are recommended.

For information about Séte and the area, stop in at the **Office de Tourisme,** 60 Grand'Rue (© **04-67-74-71-71**). Trains arrive every hour during the day from Montpellier (trip time: 20 min.), at a one-way fare of 6€.

11 av. St-Lazare. © **04-99-58-38-38.** Fax 04-99-58-38-39. www.jardindessens.com. Reservations required. Main courses 45€–85€; fixed-price lunch Tues–Fri only 50€; fixed-price dinner and Sat lunch 125€–190€. AE, MC, V. Mon–Sat noon–2pm; and 7:30–10pm. Closed 2 weeks in Jan.

Moderate

La Compagnie des Comptoirs INTERNATIONAL   Just a 5-minute walk east of the town center, and lodged behind a set of massive doors intricately sculpted by artisans in Morocco, this restaurant manages to evoke the aesthetic of the late-19th-century French colonies in, say, North Africa or Indochina. The restaurant features a large dining room seating about 130 diners, and a big outdoor terrace with flowering shrubs and a splashing fountain. The cuisine emphasizes the kind of sunny, flavorful, and pungent cuisine you find around the edges of the Mediterranean. The best examples include a succulent version of tempura of crayfish; *accras* (beignets) of crab; grilled calamari with a confit of lemon; grilled steak from bulls from the Camargue, served with red-wine sauce; and a winning collection of desserts.

51 rue François Delmas. (© **04-99-58-39-29.** www.lacompagniedescomptoirs.com. Reservations recommended. Fixed-price menus 25€–36€. AE, DC, MC, V. Wed–Fri and Sun noon–2:30m; Tues–Sun 8–11:30pm.

L'Olivier ★★ (Finds) MODERN FRENCH   This charming restaurant's cuisine is so satisfying that we consider it the finest in Montpellier outside the luxe Jardin des Sens. Chef Michel Breton, assisted by his charming wife, Yvette, cooks to perfection. The establishment seats only 20, in a subdued and rather bland modern space accented only by contemporary paintings. But you don't come to L'Olivier to look at the walls. You come for Breton's salmon with a tartare of oysters, warm monkfish terrine, roasted filet of lamb with sweetbread-studded macaroni, and haunch of rabbit stuffed with wild mushrooms. The welcome is warm and sincere.

12 rue Aristide-Olivier. (© **04-67-92-86-28.** Reservations required. Main courses 21€–27€; fixed-price lunch 21€; fixed-price dinner 38€–48€. AE, MC, V. Tues–Sat noon–2pm and 7:30–9:30pm. Closed Aug and holidays.

MONTPELLIER AFTER DARK

After the sun sets, head for **place Jean-Jaurès, rue de Verdun,** and **rue des Ecoles Laïques,** or walk down **rue de la Loge** and soak up its carnival atmosphere, watching talented jugglers, mimes, and musicians.

Le Corum (© 04-67-61-67-61), the most up-to-date theater in town, books plays, dance recitals, operas, and symphonic presentations. It's in the Palais des Congrès, esplanade Charles-de-Gaulle. For ticket information and schedules, contact the Corum or the **Opéra Comédie,** place de la Comédie (© 04-67-60-19-80).

Rockstore, 20 rue de Verdun (© 04-67-06-80-06; www.rockstore.fr), draws lots of students with 1950s rock memorabilia and live concerts. Up a flight of stairs is its disco, which pounds out techno and rock. There is no cover, except on concert nights. For the best jazz and blues in town, check out **JAM,** 100 rue Ferdinand-de-Lessops (© 04-67-58-30-30; www.lejam.com). In a noisy, smoky, and even gritty space, its regular concerts attract jazz enthusiasts from miles around. Concert tickets average 10€ to 25€.

A modern, convivial disco, known throughout the region, is **Le Pacha,** route des Plages, in the hamlet of Lattes (© 04-99-52-97-06), 4km (2½ miles) south of Montpellier. It attracts drinkers and dancers ages 23 to 40. Le Pacha is open Thursday to Saturday beginning around 11pm; on Friday and Saturday it charges a 10€ to 15€ cover, including a drink. Gays and lesbians in Lattes gather at the animated bar and disco, **La Villa Rouge,** route de Palavas (© 04-67-06-50-54).

12 NIMES ★★★

708km (440 miles) S of Paris; 43km (27 miles) W of Avignon

Nîmes, the ancient Nemausus, is a great place to view some of the world's finest Roman remains. The city grew to prominence during the reign of Caesar Augustus (27 B.C.–A.D. 14). Today it possesses one of the best preserved Roman amphitheaters in the world and a near-perfect Roman temple. The city of 135,000 is more like Provence than Languedoc, with a touch of Pamplona (Spain) here in the festivals of the *corridas* (bullfights) at the arena. The Spanish image is even stronger at night, when the bodegas fill with students drinking sangria and listening to the sounds of flamenco.

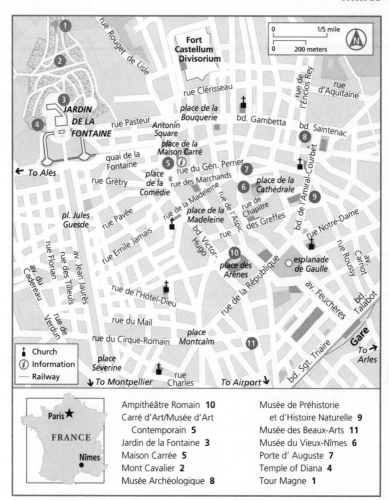

Church
Information
Railway

Ampithéâtre Romain **10**	Musée de Préhistorie
Carré d'Art/Musée d'Art	et d'Histoire Naturelle **9**
Contemporain **5**	Musée des Beaux-Arts **11**
Jardin de la Fontaine **3**	Musée du Vieux-Nîmes **6**
Maison Carrée **5**	Porte d' Auguste **7**
Mont Cavalier **2**	Temple of Diana **4**
Musée Archéologique **8**	Tour Magne **1**

ESSENTIALS

GETTING THERE The entire town center is now free of vehicular traffic. Nîmes has bus and train service from the rest of France and is near several autoroutes. It lies on the main **rail** line between Marseille and Bordeaux. Thirteen TGV trains arrive daily from Paris's Gare de Lyon; the one-way fare is 92€. For train information and schedules, call ✆ **36-35**, or visit **www.voyages-sncf.com**. The **bus station** is at rue Ste-Felicité (no street number; ✆ **04-66-38-59-43**), behind the train station. Bus information is found at a kiosk in the train station open Monday to Friday, 8:30am to 2:15pm, and 3 to 6pm, closed Saturday and Sunday. If you're **driving,** take A7 south from Lyon to the town of Orange and connect to A9 into Nîmes.

VISITOR INFORMATION   The **Office de Tourisme** is at 6 rue Auguste (© **04-66-58-38-00;** fax 04-66-58-38-01; www.ot-nimes.fr).

EXPLORING THE CITY
The Top Sights

Amphithéâtre Romain ★★★   The elliptically shaped amphitheater is a better-preserved twin of the one at Arles and is far more complete than the Colosseum of Rome. It's two stories high, each floor having 60 arches, and was built of stones fitted together without mortar. One of the best preserved arenas from ancient times, it once held more than 20,000 spectators who came to see gladiatorial combats and wolf or boar hunts. Today it's used for everything from ballet recitals to bullfights.

Place des Arènes. © **04-66-76-72-77.** Admission 7.70€ adults, 5.60€ students and children 15 and under. Tues–Sun 10am–6pm.

Carrée d'Art/Musée d'Art Contemporain   Across the square stands the modern-day twin of the Maison Carrée, a sophisticated research center and exhibition space that contains a library, newspaper kiosk, and art museum. Its understated design from 1993 was inspired by (but doesn't overpower) the ancient monument nearby. The museum's permanent expositions are often supplemented with temporary exhibits of contemporary art. *Note:* The view from this modern building's terrace allows you to rise above the roaring traffic and presents a panorama of ancient monuments and medieval churches.

Place de la Maison Carrée. © **04-66-76-35-35.** Admission 5€ adults, 3.70€ students and children 14 and under. Free the 1st Sun of each month. Tues–Sun 10am–6pm.

Maison Carrée ★★★   The pride of Nîmes, this is one of the most beautiful, and certainly one of the best preserved, Roman temples of Europe. It was built during the reign of Caesar Augustus. Set on a raised platform with tall Corinthian columns, it inspired Thomas Jefferson as well as the builders of La Madeleine in Paris. A changing roster of cultural and art exhibits is presented.

Place de la Comédie. © **04-66-21-82-56.** Free admission. Mid-Oct to mid-Mar daily 10am–5pm; mid-Mar to mid-Oct daily 9am–7pm.

Musée des Beaux-Arts   The city's largest museum contains French paintings and sculptures from the 17th to the 20th centuries, as well as Flemish, Dutch, and Italian works from the 15th to the 18th centuries. Seek out in particular one of G. B. Moroni's masterpieces, *La Calomnie d'Apelle,* and a well-preserved Gallo-Roman mosaic.

Rue Cité-Foulc. © **04-66-67-38-21.** Admission 5.10€ adults, 3.80€ students and children 16 and under. Tues–Sun 10am–6pm.

 Tips   **Your Lucky Ticket**

If you want to see all of the city's monuments and museums, consider buying a *billet global* (Forfait Monuments & Musées), sold at the ticket counter of any of the local attractions. It provides access for a 3-day period to all the cultural sites described below. The fee is 9.80€ for adults, 7.50€ for students and children 10 to 15, free for children 9 and under.

More Sights

One of the most beautiful gardens in France, **Jardin de la Fontaine** ★★, at the end of quai de la Fontaine, was laid out in the 18th century, using the ruins of a Roman shrine as a centerpiece. It was planted with rows of chestnuts and elms, adorned with statuary and urns, and intersected by grottoes and canals. The garden is open from April to mid-September daily from 7:30am to 10pm, from mid-September to March, daily from 7:30am to 6:30pm. Within the garden are the ruined **Temple of Diane** ★ and the remains of some Roman baths. Over the park, within a 10-minute walk north of the town center, is **Mont Cavalier,** a low, rocky hill on top of which rises the sturdy bulk of the **Tour Magne** ★, the city's oldest Roman monument. You can climb it for 2.70€ for adults, 2€ for students and children 14 and under. From April to October it is open daily from 10am to 7pm, November to March, daily 10am to 6:30pm. It offers a panoramic view over Nîmes and its environs.

If time allows, visit the **Musée du Vieux-Nîmes,** place aux Herbes (© **04-66-76-73-70**), housed in an Episcopal palace from the 1700s and rich in antiques, porcelain, and workday objects from the 18th and 19th centuries. Admission is free. Hours are Tuesday to Sunday 10am to 6pm.

One of the city's busiest thoroughfares, **boulevard de l'Amiral-Courbet,** leads to the **Porte d'Auguste** (Porte d'Arles)—the remains of a gate built by the Romans during the reign of Augustus. About 45m (150 ft.) to the south are the **Musée de Préhistoire et d'Histoire Naturelle** (© **04-66-76-73-45**) and the **Musée Archéologique** ★ (© **04-66-76-74-80**), in the same building at 13 bis bd. l'Amiral-Courbet. Admission is free. Hours are Tuesday to Sunday 10am to 6pm.

A Famous Roman Bridge

Outside the city, 23km (14 miles) northeast, the **pont du Gard** ★ spans the Gard River. The bridge is constructed of huge stones fitted together without mortar and stands as one of the region's most vivid reminders of its ancient glory. Consisting of three tiers of arches arranged into gracefully symmetrical patterns, it dates from about 19 B.C. Frédéric Mistral, national poet of Provence and Languedoc, recorded a legend alleging that the devil constructed the bridge with the promise that he could claim the soul of the first person to cross it. To visit it, take highway N86 from Nîmes to a point 3km (1¾ miles) from the village of Remoulins, where signs are posted.

The pont du Gard has a museum, **La Grande Expo du Pont du Gard,** B.P. 7, 30210 Vers Pont du Gard (© **04-66-37-50-99**). Four exhibits detail the bridge's construction, its function throughout the Middle Ages, and insights into its role as a symbol of the architectural savvy of ancient Rome. There's also a restaurant, cafe, and gift shop. It's open daily from May to August 9:30am to 7pm (until 6pm Feb–Apr and Sept–Oct; until 5pm Nov–Jan). The exposition opens every Monday at 1:30pm and closes at the hours noted, according to the season. It is closed the first 3 weeks in January. Admission is 12€ for adults, 9€ for persons 24 and under and students.

SHOPPING

Head to the center of town and **rue du Général-Perrier, rue des Marchands, rue du Chapître,** and the pedestrian **rue de l'Aspic** and **rue de la Madeleine.** A Sunday flea market runs from 8am to around 1pm in the parking lot of the **Stade des Costières,** site of most of the town's football (soccer) matches, adjacent to the southern edge of the boulevard *périphérique* that encircles Nîmes.

To appease your sweet tooth, go to just about any pastry shop in town and ask for the regional almond-based cookies called *croquants villaret* and *caladons*. They're great for a burst of energy or for souvenirs. One of the best purchases you can make, especially if you're not continuing east into Provence, is a *santon*. These figurines are sculpted into characters from Provençal country life and can be collected to create a unique country-French nativity scene. For a selection of *santons* in various sizes, visit the **Boutique Provençale,** 10 place de la Maison Carrée (② **04-66-67-81-71**).

WHERE TO STAY

Expensive

Imperator Concorde ★★   This hotel, with its pale pink Italianate facade, is part of the Concorde chain and is the largest and finest hotel in town—and is adjacent to Les Jardins de la Fontaine. In 2005, it underwent a major renovation that left it much improved. The artful and cozy rooms have traditional or French furniture, with fluted or cabriole legs in one or another of the Louis styles. Each unit has a first-rate private bathroom. You can order a meal in the hotel's verdant rear gardens or in a high-ceilinged dining room, L'Enclos de la Fontaine.

Quai de la Fontaine, 30900 Nîmes. ② **04-66-21-90-30.** Fax 04-66-67-70-25. www.hotel-imperator.com. 62 units. 149€–243€ double; 212€–243€ suite. AE, DC, MC, V. Parking 13€. **Amenities:** Restaurant; bar; babysitting; room service. *In room:* A/C, TV, hair dryer, minibar, Wi-Fi (free).

Moderate

Hôtel Vatel ★   Built around 1990, the hotel lies 3km (1¾ miles) north of the town center, in a cluster of buildings that includes a university and a hospital. It's efficiently staffed with students from the local hotel school, who work here as part of their on-the-job training. The rooms are streamlined, tasteful, and modern, with terraces. The modern establishment provides a level of comfort that older hotels, in more historic settings, can't provide.

140 rue Vatel, B.P. 7128, 30913 Nîmes. ② **04-66-62-57-57.** Fax 04-66-62-57-50. www.hotelvatel.com. 46 units. 130€ double; 200€ suite. AE, DC, MC, V. Free parking. From the A4 autoroute, exit at NIMES OUEST. **Amenities:** 2 restaurants; bar; pool (indoor); room service; spa. *In room:* A/C, TV, hair dryer, minibar, Wi-Fi (free).

La Maison de Sophie ★   The big draw to "Sophie's House" is the on-site presence, like a kindly matriarch in charge of a house party, of Sophie Rigon and her husband, Yves. Another strong draw is its location in the heart of Nîmes, within a 5-minute proximity to the Arenas, where *"Olé!"* resounds as toreadors taunt bulls. The building is viewed by historians as an architectural gem: Built in 1901, with public areas and bedrooms outfitted in furniture crafted in most cases between 1900 and 1930, it resembles a small Venetian *palazzo*, replete with stained glass and a scattering of marble columns in the entrance area. The lovely garden is loaded with old-species roses and irises, and even features an open-air swimming pool. The rooms aren't particularly luxurious, but each has a balcony and a small bathroom.

31 av. Carnot, 30000 Nîmes. ② **04-66-70-96-10.** Fax 04-66-36-00-47. www.hotel-lamaisondesophie. com. 7 units. 150€–250€ double; 295€ suite. AE, MC, V. Parking 10€. **Amenities:** Breakfast room; pool (outdoor). *In room:* A/C, TV, Wi-Fi (free).

New Hôtel La Baume ★ (Finds)   One of our favorite nests in Nîmes is actually the 17th-century mansion of the Marquis de la Baume. An overall sense of grandeur and a magnificent staircase that ornaments the interior courtyard are the best features. During the hotel conversion, the designers carefully preserved the original architecture, and the result is a winning combination of modern and traditional. In contrast to the stately exterior, the guest rooms are hyper-contemporary, usually in tones of soft reds, oranges, and ochers, and the tiled bathrooms are in a postmodern style evocative of Philippe Starck's work.

21 rue Nationale, 30000 Nîmes. ℂ **04-66-76-28-42.** Fax 04-66-76-28-45. www.new-hotel.com. 34 units. 140€ double; 170€ junior suite. AE, DC, MC, V. **Amenities:** Bar; room service; Wi-Fi (21€ per hr.). *In room:* A/C, TV, hair dryer, minibar.

Novotel Atria Nîmes Centre   Opened in mid-1995, this cost-conscious member of a nationwide chain occupies a desirable site in the heart of Nîmes, adjacent to the ancient arena. Its six floors wrap around a carefully landscaped inner courtyard. Each room contains a double bed, a single bed (which converts into a sofa), a well-equipped bathroom, and a wide writing desk. All the rooms are renovated, although still in a rather sterile chain format.

5 bd. de Prague, 3000 Nîmes. ℂ **04-66-76-56-56.** Fax 04-66-76-56-59. www.accor-hotels.com. 119 units. 125€–165€ double; 180€ suite. AE, DC, MC, V. Parking 11€. **Amenities:** Restaurant; bar; room service. *In room:* A/C, TV, minibar, Wi-Fi (4.50€ per hr.).

Inexpensive

Hôtel César   This three-story hotel is just across the street from the railway station and is especially convenient for Eurailpass holders on a tight budget. All rooms have been completely renovated in a basic Provençal style. They are a bit small but reasonably comfortable and a good value for the price; bathrooms, however, are cramped. The only meal served on the premises is breakfast, but the staff will direct you to several restaurants in the neighborhood.

17 av. Feuchères, 30000 Nîmes. ℂ **04-66-29-29-90.** Fax 04-66-29-05-31. 33 units. 60€ double or triple. AE, DC, MC, V. **Amenities:** Room service. *In room:* A/C, TV, Wi-Fi (free).

Hôtel l'Amphithéâtre (Value   The core of this hotel dates from the 18th century, when it was built as a private home. A stay here involves trekking to your room up steep flights of creaking stairs and navigating a labyrinth of corridors. The small rooms are deliberately old-fashioned, usually containing antiques or antique reproductions and creaky, yet comfortable, beds. Don't expect much in the way of hotel amenities. The staff long ago grew jaded to the fact that the hotel is less than perfect, but at these prices, who's complaining?

4 rue des Arènes, 30000 Nîmes. ℂ **04-66-67-28-51.** Fax 04-66-67-07-79. 15 units. 101€ double. MC, V. Closed mid-Dec to mid-Jan. *In room:* A/C (in some), TV.

WHERE TO DINE

The dining room at the **New Hôtel La Baume** (p. 128) is also a good choice.

Expensive

Alexandre (Michel Kayser) ★★★ TRADITIONAL FRENCH   The most charming restaurant around is on the outskirts of Nîmes, 8km (5 miles) south of the center. Michel Kayser oversees this elegant yet rustic domain, and adheres to classic tradition, with subtle improvements. His wife, Monique, assists him in the ultramodern dining room outfitted in tones of soft reds and ochers, with gilded highlights. Menu items are designed to amuse as well as delight the palate: *île flottante,* a playful update of old-fashioned floating island, with truffles and velouté of cèpe mushrooms; roasted pigeon stuffed with vegetable purée and foie gras; tartare of oysters and shellfish with cardamom seeds; *brandade de Nîmes,* a regional version of brandade of codfish, elevated here to gourmet standards; and filet of bull from the Camargue in red-wine sauce with *camarguais* herbs. Especially appealing is the selection of goat cheeses from the region and worthy cheeses from other parts of France. The dessert trolley is incredibly hard to resist.

Rte. de l'Aéroport de Garons. (04-66-70-08-99. www.michelkayser.com. Reservations recommended. Main courses 42€–96€; fixed-price menus 46€–124€. AE, DC, MC, V. Wed–Sun noon–1:30pm; Wed–Sat 8–9:30pm. Closed 2 weeks in Feb–Mar. From town center, take rue de la République southwest to av. Jean-Jaurès; then head south and follow signs to the airport (toward Garons).

Moderate

Nicolas PROVENÇALE   This antique restaurant is a very old-fashioned, family-style Provençal dining room presided over by chef Pascal Martin. The menu, which makes use of very fresh regional products, changes frequently. In a large dining room, rather outdated, Martin serves his specialties such as flambéed shrimp based on old-time recipes.

1 rue Poise. (04-66-67-50-47. Reservations recommended. Main courses 15€–30€; fixed-price menus 14€, 19€, and 25€. MC, V. Tues–Fri and Sun noon–2pm; Tues–Sun 7–10pm (until 10:30pm July–Aug). Closed first 2 weeks of July and Dec 24–Jan 2.

Restaurant au Chapon Fin ALSATIAN/LANGUEDOCIENNE   This tavern-restaurant stands on a little square behind St. Paul's. It has beamed ceilings, small lamps, and a black-and-white stone floor. From the a la carte menu you can order foie gras with truffles, casserole of roasted lamb and eggplant, beefsteak *péllardon* (with goat-cheese sauce), and brandade of codfish. Other menu items include several kinds of Charolais beefsteak, a platter piled high with grilled sweetbreads and grilled veal kidneys, and several different variations of savory sauerkraut.

3 rue du Château-Fadaise. (04-66-67-34-73. www.chaponfin-restaurant-nimes.com. Reservations required. All main courses 16€; fixed-price lunch 13€; fixed-price dinner 23€–30€. MC, V. Mon–Sat noon–2pm and 7:30–10pm.

Wine Bar Chez Michel (Value) TRADITIONAL FRENCH   This mahogany-paneled bar has leather banquettes evocative of an early-1900s California saloon. Choices include an array of salads and platters. At lunch order from a quick menu, including an appetizer, a garnished main course, and two glasses of wine. Typical dishes are magret of duckling and top-notch beefsteaks and fresh fish. Restaurateur extraordinaire Michel Hermet makes his own wine at vineyards associated with his family for many generations. More than 300 other varieties of wine are in stock, 15 of which are available by the glass or by the pitcher.

11 place de la Couronne. (04-66-76-19-59. Main courses 9€–24€; fixed-price lunch 14€–26€; fixed-price dinner 18€–26€. AE, MC, V. Tues–Sat noon–2pm; Mon–Sat 7pm–midnight.

NIMES AFTER DARK

Once warm weather hits, all sorts of activities take place at the arena, including concerts and theater under the stars. The Office de Tourisme has a complete listing. For popular events such as football (soccer), bullfights, and rock concerts, you can contact the **Bureau de Location des Arènes,** 4 rue de la Violette ((04-66-02-80-80). Tickets for higher-brow events, such as symphonic or chamber-music concerts, theater, and opera performances, are sold through **Le Théâtre Municipal (Le Théâtre de Nîmes),** 1 place de la Calade ((04-66-36-65-10; www.theatredenimes.com).

   Streets to explore on virtually any night of the week include **place de la Maison Carrée** and **boulevard Victor-Hugo.** From June to September, locals flock to the beach to

patronize the shanty restaurants and bars. Bus no. 6 will take you to the **Plage de la**
Corniches for nighttime partying.

If you like hanging out with students and soldiers, head to **Café Le Napoléon,** 46 bd. Victor-Hugo (© **04-66-67-20-23;** www.le-napoleon.com). Popular with the intelligentsia is the **Haddock Cafe,** 13 rue de l'Agau (© **04-66-67-86-57;** www.haddock-cafe. com), which books occasional rock concerts.

The premier jazz venue in Nîmes is **Le Deep Lounge,** 41 bis rue Emile-Jamais (© **04-66-28-11-74**). Open nightly except Monday from 5:30pm until at least 2am, it offers a boozy, smoky, permissive environment where the live musicians derive from just about anywhere. Entrance is free.

Sexy, hip **La Comédie,** 28 rue Jean-Reboul (© **04-66-76-13-66**), is the hands-down best for dancing and attracts a pretty crowd of youthful danceaholics. A little less flashy but a lot more fun, **Lulu Club,** 10 impasse de la Curaterie (© **04-66-36-28-20;** www. lulu-club.com), is the gay and lesbian stronghold in Nîmes. Open Thursday to Saturday, it is a magnet for hip and straight folk as well. A youth-oriented contender is **Le C-Cafe,** 20 rue de l'Etoile (© **04-66-21-59-22**). Open Thursday to Saturday at 11pm, the youthful clientele rocks and rolls to music from L.A. to London.

LANGUEDOC-ROUSSILLON & THE CAMARGUE

5

NIMES

Provence

Provence has been called a bridge between the past and the present, where yesterday blends with today in a quiet, often melancholy way. Peter Mayle's best-selling *A Year in Provence, Toujours Provence,* and *Encore Provence* have played no small part in the burgeoning popularity this sunny corner of southern France has enjoyed during recent years.

The Greeks and Romans filled the landscape with Hellenic theaters, Roman baths, amphitheaters, and triumphal arches. These were followed in medieval times by Romanesque fortresses and Gothic cathedrals. In the 19th century,

Provence's light and landscapes attracted illustrious painters such as Cézanne and van Gogh. Despite the changes over the years, the howling mistral, the legendary bone-chilling wind that blows through each winter, will forever be heard through the broad-leaved plane trees.

Provence has its own language and its own customs. The region is bounded on the north by the Dauphine, on the west by the Rhône, on the east by the Alps, and on the south by the Mediterranean. We'll focus in the next chapters on the part of Provence known as the glittering French Riviera or Côte d'Azur.

1 ORANGE ★★

658km (409 miles) S of Paris; 55km (34 miles) NE of Nîmes; 26km (16 miles) S of Avignon

Orange gets its name from the days when it was a dependency of the Dutch House of Orange-Nassau, not because it is set in a citrus belt. Actually, the last orange grove departed 2,000 years ago. The juice that flows in Orange today comes from its fabled vineyards, which turn out a Côtes du Rhône vintage. Many *caves* (vineyards) are spread throughout the district, some of which offer *dégustations* (wine tastings). The tourist office (see "Essentials," below) will provide you with a list.

Overlooking the Valley of the Rhône, today's Orange, with a somewhat sleepy population of about 30,000, tempts visitors with Europe's third-largest extant triumphal arch and best-preserved Roman theater. Louis XIV, who toyed with the idea of moving the theater to Versailles, said, "It is the finest wall in my kingdom."

ESSENTIALS

GETTING THERE Some 20 **trains** per day arrive from Avignon (trip time: 20 min.); the one-way fare is around 7€. From Marseille, there are 11 trains per day (trip time: 1 hr., 15 min.) for 21€ one-way. From the Gare de Lyon Paris, you can catch a TGV train to Orange; the one-way fare is 76€, and the trip takes 3 hours. For rail information, call ✆ **36-35,** or visit **www.voyages-sncf.com.** For information on bus routes, contact the **Gare Routière** (✆ **04-90-82-07-35**), place Pourtoules, behind the Théâtre Antique. If you're **driving** from Paris, take A6 south to Lyon, then A7 to Orange. The 684km (425-mile) drive takes 5½ to 6½ hours.

VISITOR INFORMATION The **Office de Tourisme** is at 5 cours Aristide-Briand (✆ **04-90-34-70-88;** fax 04-90-34-99-62; www.otorange.fr).

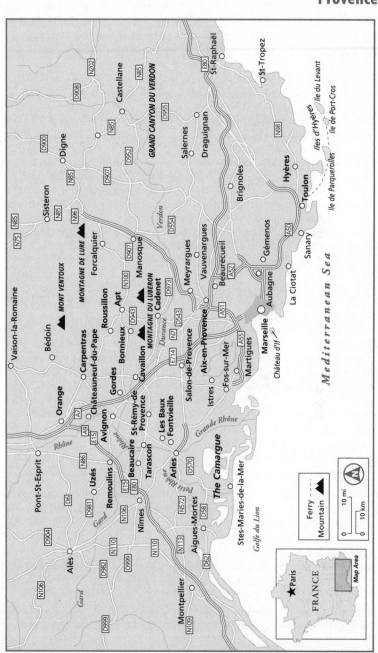

From July 11 to August 4, a drama, dance, and music festival called **Les Chorégies d'Orange** takes place at the Théâtre Antique, one of the most evocative ancient theaters in Europe. For information or tickets, visit or contact the office, 18 place Sylvain, adjacent to the theater (© **04-90-34-24-24;** fax 04-90-11-04-04; www.choregies.asso.fr).

SEEING THE SIGHTS

In the southern part of town, the carefully restored **Théâtre Antique** ★★★, place des Frères-Mounet (© **04-90-51-17-60;** www.theatre-antique.com), dates from the days of Augustus. Built into the side of a hill, it once held 8,000 spectators in tiered seats. The theater is nearly 105m (345 ft.) long, 38m (125 ft.) high, and noted for its acoustics. It's open daily: November to February 9:30am to 4:30pm, March and October 9:30am to 5:30pm, April to May and September 9am to 6pm, and June to August 9am to 7pm. Admission is 7.70€ for adults, 5.80€ for students and children 17 and under.

West of the theater stood a huge temple that, along with a gymnasium, formed one of the greatest buildings in the empire. Across the street, the **Musée Municipal d'Orange,** place du Théâtre-Antique (© **04-90-51-17-60**), displays fragments of the temple. Your ticket to the theater also admits you to the museum, which is open daily April through September 9:30am to 7pm, and October to March 9am to 5:30pm.

Even older than the theater is the **Arc de Triomphe** ★★, on avenue de l'Arc-de-Triomphe. It has decayed, but its decorations and other elements are fairly well preserved. Built to honor the conquering legions of Caesar, it rises 22m (72 ft.) and is nearly 21m (69 ft.) wide. Composed of a trio of arches held up by Corinthian columns, it was used as a dungeon in the Middle Ages.

Before leaving Orange, head for the park **Colline St-Eutrope,** adjacent to the Théâtre Antique, for a view of the valley and its mulberry plantations.

After exploring the town, drive south for 13km (8 miles) along A9 to **Châteauneuf-du-Pape,** where you can have lunch (Tues–Sun) at the **Hostellerie du Château des Fines-Roches,** route d'Avignon (© **04-90-83-70-23;** www.chateaufinesroches.com). Fixed-price menus range from 25€ to 85€. Although the *hostellerie* was built in the 19th century, its medieval features make it appear feudal. If you're pressing on to Avignon, it's only another 13km (8 miles) south along any of three highways (each marked AVIGNON).

WHERE TO STAY

Hôtel Arène ★ (Finds)   On a pedestrian street in the shade of century-old plane trees, this hotel boasts a bull's-eye location in the center of the historic district. Try to get one of the nostalgic rooms that opens onto the old square in front. A series of four antique town houses woven into a seamless whole comprise the complex. Amenities are up-to-date, and the staff is among the more courteous and helpful in town. Guest rooms are traditionally furnished with French decor, and the well-equipped executive rooms are better furnished, and, of course, more expensive.

Place de Langes, 84100 Orange. © **04-90-11-40-40.** Fax 04-90-11-40-45. www.hotel-arene.fr. 35 units. 82€–145€ double; 125€–160€ triple; 170€ junior suite. AE, DC, MC, V. Parking 8€. **Amenities:** 2 restaurants; room service; Wi-Fi (free). *In room:* TV, hair dryer, minibar, Wi-Fi (in executive rooms only; free).

Hôtel Le Louvre et Terminus (Value)   Surrounded by a garden terrace, this conservatively decorated Logis de France offers a good value, housed in a renovated building

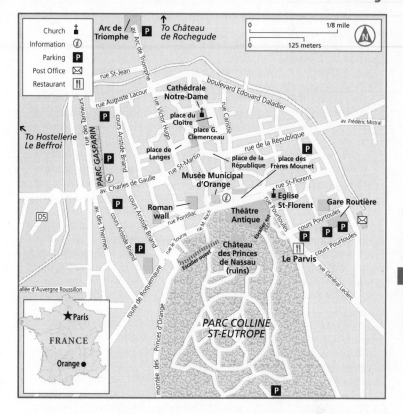

Map legend:
- Church ✝
- Information ⓘ
- Parking 🅿
- Post Office ✉
- Restaurant 🍴

Arc de Triomphe

To Château de Rochegude

0 —— 1/8 mile
0 —— 125 meters

Cathédrale Notre-Dame
boulevard Edouard Daladier
av. Frédéric Mistral
rue St-Jean
rue Auguste Lacour
place du Cloître
place G. Clemenceau
rue Caristie
rue de la République
rue Victor Hugo
rue des Tanneurs
cours Aristide Briand
PARC GASPARIN
place de Langes
rue St-Martin
place de la République
place des Frères Mounet
To Hostellerie Le Beffroi
Musée Municipal d'Orange
av. Charles de Gaulle
rue St-Florent
Eglise St-Florent
Gare Routière
D5
Roman wall
rue Pontillac
Théâtre Antique
cours Pourtoules
av. des Thermes
cours Aristide Briand
rue le Tourre
rue M. Roch
Escalier est
cours Pourtoules
Le Parvis
Château des Princes de Nassau (ruins)
Escalier ouest
rue Général Leclerc
allée d'Auvergne Roussillon
route de Roquemaure
montée des Princes d'Orange
PARC COLLINE ST-EUTROPE

★ Paris
FRANCE
Orange ●

from 1854. Don't expect grandeur: Everything is simple, efficient, and rather brusque. Bedrooms, ranging from small to medium in size, have all the basic necessities and either double or twin beds; the tiled bathrooms are small.

89 av. Frédéric-Mistral, 84100 Orange. ✆ **04-90-34-10-08.** Fax 04-90-34-68-71. www.hotel-louvre-orange.com. 32 units. 65€–115€ double; 105€–129€ suite. AE, DC, MC, V. Parking 8€ in garage. **Amenities:** Restaurant; bar, pool (outdoor). *In room:* A/C, TV, hair dryer, minibar, Wi-Fi (free).

Park Inn This is one of your best bets for general overnight comfort far from the crowds. The well-managed hotel in a 1980s building has wings that curve around a landscaped courtyard. Its well-furnished rooms are arranged around a series of gardens, the largest containing a pool. Rooms have compact modern bathrooms. The poolside restaurant serves fixed-price menus.

80 rte. de Caderousse, 84100 Orange. ✆ **04-90-34-24-10.** Fax 04-90-34-85-48. www.parkinn.com. 99 units. 89€–140€ double. AE, DC, MC, V. Free parking. Drive .8km (¹/₂ mile) west of the city center, following directions to Caderousse. **Amenities:** Restaurant; bar; pool (outdoor); room service. *In room:* A/C, TV, hair dryer, minibar, Wi-Fi (free).

Driving Les Routes de la Lavande

As characteristic of Provence as heather is of the Yorkshire moors, lavender has played a major role in this region for hundreds of years. When it was part of the Roman Empire, Provence produced the flowers to scent the public baths. In the Middle Ages, villages burned piles of the plant in the streets, in keeping with the prevalent medical theory that disease was spread by vapors in the air. But it was during the Renaissance that the current industry took root, linked to the Médicis, who padded their wealth with trade in the distillation of the flower's essential oils.

The heart of lavender production lies in Provençal fields stretching from the foothills of the Vercors mountains to the Verdon canyons and from Buech to the Luberon range. Plants grown and distilled in this area are sold under the Haute-Provence label, renowned for its quality. A drive through the region is most scenic just before the midsummer harvest, when the countryside is a purplish hue from the blossoms of the lavender plants, spread out in seemingly endless rows to the horizon. Not only can you take in the sight and scent of the flowers, but you can also tour the distilleries and farms. Some of these facilities are open only during summer when the year's harvest is undergoing distillation. Those that are open year-round offer tours. They also sell the plants themselves, as well as the essential oils and dried flowers of the plant (used in *provençale* cooking), perfumes, honey, and herbal teas.

One of the best places to visit lavender farms and distilleries is Nyons, 42km (26 miles) northeast of Orange. From Orange, take A7 northwest for 3km (1¼ miles) to Route 976 and drive northeast for 13km (8 miles) to St-Cécile-les-Vignes, where the road becomes Route 576. Continue northeast for 6km (3¾ miles) to Tulette, turn right onto Route 94, and go 22km (14 miles) northeast to Nyons. Stop at the **Office de Tourisme,** place Libération (© **04-75-26-10-35;** www.paysdenyons.com), to pick up the brochure *Les Routes de la Lavande,*

WHERE TO DINE

Le Parvis (Kids) TRADITIONAL FRENCH   Jean-Michel Berengier sets the best table in Orange, albeit in a rather austere dining room. He bases his cuisine on prime vegetables and the best ingredients from the mountains or sea. The restaurant also has a children's menu. Try escalope of braised sea bass with fennel or asparagus, or lamb with garlic cream sauce. The foie gras is a can't-miss dish. Fresh and flavorful seafood is prepared in different ways according to the season, and the staff prides itself on its dozens of preparations. The service is efficient and polite.

55 cours Pourtoules. © **04-90-34-82-00.** Reservations required. Main courses 17€–23€; fixed-price menu 25€–42€; children's menu 12€. MC, V. Tues–Sun noon–2:30pm; Tues–Sat 7:30–9:15pm. Closed mid-Nov to Dec 3 and Jan 16–Feb 3.

WHERE TO STAY & DINE NEARBY

Château de Rochegude ★★   This Relais & Châteaux member stands on 10 hectares (25 acres) of parkland. The castle is at the edge of a hill, surrounded by vineyards.

offering a brief explanation and history of lavender production and a map of the region and its production facilities, with addresses, phone numbers, and hours.

On the outskirts of Nyons, start out at the **Jardin des Arômes (Garden of Aromas),** promenade de la Digue (© **04-75-26-20-51**), with its collection of aromatic plants and lavenders; it's open round-the-clock throughout the year and charges no admission. To reach it from Nyons, follow the road signs pointing to Gap. After viewing and enjoying the scent of the living plants close by, go to **Bleu Provence,** 58 promenade de la Digue (© **04-75-26-10-42;** www. distillerie-bleu-provence.com), a family-owned distillery founded in 1926, for thyme, rosemary, lavender, and "every other spice that's Provençal." A shop on the premises sells essential oils, soaps, and unguents, and the staff will take you on a guided English or French-language tour. If you walk around the premises on your own, the visit is free; to participate in the 45-minute guided tours, the cost is 3€ per person. You must call in advance for an appointment.

In St-Nazaire-le-Desert, northeast of Nyons, you can visit **Gérard Blache,** in the village center next to the Auberge du Desert (© **04-75-27-51-08**), place de la Fontaine, a shop that sells all things lavender in July and August daily from 9:30am to 7:30pm. From here, head southeast to **Rosans,** where the distillery of the Cooperative des Producteurs de Lavande des Alpes (Lavender Cooperative of the Alps), on D94 west of Rosans (© **04-75-26-95-00**), offers short guided tours and sales of essential oils July to August, Tuesday to Saturday 9:30am to 3pm, and off season Wednesday and Saturday to Sunday upon reservation. Southwest of here is **Buis-les-Baronnies,** where the Shop Bernard Laget, in the village center on place aux Herbes (© **04-75-28-12-01;** www. bernard-laget.fr), includes lavender products among its medicinal and aromatic plants; it's open Tuesday to Saturday 9:30am to noon and 3 to 6pm.

The 12th-century turreted residence has been renovated by a series of distinguished owners, ranging from a pope to a dauphin. Each room is done in Provençal style, with fabrics and furniture influenced by the region's 18th- and 19th-century traditions. As befits a château, rooms come in many shapes and sizes, and some are quite spacious. Both the food and the service are exceptional at the château's restaurant. You can enjoy meals in the stately dining room, barbecue by the pool, and refreshments on the sunny terraces. Fixed-price lunches cost 16€ to 31€, fixed-price dinners 35€ to 85€.

26790 Rochegude. © **04-75-97-21-10.** Fax 04-75-04-89-87. www.chateauderochegude.com. 25 units. 170€–355€ double; 350€–555€ suite. AE, DC, MC, V. Free parking. Closed Nov. Take D976 13km (8 miles) north of Orange, following signs toward Gap and Rochegude. **Amenities:** Restaurant; bar; pool (outdoor); room service; tennis court. In room: A/C, TV, minibar, Wi-Fi (free).

Hostellerie Le Beffroi ★ (Finds) This hotel from 1554 draws its charm from ocher walls and original detailing on the exterior, and flowered wallpaper, heavy ceiling beams, plaster detailing, and fireplaces in the rustic interior. The elegantly furnished rooms display 19th-century antiques. Bedrooms offer fine linen on comfortable French beds, most often a double or two twins. In the garden you can order meals under a giant fig tree and dine with a view of town. The hotel, across from the chiseled fountain in the Haute-Ville sector, maintains a limited number of parking spaces.

The town itself is worth exploring, for it contains some fascinating reminders of its former Roman occupation, including Les Ruines Romaines, two areas that have been excavated—the Quartier Puymin and Quartier Villasse.

Rue de l'Evèché, 84110 Vaison-la-Romaine. ☎ **04-90-36-04-71.** Fax 04-90-36-24-78. www.le-beffroi. com. 22 units. 75€–144€ double; 130€–170€ suite. AE, DC, MC, V. Parking 10€. Closed late Jan to mid-Mar. From Orange, drive 34km (21 miles) northeast, following the signs to Vaison-la-Romaine. The hotel is in Vaison's medieval core (Cité Médiévale). **Amenities:** Restaurant (Apr–Oct); bar; pool (outdoor); Wi-Fi (free). *In room:* TV, hair dryer, minibar.

2 CHATEAUNEUF-DU-PAPE

671km (417 miles) S of Paris; 19km (12 miles) N of Avignon; 13km (8 miles) S of Orange

Near Provence's north border, the Château-du-Pape was built as the Castelgandolfo, the country seat of the French popes of Avignon, during the 14th-century reign of Pope John XXII. Today its ruins overlook the vast acres of vineyards planted by the popes, the start of a regional industry that today produces some of the world's best reds as well as an excellent white.

ESSENTIALS

GETTING THERE   To reach Châteauneuf-du-Pape, you must take one of three daily **buses** from Avignon (p. 141), a journey of less than 30 minutes. Châteauneuf does not have a bus station; you are deposited at place de la Bascule, behind the local post office. This is also where you catch buses returning to Avignon. The tourist office (see below) is the best source for schedules and information about bus access.

If you're **driving** from Avignon, head north on A7 to the intersection with Route 17, at which point you continue northwest following the signs into Châteanuef-du-Pape.

VISITOR INFORMATION   The **Office de Tourisme** is at place du Portail (☎ **04-90-83-71-08;** www.ccpro.fr). Summer hours are 9:30am to 6pm, Monday to Saturday. Winter hours are 9:30am to 12:30pm and 2 to 6pm Monday and Tuesday and Wednesday to Saturday.

A SPECIAL EVENT   Since the Middle Ages, the annual **Fête de la Véraison** has been held in early August. See details below.

WINE LURE & LORE

The local wines are distinctive in their blending of 13 varieties of grapes, grown on vines surrounded by stones that reflect heat onto them during the day and keep them warm in the cool night. As a result, the wines produced in the district's vineyards are among the most potent in France, with an alcohol content of at least 12.5% and, in many instances, as high as 15%. The region played a central role in the initiation of the Appellation d'Origine Contrôlée, France's strict quality-control system. The late Baron Le Roy de Boiseaumarie, the most distinguished of the local vintners, initiated geographical boundaries and minimum standards for the production of wines given the Châteauneuf-du-Pape label. In 1923, local producers won exclusive rights to market their Côtes du Rhônes under that label and thus paved the way for other regions to identify and protect

A useful source is **La Vinothèque,** 9 rue de la République (© **04-90-83-74-01**). A sales and marketing outlet for Madame Carre, matriarch of the Comtes d'Argelas vineyards, it's open for wine tastings and sales daily from 10am to 6pm. On the premises is La Boutique de la Vinothèque, where wine accessories (corkscrews, racks, decanters) are sold.

TOURING & TASTING THE WINES

A map posted in place du Portail (but called place de la Fontaine by just about everyone), pinpoints 22 wineries open for touring and tasting. The best known is **Domaine de Mont-Redon,** on D68 about 5km (3 miles) north of the town center (© **04-90-83-72-75;** www.chateaumontredon.fr). It offers samplings of recent vintages of reds and whites and sales of *eau-de-vie,* a clear grape liqueur produced in a limited batch annually. A noteworthy competitor is **Clos des Papes,** avenue Le Bienheureux Pierre de Luxembourg, in the town center (© **04-90-83-70-13;** www.clos-des-papes.fr), where humidified cellars produce what many connoisseurs consider the region's best wine. Both establishments prefer advance notice before your arrival.

The town's only museum devotes all its exhibition space to winemaking. The **Musée des Vieux Outils de Vignerons of the Caves du Père-Anselme,** avenue Le Bienheureux Pierre de Luxembourg (© **04-90-83-70-07;** www.brotte.com), contains the history and artifacts of local wine production, including a 16th-century wine press, winemakers' tools, barrel-making equipment, and a tasting cellar. It's open daily from mid-April to mid-September from 9am to 1pm and 2 to 7pm, and the rest of the year from 9am to noon and 2 to 6pm. Admission and tastings are free.

A WINE FESTIVAL   During 3 days in early August, the village hosts the annual **Fête de la Véraison** ★, a medieval fair. It includes tasting stalls set up by local winemakers, actors impersonating Provençaux troubadours, bear-baiters (who are much kinder to their animals than their medieval counterparts), falconers with their birds, merchants selling locally made handicrafts, battered flea market kiosks, and food. Don't expect dancing—what you'll get is a festival where the antique fountain on place du Portail spurts out wine, and vast amounts of that beverage are consumed. If you attend, you can drink all the wine you want for the price of a *verre de la Véraison.* This souvenir glass, filled on demand at any vintner who participates, costs 4€ and is sold at strategically positioned kiosks around town.

(**Finds**)   **Wine & Chocolate**

One of the newest industries in Châteauneuf is the **Chocolaterie Castelain,** whose factories and showrooms lie on the Route d'Avignon (© **04-90-83-54-71;** www.chocolat-castelain.com), about 3km (2 miles) south of town. They've become known for a popular type of black chocolate *(la ganache)* flavored with a distilled version *(vieu marc de Châteauneuf)* of the red wine produced in local vineyards. The brand name of their chocolates is **Palet des Pâpes.** The chocolates pair very well with any of the local vintages.

Hostellerie du Château des Fines-Roches ★★   This medieval-inspired manor house is from the late 19th century. Named for the smooth rocks *(fines roches)* found in the soil of the nearby vineyards, the château devotes its huge cellars to the storage of thousands of bottles of local wines. The guest rooms on the upper floors of this charming hotel are renovated and include Provençal styling with a scattering of antiques.

We highly recommend taking a meal in the restaurant here. Menu items, carefully crafted and full of flavor, include filets of red mullet prepared with aromatic herbs and garnished with its own liver marinated in vinaigrette, barigoule of crayfish tails with artichokes, filet of bull from the Camargue marinated in a particular vintage *(syrah)* of strong red wine, and roast rack of local lamb with a gratin of eggplant and sheep's cheese. The wine list focuses on local vintages, particularly those from the village.

Rte. De Sorgues, 84230 Châteauneuf-du-Pape. (𝄞 **04-90-83-70-23.** Fax 04-90-83-78-42. www.chateau finesroches.com. 11 units. 109€–309€ double. AE, DC, MC, V. Free parking. Closed Nov. From the center of town, drive 3km (2 miles) south, following the signs to Avignon. **Amenities:** Restaurant; bar; pool (outdoor); room service. *In room:* A/C, TV, hair dryer, minibar, Wi-Fi (free).

WHERE TO DINE

La Mère Germaine ★ PROVENÇALE   Named after the matriarch who established this place several generations ago, La Mère Germaine contains both a restaurant gastronomique and a simple bistro. Both enjoy sweeping panoramas from terraces where tables are set out in the summer months. Cuisine in both establishments is based on the traditions of Provence. In the bistro, you're likely to find simple platters of grilled fish, stews, casseroles, and grilled meats, but in the restaurant, cuisine is more elaborate, intricate, and tuned to the seasons. Dishes in the restaurant include zucchini flowers stuffed with mushrooms and drizzled with ratatouille juice, roasted rabbit stuffed with black-olive tapenade and fresh tomatoes, filet of turbot with *barigoule* (Provençal vinaigrette), and crispy rack of lamb scented with herbs from the surrounding *garrigue* (scrubland).

Eight simple, well-scrubbed bedrooms are available on the premises. None has a phone or elaborate amenities, but for a comfortable sojourn after a meal in the restaurant, they all offer good value and a sense of comfort and efficiency.

3 rue du Commandant Lemaitre, 84230 Châteauneuf-du-Pape. (𝄞 **04-90-83-54-37.** Fax 04-90-83-50-27. www.lameregermaine.com. Reservations recommended. In the bistro, platters 17€–23€; in the restaurant, fixed-price menus 20€–38€; gourmet menu 105€. AE, DC, MC, V. Daily noon–2pm and 7–9pm.

3 AVIGNON ★★★

684km (425 miles) S of Paris; 80km (50 miles) NW of Aix-en-Provence; 106km (66 miles) NW of Marseille

In the 14th century, Avignon was the capital of Christendom—the popes lived here instead of in Rome. The legacy left by their "court of splendor and magnificence" makes Avignon one of the most interesting and beautiful of Europe's medieval cities.

The popes are long gone, but life goes on exceedingly well without them. Avignon at any time of the year is a major stopover on the route from Paris to the Mediterranean. Lately, it has become well-known as a cultural center as artists and painters in increasing numbers have been moving here. Experimental theaters, painting galleries, and art cinemas have brought diversity to the inner city, especially rue des Teinturiers. Today this walled city of some 100,000 residents reaches its peak celebration during the famous

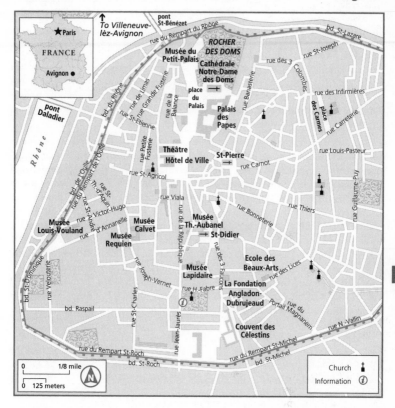

Festival d'Avignon, a 3-week stint of music, art, and theater when bacchanalia reigns in the streets.

ESSENTIALS

GETTING THERE The fastest and easiest way to get here is to **fly** from Paris's Orly Airport to **Aéroport Avignon-Caumont** (☎ 04-90-81-51-51), 8km (5 miles) southeast of Avignon (trip time: 1 hr.). Taxis from the airport to the center cost 21€. Call ☎ **04-90-82-20-20.** From Paris, TGV **trains** from Gare de Lyon take 3 hours and 30 minutes. The one-way fare is 78€. Trains arrive frequently from Marseille (70 min.; 23€) and from Arles (20 min.; 6€). For train information, call ☎ **36-35,** or visit **www. voyages-sncf.com**.

The **bus station** in Avignon is Gare Routière, 5 av. Monclar (☎ 04-90-82-07-35). The main routes connect to Arles (trip time: 1½ hr.), costing 7.10€, and Marseille (trip time: 2 hr.), costing 18€.

If you're **driving** from Paris, take A6 south to Lyon, then A7 south to Avignon. To explore the area by **bike,** go to **Provence Bike,** 52 bd. St-Roch (☎ **04-90-27-92-61;** www.provence-bike.com), which rents all sorts of bikes, including 10-speed road bikes and mountain bikes, for around 12€ to 25€ per day. A deposit of 150€ to 450€, in cash or a credit card imprint, is required.

VISITOR INFORMATION   The **Office de Tourisme** is at 41 cours Jean-Jaurès (© **04-32-74-32-74;** fax 04-90-82-95-03; www.ot-avignon.fr).

SPECIAL EVENTS   The biggest celebration is the **Festival d'Avignon,** held July 6 to July 27. The international festival focuses on avant-garde theater, dance, and music. Part of the fun is the nightly revelry in the streets. Tickets cost 5€ to 40€. Prices for rooms and meals skyrocket, so make reservations far in advance. For information, contact the **Bureaux du Festival,** Espace Saint-Louis, 20 rue du Portail Boquier, 84000 Avignon (© **04-90-27-66-50;** www.festival-avignon.com).

Palais des Papes ★★★   Dominating Avignon from a hill is one of the most famous (or notorious, depending on your point of view) palaces in the Christian world. Head-quarters of a schismatic group of cardinals who came close to toppling the authority of the popes in Rome, it is part fortress, part showplace. In 1309, Pope Clement V fled to Avignon to escape political infighting in Rome. His successor, John XXII, chose to stay in Avignon. The third Avignon pope, Benedict XII, was the one responsible for the construction of this magnificent palace. Avignon became, for a time, the Vatican of the north. During the period, dubbed "the Babylonian Captivity" by Rome, the popes held extravagant court in the palace; art and culture flourished—and so did prostitution and vice. When Gregory XI was persuaded to return to Rome in 1376, Avignon elected its own rival pope, and the Great Schism split the Christian world. The real struggle, of course, was about the wealth and power of the papacy. The reign of Avignon's antipopes finally ended in 1417 with the election of Martin V in Rome, and the papal court here was disbanded.

Chapelle St-Jean is known for its beautiful frescoes, attributed to the school of Mat-teo Giovanetti and painted between 1345 and 1348. The frescoes present scenes from the life of John the Baptist and John the Evangelist. More Giovanetti frescoes can be seen above the Chapelle St-Jean in the **Chapelle St-Martial.** The frescoes here depict the miracles of St. Martial, patron saint of Limousin.

Grand Tinel (Banquet Hall) is about 41m (135 ft.) long and 9m (30 ft.) wide, and the pope's table stood on the southern side. The **pope's bedroom** is on the first floor of the Tour des Anges. Its walls are entirely decorated in tempera with foliage on which birds and squirrels perch; bird cages are painted in the recesses of the windows. In a secular vein, the **Studium (Stag Room)**—study of Clement VI—was frescoed in 1343 with hunting scenes. Added under the same Clement, who had a taste for grandeur, the **Grande Audience (Great Audience Hall)** contains frescoes of the prophets; these are also attributed to Giovanetti and were painted in 1352.

Between two and four French-language guided tours are offered every day at schedules that vary widely according to the season and day of the week. Tours usually last 50 min-utes. Aside from the exceptions mentioned above, they are somewhat monotonous, since most of the rooms have been stripped of their once-legendary finery. Self-guided tours in English, using a hand-held audio device, are available anytime during opening hours.

Place du Palais des Papes. © **04-90-27-50-00.** www.palais-des-papes.com. Admission (including tour with guide or recording) 8.50€–11€ adults, 7€–8.50€ seniors and students, free for children 7 and under. Daily Mar 1–14 9am–6:30pm; Mar 15–June 9am–7pm; July 9am–8pm; Aug 9am–9pm; Sept 1–15 9am–8pm; Sept 16–Nov 1 9am–7pm; Nov 2–Feb 9:30am–5:45pm.

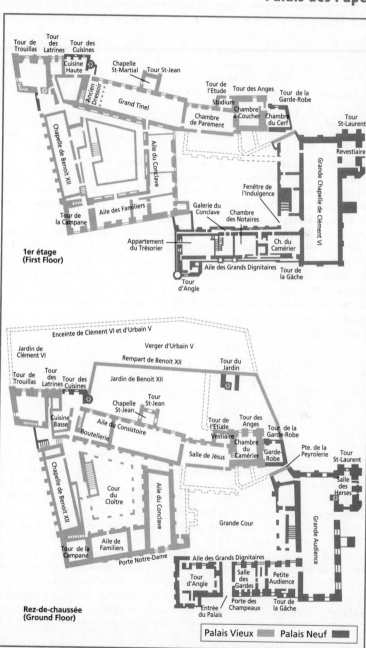

1er étage (First Floor)

Tour de Trouillas
Tour des Latrines
Tour des Cuisines
Cuisine Haute
Ancien Dressoir
Chapelle St-Martial
Tour St-Jean
Grand Tinel
Tour de l'Etude
Tour des Anges
Tour de la Garde-Robe
Studium
Chambre à Coucher
Chambre du Cerf
Tour St-Laurent
Chambre de Parement
Revestiaire
Chapelle de Benoît XII
Aile du Conclave
Grande Chapelle de Clément VI
Fenêtre de l'Indulgence
Galerie du Conclave
Chambre des Notaires
Aile des Familiers
Tour de la Campane
Appartement du Trésorier
Ch. du Camérier
Aile des Grands Dignitaires
Tour de la Gâche
Tour d'Angle

Rez-de-chaussée (Ground Floor)

Enceinte de Clément VI et d'Urbain V
Verger d'Urbain V
Jardin de Clément VI
Rempart de Benoit XII
Tour du Jardin
Tour de Trouillas
Tour des Latrines
Tour des Cuisines
Jardin de Benoit XII
Cuisine Basse
Chapelle St-Jean
Tour St-Jean
Aile du Consistoire
Tour de l'Etude
Tour des Anges
Tour de la Garde-Robe
Boutellerie
Vestiaire
Chambre du Camérier
Garde-Robe
Pte. de la Peyrolerie
Tour St-Laurent
Salle de Jésus
Salle des Herses
Chapelle de Benoît XII
Cour du Cloître
Aile du Conclave
Grande Cour
Grande Audience
Aile de Familiers
Tour de la Campane
Porte Notre-Dame
Aile des Grands Dignitaires
Tour d'Angle
Salle des Gardes
Petite Audience
Entrée du Palais
Porte des Champeaux
Tour de la Gâche

Palais Vieux   Palais Neuf

Even more famous than the papal residency is the ditty *"Sur le pont d'Avignon, l'on y danse, l'on y danse."* **Pont St-Bénézet ★★** (📞 **04-90-27-51-16**) was far too narrow for the *danse* of the rhyme, however. Spanning the Rhône and connecting Avignon with Villeneuve-lèz-Avignon, the bridge is now a ruin, with only four of its original 22 arches. According to legend, it was inspired by a vision that a shepherd named Bénézet had while tending his flock. The bridge was built between 1177 and 1185 and suffered various disasters. (In 1669, half of it fell into the river.) On one of the piers is the two-story **Chapelle St-Nicolas**—one story in Romanesque style, the other in Gothic. The remains of the bridge are open daily November to March 9:30am to 5:45pm; April to June and October 9am to 6pm; August 9am to 9pm; and July and September 9am to 8pm. Admission is 4€ for adults, 3.50€ for seniors and students, free for children 7 and under. A visit to the small chapel on the bridge is part of the overall admission fee.

It's worth at least an hour to walk through the **Quartier de La Balance,** where the Gypsies lived in the 1800s. Over the years, La Balance had grown seedy, but since the 1970s, major renovations have taken place. Start at place du Palais, going along rue de La Balance, detouring into the historically evocative rue de la Grande Fusterie and the rue des Grottes. The main interest here is the restoration of the old town houses with their renewed elegant facades, many graced with mullioned windows. In the district are some of the ramparts that used to surround Avignon, stretching for 4km (2½ miles). Built in the 14th century by the popes, these ramparts were partially restored in the 19th century by that busy restorer of medieval monuments, Viollet-le-Duc. The most intriguing section is along rue du Rempart-du-Rhône, leading east to place Crillon. After a look, you can return to place de l'Horloge via rue St-Etienne.

Cathédrale Notre-Dame des Doms ★   Near the palace is this 12th-century cathedral, containing the Flamboyant Gothic tomb of a few apostate popes. Crowning the top is a gilded statue of the Virgin from the 19th century. The cathedral's hours vary according to the schedule of religious ceremonies, but generally it's open during the hours noted below. From the cathedral, enter the promenade du Rocher-des-Doms and its garden to enjoy the view across the Rhône to Villeneuve-lèz-Avignon.

Place du Palais. 📞 **04-90-86-81-01.** Free admission. Daily 8am–9pm; hours may vary according to religious ceremonies.

La Fondation Angladon-Dubrujeaud ★   This museum, opened in 1995, contains the magnificent art collection of Jacques Doucet, renowned Parisian haute couture designer and Belle Epoque dandy and dilettante. Doucet cultivated a number of young artists, among them Picasso, Braque, Max Jacob, Marcel Duchamp, and Guillaume Apollinaire, and began to collect their early works. For decades, Doucet's heirs kept the treasure-trove a relative secret and lived in quiet splendor amid canvases by Cézanne, Sisley, Derain, Degas, and Modigliani. Today you can wander through Doucet's former abode, which is also filled with rare antiques and art objects that include 16th-century Buddhas and Louis XVI chairs designed by Jacob. Doucet died in 1929 at the age of 76, his own fortune so diminished that his nephew paid for his funeral. But his rich legacy lives on here.

5 rue Laboureur. 📞 **04-90-82-29-03.** www.angladon.com. Admission 6€ adults, 4€ students and children 14–18, 1.50€ children 7–13. Tues–Sun 1–6pm. Closed Tues in winter.

Musée Calvet ★   In an 18th-century mansion, this museum holds a fine- and decorative-art collection that features the works of Vernet, David, Corot, Manet, and Soutine, plus a collection of ancient silverware. Our favorite oil is Bruegel the Younger's *Le Cortège*

Nuptial (The Bridal Procession). Look for a copy of Bosch's *Adoration of the Magi*, plus sculptures by Camille Claudel.

65 rue Joseph-Vernet. ✆ **04-90-86-33-84.** www.musee-calvet.org. Admission 6€ adults, 3€ students, free for children 12 and under. Wed–Mon 10am–1pm and 2–6pm.

Musée du Petit-Palais This was the palace where the first two Avignon popes lived until the construction of the Palais des Papes. It holds an important collection of paintings from the Italian schools of the 13th to 16th centuries, including works from Florence, Venice, Siena, and Lombardy. Salons display 15th-century paintings done in Avignon, and several galleries are devoted to Roman and Gothic sculptures.

Place du Palais des Papes. ✆ **04-90-86-44-58.** Admission 6€ adults, 3€ students, free for children 12 and under. June–Sept Wed–Mon 10am–6pm; Oct–May Wed–Mon 10am–1pm and 2–6pm.

Musée Lapidaire ★ Behind a baroque facade, a 17th-century Jesuit church has been turned into an intriguing museum of mainly Gallo-Roman sculptures that can be viewed in less than an hour. In the museum you can trace the history of the various civilizations that have cultivated Provence. Some of the exhibitions are frightening, including the statue of a man-eating monster discovered at Noves called *Tarasque*. Fascinating Greco-Roman statues are on exhibition, including a magnificent copy of Praxiteles' **Apollo the Python Killer ★**. A large number of ancient sarcophagi and funerary art is also on show, including an unusual series of masks from Vaison.

65 rue de la République. ✆ **04-90-85-75-38.** Admission 7€ adults, 3.50€ students 13–18, free for children 12 and under. Wed–Mon 10am–noon and 2–6pm.

Musée Louis-Vouland This 19th-century mansion opening onto a lovely garden displays lavish 17th- and 18th-century antiques and objets d'art from Avignon. The collection includes Sèvres porcelain, the *comtesse* du Barry's tea set, great tapestries from Aubusson and Gobelins, glittering chandeliers, and commodes to equal those at Versailles. Our favorites are the Louis XV inkpots with silver rats holding the lids.

17 rue Victor-Hugo. ✆ **04-90-86-03-79.** www.vouland.com. Admission 6€ adults, 4€ students and ages 3–12. July–Sept Tues–Sun noon–6pm; Oct–June Tues–Sun 2–6pm. Closed Feb.

Musée Requien For aficionados only, this offbeat museum can easily take up an hour of your time. Located next to the Musée Calvet, it was named after the naturalist Espirit Requien (1788–1851), who was largely responsible for the nucleus of the collection. The museum houses one of the most important natural history libraries in France but is most often visited for its **herbarium ★**, containing some 200,000 specimens gathered by botanists from around the world. To round out the collection is a parade of exhibits that trace the geology, zoology, and botany of Provence.

67 rue Joseph-Vernet. ✆ **04-90-82-43-51.** www.museum-avignon.org. Free admission. Tues–Sat 9am–noon and 2–6pm.

SHOPPING

Mistral Les Indiens de Nîmes, 19 rue Joseph-Vernet (✆ **04-90-86-32-05**), duplicates 18th- and 19th-century Provençal fabric patterns. Fabrics are available by the meter or as clothing for men, women, and children. Kitchenware and furniture inspired by Provence and the steamy wetlands west of Marseille are also for sale.

The clothing at **Souleiado,** 5 rue Joseph Vernet (✆ **04-90-86-47-67**), derives from traditional Provençal costumes. Most of the clothing is for women. Fabrics are for sale by the meter. The name means "first ray of sunshine after a storm."

Hervé Baume, 19 rue Petite Fusterie (☎ **04-90-86-37-66**), is for those who yearn to set a Provençal table. The store is piled high with a little bit of everything—from Directoire dinner services to French folk art to handblown crystal lamps. **Jaffier-Parsi,** 42 rue des Fourbisseurs (☎ **04-90-86-08-85**), is known for its copper saucepans from the Norman town of Villedieu-les-Poêles, which has been making them since the Middle Ages. If you're seeking a new perspective on Provençal pottery, go to **Terre è Provence,** 26 rue de la République (☎ **04-90-85-56-45**). You can pick up wonderful kitsch—perhaps terra-cotta plates decorated with three-dimensional cicadas.

Most markets in Avignon are open 6am to 1pm. The biggest covered market with 40 different merchants is **Les Halles,** place Pie, open Tuesday to Sunday. Other smaller **food markets** are on place Parking des Italiens on Sunday, and on place St-Chamand also on Sunday. The **flower market** is on place des Carmes on Saturday, and the **flea market** is in the same place on Sunday.

WHERE TO STAY

Very Expensive

La Mirande ★★★ In the heart of Avignon behind the Palais des Papes, this 700-year-old town house is one of France's grand little luxuries. In 1987, Achim and Hannelore Stein transformed it into a citadel of opulence. The hotel displays 2 centuries of decorative art, from the 1700s Salon Chinois to the Salon Rouge, with striped walls in Rothschild red. Room no. 20 is the most sought after—its lavish premises open onto the garden. All rooms are stunning, with exquisite decor, hand-printed fabrics on the walls, antiques, and bedside controls. The restaurant, among the finest in Avignon, deserves its one Michelin star.

4 place de la Mirande, 84000 Avignon. ☎ **04-90-85-93-93.** Fax 04-90-86-26-85. www.la-mirande.fr. 25 units. 310€–540€ double; 660€–850€ suite. AE, DC, MC, V. Parking 22€. **Amenities:** Restaurant; bar; babysitting; room service; rooms for those w/limited mobility. *In room:* A/C, TV, hair dryer, minibar, Wi-Fi (free).

Expensive

Hôtel d'Europe ★★★ This deluxe hostelry, in operation since 1799, is almost the equal of La Mirande (see above), though slightly less expensive. The grand hall and salons contain antiques, and the good-size guest rooms have handsome decor and period furnishings. Two suites are on the roof, with views of the Palais des Papes. Overall, accommodations are comfortable, with touches of Gallic charm. The spacious bedrooms are handsomely equipped, and each has an immaculate bathroom. The restaurant, which specializes in traditional French and *provençale* cuisine, is one of the best in Avignon.

12 place Crillon, 84000 Avignon. ☎ **04-90-14-76-76.** Fax 04-90-14-76-71. www.heurope.com. 44 units. 175€–480€ double; 655€–820€ suite. AE, DC, MC, V. Parking 15€. **Amenities:** Restaurant; bar; babysitting; room service. *In room:* A/C, TV, hair dryer, minibar, Wi-Fi (free).

Moderate

Hôtel Bristol In the center of Avignon, on one of the principal streets leading to the landmark place de l'Horloge and the Palais des Papes, the Bristol is one of the town's better bets. A traditional hotel, it offers comfortably furnished well-maintained rooms, most with twin beds. Breakfast is the only meal served. Though it's not the most atmospheric place, it offers good, solid value in an expensive city.

44 cours Jean-Jaurès, 84000 Avignon. ☎ **04-90-16-48-48.** Fax 04-90-86-22-72. www.bristol-hotel-avignon.com. 67 units. 81€–97€ double; 133€–179€ suite. AE, DC, MC, V. Parking 11€. **Amenities:** Bar; room service. *In room:* A/C, TV, hair dryer, minibar, Wi-Fi (in some, 4.50€ per hour).

Hôtel Clarion Cloître St-Louis ★ This hotel is in a former Jesuit school built in the 1580s. Much of the original premises remains, including the baroque facade, the wraparound arcades, and the soaring ceiling vaults. Guest rooms are more functional; in fact, they're rather dull as a result of renovations. Rooms range from medium-size to spacious, and some have sliding glass doors overlooking the patio.

20 rue du Portail Boquier, 84000 Avignon. ✆ **800/CLARION [252-7466]** in the U.S., or 04-90-27-55-55. Fax 04-90-82-24-01. www.cloitre-saint-louis.com. 80 units. 100€–210€ double; 250€–350€ suite. AE, DC, MC, V. Parking 10€–15€. **Amenities:** Restaurant; bar; pool (outdoor); room service; Wi-Fi (free). *In room:* A/C, TV, hair dryer, minibar.

Hôtel du Palais des Papes From the twin terraces of this simple but well-established hotel, you can enjoy views of the clock tower (overlooking the place de l'Horloge) and the Palais des Papes alike. Few other hotels have such a central location and only a handful are able to boast construction that was completed in series between the 15th century and the 1920s. You access the three floors via a corkscrew stone staircase that, in addition to exposed stone walls, massive ceiling beams, and wrought-iron bedsteads, evokes a modern twist on the Middle Ages (which fortunately includes neatly tiled bathrooms). The hotel has two dining rooms: one medieval-looking, with a big fireplace, and the other slightly more modern. Cuisine is *provençale* and French, flavorful, and served in generous portions. The hotel and its restaurant have been operated for many previous generations by the Donche-Gay family, who are almost always on-site.

3 place du Palais, 84000 Avignon. ✆ **04-90-86-04-13.** Fax 04-90-27-91-17. www.hotel-avignon.com. 27 units. 72€–98€ double; 120€–133€ junior suite. AE, MC, V. Parking 8€ per night in a nearby municipal parking lot. **Amenities:** Restaurant; bar. *In room:* A/C (in some), TV, Wi-Fi (free).

Hôtel Mercure Cité-des-Papes Nearly adjacent to the Palais des Papes, this five-story modern building offers solid, comfortable, though not particularly stylish, bedrooms. Views from many windows extend over the place de l'Horloge. While the hotel has no restaurant, its central location makes it easy to dine out.

1 rue Jean-Vilar, 84000 Avignon. ✆ **04-90-80-93-00.** Fax 04-90-80-93-01. www.mercure.com. 89 units. 125€–170€ double. AE, DC, MC, V. Parking 5.80€. **Amenities:** Restaurant; babysitting; bar. *In room:* A/C, TV, hair dryer, minibar, Wi-Fi (4.50€ per hr.).

La Banasterie ★ (Finds) Parisian owners Françoise and Jean-Michel operate one of the most stylish B&Bs in Avignon in a building that preserves the stone walls and architectural details of another age. The guesthouse is elegantly decorated, with each room decorated differently. The hosts also share a devotion to *chocolat:* All the bedrooms are named for famous names of different chocolates, and excellent hot cocoa in the evening and fine chocolates on your pillow round out the day. In the center of town, the B&B lies on a hard-to-find side street by the Palais des Papes.

11 rue de la Banasterie, 84000 Avignon. ✆/fax **04-32-76-30-78.** www.labanasterie.com. 5 units. 100€ double; 160€ suite. Rates include continental breakfast. No credit cards. **Amenities:** Breakfast room. *In room:* A/C, TV, hair dryer, Wi-Fi (free).

Lumani ★ (Finds) Artist-owners Elizabeth and Jean have restored this 1800s manor house and decorated it with style. Each room has a distinct personality and is decorated with taste and comfort in mind. Old architectural features are blended with modern comfort. The lovely courtyard is shaded by centuries-old plane trees. Dining is available by reservation only, costing 30€ per person, with a minimum of six diners required.

37 rue du Rempart St-Lazare, 84000 Avignon. ✆ **03-90-82-94-11.** www.avignon-lumani.com. 5 units. 100€–170€ double. MC, V. **Amenities:** Dining room. *In room:* No phone.

Villa Agapè ★   In the town center near the papal palace, this small hotel occupies two elegantly restored 17th-century buildings. The villa surrounds a spacious, flowery terrace. Inside the air-conditioned house, guests can enjoy the spectacular lounge-library. Bedrooms are spacious and sunny, decorated with quality furnishings in a Provençal style. The family rooms, which open onto a private terrace, can hold four comfortably. A delicious breakfast can be served alfresco on the terrace.

13 rue St-Agricol. 84000 Avignon. ✆ **04-90-85-21-92.** Fax 06-07-98-71-30. www.villa-agape.com. 3 units. 100€–150€. Rates include continental breakfast. No credit cards. **Amenities:** Breakfast room; pool (outdoor). *In room:* Wi-Fi (free).

Inexpensive
Hôtel d'Angleterre   This three-story Art Deco structure in the heart of Avignon is the city's best budget hotel, with the advantage of being located inside the city ramparts. Built in 1929 of gray stone, it emulates the style that local builders imagined was characteristic of English houses. The rooms are small, but comfortably furnished. Only breakfast is served, and except for a laundry service, amenities hardly exist.

29 bd. Raspail, 84000 Avignon. ✆ **04-90-86-34-31.** Fax 04-90-86-86-74. www.hoteldangleterre.fr. 39 units. 60€–85€ double. AE, MC, V. Free parking. Closed Dec 19–Jan 19. *In room:* A/C, TV, Wi-Fi (free).

Hôtel le Médiéval   About 3 blocks south of the Palais des Papes, this town house from the late 1600s is uncomplicated and well maintained. Under beamed ceilings, the comfortable guest rooms are medium-size to spacious. Most peaceful are the units that overlook the inner courtyard, with its pots of flowers and shrubs. Those that overlook a congested medieval street corner might be noisier, but they have a rough-and-ready charm of their own.

15 rue Petite Saunerie, 84000 Avignon. ✆ **04-90-86-11-06.** Fax 04-90-82-08-64. www.hotelmedieval. com. 35 units. 66€–73€ double. Extra bed 8€. MC, V. Closed Dec 22–Feb 3. **Amenities:** Room service. *In room:* TV, hair dryer, Wi-Fi (4.50€ per hr.).

WHERE TO DINE
Expensive
Brunel PROVENÇALE   This flower-filled restaurant is in the heart of Avignon. The managing Brunel family offers such superb dishes as monkfish with anise-flavored butter; confit of lamb couscous; and tuna steak with coulis of capers and onions. Artichoke hearts accompany grilled John Dory, and even the pigs' feet are sublime. The desserts are prepared fresh daily. You can order house wines by the carafe.

46 rue de La Balance. ✆ **04-90-85-24-83.** Reservations required. Main courses 13€–20€ lunch, 28€–35€ dinner; fixed-price menu 28€–33€. AE, MC, V. Tues–Sat noon–1:30pm and 7:30–9pm (Mon–Sat in July). Closed first 2 weeks in Aug and Dec 20–Jan 6.

Christian Etienne ★★★ PROVENÇALE   The stone house containing this restaurant was built in 1180, around the same time as the Palais des Papes (which happens to be next door). The dining room contains early-16th-century frescoes honoring the marriage of Anne de Bretagne to the French king in 1491. Owner Christian Etienne's fixed-price menus feature themes: Two present seasonal tomatoes, mushrooms, or other vegetables; one offers preparations of lobster; and the priciest relies on the chef's imagination *(menu confiance)* for unique combinations. In summer, look for the vegetable menu entirely based on ripe tomatoes. The vegetable menus aren't completely vegetarian; they're flavored with meat, fish, or meat drippings. A la carte specialties include filet of

perch with Châteauneuf-du-Pape, filet of venison with foie gras, and a dessert of fennel
sorbet with saffron-flavored English cream sauce.

10 rue Mons. ✆ **04-90-86-16-50.** www.christian-etienne.fr. Reservations required. Main courses 28€–45€; fixed-price lunch 35€–120€; fixed-price dinner 65€–120€. AE, DC, MC, V. Tues–Sat noon–1:15pm and 7:30–9:15pm. Closed first 2 weeks in Aug and Dec 20–Jan 6.

Hiély-Lucullus ★★ FRENCH   This Relais Gourmand property is formidable competition for Christian Etienne (see above) as Avignon's most outstanding restaurant. The Belle Epoque decor enhances the grand cuisine. Market-fresh products go into such innovative dishes as crayfish-stuffed ravioli flavored with fresh sage and served with pumpkin sauce, filet of female venison with tangy honey sauce, and escalope of sautéed foie gras on toasted rye bread. Lots of fresh fish is imported daily and cooked to perfection. The *pièce de résistance* is *agneau des Alpilles grillé* (grilled Alpine lamb). Dessert may be vanilla-bourbon cream in puff pastry. Carafe wines include Tavel Rosé and Châteauneuf-du-Pape.

5 rue de la République. ✆ **04-90-86-17-07.** Reservations required. Main courses 25€–40€; fixed-price menu 35€–95€. AE, MC, V. Daily noon–2pm and 7–10pm.

Moderate

La Fourchette ★ (**Value**) FRENCH   This bistro offers creative cooking at a moderate price. Its two airy dining rooms have large bay windows that flood the inside with light. You may begin with fresh sardines flavored with citrus, ravioli filled with haddock, or parfait of chicken livers with spinach flan and confit of onions. For a main course, we recommend monkfish stew with endive or daube of beef with gratin of macaroni. Don't come here on the weekends: It will be closed.

7 rue Racine. ✆ **04-90-85-20-93.** Fixed-price lunch 26€–28€; fixed-price dinner 32€. MC, V. Mon–Fri 12:15–1:45pm and 7:15–9:45pm. Closed 3 weeks in Aug. Bus: 11.

Numéro 75 ★★ FRENCH   Centrally located on a narrow street that connects with the better-known rue des Teinturiers, this restaurant is close to Avignon's main fruit and vegetable market *(le grand marché des Halles)* in the town's historic core. It occupies what was built during the 19th century as the private home of distiller Jules Pernod, creator of the anisette liqueur that bears his name today. Within a contemporary dining room that opens onto a restful garden studded with century-old trees, you'll appreciate the flavorful but unpretentious cuisine of chef Robert Brunel. Don't expect a wide choice of menu items; the list is tailored every day to a limited array of dishes made from very fresh ingredients that change with the seasons. These are stylishly but informally configured into an assortment of *plats du jour,* slightly more substantial and formal-looking *suggestions du chef,* and full-fledged *formulas* (fixed-price menus). The finest examples include a platter of grilled and very fresh fish; a crème brûlée of gooseliver; grilled lamb served "in the style of province," with stewed peppers and tomatoes; and a poached filet of seawolf with stewed hearts of artichokes.

75 rue Guillaume Puy. ✆ **04-90-27-16-00.** www.numero75.com. Reservations recommended. Lunch main courses 10€–16€; fixed-price lunch 17€; fixed-price dinners 33€. MC, V. May–June and Aug–Oct Mon–Sat noon–2pm and 8–10pm; Nov–Apr Mon–Fri noon–2pm, Tues–Sat noon–10pm; July daily noon–2pm and 8–10pm.

Piedoie ★ (**Finds**) MODERN FRENCH   In an intimate yellow-and-ocher-colored dining room behind the city ramparts, this place is the creative statement of its namesake, Thierry Piedoie, a chef who takes his food seriously. Menu items change with the seasons and availability of ingredients, but are likely to include a warm tartlet of asparagus tips and Serrano ham; a platter with smoked Scottish salmon, black Provençal olives, and herb salad; sweetbreads with glazed ginger and a confit of lemons; and filet of sole served with sesame seeds and grapefruit segments.

26 rue des Trois-Faucons. (℃ **04-90-86-51-53.** www.restaurant-gastronomique-avignon.fr. Reservations recommended. Main courses 23€; fixed-price menus 17€–49€ lunch, 25€–49€ dinner. MC, V. Thurs–Sun and Tues noon–1:30pm and 7:15–9:30pm. Closed 2 weeks in Feb and 2 weeks in Nov.

NEARBY ACCOMMODATIONS & DINING

Auberge de Cassagne ★★   This could be your best bet for food and lodging in the greater Avignon area. The hotel, set in a park, is an enchanting little Provençal inn. The country-style rooms, most of which are connected by the pleasant, tree-studded inner courtyard, have been recently renovated and feature fine Provençal linens. The cuisine is exceptionally good, much of it in the style of Paul Bocuse. You can enjoy your meals in an elegantly rustic dining room or at a table in the garden. The kitchens feature dishes such as a duo of turbot and salmon served with a ragout of mushrooms, foie gras braised in port wine, and tagliatelle with a confit of tomatoes and olive oil.

450 allée de Cassagne, Rte. de Vèdene (D62), Le Pontet, 84130 Avignon. (℃ **04-90-31-04-18.** Fax 04-90-32-25-09. www.aubergedecassagne.com. 49 units. 179€–409€ double; 419€–629€ suite. AE, DC, MC, V. Free parking. Take N7 and D62 for 6km (4 miles) northeast. **Amenities:** Restaurant; babysitting; bar; nearby golf course; health club w/Jacuzzi & sauna; Internet (free); pool (indoor); room service. *In room:* A/C, TV, hair dryer, minibar.

Hostellerie de l'Abbaye de la Celle ★★   One of France's most famous chefs, Alain Ducasse, is the owner of this idyllic Provençal inn. It lies in the hamlet of La Celle, midway between Nice and Avignon, on rocky, rolling land, a short walk from an 18th-century monastery—the architectural highlight of the village. Ducasse has set out to create an inn that lives up to one's fantasy of Provence: a dining room featuring simple and delicious cooking, and individually decorated rooms that evoke what you might have found within a distinguished Mediterranean villa. Five of them are within an annex that Ducasse commissioned in 1999; the others are within an ocher-sided manor house that was built in 1745 as one of the outbuildings of the nearby monastery.

Place du Général-de-Gaulle, 83170 La Celle. (℃ **04-98-05-14-14.** Fax 04-98-05-14-15. www.abbaye-celle. com. 10 units. 250€–400€ double; 340€–450€ suite. AE, DC, MC, V. Free parking. From Avignon, take the A8 Autoroute in the direction of Toulon, then exit at Brignoles, and follow the signs to La Celle. It's a total distance of 35km (22 miles) and takes about 40 min. each way. **Amenities:** Restaurant; bar; babysitting; pool (outdoor); Wi-Fi (free). *In room:* A/C, TV/VCR, CD player, hair dryer, minibar.

AVIGNON AFTER DARK

Near the Palais des Papes is **Le Grand Café,** La Manutention (℃ **04-90-86-86-77**), a restaurant-bar-cafe that just may become your favorite watering hole. Behind the Palais des Papes, it's in an entertainment complex in a former military supply warehouse. The dance-club standby is **Les Ambassadeurs,** 27 rue Bancasse (℃ **04-90-86-31-55**); it's more animated than its competitor, **Piano Bar Le Blues,** 25 rue Carnot (℃ **04-90-85-79-71;** www.leblues.com). Nearby is a restaurant, **Red Zone,** 27 rue Carnot (℃ **04-90-27-02-44;** www.redzonebar.com), that books live performances in the bar area by whatever band happens to be in town.

   Winning the award for most unpronounceable name is **Le Woolloomooloo** (it means "black kangaroo" in an Australian Aboriginal dialect), 16 bis rue des Teinturiers (℃ **04-90-85-28-44;** www.woolloo.com/gb). The bar and cafe complement a separate room devoted to French cuisine and a changing roster of Asian, African, and South American cuisine. An alternative is **Bokao's Café,** 9 quai St-Lazare (© **04-90-82-47-95;** www.bokaos.fr), a restaurant and disco. The most viable option for lesbians and gays is **L'Esclave,** 12 rue de Limas (© **04-90-85-14-91;** www.esclavebar.com), a bar and disco that are the focal point of the city's gay community.

VISITING VILLENEUVE-LEZ-AVIGNON ★

The modern world is impinging on Avignon, but across the Rhône, the Middle Ages slumber on. When the popes lived in exile at Avignon, cardinals built palaces *(livrées)* across the river. Many visitors prefer to stay or dine here rather than in Avignon. Villenueve-lez-Avignon lies just across the Rhône from Avignon and is easiest to reach on bus no. 11, which crosses the **pont Daladier.**

For information about the town, contact the **Office de Tourisme,** 1 place Charles David (© **04-90-25-61-33;** fax 04-90-25-91-55; www.villeneuvelesavignon.fr/tourisme).

Cardinal Arnaud de Via founded the **Eglise Notre-Dame,** place Meissonier (© **04-90-25-46-24**), in 1333. Other than its architecture, the church's most popular attraction is an antique copy (by an unknown sculptor) of Enguerrand Charonton's *Pietà,* the original of which is in the Louvre. The church is open April to September daily 10am to 12:30pm and 2 to 6:30pm; October to March daily 10am to noon and 2 to 5pm. Admission is free.

Chartreuse du Val-de-Bénédiction Inside France's largest Carthusian monastery, built in 1352, you'll find a church, three cloisters, rows of cells that housed the medieval monks, and rooms depicting aspects of their daily lives. Part of the complex is devoted to a workshop (the Centre National d'Ecritures et du Spectacle) for painters and writers, who live in the cells rent-free for up to a year to pursue their craft. Photo and art exhibits take place throughout the year.

Pope Innocent VI (whose tomb you can view) founded this Charterhouse, which became the country's most powerful. The 12th-century graveyard cloister is lined with cells where the fathers prayed and meditated.

Rue de la République. © **04-90-15-24-24.** www.chartreuse.org. Admission 6.50€ adults, 4.50€ students, free for children 17 and under. Mon–Fri 9:30am–5pm; Sat–Sun 10am–5pm.

Tour Philippe le Bel Philippe the Fair constructed this tower in the 13th century, when Villeneuve became a French possession; it served as a gateway to the kingdom. With stamina, you can climb to the top for a view of Avignon and the Rhône Valley.

Rue Montée-de-la-Tour. © **04-32-70-08-57.** Admission 2€ adults, 1.50€ students and children 12–17, free for children 11 and under. Apr–Sept daily 10am–12:30pm and 2–6pm; Mar and Oct–Nov Tues–Sun 10am–noon and 2–7pm. Closed Dec–Feb.

Where to Stay & Dine in Villeneuve-lèz-Avignon

Best Western La Magnaneraie ★★ One of the most charming accommodations in the region is this 15th-century country house on a hectare of gardens, under the direction of Gérard and Eliane Prayal. Tastefully renovated, the place is furnished with antiques and good reproductions. Many guests who arrive for only a night remain for many days to enjoy the good food and atmosphere, garden, tennis court, and landscaped pool. Madame Prayal's cuisine is excellent: Menu items might include zucchini flowers stuffed with mushroom-and-cream purée, feuilleté of foie gras and truffles, croustillant of red snapper with basil and olive oil, and rack of lamb with thyme. Dessert might be gratin of seasonal fruits with sabayon of lavender-flavored honey.

37 rue Camp-Bataille, 30400 Villeneuve-lèz-Avignon. ℂ **04-90-25-11-11.** Fax 04-90-25-46-37. www. bestwestern.com. 32 units. 139€–249€ double; 195€–455€ suite. AE, DC, MC, V. Free parking. **Amenities:** Restaurant; bar; babysitting; pool (outdoor); room service; tennis court (lit). *In room:* A/C, TV, hair dryer, minibar, Wi-Fi (free).

Hôtel de l'Atelier The name of this 16th-century house (which translates as "the workshop") derives from the weaving machines that produced fabrics here during the 1950s. Since 2003, it has been the domain of Gérard and Annick Burret, who outfit their rooms in as romantic and nostalgic a style as possible. A rear garden with potted orange and fig trees provides fruit for breakfast. A stone fireplace in the lounge blazes on cold winter nights. Continental breakfast is the only meal served. You'll find the hotel in the heart of Villeneuve-lèz-Avignon, a 2-minute walk from the Pierre de Luxembourg museum.

5 rue de la Foire, 30400 Villeneuve-lèz-Avignon. ℂ **04-90-25-01-84.** Fax 04-90-25-80-06. www. hoteldelatelier.com. 23 units. 56€–109€ double; 94€–127€ triple. AE, MC, V. Parking 9€ in nearby garage. **Amenities:** Room service. *In room:* TV, hair dryer, Wi-Fi (free).

Le Prieuré ★★★ This charming, well-managed property was converted from a 1322 cardinal's residence. Roger Mille purchased it in 1943, and since then it has been run by three generations of his family. Adjacent to the village church, it has an ivy-covered stone exterior, with green shutters, a tiled roof, and rustic but plush public rooms. The choice of bedrooms includes those in the main house (the old priory), which are a bit small but filled with antique charm; or those in the modern annex by the swimming pool, which are much more spacious and offer better views. Whatever your assignment, you'll be rewarded with grand style and luxe living. One of the finest Relais & Châteaux properties in the south of France, "the Priory" remains the first choice for those with traditional taste who demand the very best wherever they travel.

Tables at the in-house restaurant are eagerly booked, as Le Prieuré has long been known for the excellence of its cuisine and the charm of its setting. June through September, lunch, featuring an array of dishes, especially freshly made salads, is served on a luxurious terrace adjacent to the pool.

7 place du Chapitre, 30400 Villeneuve-lèz-Avignon. ℂ **04-90-15-90-15.** Fax 04-90-25-45-39. www. maisondebaumaniere.com. 39 units. 205€–315€ double; 410€–530€ apt. AE, DC, MC, V. Free parking. **Amenities:** Restaurant; bar; pool (outdoor); 2 tennis courts (lit). *In room:* A/C, TV, hair dryer, minibar, Wi-Fi (free).

---

4 UZES ★

682km (424 miles) S of Paris; 39km (24 miles) W of Avignon; 51km (32 miles) NW of Arles

Set amid the severe though charming countryside along the foot of the ancient Massif Central, this scenically beautiful village sits on a limestone plateau, straddling the line between Provence and the Garrigues region. The town is dominated by the famous and long-standing House of Uzès, home of France's highest-ranking ducal family, who still live in the ducal palace of Le Duché.

Jean Racine lived here in 1661, sent by his family to stay with an uncle, the vicar general of Uzès, in hopes that his dramatic ambitions might be dispelled. They weren't, and he went on to claim his place as one of France's great dramatists/poets. More recently, Uzès was the setting of Jean-Paul Rappeneau's version of *Cyrano de Bergerac*, in which Gérard Depardieu played the part of the soldier-poet.

In 1962, the village was named one of France's 500 *villes d'art* and has since taken good advantage of preservation funds for restoration of its historic district. However, the designation has been viewed as a mixed blessing since many visitors, notably Parisians taking a break from city life, have since discovered the charms of the village.

ESSENTIALS

GETTING THERE As Uzès has no train station, **train** passengers must get off at Avignon or Nîmes (both are a 1-hr. bus ride away). For rail schedules and information, call ℂ **36-35,** or visit **www.voyages-sncf.com.** About eight **buses** a day run from both places. For bus information, contact the **Gare Routière d'Uzès,** avenue de la Libération, through the tourist office (ℂ **04-66-22-68-88**). By **car** from Avignon, take N100 west to the intersection with D981, following the signs northwest into Uzès.

VISITOR INFORMATION The **Office de Tourisme** is on place Albert-1er (ℂ **04-66-22-68-88;** www.uzes-tourisme.com).

SPECIAL EVENTS The well-attended **Nuits Musicales d'Uzès** (ℂ **04-98-38-09-09**) draws musicians of many stripes and talents from all over the world to a series of musical concerts performed at various venues throughout the town. The event takes place during the second half of July, with tickets costing from 15€ to 100€ per performance, depending on seating arrangements. Tickets for these events, along with announcements of concerts, are available at the tourist office.

SEEING THE SIGHTS

In the old part of town, every building is worth a moment or two of consideration. The asymmetrical **place aux Herbes** is defined by the medieval homes and sheltered walkways along its edges and is a pleasant square for a stroll. The **Cathédrale St-Théodorit,** place de l'Evêché (ℂ **04-66-22-13-26**), still uses its original 17th-century organ, a remarkable instrument of 2,772 pipes. The cathedral is open daily from 8am to 7pm. If you're lucky enough to be here during the last 2 weeks of July, you can attend an organ concerts of the Nuits Musicales d'Uzès festival (see above). Adjacent is the circular six-story **Tour Fenestrelle,** all that remains of the original 12th-century cathedral that was burned down by the Huguenots. It's closed to the public.

Le Duché ★ The palace is a massive conglomeration of styles, the result of nearly continuous expansion of the residence in direct correlation to the rising wealth and power of the duke and duchess. The Renaissance facade blends Doric, Ionic, and Corinthian elements. Easily seen from below is the Tour de la Vicomté, a 14th-century watchtower recognizable by its octagonal turret.

Large segments of the compound, most notably its sprawling annex, are occupied by the Duc and Duchesse de Crussol d'Uzès and cannot be visited. You can climb the winding staircase in the square 11th-century Tour Bermonde for a sweeping view over the countryside from its elevated terrace. The 11th-century cellar, noted for its huge dimensions and vaulted ceilings, contains casks of wine from the surrounding vineyards. Tours of the site end with a *dégustation* of the reds and rosés of the Cuvée Ducale. The building's showcase apartments include a dining room with Louis XIII and Renaissance furnishings, a great hall (Le Grand Hall) done in the style of Louis XV, a large library that includes family memoirs, and the 15th-century Chapelle Gothique. Visits are usually part of an obligatory French-language tour, but you can follow the commentary with an English-language pamphlet.

Place du Duché. ✆ **04-66-22-18-96.** www.duche-uzes.fr. Admission 15€ adults, 11€ students and teens 12–16, 5€ children 7–11, free for children 6 and under. Sept–June daily 10am–noon and 2–6pm; July–Aug daily 10am–12:30pm and 2–6:30pm.

WHERE TO STAY

Hôtel du Général Entraigues ★ (Value)   The core of this hotel is a 15th-century manor house expanded into two separate buildings, and much of it still looks as it did 300 years ago. It's nestled in a Mediterranean garden facing the cathedral. Room furnishings vary from old-fashioned to modern contemporary. All of the rooms are of decent size, often with exposed beams and antiques. However, the most expensive accommodations are very large with private balconies and painted beamed ceilings from the 1600s. The rooftop bar with a shallow pool opens onto views of the cathedral. Check out the restaurant's view of the underside of the pool. Like Marie d'Agoult (see below), d'Entraigues is imbued with the charm of yesterday, but the comfort isn't as lavish here. D'Entraigues's strongest selling point is in its remarkable price.

Place de L'Evêché, 30700 Uzès. ✆ **04-66-22-32-68.** Fax 04-66-22-57-01. www.hoteldentraigues.com. 35 units. 70€–185€ double. AE, DC, MC, V. Parking 10€. **Amenities:** Restaurant; bar; shallow pool (outdoor); room service. *In room:* A/C (in most), TV, hair dryer, minibar, Wi-Fi (4.50€ per hr.).

Hôtel Marie d'Agoult (Château d'Arpaillargues) ★★   The foundations of this hotel are believed to date from a 3rd-century fortress, making it as old as the Gallo-Roman occupation of Provence. The site was also a silkworm hatchery when this area was involved in the silk trade. The combination of rough and chiseled stone construction you see today is from the late 1600s and early 1700s. The hotel is named for a former occupant, Marie d'Agoult, mistress of Franz Liszt and mother of Richard Wagner's wife, Cosima. The place offers a sleepy insight into a long ago way of life. The rooms, on the ground floor, have vaulted ceilings with exposed brick. Each bedroom comes with a small, but tidy, bathroom.

Arpaillargues, 30700 Uzès. ✆ **04-66-22-14-48.** Fax 04-66-22-56-10. www.chateaudarpaillargues.com. 27 units. 100€–190€ double; 150€–290€ suite. AE, DC, MC, V. Closed Oct to mid-Nov. Drive 4km (2¹⁄₂ miles) west of Uzès, following the signs to Andouze-Arpaillargues. **Amenities:** Restaurant; bar; pool (outdoor); room service; tennis court (lit). *In room:* A/C (in some), TV, hair dryer, minibar, Wi-Fi (4.50€ per hr.).

La Maison ★ (Finds)   More and more visitors are discovering this little village lying 7km (4½ miles) south of Uzès and reached along D979. This stone-built house, now run as a B&B, is the epitome of Provençal charm and grace. It is an 18th-century *maison de village*—hence its name—right in the center of the village of Blauzac. Its walled swimming pool, fronted with oleander and olive trees, immediately won our hearts. The French country–style bedrooms are studies in old-fashioned Provençal taste and comfort. The Ferrara room, with its understated charm, was our favorite, although each of the accommodations is inviting with an original decor. As you walk down the streets of Blauzac, you'll spot the green shutters and small green door of this house. Just don't tell anybody about your discovery: You wouldn't want the place to become overrun.

Place de l'Eglise, 30700 Blauzac. ✆ **04-66-81-25-15.** www.chambres-provence.com. 5 units. 115€–195€ double. Extra bed 15€. Rates include breakfast. AE, MC, V. **Amenities:** Bar; lounge; pool (outdoor). *In room:* TV, Wi-Fi (free).

WHERE TO DINE

If you'd like to dine in town, consider the **Jardins de Castille,** the restaurant of the Hôtel du Général Entraigues (see above). However, the area's best place to dine is in the hamlet

Le Bec à Vin MEDITERRANEAN   In a 12th-century building in the heart of Uzès,
you can enjoy thoughtful service and a well-seasoned roster of mostly Mediterranean
dishes. Menu items include roasted breast of duckling with cherry sauce; a brochette of
scallops served with braised leeks and cinnamon sauce; thin sliced chicken cutlets cooked
in a salt crust flavored with cocoa; and roasted monkfish served with a fennel flan. A
comprehensive selection of cheeses is offered from the trolley, and a particularly succulent
dessert is a frozen white-chocolate soufflé served with a whiskey-flavored cream sauce.
The courtyard contains a scattering of summertime tables and a pair of verdant fig trees.

6 rue Entre les Tours. (℗ **04-66-22-41-20.** Reservations required. Main courses 17€–27€; set menus
15€–30€. AE, MC, V. Mar–June and Sept–Jan Wed–Sun noon–2pm, Tues–Sun 7:30–10pm; July–Aug daily
noon–2pm and 7:30–10pm. Closed Nov and Feb.

5 ARLES ★★★

724km (450 miles) S of Paris; 35km (22 miles) SW of Avignon; 89km (55 miles) NW of Marseille

Often called the soul of Provence, this town on the Rhône attracts art lovers, archaeolo-
gists, and historians. To the delight of visitors, many of the luminous vistas of van Gogh's
paintings remain. The painter left Paris for Arles in 1888, the same year he cut off part
of his left ear. He painted some of his most celebrated works here, including *Starry Night,
The Bridge at Arles, Sunflowers,* and *L'Arlésienne.*

The Greeks are said to have founded Arles in the 6th century B.C. Julius Caesar established a Roman colony here; Constantine the Great named it the second capital of his
empire in A.D. 306, when it was known as "the little Rome of the Gauls." Arles was
incorporated into France in 1481.

Though Arles doesn't possess as much charm as Aix-en-Provence, it's still rewarding to
visit, with first-rate museums, excellent restaurants, and summer festivals. The city today,
with a population of 55,000, isn't quite as lovely as it was when Picasso lived here, but it
has enough of the antique Provence charm to keep its appeal alive.

ESSENTIALS

GETTING THERE   Hourly **trains** connect Arles and Avignon (20 min.; 6€–8€), Marseille (50 min.; 13€), and Nîmes (20 min.; 7.30€). For rail schedules and information,
call (℗ **36-35,** or visit **www.voyages-sncf.com.** About four **buses** per day make the trip
from Aix-en-Provence (trip time: 1 hr., 45 min.). For bus information, call (℗ **08-10-00-
08-16.** If **driving,** head south along D570 from Avignon.

VISITOR INFORMATION   The **Office de Tourisme,** where you can buy a *billet global* is
on esplanade Charles-de-Gaulle ((℗ **04-90-18-41-20;** fax 04-90-18-41-29; www.arles.org).

GETTING AROUND   If you'd like to get around by bicycle, head for **Magasin Payan,**
18 av. De Général Vincent ((℗ **04-66-22-13-94**). All bikes rent for 15€ per day. Or seek out
Cycles Peugeot, 15 rue du Pont ((℗ **04-90-96-03-77**), which rents bikes at 30€ per day.

EXPLORING THE TOWN

Arles is full of Roman monuments. **Place du Forum,** shaded by trees, is around the old
Roman forum. The Café de Nuit, immortalized by van Gogh, once stood on this square.
You can see two Corinthian columns and fragments from a temple at the corner of the

Hôtel Nord-Pinus. Three blocks south is **place de la République,** dominated by a 15m-tall (50-ft.) blue porphyry obelisk. On the north is the **Hôtel de Ville (town hall)** from 1673, built to Mansart's plans and surmounted by a Renaissance belfry.

Eglise St-Trophime ★

This church is noted for its 12th-century portal, one of the finest achievements of the southern Romanesque style. Frederick Barbarossa was crowned king of Arles here in 1178. In the pediment, Christ is surrounded by the symbols of the Evangelists. The cloister, in Gothic and Romanesque styles, is noted for its medieval carvings.

East side of place de la République. ✆ **04-90-96-07-38**. Free admission to church; cloister 3.50€ adults, 2.60€ students and children 12–18, free for children 11 and under. Church daily 8:30am–6:30pm. Cloister Nov–Feb daily 10am–5pm; Mar–Apr and Oct daily 9am–6pm; May–Sept daily 9am–6:30pm. Closed Jan 1, May 1, Nov 1, and Dec 25.

Les Alyscamps ★

This is one of the most famous necropolises of the western world. Its fame began when Genesius, a Roman civil servant, refused to write down an edict calling for persecution of Christians. For this, he was beheaded in 250; later he was made a saint when it was said that miracles began to happen on this site. In time, as the fame of Les Alyscamps spread throughout the Christian world, more of the faithful wanted to be buried here, and coffins were shipped down the Rhône. By the 10th century, the legend spread that the heroes of Roncevaux—Roland and Olivier—were also entombed here, which brought the place even more fame. Dante even mentioned it in his *Inferno*.

In the Middle Ages, 19 churches and chapels occupied this site. After the Renaissance, the graveyard was desecrated: Tombs were removed and stones were taken to construct other buildings. For an evocative experience, walk down L'Allée des Sarcophages, where 80 generations have been buried over 2,000 years. The lane is lined with sarcophagi under tall poplar trees.

Rue Pierre-Renaudel. ✆ **04-90-49-36-87**. Admission 3.50€ adults, 2.60€ children 12–18, free for children 11 and under. Nov–Feb daily 10am–noon and 2–4:30pm; Mar–Apr and Oct daily 9:30am–noon and 2–5:30pm; May–Sept daily 9am–6pm. Closed Jan 1, May 1, Nov 1, and Dec 25.

Musée de l'Arles et de la Provence Antiques ★★

Less than a kilometer (½ mile) south of town within a hypermodern setting built in 1995, you'll find one of the world's most famous collections of Roman Christian sarcophagi, plus a rich ensemble of sculptures, mosaics, and inscriptions from the Augustinian period to the 6th century A.D. Eleven detailed models show the region's ancient monuments as they existed in the past.

Presqu'île du Cirque Romain. ✆ **04-90-18-88-88**. Admission 5.50€ adults, 4€ students and children 17 and under. Apr–Oct daily 9am–7pm; Nov–Mar daily 10am–5pm. Closed Jan 1, May 1, Nov 1, and Dec 25.

Musée Réattu ★

This collection, which belonged to the local painter Jacques Réattu, has been updated recently with works including etchings and drawings by Picasso. Other pieces are by Alechinsky, Dufy, and Zadkine. Note the Arras tapestries from the 16th century.

10 rue du Grand-Prieuré. ✆ **04-90-49-37-58**. Admission 4€ adults, 3€ students and children 12–18, free for children 11 and under. May–Sept daily 10am–noon and 2–6:30pm; Mar–Apr and Oct daily 10am–noon and 2–5pm; Nov–Feb daily 1–5:30pm.

Museon Arlaten ★

The museum was founded by Frédéric Mistral, the Provençal poet who led a movement to establish modern Provençal as a literary language, using the money from his Nobel Prize for Literature in 1904. This is really a folklore museum, with regional costumes, portraits, furniture, dolls, a music salon, and a room devoted to

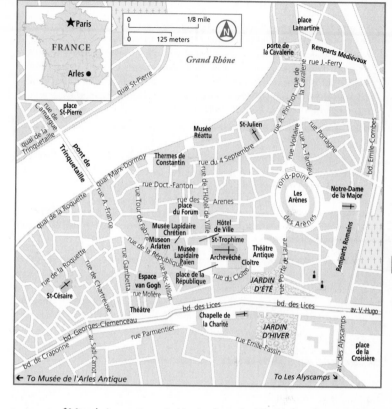

← To Musée de l'Arles Antique

To Les Alyscamps ↘

mementos of Mistral. Among its curiosities is a letter (in French) from President Theodore Roosevelt to Mistral, bearing the letterhead of the Maison Blanche in Washington, D.C.

29 rue de la République. © **04-90-93-58-11.** Admission 1€. June–Aug daily 9:30am–12:30pm and 2–6pm; Sept and Apr–May Tues–Sun 9:30am–noon and 2–5pm; Oct–Mar Tues–Sun noon–4:30pm.

Théâtre Antique/Amphithéâtre (Les Arènes) ★★ These are the city's two great classical monuments. The Roman theater, begun by Augustus in the 1st century, was mostly destroyed and only two Corinthian columns remain. Here the famous *Venus of Arles* was discovered in 1651. A copy of a masterpiece of Hellenistic statuary, it was broken into three pieces and armless when discovered. Arles offered it to Louis XIV, who had it restored, and today it is in the Louvre. To reach the theater, take rue de la Calade from the city hall.

Nearby, also built in the 1st century, the Amphitheater seats almost 25,000 and still hosts bullfights in summer. The government warns you to visit the old monument at your own risk, since the stone steps are uneven and much of the masonry is worn down to the point where it might be a problem for seniors or for those with disabilities. For a

> ### (Finds)   Les Olivades
>
> In a somewhat isolated location 12km (7¹/₂ miles) north of Arles, **Les Olivades Factory Store,** chemin des Indienneurs, St-Etienne-du-Grès (© **04-90-49-18-04**), stands beside the road that's signposted to Tarascon and Avignon. Because of the wide array of art objects and fabrics inspired by the traditions of Provence, it's worth your while to make a trek out here. Fabrics, dresses, shirts for men and women, table linens, and fabric by the yard are all available at retail outlets of the Olivades chain throughout Provence, but here the selection is a bit cheaper and more diverse.

good view, you can climb the three towers that remain from medieval times when the amphitheater was turned into a fortress. Note that the theater and Les Arènes maintain the same hours and the same fluid scheduling as Eglise St-Trophime.

Théâtre Antique: Rue du Cloître. © **04-90-49-36-74.** Admission 3€ adults, 2.20€ students and children 12–18, free for children 11 and under. Amphitheater: Rond-pont des Arènes. © **04-90-49-36-86.** 5.50€ adults, 4€ students and children 18 and under. May–Sept daily 9am–7pm; Mar–Apr and Oct daily 9am–6pm; Nov–Feb daily 10am–5pm.

Thermes de Constantin   Near the banks of the Rhône is the entrance to 4th-century Roman baths, which have been partially restored with characteristic bands of brickwork. The baths or thermae are all that remain of a once grand imperial palace that stood here, Palais Constantin. These baths are the largest that remain in Provence. Dating from Constantine's era, the ruins of the baths measure 45 to 98m (148–322 ft.). You enter by the tepidarium, going through the caldarium, with its remaining hypocaust. Allow about half an hour to inspect the ruins.

Rue Dominique-Maisto. © **04-90-49-31-32.** 3€ adults, 2.20€ children.

WHERE TO STAY
Expensive
Grand Hôtel Nord-Pinus ★   Few other hotels in town evoke Provence's charm as well as this one, which originated as a bakery at the turn of the 20th century. Occupying a town house on a tree-lined square in the heart of Arles, it has public rooms filled with antiques, an ornate staircase with wrought-iron balustrades, and many of the trappings you'd expect in an upscale private home. Guest rooms are glamorous, even theatrical; they come in a range of shapes, sizes, and decors, and are filled with rich upholsteries and draperies arranged artfully beside oversize French doors. Many bullfighters and artists have stayed here—their photographs, as well as a collection of safari photos by Peter Beard, decorate the public areas. The atmosphere extends to the sophisticated on-site restaurant **Brasserie Nord-Pinus** (p. 161).

14 place du Forum, 13200 Arles. © **04-90-93-44-44.** Fax 04-90-93-34-00. www.nord-pinus.com. 26 units. 160€–295€ double; 570€ suite. AE, DC, MC, V. Parking 17€. **Amenities:** Restaurant; bar; room service. *In room:* TV.

Hôtel Jules César ★★★   This 17th-century Carmelite convent is now a stately country hotel with one of the best restaurants in town. Although it's in a noisy neighborhood, most rooms face the unspoiled cloister. You'll wake to the scent of roses and the sounds of birds singing. Throughout, you'll find a blend of neoclassical architecture and modern amenities. The decor is luxurious, with antique Provençal furnishings. The interior rooms are the most tranquil and the darkest, though enlivened by bright fabrics. Most of the downstairs units are spacious; the upstairs rooms are small but have a certain old-world charm. The rooms in the modern extensions are comfortable but lack character. The restaurant, **Restaurant Lou Marquès** (p. 162), is a highly recommended local favorite.

9 bd. des Lices, 13631 Arles Cedex. ℂ **04-90-52-52-52.** Fax 04-90-52-52-53. www.hotel-julescesar.fr. 58 units. 160€–250€ double; 300€–385€ suite. AE, DC, MC, V. Parking 13€. Closed Nov 2–Mar. **Amenities:** Restaurant; bar; babysitting; room service. *In room:* TV, hair dryer, minibar, Wi-Fi (10€ per hr.).

L'Hôtel Particulier ★★ (Finds)   Occupying an 18th-century pavilion, this was the last of the grand private town houses built in the center of Arles. It may not be as grand as the Jules César, but it has become a formidable challenger to the Nord Pinus despite its small size. Behind its monumental gate, you'll encounter ancient yew trees and a courtyard with teak lounges and a limestone-built *bassin* which contains a lap pool. Guests congregate here for morning coffee or the first aperitif of the evening. The hosts are among the most gracious we've encountered in town. Imagine—fresh rose petals scattered on your breakfast table! Each bedroom is decorated individually and elegantly, some with four-poster beds and draped canopies. The furnishings are Provençal antiques or tasteful reproductions.

4 rue de la Monnaie, 13200 Arles. ℂ **04-90-52-51-40.** Fax 04-90-96-16-70. www.hotel-particulier.com. 8 units. 189€–239€ double; 229€–389€ suite. AE, DC, MC, V. Parking 19€. **Amenities:** Restaurant (guests only); small pool (outdoor); room service; spa. *In room:* A/C, TV, minibar, Wi-Fi (in some; free).

Moderate

Hôtel d'Arlatan ★★   Near place du Forum, this hotel occupies the former residence of the *comtes* d'Arlatan de Beaumont and has been managed by the same family since 1920. It was built in the 15th century on the ruins of an old palace begun by Constantine—in fact, one of the walls is from the 4th century. Rooms are furnished with Provençal antiques and reproductions, with patterned wallpaper and, in some rare instances, tapestries in the style of Louis XV and Louis XVI. The most appealing rooms overlook the garden. This was a former private residence, so accommodations range from small (on the upper floors) to more spacious on the ground floor.

26 rue du Sauvage, 13100 Arles. ℂ **04-90-93-56-66.** Fax 04-90-49-68-45. www.hotel-arlatan.fr. 47 units. 85€–155€ double; 175€–245€ suite. AE, MC, V. Parking 13€–16€. Closed Jan. **Amenities:** Bar; babysitting. *In room:* A/C, TV, minibar, Wi-Fi (10€).

Hotel de l'Amphithéâtre   Originally built in the 1600s, this hotel is ideally situated midway between the ancient Roman amphitheater and the Roman theater. Today, it's on the short list of the city's centrally located and particularly charming hotels. The antique atmosphere is filled with hand-hewn wooden ceiling beams; bright fabrics, which usually include tones of red; soft lighting; reproductions of Provençal or rococo furniture; and bedrooms that feature in some cases sweeping views out over the terra-cotta roofs of historic Arles. Our preferred nest here is the Belvedere Suite, a rooftop eyrie whose windows offer 360-degree views over the town.

5–7 rue Diderot, 13200 Arles. ℂ **04-90-96-10-30.** Fax 04-90-93-98-69. www.hotelamphitheatre.fr. 28 units. 95€ double; 125€–155€ suite. AE, MC, V. Parking 5.50€. **Amenities:** Babysitting. *In room:* A/C, TV, fridge, hair dryer, Wi-Fi (free).

Mireille ★ On the right bank of the Rhône River on the outskirts of Arles, this charming hotel is an oasis of tranquillity. Set in two joined houses, it features a poolside terrace lined with mulberry trees. Spacious bedrooms are warmly decorated in typical Provençal style. On-site is a little shop selling products of Provence, such as tapenade, *herbes de provence,* regional wines, and jams, all of good quality. At the restaurant, you can dine inside or out, sampling the specialties of the region.

2 place St-Pierre at Trinquetaille, 13200 Arles. ✆ **04-90-93-70-74.** Fax 04-90-93-87-28. www.hotel-mireille.com. 34 units. 89€–150€ double; 99€–185€ triple or quad. AE, DC, MC, V. **Amenities:** Restaurant; bar; pool (outdoor); room service. *In room:* A/C, TV, hair dryer, Wi-Fi (free).

Inexpensive

Acacias (Value) In high-priced Arles, this hotel comes as a real discovery. It lies in the Cavaliere district of the city at the doorway to the historic center and only a few minutes' walk from the rail station. Its facade is rather band-boxy, but inside personal decoration adds warmth. The public areas are more inviting than the bedrooms, which tend to be minimalist. However, they are bright, furnished with a very contemporary look, and well maintained. The location is in a noisy part of Arles, but the rooms are soundproof.

2 rue de la Cavaliere, 13200 Arles. ✆ **04-90-96-37-88.** Fax 04-90-96-32-51. www.hotel-acacias.com. 33 units. 51€–76€ double; 80€–100€ quad. AE, MC, V. Free parking. **Amenities:** Breakfast room. *In room:* A/C, TV, hair dryer, Wi-Fi (free).

Hôtel Calendal ★ (Value) Because of its reasonable rates, the Calendal is a bargain hunter's favorite. On a quiet square near the arena, it offers high-ceilinged accommodations decorated in bright colors. Most rooms have views of the hotel's garden, filled with palms and palmettos. The restaurant has a limited menu featuring omelets, soups, and platters.

5 rue Porte de Laure, 13200 Arles. ✆ **04-90-96-11-89.** Fax 04-90-96-05-84. www.lecalendal.com. 38 units. 99€–119€ double; 149€ suite. AE, DC, MC, V. Parking 8€. Bus: 4. **Amenities:** Restaurant; bar; room service; spa. *In room:* A/C, TV, hair dryer, Wi-Fi (free).

Hôtel de la Muette A short walk from the city's ancient Roman arena, this hotel occupies an old building that has been an inn since the 1100s. Extensively renovated and restored, it presents a severe-looking stone facade to the outside world and an interior that retains the ancient ceiling beams and rough-textured masonry walls. Many coats of white paint and traditional Provençal fabrics in bright hues of maize, red, and blue add cheer. Overall, the place is comfortable, if a bit cramped, representing good value for the money.

15 rue des Suisses, 13200 Arles. ✆ **04-90-96-15-39.** Fax 04-90-49-73-16. www.hotel-muette.com. 18 units. 54€–65€ double; 74€–90€ quad. AE, MC, V. Parking 7€. **Amenities:** Breakfast room. *In room:* TV, fridge, hair dryer, minibar, Wi-Fi (free).

Hôtel Le Cloître (Value) This hotel, between the ancient theater and the cloister, offers great value. Originally part of a 12th-century cloister, it still has its original Romanesque vaultings. You'll find a rich Provençal atmosphere, pleasant rooms with high ceilings, and subtle references to the building's antique origins. Guest rooms are small and lean on amenities except for phones. Some units have TVs available for a supplemental charge of 4.50€ per day; otherwise, there's a TV lounge.

16 rue du Cloître, 13200 Arles. www.hotelcloitre.com. ✆ **04-90-96-29-50.** Fax 04-90-96-02-88. 30 units. 50€–80€ double. AE, MC, V. Parking 5€. Closed Nov 1–Mar 10. *In room:* A/C, TV (in some).

Moderate

Brasserie Nord-Pinus ITALIAN/PROVENÇALE   Here you will find accouterments not duplicated in any other hotel. Terraces surround the complex on all sides, and an ancient Roman column (part of the ancient Temple of Constantine) rises from one edge of the terrace. The Corrida Bar features photos of the grand painters who made the bar their hangout in the 1950s, along with an artistically and historically important collection of valuable African wildlife photos taken by Peter Beard, a long-ago friend of Karen Blixen. It's hot, artsy, sensual, a bit imperial, comfortable, and very grand. The decor of the restaurant is vaguely baroque, filled with paneling and mirrors, with a '50s-era decor that no one wants to change. The cuisine is one of the lightest and most sophisticated in town, employing top-notch chefs to prepare dishes based on the best of seasonal shopping. The menus change frequently but are generally a delight. The food is colorful, spicy, and artfully arranged on platters.

In the Grand Hôtel Nord-Pinus (p. 158), Place du Forum. ✆ **04-90-93-58-43.** Reservations recommended. Main courses 15€–18€; fixed-price lunch 22€–28€. AE, DC, MC, V. May–Sept Mon–Sat noon–3pm and 7–10:30pm; Oct–Apr Tues–Sat noon–2pm and 7–10pm.

La Charcuterie DELI/PROVENÇALE   This charcuterie opened in the war year of 1942 when the Nazis occupied most of France. The little deli thrived in a small space and now has been turned into one of the most beloved bistros in Arles. The old pig figurines are still there but the owners, François Colcombet and his wife Regoyya, have added such flourishes as red velvet banquettes. They have created what they call a *bistro des copains*— a bistro just for friends.

The menu is small and is prepared by Regoyya, an Arlesian. She is not a vegetarian, and the menu showcases enough meat and poultry to satisfy a dinosaur. Her specialty is Charlois beef or rack of lamb, among the best seasoned and most tender meats in town, and she also does a wonderful grilled duck breast. In honor of their former business, the couple still serves an *assiette anglaise*, a lavish spread of deli meats and warm *saucisson* of Lyon studded with pistachio nuts.

51 rue des Arènes. ✆ **04-90-96-56-96.** www.lacharcuterie.camargue.fr. Reservations recommended. Main courses 9€–17€; fixed-price menus 15€–24€. MC, V. Tues–Sat noon–2:30pm and 7–9pm.

La Gueule du Loup FRENCH/PROVENÇALE   Named for its founder, who, according to local legend, grew to resemble a wolf as he aged, this cozy, well-managed restaurant occupies a stone-fronted antique house in the historic core of Arles, near the ancient Roman arena. Today it's owned by members of the Allard family, who prepare serious gourmet-style French food that's more elaborate than the cuisine at many competitors. The best examples include hearty filet of bull braised in red wine, monkfish in saffron sauce, roasted cod with green and sweet red peppers in saffron sauce, and superb duckling cooked in duck fat and served with flap mushrooms. Reservations are important—the cozy room seats only 30.

39 rue des Arènes. ✆ **04-90-96-96-69.** Reservations recommended. Main courses 24€–39€; fixed-price lunch 12€–29€; fixed-price dinner 22€–29€. MC, V. Tues–Sun noon–2pm and 7–10:30pm. Closed 1 week in Nov and mid-Jan to mid-Feb.

L'Atelier de Jean Luc Rabanel ★★★ (**Finds**) MEDITERRANEAN   This restaurant is devoted to the most savory tapas in the region and is unique to the area. Chef Jean Luc Rabanel harvests ingredients from his organic cottage garden right before cooking, creating an original and personalized cuisine. He cultivates many varieties of the same vegetable to create a palette of different textures and flavors. You may be served a type of aubergine (eggplant) you've never tasted before, or perhaps a "surprise" tomato. Monsieur Rabanel creates a different menu every day—you never know what you're going to be served.

7 rue des Carmes. ✆ **04-90-91-07-69.** Reservations required. Fixed-price lunch 85€; fixed-price dinner 85€–150€. AE, MC, V. Wed–Sun noon–2pm and 7–9pm. Closed Feb 23–Mar 5.

Restaurant Lou Marquès ★★ PROVENÇALE   Lou Marquès, at the Hôtel Jules-César, has the best reputation in town. Seating is in the formal dining room or on the terrace. The cuisine features creative twists on *provençale* specialties. A first course could be *queues de langoustine en salade vinaigrette d'agrumes et basilic* (crustaceans and salad with citrus-and-basil vinaigrette) or *risotto de homard aux truffes* (lobster risotto with truffles). As a main course, try *pavé de loup en barigoule d'artichaut et à la sauge* (a thick slice of wolf fish with sage-stuffed artichokes) or *filet mignon de veau et ragoût fin de cèpes et salsifis* (veal with a stew of mushrooms and salsify, a long-forgotten oyster-flavored vegetable). For a light dessert, try *biscuit glacé au miel de lavande* (a small cake glazed with lavender honey).

At the Hôtel Jules César (p. 158), 9 bd. des Lices. ✆ **04-90-52-52-52.** Reservations recommended. Main courses 26€–34€; fixed-price lunch 21€–28€; fixed-price dinner 40€–75€. AE, DC, MC, V. Tues–Fri and Sun noon–1:30pm; Tues–Sat 7–9:30pm. Closed Nov 12–Dec 24.

ARLES AFTER DARK

Because of its relatively small population (around 50,000), Arles doesn't offer as many nightlife options as Aix-en-Provence, Avignon, Nice, or Marseille. The town's most appealing choice is the bar-cafe-music hall **Le Cargo de Nuit,** 7 av. Sadi-Carnot (✆ **04-90-49-55-99;** www.cargodenuit.com). Open Wednesday to Saturday night, it's a club that later has live music—salsa, jazz, rock 'n' roll, whatever—and then disco dancing until 3am. Cover ranges from 8€ to 25€.

The town's most animated cafe, where most singles go, is **Le Café van Gogh,** 11 place du Forum (✆ **04-90-96-44-56**). Overlooking an attractive plaza, it features live music and an ambience that the almost-young and the restless refer to as *super-chouette,* or "super cool."

---

6 LES BAUX ★★★

715km (444 miles) S of Paris; 19km (12 miles) NE of Arles; 80km (50 miles) N of Marseille and the Mediterranean

Cardinal Richelieu called Les Baux a "nesting place for eagles." In its lonely position high on a windswept plateau overlooking the southern Alpilles, Les Baux seems to be part of the mysterious, shadowy rock formations themselves.

Once it was the citadel of the powerful seigneurs of Les Baux, who ruled with an iron fist and sent their conquering armies as far as Albania. In medieval times, the flourishing culture of Les Baux attracted troubadours from all over Europe to the "court of love." Later, Les Baux was ruled by the notorious "Scourge of Provence," Raymond de Turenne, who sent his men throughout the land to kidnap people. If a victim's friends and family could not pay ransom, the poor wretch was forced to walk a gangplank over the cliff's edge.

When Les Baux became a Protestant stronghold in the 17th century, Richelieu, fed up with its constant rebellion against Louis XIII, commanded his armies in 1632 to destroy the "eagle's nest." Today the castle and ramparts are a mere shell, though you can see remains of great Renaissance mansions.

Now the bad news: Because of the beauty and drama of the area, Les Baux is virtually overrun with visitors; it's not unlike Mont-St-Michel in that respect.

ESSENTIALS

GETTING THERE   There is no rail service; by **train,** most passengers get off at Arles. **Bus** service has been discontinued. Taxis in Arles (© 06-80-27-60-92) will take you to Les Baux for around 30€; be sure to agree upon the fare in advance. Les Baux is best reached by **car.** From Arles, take the express highway N570 northeast until you reach the turnoff for a secondary road (D17), which will lead you northeast to Fontvieille. From here, just follow the signs east into Les Baux.

VISITOR INFORMATION   The **Office de Tourisme** (© 04-90-54-34-39; fax 04-90-54-51-15; www.lesbauxdeprovence.com) is on Maison du Roy, near the northern entrance to the old city.

EXPLORING THE AREA

Les Baux has two differing characters: the inhabited and carefully preserved medieval village and the evocative ruins of its fortress, the "dead" village. Visitors enter the city through the 19th-century **Port Mage,** but in medieval times, the monumental Porte Eyguières was the only entrance to the fortified city.

From place St-Vincent are sweeping views over the Vallon de la Fontaine. This is the site of the 12th-century **Eglise St-Vincent** (no phone), with its beautiful campanile, called La Lanterne des Morts (Lantern of the Dead). The stained-glass windows were a gift from Rainier of Monaco, in his capacity as the marquis des Baux. They are modern, based on designs of French artist Max Ingrand. The church is open April to October daily from 9am to 6:30pm, November to March daily 10am to 5:30pm. **Yves Brayer Museum,** at the intersection of rue de la Calade and rue de l'Eglise (© 04-90-54-36-99), holds a retrospective collection of the works of Yves Brayer (1907–90), a figurative painter and Les Baux's most famous native son (he's buried in the village cemetery). He painted scenes of Italy, of Morocco, and, in Spain, of many bullfights, working mainly in shades of red, ocher, and black. Brayer also decorated the restored 17th-century La Chapelle des Pénitents Blancs, which stands close to the Church of St. Vincent, with frescoes of the Annunciation, the Nativity, and Christ in Majesty. The museum is open April to September daily from 10am to 12:30pm and 2 to 6:30pm; off-season hours are Wednesday to Monday from 10am to 12:30pm and 2 to 5:30pm (closed Jan to mid-Feb). Admission is 4€ for adults, 2.50€ for students and children 12 and under.

The Renaissance-era **Hôtel de Manville,** rue Frédéric-Mistral, functions today as the Mairie (Town Hall). Only its courtyard is open to visitors. The ancient town hall on place Louis Jou now contains the **Musée des Santons** (© 04-90-54-34-39), a collection of antique crêche figures. It's open April to October daily from 9am to 7pm, November to March daily from 9am to 5pm. In the Renaissance-era Hôtel Jean-de-Brion, rue Frédéric-Mistral (© 04-90-69-88-03 or 90-54-34-17), is the **Fondation Louis Jou,** which can be visited only by special arrangement. It has engravings and serigraphs by the artist. The 1569 **Hôtel des Porcelles** contains a collection of contemporary artists who have worked in Les Baux and in Provence.

Moments A Drive Through Hell

Below Les Baux is a jagged and irregular gorge, *Val d'Enfer* (**Valley of Hell**). You can access the valley by D27 and D78G and drive through this bleak and rugged scenery. Centuries ago, caves in the gorge were inhabited by humans. The gorge is the source of many Provençal legends—witches, sprites, and fairies are said to live in the caves.

On your way to the valley, you can stop at the **Cathédrale d'Images** ★★ (© 04-90-54-38-65; www.cathedrale-images.com), off Route du Val d'Enfer (D27), a kilometer (half-mile) north of the village, in a former quarry. Photographer Albert Plecy converted this dark, cavernous space of large, square limestone columns and high-arched ceilings into a three-dimensional palette for an interactive experience with frescoes of the Italian Renaissance. Forty-eight strategically placed projectors splash images from the frescoes in all directions: You might walk across a projection of a full fresco, while on the wall next to you a close-up of an infant's face from the scene is enlarged and displayed, and above you the dueling men in the back of the fresco are plucked out and brought into focus. The moving display, in synchronization with well-chosen musical pieces from the era, is 30 minutes long, though you can stay longer and watch the loop replay. It's open daily from 10am to 6pm; closed January 2 to February 8. Admission is 7.50€ for adults, 3.50€ for children 17 and under.

Château des Baux The grounds of the château encompass a complex of evocative, mostly ruined buildings, which were carved out of the rocky mountain peak. Also called *la ville morte* (the "ghost village") or La Citadelle, the Château des Baux is at the upper (northern) end of Les Baux. It's accessible via the rue du Château, at the Hôtel de la Tour du Brau, which contains a small archaeological and lapidary museum. Inside the compound is the ruined château des Baux with its tower-shaped *donjon* and surrounding ramparts, and the two towers, Tour Paravel and Tour Sarascenes. The collection of replicated medieval siege engines was built from the original plans. The ruined chapel of St-Blaise houses a little museum devoted to the olive. The site of the former castle covers an area at least five times that of the present village of Les Baux. As you stand here you can look out over the *Val d'Enfer* (Valley of Hell) and even glimpse the Mediterranean in the distance.

North end of Les Baux, via the rue de Château. © 04-90-54-55-56. www.chateau-baux-provence.com. Admission 7.70€ adults, 5.70€ students and children ages 7–17, 23€ family. July–Aug daily 9am–8:30pm; Sept–Oct daily 9:30am–6pm; Nov–Feb daily 9:30am–5pm; Mar–June daily 9:30am–6:30pm.

WHERE TO STAY

Note that **La Riboto de Taven** (see "Where to Dine," below) also rents rooms.

Very Expensive

Oustau de Baumanière ★★★ This Relais & Châteaux is one of southern France's legendary hotels. Raymond Thuilier bought the 14th-century farmhouse in 1945 and, by the 1950s it was a rendezvous point for the glitterati. Managed today by its founder's grandson, it's no longer as glitzy, but the three stone houses draped in flowering vines are still charming. The plush rooms evoke the 16th and 17th centuries. No two units are alike, although all contain large sitting areas. If the main building has no vacancies, the hotel will assign you to one of the annexes. Request Le Manoir, the most appealing.

In the stone-vaulted dining room, the chef serves specialties such as ravioli of truffles with leeks, *rossini* (stuffed with foie gras) of veal with fresh truffles, and roast duckling with olives. The award-winning *gigot d'agneau* (lamb) *en croûte* has become this place's trademark. Fixed-price menus cost 120€ to 175€.

Les Baux, 13520 Maussane-les-Alpilles. (?) **04-90-54-33-07.** Fax 04-90-54-40-46. www.oustaudebaumaniere. com. 30 units. 230€–410€ double; 380€–555€ suite. AE, DC, MC, V. Closed Jan 4–Feb 5. Restaurant closed Wed all day and Thurs at lunch Oct–Mar. **Amenities:** Restaurant; babysitting; pool (outdoor); room service. *In room:* A/C, TV, hair dryer, minibar, Wi-Fi (free).

Expensive

La Cabro d'Or ★★★   This is the less famous, less celebrated sibling of the nearby Oustau de Baumanière (see above). You'll find some of the most comfortable accommodations in the region in these five low-slung stone buildings. The original building, a farmhouse, dates from the 18th century. The guest room decor evokes old-time Provence with art and antiques. Some rooms have sweeping views over the countryside. The dining room sits in a much-altered agrarian building from the 1800s. The massive ceiling beams are works of art in their own right.

The restaurant is flanked by a vine-covered terrace with views of a pond, garden, and rocky and barren landscape that has been compared to the surface of the moon. The cuisine, although not on the level of Oustau de Baumanière's, is sublime—light and flavorful, with an emphasis on fresh produce. Specialties include a thick roasted slice of duckling foie gras served with lemon-flavored quince sauce and red port wine, carpaccio of red mullet flavored with olive oil and sea salt, and a lasagna of scallops served with strips of Serrano ham. Main courses range from 45€ to 47€; the restaurant also features a fixed-price *menu du jour* for 110€.

13520 Les Baux de Provence. (?) **04-90-54-33-21.** Fax 04-90-54-45-98. www.lacabrodor.com. 31 units. 160€–300€ double; 320€–470€ suite. Off-season discounts (about 25%) available. Half-board 80€ per person. AE, DC, MC, V. Closed mid-Nov to Dec 21. **Amenities:** Restaurant; bar; babysitting; pool (outdoor); 2 tennis courts (lit). *In room:* A/C, TV, hair dryer, minibar, Wi-Fi (free).

Moderate

Auberge de la Benvengudo ★   In a quiet location about 1.5km (1 mile) south of town, this auberge is a 19th-century farmhouse surrounded by sculptured shrubbery, towering trees, and parasol pines. The property has an outdoor pool, a tennis court, and a terrace filled with the scent of lavender and thyme. About half the rooms are in the original building, above the restaurant, and the rest are in an attractive stone-sided annex. All are sunny and well maintained. Each has a private terrace or balcony, and some have antique four-poster beds.

Vallon de l'Arcoule, rte. d'Arles, 13520 Les Baux. (?) **04-90-54-32-54.** Fax 04-90-54-42-58. www.benvengudo. com. 26 units. 105€–200€ double; 155€–370€ suite. AE, MC, V. Parking 13€. Closed Nov 1–Mar 15. Take RD78 for 1.5km (1 mile) southwest of Les Baux, following signs to Arles. **Amenities:** Restaurant; babysitting; pool (outdoor); room service; tennis court (lit). *In room:* A/C, TV, hair dryer, Wi-Fi (in some; free).

Mas de L'Oulivié ★★   This complex of traditional Provençal buildings capped with terra-cotta roofs is 1.6km (about a mile) from town. Lounges have beamed ceilings, terra-cotta floor tiles, and comfortable furnishings. The high-ceilinged bedrooms have casement doors that open onto the garden. The units vary in size and shape—some are quite spacious—with a correspondingly wide difference in price. Breakfast and lunch are the only meals served.

13520 Les Baux de Provence. ✆ **04-90-54-35-78.** Fax 04-90-54-44-31. www.masdeloulivie.com. 27 units. 110€–260€ double; 340€–470€ suite. AE, DC, MC, V. Closed Nov to early Mar. **Amenities:** Restaurant; bar; babysitting; pool (outdoor); tennis court (lit). *In room:* A/C, TV, hair dryer, Internet (free), minibar.

Inexpensive

Hostellerie de la Reine-Jeanne (Value)   In the heart of the village, this warm, well-scrubbed inn is the best bargain in Les Baux. You enter through a typical French bistro. All the guest rooms are spartan but comfortable, and three have terraces. Bathrooms are cramped and relatively modest.

Grand-Rue, 13520 Les Baux. ✆ **04-90-54-32-06.** Fax 04-90-54-32-33. www.la-reinejeanne.com. 10 units. 50€–70€ double; 100€ apt for 4. AE, MC, V. Closed Jan 15–31 and Nov 15–30. **Amenities:** Restaurant; bar; room service. *In room:* A/C, TV.

WHERE TO DINE

A cafe near place St-Vincent offers refreshments and panoramic views: the **Hostellerie de la Reine Jeanne,** rue Frédéric-Mistral (✆ **04-90-54-32-06**). Note also the excellent dining room of **Oustaù de Baumanière** (p. 164).

La Riboto de Taven ★★★   Known for its flawless cuisine and market-fresh ingredients, this is one of the great restaurants of the area, a rival of La Cabro d'Or. The 1835 farmhouse outside the medieval section of town has been owned by two generations of the Novi family. Brawny flavors and the heady perfumes of Provençal herbs characterize chef Jean-Pierre Novi's cuisine. Menu items may include sea bass in olive oil; fricassee of mussels flavored with basil; lamb *en croûte* with olives; or perhaps, in late autumn and winter, medallions of roebuck served with caramelized root vegetables; plus homemade desserts. The menu changes virtually every day and always features an intelligent and tasteful use of local ingredients and produce.

A small hotel is associated with the restaurant. Accommodations include four rooms within the thick walls of the main *mas* (Provençal farmhouse), costing 160€ to 240€, and two "cave-dweller junior suites" that have been shoehorned into the grottoes at the far end of the establishment's garden, and which look out across the ravine toward the once-fortified citadel of Les Baux. These go for 280€. Each of the accommodations is gracefully accessorized with Provençal-style furniture, and each contains a minibar, phone, TV, hair dryer, and bathroom with a tub/shower combo. The property has an outdoor swimming pool.

Le Val d'Enfer, 13520 Les Baux. ✆ **04-90-54-34-23.** Fax 04-90-54-38-88. www.riboto-de-taven.fr. Reservations required. Fixed-price menu 56€. AE, MC, V. Thurs–Tues 7:30–9:30pm. Closed Nov–Jan.

7 ST-REMY-DE-PROVENCE ★

705km (438 miles) S of Paris; 26km (16 miles) NE of Arles; 19km (12 miles) S of Avignon; 13km (8 miles) N of Les Baux

We're not alone in our enthusiasm for St-Rémy, for we've spotted Princess Caroline here several times. Nostradamus, the famous French physician/astrologer, was born here in 1503. In 1922, Gertrude Stein and Alice B. Toklas found St-Rémy after "wandering

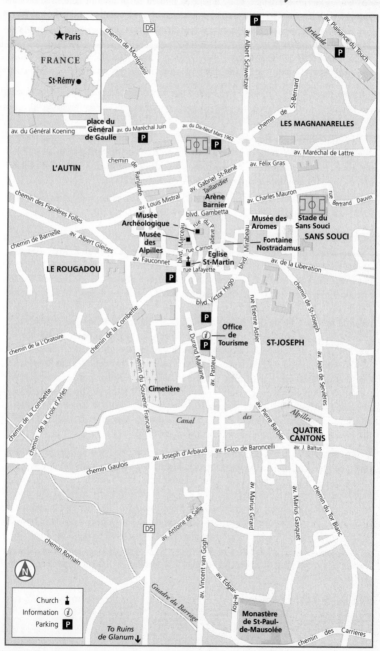

around everywhere a bit," as Ms. Stein wrote to Cocteau. But mainly St-Rémy is associated with Vincent van Gogh: He committed himself to an asylum here in 1889 after cutting off his left ear. His "cell" was later occupied by an interned German during World War I—Albert Schweitzer. Between moods of despair, van Gogh painted such works as *Olive Trees* and *Cypresses.*

Come to sleepy St-Rémy today not only for its history and sights, but for an experience of Provençal small-town living that you won't find in Aix or Avignon. It's a market town of considerable charm and attracts the occasional celebrity who "hides out" here away from the hordes.

ESSENTIALS

GETTING THERE   St-Rémy has no train station. Local **buses** from Avignon (four to nine per day) take 40 minutes and cost around 4€ one-way. In St-Rémy, buses pull into the place de la République in the town center. For bus information, call ✆ **04-90-82-07-35.** If you're **driving,** head south from Avignon along D571.

VISITOR INFORMATION   The **Office de Tourisme** is on place Jean-Jaurès (✆ **04-90-92-05-22;** fax 04-90-92-38-52; www.saintremy-de-provence.com).

SEEING THE SIGHTS

The cloisters of the asylum at the 12th-century **Monastère de St-Paul-de-Mausolée** ★★, avenue Edgar-le-Roy (✆ **04-90-92-77-00**), were made famous by the paintings of Vincent van Gogh, who was confined here from 1889 to 1890. Still a psychiatric hospital, the former monastery is east off D5, a short drive north of Glanum (see below). Visitors can tour a replica of van Gogh's cell and a treatment room, which manage to convey the painful isolation in which he produced the *Starry Night* and other paintings that established his genius and appeal only after his death. Most moving is the self-guided walking tour that uses homespun placards of his artworks to mark the very spot in which he painted them. It's also worth coming to experience the sense of sanctuary that pervades the Romanesque chapel and the cloisters, with their circular arches and columns, and beautifully carved capitals. The cloisters are open April to September daily 9:30am to 7pm, and October to December and February to March daily 10:15am to 5pm. Closed in January. Admission is 4€ adults, 3€ students and children 12 to 16. It's free for kids 11 and under. Adjacent to the church, you'll see a commemorative bust of van Gogh.

Ruines de Glanum ★   A Gallo-Roman settlement thrived here during the final days of the Roman Empire. Its monuments include a triumphal arch from the time of Julius Caesar, along with a cenotaph called the Mausolée des Jules. Garlanded with sculptured fruits and flowers, the arch dates from 20 B.C. and is the oldest in Provence. The mausoleum was raised to honor the grandsons of Augustus and is the only extant monument of its type. In the area are entire streets and foundations of private residences from the 1st-century town, plus some remains from a Gallo-Greek town of the 2nd century B.C.

Av. Vincent-van-Gogh. ✆ **04-90-92-23-79.** Admission 7€ adults, 5.50€ students and ages 18–25, free for children 17 and under. Apr–Aug daily 10am–6:30pm; Sept–Mar Tues–Sun 10:30am–5pm. From St-Rémy, take D5 1.5km (1 mile) south, following signs to LES ANTIQUES.

WHERE TO STAY
Expensive
Domaine de Valmouriane ★★   This is a country-house hotel that occupies a century-old farmhouse. Set on rocky, sun-flooded land, it offers charming, antiques-dotted

accommodations, each with flowered upholsteries and a reference to whatever Provençal writer it was named after. A sense of nostalgia for bygone eras and tremendous charm permeates throughout. Madame Capel, the German-born owner, attends to dozens of small details. The establishment's focal point is a flowering terrace near the dining room, where Pierre Walter prepares spectacular meals.

Petite rte. Des Baux (D27), 13210 St-Rémy-de-Provence. (℃) **04-90-92-44-62.** Fax 04-90-92-37-32. www. valmouriane.com. 145€–280€ double; 230€–340€ suite. AE, MC, V. From St-Rémy, drive 5km (3 miles) from the center, following the signs to Beaucaire/Tarascon, and then, after reaching the D27, follow signs to Les Baux. **Amenities:** Restaurant; bar/tearoom; babysitting; Jacuzzi; pool (outdoor); tennis court (lit); Wi-Fi (free). *In room:* A/C, CD player, hair dryer, minibar.

Hostellerie du Vallon de Valrugues ★★★   Surrounded by a park, this hotel has the best accommodations and restaurant in town. Constructed in the 1970s, it resembles a fantasy version of an ancient Roman villa. Owner Jean-Michel Gallon offers beautiful rooms and suites with marble bathrooms. The property has a putting green, and guests have access to horseback riding. The restaurant's terrace is as appealing as its cuisine, which is winning praise for innovative light dishes, such as John Dory with truffles, and frozen nougat with confit of fruits. Fixed-price menus are 58€ to 85€; a children's menu is 20€.

Chemin Canto-Cigalo, 13210 St-Rémy-de-Provence. (℃) **04-90-92-04-40.** Fax 04-90-92-44-01. www. vallondevalrugues.com. 52 units. 190€–310€ double; 310€–1,310€ suite. AE, MC, V. Closed mid-Jan to mid-Feb. **Amenities:** Restaurant; bar; babysitting; exercise room; room service; sauna; 2 tennis courts (lit). *In room:* A/C, TV, hair dryer, minibar, Wi-Fi (free).

Le Château des Alpilles ★★★   For luxury and refinement, this is the only château in the area that can equal Vallon de Valrugues (see above). It sits in the center of a tree-studded park 2km (1¼ miles) from the center of St-Rémy. The Pichot family built it in 1827, and it has since housed Chateaubriand and other luminaries. When Françoise Bon converted the mansion in 1980, she wanted to create a "house for paying friends." The rooms combine an antique setting with plush upholstery, rich carpeting, and vibrant colors with a garden graced with majestic magnolias. Whimsical accessories grace each guest room, such as a pair of porcelain panthers flanking one of the mantels, and travertine-trimmed bathtubs. Units in the 19th-century annex are as comfortable as those in the main house.

Ancienne rte du Grès, 13210 St-Rémy-de-Provence. (℃) **04-90-92-03-33.** Fax 04-90-92-45-17. www. chateaualpilles.com. 21 units. 180€–320€ double; 260€–340€ suite. AE, DC, MC, V. Closed early Jan to mid-Mar. **Amenities:** Restaurant; bar; pool (outdoor); room service; 2 tennis courts (lit). *In room:* A/C, TV, hair dryer, minibar.

Mas de Cornud ★ (**Finds**)   The setting is a severely dignified, carefully renovated Provençal farmhouse, built 250 years ago and converted between 1985 and 1993 into the well-managed inn you'll see today. American-born David Carpita and his Egyptian-born wife, Nito, maintain a building loaded with regional memorabilia and antiques, along with artifacts from the rest of the world. Accommodations are cozy, high-ceilinged, and charming, with many yards of cheerful fabrics, a whimsical sense of nostalgia, and sometimes antique ceiling beams. The Carpitas maintain a high-caliber on-site cooking school, whose participants sometimes fill the hotel to capacity. These weeklong sessions occur during 4 weeks scattered throughout the year.

Petite rte. De Baux, 13210 St-Rémy-de-Provence. (℃) **04-90-92-39-32.** Fax 04-90-92-55-99. www.mascornud. com. 7 units. 150€–230€ double. Rates include breakfast. No credit cards. Closed Nov–Mar. From St-Rémy, follow D99 to the D27 and then D31, following the signs to Mas de Cornud, driving 3km (2 miles) west of St-Rémy. **Amenities:** Restaurant; bar; babysitting; pool (outdoor). *In room:* A/C, no phone, Wi-Fi (free).

Château de Roussan ★★ (Finds)   Although other château hotels are more stylish, this one is more evocative of another time. Its most famous resident, the psychic Nostradamus, lived in an outbuilding a few steps from the front door. Today, you'll pass beneath an archway of 300-year-old trees leading to the neoclassical facade, built in 1701. History will envelop you as you wander the grounds, especially when you come upon the sculptures lining a stream-fed basin. At press time, this hotel was still under renovation, with an opening set for late in 2009. Search the website (see below) for a phone contact and the posting of rates and amenities when it opens.

Rte. de Tarascon, 13210 St-Rémy-de-Provence. www.chateauderousson.com. 20 units. From the center, head in the direction of Tarascon (D99) for 2km (1¼ miles).

Le Mas des Carassins ★ (Finds)   Van Gogh and Nostradamus used to walk by the front door of this property, on which the present *mas* was constructed in the mid-1880s. The most tranquil oasis in St-Rémy, this hotel is surrounded by gardens planted with century-old olive trees, lavender, rosemary, bay trees, and thyme. Sit in the thoughtfully placed chairs to enjoy the bubbling waters of the fountains and small pools. Each bedroom is beautifully decorated, the beds often with canopied covers. Rooms open onto views of the gardens or the distant Alps. The public areas are furnished in the style of a typical upmarket Provençal private home, great for lingering or reading. Excellent *provençale* and Mediterranean cuisine is served in the restaurant. The only trouble in checking into this place is that you may not want to leave.

1 Chemin Gaulois, 13210 St-Rémy-de-Provence. ✆ 04-90-92-15-48. Fax 04-90-92-63-47. www.masdes carassins.com. 14 units. 126€–189€ double; 178€–212€ suite. MC, V. **Amenities:** Restaurant; bar; room service. *In room:* A/C, TV, hair dryer, Internet (free), minibar.

Inexpensive

Hôtel du Soleil   In 1965, a private home was converted into this amiable, unpretentious hotel, set in a garden with grand trees and a wrought-iron gazebo, a mere 4-minute walk south of the town center. Inside, the ceiling beams and Provençal accessories evoke the region around you. Guest rooms are simple but convenient, with tasteful furnishings and small, tiled bathrooms (some tub and shower alike). You'll want to spend part of your time beside the pool.

35 av. Pasteur, 13210 St-Rémy-de-Provence. ✆ 04-90-92-00-63. Fax 04-90-92-61-07. www.hotelsoleil. com. 24 units. 64€–80€ double; 110€ suite. AE, DC, MC, V. Closed mid-Nov to early Mar. **Amenities:** Bar; pool (outdoor); room service. *In room:* TV, hair dryer, Wi-Fi (free).

Hôtel van Gogh   Set 20m (67 ft.) east of the town's historic center, beside the highway leading to Cavaillon, this is a low-slung and pleasant hotel covered with ivy. Built in 1974 and renovated several times since then, it offers a reception area with a fireplace, parquet floors, and traditional furniture; clean bedrooms with a minimum of furniture; and small bathrooms. Breakfast, which is served on a backyard veranda with a striped canopy, is the only meal served.

1 av. Jean Moulin, 13210 St-Rémy de Provence. ✆ 04-90-92-14-02. Fax 04-90-92-09-05. www.hotel-vangogh.com. 21 units. 65€–85€ double. AE, MC, V. Free parking. **Amenities:** Bar; pool (outdoor); room service. *In room:* A/C (in some), TV, hair dryer, Wi-Fi (free).

WHERE TO DINE

great dining choice is also the restaurant at **Vallon de Valrugues** (p. 169).

Bistro d'Eygalières ★★ PROVENÇALE   Serious foodies visiting St-Rémy-de-Provence make the 10km (6¼-mile) journey southeast to the tranquil village of Eygalières, which is surrounded by the countryside of the Alpilles, looking out over fields of olive groves and vineyards. Here you can experience the superb cuisine of Belgian Wout Bru. He prepares some of the most satisfying dishes in the area, including lobster lasagna with confit tomatoes and thyme butter. You might begin with a smoked duckling foie gras with a compote of figs or a velvety king crab mousse with truffles. Other main courses include roast pigeon flavored with cardamom or steamed sea bass perfumed with fresh thyme.

If you'd like to stay over, Bru offers two beautifully furnished bedrooms and suites over the restaurant, costing 130€ to 150€.

Rue de République, 13810 Eygalières. ⓒ **04-90-90-68-34.** Fax 04-90-90-60-37. www.chezbru.com. Main courses 48€–50€; fixed-price menu 130€–150€. AE, DC, MC, V. June–Sept daily 12:30–2:30pm and 7:30–9:30pm; Oct–May Wed–Sun 12:30–2:30pm; Mon–Sat 7:30–9:30pm. Closed 2 weeks in Nov.

Charmeroy Maison de Gouts TEA/PASTRIES   Charming, intimate, and restful, this attractive tearoom dispenses relaxation along with savory cups of genuinely unusual teas. Operated with flair by a bilingual local resident, Madame Fabienne Charmeroy, it's a cozy spot on the boulevard that encircles the old town, near the Fountaine de la Liberté, midway between the Musée Jouenne and the Musée Floram.

The pastries sold here are usually linked to the herbs and fruits of the region, with an emphasis on using whatever *provençale* products are fresh at the time. Especially tempting are the tarts layered with slices of pear, prune, apricot, and lemon. Many of the teas are custom-blended by Madame Charmeroy to reflect some aspect of Provence. Examples include a version named after Nostradamus, based on a 16th-century recipe using grapes and cinnamon that might have been consumed by the psychic himself. Other versions combine raspberries, orange blossoms, herbs from the Alpilles, edible orchids, white grapes, vanilla, figs, and apples into blends with names such as Chung Hao, Fancy Oolang Black Dragon, and Gunpowder Green.

26 bd. Mirabeau. ⓒ **04-32-60-01-23.** www.charmeroy.com. Pots of tea 3.70€–6.10€ each; pastries and ice cream 5.50€ each. No credit cards. Mar–Dec Tues–Sun 10:30am–12:30pm and 3–7pm; Jan–Feb Fri–Sat 10:30am–12:30pm and 3–7pm.

La Maison Jaune ★★ FRENCH/PROVENÇALE   The most enduringly popular restaurant in St-Rémy is in the former residence of an 18th-century merchant. Today, in a pair of dining rooms occupying two floors, you'll appreciate cuisine prepared and served with flair by François and Catherine Perraud. In nice weather, additional seats are on a terrace overlooking the Hôtel de Sade. Menu items include pigeon roasted in wine from Les Baux; grilled sardines served with candied lemon and raw fennel; artichoke hearts marinated in white wine and served with tomatoes; and succulent roasted rack of lamb served with tapenade of black olives and anchovies.

15 rue Carnot. ⓒ **04-90-92-56-14.** www.franceweb.org/lamaisonjaune. Reservations required. Fixed-price menu 36€–66€. No credit cards. Tues–Sun noon–1:30pm; Tues–Sat 7:30–9pm. Closed Dec–Jan.

Le Jardin de Frédéric ★ PROVENÇALE   Charming, with a good-humored atmosphere, this restaurant occupies a green-painted villa that was built on the site of a garden where Frédéric Mistral, "national poet" of Provence, wrote part of his opus. Menu items are innovative and reflect culinary techniques from local sources and the grand restaurants of faraway Paris alike. Savor the seductive, succulent soufflé of codfish, served with saffron and garlic sauce, or carpaccio of duckling with foie gras. Try the tender rack of Sisteron lamb with a creamy garlic sauce, or filet of sea bass with basil sauce. Dessert might be a chocolate mousse with vanilla sauce. In summer, the dining room expands outside into the open air.

8 bd. Gambetta. (℃ **04-90-92-27-76.** Reservations required. Main courses 15€–23€; fixed-price menus 21€–29€; fixed-price lunch 16€. MC, V. Tues–Sun noon–2pm; Mon–Sat 7:30–9:30pm. Closed Feb.

8 GORDES ★

713km (443 miles) SE of Paris; 35km (22 miles) E of Avignon; 16km (10 miles) NE of Cavaillon; 64km (40 miles) N of the Marseille airport

Gordes is a colorful village whose twisted, narrow cobblestone streets circle a rocky bluff above the Imergue Valley. By the turn of the 20th century, as its residents migrated toward cities and factory jobs, it suffered from the kind of attrition that was affecting agrarian communities all over Europe.

The 12th-century village was saved by modern art. Cubist painter André Lhote discovered the hamlet in 1938, and renowned artists such as Marc Chagall began visiting and summering here. The late Victor Vasarély, one of the founders of op art, became its most famous full-time resident.

ESSENTIALS

GETTING THERE   Gordes has no rail station. **Trains** arrive at nearby Cavaillon, where taxis wait at the railway station; the trip into Gordes costs around 25€. For rail information and schedules in Cavaillon, call ℃ **36-35,** or visit **www.voyages-sncf.com.** There are no local buses. By **car** from Avignon, take Route 100 east to the intersection to D2, at which point you head north following the signs into Gordes. The village itself is closed to cars, but large parking lots are along its edge.

VISITOR INFORMATION   The **Office de Tourisme** is in the Salle des Gardes du Château, place du Château (℃ **04-90-72-02-75;** www.gordes-village.com).

SEEING THE SIGHTS

Dominating the skyline, the **Château de Gordes** is a fortified 12th-century structure whose dramatic silhouette contributed to the town's nickname as "the Acropolis of Provence." The château was really a fortress with crenelated bastions and round towers in each of its four corners. This is home to the **Musée du Château de Gordes** (℃ **04-90-72-02-75**), site of a collection of works by Flemish-born painter Pol Mora. This collection may be replaced with the *oeuvres* of other painters during the lifetime of this edition of this guide, including some by surrealist and geometric master Vasarély. It's open daily from 10am to noon and 2 to 6pm. Adults pay 4€ admission; students and youth ages 10 to 17 pay 3€. Entrance is free for children 10 and under.

Some 4km (2½ miles) south of the village, surrounded by a rocky, arid landscape that supports only stunted olive trees and gnarled oaks (the Provençaux refer to this type of terrain as *la garrigue*), stands the **Moulin des Bouillons,** route de St-Pantaléon (℃ **04-90-72-22-11**), an olive-oil mill so ancient it was mentioned in the 1st-century writings of Pliny the Elder. It's now owned by the stained-glass artist Frédérique Duran, and its interior still has the original Roman floors and the base of the olive press. The

complex is open Wednesday to Monday from 10am to noon and 2 to 6pm. A ticket
granting admission to the mill costs 5€ adults, 3.50€ ages 12 and under.

Cousin to the *trullis* of Italy are the reconstructed *bories* in the **Village des Bories,** Les
Savournines (© **04-90-72-03-48**), 3km (2 miles) southwest of town. These mysterious
structures are composed of thin layers of stone that spiral upward into a dome. The
substantial buildings were constructed without mortar and are surrounded by stone
boundary walls of similar construction. Their origin and use are mysteries—some sources
claim they're Neolithic. What is known is that they were inhabited until the early 1800s.
Their form suggests they were developed by shepherds and goat herders as shelter for
themselves and their flocks. To get here, take D15, veering right beyond a fork at D2. A
sign marks another right turn toward the village, where you must park and walk 45
minutes to visit the site. The village is open daily from 9am to 7:30pm. Admission is
5.50€ for adults and 3€ for children 17 and under.

Founded in 1148, the **Abbaye Notre-Dame de Sénanque** ★, a Cistercian monastery
4km (2½ miles) north of Gordes on D15/D177 (© **04-90-72-05-72;** www.senanque.
fr), sits in isolation surrounded by lavender fields. It was abandoned during the Revolution, reopened in the 19th century, closed again in 1969, and reopened yet again (by the
Cistercians) in 1988. The influential 20th-century writer and Catholic theologian
Thomas Merton can be counted among those who found peace here. One of Provence's
most beautiful medieval monuments, it's open Monday to Saturday from 10am to noon
and 2 to 6pm, and Sunday from 2 to 6pm. Admission costs 7€ for adults and 3€ for
persons ages 6 to 18. It's free for children 5 and under. Be aware that this is a working
monastery, not merely a tourist site. You can attend any of five Masses per day, buy
religious souvenirs and texts in the gift shop, and generally marvel at a medieval setting
brought back to life.

WHERE TO STAY

Hôtel La Bastide de Gordes ★★ This manor house dates from the 17th century.
After World War II, it was enlarged to become the headquarters for the town's gendar-
merie, and in 1988, it was transformed into a hotel. Some rooms have views over the
valley of the Luberon. Bedrooms are luxurious and tasteful, with contemporary, antique,
and reproduction furnishings and soft colors. Known for its inventive and creative cuisine, the on-site restaurant, Olivier Bouzon, is named for its chef and is a worthy choice
even if you're not a guest of the hotel. Against a backdrop of old-fashioned Provençal
elegance, market-fresh ingredients concocted into sublime dishes are served to an appreciative clientele with discerning palates.

Le Village, 84220 Gordes. © **04-90-72-12-12.** Fax 04-90-72-05-20. www.bastide-de-gordes.com. 41
units. 245€–455€ double; 315€–865€ suite. AE, MC, V. Free parking. Closed Jan to mid-Feb. **Amenities:**
Restaurant; bar; babysitting; health club & spa; 2 pools (outdoor). *In room:* A/C, TV, hair dryer, minibar,
Wi-Fi (10€ per hr.).

Hôtel Le Gordos Set within a prosperous-looking residential neighborhood about a
kilometer (½ mile) southwest of the town center, this hotel was established in the early
1990s within the stone-sided shell of a several-hundred-year-old Provençal *mas.* Surrounded by shrubbery and capped with terra-cotta tiles, it's a less expensive version of its
plusher sibling, Hôtel La Bastide de Gordes (see above). Inside is a smooth and seamlessly
comfortable decor that's light, airy, and traditional. Bedrooms are simple but appealing,
with lots of sunlight and pale colors. The establishment's social center is a swimming pool
set into the garden, where breakfast is served.

Rte. de Cavaillon, 84220 Gordes. ☎ **04-90-72-00-75.** Fax 04-90-72-07-00. www.hotel-le-gordos.com. 19 units. 119€–240€ double. AE, MC, V. Free parking. Closed Mar. From the center of Gordes, follow the signs to Cavaillon and travel 1km (¹/₂ mile) southwest. **Amenities:** Babysitting; pool (outdoor); tennis court (lit). *In room:* A/C, TV, hair dryer, Wi-Fi (10€ per hr.).

Hôtel Les Bories ★★★   This is Gordes's best accommodations, a modern hotel clad in rough stone and built around the core of an old Provençal *mas*. It takes advantage of its hillside setting, offering vistas from the dining terrace, outdoor pool and terrace, glass-fronted lobby, and indoor pool. The garden's plantings of olive, holm oak, and lavender tie it to the valley. The decor was inspired by high-tech Milanese design, with streamlined furniture, tile floors, and Oriental rugs in public spaces and the spacious guest rooms alike. The cozy dining room is in a nook rising into a craggy stone vault, and the matching fireplace is topped by a mantle of massive rugged beams.

Rte. de l'Abbaye de Sénanque, 84220 Gordes. ☎ **04-90-72-00-51.** Fax 04-90-72-01-22. www.hotelles bories.com. 34 units. 215€–430€ double; 498€–820€ suite. AE, DC, MC, V. Closed Jan–Feb. From town, drive 2.4km (1¹/₂ miles) north, following the signs to Abbaye de Sénanque or Venasque. **Amenities:** Restaurant; bar; babysitting; health club w/Jacuzzi; 2 pools (indoor & outdoor). *In room:* A/C, TV, hair dryer, minibar, Wi-Fi (free).

Le Mas de Garrigon ★ (Finds)   Nine kilometers (5½ miles) east of Gordes, and 35km (22 miles) west of Avignon, Le Mas de Garrigon occupies a gracious building that owner Christiane Druart custom-built in 1979, using antique building materials. Opening onto a view of the Luberon, each room has a different, usually monochromatic, color scheme and a rustic but elegant decor. In winter, guests enjoy crackling fires and classical music; in summer, they take advantage of the surrounding outdoor activities, such as tennis, canoeing, mountain biking, or horseback riding. The excellent in-house restaurant serves *provençale* and Mediterranean cuisine, but only to hotel residents, who pay 46€ each for a full evening meal. (It's open only for dinner.) Four of the rooms are air-conditioned, and all rooms have a private terrace. Note that the hotel closes briefly in the winter season. Be sure to call ahead if you are planning a visit for November to January.

Rte. de St. Saturnin d'Apt, 84220 Gordes. ☎ **04-90-05-63-22.** Fax 04-90-05-70-01. www.masdegarrigon-provence.com. 9 units. 157€–167€ double; 185€ suite. Rates include breakfast. AE, DC, MC, V. Free parking. From Gordes, follow the signs to St-Saturnin d'Apt. **Amenities:** Restaurant (for hotel guests only); pool (outdoor); room service. *In room:* A/C, TV, minibar, Wi-Fi (10€).

Le Mas du Loriot ★ (Finds)   This haven of tranquillity is an undiscovered gem, set on the southern slopes of Monts du Vaucluse in the heart of Lubéron Regional Nature Park, between Gordes and Roussillon. The house opens onto views of the mountains. All the rooms are on the ground floor, each with a private terrace that takes advantage of the views. Furnishings are modern. The swimming pool is surrounded by lavender and pine trees. Local produce is used in top-rate cuisine that is full of robust country flavor.

Rte. de Joucas, 84220 Murs-en-Provence (8km/5m E of Gordes). ☎ **04-90-72-62-62.** www.masduloriot. com. 8 units. 180€–208€ half-board for 2. MC, V. Closed Nov 16–Mar 26. **Amenities:** Restaurant; bar; pool (outdoor). *In room:* TV, hair dryer, minibar, Wi-Fi (in some; free).

WHERE TO DINE

The area's best cuisine is served at the **Hôtel Les Bories** (above).

Le Bouquet de Basilic ★ (Value) PROVENÇALE   Ignore the tacky souvenir shop in front and proceed deeper into this restaurant, which has some of the best and most affordable *provençale* dishes in this tourist-trodden town. A leafy terrace offers a cool refuge on a scalding Provençal day. Sicilian Marianne Galante has a wonderful, distinctive spin on

Mediterranean dishes, including the daily specialties she posts on a blackboard menu. She grows her own garlic, and her olive oil is locally pressed. Dig in and try almost anything, especially her tagliatelle with fresh tomatoes, garlic, and the fresh basil from which the restaurant takes its name. Galante even makes a "hamburger" out of smoked salmon.

Rte. de Murs. © **04-90-72-06-98.** Reservations recommended. Main courses 9.50€–18€; fixed-price menu 20€. MC, V. Thurs–Tues 12:15–2:30pm and 7–9:30pm.

Le Mas Tourteron PROVENÇALE   On the outskirts of the village of Les Imberts, this restaurant occupies an 18th-century Provençal *mas* whose cherry trees and vines still produce good fruit. It has a sun-flooded dining room, with additional seating that spills over into the verdant garden. The menu is based on fresh ingredients and includes cassoulet of asparagus and herbs with a medley of other (strictly seasonal) ingredients, charlotte of lamb with Provençal herbs, and a *tarte à l'envers* (upside-down tart) of roast rabbit with black-olive tapenade. Things here are small-scale and just a wee bit fussy, but overall, the food is very good and the staff is friendly.

Chemin de St-Blaise, Les Imberts. © **04-90-72-00-16.** Reservations required. www.mastourteron.com. Fixed-price menu 38€–45€. MC, V. Daily 7:30–9:30pm; Sun noon–2pm. Closed Jan–Feb. Take D2 for 6km (4 miles) southwest of Gordes.

Les Cuisine du Château ★ PROVENÇALE   An especially appealing restaurant in Gordes occupies the town's *épicerie* (food market), originally built in the 1850s. Today Justine Cairel manages a kitchen staff and a limited number of seats (only 26) within a restaurant noted for its coziness and Provençal charm. Additional seating is offered on two outdoor terraces, set against the front and back of the restaurant. Expect furniture crafted from old wine cases and a changing array of paintings by local artists, many of which are for sale. The menu focuses on regional ingredients and time-tested recipes. Your meal might begin with a platter of stuffed baby vegetables or a chilled slab of fresh-made foie gras. Roasted rack of lamb with Provençal herbs is an excellent choice, or perhaps a garlicky version of aioli of codfish. Desserts here are best showcased as part of an *assiette gourmande*, wherein a selection of the pastry chef's most appealing creations are artfully arranged on the same dessert platter.

Place du Château. © **04-90-72-01-31.** Reservations recommended. Main courses 17€–20€; fixed-price menu 24€–29€. MC, V. Wed–Mon noon–2:30pm and 7–9pm. Closed Nov to mid-Dec and early Jan to early Mar.

---

9 ROUSSILLON & BONNIEUX ★

These villages lie so close to each other that you can visit both in a long morning or afternoon.

ROUSSILLON

45km (28 miles) E of Avignon; 10km (6 miles) E of Gordes

Color—17 shades of ocher, to be more precise—has proven to be this village's lifeblood. The area's rich deposits of ocher have been valued ever since Roman times; beginning in the late 1700s, Roussillon's ocher powders were shipped around the world from Marseille. Though the mining industry has dried up, hordes of artists and visitors still flock here to marvel at and be inspired by the gorgeous ranges of the vibrant warm tones. Roussillon also served as a giant laboratory of sorts for the famous American sociologist Laurence William Wylie, who packed up his family and moved here for a year to study the village's complex life of work and play, love and family feuds, and simple day-to-day existence. He published his study as *A Village in the Vaucluse* in 1957.

Essentials

GETTING THERE   No trains or buses service Roussillon. To **drive** from Avignon, drive east on N7 to D973, and then to D22. Finally, turn north on D149 and follow the signs to Roussillon. The trip takes about 45 minutes.

VISITOR INFORMATION   The **Office de Tourisme** is on place de la Poste (© **04-90-05-60-25;** www.rousillon-provence.com).

Seeing the Sights

Take time to explore the narrow, steep streets, soaking in the rusts, reds, and ochers of the stone used in the construction of the houses. From the **Castrum,** at the high point along rue de l'Eglise, you'll see a magnificent vista. Face north and gaze across the Vaucluse plateau and to Mont Ventoux. Turn south to see the Coulon valley and the Grand Luberon.

You can reach the **old ocher quarries,** with their exposed, sunburned rocks, by taking a 40-minute scenic walk east of the village. Paths to the quarries start at the tourist office (see "Essentials," above). The huge red cliffs of **Chaussée des Géants** comprise another panorama. To view them, take the path southeast of the tourist office. The walk is about 45 minutes and includes a great look back at Roussillon.

About 5km (3 miles) south of town on D149 is the **pont Julien.** Built more than 2,000 years ago, this three-arched Roman engineering feat of precisely hewn stone spans the Calavon River without the use of any mortar. It's thought to have been named in honor of the nearby Roman town of Apta Julia, known today as Apt.

Where to Stay

Le Clos du Buis ★ (**Finds**)   Set on the northern outskirts of the small town of Bonnieux, within a garden centered on a copse of small trees *(les buis),* this small-scale bed-and-breakfast is housed within a late-18th-century stone-fronted Mediterranean-style villa. The hotel has very few amenities, other than a small swimming pool in the garden that functions as the most social spot on-site. Bedrooms are plain but comfortable, often with rough-hewn ceiling beams, sweeping views over the Luberon countryside, white walls, and splashes of jewel-toned color. Life here is simple, old-fashioned, and charming.

Rue Victor Hugo, 84480 Bonnieux. © **04-90-75-88-48.** Fax 04-90-75-88-57. www.leclosdubuis.com. 8 units. 92€–120€ double. Rates include breakfast. MC, V. Free parking. Closed Dec–Feb. **Amenities:** Pool (outdoor). *In room:* A/C, no phone, Wi-Fi (free).

Le Mas de la Tour   The history of this *mas* on the outskirts of town dates back some 800 years. It has been renovated to add modern amenities, including a large enticing pool. The rooms run the gamut from matchbox-size to palatial. The smaller ones have exterior entrances and are somewhat reminiscent of those found in simple motels; the larger ones have bathtubs and terraces.

84400 Gargas. © **04-90-74-12-10.** Fax 04-90-04-83-67. www.mas-de-la-tour.com. 32 units. 58€–127€ double. MC, V. Closed Oct to early May. From Gargas, drive 3km (2 miles) south, following the signs to Apt. **Amenities:** Restaurant; bar; pool (outdoor). *In room:* TV, Wi-Fi (free).

Where to Dine

David PROVENÇALE   The town's most popular restaurant offers an airy dining area and panoramic views of the red cliffs and hills of the Vaucluse. In the warmer months, dining is *en plein-air* on the flowered terrace. The talented chef/owner Jean Luc Labonie is an innovative restaurateur who takes pride in his art. His best dishes include a rice casserole of scallops and spinach, grilled country lamb flank rubbed with rosemary and served with an assortment of seasonal vegetables, and a tender beef filet with dark morel sauce. The light homemade fruit sorbets are a perfect end to a satisfying meal.

Place de la Poste. ☏ **04-90-05-60-13.** Reservations recommended. Main courses 28€; fixed-price menus 33€–65€. AE, MC, V. Thurs–Sun and Tues 12:30–2pm; Mon–Tues, Thurs, and Sat 7:30–9pm. Closed mid-Nov to mid-Dec.

Le Bistro de Roussillon PROVENÇALE   Here's a place where the vibrancy of a fast-paced Paris bistro collides with relaxed Provençal *savoir-vivre.* The result is a superlative ambience of hearty meals, intriguing chatter, and festive, friendly service. The bistro has one intimate dining room and two terraces—one with a vista of valley and hills and the other facing the square. The menu varies from light salads to regional fare such as *daube* (a traditional beef-and-vegetable stew often served over pasta), roast rack of pork with honey and spices, and grilled filet of hogfish.

Place de la Mairie. ☏ **04-90-05-74-45.** Reservations recommended. Main courses 14€; fixed-price menu 22€. MC, V. Daily noon–3pm and 7–9pm. Closed Nov.

BONNIEUX
11km (7 miles) S of Roussillon; 45km (28 miles) N of Aix-en-Provence

This romantic hill town, nestled in the heart of the Petit Luberon, commands views of nearby Roussillon, the whole Coulon Valley, and the infamous Château de Lacoste, whose ruins bear testament to the life of its disturbed owner, Donatien Alphonse François, *comte* de Sade (also known as the marquis de Sade), who lived there in the 1770s. The celebrated marquis, who gave us the term *sadism,* died in a lunatic asylum. Because of the danger of falling stones, the ruins of the château cannot be visited—even by the most devoted aficionados of de Sade—but merely admired from afar.

Strategically located between Spain and Italy, Bonnieux has had a bloody history of raids and battles since its beginnings in Roman times, when it stood closer to the valley floor. To better defend itself, the town was moved farther up the hill during the 1200s, when it also received sturdy ramparts and sentry towers. In the 16th century, Bonnieux grew into a Catholic stronghold and often found itself surrounded by Protestants who were suspicious and jealous of its thriving economy. Since its streets were lined with mansion after mansion belonging to prominent bishops, allegations swirled around that the town received particular "favors" to bolster its standing. Envy and zeal got the best of the Protestants, and they eventually laid siege to the town, killing approximately 3,000 of the 4,000 inhabitants. Even though Bonnieux is the largest hill town in the area, its population never truly recovered and continues to hover around 1,500.

Essentials
GETTING THERE   There is no train or bus service. From Roussillon, **drive** south along D149 directly to Bonnieux. The trip takes about 15 minutes.

VISITOR INFORMATION   The **Office de Tourisme** is at 7 place Carnot (☏ **04-90-75-91-90**).

Seeing the Sights
You'll most likely want to work with gravity and not against it when exploring this steep village. Start at the summit with the **Vieille Eglise (Old Church)** and its cemetery. The grounds of stately cedars surrounding this Romanesque church, which dates from the

The Libertine Trail of the Marquis de Sade

Denounced by some and a cult figure to others even today, Donatien Alphonse François, *comte* de Sade (1740–1814), is, of course, better known as the "marquis de Sade." The word *sadism* was coined from his name, and this "freest spirit who ever was" led a life devoted to an unleashed libido. By 1764, a police alert advised brothel madams to "refrain from providing the marquis with girls to go to any private chambers with him." Because of his prolonged sexual orgies that combined various kinds of torture (willing or unwilling), and especially because he recorded his controversial ideas for public consumption, he was often in and out of prison.

The marquis and his wife, the very plain but very wealthy Renée-Pélagie de Montreuil, hated Paris and court life and sought a secluded place in the country for their family of three. His wife, who was at first totally devoted to him, apparently overlooked his "deviant behavior," and so he was supposedly a "happily married man."

The marquis grew up in the area around Lacoste. Banished from home because of his violent rages, he spent 6 years of his childhood with his uncle, the noted cleric/scholar Abbé de Sade (who also happened to be a libertine) at the Abbé's castle at Saumane-de-Vaucluse, halfway between Lacoste and Mazan.

This crenelated fortress was a gift from the popes at Avignon, and it still stands in the hilltop village of Saumane-de-Vaucluse, to the west of Lacoste. The castle has been restored, and you can visit it. It is believed that the fictional Château de Silling, depicted in *The 120 Days of Sodom*, was based on this castle, where "all that the cruelest art and most refined barbarity could invent in the way of atrocity" was concealed for orgies and torture.

When the marquis returned to Paris, he attended the prestigious Lycée Louis Le Grand, where flagellation was the school's accepted form of punishment. He related to this on an erotic level, and the experience was the catalyst for his lifelong exploration of the pain of pleasure and the pleasure of pain.

De Sade country really begins some 40km (25 miles) east of Avignon and not far from Ménerbes. The little village of Lacoste, surmounted by the marquis's ancestral castle, exists in a kind of time pocket, with a population that is about the same as it was back in the days of history's most articulate libertine. The château itself (not open to the public) isn't in good shape—just a moat, a few walls, some ramparts, and a scattering of rooms. More interesting is the

1100s, provide the best vantage point from which to view the valley's hill towns. Hours of this church are erratic, corresponding to the whims of the priest who performs Mass here at irregular intervals. Farther down the incline is the **Musée de la Boulangerie,** 12 rue de la République (© **04-90-75-88-34**), dedicated to the authentic portrayal of the art of French breadmaking. Exhibits show all stages of the process, from planting and harvesting the grain to the final mixers and ovens that turn the flour, water, salt, and yeast mixture into warm, crusty loaves. The museum is open April to October Wednesday to panoramic view—on a clear day, you can even see Bonnieux. As you stand here, it's easy to imagine the marquis's world of tortured damsels and debauched noblemen coming alive again in such a remote spot in a foreboding landscape.

Though he spent 1771 worrying about "garden, farmyard, cheeses, and firewood," in 1772 the marquis found himself deep in trouble. His manservant, Latour, had arranged for four girls to meet with the marquis. De Sade had prepared some sweets whose sugar had been soaked in extract of Spanish fly (an actual aphrodisiac); later, some of the girls complained to the police that they'd been poisoned and accused Latour and de Sade of homosexual sodomy. The marquis fled but in *absentia* was found guilty of poisoning and sodomy. The punishment under law was decapitation—de Sade and Latour were later executed in effigy at Aix-en-Provence.

In 1778, de Sade's days of indulgence came to an end. His mother-in-law, outraged at his behavior, had him legally imprisoned for life. He wrote his novels, including *Justine* and the *120 Days of Sodom*, in prison. Freed in 1790 following the onset of the Revolution, he found that his wife had finally abandoned him forever. Napoleon ordered that the marquis be placed in a mental institution, where he died in 1814 at age 74, leaving scores of unpublished manuscripts that were not to see print for more than a century.

In time, this "abominable assemblage of all crimes and obscenities" won an adoring public. Sadists looked to him as the father of their cult. Foreigners attracted to the marquis's reputation have turned Lacoste into a lively place. An American art school was founded here in the 1970s, and—surprise, surprise—many locals are proud of their hometown boy. A small theater has been built in a stone quarry just below the château, and so the marquis's long-cherished wish to make Lacoste into a mecca for thespians has come true. **Théâtre de Lacoste** now draws some 1,600 patrons at a time, equaled in size in the region only by Avignon's outdoor theater. Believe it or not, one recent production dramatized a fictional love affair between the marquis and St. Theresa of Avila. Don't expect comfort or even high-tech acoustics when you come to a production at this theater: seats are on stone ledges, and the audience is subject to the vagaries of wind and weather. For information about tickets and performances, contact the Mairie (Town Hall) of Lacoste at ✆ **04-90-75-83-12** or 90-06-11-36.

Monday 10am to 12:30 and 2:30 to 6pm. Admission is 3.50€ for adults and 1.50€ for seniors and students (free 12 and under).

At the lower extreme of town, clearly signposted from the center, is the **Eglise Neuve (New Church),** from the late 1800s. Many people find the architecture of this church to be less than inspiring. Visit it, however, to admire the four beautiful panels from the Old Church. They date from the 1500s and are painted in the brightly colored German style to show the intensity of the Passion of Christ. It's open daily from 9am to 7pm.

Auberge de l'Aiguebrun ★ Finds   Come here to relax in one of the most tranquil settings in Provence and soak up that special, surreal sunlight. Artists and lovers seek out this remarkable 19th-century manor house enclosed by the Luberon hills and a mountain river. The intimate guest rooms that look out over the river or hills are individually decorated in the Provençal style. In the public rooms, attention is lovingly paid to every detail, from the crackling fire on cooler evenings to the soft and classical music wafting from room to room. The hotel also has a superb restaurant with its own garden; it's open Thursday to Monday (closed Wed at lunchtime).

Off D943, 84480 Bonnieux. © **04-90-04-47-00.** Fax 04-90-04-47-01. www.aubergedelaiguebrun.fr. 170€–204€ double; 270€–314€ suite. Rates include breakfast. AE, MC, V. Free parking. Closed Dec–Feb. From town, drive 6km (4 miles) southeast, following the signs to Lourmarin. **Amenities:** Restaurant; bar; babysitting; pool (outdoor). *In room:* A/C, TV, hair dryer, Wi-Fi (free).

Where to Dine

You can also consider dining at the inn listed above.

La Ferme de Capelongue ★★ PROVENÇALE   Above the village of Bonnieux, this restored farmhouse stands opposite the Bastide. You wander into its large garden with a swimming pool before being encased within the old stone walls. From here, panoramic views of the Lubéron mountains unfold. Rated four stars by the government, the old Provençal farmhouse is filled with charm and a minimalist decor. Its on-site gourmet restaurant is rated two stars in the Michelin guide. Each of the beautifully furnished bedrooms is named after a famous character in the literary heritage of Provence. The furnishings are in white and cream, traditional for this part of France.

Lieu dit Croupatiere, 84480 Bonnieux. © **04-90-75-89-78.** Fax 04-90-75-93-03. www.capelongue.com. 17 units. 280€ double; 350€ quad; 390€ for 6. AE, DC, MC, V. **Amenities:** Restaurant; bar; pool (outdoor); room service. *In room:* A/C, TV, hair dryer, minibar, Wi-Fi (in some; free).

Le Bastide de Capelongue ★★★ CONTINENTAL   One of the great restaurants of Provence, this citadel of haute cuisine, operated by its owner-chef Edouard Loubet, has made sleepy little Bonnieux a place of gastronomic pilgrimage. His is an expert, beguiling cuisine—he's known as "an alchemist of authentic flavors"—that turns the simplest of dishes into something special. He dazzles with such dishes as white sausage of truffled chicken with pistachio nuts and celeriac spaghetti or a rack of lamb with wild thyme. He grills Alpilles pigeon and serves it with a succulent essence of rocket *jus* and a tartlet of offal decorated with flowers from chives. The chef takes as much care with his desserts as he does with his main courses—take the crisp praline of bitter chocolate perfumed with absinthe and served with lemon verbena ice cream.

If you'd like to stay over, the restaurant rents 16 beautifully furnished and elegant bedrooms costing from 190€ to 380€ for a double.

Rte. de Lourmarin (via D232). © **04-90-75-89-78.** www.capelongue.com. Reservations required as far in advance as possible. Main courses 46€–64€. AE, DC, MC, V. Daily noon–2pm and 7:30–10pm. Closed Nov 16–Mar 14.

Le Fournil PROVENÇALE   Charming and completely without pretension, this restaurant occupies the premises of a clean, dry, well-swept cave opening on a small-scale square graced with a 12th-century fountain. The inventive chefs, Guy Malbec and Jean-Christophe Lèche, have given recipes of long standing a new and livelier taste. The menu varies with the season and the inspiration of the chefs but might include crispy-skinned stuffed guinea fowl with baby vegetables, a confit of fruit, and parsley sauce; a platter of

roasted and grilled baby goat, featuring two cooking techniques on one platter, with a **181**
confit of lemon; and filet of monkfish with sweet garlic and served with a purée of potatoes and olive oil. The wine list contains 35 to 40 selections, mainly regional choices such
as Côtes du Rhône and Côte de Luberon.

5 place Carnot. ☎ **04-90-75-83-62.** Reservations recommended. Main courses 22€; fixed-price menus
22€–28€ at lunch, 42€ at dinner. MC, V. Apr–Sept Wed–Fri and Sun noon–2pm, Tues–Sun 7–10pm; Oct–
Mar Wed–Sun 12:30–1:45pm and 7:30–9:45pm. Closed Nov 25–Dec 20 and Jan 15–Feb 15.

---

10 APT

52km (32 miles) W of Avignon; 52km (32 miles) N of Aix-en-Provence; 726km (451 miles) S of Paris

Known as *Colonia Apta Julia,* this was an important Gallo-Roman city and today is a
bustling market town. Ignore the modern industrial area and head for the Vieille Ville to
capture the beauty of Apt. Here you can walk long, narrow streets that wind between old
houses, where every nook and cranny offers something waiting to be discovered.

Apt is known for its wines—it's a region of the Rhône Valley where the grapes that go
into Côte de Luberon and Côtes de Ventoux are grown. It is also known for its basket-
and wickerwork and has been a producer of hats since the 17th century. Others know it
as the capital of *fruit-confits,* the crystallized fruit so beloved in Provence.

The old Roman city faded into history and was eventually deserted and covered by silt
from the river and the hillsides. Roman remains are still buried around 5 to 10m (16–33
ft.) below the current town.

ESSENTIALS

GETTING THERE   Apt has no railway station. From Avignon, five **buses** per day make
the 75-minute trek to Apt; a one-way ticket is 8.20€. Bus passengers are deposited in a parking lot beside the **Route de Digne** (☎ **04-90-74-20-21**), at the eastern periphery of town.
    The best way to reach Apt is by **driving;** follow the N100 east from Avignon.

VISITOR INFORMATION   The **Office de Tourism** is at 20 av. Philippe-de-Girard
(☎ **04-90-74-03-18;** www.ot.apt.fr).

EXPLORING THE AREA

Apt, capital of Le Luberon, proclaims itself "the world capital of crystallized fruits." The
town is filled with confiseurs selling this treat (see "shopping," below). The best time to
visit Apt is for its Saturday-morning market centered on **place de la Bouquerie,** voted
one of the 100 most appealing village markets in France. The streets are packed with
market stalls and temporary shops. Lavender growers, purveyors of goat cheese, potters,
local beekeepers, and craftspeople who look like leftovers from the 1960s invade the town
to peddle their wares. The Tour de l'Horloge, dating from the 1500s and straddling the
rue des Marchands, is a particularly active area for the Saturday market. On market days,
the town fills with jazz musicians, barrel-organ players, stand-up comics, and what one
local merchant calls "assorted freaks."

Cathédrale Ste-Anne   This major monument is known for its ancient two-level crypt.
According to legend, the bones of the legendary Ste-Anne, mother of the Virgin Mary, were
miraculously discovered in this crypt in the 8th century, occasioning the building of the
cathedral. Her life is depicted in a beautiful set of 14th-century stained-glass windows at
the end of the apse. Her shroud is also displayed among the reliquaries of the treasury.

Scholars speculate that Anne was not the biblical figure, but a dim memory of the primeval Pan-European mother goddess sometimes known as Ana or Anna Perenna to the Romans.

In the 13th century, the present church was enlarged, and in the 18th century the floor was raised and the broken barrel vault turned into a higher ogee vault. The oldest part of the cathedral is the tower crypt, which still has both a funerary monument honoring a priest in the time of Apia Julia and Carolingian flagstones. The church and treasury are filled with rare ecclesiastical artifacts. In the chapel of St. John the Baptist is an early Christian marble sarcophagus from the Pyrenees. Among the treasures in the sacristy are 11th- and 12th-century manuscripts, elaborate vestments, and an 11th-century Arab standard brought back from the First Crusade. The nave is adorned with scenes from the life of Christ, painted by Pierre and Christophe Delpech in the 18th century.

To see the Sacristy, you must ask Claude Pion, the church caretaker. She is constantly on-site during open hours (see below) and will open it according to the schedule of daily Masses or the priorities of the priests. If she does, a donation to the maintenance of the church is appreciated.

Vieille Ville. ✆ **04-90-04-85-44.** www.apt.cathedrale.com. free admission. Mon–Fri noon–2:30pm and 3–6pm; Sun 2:30–6pm. Ask the caretaker for entrance to the Sacristy.

Hôtel Colin d'Albertas The lavish 17th-century baroque interior of this building contains some of the most spectacular plaster- and stuccowork in the region and is a museum in its own right.

Rue de la République. ✆ **04-90-74-02-40.** Tours 5€ adults. July–Aug Thurs only 11am–4pm.

Musée Archéologique The town's major museum contains Roman objects found in local excavations, including pieces of mosaics, sarcophagi, coins, and even oil lamps from the 2nd century B.C. It also displays sacred and decorative art by faïence makers from the 17th and the 19th centuries.

Place Carnot. ✆ **04-90-74-95-30.** Admission 2€ adults, 1€ students and children. Call ahead for an appointment.

ⓘ Tips   Outdoors in Lubéron National Park

Apt is one of the gateways to the vast **Lubéron National Park.** The area covers 1,200 sq. km (463 sq. miles), encompassing several villages and many desolate forests. Maybe you'll come across an abandoned farmhouse. If you read Peter Mayle's *A Year in Provence,* perhaps you'll fall in love with one and decide to restore it.

The **information office** for the park is in an 18th-century house, La Maison du Parc, 1 place Jean-Jaurès (✆ **04-90-04-42-00**). The office provides maps, details of hiking trails in the park, and other outdoor activities in the area. Otherwise, the tourist office in Apt (see above) will provide information as well as useful maps. Much of the land in the Lubéron area is privately owned, but trails in the park are open to the public. On-site is a small **Museum of Paleontology,** of only specialist interest. Admission is free, and it's open May to October Monday to Saturday from 8:30am to noon, and the rest of the year Monday to Friday from 1:30 to 6pm. No buses or taxis serve the area. You'll have to explore by car or by foot. To reach the park from Apt, take D48 southeast to the village of Saignon or else D943 southwest, following the signs to Bonnieux (p. 177).

The large town is filled with confiseurs selling candied fruits. The best are **Confiserie Marcel Richaud,** 112 quai de la Liberté (© **04-90-74-13-56**), and **Confiseur Le Coulon/Jean Ceccon,** 24 quai de la Liberté (© **04-90-74-21-90**).

WHERE TO STAY & DINE

Auberge de la Loube ★ (Finds) PROVENÇALE Small, personalized, and charming, this is the century-old domain of Provençal chef and entrepreneur Maurice de la Loube. On the outskirts of an agrarian hamlet known for its rolling hills and authentic Luberon flavor, it offers delicious cuisine and a look at a slower, more relaxed lifestyle. The house has a terrace in front, with dining tables and views that sweep over the countryside. Main courses, often focusing on perfectly roasted local lamb with just the right amount of Provençal seasoning, are succulent and generous, but the real culinary charm of the place might lie in the flavor and variety of Monsieur de la Loube's starters. Several of these will be carried to your table in a wicker basket and laid out with fanfare on your table. They're likely to include poached asparagus in vinaigrette sauce, tapenade of local olives, brandade of codfish, braised carrots with aioli, and eggplant "caviar."

The dining room is charming, outfitted with mirrors, small lamps that cast a warm glow on the thick ocher-colored walls, and vases of flowers. Ask (either before or after your meal) to view the approximately 19 antique carriages, many of them made in the United States and imported here during the early 20th century, that are stored in a nearby outbuilding. Collecting them is the personal hobby of Monsieur de la Loube and a source of enormous personal pride. *Warning:* Watch for unexpected closings.

Quartier de la Loube, Buoux. © **04-90-74-19-58.** Reservations recommended. Main courses 18€; fixed-price menus 23€–33€. No credit cards. Tues–Wed and Fri–Sun noon–1:30pm and 7–9:30pm. Closed Jan–Feb. Located 8km (4¹/₂ miles) south of Apt; from Apt, follow signs to Buoux.

Domaine des Andéols ★★ PROVENÇALE Established in 2003, this hyper-upscale country inn is associated, at least insofar as its marketing campaigns, with French super-chef Alain Ducasse, who "anointed" the present chef (Laurent Poulet) with a prolonged exposure to his culinary techniques, and who drops in for a (rare) site inspection. The restaurant, permeated with the spirit of "Le Ducasse," has attracted clients who have included, among others, former design mogul Pierre Cardin. The kitchen here makes its own olive oil and uses produce, including apricots and cherries, from its own gardens. Don't expect folkloric decor or rusticity though, since the place gleams with a chic modern feel, and includes Mies van der Rohe leather lounges, Andy Warhol serigraphs, and an overall decor that's about as high-design as you're likely to find anywhere. It's all set 40km (25 miles) southeast of Avignon in rolling countryside. Here, surrounded by lakes, gardens, and orchards, owners Olivier and Patrizia Massart have gathered paintings, furniture, and sculpture from their global travels to decorate their exotic accommodations. For rent are nine stone-sided town houses, each set end-to-end, with between one and three elegant bedrooms. Each bedroom has its own kitchenette. Two of the units include private outdoor pools of their own. French critics have hailed this hotel as "the most progressive in southern France."

Les Andéols, 84490 Saint-Saturnin-les-Apt. © **04-90-75-50-63.** Fax 04-90-75-43-22. www.domaine desandeols.com. 9 units. 260€–350€ junior suite; 350€–770€ superior suite. AE, MC, V. Free parking. From Avignon, drive 40km (25 miles) to the southeast, following first the signs to Apt, and then the signs to St-Saturnin-les-Apt. **Amenities:** Restaurant; 2 pools (indoor & outdoor); room service; sauna. *In room:* TV, hair dryer, minibar, Wi-Fi (free).

Relais de Roquefure PROVENÇALE (Value Lying 6km (3½ miles) north of the center, this Logis de France country hotel in the Luberon Nature Reserve is the finest place to stay in the area. It offers good food and a good night's sleep, all at a fair price. Philippe Rousset, the owner, is a hospitable host. Rooms are small but comfortable, with fine, soft beds and small bathrooms. In summer, guests can sit under the shade trees. The food is some of the best in the area, emphasizing regional produce.

Along N100, 84400 Apt. ✆ **04-90-04-88-88.** Fax 04-90-74-14-86. www.relaisderoquefure.com. 16 units. 61€–118€ double. Half-board 134€–190€ double. MC, V. Closed Dec–Jan. **Amenities:** Restaurant; bar; pool (outdoor). *In room:* TV, hair dryer, Wi-Fi (free).

11 SALON DE PROVENCE

47km (29 miles) SE of Avignon; 37km (23 miles) NW of Aix-en-Provence; 53km (33 miles) NW of Marseille

The hometown of Nostradamus is in between Aix-en-Provence and Avignon, and makes an excellent stopover between these towns. Today a busy modern town, it grew up as a fortified hilltop fortress centering on Château de l'Empéri. With a population of some 35,000, it has been a center of the olive oil industry since the 15th century, although it owes much of its prosperity to the French Air Force's officer training school centered here.

Salon de Provence was the birthplace of Adam de Craponne (1527–76), creator of the famous canal that irrigates the region of Crau and bears his name.

ESSENTIALS

GETTING THERE **Train** connections, about seven a day from Avignon, are the best and most direct (40 min. each way). Train connections from Aix are less convenient and require a transfer in Marseille. For more information, call ✆ **36-35,** or visit **www. voyages-sncf.com.** From Aix-en-Provence, about seven daily **buses** (trip time: 30–45 min.) make the trip to downtown Salon de Provence's place Morgan. For bus information, call ✆ **08-91-02-40-25.**

If you're **driving,** Salon de Provence is strategically located at the junction of highways connecting Avignon with Aix-en-Provence (N7), and Marseille with Arles and Nîmes (N113), as well as the A7 and A54 autoroutes.

VISITOR INFORMATION The **Office de Tourisme** is at 56 cours Gimon (✆ **04-90-56-27-60;** www.visitsalondeprovence.com). Hours are July and August Monday to Saturday 9:30am to 6:30pm, Sunday 9:30am to 12:30pm. The rest of the year, hours are Monday to Saturday 9:30am to 12:30pm and 2 to 6pm.

EXPLORING THE TOWN

A major attraction is the **Fontaine Moussue** on the place Crousillat just outside the Porte de l'Horloge. Covered by a thick mound of moss, this much-photographed fountain dates from the 18th century. It is surrounded by plane trees planted to commemorate events over the centuries. One was planted in 1799 to mark the end of the Revolution; another was planted in 1919 to mark the end of World War I.

Château de l'Empéri This 10th-century château is surrounded by ancient circular walls. You can enter through the 17th-century Porte de l'Horloge or the Porte Bourg Neuf. The château is one of the most beautiful in Provence, with its courtyards, towers, and walls. Once this was the residence of the archbishops of Arles, lords of Salon. Both François I, in 1516, and Marie de Médici, in 1600, visited and stayed here. From 1831, it was used as a barracks and was severely damaged in an earthquake in 1909, but over the years it has been gradually and attractively restored.

The château houses the Musée de Art et d'Histoire Militaire, with a collection of more than 20,000 artifacts, including military uniforms, weapons, waxwork figures, and military flags. The museum covers the era from Louis XIV, the Sun King, up to France's entry into World War I.

Montée du Puech. (𝄫 **04-90-56-22-36.** Admission 3.05€ adults, 2.30€ children 7–18, free for ages 6 and under. Wed–Mon 10am–noon and 2–6pm. Closed May 1, Nov 1, Oct 12, Dec 24–25, and Jan 1.

Musée Grevin de la Provence   In this wax museum, lifelike tableaux attempt to re-create 2,600 years of the history of Provence. That history is displayed in part in the exhibition of some 15 historical paintings, one of which depicts the fabled marriage of Gyptis and Protis. Their marriage sealed the union of the Phocaeans with the Celtic-Ligurians. The exhibits go up to the 20th century, including scenes from the cinema. The museum is hardly Madame Tussaud's and it's a bit kitschy; but families with children in tow might find it worth a half-hour visit.

Place de Centuries. (𝄫 **04-90-56-36-30.** Admission 3.05€ adults, 2.30€ students and ages 17 and under. Mon–Fri 9am–noon and 2–6pm; Sat–Sun 2–6pm.

Musée Nostradamus ⌈Overrated⌉   Nostradamus (1503–66), who was born in St-Rémy-de-Provence, spent the last 19 years of his life at this little house close to the château. It's now a museum devoted to him and his famous enigmatic predictions of the future. A series of fairly unconvincing tableaux depicts scenes from his life, with a rambling commentary on portable CD players.

Nostradamus was born into a family of converted Jews and trained as a doctor in Montpellier. He treated plague victims in Lyon and Aix. He married a woman from Salon in 1547 and settled here, where he studied astrology, publishing almanacs and inventing new recipes for cosmetics. Written in the future tense, his *Centuries* in rhyming quatrains was published in 1555, bringing him instant celebrity. Nostradamus is buried in the interesting 14th-century Eglise St-Laurent, which lies just to the north of the town center.

11 rue Nostradamus. (𝄫 **04-90-56-64-31.** Admission 3.05€, 2.30€ students and ages 17 and under. Mon–Fri 9am–noon and 2–6pm; Sat–Sun 2–6pm.

SHOPPING

Salon de Provence maintains two small-scale artisans that continue to make soap the old-fashioned way, in limited batches, by hand. They are **Rampal,** 71 rue Félix Pyat (𝄫 **04-90-56-07-28**), and **Marius Fabre,** avenue Paul Bourrat (𝄫 **04-90-53-24-77;** www.marius-fabre.fr). Visits to the first are conducted only by appointment; visits to the second are possible only on Monday and Thursday at 10:30am.

WHERE TO STAY

Abbaye de Sainte-Croix ★★   No hotel in the region can claim origins as authentic and charming as this ancient one-time monastery from the 1100s, 4km (2½ miles) north of the city center. A Relais & Châteaux hotel, it lies behind thick stone walls, with most of its original arches and vaults, and a severely dignified, sometimes forbidding kind of grandeur evocative of the Middle Ages. The generally spacious bedrooms feature a simple elegance: lovely old furniture, terra-cotta floors, and sometimes spectacular views over fields of lavender and rugged hills. The place is more famous as a restaurant than as a hotel—see "Where to Dine," below.

Val de Cuech, 13300 Salon de Provence. (℗ **04-90-56-24-55.** Fax 04-90-56-31-12. www.hotels-provence. com. 25 units. 185€–377€ double; 475€–509€ suite. AE, DC, MC, V. Free parking. Closed Nov to mid-Mar. **Amenities:** Restaurant; bar; babysitting; pool (outdoor); room service. *In room:* A/C, TV, hair dryer, minibar, Wi-Fi (free).

Hôtel d'Angleterre   Set on the northwestern fringe of the peripheral boulevard (cours Carnot) that flanks the edge of town (a 10-min. walk from the center), this is a conservative, three-story hotel with roots in British tourism during the early 1900s. Everything has been radically modernized from its original turn-of-the-20th-century charm, with touches of kitsch and an overwhelming sense of bourgeois propriety. One of the few appealing touches is the circular skylight in the breakfast room. Come here for the relatively low rates, as bedrooms are spartan and not particularly cozy. They range from small to medium and are reasonably comfortable; bathrooms are cramped.

98 Cours Carnot, 13300 Salon de Provence. (℗ **04-90-56-01-10.** Fax 04-90-56-71-75. www.hotel-angleterre. biz. 26 units. 52€–64€ double; 67€ triple. AE, MC, V. Parking 7€. Closed Dec 24–Jan 2. **Amenities:** Lounge. *In room:* A/C, TV, hair dryer, Internet (free).

WHERE TO DINE

Abbaye de Sainte-Croix ★★★ FRENCH/PROVENÇALE   In the hotel of the same name (p. 185), this restaurant serves the best food in the region. Part of its appeal comes from its architecture of medieval soaring vaults, as well as the view from the terrace of the low hills of the Alpilles. The changing seasons inspire the menu here: Dishes include lobster salad with a walnut-oil vinaigrette; sliced sea wolf with a fondant of green and red peppers, basil, and locally produced olives and olive oil; thin-sliced roasted lamb with truffles from the Luberon in clarified butter; turbot with morels; and aiguillette of duck with a tapenade of olives.

Val de Cuech, 13300 Salon de Provence. (℗ **04-90-56-24-55.** Reservations recommended. Main courses 30€–45€; fixed-price menus 42€ lunch, 63€–105€ dinner. AE, MC, V. Tues–Sun noon–2pm; Wed–Mon 7:30–9pm. Closed Nov to mid-Mar.

Mas du Soleil (Restaurant Francis Robin) ★ FRENCH/MEDITERRANEAN In an 1850s stone-sided farmhouse, the ocher-colored facade of this inn is a 5-minute walk from the center of town. The critically acclaimed cuisine of Francis Robin changes according to the season and the availability of the ingredients. Menu items include such treats as a rosemary-infused rack of lamb for two, filet of beef layered with escalope of foie gras, and a medley of grilled Mediterranean fish. One tempting main course that the chef is particularly proud of is a *civet* (stew) of lobster. Dining room windows overlook a swimming pool in the garden.

An upper floor contains 10 well-maintained bedrooms outfitted with flowered wallpaper and traditional furniture. Each has a bay window overlooking the garden and terrace or a private patio. Rates are 106€ to 267€ for a double.

38 chemin St-Côme, Salon de Provence. (℗ **04-90-56-06-53.** www.lemasdusoleil.com. Reservations recommended. Main courses 22€–37€; fixed-price menus 33€–87€. AE, DC, MC, V. Tues–Sun noon–2pm; Tues–Sat 7:30–9:30pm.

12 AIX-EN-PROVENCE ★★

755km (469 miles) S of Paris; 80km (50 miles) SE of Avignon; 32km (20 miles) N of Marseille; 175km (109 miles) W of Nice

The most charming center in all Provence, this faded university town was once a seat of aristocracy, its streets walked by counts and kings. Founded in 122 B.C. by a Roman general, Caius Sextius Calvinus, who named it *Aquae Sextiae* after himself, Aix (pronounced "ex") has been, in turn, a Roman military outpost, a civilian colony, the administrative capital of a later Roman Empire province, the seat of an archbishop, and the official residence of the medieval *comtes* de Provence. After the union of Provence with France, Aix remained until the Revolution a judicial and administrative headquarters.

Paul Cézanne, the celebrated son of this old capital city of Provence, immortalized the countryside nearby. Just as he painted it, Montagne Ste-Victoire looms over the town today, though a string of high-rises has now cropped up on the landscape.

The Université d'Aix has been attracting international students since 1413. Today absinthe has given way to pastis in the many cafes scattered throughout the town.

This city of some 150,000 is reasonably quiet in winter, but active and bustling when the summer hordes pour in. Summer brings frequent cultural events, ranging from opera to jazz, June through August. Increasingly, Aix is becoming a "bedroom community" for urbanites fleeing Marseille after 5pm.

ESSENTIALS

GETTING THERE Twenty-seven **trains** arrive daily from Marseille; the trip takes 45 minutes and costs 7€ one-way. Twenty-five trains arrive from Nice; the trip takes 3 to 4 hours and costs 36€ one-way. From Cannes, 25 trains make the trip a day (3½ hr.), costing 35€ one-way. High-speed TGV trains arrive at Vitroll, 5.5km (3½ miles) west of Aix. For more information, call ✆ 36-35, or visit **www.voyages-sncf.com**. **Buses** from Marseille arrive every 10 minutes; from Avignon, five times a day; and twice a day from Nice. For more information, call ✆ 08-91-02-40-25. If you're **driving** from Avignon or other points north, take A7 south to RN7 and follow it into town. From Marseille and points south, take A51 north into town.

To explore the region by bike, head for **La Rotondo,** 2 av. Des Belges (✆ 04-42-26-78-92), a short walk northeast of the cours Mirabeau. Here you can rent 10-speed racing bikes or more durable mountain bikes for 20€ per day. You must leave a deposit—your passport or driver's license, or cash or monetary objects worth the value of the bike, usually 300€.

VISITOR INFORMATION The **Office de Tourisme** is at 2 place du Général-de-Gaulle (✆ 04-42-16-11-61; fax 04-42-16-11-62; www.aixenprovencetourism.com).

SPECIAL EVENTS Aix celebrates the performing arts, more than any other city in southwestern France. At least four summer festivals showcase music, opera, and dance, including the **Aix en Musique** (✆ 04-42-21-69-69; www.aixenmusique.fr), all summer long, which focuses on symphonic and chamber music, and **Festival International d'Art Lyrique & de Musique** (✆ 04-42-17-34-34; www.festival-aix.com) in late July, which attracts musicians from all over the world.

Aix's main street, **cours Mirabeau** ★★, is one of Europe's most beautiful. Plane trees stretch across the street like umbrellas, shading it from the hot Provençal sun and filtering the light into shadows that play on the rococo fountains below. Shops and sidewalk cafes line one side of the street; sandstone *hôtels particuliers* (mansions) from the 17th and 18th centuries fill the other. The street begins at the 1860 fountain on place de la Libération, which honors Mirabeau, the revolutionary and statesman. A ring of streets, including boulevard Carnot and cours Sextius, circles the heart of the old quarter (Vieille Ville, or Old Town). Inside this *périphérique* is the pedestrian zone.

After touring Aix, you may consider a side trip on D10 15km (9⅓ miles) east to the **Château de Vauvenarges,** the privately owned site of Pablo Picasso's last home. You can't visit the château's interior, but Picasso and one of his wives, Jacqueline Roche, are buried nearby. Stop for a meal at **Au Moulin de Provence,** rue des Maquisards (© **04-42-66-02-22**), across the road from the château.

Atelier de Cézanne Cézanne was the major forerunner of cubism. This house, surrounded by a wall and restored by American admirers, is where he worked. Repaired in 1970, it remains much as Cézanne left it in 1906, "his coat hanging on the wall, his easel with an unfinished picture waiting for a touch of the master's brush," as Thomas R. Parker wrote.

9 av. Paul-Cézanne (outside town). © **04-42-21-06-53.** Admission 5.50€ adults, 2€ students and children 13–25, free 12 and under. Apr–June and Sept daily 10am–noon and 2:30–6pm; July–Aug daily 10am–6pm; Oct–Mar daily 10am–noon and 2–5pm. Closed Jan 1, May 1, and Dec 25.

Cathédrale St-Sauveur ★ The cathedral of Aix is dedicated to Christ under the title St-Sauveur (Holy Savior or Redeemer). Its baptistery dates from the 4th and 5th centuries, and the complex as a whole has seen many additions. It contains a 15th-century Nicolas Froment triptych, *The Burning Bush.* One side depicts the Virgin and Child, the other, Good King René and his second wife, Jeanne de Laval.

Place des Martyrs de la Résistance. © **04-42-23-45-65.** Free admission. Daily 9am–noon and 2–6pm. Mass Sun 10:30am and 7pm.

Chapelle Penitents-gris (Chapelle des Bourras) This 16th-century chapel honoring St. Joseph was built on the ancient Roman Aurelian road linking Rome and Spain. Herbert Maza, founder and former president of the Institute for American Universities, restored the chapel. M. Borricand, rector of a group of local ecclesiastics, arranges visits.

15 rue Lieutaud. © **04-42-26-26-72.** Free admission; donations welcome. Visits by reservation only.

Musée des Tapisseries ★ Three series of tapestries from the 17th and 18th centuries line the gilded walls of this former archbishop's palace. The prelates decorated the palace with *The History of Don Quixote,* by Natoire; *The Russian Games,* by Leprince; and *The Grotesques,* by Monnoyer. The museum also exhibits rare furnishings from the 17th and 18th centuries.

28 place des Martyrs de la Résistance. © **04-42-23-09-91.** Admission 2.50€ adults, free for ages 24 and under. Wed–Mon 10am–12:30pm and 1:30–5pm. Closed Jan.

Musée Granet (Musée des Beaux-Arts) A former director once claimed that the walls of this museum "would never be sullied by a Cézanne." Fortunately, that's not true—the museum owns eight paintings by Cézanne, although none of them are major

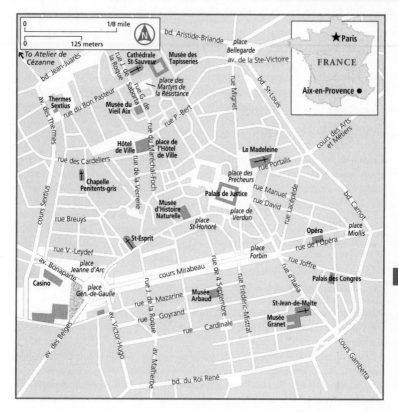

works. The great painter had a famously antagonistic relationship with the people of Aix. The museum is housed in the former center of the Knights of Malta and contains works by Van Dyck, van Loo, and Rigaud; portraits by Pierre and François Puget; and an interesting *Jupiter and Thetis* by Ingres. Ingres also did an 1807 portrait of the museum's namesake, François Marius Granet. Granet's own works abound.

Place St-Jean-de-Malte (up rue Cardinale). © **04-42-52-88-32.** Admission 4€ adults, free for ages 24 and under. June–Sept 11am–7pm; Oct–Apr noon–6pm. Closed Jan 1, May 1 and 21, July 14, Aug 15, Nov 1 and 11, and Dec 25 and 31.

SHOPPING

For the best selection of art objects and fabrics inspired by the traditions of Provence, head to **Les Olivades,** 15 rue Marius-Reinaud (© **04-42-38-33-66**). It sells fabrics, shirts for women and men, fashionable dresses, and table linens.

Opened more than a century ago, **Bechard,** 12 cours Mirabeau (© **04-42-26-06-78**), is the most famous bakery in town. It takes its work so seriously that it refers to its underground kitchens as a *laboratoire* (laboratory). Most of the delectable pastries are made fresh every day.

Founded in 1934 on a busy boulevard just east of the center of town, **Santons Fouque,** 65 cours Gambetta, route de Nice (© **04-42-26-33-38;** www.santons-fouque. com), stocks the largest assortment of *santons* (wooden figurines of saints) in Aix. More than 1,900 figurines are cast in terra cotta, finished by hand, and painted according to 18th-century models. Each of the trades practiced in medieval Provence is represented, including shoemakers, barrel makers, coppersmiths, and ironsmiths, poised to welcome the newborn Jesus. Figurines range in price from 10€ to 950€.

WHERE TO STAY

In Aix

Very Expensive

Villa Gallici ★★★   This elegant inn is relentlessly chic and stylishly decorated by its creators (architects and interior designers Messrs Dez, Montemarco, and Jouve). Each room has an individualized decor; and some feature a private terrace or garden. Beds are hung with "waterfalls" of sprigged and striped cotton, mattresses are decadently comfortable, and towels are predictably plush. The villa sits in a large enclosed garden in the heart of town, close to one of the best restaurants, **Le Clos de la Violette** (p. 192), and a 5-minute walk from the town center. Despite its grand reputation as a place that requires ironbound advance reservations and where famous people bask in sybaritic anonymity, some of the staff are not as polished as they might be. But that is only a minor distraction in an otherwise well-orchestrated symphony.

Av. de la Violette (impasse des Grands Pins), 13100 Aix-en-Provence. © **04-42-23-29-23.** Fax 04-42-96-30-45. www.villagallici.com. 22 units. 230€–780€ double; 440€–945€ suite. AE, DC, MC, V. Closed Jan. **Amenities:** Restaurant; bar; babysitting; pool (outdoor); room service. *In room:* A/C, TV, hair dryer, minibar, Wi-Fi (free).

Expensive

Hôtel Cézanne ★★   Named in honor of the painter, this is the first boutique hotel to open in Aix-en-Provence. The light-filled rooms and suites pay homage to the paintings of Cézanne. The bedrooms are spacious and up-to-date, from the "tropical" showers to free cold drinks in the minibar. Breakfast, served until noon, might include smoked salmon and champagne. The hotel is not only up-to-date, but also innovative and colorful with a strong sense of design. What we like most is how the sunlight seems to caress the mother-of-pearl inlaid walls, on which the light almost dances, as in a Cézanne painting.

40 av. Victor-Hugo, 13100 Aix-en-Provence. © **04-42-91-11-11.** Fax 04-42-91-11-10. www.hotelaix.com/cezanne. 55 units. 155€–175€ double; 220€–240€ junior suite; 310€ suite. AE, MC, V. **Amenities:** Bar; babysitting; room service. *In room:* A/C, TV, minibar, Wi-Fi (free).

Hôtel des Augustins ★   Converted from the 12th-century Grands Augustins Convent, this hotel has been beautifully restored, with ribbed-vault ceilings, stained-glass windows, stone walls, terra-cotta floors, and Louis XIII furnishings. The reception desk is in a chapel, and oil paintings and watercolors decorate the public rooms. Before its transformation into a hotel in 1892, this site won a place in history by sheltering the excommunicated Martin Luther on his return from Rome. Guest rooms are spacious and soundproof—two with terraces. They possess a severe kind of monastic dignity, with dark-grained wooden furniture and high ceilings. Touches of luxury, however, appear in the firm, very comfortable mattresses and big bathrooms. Breakfast is the only meal served.

⌐ rue de la Masse, 13100 Aix-en-Provence. © **04-42-27-28-59.** Fax 04-42-26-74-87. www.hotel-augustins. ⌐⌐ units. 99€–250€ double. AE, MC, V. **Amenities:** Breakfast room. *In room:* A/C, TV, minibar, Wi-Fi

Hôtel Pigonnet ★★ This pink-sided Provençal mansion on the edge of town is surrounded by gardens and memories of Paul Cézanne, who used to visit. The high-ceilinged bedrooms contain antique and reproduction French Provincial furnishings, elaborate curtains, and a pervasive sense of country elegance. Breakfast is served on a colonnaded veranda overlooking a reflecting pool in the courtyard. In summer, the in-house restaurant expands outward into the garden, and features such dishes as a terrine of house-made foie gras, roasted Provençal lamb in a honey-flavored rosemary sauce, and a roulade of chicken with crayfish in shellfish sauce.

5 av. du Pigonnet, 13090 Aix-en-Provence. ✆ **04-42-59-02-90.** Fax 04-42-59-47-77. www.hotelpigonnet. com. 49 units. 160€–330€ double; 220€–600€ suite. AE, DC, MC, V. Free parking. **Amenities:** Restaurant; bar; babysitting; exercise room; pool (outdoor); room service. *In room:* A/C, TV, hair dryer, minibar, Wi-Fi (free).

28 à Aix ★★★ Ⓕ**inds** This *hotel particulier* is as good as it gets if you want to live in a small, sumptuously decorated townhouse created from a restored 17th-century man-sion. With its voluptuous little garden out back, it's like living in a jewel box, complete with a rococo salon for afternoon tea. Its sophisticated owners have created this oasis of charm, tranquillity, style, and comfort, only steps away from Cours Mirabeau. You're able to enjoy light lunches and pastries near the fireplace or outside in the sunny garden. Perfection rules: Even the air is scented.

28 rue du 4 Septembre, 13100 Aix-en-Provence. ✆ **04-42-54-82-01.** Fax 04-42-53-10-13. www.28aix. com. 4 units. 250€–500€ double. Rates include breakfast. MC, V. Parking 20€. **Amenities:** Breakfast lounge; room service. *In room:* A/C, TV, hair dryer, minibar, Wi-Fi (free).

Moderate

Grand Hôtel Nègre Coste This hotel, an 18th-century former town house, is so popular with the musicians who flock to Aix for the summer festivals that it's difficult to get a room at any price. Such popularity is understandable. Flowers cascade from jar-dinières, and 18th-century carvings surround the windows. A wide staircase, marble portrait busts, and a Provençal armoire grace the interior. The medium-size soundproof rooms contain antiques. The higher floors overlook cours Mirabeau or the old city.

33 cours Mirabeau, 13100 Aix-en-Provence. ✆ **04-42-27-74-22.** Fax 04-42-26-80-93. www.hotelnegre coste.com. 37 units. 90€–145€ double. AE, DC, MC, V. Parking 10€. **Amenities:** Room service. *In room:* A/C, TV, hair dryer, minibar, Wi-Fi (10€).

Résidence Rotonde A contemporary hotel in the town center, the Rotonde pro-vides streamlined accommodations. Occupying part of a residential building, it has an open spiral cantilevered staircase. The rooms have ornate wallpaper, Nordic-style beds, and sufficiently comfortable mattresses. Bathrooms are a bit small but adequate. Break-fast is the only meal available at the hotel.

15 av. des Belges, 13100 Aix-en-Provence. ✆ **04-42-26-29-88.** Fax 04-42-38-66-98. www.hotel-rotonde. com. 41 units. 90€–165€ double; 185€ suite. AE, DC, MC, V. Parking 9€. **Amenities:** Breakfast room; bar. *In room:* A/C, TV, Internet (free), minibar.

Inexpensive

Hôtel des Quatre Dauphins This 18th-century town house is a short walk from place des Quatre Dauphins and the cours Mirabeau. Some original motifs have survived through frequent modernizations. The medium-size rooms were refurbished in simpli-fied Provençal style, some with painted ceiling beams and casement windows overlooking the street. You can have breakfast in your room or in a small salon.

54 rue Roux-Alphéran, 13100 Aix-en-Provence. ✆ **04-42-38-16-39.** Fax 04-42-38-60-19. 13 units. 65€–100€ double. AE, MC, V. **Amenities:** Room service. *In room:* A/C, TV, Wi-Fi (5€).

Hôtel La Caravelle (Value) Not everything in this hotel is state of the art, but because of the old-fashioned setting (an 18th-c. town house loaded with personalized quirks), a collection of 18th- and 19th-century antiques, and upscale, historically appropriate upholsteries, many clients don't seem to mind. Located in the Mazarin quarter, on the side of the cours Mirabeau that's less frequently visited by foreign visitors, it has touches of nostalgia that many locals associate with old-time Provence. The annex, which lies about 7.6m (25 ft.) away, near an antique church, holds most of the suites, each of which has a simple kitchenette.

29 bd. du Roi-René (at cours Mirabeau), 13100 Aix-en-Provence. ✆ **04-42-21-53-05.** Fax 04-42-96-55-46. www.lacaravelle-hotel.com. 31 units. 65€–90€ double. AE, DC, MC, V. Parking 8€. **Amenities:** Room service. *In room:* A/C, TV, minibar, Wi-Fi (free).

Le Manoir (Value) One of the best economy options in the heart of the old city of Aix is in a converted abbey in a tranquil location with a private garden. The original cloister dated from the 14th century, but it was reconstructed in the 16th century. In 1980 its owners restored the abbey and converted it into a well-run hotel, offering one of the best deals in Aix. The bedrooms are decorated with antiques, some from the reign of Louis XIII, others from the period of Louis XV. Rooms also come in the Empire style; others have no discernible decor at all, but look as if they were decorated by your Provençal grandmother, assuming you had such a relative. Breakfast is served under a vaulted cloister.

8 rue d'Entrecasteaux, 13100 Aix-en-Provence. ✆ **04-42-26-27-20.** Fax 04-42-27-17-97. www.hotelmanoir. com. 40 units. 62€–92€ double; 85€–92€ triple; 102€ quad. AE, DC, MC, V. Free parking. **Amenities:** Breakfast room. *In room:* TV.

In Meyrargues

Château de Meyrargues ★★ This 12th-century château is one of France's oldest fortified sites, having been a Celtic outpost in 600 B.C. Once the lords of Les Baux lived here; now it's an award-winning holiday retreat. The entrance is imposing, with twin stone towers flanking a sweeping set of balustraded steps. From its terraces and rooms you can enjoy a panoramic view of the valley of the Durance. The spacious accommodations feature canopied beds, fabrics inspired by Provençal designs, antiques, and tiled bathrooms.

Meals are served in a baronial-looking dining room with a large fireplace, near a bar with a private terrace. Fixed-price menus at 49€ to 59€ tend to emphasize grilled fish and roasted versions of Provençal lamb. The château is surrounded by 6 hectares of private terrain, where patches of verdant gardens are interspersed with a swimming pool and lots of rocky outcroppings.

13650 Meyrargues. ✆ **04-42-63-49-90.** Fax 04-42-63-49-92. www.chateau-de-meyrargues-abesalles. com. 11 units. 115€–220€ double; 241€–310€ suite. AE, DC, MC, V. From Aix, take A51 for 17km (11 miles) northeast, following the signs for Sisteron and Pertuis; get off at exit 14, and then follow the signs to the château. **Amenities:** Restaurant; bar; pool (outdoor); room service; Wi-Fi (free). *In room:* A/C, TV, hair dryer, minibar.

WHERE TO DINE

Expensive

Le Clos de la Violette ★★★ MODERN FRENCH This innovative restaurant is a few steps from **Villa Gallici** (p. 190) in an elegant neighborhood that most visitors reach by taxi. The Provençal villa has an octagonal reception area and several dining rooms. The stylish, seasonal dishes highlight the flavors of Provence. A stellar example of the innovative cuisine is an appetizer of mousseline of potatoes with sea urchins and fish roe. An elegant dish is braised sea wolf with crisp fried shallots and a "cappuccino" of spicy Spanish sausages. Delightful rack of suckling lamb is stuffed with carrots and chick-peas and served under an herb-flavored pastry crust. For dessert, try multilayered sugar cookies with hazelnut and vanilla-flavored cream sauce and thin slices of white chocolate, or a "celebration" of Provençal figs—an artfully arranged platter containing a galette, tart, parfait, and sorbet.

10 av. de la Violette. ✆ **04-42-23-30-71.** www.closdelaviolette.fr. Reservations required. Main courses 46€–49€; fixed-price lunch 50€; tasting menu 130€. AE, MC, V. Tues–Sat noon–1:30pm and 7:30–9:30pm. Closed Aug 1–20.

Le Passage MEDITERRANEAN   Owner/manager Reine Sammut has transformed a 19th-century candy factory into a contemporary brasserie in the nucleus of Aix. You'll find two large dining rooms plus a sprawling outdoor terrace. Walls are accented with paintings, each of which is for sale. The atmosphere is friendly and intimate, with lots of care behind every dish served. Menu items are linked to the seasons and change often, but staples include *les petits farcis* (vegetables stuffed and deep-fried) served with a tomato-basil sauce; a carpaccio of John Dory with a vanilla-flavored olive sauce; marinated and grilled filet of beef with large-cut french fries and a wasabi-flavored mayonnaise; and a filet of roasted *daurade* with green asparagus. One of the best desserts in Aix is a featured specialty here: raspberry-flavored crème brûlée with fig chutney. Also on-site are a bookshop, a tea-room, a wine boutique, and a cooking school. Note that this restaurant has two entrances.

6 bis rue Mazarine and 10 rue Villas. ✆ **04-42-37-09-00.** www.le-passage.fr. Reservations recommended. Main courses 12€–30€; fixed-price menus 25€–35€. AE, MC, V. Daily 10am–midnight.

Pierre Reboul ★★★ MODERN FRENCH   In the heart of the old town, this elegant modern restaurant specializes in the innovative cuisine of master chef Pierre Reboul. Reboul reinvents the classics, claiming, "I give a playful decoration to each plate but I never forget that quality ingredients and taste are essential." For "nibbles," he suggests pan-seared foie gras with passion fruit or goat cheese and profiteroles of herring with rocket sorbet. For a main, opt for the smoked sea bass from Brittany with stewed cabbage or lamb with celeriac under a cheesy crust. A first for us is Roquefort cheese and a banana tempura in cocoa juice.

11 Petite Rue St. Jean. ✆ **04-42-20-58-26.** Reservations required. www.restaurant-pierre-reboul.com. Fixed-price menu 39€, 78€, and 120€. AE, DC, MC, V. Tues–Sat noon–1:30pm and 7:30–9:30pm.

Moderate

Brasserie Les Deux Garcons PROVENÇALE   Patrons don't necessarily come here for the rather standard fare, but rather for the atmosphere of a brasserie founded in 1792. Emile Zola and Cézanne used to dine here, as has everybody from Picasso to Sir Winston Churchill. On a winter's night the piano bar upstairs is the coziest rendezvous in Aix, attracting jazz lovers. In summer linen-draped sidewalk tables open onto Cours Mira-beau. *Provençale* fare includes *daube de boeuf à la provençale* (stewed beef marinated in a garlic purée), roast goose, wild rabbit, and the fresh fruits and vegetables of the season.

53 Cours Mirabeau. ✆ **04-42-26-00-51.** www.les2garcons.abcsalles.com. Reservations recommended. Main courses 14€–36€; fixed-price menu 28€. AE, MC, V. Daily 11am–3pm and 7pm–midnight.

Chez Maxime GRILL/PROVENÇALE   Set in the heart of Aix's pedestrian shopping zone, this likeable restaurant has a Provençal ambience created by bordeaux-colored banquettes, salmon-colored walls, and tables shaded by an enormous linden tree. The menu features a succulent array of a dozen grills, beefsteaks, and fresh fish, as well as a main course laced with saffron and the flavors of the sea, a *marmite* (stewpot) *de la mer.*

Also appealing is house-made foie gras of duckling, a kind of pâté made from beef and Provençal herbs known as *caillette de province,* and such desserts as a *fondant au chocolat.* The wine list features dozens of vintages, many of them esoteric bottles from the region.

12 place Ramus. ℂ **04-42-26-28-51.** www.restaurant-chezmaxime.com. Reservations recommended. Main courses 12€–20€; fixed-price lunch 15€; fixed-price dinner 21€–36€. MC, V. Tues–Sat noon–2pm; Mon–Sat 7–10pm. Oct–Mar closed Sun–Mon.

Inexpensive

Le Bistro Latin ★★ (Value) PROVENÇALE   This is the best little bistro in Aix-en-Provence for the price. We've enjoyed the classic cuisine on all our visits. Guests dine in two intimate rooms: a street-level space and a cellar decorated in Greco-Latin style. The staff is young and enthusiastic, taking special pride in their fixed-price menus. Try chartreuse of mussels, a meat dish with spinach-and-saffron cream sauce, scampi risotto, or crepe rack of lamb in an herbed crust.

18 rue de la Couronne. ℂ **04-42-38-22-88.** Reservations recommended. Main courses 14€–20€; fixed-price lunch 16€; fixed-price dinner 16€–35€. MC, V. Thurs–Tues noon–2pm and 7–10:30pm.

AIX AFTER DARK

An easy-to-reach bar that manages to be convenient and hip at the same time lies almost directly across from the city's tourist office: **La Rotonde,** Place Jeanne d'Arc (ℂ **04-42-91-61-70;** www.larotonde-aix.com). Open daily from 8am until at least 2am, it functions as a bar, cafe, and rendezvous point for friends and business associates throughout the day and evening.

People between the ages of 20 and 30 who enjoy animated bar scenes and loud electronic music head for **Le Mistral,** 3 rue Frédéric-Mistral (ℂ **04-42-38-16-49**), where techno and house music blares long and loud, all for a cover charge of around 16€ to 20€—unless you happen to be gorgeous and female, in which case you'll get in free, and, depending on the mood of the staff, you may even receive a free glass or two of champagne.

For jazz by a changing roster of visiting musicians, head for the **Scat Club,** 11 rue de la Verrerie (ℂ **04-42-23-00-23**), a smoky jazz den that's the preferred venue for patrons in their late 30s and 40s. Open Tuesday to Sunday, it maintains notoriously late hours, with live music often not beginning until around midnight. And last but certainly not least is Aix's body-shop bar, **La Joia** (ℂ **06-80-35-32-94;** www.joia-club.com), route de l'Enfant, in the hamlet of Les Milles, 8km (5 miles) south of Aix (to get there, follow the signs to Marseille). On-site you'll find a restaurant, several bars, an outdoor swimming pool (the kind where you may opt to jump in topless), a dance floor with indoor and outdoor sections alike, and a venue that's more hip than it is chic. Know in advance that long lines await on Fridays and Saturdays. Entrance usually costs 12€ to 18€, unless you're a star or self-enchanted enough to convince the doorman that you are, in which case, the velvet ropes may miraculously open without charge, like the Red Sea before Moses.

13 MARSEILLE ★★★

771km (479 miles) S of Paris; 187km (116 miles) SW of Nice; 31km (19 miles) S of Aix-en-Provence

Bustling Marseille, with more than a million inhabitants, is the second-largest city in France (its population surpassed that of Lyon in the early 1990s) and France's premier port. It's been called France's New Orleans. A crossroads of world traffic—Dumas called

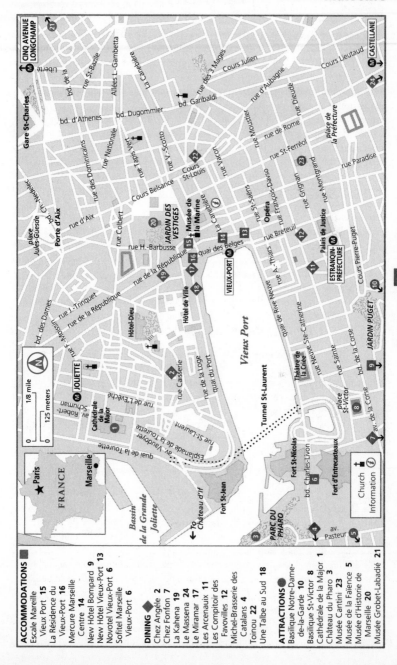

ACCOMMODATIONS ■

Escale Marseille
Vieux Port **15**
La Résidence du
Vieux-Port **16**
Mercure Marseille
Centre **14**
New Hôtel Bompard **9**
New Hôtel Vieux-Port **13**
Novotel Vieux-Port **6**
Sofitel Marseille
Vieux-Port **6**

DINING ◆

Chez Angèle **2**
Chez Fonfon **7**
La Kahena **19**
Le Massena **24**
Le Miramar **17**
Les Arcenaulx **11**
Les Comptoir des
Favouilles **12**
Michel-Brasserie des
Catalans **4**
Toinou **22**
Une Talbe au Sud **18**

ATTRACTIONS ●

Basilique Notre-Dame-
de-la-Garde **10**
Basilique St-Victor **8**
Cathédrale de la Major **1**
Château du Pharo **3**
Musée Cantini **23**
Musée de la Faïence **5**
Musée d'Historie de
Marseille **20**
Musée Grobet-Labadié **21**

it "the meeting place of the entire world"—the city is ancient, founded by Greeks from the city of Phocaea, near present-day Izmir, Turkey, in the 6th century B.C. Marseille is a place of unique sounds, smells, and sights. It has seen wars and much destruction, but trade has always been its raison d'être.

Perhaps its most common association is with the national anthem of France, "La Marseillaise." During the Revolution, 500 volunteers marched to Paris, singing this rousing song along the way. The rest is history.

Although in many respects Marseille is big and sprawling, dirty and slumlike in many places, much elegance and charm exists here as well. The Vieux Port, the old harbor, is especially colorful, compensating to an extent for the dreary industrial dockland nearby. Marseille has always symbolized danger and intrigue, and that reputation is somewhat justified. However, the city is experiencing a renaissance, and because it is now so easily reached by train from Paris, there is much hope for its economic future. Since the 1970s, a great deal of Marseille's economy has revolved around thousands upon thousands of North and sub-Saharan Africans who have poured into the city, creating a lively medley of races and creeds. One-quarter of the present population of Marseille is of North African descent.

Marseille today actually occupies twice the amount of land space as Paris, and its age-old problems remain, including drug industry, smuggling, corruption (often at the highest levels), the Mafia, and racial tension. Unemployment, as always, is on the rise. But in spite of all these difficulties, it's a bustling, fascinating city unlike any other in France. A city official proclaimed recently that "Marseille is the unbeloved child of France. It's attached to France, but has the collective consciousness of an Italian city-state, such as Genoa or Venice."

ESSENTIALS

GETTING THERE The **airport** (© 04-42-14-14-14), 27km (17 miles) northwest of the city center, receives international flights from all over Europe. From the airport, blue-and-white minivans *(navettes)* make the trip to Marseille's St-Charles rail station, near the Vieux Port, for 8.50€. The minivans run daily every 20 minutes from 6am (hourly) or to the arrival of the last flight.

Marseille has **train** connections from all over Europe, with especially good connections to and from Italy. The city is the terminus for the TGV bullet train, which departs daily from Paris's Gare de Lyon (trip time: 3 hr., 15 min.; one-way fare 50€–95€). Some Parisians plan a day trip to the Mediterranean beaches at Marseille, returning to the City of Light for dinner. Local trains leave Paris almost every hour, making a number of stops before reaching Marseille. For information, call © **36-35,** or visit **www.voyages-sncf. com.** **Buses** serve the Gare Routière, place Victor Hugo (© 04-91-08-16-40), adjacent to the St-Charles railway station. Five buses arrive from Avignon a day. Tickets are 15€ and the trip takes 2 hours. Buses arrive from Aix-en-Provence every 20 minutes, a one-way ticket costing 4.60€ (trip time: 35 min.).

If **driving** from Paris, follow A6 south to Lyon, then continue south along A7 to Marseille. The drive takes about 7 hours. From Provence, take A7 south to Marseille.

VISITOR INFORMATION The **Office de Tourisme** is at 4 la Canebière (© **04-91-13-89-00;** fax 04-91-13-89-20; www.marseille-tourisme.com; Métro: Vieux Port).

GETTING AROUND Marseille has an adequate **Métro** (subway or underground) system in the center of town. All Métro and bus lines are run by *RTM,* 6 rue des Fabres

Ⓜ Moments Exploring the Massif des Calanques

You can visit the **Massif des Calanques,** a wild and rugged terrain, from either Marseille or Cassis. This craggy coastline lies between the two ports, directly south of Marseille and to the west of Cassis. With its highest peak at 555m (1,850 ft.), the Calanques stretch for some 20km (12 miles) of dazzling limestone whiteness. This is one of France's great natural beauties.

Exactly what is a *calanque?* The word comes from the Provençal *cala,* meaning "steep slopes." Nature has cut coastal valleys into solid rock, creating steep inlets. Most of these gorges extend less than a kilometer inland from the Mediterranean. They're similar to fiords, created by glaciers, but these gorges have been created by the raging sea. The needlelike rocks and cliff faces overhanging the sea attract rock climbers and deep-sea divers.

The highlight of the Calanques is **Sormiou,** with its beach, seafood eateries, and small harbor. Sormiou is separated from another small but enchanting settlement at Morgiou by **Cap Morgiou,** which offers a panoramic belvedere with splendid views of both the Calanques and the eastern side of the massif. The **Morgiou** has tiny inlets for swimming.

PROVENCE

6

MARSEILLE

(© **04-91-91-92-10;** French-only website: www.rtm.fr). Tickets, sold at all bus and Métro stations, are good for 1 hour for travel on the bus or subway, costing 1.70€. You can buy tickets on the bus or at a Métro entrance with exact change. The best deal is a 24-hour **day pass** for 4.50€, sold at the tourist offices, or at bus or Métro stations. Another deal is a **Carte Liberté,** 6€ to 12€ for 5 to 10 trips, respectively. The most useful Métro lines are no. 1 and no. 2 which take you to the rail station; no. 1 also goes to the Vieux Port (the old port), the most intriguing district for sightseeing.

EXPLORING THE CITY

Many visitors never bother to visit the museums, preferring to absorb the unique spirit of the city as reflected by its busy streets and at its sidewalk cafes, particularly those along the main street, **La Canebière.** Known as "can of beer" to World War II GIs, it's the spine and soul of Marseille, but the seediest main street in France. Lined with hotels, shops, and restaurants, the street is filled with sailors of every nation and a wide range of foreigners, especially Algerians, some of whom live in souklike conditions. La Canebière winds down to the **Vieux Port** ★★, dominated by the massive neoclassical forts of St-Jean and St-Nicholas. The port is filled with fishing craft and yachts and is ringed with seafood restaurants.

Motorists can continue along to the **corniche Président-J.-F.-Kennedy,** a promenade running for about 5km (3 miles) along the sea. You pass villas and gardens along the way and have a good view of the Mediterranean. To the north, the **Port Moderne** (also known simply as "La Joliette," or "the gateway to the East") is a man-made labyrinth of nautical engineering. Its construction began in 1844, and a century later, the Germans destroyed it. Today it's one of the Mediterranean's busiest ports.

Basilique Notre-Dame-de-la-Garde This landmark church crowns a limestone rock overlooking the southern side of the Vieux Port. It was built in the Romanesque-Byzantine style popular in the 19th century and topped by a 9m (30-ft.) gilded statue of the Virgin. Visitors come for the view—best at sunset—from its terrace. Spread out before you are the city, the islands, and the sea.

Rue Fort-du-Sanctuaire. ✆ **04-91-13-40-80.** www.notredamedelagarde.com. Free admission. Daily 7am–7pm. Métro: Vieux Port.

Basilique St-Victor ★ This semifortified basilica was built above a crypt from the 5th century, when St. Cassianus founded the church and abbey. You can visit the crypt, which also reflects work done in the 10th and 11th centuries.

Place St-Victor. ✆ **04-96-11-22-60.** Admission to crypt 2€. Church daily 9am–7pm. Crypt daily 9am–7pm. Head west along quai de Rive-Neuve (near the Gare du Vieux Port). Métro: Vieux Port.

Cathédrale de la Major This was one of the largest cathedrals (some 135m/443 ft. long) built in Europe in the 19th century. It has mosaic floors and red-and-white marble banners, and the exterior is in a bastardized Romanesque-Byzantine style. The domes and cupolas may remind you of Istanbul. This vast pile has almost swallowed its 12th-century Romanesque predecessor, built on the ruins of a Temple of Diana.

Place de la Major. ✆ **04-91-90-52-87.** Free admission. Hours vary. Métro: Vieux Port.

Friche la Belle de Mai This is an offbeat attraction, a government-sponsored artists' building in a converted tobacco factory by the train station. Local artists refer to it as a "living laboratory," where all kinds of artistic freedom is expressed (and we truly mean that). From the visual arts to the digital arts, the center is a never-ending spectacle of painting, theater, dance, music, and film. About 60 houses of art are located here, with about 400 professional artists in all fields participating. It is a one-stop destination for "culture vultures."

41 rue Jobin. ✆ **04-95-04-95-04.** www.lafriche.org. Free admission. Mon–Sat 10am–noon and 1–6pm. Bus: 49B to Belle de Mai Maternité (get off at Jobin/Pautrier).

Musée Cantini The temporary exhibitions of contemporary art here are often as good as the permanent collection. This museum is devoted to modern art, with masterpieces by Derain, Marquet, Ernst, Masson, Balthus, and others. It also owns a selection of works by important young international artists.

19 rue Grignan. ✆ **04-91-54-77-75.** Admission 2€ adults, 1€ students, free for seniors and children 9 and under. Oct–May Tues–Sun 10am–5pm; June–Sept Tues–Sun 11am–6pm.

Musée de la Faïence This museum contains one of the largest collections of porcelain in France. Its collections date from Neolithic times to the present. Especially numerous are the delicate and richly ornate ceramics that graced the tables of local landowners during the 18th and 19th centuries. The museum is about 5km (3 miles) south of the center of Marseille, in a stately manor house (Château Pastré) that was built by a local ship owner in 1864.

In the Château Pastré, 157 av. de Montredon. ✆ **04-91-72-43-47.** Admission 2€. June–Sept Tues–Sun 10am–6pm; Oct–May Tues–Sun 10am–5pm.

Musée d'Histoire de Marseille Visitors may wander through an archaeological garden where excavations are going on, as scholars learn more about the ancient town of Massalia, founded by Greek sailors. To help you more fully realize the era, audiovisual

PROVENCE

6

MARSEILLE

exhibits and a free exhibition room set the scene. A medieval quarter of potters has been discovered and is open to the public. You can also see what's left of a Roman shipwreck excavated from the site.

Centre Bourse, sq. Belsunce. ⓒ **04-91-90-42-22.** Admission 2€ adults, 1.50€ students and children 11–18, free for children 10 and under. Mon–Sat noon–7pm. Métro: Vieux Port.

Musée d'Histoire Naturelle   If you have the time to spare and you are already visiting Palais Longchamp, consider ducking into this museum for a half-hour or so. It is usually visited jointly with the more important Musée des Beaux-Arts. The museum lies in the right wing of the Palais Longchamp and offers a parade of the fossilized remains of the animals of Provence. The museum illustrates 400 million years of the natural history of Provence in its exhibits, including a safari section that shows the diversity of animals throughout the world. Of special interest to botany lovers is a gallery showcasing regional flora and fauna. On the lowest level, a Mediterranean aquarium is devoted to fish from five oceans.

In the Palais Longchamp, place Bernex. ⓒ **04-91-14-59-50.** www.museum-marseille.org. Admission 2€ adults, 1€) students and ages 10–16, free for children 9 and under. Tues–Sun 10am–5pm.

Musée Grobet-Labadié ★   This collection, bequeathed to the city in 1919, includes Louis XV and Louis XVI furniture, as well as an outstanding collection of medieval Burgundian and Provençal sculpture. Other exhibits showcase 17th-century Gobelin tapestries; 15th- to 19th-century German, Italian, French, and Flemish paintings; and 16th- and 17th-century Italian and French faïence.

140 bd. Longchamp. ⓒ **04-91-62-21-82.** Admission 2€ adults, 1€ students and children 11–18, free for children 10 and under. June–Sept Tues–Sun 11am–6pm; Oct–May Tues–Sun 10am–5pm. Closed public holidays. Métro: Cinq av. Longchamp.

Panoramic Views

Although the architecture of the **Basilique Notre-Dame-de-la-Garde,** rue Fort-du-Sanctuaire (p. 198; ⓒ **04-91-13-40-80**), shows France's Gilded Age at its most evocative, visitors come here not so much for the church as for the view—best appreciated at sunset—from its terrace. The church is open daily from 7am to 7pm.

Another panoramic view is from **Parc du Pharo,** a promontory facing the entrance to the Vieux Port. Most people visit this park to escape the urban congestion of Marseille, but if you're in the mood for some history, check out the gray stone facade of the **Château du Pharo** (ⓒ **04-91-14-64-95**). Built in the 1860s by Napoleon III for his empress, Eugénie (who is reputed not to have liked it and seldom visited), it's owned and maintained by the city of Marseille as a convention center and—less frequently—as a concert hall. The building has no regular hours, but if nothing is going on, you can enter the lobby and ask for a quick glance at the Salon des Génies.

Boating to Château d'If ★★

From quai des Belges at the Vieux Port, you can take a 20-minute motorboat ride to **Château d'If** for 10€ round-trip. Boats leave every 30 to 45 minutes, depending on the season. For information, contact the **Frioul If Express,** quai des Belges (ⓒ **04-91-46-54-65;** www.frioul-if-express.com). On the sparsely vegetated island of Château d'If (ⓒ **04-91-59-02-30** for information), François I built a fortress to defend Marseille. The site later housed a prison, where carvings by Huguenot prisoners can still be seen. Alexandre Dumas used the château as a setting for the fictional adventures of *The Count of Monte Cristo.* The château's most famous association—with the legendary Man in the

Iron Mask—is also apocryphal. The château is open Tuesday to Sunday from 9am to 5:30pm (until 6:30pm Apr–Sept). Adults pay 5€ to enter the island or 3.50€ for ages 18 to 25; free for those 17 and under.

SHOPPING

Only Paris and Lyon can rival Marseille in breadth and diversity of merchandise. Your best bet is a trip to the Vieux Port and the streets surrounding it for a view of the folkloric objects that literally pop out of the boutiques.

ART & ANTIQUES   Marseille has a handful of well-respected art galleries. Antiques from around Provence are sold at **Antiquités François-Décamp,** 302 rue Paradis (© **04-91-81-18-00**).

FASHION   You don't normally think of Marseille as a place of fashion, but the local fashion industry is booming. The fashion center is found along **cours Julien,** with dozens of boutiques and ateliers. Much of the clothing reflects North African influences, although a vast array of French styles are for sale as well.

For hats, at **Felio,** 4 place Gabriel-Péri (© **04-91-90-32-67**), you'll find large-brimmed numbers that would've thrilled ladies of the Belle Epoque or guests at a stylish wedding inspired in the 1920s by Lanvin. It also carries a selection of *casquettes Marseillaises* (developed for men as protection from the *soleil du Midi*) and berets that begin at 25€.

FOLKLORE & SOUVENIRS   Especially popular are *santons* (carved wooden crèche figurines). The best place for acquiring these is just above the Vieux Port, behind the Théâtre National de la Criée. At **Ateliers Marcel Carbonel,** 47 rue Neuve-Ste-Catherine (© **04-91-54-26-58;** www.santonsmarcelcarbonel.com), more than 600 figures, available in half a dozen sizes, sell at prices beginning at 10€.

All the souvenir shops along the pedestrian **rue St-Féréol,** running perpendicular to La Canebière, sell folkloric replicas of handicrafts from Old Provence, including the cream-colored or pale-green bars of the city's local soap, **savon de Marseille.** Infused with a healthy dollop of olive oil, it's known for its kindness to skin dried out by the sun and mistral. A large selection is available at **La Savonnerie du Sérail,** 50 bd. Anatole de la Forge (© **04-91-98-28-25;** www.savon-leserail.com).

FOOD & CHOCOLATE   At **Amandine,** 69 bd. Eugène-Pierre (© **04-91-47-00-83**), a photograph or a work of graphic art can be reproduced in various shades of chocolate on top of a delicious layer cake in any flavor you specify in advance. If you don't happen to have your scrapbook with you, you can buy a cake emblazoned with scenes of the Vieux Port. More traditional pastries and chocolates are found at **Puyricard,** 25 rue Francis-Davso (© **04-91-54-26-25;** www.puyricard.fr), with another location at 155 rue Jean-Mermoz (© **04-91-77-94-11**). The treats available here include chocolates stuffed with almond paste *(pâté d'amande)* or *confits de fruits,* along with a type of biscuit called *une Marseillotte.*

Since medieval times, Marseille has thrived on the legend of Les Trois Maries—three saints named Mary who, assisted by awakened-from-the-dead St. Lazarus, reportedly came ashore at a point near Marseille to Christianize ancient Provence. In commemoration of their voyage, small boat-shaped cookies called *les navettes* are flavored with secret ingredients (that include orange zest, orange-flower water, and sugar), and are forever associated with Marseille. You can find them throughout the city, notably at **Le Four des Navettes,** 136 rue Sainte (© **04-91-33-32-12;** www.fourdesnavettes.com). It opened in 1791 and is dedicated to perpetuating the city's most cherished medieval myth and ferociously guarding the secret of how the pastries are made. The boat-shaped cookies are sold for 17€ per dozen.

One of the city's most sophisticated emporiums for takeout food is **La Fromagerie Marrou,** 2 bd. Baille (© **04-91-78-17-68**). Established in 1902 and known as one of the most comprehensive upscale food stores in Marseille, it sells more than just cheeses: You will also find meats, baked goods, deli items, wines, liqueurs, foie gras, and caviar. With a main branch at 2 bd. Baille, the shop maintains secondary branches at 475 rue Paradis and 15 place Castellane.

A MARSEILLE MALL   Looking for something that approximates, with a Provençal accent, a sun-flooded mall in California? Head for the most talked-about real-estate development in the city's recent history, **L'Escale Borély,** avenue Mendès-France. Within a 25-minute transit trip (take the Métro to rond-point du Prado and then transfer to bus no. 19) south of Marseille, it incorporates shops, cafes, bars, and restaurants. Note the newest fad from your seat on a terrace as you sip pastis: in-line skating. For more on L'Escale Borély, see "Marseille After Dark" on p. 208.

WHERE TO STAY
Very Expensive
Le Petit Nice ★★★   This is the best hotel in Marseille, with the finest restaurant. The residence opened in 1917 when the Passédat family joined two villas. The narrow approach takes you past what looks like a row of private villas, in a secluded area below the street paralleling the beach. Rooms are decorated with tasteful fabrics and quality carpeting, and all come equipped with fine beds. Units in the main house are modern and even avant-garde—four units were inspired by cubism and have geometric appointments and bright colors. The spacious Marina Wing across from the main building offers individually decorated rooms in the antique style, opening onto sea views. Marble bathrooms are quite sumptuous and come with deluxe toiletries.

The beautiful glass-enclosed restaurant has a view of the shore and the rocky islands off the coast. In summer, dinner is served in the garden facing the sea. It's run by Gerald Passédat, whose imaginative culinary successes include sliced sea wolf in the style of the Passédat family matriarch, Lucy; vinaigrette of *rascasse* (hogfish); and sea devil with saffron and garlic.

Corniche Président-J.-F.-Kennedy/Anse-de-Maldormé, 13007 Marseille. © **04-91-59-25-92.** Fax 04-91-59-28-08. www.petitnice-passedat.com. 16 units. 250€–640€ double; 500€–1,090€ suite. AE, DC, MC, V. Free parking. Métro: Vieux Port. **Amenities:** Restaurant; bar; babysitting; bikes; pool (outdoor). *In room:* A/C, TV, hair dryer, minibar, Wi-Fi (free).

Ⓣⁱᵖˢ   **A Day at the Beach**

Bus no. 83 leaves from the Vieux Port heading for the public beaches outside Marseille. This bus takes you to **Plage du Prado** and **Plage de la Corniche,** the best bets for swimming and sunning. The sands are a bit gray and sometimes rocky, but the beaches are wide and the water is generally clear. These beaches are set against a scenic backdrop of the cliffs of Marseille.

Sofitel Marseille Vieux Port ★★★ This government-rated four-star hotel lacks the glamour and style of Le Petit Nice, but it is the highest-rated lodging in the city center. A glistening, modern palace, it stands above the embankments of the old port. Some guest rooms have panoramic views of the Vieux Port; others look out on the boulevard. Rooms are up-to-date, comfortable, and furnished in Provençal style. All are fairly generous in size. This hotel and its corporate sibling, the Novotel Vieux Port (see below), are in the same building and share a staff and dining facilities.

36 bd. Charles-Livon, 13007 Marseille. ✆ **04-91-15-59-00.** Fax 04-91-15-59-50. www.accorhotels.com. 134 units. 265€–400€ double; 595€–1,200€ suite. AE, DC, MC, V. Parking 16€. Métro: Vieux Port. **Amenities:** Restaurant; bar; babysitting; room service. *In room:* A/C, TV, hair dryer, Internet (9.90€), minibar.

Villa Massalia Concorde Marseille ★ Near the Borély racetrack and Parc Chanot, this hotel lies in an upmarket residential district of the city. With a rather stunning modern design, it showcases such materials as real oak, feather bedding, and leather. It is close to several sandy beaches, and is ideal for the business traveler and vacationer alike. The hotel is elegantly and warmly decorated with fine natural materials. Bedrooms are sleek and modern, with all the latest gadgets.

17 place Louis Bonnefon, 13008 Marseille. ✆ **04-91-72-90-00.** Fax 04-91-72-90-01. www.concorde-hotels.com. 140 units. 164€–325€ double; 305€–690€ suite. AE, DC, MC, V. **Amenities:** Restaurant; bar; pool (outdoor); room service. *In room:* A/C, TV, hair dryer, minibar, Wi-Fi (free).

Moderate

Hôtel Le Corbusier ★ (Finds) The radical designs of Swiss-born architect, Le Corbusier (aka Charles-Edouard Jeanneret, 1887–1965), have long been associated with Marseille. In 1952, in a location 2km (1¼ miles) south of Marseille's Vieux Port, he designed the Unité d'Habitation (it's also known as La Cité Radieuse), a multifunctional, nine-story building that combines shops and apartments for 1,500 residents. Within his original plan was a provision for a hotel which, beginning in 1959, opened its doors for business to the general public from the building's third and fourth floors.

The husband-and-wife team of Alban and Dominique Gérardin has worked hard to strip the hotel back to the original combination of expressionism and functionalism for which Le Corbusier is known. They've zealously retained a handful of their studios' original kitchens, each designed by Le Corbusier's now-celebrated collaborator Charlotte Perriand (none of them actually works, but they're highly prized as minimalist statements nonetheless), and outfitted the hotel with the kind of Apartan, functional, and often metallic furniture, lighting fixtures, and accessories of which the great designer would have approved. The smallest units evoke cruise ship cabins; larger units are more airy and congenial, some with their (nonworking) original kitchens. On the premises is a restaurant, **Le Ventre de l'Architect** (the **Architect's Stomach;** p. 206).

On the 3rd and 4th floors of "Le Cité Radieuse," 280 bd. Michelet, 13008 Marseille. ✆ **04-91-16-78-00.** www.hotellecorbusier.com. 21 units. 94€–114€ double; 120€ suite. DC, MC, V. Bus: 21. **Amenities:** Restaurant; bar; exercise room; wading pool. *In room:* A/C, TV, fridge, Wi-Fi (9.90€).

La Résidence du Vieux Port This old hotel has a touch of raffish charm and an unbeatable location directly beside the harbor. Guest rooms have loggia-style terraces opening onto the port; the rooms are simple but serviceable, each with a small bathroom.

18 quai du Port, 13001 Marseille. ✆ **04-91-91-91-22.** Fax 04-91-56-60-88. www.hotelmarseille.com. 50 units. 103€–154€ double; 165€ suite. AE, DC, MC, V. Parking 8€. Métro: Vieux Port. **Amenities:** Cafe; bar; room service. *In room:* A/C, TV, hair dryer, minibar.

Mercure Marseille Centre   One of the most modern hotels in town, this bronze building looks out over the Greco-Roman ruins of the Jardin des Vestiges, a 2-minute walk from the Old Port and near a collection of boutiques, the Centre Bourse. The well-kept rooms are furnished in a functional chain-style format, with twin or double beds. Tiled bathrooms are compact but have adequate shelf space. The on-site restaurant is popular with Marseille's shoppers. Many staff members speak English.

Rue Neuve-St-Martin, 13001 Marseille. ✆ **04-96-17-22-22.** Fax 04-96-17-22-33. www.mercure.com. 199 units. 120€–165€ double; 200€ suite. AE, DC, MC, V. Parking 12€. Métro: Colbert. **Amenities:** Restaurant; bar; room service. *In room:* A/C, TV, hair dryer, minibar, Wi-Fi (9.90€).

New Hôtel Vieux-Port (Value)   Located close to the port, this hotel lies in a six-story, turn-of-the-20th-century building. It offers comfortable rooms and a hardworking, English-speaking staff. Rooms that overlook the port are outfitted in a traditional way; the more contemporary-looking accommodations look out over the commercial neighborhood nearby. This hotel offers exceptional value for Marseille, although most of the accommodations are small. Each comes with twin or double beds; bathrooms are compact but well maintained.

3 bis rue Reine-Elisabeth, 13001 Marseille. ✆ **04-91-99-23-23.** Fax 04-91-90-76-24. www.new-hotel. com. 42 units. 160€–260€ double. Children 10 and under stay free in parent's room. AE, DC, MC, V. Parking 12€. Bus: 83. Métro: Vieux Port. **Amenities:** Bar; exercise room. *In room:* A/C, TV, hair dryer, minibar, Wi-Fi (13€).

Novotel Vieux Port (Value)   In the same building as the Sofitel (p. 202), the Novotel broke off from its more upscale affiliate in 1987. Services are less extensive, amenities less plush, and spaces a bit more cramped than at the Sofitel; but because this is one of the most reasonably priced hotels in town, no one seems to mind. The few rooms overlooking the old port tend to fill up first. Each unit is outfitted in chain-hotel style and comes with a small, well-equipped bathroom.

36 bd. Charles-Livon, 13007 Marseille. ✆ **04-96-11-42-11.** Fax 04-96-11-42-20. www.accorhotels.com. 110 units. 115€–190€ double. AE, DC, MC, V. Parking 16€. Métro: Vieux Port. **Amenities:** Restaurant; bar; babysitting; exercise room; pool (outdoor); room service. *In room:* A/C, TV, hair dryer, minibar, Wi-Fi (9.90€).

Inexpensive

Escale Marseille Vieux Port   This hotel evokes the grandeur of 19th-century life in Marseille. It's less than 2 blocks from the Vieux Port, in the heart of town. The sun and mistrals of many seasons have battered the Beaux Arts facade, decorated with ornate corbels and cornices. Renovations have stripped the guest rooms of some of their old-fashioned charm, but have left efficient, soundproof spaces. Each unit has a compact bathroom. Breakfast is the only meal served, but the neighborhood abounds with dining options.

5 la Canebière, 13001 Marseille. ✆ **04-91-90-61-61.** Fax 04-91-90-95-61. www.oceanianhotels.com. 45 units. 98€–115€ double; 140€ suite. AE, DC, MC, V. Parking in nearby public lot 12€. **Amenities:** Room service. *In room:* A/C, TV, hair dryer, minibar, Wi-Fi (9.90€).

New Hôtel Bompard   This tranquil retreat, built after World War II, lies atop a cliff along the corniche, about 3km (2 miles) east of the Vieux Port. Partly because of its garden, it may remind you of a well-appointed private home. A Provençal *mas* (farmhouse) in the garden holds four large rooms that are more luxurious and atmospheric than those in the main building. Some of the beds are baldachin-style (canopied); floors have Provençal tiles; and furnishings are romantic. Rooms in the main building are cheap, modern, and streamlined.

2 rue des Flots Bleus, 13007 Marseille. ☎ **04-91-99-22-22.** Fax 04-91-31-02-14. www.new-hotel.com. 49 units. 95€–149€ standard double; 145€–215€ Provençal *mas* double. AE, DC, MC, V. Free parking. Bus: 61 or 83. **Amenities:** Restaurant; bar; pool (outdoor); room service. *In room:* A/C, TV, hair dryer, minibar, Wi-Fi (13€).

WHERE TO DINE
Expensive

Chez Fonfon ★ (Finds) PROVENÇALE/FRENCH   This is one of the legendary restaurants of Marseille, with a clientele of famous actors that included John Wayne and Yves Montand in the 1950s and 1960s, and a bevy of newer, mostly French stars during the late 1990s. Its founder, a formidable but funny chef named Fonfon, died in 1998, and since then, the place has been capably handled by his great-nephew, Alexandre Pinna. The location directly fronts the Port du Vallon des Auffes, a harbor for fishing boats that's within a 20-minute walk east of the more famous Vieux Port. The decor is inspired by the furnishings and colors of the midsummer Provençal landscape, and the cuisine has an earthy, savory quality that many Marseillais remember from their childhoods. Examples include a savory bouillabaisse; all kinds of fish, sometimes grilled, sometimes baked in a salt crust and served on a slab of hot stone; and different variations of Provençal lamb. Starters include fish soup, a medley of stuffed vegetables (*les petits farcis*), and fresh baby octopus, either grilled or fried.

140 rue du Vallon des Auffes, Port du Vallon des Auffes. ☎ **04-91-52-14-38.** www.chez-fonfon.com. Reservations recommended. Main courses 26€–47€; fixed-price menus 42€–55€. AE, DC, MC, V. Tues–Sat noon–1:45pm; Mon–Sat 7:15–9:45pm. Closed 2 weeks in Jan. Métro: Vieux Port.

L'Epuisette ★ PROVENÇALE/MEDITERRANEAN   For your bouillabaisse fix, head for this bluff at the mouth of an inlet in the fishing port of Vallon des Auffes, half a mile from the center of Marseille. Here you can have your bouillabaisse at the old port and understand why Dumas, Zola, and Standhal smacked their lips over this succulent dish. The restaurant, which has been entrancing diners for more than half a century, also has other goodies on the menu, notably gazpacho of zucchini with fresh mint or a ravioli of lobster with a tarragon-perfumed mousse. Monkfish, "the poor man's lobster," comes with young purple flowering artichokes. For dessert, why not the coffee-flavored upside down layer cake with peanut ice cream and an espresso sauce?

Vallon des Auffes, Marseille. ☎ **04-91-52-17-82.** Reservations recommended. www.1-epuisette.com/contact_an.html. Main courses 30€–42€; fixed-price menus 45€, 65€, and 95€. MC, V. Tues–Sat noon–2pm and 7:30–10:30pm. Closed Aug 4–Sept 2.

Le Miramar ★★★ SEAFOOD   Except for Le Petit Nice (p. 201), Le Miramar offers the grandest dining in Marseille, as it is linked to a terrace overlooking Marseille's Notre-Dame-de-la-Garde. Diners sit in a room graced with frescoes of underwater life and big windows that open onto the Vieux Port. Bouillabaisse aficionados flock here to savor what will surely be a culinary highlight of your trip. Actually, it's traditionally two dishes, a saffron-tinted soup followed by the fish poached in the soup. It's eaten with *une rouille*, a sauce of red chilies, garlic, olive oil, egg yolk, and cayenne. The version served here involves lots of labor and just as much seafood.

12 quai du Port. ☎ **04-91-91-10-40.** www.bouillabaisse.com. Reservations recommended. Main courses 31€–48€; bouillabaisse from 58€ per person (minimum 2). AE, DC, MC, V. Tues–Sat noon–2:30pm and 7–9:30pm. Métro: Vieux Port.

Michel-Brasserie des Catalans ★ SEAFOOD   Although it's decorated with shel-lacked lobsters and starfish, this restaurant established in 1946 serves a fine bouillabaisse. Just beyond the Parc du Pharo, next to the Old Port, it's one of the best old-time restau-rants in town. The cooking emphasizes the taste of the seafood rather than fancy sauces. In addition to the bouillabaisse, it offers a good *bourride* (fish stew with aioli sauce). The waiter brings you an array of fresh fish from which you make your selection. The atmo-sphere is appealingly insouciant.

6 rue des Catalans. ✆ **04-91-52-30-63.** Reservations recommended. Main courses 33€–55€. AE, MC, V. Daily noon–1:30pm and 8–9:30pm. Bus: 81 or 83.

Une Table au Sud ★★★ MODERN PROVENÇALE   One floor above street level, in a modern dining room with views of the Vieux Port, this restaurant serves the most creative cuisine in Marseille. The historically important 19th-century building has sculpted lion heads embellishing its facade. Chef de cuisine Lionel Levy and his wife, Florence, the *maître d'hôtel,* are the creative forces here. Their cuisine changes daily according to the ingredients available at local markets. Menu items include a creamy soup made from chestnuts and sea urchins, and a thick slice of a local saltwater fish known as *denti* served with flap mushrooms and chicken stock; mullet served with saf-fron and herb risotto; and roasted squab with arabica coffee–flavored juices. Depending on the mood of the chef, desserts may include pineapple *dacquoise* (stacked meringue dessert) served with vanilla-flavored whipped cream.

1 quai du Port. ✆ **04-91-90-63-53.** www.unetableausud.com. Reservations recommended. Fixed-price lunch 37€–47€; fixed-price dinner 52€–105€. AE, MC, V. Tues–Thurs noon–2pm and 7:30–10:30pm; Fri-Sat noon–2pm and 7:30pm–midnight. Closed Aug and Dec 21–26. Métro: Vieux Port.

Moderate

Le Massena SEAFOOD   The atmosphere is rough-edged but civil at this bustling Marseille-style brasserie. A red-and-white color scheme, views of a fountain through large windows, and the bustling square outside contribute to an exotic, savory experience care-fully tuned to the rhythms of this port city. Fast-talking, local staff take orders for dishes that include a well-flavored version of *bourride* (garlic-flavored fish soup); bouillabaisse (the most expensive main course on the menu); *gigot de lotte* (monkfish stewed in cream sauce with fresh vegetables); platters of grilled fish served simply, perhaps with lemon sauce; and scallops cooked with morels.

19 place Castellane. ✆ **04-91-78-18-10.** Reservations recommended. Main courses 8€–35€; set-price menu 18€. MC, V. Mon–Sat noon–3pm and 7–11pm. Métro: Catellane.

Le Ruhl ★★ **Finds** SEAFOOD   Since 1940, this restaurant has offered two versions of bouillabaisse that continue to wow gastronomes. Set about 3km (2 miles) east of the Vieux Port, across the boulevard from a rocky stretch of seacoast, it offers two blue-and-white dining rooms, lots of varnished mahogany and polished brass, and seats that never come without some kind of sea view. Alex Galligani, the owner, once drafted the *Charte de la Bouillabaisse Marseillaise,* which stipulates that a proper bouillabaisse must contain at least four types of fish, which may include gurnard, John Dory, anglerfish, chapon, conger, and scorpion fish. All of these are present within the standard-issue *bouillabaisse de pecheur* served here; the *bouillabaisse homard* has chunks of lobster meat as well. The other distinctive specialty of this place is grilled fish, almost every kind that lives in the Mediterranean; a display of the raw ingredients greets you near the restaurant's entrance.

269 Corniche Président-J.-F.-Kennedy. ✆ **04-91-52-01-77.** www.bouillabaissemarseille.com. Reservations recommended. Main courses 19€–28€; bouillabaisse 45€. MC, V. Daily noon–2:30pm and 8–10pm. Métro: Vieux Port, then take bus for 3km (2 miles) east.

Les Arcenaulx ★ (Finds) PROVENÇALE   This architectural oddity serves memorable cuisine. The navies of Louis XIV built these stone warehouses near the Vieux Port; today they house this restaurant and two bookstores, all run by the charming sisters Simone and Jeanne Laffitte. Their *provençale* cuisine comes with a Marseillais accent: roasted pigeon or duckling with caramelized quince; roasted scallops with hearts of violet artichokes; *daurade* (bream) roasted whole "on its skin"; and filet of beef *rossini*, layered with foie gras. Equally tempting are artichokes *barigoule* (loaded with aromatic spices and olive oil) and a worthy assortment of *petites légumes farcies* (Provençal vegetables stuffed with chopped meat and herbs).

25 cours d'Estienne d'Orves. ✆ **04-91-59-80-30.** www.jeanne-lafitte.com. Reservations recommended. Main courses 18€–34€; fixed-price menu 27€–55€. AE, DC, MC, V. Mon–Sat noon–2pm and 8–11pm. Closed Aug 15–22 and Dec 27–Jan 3. Métro: Vieux Port.

Le Ventre de l'Architect FRENCH   With a westward-facing view of the sea and the setting sun, this restaurant lies in a building designed by Le Corbusier between 1952 and 1954, and considered at that time one of the most revolutionary designs in Europe. You'll benefit from both an architecturally historic setting and menu items which are creative, imaginative, and—if you understand a bit of French—described in ways that would have pleased a 19th-century Impressionistic poet. Examples include cream of pumpkin soup; a "pillow" of foie gras "draped" with slices of Serrano ham; a "waltz" of jumbo shrimp with scallops, served with pink risotto; beef medallions "rolled together" with cured ham and served with "herbs from the chef's garden"; and veal chops with braised endives and a purée of violets.

In the Hôtel Le Corbusier (p. 202), on the 3rd floor of "La Cité Radieuse," 280 bd. Michelet. ✆ **04-91-16-78-23.** Main courses 28€–33€; fixed-price lunch 28€; fixed-price dinner 50€. DC, MC, V. Tues–Sat noon–2pm and 8–11pm. Bus: 21.

Toinou SEAFOOD   In a massive building overshadowing every other structure nearby, this landmark restaurant serves more shellfish than any other restaurant in Marseille. Inside, a display of more than 40 species of shellfish is laid out for inspection by some of the canniest judges of seafood in France—Toinou's customers. Dining rooms are on three floors, served by a waitstaff who are very entrenched in their *Marseillais* accents and demeanors. Don't come here unless you're really fond of shellfish, any species of which can be served raw or cooked. The wine list is extensive, with attractively priced whites from such regions as the Loire Valley.

3 cours St-Louis, 1e. ✆ **04-91-33-14-94.** www.toinou.com. Reservations recommended. Main courses 15€–33€; fixed-price shellfish platter for two 42€. DC, MC, V. Daily 11:30am–11pm. Métro: Vieux Port.

Inexpensive

Chez Angèle PROVENÇALE/PIZZA   A local friend guided us here, and though most of Marseille's cheap eating places aren't recommendable, this one is worthwhile if you're watching your euros. Small and unpretentious, with a raffish kind of amiability on the part of the owner, it's a pizzeria-restaurant, with a menu more comprehensive than usual. Pizzas (the best are pistou, fresh seafood, or crepes), well-prepared ravioli, tagliatelle, and grilled shrimp, squid, and daurade Provençal style are available. For

something really ethnic, ask for Francis's version of *pieds et paquets,* a country recipe **207**
savored by locals—equal portions of grilled sheep's foot and sheep's intestines stuffed
with garlic-flavored bread crumbs, herbs, and chopped vegetables. Note that this place
lies on the route between Marseille and Aix.

50 rue Caisserie. ✆ **04-91-90-63-35.** Reservations recommended. Pizzas, pastas, and salads 9.50€–27€;
fixed-price menu 13€–19€. MC, V. Mon–Sat noon–2:30pm; Sun–Fri 7:30–11:30pm. Closed July 20–Aug 20.
Métro: Vieux Port.

La Kahena TUNISIAN   This is one of the busiest and most-respected Tunisian restaurants in a city loaded with worthy competitors. Established in 1976 and set close to
the Vieux Port, it's an enclave of savory North African aromas: minced or grilled lamb,
tomatoes, eggplant, herbs, and couscous, so beloved by Tunisian expatriates. The menu
lists 10 varieties of couscous, including versions with lamb, chicken, fish, the savory
sausages known as *merguez,* and a "complete" version that includes a little bit of each of
those ingredients. Also look for *méchouia,* a succulent version of roasted lamb. The restaurant's name, incidentally, derives from a 6th-century-B.C. Tunisian princess who was
legendary for uniting all the Berber tribes of North Africa.

2 rue de la République. ✆ **04-91-90-61-93.** Reservations recommended. Main courses 9€–16€. MC, V.
Daily noon–2:30pm and 7:30–11pm. Métro: Vieux Port.

Le Comptoir des Favouilles PROVENÇALE   On the opposite side of the building
from Les Arcenaulx (p. 206), this restaurant occupies a former dorm for prisoners who
were forced to row the ornamental barges of Louis XIV during his inspections of Marseille's harbor. Today, it contains chandeliers, plush carpets, antiques, massive rocks and
thick beams. You'll get a lot for your money; prices are relatively reasonable and ingredients very fresh. *Provençale* dishes include succulent baked sea wolf prepared as simply as
possible—with herbs and olive oil. Particularly noteworthy is bouillabaisse (which, at
50€ per person is the most expensive main course on the otherwise inexpensive menu),
and a delicious combination of saltwater crayfish with foie gras. Desserts usually include
roasted figs served with sweet dessert wine.

44 rue Sainte. ✆ **04-96-11-03-11.** Reservations recommended. Main courses 12€–19€. AE, DC, MC, V.
Mon–Fri noon–2:30pm; Mon–Sat 7:30–10:30pm. Métro: Vieux Port.

NEARBY ACCOMMODATIONS & DINING

Relais de la Magdeleine ★ (Finds)   In a stone-sided, early-18th-century country
mansion at the foot of the Ste-Baume mountain range, this hotel is surrounded by
large homes, open fields, and woodlands, yet still near the beach. It's not far from the
venerated spot where, according to medieval legend, Mary Magdalene is believed to
have died. The inn has striking architectural details: Note a carving of St. Roch with
his dog above the entrance. The upscale decor features antiques and worthy reproductions. Guest rooms are individually furnished, in Directoire, Provençal, and Louis
styles.

The relais also serves savory meals. Specialties include lamb cooked with Provençal
honey and thyme, and filet of sole Beau with red-wine butter and a fondue of leeks.

Rte. d'Aix, 13420 Gemenos. ✆ **04-42-32-20-16.** Fax 04-42-32-02-26. www.relais-magdeleine.com. 28
units. 120€–170€ double; 200€–220€ suite. AE, MC, V. Free parking. Closed Nov 15–Mar 15. Head east of
Marseille for 24km (15 miles) along A50. **Amenities:** Restaurant; bar; nearby golf & tennis; pool (outdoor).
In room: A/C, TV, hair dryer, Internet (free).

PROVENCE

6

MARSEILLE

For an amusing and relatively harmless exposure to the town's saltiness, walk around the **Vieux Port,** where cafes and restaurants angle their sightlines for the best view of the harbor.

L'Escale Borély, avenue Mendès-France, is a modern-day equivalent of the Vieux Port. It's a waterfront development south of the town center, only 20 minutes away (take bus no. 83 or 19). About a dozen cafes and restaurants of every possible ilk serve many cuisines. They offer views of in-line skaters on the promenade in front and the potential for conversation with friendly strangers, with less likelihood of street crime.

Unless the air-conditioning is powerful, Marseille's dance clubs produce a lot of sweat. Close to Vieux Port, you can dance and drink at the **Metal Café,** 20 rue Fortia (© **04-91-54-03-03**), where 20- to 50-year-olds listen to R&B, house, and techno music recently released in London and Los Angeles. Or try the nearby **Trolley Bus,** 24 quai de Rive-Neuve (© **04-91-54-30-45;** www.letrolley.com), best known for its techno, house, hip-hop, jazz, and salsa.

If you miss free-form modern jazz and don't mind taking your chances in the less-than-savory neighborhood adjacent to the city's rail station (La Gare St-Charles—take a taxi there and back), consider dropping into **La Cité de la Musique** (also known as **La Cave à Jazz**), 4 rue Bernard-du-Bois (© **04-91-39-28-28;** www.citemusique-marseille. com). Other nightlife venues in Marseille evoke Paris, but with lots of extra *méridional* (southern) spice thrown in for flavor. Three Marseillais bars that we found particularly intriguing include **Le Pharaon,** Place de l'Opéra (© **04-91-54-09-89;** Métro: Vieux Port), a cozy enclave of deep sofas and armchairs, and soft lighting. Somewhat more bustling and animated is **l'Exit,** 12 quai de Riveneuve (© **04-91-54-29-43;** Métro: Vieux Port), a bar with a terrace that profits from Marseille's sultry nights and two floors of seething nocturnal energy. And for a bar that prides itself on its wide array of complicated cocktails and tapas, as well as a lot of attractive 30-somethings, consider **l'Interdit,** 9 rue Molière (© **06-22-99-51-25;** Métro: Vieux Port). A place that's loaded with razzmatazz and appealing for both its dance floor and its cabaret acts is **Le Circus,** 5 rue du Chantier (© **04-91-33-77-22;** www.lecircus.fr; Métro: Vieux Port). A fee of 15€ gets you entrance into the overall compound, after which you can visit any aspect of the place (cabaret vs. dance floor) that appeals to you at the time.

The gay scene is Marseille isn't as crowded, or as intriguing as in Nice, but its premier gay bar, the **Get Bar-MP Bar,** 10 rue Beauvau (© **04-91-33-64-79;** www.get-bar.com), benefits from a long history of being the town's gay bar of record. It's open Tuesday to Sunday 7pm to 3am. An equally valid, and equally gay, option is the **New Can Can,** 3–5 rue Sénac (© **04-91-48-59-76;** www.newcancan.com), a broad and sprawling bar-and-disco venue that, at least in Marseille, seems to be everybody's favorite dance-club venue. Technically, the place identifies as mostly gay, but frankly, it gets so many heterosexuals that the gender-specific definitions that dominate many of the town's other nightclubs are—at least here—practically moot. One or another of its subdivisions tends to open nightly at around 8:30pm, with other components of the place going online one by one, until by the weekend, it blossoms into full electronic bloom. It is open Thursday to Sunday 11pm until dawn. Cover charge is free except on Friday and Saturday nights. On Friday it's free until midnight. On Saturday a 15€ entrance is charged.

835km (519 miles) S of Paris; 127km (79 miles) SW of Cannes; 68km (42 miles) E of Marseille

This fortress and modern town is the principal naval base of France: the headquarters of the Mediterranean fleet, with hundreds of sailors wandering the streets. With its beautiful harbor, it's surrounded by hills crowned by forts. A large breakwater protects the port on the east, and the great peninsula of Cap Sicié is on the west. Separated by the breakwater, the outer roads are known as the Grande Rade, and the inner roads are the Petite Rade. On the outskirts is a winter resort colony. Like Marseille, the population of Toulon has grown because of the large influx of people from North Africa, especially French-speaking Algeria, which was once a part of France.

Note that racial tension here has been worsened by the closing of the shipbuilding yards. Tourists face no more particular danger than one would find in any Mediterranean port, be it Barcelona or Genoa. However, caution at night is always advised, especially in the immediate port area.

Park your vehicle underground at place de la Liberté; then go along boulevard des Strasbourg, turning right onto rue Berthelot. This will take you into the pedestrian zone in the core of the old city, centered on the rue d'Alger. This area is filled with shops, hotels, restaurants, and cobblestone streets but can be dangerous at night. The best beach, Plage du Mourillon, is 2km (1¼ miles) east of the heart of town.

ESSENTIALS

GETTING THERE **Trains** arrive from Marseille every 5 to 30 minutes (trip time: 1 hr.); the one-way fare is 13€. Trains also arrive frequently from Nice (trip time: 1 hr., 45 min.) and Cannes (trip time: 80 min.). For information, call *©* **36-35,** or visit **www. voyages-sncf.com**.

Three **buses** per day arrive from Aix-en-Provence (trip time: 1 hr., 15 min.); the fare is about 15€ one-way. For information, call **Sodetrav** (*©* **08-25-00-06-50**). If you're **driving** from Marseille, take A50 east to Toulon. When you arrive, park your car and get around on foot—the Vieille Ville (Old Town) and most attractions are easy to reach.

GETTING AROUND A municipal **bus** system serves the town as well. A bus map is available at the tourist office. Buses depart from the main terminal on Place de l'Europe next to the train station. Intercity bus tickets cost 1.50€. Several companies sell tickets, including **Sodetrav,** 4 bd. Pierre Toesca (*©* **04-93-92-26-41**), located opposite the bus terminal. The office here is open daily 6am to 12:30pm and 2 to 6pm. For information, call **Le Réseau Mistral** at *©* **04-94-03-87-03.**

VISITOR INFORMATION The **Office de Tourisme** is at place Raimu (*©* **04-94-18-53-00;** fax 04-94-24-77-39; www.toulontourisme.com).

EXPLORING THE TOWN

In **Vieux Toulon,** between the harbor and boulevard de Strasbourg (the main axis of town), are many remains of the port's former days. A colorful food market, conducted Tuesday to Sunday from 8am to 1pm, **Le Marché du Cours Lafayette** spills onto the streets around cours Lafayette. Also in old Toulon is the **Cathédrale Ste-Marie-Majeure** (*©* **04-94-92-28-91**), built in the Romanesque style in the 11th and 12th centuries, and expanded in the 17th. The badly lit nave is Gothic; the belfry and facade are from the 18th century. It's open daily from 7:30am to noon and 2:30 to 7pm.

In contrast to the cathedral, tall modern buildings line quai Stalingrad, opening onto **Vieille d'Arse.** On place Puget, look for the *atlantes* **(caryatids),** figures of men used as columns. These figures support a balcony at the **Hôtel de Ville (City Hall)** and are also included in the facade of the naval museum.

Musée de la Marine, place du Ingénieur-Général-Monsenergue (② **04-94-02-02-01**), contains figureheads and ship models. Year-round, it's open daily 10am to 6pm. Closed Tuesday September to June. Admission is 5€ for adults, 3.50€ for students, free for ages 17 and under.

Musée de Toulon, 113 bd. du Maréchal-Leclerc (② **04-94-36-81-00**), displays works from the 16th century to the present, including Provençal and Italian paintings and religious works. The latest acquisitions include New Realism pieces and minimalist art. It's open Tuesday to Sunday noon to 6pm; admission is free.

Panoramas & Views

After you've covered the top attractions, we suggest taking a drive an hour or two before sunset along the **corniche du Mont-Faron.** This scenic boulevard along the lower slopes of Mont Faron affords views of the busy port, the town, the cliffs, and, in the distance, the Mediterranean.

Earlier in the day, consider boarding a **téléphérique,** or funicular (② **04-94-92-68-25**), near the **New Hôtel La Tour Blanche** (see below). It operates Tuesday to Sunday 9:30am to noon and 2 to 6:30pm (closed mid-Nov to Feb 3); the round-trip costs 6.50€ for adults, 4.80€ for children 4 to 10 years old. At the top, enjoy the view and then visit the **Memorial du Débarquement en Provence,** Mont Faron (② **04-94-88-08-09**), which documents the Allied landings in Provence in 1944, among other events. It's open in summer daily 10am to noon and 2 to 4:30pm; from mid-September to June, it's open Tuesday to Sunday 10am to noon and 2 to 4:30pm. Admission is 4€ for adults, 1.60€ for children 8 to 16.

WHERE TO STAY

Hôtel La Corniche An attractive hotel near the town's beaches, with an interior garden, La Corniche offers a pleasant staff and comfortable accommodations. Those at the front have sea views and loggias, and are more expensive. Rooms are decorated in Provençal style. You'll find this place in the neighborhood known as Le Mourillon, a 15-minute walk from the congested commercial center of Toulon.

17 Littoral Frédéric-Mistral (at Le Mourillon), 83000 Toulon. ② **800/528-1234** in the U.S., or 04-94-41-35-12. Fax 04-94-41-24-58. www.hotel-corniche.com. 23 units. 80€–150€ double; 150€–250€ junior suite. AE, DC, MC, V. Parking 12€. **Amenities:** Bar; room service. *In room:* A/C, TV, hair dryer, Internet (free), minibar.

New Hôtel La Tour Blanche With excellent accommodations, terraced gardens, and a pool, this 1970s hotel is one of the best in Toulon. It lies in the hills about 1.5km (1 mile) north of the center of town, which gives it sweeping views of the port and sea even from the lower floors. Many rooms, especially those overlooking the bay, have balconies. All are comfortably and simply outfitted in international modern style. The compact bathrooms have showers, but only half have tub/shower combinations. Some units have dataports. The restaurant, Les Terrasses, has a panoramic view.

Bd. de l'Amiral-Vence, Mont Faron, 83000 Toulon. ② **04-94-24-41-57.** Fax 04-94-22-42-25. www.new-hotel.com. 75 units. 90€–125€ double. AE, DC, MC, V. Free parking. Bus: 40. From the town center, follow signs to the Mont Faron téléphérique, and you'll pass the hotel en route. **Amenities:** Restaurant; bar; pool (outdoor); room service. *In room:* A/C, TV, hair dryer, Wi-Fi (9.90€).

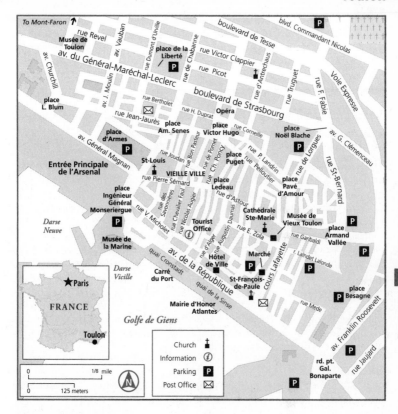

To Mont-Faron ↑
Musée de Toulon
rue Revel
av. Vauban
rue Dumont d'Urville
place de la Liberté
rue de Chabanne
boulevard de Tesse
blvd. Commandant Nicolas
rue Victor Clappier
rue d'Antrechaus
rue Picot
Voie Express
av. du Général-Maréchal-Leclerc
av. Churchill
av. J. Moulin
rue Bertholet
place L. Blum
boulevard de Strasbourg
rue F. Fabié
rue Truquet
rue Jean-Jaurès
rue H. Duprat
Opéra
place Am. Senes
place Victor Hugo
rue Corneille
place Noël Blache
av. G. Clémenceau
place d'Armes
av. Général Magnan
rue Joudan
rue Bon Pasteur
rue de Pomet
place Puget
rue P. Landrin
rue Pelloutier
rue de Lorgues
rue St-Bernard
St-Louis
VIEILLE VILLE
rue Ch. Poncy
place Ledeau
place Pavé d'Amour
Entrée Principale de l'Arsenal
rue Pierre Sémard
rue des Savonnières
rue Chevalier Paul
rue Nicolas Aujier
rue d'Astour
place Ingénieur Général Monseriergue
rue V. Micholet
rue Augustin Daumas
Cathédrale Ste-Marie
Musée de Vieux Toulon
place Armand Vallée
Darse Neuve
Musée de la Marine
quai Cronstadt
Tourist Office
rue d'Alger
rue E. Zola
rue Garibaldi
r. Laindet Lalonde
Darse Vieille
Carré du Port
Hôtel de Ville
Marché
cours Lafayette
Paris
FRANCE
Toulon
av. de la République
quai de la Sinse
St-François-de-Paule
place Besagne
Golfe de Giens
Mairie d'Honor Atlantes
rue Mede
av. Franklin Roosevelt
Church †
Information ⓘ
Parking P
Post Office ✉
0   1/8 mile
0   125 meters
rd. pt. Gal. Bonaparte
rue Jaujard

PROVENCE
6
TOULON

WHERE TO DINE

L'Arbre Rouge ★ SOUTHERN FRENCH   The cuisine here is memorable, and the restaurant is the finest for miles. It's in the town center, in a nondescript building whose thick walls hint at its age. The menu changes with the seasons but might include foie gras of duckling with salty caramel sauce; eggplant with roasted lamb served with coriander sauce; and a dessert confection consisting of semi-baked, ultra-moist chocolate cake with mint-flavored cream sauce. The fixed-price menu includes a choice of three appetizers, three main courses, and three desserts.

25 rue Denfert-Rochereau. ✆ **04-94-92-28-58.** Reservations recommended. Main courses 14€–22€; fixed-price menu 21€–29€. AE, MC, V. Mon–Fri noon–2:30pm; Fri–Sat 7:15–9:30pm. Closed first 2 weeks of Sept. Bus: 1 or 21.

TOULON AFTER DARK

The temporary home of thousands of sailors is bound to have a nightlife scene that's earthier, and a bit raunchier, than those of equivalent-size towns elsewhere. A rough-and-ready bar for stiff drinks, live music, and a complete lack of pretension is **Le Bar 113,** 113 av. de Infanterie de la Marine (✆ **04-94-03-42-41**). At **Bar à Thym,** 32 bd. Cuneo

(© **04-94-41-90-10**), everybody enjoys drinking beer, gossiping, and listening to live music.

Toulon is also home to one of the region's best-known gay discos, **Boy's Paradise,** 1 bd. Pierre-Toesca (© **04-94-09-35-90;** www.boysparadise83.com), near the train station. Adjacent to the port is the gay **Bar La Lampa,** Port de Toulon (© **04-94-03-06-09**), where tapas and live music accompany lots of beer and wine or whiskey.

---

15 HYERES ★

852km (529 miles) S of Paris; 100km (62 miles) SE of Aix-en-Provence; 122km (76 miles) SW of Cannes; 18km (11 miles) E of Toulon

The broad avenues of Hyères, shaded by date palms, still evoke the lazy Belle Epoque. The full name of the town is Hyères-les-Palmier, as it is known for its production of palm trees. Believe it or not, many of these trees are exported to the Middle East.

Hyères is the oldest resort along the Côte d'Azur, having once been frequented by the likes of Queen Victoria, Napoleon, Leo Tolstoy, and Robert Louis Stevenson. It was particularly popular with the British before 1939. It has changed so little from its heyday that many French film directors, including Jean-Luc Godard *(Pierrot le Fou)* and François Truffaut, who shot his last film here (*Vivement Dimanche,* released as *Confidentially Yours* in the U.S.), have used it as locations for period pieces. Today it lives off its past glory and its memories.

As a visitor, you'll find the most interesting section of Hyères to be the Vieille Ville, which lies 5km (3 miles) inland from the sea on a hill. Try to arrive early to attend a bustling morning market around place Massillon. The more modern town and the nucleus of the 19th-century resort stretch toward the sea.

ESSENTIALS

GETTING THERE **Flights** from Paris arrive at the Toulon-Hyères airport, which lies between the town center and the beach. For flights, call © **04-42-14-14-14.** Rail connections are fairly easy, as Hyères lies on the main Nice-Lyon-Paris line. Nine local **trains** a day connect Hyères with Toulon; a one-way ticket costs 8.50€. For information, call © **36-35,** or visit **www.voyages-sncf.com.**

Buses for Hyères depart Place de l'Europe in Toulon, Monday to Saturday only; the trip takes 40 minutes. Bus information is available from **Sodetrav** (© **04-93-92-26-41**) at 4 bd. Pierre Toesca, opposite the bus terminal in Toulon. Hyères does not have a bus station, only a bus stop.

If you're **driving,** A5 goes through Toulon to Marseille and points north and west; A57 goes northeast to join A8, the autoroute between Nice and Aix-en-Provence.

VISITOR INFORMATION Contact the **Office de Tourisme,** 3 av. Ambroise Thomas, Hyères (© **04-94-01-84-50;** www.hyeres-tourisme.com), or the **Office de Tourisme,** place Raimu, Toulon (© **04-94-18-53-00;** www.toulontourisme.com).

EXPLORING THE AREA

The land lying between the city and the sea is unattractive, and the beaches are a bit polluted; but swimming is possible, notably at **Hyères-Plage. Port d'Hyères** has a yacht marina. We find the parks and old town more interesting than the beachfront.

Heading into town from the beach, go along the wide **avenue Gambetta** shaded by double rows of palms. At the end of Gambetta, continue along rue Rabaton to **place Massillon,** the beginning of the Old Town and the site of many good terrace cafe-restaurants. The daily market also takes place here. The 12th-century **Tour St-Blaise,** which stands on the square, was once a command post of the Knights Templar.

Above place Massillon is a warren of intriguing old streets climbing the hillside. Many are cobblestoned and bordered by stone walls, with an abundance of flowers in summer. Look for the medieval arched *portes.* Most of the Vieille Ville houses have been restored, often painted in lovely pastels with contrasting shutters and doors.

Parts of the 12th-century ramparts have survived, although most of them have been torn down. All that remains of the south "curtain wall" are **Porte-St-Paul,** next to the Collegiate Church, and **Porte Baruc.** A trio of lovely old towers has survived from the north curtain wall.

Steep, narrow streets lead up behind Tour St-Blaise to the 18th-century **Le Collegiale St-Paul,** place St-Paul (© **04-94-01-84-50**). In the Romanesque narthex are 400 fragments from the Church of Notre-Dame-de-Consolation, destroyed in bombing raids in 1944. The Gothic nave dates from the 15th and 16th centuries. The church is flanked by an elegant turreted Renaissance house constructed above one of the medieval city gates. The church is open Wednesday to Monday, April to October from 4 to 7pm. November to March, it is open Wednesday to Sunday, 10am to noon and 2 to 5:30pm.

Artifacts left behind by the Greeks and Romans can be examined at the **Musée Municipal,** place Lefebvre (© **04-94-00-11-30**). The museum is often the venue for special exhibitions. Entrance is free, and it is open Tuesday and Friday 2 to 6pm; Wednesday and Saturday 10am to 6pm, and Thursday 1 to 7pm.

The main attraction of the town is **Parc St-Bernard,** on the hill above Hyères. It is open year-round daily from 8am to 6:30pm. To reach the park, go up rue Saint Esprit to where it becomes rue Barbacane. Charles and Marie-Laure de Noailles, great patrons of the arts, commissioned a modern cubist-style villa here in 1924 and brought in garden designer Gabriel Guevrekian, who created an extensive garden in the shape of an isosceles triangle, pointing away from the end of the villa. The Noailles played a role in nurturing the avant-garde artists of the Jazz Age, including F. Scott Fitzgerald. Edith Wharton was a devoted friend of the family. The villa is currently being restored, but you can visit the terraced gardens and relax on benches shaded by olive trees and pines. Above in the villa, in a separate compound of its own, are the ruins of **Château d'Hyères,** above the medieval Old Town. Signposts and arrows lead visitors on a self-guided walk through the ruins, which have unrestricted access.

WHERE TO STAY

Hôtel du Soleil   The foundations of this hotel date from the 11th century, when they were lodgings for the guards who defended the once-formidable fortress of Hyères. What you'll see, however, dates from around 1900—a boxy-looking *bastide* (masonry building) atop the old foundations. Over the years, a sheathing of ivy has softened the angles a bit, and the interior has been kept up to date with frequent modernizations. Bedrooms are cozy, if somewhat small, with Provençal furniture and casement windows; from the back are views of the sea, and in front are views of upscale villas on a nearby hill. Breakfast is the only meal served, although several places to eat (including the Bistrot de Marius, below) lie within a 3-minute walk.

Rue du Rempart (place Clemenceau), 83400 Hyères. © **04-94-65-16-26.** Fax 04-94-35-46-00. www.hotel dusoleil.com. 22 units. 50€–120€ double. AE, DC, MC, V. **Amenities:** Breakfast room. *In room:* TV, Wi-Fi (free).

Ibis Thallassa   This hotel is located between the coastal road and the beach, on the eastern edge of the land bridge that stretches between the French mainland and the Gien peninsula. Designed in a horseshoe shape, with the open end of the U facing the beach, the hotel places emphasis on resort life. Guest rooms are decent-size and decorated in a standardized format that includes one double bed and one single bed, a writing table, and a soothing color scheme of blue-gray. Bathrooms are motel standard, with tidy maintenance. Another Ibis hotel is located downtown.

Allée de la Mer, La Capte, 83400 Hyères-Plage. ✆ **04-94-58-00-94.** Fax 04-94-58-09-35. www.accou thalassa.com. 95 units. 75€–139€ double. AE, DC, MC, V. **Amenities:** Restaurant; bar; health club & spa; pool (outdoor). *In room:* A/C, TV, hair dryer, Wi-Fi (free).

WHERE TO DINE

Bistrot de Marius PROVENÇALE/SEAFOOD   Set almost adjacent to the Tour des Templiers, this restaurant dates from 1906, when it was established in a building whose foundations date from the 13th century. Its trio of dining rooms (one is upstairs) has exposed stone and paneling, and a sense of historical charm. Fish, especially grilled sea bass, monkfish, dorado, and tuna, are specialties here, along with mussels and oysters. Sauce choices include *marchand de vin* (a red wine–based sauce), and lemon-butter and basil-flavored vinaigrette. A succulent version of bouillabaisse, priced at 44€, is a meal in itself, although you can also choose from a limited selection of chicken, veal, and beef.

1 place Massillon. ✆ **04-94-35-88-38.** Reservations recommended. Main courses 13€–24€; fixed-price menus 19€–32€. AE, DC, MC, V. Wed–Sun noon–2pm and 7–10pm (daily July–Aug). Closed Nov 15–Dec 15 and last 2 weeks of Jan.

Le Jardin MODERN MEDITERRANEAN   Set directly across the street from the Town Hall *(Mairie)* of Hyère, this restaurant takes gardening, and its name, seriously. During most of the year, the retractable roof, a motorized contraption of folding plastic panels, remains open to night breezes, as doors and windows and outdoor tables show-case the venerable plantings of a mature garden ringed with crab apple, orange, and palm trees. The London-trained owner, Mr. Cheval, speaks perfect English, and welcomes a young and young-at-heart crowd who keep the place convivial. The menu derives from the northern and southern edges of the Mediterranean, and can include a salad of grilled scallops with ginger; a platter of *crudités* accessorized with both anchovy paste and a tapenade of olives; a genuinely wonderful version of octopus stew cooked in red wine *(daube de pulpe);* a tagine of the day (during our visit, it featured roasted lamb with prunes, slow-cooked in a clay pot in the Moroccan style); and a grilled filet of bluefin tuna served with wasabi-flavored mashed potatoes.

19 av. Joseph Clotis. ✆ **04-94-35-24-12.** Reservations recommended. Main courses 9€–22€. AE, MC, V. Mon–Thurs noon–2:30pm; Fri–Sat noon–11pm. Closed Dec 15–Jan 24.

16 ILES D'HYERES ★

39km (24 miles) SE of Toulon; 119km (74 miles) SW of Cannes

Off the Riviera in the Mediterranean is a little group of islands enclosing the southern boundary of the Hyères anchorage. During the Renaissance they were called the Iles d'Or, from the golden glow sometimes given off by the rocks in the sunlight. Nothing in the islands today will remind you of the turbulent time when they were attacked by pirates and Turkish galleys, or even of the Allied landings here in World War II.

Mass tourism has arrived on these sun-baked islands, with some of the tackiness that goes with it. Cars are forbidden on all three major islands, and vehicles cannot be transported on any of the ferryboats. Expect a summer holiday spirit not unlike a Gallic version of Nantucket, with thousands of midsummer day-trippers arriving, often with children, for a day of sun, sand, and people-watching.

Which island is the most appealing? Ile des Porquerolles is the most beautiful. Thinking of heading to Le Levant? You might want to steer clear—only 25% of the island is accessible to visitors, as three-quarters of it belongs to the French army, and it is used frequently for testing missiles.

Note: Héliopolis, a section of Ile du Levant, is home to the oldest nudist colony in Europe. Islanders and visitors go *au naturel* on the beaches. Many of the more daring visitors also don't wear a lot of clothing in the village.

ESSENTIALS

GETTING TO ILE DE PORQUEROLLES   Ferryboats leave from several points along the Côte d'Azur. The most frequent, convenient, and shortest trip is from La Tour Fondue on the peninsula of Giens, a 32km (20-mile) drive east of Toulon. Depending on the season, there are 4 to 20 departures a day. The round-trip fare for the 15-minute crossing is 16€ or 14€ for ages 4 to 10. For information, call the **Transports Maritimes et Terrestres du Littoral Varois,** La Tour Fondue, 83400 Giens (© **04-94-58-21-81**). The next-best option is the ferryboat from Toulon, but only between June and September. Other options, each of them also available only between June and September, involve taking one of the ferries maintained by the **Compagnie Maritime des Vedettes Ile d'Or & Le Corsaire** (© **04-94-71-01-02**). Their ferryboats offer crossings from either of *Les Gares Maritimes* in Le Lavandou and Cavalaire.

On any of the venues noted above, round-trip fares to the Ile de Porquerolles cost 32€ for adults and 25€ for children 4 to 11.

GETTING TO ILE DE PORT-CROS   The most popular ferry route to the island is the 35-minute crossing that departs from Hyères between four and seven times daily, depending on the season. (Oct–Mar, there are only three crossings per week.) For information, contact the **Compagnie Maritime des Vedettes** (© **04-94-71-01-02**). Round-trip fares cost 25€ for adults and 21€ for children 4 to 11. The same company, for approximately the same price, also offers crossings to Port-Cros from Cavalaire, but only between April and September. For no additional fee, vessels will drop passengers at the military installations at Le Levant.

VISITOR INFORMATION   Other than temporary, summer-only kiosks without phones that distribute brochures and advice near the ferry docks in Porquerolles and Port-Cros, the islands do not operate tourist bureaus. The offices in Hyères and Toulon try to fill in the gaps. Contact the **Office de Tourisme,** 3 av. Ambroise Thomas, Hyères (© **04-94-01-84-50**), or the **Office de Tourisme,** place Raimu, Toulon (© **04-94-18-53-00**).

ILE DE PORQUEROLLES ★

This is the largest and westernmost of the Iles d'Hyères. It has a rugged south coast, but the north strand, facing the mainland, is made up of sandy beaches bordered by heather, scented myrtles, and pine trees. The island is about 8km (5 miles) long and 2km (1¼ miles) wide, and is 5km (3 miles) from the mainland.

The population is only 400. The island is said to receive 275 days of sunshine annually. It's a land of rocky capes, pine forests twisted by the mistral, sun-drenched vineyards, and pale-ocher houses. The "hot spots," if any, are the cafes around **place d'Armes** where everybody gathers.

The island has had a violent history of raids, attacks, and occupation by everybody from the Dutch, English, and Turks to the Spaniards. Ten forts, some in ruins, testify to a violent past. The most ancient is **Fort Ste-Agathe,** built in 1531 by François I. In time it was a penal colony and a retirement center for soldiers of the colonial wars.

The French government in 1971 purchased the largest hunk of the island and turned it into a national park and botanical garden.

Where to Stay & Dine

Hotel et Residence Les Medes ★ In the center of the village is this tranquil choice set in a large private garden with a sun deck. Well-furnished rooms, studios, and apartments are suitable for two to four guests; each is provided with a kitchenette. Many of the accommodations contain bunk beds for children. The more desirable units open onto private terraces with a view. The location is 400m (1,312 ft.) from Courtade Beach and only a short walk from the wharf. Guests gather in the lounge with its bar, fireplace, library, and public Internet. Main courses in the restaurant range from 16€ to 23€ and include *provençale* food and international specialties such as rabbit with chocolate, various fresh fish, and a spicy tagine Moroccan style. The chefs even offer kangaroo meat from Australia.

2 rue de la Douane, 83400 Porquerolles. ✆ **04-94-12-41-24.** Fax 04-94-58-32-49. www.hotel-les-medes. fr. 30 units. 96€–379€ double. MC, V. Closed Nov 8–Dec 26. **Amenities:** Restaurant; bar. *In room:* A/C, TV, phone.

Mas du Langoustier ★★ In a large park on the island's western tip, this tranquil resort hotel is an old *mas* with a view of a lovely pine-ringed bay. Employees greet guests in a covered wagon by the jetty. Guest rooms done in antique Provençal style are the most elegantly decorated on the island. Should you visit for a meal, the menu is the finest in the Hyère islands, offering mainly seafood in a light nouvelle style. Try *loup* (wolf fish) with Noilly Prat in puff pastry, or tender kid with dried tomatoes roasted in casserole. You can drink and dine on the terraces.

83400 Porquerolles. ✆ **04-94-58-30-09.** Fax 04-94-58-36-02. www.langoustier.com. 50 units. 179€–264€ double; 269€–314€ suite. Rates include half-board. MC, V. Closed late Sept to late Apr. **Amenities:** 2 restaurants; bar; pool (outdoor); room service. *In room:* A/C, TV, minibar.

ILE DE PORT-CROS ★

Lush subtropical vegetation reminiscent of the Caribbean makes this a green paradise, 5km (3 miles) long and 2km (1¼ miles) wide. The most mountainous of the archipelago, Port-Cros has been a French national park since 1963. A fire in 1892 devastated the island, which now abounds with pine forests and ilexes. Birders flock here to observe nearly 100 different species. Day-trippers can explore the many marked trails. The most popular and scenic is *sentier botanique;* the more adventurous and athletic take the 10km (6-mile) *circuit historique* (bring a packed lunch). Divers follow a 274m (900-ft.) trail from Plage de la Palud to the islet of Rascas, where a plastic guide sheet identifies the underwater flora. Thousands of pleasure craft call here annually, which does little to help the island's fragile environment.

Le Manoir ★   This is the only bona fide hotel on the island, but despite lack of competition, its owners work hard to make their guests as comfortable as possible. Originally, it functioned as the grandiose home of the family that owned the entire island. Today, the hotel consists of an 18th-century architectural core, plus an annex that contains most of the guest rooms. Accommodations are simple, and bathrooms come equipped with tub/shower combinations. Some rooms have air-conditioning. The restaurant serves lobster-and-fish terrine, several seasoned meats, and fresh local fish with baby vegetables, as well as regional goat cheese and velvety mousses. A fixed-price menu costs 54€.

83400 Ile de Port-Cros. (✆ **04-94-05-90-52.** Fax 04-94-05-90-89. lemanoir.portcros@wanadoo.fr. 22 units. 160€–200€ double; 190€–225€ suite. MC, V. Closed Oct–Apr. **Amenities:** Restaurant; bar; pool (outdoor); room service. *In room:* A/C, hair dryer.

---

17 GRAND CANYON DU VERDON ★

Trigance: 72km (45 miles) S of Digne-les-Bains, 20km (12 miles) W of Castellane, 43km (27 miles) NW of Draguignan, 85km (53 miles) E of Manosque; La-Palud-sur-Verdon: 64km (40 miles) S of Digne-les-Bains, 25km (16 miles) W of Castellane, 60km (37 miles) NW of Draguignan, 66km (41 miles) E of Manosque

Over the centuries, the Verdon River, a tributary of the Durance, has cut Europe's biggest canyon into the surrounding limestone plateau. The canyon runs from pont de Soleils to Lac Ste-Croix, a distance of 21km (13 miles) east to west. The upper section of the gorge, to the east, is between 210 and 1,605m (700–5,350 ft.) wide; the lower section narrows to between 6 and 105m (20–350 ft.). The gorge's depth varies from 263m (875 ft.) at one point to 750m (2,500 ft.).

Vertiginous roads wind along both rims of the canyon, giving you the opportunity to pull over at any of several scenic belvederes. Among the best of these is the Balcon de la Mescla, the first stop traveling west from Trigance on the canyon's south side, where the sheer cliffs drop 270m (900 ft.) to the river. A short distance away is Falaise de Cavaliers (Horseman's Cliff), dropping 323m (1,075 ft.) and signaling the beginning of the Corniche Sublime, where the gorge plunges to 428m (1,425 ft.) along a stretch running west to Aiguines. In between these scenic stops, you can actually drive across the canyon on the dramatic pont de l'Artuby, a single-arched, 120m-long (400-ft.) span, 638m (2,125 ft.) above the river.

Ancient villages cling to rocky outcroppings along the two rim roads. At Aiguines, a private castle flanked by four turrets dominates the skyline. On Route 19, 9km (5½ miles) north of the canyon on its western end, sits Moustiers-Ste-Marie, a medieval village of potters who sell their wares—but beware, prices here are celestial, especially in July and August, when tourist dollars are easy to come by.

ESSENTIALS

GETTING THERE   From the Riviera, follow A85 for 84km (52 miles) northwest from Cannes to Castellane; then take Route 952 west to the intersection with Route 955 and proceed along 955 south to Trigance, about 20km (13 miles). From here, continue south to Route 71, 3km (1¾ miles) away, and take a left to travel west along the southern edge of the canyon. At Les-Salles-sur-Verdon, on the banks of Lac St-Croix, turn right on D957 and drive north, crossing the Verdon where it flows into Lac St-Croix; then, just south of Moustiers-Ste-Marie, turn right again on Route 952 to trace the north side of the canyon back to the east.

VISITOR INFORMATION Information about how best to take advantage of the region's natural beauty and sporting options, as well as information on events, is available from the tourist offices of the three largest settlements in the canyon. They include the Office de Tourisme de Castellane, 04120 Castellane (© **04-92-83-61-14;** www.castellane.org), and the Office de Tourisme de Moustiers Ste-Marie, 04360 Moustiers-Ste-Marie (© **04-92-74-67-84;** www.mousiers.fr). Smaller than either of the other two, and open mostly in midsummer, is the Office de Tourisme d'Esparron, 04800 Esparron (© **04-92-77-15-97**).

EXPLORING THE CANYON

Activities available in the canyon include guided hikes from the **Bureau des Guides,** 04120 La-Palud-sur-Verdon (© **04-92-77-30-50**). Canoeing and kayaking are available through the **Aqua Viva Est,** La Piscine, 04120 Castellane (© **04-92-83-75-74;** www.aquavivaest.com), and the **Club Nautique,** 04800 Esparron (© **04-92-77-15-25**). Rafting trips are conducted by **Acti Raft,** 04120 Castellane (© **04-92-83-76-64**). All three of these organizations operate in full swing between May and early September. The rest of the year, they operate with skeleton staffs, usually via answering machine and fax.

A deservedly popular walk that showcases the area's scenery is a 2-hour round-trip trek launched at the parking lot at Samson Corridor. The route is clearly marked as it bends its way to a tunnel after Point Sublime. Continue your trek to a footbridge spanning the Baou River. After crossing it, go straight ahead through another two tunnels until you reach a belvedere with a panoramic sweep of the Trescare Chaos. For transit through the tunnels, carry along a flashlight.

A more strenuous 6- to 8-hour hike starts at the Chalet de la Maline on the Crest Road and goes for about 15km (9⅓ miles) to Point Sublime. The footpath is marked with arrows. Again, you'll need a flashlight, but this trek is so long that food and water are also recommended. Before heading out, call © **04-92-83-61-62** to make arrangements with the most reliable of the local taxi dispatchers (Taxis Vincent) to arrange for a taxi to pick you up at a designated time after you reach Point Sublime. The cost of such transport by taxi from Port Sublime back to, say, Castellane, is 12€ per person. Be warned in advance that arrangements like this with the local taxi operators are easiest between late May and September. The rest of the year, taxis (and virtually everything else in the region) operates at very low gear.

WHERE TO STAY

Auberge Point-Sublime This hotel offers simple, unpretentious rooms, each with congenially battered, old-fashioned (but not antique) furniture. Bedrooms are small and without particular style, although each has a comfortable mattress, plus a somewhat cramped bathroom. You do get views over the gorge and a convenient location, 2km (1¼ miles) south of the Couloir Samson, the point where many trekkers exit from hikes in the nearby gorge. The restaurant serves *provençale* fixed-price meals. Specialties are civets of both rabbit and lamb, a truffle-studded omelet, and crayfish with truffles. Staff here is unusually bossy, insisting that residents consume at least one meal a day on-site.

04120 Point Sublime, Rougon. © **04-92-83-60-35.** Fax 04-92-83-74-31. 15 units. 61€ double. MC, V. Closed Oct–Mar. From Castellane, drive 19km (12 miles) north toward Moustiers-Ste-Marie; it's beside the road on the distant outskirts of Rougon. **Amenities:** Restaurant; bar. *In room:* TV, Wi-Fi (free).

Bastide de Moustiers ★★★ Very near the Gorges du Verdon, in a village of pottery makers, Alain Ducasse, arguably hailed as the world's greatest chef, has opened an informal inn of charm and grace. The property once belonged to a master potter, and the country house is filled with the celebrated Moustiers earthenware. The inn is surrounded by tree-studded grounds covering 4 hectares (10 acres). Aided by local artisans, the inn has been beautifully restored and each room individually designed. Accommodations are filled with the rewards of Ducasse's antiques-hunting expeditions. Bathrooms are luxurious—one bathroom, for example, was designed by the famous Philippe Starck.

Even if you're not staying here, consider making a reservation for a meal here. The aroma of the flavors of Provence and the Mediterranean emerge from the kitchen, and much homegrown produce is used, including provisions from the inn's own vegetable garden. Fixed-price menus begin at 46€ to 61€.

Chemin de Quinson, 04360 Moustiers Sainte-Marie. (**©** **04-92-70-47-47.** Fax 04-92-70-47-48. www. bastide-moustiers.com. 12 suites. 190€–400€ double. AE, DC, MC, V. **Amenities:** Restaurant; bar; pool (outdoor); room service. *In room:* A/C, TV/DVD, hair dryer, minibar.

Château de Trigance ★   This Relais & Châteaux property is the district's best hotel, rising on a rocky spur above a hamlet of fewer than 120 full-time inhabitants; it occupies the core of a 9th- and 10th-century fortress. Virtually every window has views over the Provençal plain. The rooms contain strong hints of their medieval origins including baldachin-style beds.

The dining room is unusual: Originally used to store weapons, it has a vaulted ceiling that was, in accordance with the era's techniques, built without groins or a central key. A wooden form was constructed and carefully chiseled stones were fitted into position on top. When complete, the form was burned away and the vaulting remained—somewhat precariously until it was shored up with additional mortar. The fare is intensely cultivated: "marbled" foie gras of duckling with artichoke hearts; pressed leeks with smoked salmon, crayfish, and sweet-and-sour sauce; and roasted leg of lamb "en surprise" with a "spaghetti" of zucchini and cream of garlic *en confit.* Menus cost 30€ to 48€. A parking lot near the entrance of the hotel saves you the arduous hike up the medieval-looking steps that were once the only route of access.

83840 Trigance, Var. (**©** **04-94-76-91-18.** Fax 04-94-85-68-99. www.chateau-de-trigance.fr. 10 units. 115€–175€ double; 195€ junior suite. AE, DC, MC, V. Free parking. Closed Nov 1 to early Apr. **Amenities:** Restaurant; bar; room service. *In room:* TV.

Hôtel du Grand Canyon de Verdon ★ (**Finds**)   This is the most charming hotel along the south bank of the Verdon canyon. It's on a rocky outcropping above the precipice, vertiginously close to the edge, and exists only because of the foresight of the grandfather of the present owner. In 1946, on holiday in Provence from his home in the foggy northern French province of Pas de Calais, he fell in love with the site, opened a brasserie, and secured permission to build a hotel here. In 1982, his grandson, Georges Fortini, erected the present two-story hotel. Rooms are simple and small, but comfortable, with light-grained wood and off-white walls. Set on a 4-hectare (10-acre) tract on the Corniche Sublime, the hotel features a glassed-in restaurant overlooking a 322m (1,075-ft.) drop to the canyon bottom.

Falaise des Cavaliers, 83630 Aiguines. (**©** **04-94-76-91-31.** Fax 04-94-76-92-29. 13 units. 120€–130€ double. Rates include half-board. AE, MC, V. Closed Oct to mid-Apr. **Amenities:** Restaurant; bar. *In room:* TV, hair dryer, minibar.

Hôtel Les Gorges du Verdon   This hotel is in the heart of La-Palud-sur-Verdon (pop. 250; altitude 914m/3,000 ft.), about 6km (4 miles) west of the canyon edge. Though you won't be able to see the canyon from the windows, views over the rugged countryside stretch out on virtually every side. The recently upgraded rooms have elaborate curtains that soften their modern angularity. Overall, the rooms aren't exactly plush; but since most guests opt to spend their days in the great outdoors, no one really seems to care. Most rooms have a private terrace or balcony overlooking a scenic landscape. Some are entered from a landing with a staircase leading down into the room, creating a mezzanine effect.

Half-board is obligatory in midsummer. Well-prepared meals include duck thigh stuffed with mushrooms, grilled whole sea bass with anise-flavored butter, and Provençal lamb chops with tarragon-flavored butter sauce.

04120 La-Palud-sur-Verdon. (©) **04-92-77-38-26.** Fax 04-92-77-35-00. www.hotel-du-gorges-de-verdon. fr. 30 units. 135€–180€ double; 225€–370€ suite. MC, V. Free parking. Closed late Oct to Easter. **Amenities:** Restaurant; bar; babysitting; pool (outdoor); room service; steam room; tennis court (lit). *In room:* TV, hair dryer, Wi-Fi (free).

Hôtel Le Vieil Amandier   At the edge of town, this hotel offers clean, uncomplicated guest rooms and a dining room with straightforward but thoughtfully prepared cuisine. Half the rooms face the pool and get southern light; the remainder are just as comfortable but without views. The largest is the rustic and woodsy no. 6; nos. 3 and 4 are more Provençal, and the others are blandly international. Your hosts are Cécile and Bernard Clap (Bernard is the hamlet's mayor). They maintain a pleasant, unpretentious restaurant where lunch and dinner are served daily. Cuisine is artful and flavorful, featuring good value for the money. Menu items include profiteroles of goat cheese with chives and olive oil, duckling with myrtle leaves and garlic, and rack of lamb in puff pastry served with fine-textured ratatouille.

83840 Trigance, Var. (©) **04-94-76-92-92.** Fax 04-94-85-68-65. http://levieilamandier.free.fr. 12 units. 65€–99€ double. AE, DC, MC, V. Free parking. Closed mid-Oct to Apr 1. **Amenities:** Restaurant; bar; pool (outdoor); spa. *In room:* TV, hair dryer, Wi-Fi (free).

WHERE TO DINE

Many of the inns recommended above, are also the finest places to dine—notably the **Château de Trigance.**

Les Santons ★ FRENCH/PROVENÇALE   One of the region's most charming restaurants occupies a stone-sided, 12th-century house adjacent to the village church. The cozy dining room filled with 19th-century paintings and antique pottery holds fewer than 20 seats. A terrace with flowering plants doubles the seating space during clement weather. Examples of the fare include homemade noodles studded with truffles and chunks of foie gras, chicken roasted with lavender-scented honey and Provençal spices, and Sisteron lamb roasted with honey and spices and served with an herb-scented ratatouille and *gratin dauphinoise* (potatoes with grated cheese).

Place de l'Eglise, 04360 Moustiers-Ste-Marie, Alpes-de-Haut-Provence. (©) **04-92-74-66-48.** www. lessantons.com. Reservations recommended. Main courses 15€–23€; fixed-price menus 26€–35€. AE, MC, V. Mon noon–2pm; Wed–Sun noon–2pm and 7:30–9:30pm. Closed Nov–Feb.

7

The Western Riviera: From St-Tropez to Cannes to Cap d'Antibes

The western part of the Côte d'Azur begins at glittering St-Tropez and ends at the even more elegant Cap d'Antibes. In between are mostly middle-class resort towns, such as St-Raphaël, scattered along a coast that also features the wild and desolate landscape of the Massif de l'Estérel.

Ste-Maxime and Fréjus offer some of the area's best budget accommodations, having been taken over by French families in search of a holiday getaway on the once-exclusive coast.

The area does, of course, embrace Cannes, the most famous resort in the region because of the glitz and glamour surrounding its film festival, which overflows into the upscale La Napoule-Plage, home of the Clews Museum.

Inland, the terrain climbs away from the coast to the hillside communities of Grasse, with its perfume distilleries, and Mougins, a charming old village and culinary center that makes for a romantic retreat. Food also lures gastronomes to Golfe-Juan, which features one of the region's best restaurants, Chez Tétou, a stop for a rich bowl of bouillabaisse.

Nightlife is the focus of neighboring Juan-les-Pins, attracting spirited adventurers to its all-night jazz clubs and discos. Nearby Vaullaris hosts Galerie Madoura, a pottery firm with exclusive rights to reproduce Picasso's earthenware designs. Antibes also profits from its association with Picasso by the museum dedicated to his life and work. This largely middle-class resort gives way to Cap d'Antibes, the peninsular resort that's as tony today as when F. Scott Fitzgerald used it as the setting for his novel *Tender Is the Night*.

1 ST-TROPEZ ★★

874km (543 miles) S of Paris; 76km (47 miles) SW of Cannes

Sun-kissed lasciviousness is rampant in this carnival town, but the true Tropezian resents the fact that the port has such a bad reputation. "We can be classy, too," one native has insisted. Creative people in the lively arts along with ordinary folk create a volatile mixture. One observer said that St-Tropez "has replaced Naples for those who accept the principle of dying after seeing it. It's a unique fate for a place to have made its reputation on the certainty of happiness."

St-Tropez—this palimpsest of nostalgia—was popularized by sex symbol Brigitte Bardot in *And God Created Woman*, but it had long since attracted the famous. Colette lived here for many years. Even the late diarist Anaïs Nin, confidante of Henry Miller, posed for a little cheesecake on the beach here in 1939 in a Dorothy Lamour–style bathing suit. Earlier, St-Tropez was visited by Matisse, Signac, and Bonnard, and even Maupassant before he died of syphilis.

Artists, composers, novelists, and the film colony come to St-Tropez in summer. Trailing them is a line of humanity unmatched anywhere else on the Riviera for sheer flamboyance. Chic people anchor their yachts here in summer but disappear long before the dreaded mistral of winter.

In 1995, Bardot pronounced St-Tropez dead—"squatted by a lot of no-goods, drugheads, and villains"—and swore she'd never go back, at least in summer. But 1997 saw her return, as headlines in France flashed the news that St-Tropez was "hot once again." Not only Bardot, but other celebrities have been showing up, including Oprah Winfrey, Don Johnson, Quincy Jones, Barbra Streisand, Jack Nicholson, Robert De Niro, Sean "P. Diddy" Combs, and even Elton and Sly (not together!).

ESSENTIALS

GETTING THERE The nearest rail station is in St-Raphaël, a neighboring resort. At St-Raphaël's Vieux Port, **boats** leave the Gare Maritime de St-Raphaël, rue Pierre-Auble (© **04-94-95-17-46**), for St-Tropez (trip time: 50 min.) on Tuesday and Saturday. The one-way fare is 13€. Year-round, 10 to 15 Sodetrav **buses** per day leave from the Gare Routière in St-Raphaël (© **04-94-97-88-51**) for St-Tropez. The trip takes 1½ to 2¼ hours, depending on the bus and the traffic, which during midsummer is usually horrendous. A one-way ticket costs 12€. Buses run directly to St-Tropez from Toulon and Hyères and from the nearest airport, at Toulon-Hyères, 56km (35 miles) away.

If you **drive,** note that parking in St-Tropez is very difficult, especially in summer. You can park in the **Parking des Lices** (© **04-94-97-34-46**), beneath place des Lices; enter on avenue Paul-Roussel. Designed for 300 cars, this lot charges 2.20€ per hour. A 24-hour sojourn costs 34€ in summer; winter visitors enjoy a slight reduction—to 23€. Many visitors with expensive cars prefer this lot, because it's more secure than any other. Charging the same rates, a new garage, **Parking du Nouveau Port,** avenue Charles de Gaulle (© **04-94-97-40-31**), stands at the waterfront. Every municipal engineer in St-Tropez has worked hard to funnel incoming traffic toward either of these two underground garages. To get here from **Cannes,** drive southwest along the coastal highway, turning east when you see signs pointing to St-Tropez.

VISITOR INFORMATION The **Office de Tourisme** is on quai Jean-Jaurès (© **04-94-97-45-21;** fax 04-94-97-82-66; www.ot-saint-tropez.com).

OUTDOOR PURSUITS
A Day at the Beach

The hottest Riviera beaches are at St-Tropez. The best for families are closest to the center, including the **Plage de la Bouillabaisse** and **Plage des Graniers.** More daring are the 9.5km (6-mile) crescents at **Plage des Salins** and **Plage de Pampelonne,** some 3km (1¾ miles) from the town center. At Pampelonne about 35 businesses are on a 4.8km (3-mile) stretch, located about 10km (6¼ miles) from St-Tropez. The concessionaire that's noted as an all-gay venue is the **Aqua Club,** Plage de Pampelonne (© **04-94-79-84-35;** www.aquaclub.fr). You'll need a car, bike, or scooter to get from town to the beach. Parking is 6€ for the day. Famous hedonistic spots along Pampelonne include the cash-only club **La Voile Rouge** (© **04-94-79-84-34**), which features bawdy spring-break-style entertainment. This is the most outrageous, the sexiest, and the most exhibitionist (not for children) of the beaches of St-Tropez. Also thriving are **Club 55,** 55 bd. Patch, Plage de Pampelonne (© **04-94-55-55-55**), and **Nikki Beach,** Plage de Pampelonne (© **04-94-79-82-04;** www.nikkibeach.com/sttropez). Maintained by an American from Miami, Nikki Beach is

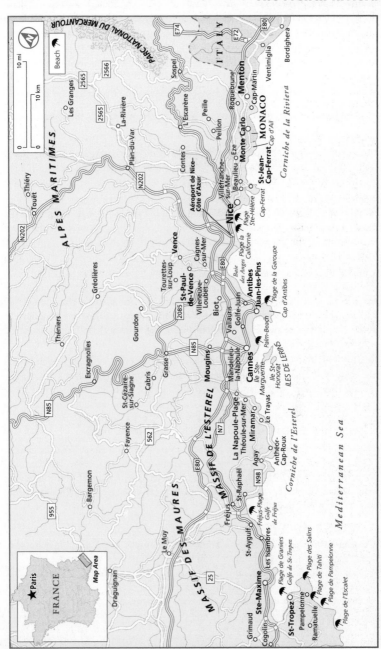

10 mi
10 km

Beach

PARC NATIONAL DU MERCANTOUR

E74
E72
E80

ITALY

Bordighera
Ventimiglia
Menton
Cap-Martin
Roquebrune
Monte Carlo
MONACO
Cap d'Ail
St-Jean-
Cap-Ferrat
Beaulieu
Èze
Villefranche-
sur-Mer
Cap-Ferrat
Corniche de la Riviera

Sospel
2566
L'Escarène
Peille
Peïllon
Contes
Plan-du-Var
La-Rivière
2565
2565
Les Granges
2565
Thiéry
Touët
N202

ALPES MARITIMES

N202

N202

Aéroport de Nice-
Côte d'Azur
Nice
Plage
Ste-Hélène
Plage la
Californie
Baie
des Anges
Plage la
Garoupe
Cap d'Antibes

Théniers

Gréolières

Tourettes-
sur-Loup
Vence
Cagnes-
sur-Mer
St-Paul-
de-Vence
Villeneuve-
Loubet
2085
E80
Biot
Vallauris
Golfe-Juan
Antibes
Juan-les-Pins
Plage de la Garoupe

Gourdon
Escragnolles
Grasse
N85
Mougins
Cannes
Île Ste-
Marguerite
Île St-
Honorat
ÎLES DE LÉRINS
Palm-Beach
Mandelieu-
la-Napoule

Cabris
St-Cézaire-
sur-Siagne
MASSIF DE L'ESTEREL

Fayence
562
N7
La Napoule-Plage
Théoule-sur-Mer
Le Trayas
Miramar
Corniche de l'Esterel

Bargemon
955
E80
St-Raphaël
N98
Agay
Anthéor-
Cap-Roux

Le Muy
Fréjus
Fréjus-Plage
Golfe
de Fréjus

MASSIF DES MAURES

St-Aygulf
Les Issambres
25

Draguignan

Ste-Maxime
Plage de Graniers
Golfe de St-Tropez
Plage des Salins
Plage de Tahiti

Grimaud
Cogolin
St-Tropez
Pampelonne
Ramatuelle
Plage de Pampelonne
Plage de l'Escalet

Mediterranean Sea

Map Area
Paris
FRANCE

wild, frenetic, uninhibited, and about as Floridian a venue as you're likely to find in the south of France. **Plage des Jumeaux** (© **04-94-55-21-80**) is another active beach; it draws many families with young kids because it has playground equipment. **Marine Air Sport** (© **04-94-97-89-19**; www.marine-air-sport.com) rents boats; **Sun Force** (© **04-94-79-90-11**; www.sunforce.fr) rents jet skis, scooters, water-skiing equipment, and boats.

Notoriously decadent **Plage de Tahiti** occupies the north end of the 5.5km-long (3½-mile) Pampelonne, lined with concessions, cafes, and restaurants. It's a strip of golden sand long favored by exhibitionists wearing next to nothing (or nothing) and cruising shamelessly. If you ever wanted to go topless, this is the place to do it. Gay men tend to gravitate to **Coco Beach** in Ramatuelle, about 6.5km (4 miles) from the center of St-Tropez.

Staying Active

BICYCLING & MOTOR-SCOOTERING One of the best outfitters is **Rolling Bikes,** 14 av. Général Leclerc (© **04-94-97-09-39**). Deposits, depending on the model, range from 740€ to 1,400€. Rentals are for 24 hours, scooter rentals costing from 40€ to 60€, with motorcycle rentals going for 120€.

BOATING The highly recommended **Suncap Company,** 15 quai de Suffren (© **04-94-97-11-23**; www.suncap.fr), rents boats 5.5 to 12m (18–39 ft.) long. Larger ones come with a captain at the helm. Prices begin at 1,500€ per day.

GOLF The nearest golf course, at the edge of Ste-Maxime, across the bay, is the **Golf Club de Beauvallon,** boulevard des Collines (© **04-94-96-16-98**), a popular 18-hole course. Sprawling over a rocky, vertiginous landscape that requires a golf cart and a lot of exertion is the Don Harradine–designed **Golf de Ste-Maxime-Plaza,** route du Débarquement, Ste-Maxime (© **04-94-55-02-02**). It welcomes nonguests; phone to reserve tee times. Greens fees at both golf courses cost 85€ for 18 holes per person, and 45€ for 9 holes, year-round.

SCUBA DIVING A team of dive enthusiasts will show you the azure-colored depths off the coast of St-Tropez from the *Octopussy I* and *II.* Both are aluminum-sided, yellow-painted dive boats. They're based year-round in St-Tropez's Nouveau Port. For reservations and information, contact *Les Octopussys,* quartier de Bertaud, Gassin, 83900 St-Tropez (© **04-94-56-53-10**; fax 04-94-56-46-59). For a look at the boats, head down to the Nouveau Port, where they usually tie up when not out to sea.

TENNIS Anyone who phones in advance can use the eight courts (artificial grass or "Quick," a form of concrete) at the **Tennis-Club de St-Tropez,** route des Plages, St-Claude (© **04-94-97-15-52**), less than a kilometer (about ½ mile) from the resort's center. Open year-round, the courts rent for 20€ per hour for green set, 25€ per hour for clay set, from 9am to 8pm.

SEEING THE SIGHTS

Château Suffren is east of the port at the top end of quai Jean-Jaurès. Home to occasional art exhibits, it was built in A.D. 980 by Comte Guillaume I of Provence.

Near the junction of quai Suffren and quai Jean-Jaurès stands the bronze **Statue de Suffren,** paying tribute to Vice-Admiral Pierre André de Suffren. This St-Tropez native became one of the greatest sailors of 18th-century France, though he's largely forgotten today. In the Vieille Ville, one of the most interesting streets is **rue de la Miséricorde.** It's lined with boutiques set in stone houses. This street evokes medieval St-Tropez better than any other in town. At the corner of rue Gambetta is the **Chapelle de la Miséercorde,** with a blue, green, and gold tile roof.

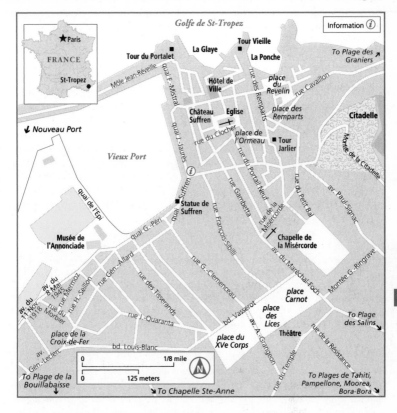

Three kilometers (2 miles) east of St-Tropez, **Port Grimaud** ★ makes an interesting outing. From St-Tropez, drive 4km (2½ miles) west on A98 to Route 98, and then 1.5km (1 mile) north to the Port Grimaud exit. If you approach the village at dusk, when it's bathed in Riviera pastels, it looks like a hamlet from the 16th century. But this is a mirage. Port Grimaud is the dream of its promoter, François Spoerry, who carved it out of marshland and dug canals. Flanking these canals, fingers of land extend from the square to the sea. The homes are Provençal style, many with Italianate window arches. Boat owners can anchor at their doorsteps. One newspaper called the port "the most magnificent fake since Disneyland." Most shops and restaurants in Port Grimaud are closed between October and March.

Musée de l'Annonciade (Musée St-Tropez) ★★   Near the harbor, this museum occupies the former chapel of the Annonciade. It houses one of the Riviera's finest modern-art collections of post-Impressionist masters. Many of the artists, including Paul Signac, depicted the port of St-Tropez. The collection includes such works as van Dongen's *Women of the Balustrade,* and paintings and sculpture by Bonnard, Matisse, Braque, Dufy, Utrillo, Seurat, Derain, and Maillol.

Place Grammont. ✆ **04-94-97-04-01.** Admission 5.50€ adults, 3.50€ children 11 and under. June–Sept Wed–Mon 10am–noon and 3–7pm; Oct and Dec–May Wed–Mon 10am–noon and 2–6pm. Closed Nov.

SHOPPING

St-Tropez is dense with stylish shops, but has no specific shopping street. Most shops are tucked in out-of-the-way corners of the Old Town. Big names include Hermès, Sonia Rykiel, and Dior. **Galeries Tropéziennes,** 56 rue Gambetta (✆ **04-94-97-02-21**), crowds hundreds of gift items—some worthwhile, some silly—into its showrooms near place des Lices. The merchandise is Mediterranean, breezy, and sophisticated.

Olives and wood from the trees that produce them have always been prized in Provence. For carvings made from the wood, head to **Autour des Oliviers,** 2 place de l'Ormeau (✆ **04-94-97-64-31**), which stocks large inventories of kitchen utensils, bread boards, carved crucifixes, pottery, trays, platters, ornaments, and gift items carved from the yellow-and-brown wood. It also stocks salt from the Camargue and a wide array of French olive oils.

And even chic St-Tropez has **Le Dépot,** boulevard Louis-Blanc (✆ **04-94-97-80-10**), which sells secondhand designer clothes by the likes of Hermès, Moschino, Gaultier, and Chanel. Some of the merchandise even has its original tags.

An **outdoor market** with food, clothes, and *brocante* takes place on Tuesday and Saturday mornings on place des Lices. This is one of the best Provençal markets in the south of France, with more than 100 vendors selling everything from tableware to home-made bread. The fish, vegetable, and flower market is down a tiled alley (place aux Herbes) behind the tourist office. It operates daily 8am to noon in summer and Tuesday to Sunday 8am to noon in winter.

WHERE TO STAY

Very Expensive

Hôtel Byblos ★★★   The builder said he created "an anti-hotel, a place like home." That's true if your home resembles a palace in Beirut and has salons decorated with Phoeni-cian gold statues from 3000 B.C. On a hill above the harbor, this complex encompasses intimate patios and courtyards. It's filled with antiques and rare objects such as polychrome carved woodwork, marquetry floors, and a Persian-rug ceiling. Every room is unique, and all have elegant beds. Unusual features might include a fireplace on a raised hearth or a bed recessed on a dais. The rooms range in size from medium to spacious, often with high ceil-ings and antiques or reproductions. Some units have such special features as four-posters with furry spreads or sunken whirlpool baths. Le Hameau, a stylish annex, contains 10 duplex suites built around a small courtyard with an outdoor spa. Some rooms have balco-nies overlooking an inner courtyard; others open onto a flowery terrace. One of the restau-rants, **Spoon Byblos** (p. 231), is run by the famed Chef Alain Ducasse; the lobby-level nightclub (p. 232) is one of France's most famous nightspots.

Av. Paul Signac, 83990 St-Tropez. ✆ **04-94-56-68-00.** Fax 04-94-56-68-01. www.byblos.com. 96 units, 10 junior suites. 410€–850€ double; 760€–2,500€ suite. AE, DC, MC, V. Parking 30€. Closed mid-Oct to mid-Apr. **Amenities:** 2 restaurants; 2 bars; babysitting; concierge; health club & spa; pool (outdoor); room service. *In room:* A/C, TV, hair dryer, minibar, Wi-Fi (free).

Hôtel Le Yaca ★   Life here is *la dolce vita.* Built in 1722 off a narrow street in the old part of town, this was the first hotel in St-Tropez. Colette lived for a few weeks here in 1927, and before that it was the temporary address of pre-Impressionists such as Paul Signac. The high-ceilinged reception area and many of the rooms overlook a flower-filled inner courtyard. All the rooms were renovated in the early part of the millennium, and those on the upper level have terra-cotta floor tiles and massive ceiling timbers. Each has a comfortable bed, utilitarian furniture, and high ceilings, and most have a roomy bathroom.

1 bd. d'Aumale, 83900 St-Tropez. © **04-94-55-81-00.** Fax 04-94-97-58-50. www.hotel-le-yaca.fr. 28 units. 270€–650€ double; 790€–1,550€ suite. AE, DC, MC, V. Parking 20€. Closed mid-Oct to mid-Apr. **Amenities:** Restaurant; bar; babysitting; pool (outdoor); room service. In room: A/C, TV, hair dryer, minibar, Wi-Fi (free).

Hôtel Villa Belrose ★★ (Finds) Small-scale and *luxe,* Hôtel Villa Belrose is set within a sloping garden in Gassin, an upscale residential neighborhood within a 10-minute drive northwest of St-Tropez. It was built in 1997 in an ocher-and-white-walled replica of a rambling private villa, with views that sweep from most of the bedrooms out over the gulf of St-Tropez. Bedrooms in this hideaway are lavishly and opulently accessorized with fine linens and lots of upscale toiletries in the bathrooms, but there's no disguising the fact that they fall midway along the spectrum of being either cozy or cramped, depending on your point of view. In many cases, glass doors open onto private terraces, a well-landscaped garden with plenty of botanical surprises and charm, and those magnificently ethereal views. Much of the establishment's identity derives from its elegant restaurant, open daily for lunch and dinner to nonresidents with reservations in advance. Chef Thierry Thiercelin prepares fixed-price menus that focus on Mediterranean cuisine that's as chic as St-Tropez itself.

Gassin, St-Tropez. © **04-94-55-97-97.** Fax 04-94-55-97-98. www.villabelrose.com. 40 units. 380€–850€ double; 1,100€–2,400€ suite. Half-board from 300€ per person per day. AE, DC, MC, V. Free outdoor parking; indoor parking 30€. Closed Nov–Apr. **Amenities:** Restaurant; babysitting; health club & spa; pool (outdoor); room service. In room: A/C, TV, hair dryer, minibar, Wi-Fi (free).

La Bastide de St-Tropez ★★★ Near the landmark place des Lices, this tile-roofed replica of a Provençal manor house looks deliberately severe, but the interior is opulent. It contains a monumental staircase leading from a sun-filled living room to the upper floors. The guest rooms are named according to their individual decor: Rose of Bengal, Fuchsia, or Tangerine Dawn. Each has a terrace or private garden, and some have Jacuzzis. Several, however, are quite small. The soft beds under fine quilting with matching draperies are among the most luxurious in St-Tropez. The well-appointed bathrooms have deluxe toiletries. The hotel is noted for its restaurant, L'Olivier.

Rte. des Carles, 83990 St-Tropez. © **04-94-55-82-55.** Fax 04-94-97-21-71. www.bastide-saint-tropez. com. 26 units. 250€–550€ double; 335€–850€ suite. AE, DC, MC, V. Free parking. Closed Jan. **Amenities:** Restaurant; bar; babysitting; pool (outdoor); room service. In room: A/C, TV, hair dryer, minibar, Wi-Fi (20€).

La Réserve Ramatuelle ★★★ A secret hideaway with a deluxe spa right near St-Tropez is attracting the glitterati to its precincts. All the accommodations are gorgeous, especially the classic Provençal villas with pools set in landscaped gardens. The property opens onto views of the Mediterranean as far as the eye can see. A hedonistic atmosphere permeates the place; the 4-day rejuvenation program at the spa is the height of sybaritic indulgence.

Chemin de la Quessine, 83350 Ramatuelle. © **04-94-44-94-44.** Fax 04-94-44-94-45. www.lareserve-ramatuelle.com. 23 units, 12 villas. 550€–750€ double; 1,050€–1,400€ suite; from 15,000€ villa for 1 week. AE, DC, MC, V. **Amenities:** Restaurant; bar; concierge; health club & spa; 2 pools (indoor & outdoor); room service. In room: A/C, TV, hair dryer, minibar, Wi-Fi (free).

Pastis Hotel-St-Tropez ★★ (Finds) Two expat Brits, John and Pauline Larkin, have taken a portside Provençal house and transformed it into a chic little inn. They have decorated it in a sophisticated eclectic style, even including their collection of framed albums of the Sex Pistols and the Rolling Stones. The courtyard pool is the focal point for socializing guests sipping aperitifs. The rooms are also furnished in an eclectic mix, and each unit comes with a spacious bathroom as well as a balcony or breakfast terrace. Some accommodations are large enough for extra beds or cots. Indian rugs, Chinese armoires, and beds adorned with Provençal *boutis* spreads enhance the warm, intimate ambience. Although the hotel doesn't have a restaurant, the staff prepares breakfast and light lunches for guests, or even a little supper for those arriving late. Best-selling author Peter Mayle, whose writings have drawn thousands to visit Provence, occasionally drops by this boutique hotel.

61 av. du Général Leclerc. 83990 St-Tropez. ✆ 04-98-12-56-60. Fax 04-94-96-99-82. www.pastis-st-tropez.com. 9 units. 250€–600€ double. AE, MC, V. Free parking. **Amenities:** Pool (outdoor). *In room:* A/C, TV.

Résidence de la Pinède ★★★ This hotel is St-Tropez's only rival to the Byblos, and, though just as luxurious and offering an even finer cuisine, it tends to have a more serious and staid clientele. This Relais & Châteaux hotel was built in the 1950s around a rustic stone-sided tower once used to store olives. Jean-Claude and Nicole Delion are the owners of this luxurious place on the seaside. The airy, spacious rooms open onto balconies or terraces with a view over the bay of St-Tropez. The stylish but offhand staff seems constantly overburdened.

Plage de la Bouillabaisse, 83990 St-Tropez. ✆ 04-94-55-91-00. Fax 04-94-97-73-64. www.residencepinede.com. 39 units. 395€–915€ double; 800€–1,910€ suite. AE, DC, MC, V. Free parking. Closed early Oct to May 2. **Amenities:** Restaurant; bar; babysitting; pool (outdoor); room service. *In room:* A/C, TV, hair dryer, minibar, Wi-Fi (free).

Expensive

Hôtel La Maison Blanche ★ Originally designed as a private villa late in the 19th century, this small and elegant government-rated four-star hotel enjoys a superbly convenient location directly astride the most visible square in St-Tropez, the place des Lices. Expanded since its original construction, it exudes an air of whitewashed elegance that's hard to find in St-Tropez. Charming details include the in-house bar that serves only champagne and an 18th-century fountain that was found on-site. La Maison Blanche is in close proximity to the Port of St-Tropez and is a 3-minute walk from the sea and beach. The rooms are comfortable and stylish, but contain very few mainstream amenities. In light of the resources of St-Tropez that lie in virtually every direction, no one seems to mind.

Place des Lices, 83990 St-Tropez. ✆ 04-94-97-52-66. Fax 04-94-97-89-23. www.hotellamaisonblanche.com. 9 units. 180€–460€ double; 350€–890€ suite. Extra bed 60€–90€. AE, DC, MC, V. **Amenities:** Champagne bar. *In room:* A/C, TV, hair dryer, Wi-Fi (free).

Hôtel La Mandarine ★ You definitely get glamour here. La Mandarine is built in the Provençal style with strong angles, thick stucco walls, a tile roof, and patios. The hotel was designed to look like a small village. Rooms are luxuriously furnished and open onto one or more terraces; some of the suites offer as many as three terraces. Fine linens and elegant fabrics grace the comfortable beds. Beautifully maintained bathrooms are tiled and equipped with luxury toiletries.

Rte. de Tahiti, 83990 St-Tropez. ✆ 04-94-79-06-66. Fax 04-94-97-33-67. www.hotellamandarine.com. 43 units. 255€–440€ double; from 575€ suite. AE, MC, V. Free parking. Closed Oct 15–May 15. Take the road leading to Plage de Tahiti; it's just off the road, 1km (¹/₂ mile) southeast of the center. **Amenities:** Restaurant; bar; babysitting; pool (outdoor); room service. *In room:* A/C, TV, minibar, Wi-Fi (free).

Hôtel La Mistralée ★ (Finds)   With architecture dating to 1850, this charming hotel is in the heart of St-Tropez, 2 minutes from the Vieux Port. The decor exudes baroque sophistication, especially in the gold-and-bronze drawing room where high ceilings, Corinthian columns, and stained glass dominate. Outside, the Oriental-themed garden is no less elegant, filled with palm, lemon, and orange trees as well as bamboo and papyrus plants. All 10 rooms are decorated in different themes, from a Chanel-fashion-inspired one to a Chinoise room. The restaurant further develops Mistralée's slight obsession with Asia: Chef Pascale Bouissie offers *provençale* cooking with a Chinese flair.

1 av. du Général Léclerc, 83990 St-Tropez. ✆ **04-98-12-91-12.** Fax 04-94-43-48-43. www.hotel-mistralee. com. 10 units. 230€–600€ double; 370€–790€ suite. Extra bed 80€. AE, MC, V. Parking 20€. **Amenities:** Restaurant; pool (outdoor); sauna. *In room:* A/C, TV, minibar, Wi-Fi (free).

Hôtel La Ponche ★★   The same family has run this hotel for more than half a century. Overlooking the port, this cozy nest has long been a favorite of ours, as it's the most discreet, most charming, and least celebrity-flashy establishment in town, making Byblos look nouveau riche and a bit strident. The hotel is filled with the original airy paintings of Jacques Cordier. The redecorated rooms are well equipped and open onto sea views. Each floor holds two or three rooms. Sun-colored walls with subtle lighting lend a homey feeling. The beds are elegantly appointed with linen and quality mattresses.

Port des Pêcheurs, 83990 St-Tropez. ✆ **04-94-97-02-53.** Fax 04-94-97-78-61. www.laponche.com. 18 units. 195€–460€ double; 225€–590€ suite. AE, MC, V. Parking 21€. Closed Nov to mid-Feb. **Amenities:** Restaurant; bar; babysitting; room service. *In room:* A/C, TV, hair dryer, minibar, Wi-Fi (free).

L'Hôtel des Lices ★   One consistently reliable bet for lodgings in St-Tropez is this modern hotel in its own small garden, close to place des Lices. The tastefully furnished rooms are tranquil and comfortable, overlooking either the outdoor pool or the garden; their rates vary widely according to season, size, and view. Breakfast is the only meal served, although afternoon snacks are provided beside the pool.

135 av. Augustin-Grangeon, 83993 St-Tropez. ✆ **04-94-97-28-28.** Fax 04-94-97-59-52. www. hoteldeslices.com. 42 units. 130€–260€ double; 260€–385€ suite. AE, MC, V. Free parking. Closed Nov 3–Feb. **Amenities:** Restaurant; bar; babysitting; pool (outdoor); room service. *In room:* A/C, TV, Wi-Fi (free).

Moderate

Hôtel Ermitage ★ (Value)   This attractively isolated hotel amid the rocky heights of St-Tropez was built in the 19th century as a private villa. Today its red-tile roof and green shutters shelter a plush hideaway. A walled garden is illuminated at night, and a cozy corner bar near a wood-burning fireplace takes the chill off blustery evenings. The guest rooms offer good value for St-Tropez. They are pleasantly but simply furnished, with efficiently organized and well-maintained bathrooms.

Av. Paul-Signac, 83990 St-Tropez. ✆ **04-94-97-52-33.** Fax 04-94-97-10-43. 27 units. 120€–220€ double. AE, DC, MC, V. **Amenities:** Bar; babysitting; room service. *In room:* TV.

Hôtel La Tartane ★   This small hotel lies between the center of St-Tropez and the Plage des Salins, about a 3-minute drive from each. After a comprehensive upgrade, its government rating jumped from three stars to four, accompanied by a big hike in prices. It has a heated stone-rimmed pool in the garden, attractively furnished public rooms with terra-cotta floors, and attentive, hardworking management. The midsize guest rooms are bungalows surrounding the pool. Breakfasts are elaborate.

Rte. des Salins, 83990 St-Tropez. ✆ **04-94-97-21-23.** Fax 04-94-97-09-16. www.latartane.fr. 28 units. 275€–670€ double; 600€–935€ suite. AE, DC, V. Closed mid-Oct to mid-Apr. **Amenities:** 2 restaurants; bar; pool (outside); spa. *In room:* A/C, TV, hair dryer, minibar, Wi-Fi (free).

Tips   **An Undiscovered Fishing Village**

More and more frugal visitors are fleeing the high prices of St-Tropez and heading for Sanary-sur-Mer, a tiny fishing village 80km (50 miles) southwest of St-Tropez. The French themselves come here for their vacations, leaving the more famous mecca for the tourists. Wednesday is grand market day at Sanary, as 300 vendors hawk their wares, selling everything from strawberries to foie gras. Drop in at the portside cafe, **Coquillages Philippe,** 8 place de la Tour (✆ **06-23-95-77-56**), a shellfish bar with ultra-fresh oysters. Here is your chance to try the famous sea urchin. On another front, **L'En K Fé,** 4 rue Louis Blanc (✆ **04-94-74-66-57**), is known for its Moroccan tagine of chicken with dates. For a hotel, check out **Hotel de la Tour,** 24 quai Général de Gaulle (✆ **04-94-74-10-10**), run by the Mercier family. Rooms are simple but have a view of the harbor, costing 80€ to 108€ for a double.

Hôtel Sube   If you want to be right on the port in a perfect ship- and celebrity-watching location, this might be your first choice. It's directly over the Café de Paris bar in the center of a shopping arcade. The two-story lounge has a beamed ceiling and a glass front, allowing a great view of the harbor. The French Provincial–style rooms aren't large but are comfortable. The more expensive units have scenic views of the port.

15 quai Suffren, 83900 St-Tropez. ✆ **04-94-97-30-04.** Fax 04-94-54-89-08. www.hotel-sube.com. 28 units. 125€–310€ double. AE, MC, V. Parking nearby 30€. **Amenities:** Cafe; bar. *In room:* A/C, TV.

Inexpensive

Hôtel Lou Cagnard ★ **Value**   This pleasant roadside inn, with a tile roof and green shutters, offers quiet rooms in the rear overlooking the garden. Monsieur and Madame Yvon are the hardworking owners, explaining to newcomers the translation of the name of their hotel (*Lou Cagnard,* in Provençal dialect, means "The hot, burning sun"). They extend a warm welcome to their guests. Although nothing is grand about the bedrooms, they are comfortable, with fine mattresses and well-maintained bathrooms with adequate shelf space. This hotel is a bargain in pricey St-Trop.

18 av. Paul-Roussel, 83990 St-Tropez. ✆ **04-94-97-04-24.** Fax 04-94-97-09-44. www.hotel-lou-cagnard. com. 19 units. 54€–130€ double. MC, V. Free parking. Closed Nov 1–Dec 26. **Amenities:** Lounge. *In room:* A/C, TV, Wi-Fi (free).

WHERE TO DINE

The **Résidence de la Pinède** (p. 228) serves flavor-filled *provençale* dishes.

Expensive

Colors ★ GRILL/SUSHI   Relatively new on the St-Tropez dining scene, this restaurant offers a verdant garden setting and one of the town's very few wood-burning ovens, on which a succulent array of fresh meat and fish is slowly cooked. Here, amid a decor of—you guessed it—strong colors, you can enjoy grilled filet steaks, rib-eyes, and such fresh fish as sea bass. Most are accompanied with creamy house-style mashed potatoes and fresh vegetables.

3 rue du Temple. ✆ **04-94-97-00-15.** Reservations required July–Aug. Main courses 25€–30€; sushi assortment 29€. AE, MC, V. Daily 7:30pm–1am. Closed mid-Oct to mid-Mar.

Le Girelier ★ PROVENÇALE   The Rouets own this portside restaurant whose blue- 231
and-white color scheme has become a trademark. They serve grilled fish in many versions, as well as bouillabaisse (only for two). Also on the menu are brochette of monkfish, a kettle of spicy mussels, and *pipérade* (a Basque omelet with pimentos, garlic, and tomatoes). Most dishes are moderately priced.

Quai Jean-Jaurès. ✆ **04-94-97-03-87.** Main courses 21€–50€; fixed-price menu 39€. AE, DC, MC, V. Daily noon–6pm and 7–11pm. Closed Nov 1–Mar 30.

Leï Mouscardins ★★★ FRENCH/PROVENÇALE   This restaurant, located at the end of St-Tropez's harbor, has won awards for culinary perfection. The dining room is decorated in formal Provençal style; an adjoining sunroom sits under a canopy. We recommend *moules* (mussels) *marinières* for an appetizer. On the menu are a celebrated Côte d'Azur fish stew, *bourride provençale,* and an unusual main-course specialty, crushed chestnuts garnished with morels, crayfish, and truffles. The fish dishes are excellent, particularly sauté of monkfish, wild mushrooms, and green beans. Dessert specialties are soufflés made with Grand Marnier or Cointreau.

1 rue Portalet. ✆ **04-94-97-29-00.** Reservations required. Main courses 28€–115€; fixed-price lunch 60€. AE, DC, MC, V. June–Sept daily noon–2pm and 7:30–10pm; Oct–May Wed–Mon noon–2pm and 7:30–9:30pm.

Spoon Byblos ★★ FRENCH/INTERNATIONAL   This is one of the many entrepreneurial statements by Alain Ducasse, considered by some to be the world's greatest chef—or at least the most acclaimed. The cuisine here draws special inspiration from the food of Catalonia, Andalusia, and Morocco; and Byblos offers more than 300 wines from around the world. Background music ranges from hip-hop to the hits of the '70s. The restaurant opens onto a circular bar made of blue-tinted glass and polished stainless steel. It's all terribly fashionable, although you may grow a bit weary of its self-conscious sense of chic after an hour or two within its ultradesigned premises. Dig into shrimp and squid consommé with a hint of jasmine and orange, or spicy king prawns on a skewer. Then try delectable lamb couscous or spit-roasted John Dory. You may top off a meal with the chef's favorite cheesecake or a slice of Neapolitan with the taste of strawberry, vanilla, and pistachio.

In the Hôtel Byblos (p. 226), av. Paul-Signac. ✆ **04-94-56-68-20.** Reservations required. Main courses 32€–49€; fixed-price menu 89€. AE, DC, MC, V. July–Aug daily 8pm–12:30am; mid-Apr to June and Sept to mid-Oct daily 8–11pm. Closed mid-Oct to mid-Apr.

Villa Romana ★ ITALIAN   This is where the St-Tropez party scene breaks for dinner; it's behind place des Lices, close to the nightclub Les Caves du Roy. The Italian cuisine here hardly ranks with the best you've ever had, but watching the (often scantily clad) patrons makes for the most amusing dinner in town. The place looks like Hugh Hefner designed it for his Playboy Mansion. Tycoons, wannabes, tabloid celebrities, and yachties look up as each new diner enters. When we went, it seemed a particular Italophile celebrity enjoyed the grilled calamari and the beef filet with summer truffles more than we did. We think your best bet is one of the homemade pastas or the catch of the day. In summer wear your skimpiest attire (that goes for men and women alike).

Impasse des Conquetes (near the corner of av. Paul Roussel, a short walk southwest of Place des Lices). ✆ **04-94-97-15-50.** Reservations required. Main courses 24€–75€; pizzas 20€–35€. MC, V. Easter to early Oct Thurs–Sun 8–11:30pm.

Auberge des Maures PROVENÇALE   One of our favorite cost-conscious restaurants in an otherwise very expensive town lies close to one end of the all-pedestrian rue Allard. The seating capacity doubles when the roof is rolled away in good weather and tables are set up in the garden with views of the moon, stars, splashing fountains, and ornamental shrubbery. Murals of the Provence countryside highlight the stone walls. The hardworking staff in the kitchen are on display as they churn out tempting platters completely based on seasonal, all-fresh ingredients. Menu items include grilled versions of many kinds of fresh fish and meat, and often taste best when preceded with starters such as *panache provençale,* with piled deep-fried zucchini blossoms; hearts of artichoke *barigoule;* and a medley of *petits farcis* (stuffed vegetables).

4 rue du Docteur Boutin. ⓒ **04-94-97-01-50.** www.aubergedesmaures.com. Reservations recommended. Main courses 40€–60€; fixed-price menu 49€. AE, DC, MC, V. Daily 7:30pm–1am. Closed Nov–Mar.

Chez Joseph/Le Petit Joseph ★ PROVENÇALE   These side-by-side restaurants are serviced by the same kitchen, and the menus are quite similar. Le Petit Joseph is quieter and more romantic, with low-beamed ceilings, an Asian decor, and cozy banquettes. Chez Joseph, where you sit with other patrons at long tables, tends to be completely booked and packed at 10pm. Both restaurants offer outdoor seating, but Le Petit has just a few tables; Chez features a large terrace. The traditional yet creatively presented cuisine emphasizes fish, with menu changes often. For dessert, the *parfait léger* is a treat—vanilla custard with chocolate powder on a cherry crumble with a scoop of cherry-vanilla ice cream and fresh fruit.

1 place de l'Hôtel-de-Ville. ⓒ **04-94-97-01-66.** www.joseph-saint-tropez.com. Reservations recommended at Chez Joseph. Main courses 29€–155€; fixed-price lunch 39€. AE, MC, V. Daily noon–2pm and 7:30pm–midnight.

Chez Maggi ★★ PROVENÇALE/ITALIAN   St-Tropez's most flamboyant gay restaurant and bar also draws straight diners and drinkers. At least half its floor space is devoted to a bar, where patrons range in age from 20 to 60. Consequently, cruising at Chez Maggi, in the words of loyal patrons, is *très crazée* and seems to extend for blocks in every direction. Meals are served in an adjoining dining room. Menu items include chicken salad with ginger; goat-cheese salad; *petits farcis provençale* (vegetables stuffed with minced meat and herbs); brochettes of sea bass with lemon sauce; and chicken curry with coconut milk, capers, and cucumbers.

7 rue Sibille. ⓒ **04-94-97-16-12.** Reservations recommended. Main courses 16€–32€. MC, V. Apr–Sept daily 7pm–3am; Oct–Mar Thurs–Sat 7pm–2am.

ST-TROPEZ AFTER DARK

On the lobby level of the Hôtel Byblos (p. 226), **Les Caves du Roy,** avenue Paul-Signac (ⓒ **04-94-97-16-02**), is the most self-consciously chic nightclub in St-Tropez and the most famous in France. Entrance is free, but drink prices begin at a whopping 18€. It's open nightly from May to late September from 11:30pm until dawn. **Le Papagayo,** in the Résidence du Nouveau-Port, rue Gambetta (ⓒ **04-94-97-95-95**), is one of the largest nightclubs in town. The decor was inspired by the psychedelic 1960s. Entrance is between 15€ and 18€ and includes one drink.

Adjacent to Le Papagayo is a club whose upscale male and female patrons may be equally at home in Les Caves du Roy: **Le VIP Room,** in the Résidence du Nouveau-Port (ⓒ **04-94-97-14-70;** www.viproom.fr); they pay between 14€ and 15€ per cocktail for the chance to (demurely or not) whoop it up. The club is all steel, chrome, mirrors, and glass. Expect an active bar area, dance floor, and the kind of social posturing and preening that can be amusing—or not.

Le Pigeonnier, 13 rue de la Ponche (© 04-94-97-84-26), rocks, rolls, and welcomes a crowd that's mostly gay or lesbian, and between 20 and 50. Most of the socializing revolves around the long, narrow bar, where patrons from all over Europe seem to enjoy chitchat. There's also a dance floor. For another gay hot spot, check out the action at **Chez Maggi** (p. 232).

Below the Hôtel Sube, the **Café de Paris,** sur le Port (© 04-94-97-00-56), is one of the most popular hangouts. The utilitarian room has early-1900s globe lights, an occasional 19th-century bronze artifact, masses of artificial flowers, and a long zinc bar. The crowd is irreverent and animated. The reporter Leslie Maitland aptly captured the crowd attracted to **Café Sénéquier,** sur le Port (© 04-94-97-20-20): "What else can one do but gawk at a tall, well-dressed young woman who appears *comme il faut* at Sénéquier's with a large white rat perched upon her shoulder, with which she occasionally exchanges little kisses, while casually chatting with her friends." The cafe is historic, venerable, and snobbish, and, at its worst, off-puttingly stylish.

Le Bar du Port, quai Suffren, adjacent to the Café de Paris (© 04-94-97-00-54), is breezy, airy, and almost obsessively hip and self-consciously trendy. This cafe-bar attracts a consistently young clientele. Expect lots of table-hopping, stylishly skimpy clothing, recorded music that may make you want to get up and dance, and insights into what's really going on in the minds of French 20-somethings.

If your idea of a night out is sitting in a cafe drinking wine, you can "hang out" at such joints as **Kelly's Irish Pub,** quai F. Mistral, at the bottom end of the Vieux Port (© 04-94-54-89-11), which draws a mostly foreign crowd. The tavern is casual, not chic. If you're nostalgic for St-Germain-des-Prés, head for the old-fashioned **Le Café,** place des Lices (© 04-94-97-44-69; www.lecafe.fr), with its famous zinc bar. Its glory lies in its location and not because of any innate value as a warm and cozy cafe—actually, it's both a bistro-restaurant and cafe today.

2 STE-MAXIME

24km (15 miles) SW of St-Raphaël; 61km (38 miles) SW of Cannes

Ste-Maxime is just across the gulf from glitzy St-Tropez, but its atmosphere is much more sedate. Young families are the major vacationers here, though an occasional refugee from across the water will come over to escape the see-and-be-seen crowd. The town is surrounded by the red cliffs of the Massif des Maures, protecting it from harsh weather. However, the wide stretches of sand and the cafe-lined promenades lure travelers to spend their days basking in the sun. More active vacationers might want to try windsurfing or water-skiing in the calm waters, or even golfing. The 16th-century fort was built by the monks of Lérins (who also named the port) and houses a museum. The best thing about Ste-Maxime is the price—though the town isn't as in vogue as St-Tropez, it's fun, affordable, and—according to locals—a lot less decadent.

ESSENTIALS

GETTING THERE Access to the nearest railway station is at St-Raphaël. For information about the **buses** that run frequently between St-Raphaël and Ste-Maxime, and from

Tips   **Wheeling Around Ste-Maxime**

A great way to explore Ste-Maxime is on two wheels with some wind in your hair. Consider visiting **Rent Bike,** 13 rue Magali (② **04-94-43-98-07**), which rents bikes and mopeds. Mountain bikes are 12€ per day, with a 150€ deposit; mopeds are 37€, with a 760€ deposit.

Ste-Maxime on to St-Tropez, call **Sodetrav** (② **04-94-54-62-36**). One-way passage between Ste-Maxime and either St-Raphaël or St-Tropez costs between 5€ and 7€ per person. If you're headed to Ste-Maxime from St-Tropez anytime between February and December, a frequent ferryboat service (transit time: 20 min.) costs 6.60€ per person, each way. For information about these boats, contact **Les Bâteaux Verts,** quai L.-Condroyer (② **04-94-49-29-39;** www.bateauxverts.com). If you're **driving** from Cannes, follow coastal road N98 southwest into Ste-Maxime.

VISITOR INFORMATION   The **Office de Tourisme** is on 1 promenade Simon-Lorière (② **04-94-55-75-55**).

A DAY AT THE BEACH

Beaches are the main attraction here. Of the four nearby, two are an easy walk from the town center. Across the road from the casino is **Plage du Casino**—we advise avoiding it because of the fumes from the nearby roadway, the narrow sands, and the hordes of sunbathers. A better bet is **Plage de la Croisette,** a wider, nominally less-congested expanse that's a 2-minute walk west of Plage du Casino. The most appealing beaches are **Plage de la Nartelle** and the adjacent **Plage des Eléphants,** with broad expanses of clean, fine-textured light-beige sand about 2km (1¼ miles) west of town. To reach them, follow signs along the coastal road pointing to St-Tropez. Here you can rent a mattress for sunbathing from any of several concessionaires for around 12€ to 15€, depending on the beach.

SEEING THE SIGHTS

Start with the 16th-century **La Tour Carrée des Dames (Dames Tower)** at place des Aliziers. It was originally a defensive structure; today it's home to the **Musée des Traditions Locales,** place de l'Eglise (② **04-94-96-70-30**), with exhibits on the area's history and tradition. The museum is open Wednesday to Monday during July and August from 10am to noon and 3 to 6pm, and September to June from 10am to noon and 3 to 6pm only. Admission is 2.50€ for adults and 1€ for children 11 and under.

Facing the tower is the **Eglise Ste-Maxime,** place des Aliziers (② **04-94-49-06-67**), with a green marble altar from the former Carthusian monastery of La Verne in the Massif des Maures. The choir stalls date from the 15th century.

St-Maxime hosts various markets. On Thursday, a **crafts market** is held on and around place du Marché; on Friday morning (8am–noon), vendors sell a variety of **knickknacks** on place Jean-Mermoz. In the pedestrian streets of the old town, an **arts-and-crafts fair** takes place daily in summer from 5 to 11pm.

Outside town are several worthy sights. About 10km (6 miles) north on the road to Muy (Rte. de Muy) is the **Musée du Phonographe et de la Musique Méchanique** (② **04-94-96-50-52**). This extensive display of audio equipment is the result of one woman's 40-year obsession. Sometimes she gives personal tours. In the museum is one of Edison's original "talking machines" and an audiovisual panthographe used to teach foreign languages in 1913. The museum is open Easter to late September only, Wednesday to Sunday 10am to noon and 3:30 to 6pm. During July and August, it's open from 10am to noon and from 4 to 6:30pm. Admission is 3€ for adults and 1.50€ for children 5 to 12 years.

If you're a nature lover, follow the signs along boulevard Bellevue for 1.5km (1 mile) north of town to the little town of **Sémaphore.** Here you'll find panoramic views along many hiking trails that wind along the coast or into the mountains, reaching an altitude of 120m (400 ft.). The tourist office has maps, or you can head for the Sentier du Littoral (Chemin des Douaniers), a trail that meanders along the coast toward St-Tropez and has access to the sea at almost all points along the way.

WHERE TO STAY

Although hotels are less expensive here than in the neighboring towns, you might find that you must pay for half-board in July and August. Most places are closed in winter, but May, June, and September are great times to find a good deal.

Expensive

Hôtel La Belle Aurore ★★ La Belle Aurore is on its own private beach and is one of the finest addresses in the area for the cost. If it has a serious challenger, it's Les Santolines (see below). Each of the well-furnished guest rooms has a terrace overlooking the sea; the breezes keep the inside temperature comfortable. Tiled bathrooms are small and tidy.

5 bd. Jean-Moulin, 83120 Ste-Maxime. ✆ 04-94-96-02-45. Fax 04-94-96-63-87. www.belleaurore.com. 17 units. 195€–325€ double; 370€–570€ suite. AE, DC, MC, V. Parking 6€–15€. Closed Oct 15 to late Mar. **Amenities:** Restaurant; pool (outdoor); room service. *In room:* A/C, TV, hair dryer, minibar, Wi-Fi (free).

Moderate

Best Western Hôtel Montfleuri ★ (Finds) This hotel on a hillside in a quiet residential neighborhood opens onto a superb view of the Gulf of St-Tropez. The large guest rooms have fine linen, twin or double beds, and a small bathroom. All of the accommodations facing the ocean have their own private terraces. The hotel restaurant serves "family cooking" *provençale* style in a pleasant garden.

3 av. Montfleuri, 83120 Ste-Maxime. ✆ 800/528-1234 in the U.S. and Canada, or 04-94-55-75-10. Fax 04-94-49-25-07. www.montfleuri.com. 30 units. 60€–215€ double; 100€–265€ suite. AE, DC, MC, V. Closed Nov 5–Dec 23 and Jan 5–Mar 1. **Amenities:** Restaurant; bar; pool (outdoor). *In room:* A/C, TV, hair dryer, minibar, Wi-Fi (free).

Hôtel La Croisette ★ This charming hotel is surrounded by its own lush garden and has an intimate aura, lying 200m (656 ft.) from the beach. Room rates vary according to view—those with a balcony and sea view are most expensive; those that open onto the garden are less. Homey and cozy, they are decorated in a provincial southern style; the tiled bathrooms are tidy. Maintenance here is high quality.

2 bd. des Romarins, 83120 Ste-Maxime. ✆ 04-94-96-17-75. Fax 04-94-96-52-40. www.hotel-la-croisette. com. 19 units. 84€–174€ double. AE, MC, V. Closed Nov–Apr 1. **Amenities:** Bar; babysitting; room service. *In room:* A/C, TV, hair dryer, minibar, Wi-Fi (free).

Hôtel Les Santolines ★★ This is an excellent choice for those who want to remove themselves from the crowds. Les Santolines is 10 minutes from the busy center area but still close to the beach. The building is arranged around a grassy courtyard that has an outdoor pool and the town's most inviting *jardin fleuri* (flower garden). Rooms are comfortable and private; most have balconies. The look is very French Provincial. Some bathrooms are rather dramatically tiled in sea blue, and all have double basins.

Quartier de la Croisette, 83120 Ste-Maxime. ✆ **04-94-96-31-34.** Fax 04-94-49-22-12. www.hotel-les-santolines.com. 13 units. 78€–148€ double. AE, MC, V. Free parking. **Amenities:** Restaurant; bar; babysitting; pool (outdoor). *In room:* A/C, TV, hair dryer, minibar, Wi-Fi (free).

Inexpensive

Hôtel de la Poste   This modern hotel's location in the town center, convenient to the beach and shopping, makes up for what it lacks in personality. The inside of this Logis de France hotel is cool and comfortable, with a quiet lounge and pleasant bar. Guest rooms are clean and comfortably furnished. At lunchtime snacks are served. The staff is friendly and always happy to help you decide how to spend your day.

11 bd. Frédéric-Mistral, 83120 Ste-Maxime. ✆ **04-94-96-18-33.** Fax 04-94-55-58-63. www.hotelleriedusoleil.com. 28 units. 70€–190€ double; 120€–225€ suite. AE, DC, MC, V. **Amenities:** Bar; babysitting; pool (outdoor); room service; solarium. *In room:* A/C, TV, hair dryer, minibar, Wi-Fi (10€ per hr.).

Hôtel Le Chardon Bleu   Situated 10m (33 ft.) from the beach, Le Chardon Bleu is also close to the pedestrian area and the casino. The hotel has a garden where you can enjoy the aroma of the flowers. The well-maintained rooms are comfortable and inviting, though the furnishings are standard; all rooms have small balconies. Bathrooms are tiled and compact.

29 rue de Verdun, 83120 Ste-Maxime. ✆ **04-94-55-52-22.** Fax 04-94-43-90-89. www.aubergedu chardonbleu.fr. 25 units. 60€–87€ double. AE, DC, MC, V. **Amenities:** Lounge. *In room:* A/C, TV, minibar.

WHERE TO DINE

La Gruppi FRENCH/PROVENÇALE   Earthy and amusing (La Gruppi is the Provençal word for a miniature trough used to feed barnyard animals), this restaurant has thrived on the promenade adjacent to the sea ever since the Lindermanns opened it in the 1960s. Bay windows illuminate dining rooms on two floors, decorated with rattan furnishings. The deluxe version of the establishment's savory bouillabaisse must be ordered a day in advance; otherwise, you get a simplified version, which the chefs refer to as a *soupe de poisson*. Other menu items are seafood platters; herbed and roasted lamb from Sisteron; veal; chicken; and all the vegetarian bounty of Provence. If you opt for fish, a staff member will carry a basket filled with the best of the day's catch for your inspection and advise you on their respective merits. One particularly succulent example is braised sea wolf in champagne sauce.

82 av. Charles-de-Gaulle. ✆ **04-94-96-03-61.** Reservations recommended. Main courses 25€–30€; fixed-price menus 23€–32€. AE, MC, V. Tues and Thurs–Sun noon–2pm; daily 7–11pm. Closed 2 weeks in Dec.

Restaurant Sans Souci FRENCH/PROVENÇALE   Ever since Philippe Sibilia's Italian-born grandfather opened this place in 1953, it's always served reliably great food. In a turn-of-the-20th-century building next to the church, it has a Provence-inspired decor with ceiling beams and old-time accessories. Menu items prepared by the good-humored owner are concocted from fresh ingredients and years of practice. Examples are pan-fried Provençal veal, sea wolf with fennel, octopus salad, filet of hake with basil, and one of our favorite dishes anywhere, noisettes of lamb with a tapenade of olives, enhanced with pulverized anchovies and a hint of fresh cream.

58 rue Paul-Bert. ✆ **04-94-96-18-26.** Reservations recommended. Main courses 9€–19€; fixed-price menus 24€–27€; fixed price lunch 14€. V. Sept–June Tues–Sun noon–2pm and 7–10:30pm; July–Aug 7–11pm.

3 FREJUS ★

3km (2 miles) W of St-Raphaël; 14km (8³/₄ miles) NE of St-Tropez

Fréjus was founded by Julius Caesar in 49 B.C. as Forum Julii; later, under Augustus's rule, it became a key naval base. The warships with which Augustus defeated Antony and Cleopatra at the battle at Actium were built here in 31 B.C. By the Middle Ages, however, the port had declined. It began to silt up from disuse and was eventually filled in. Today the port lies more than 3km (2 miles) inland.

Remnants from Roman times still stand in the Vieille Ville, including parts of an arena and a theater. An interesting section also dates to medieval times called the "Cité Episcopale." The baptistery is one of France's oldest ecclesiastical buildings.

In more recent times, Fréjus has again expanded toward the water. The beach area, Fréjus Plage, tends to blend into St-Raphaël. The two towns are often considered a single holiday destination, though serious beachgoers often opt to stay in St-Raphaël, where the hotels are closer to the water and cheaper.

ESSENTIALS

GETTING THERE   From the main station at St-Raphaël, several **trains** a day arrive at a small train station in Fréjus on rue Martin-Bidoure. Call ✆ **36-35,** or visit **www.voyages-sncf.com**. The beach is a shorter walk (about 15 min.) from the St-Raphaël station than from the Fréjus station.

Aglobus (✆ **04-94-95-16-71**), which functions in cooperation with **Estérel Bus** (✆ **04-94-53-78-46**), operates routes throughout Provence and the Riviera, including a bus service into Fréjus from St-Raphaël every 30 minutes. Buses arrive at the **Fréjus Gare Routière,** place Paul-Vernet (✆ **04-94-83-87-63**), at the east end of the town center. One-way tickets cost 3.25€. **Sodetrav** buses (✆ **04-94-95-24-82**) en route to St-Tropez from St-Raphaël stop along the coast in Fréjus.

To reach Fréjus from St-Raphaël, take the N98 west to the intersection with D7, at which point you cut north for a short distance.

GETTING AROUND   Rent mopeds at **Action 2 Roues,** 18 av. Des Portes-du-Soleil (✆ **04-94-44-48-34**). Prices range from 25€ to 40€ depending on the model, and credit card deposits are required. **Cycles Patrick Beraud,** 337 rue de Triberg (✆ **04-94-51-20-20;** www.cyclesberaud.fr), rents the pedal-powered version of two-wheeled transportation. Expect to pay 12€ to 25€, plus a security deposit.

VISITOR INFORMATION   The **Office de Tourisme** is at 325 rue Jean-Jaurès (✆ **04-94-51-83-83;** www.frejus.fr).

SPECIAL EVENTS   The **Fête des Plantes** is held annually in the park of the Villa Aurélienne (see below), during a 3-day period in late March and April. For information, call ✆ **04-94-51-83-83** or contact the local tourist office.

EXPLORING THE TOWN
The Top Sights

If you want to visit several sites in the area, you can purchase a **Fréjus Pass** for 4.60€ for adults or 3.10€ for ages 12 to 18, free for ages 11 and under. The best preserved of the ruins is the **Amphithéâtre (Les Arènes)** ★, rue Henri-Vadon (✆ **04-94-51-34-31**). In Roman times, it held up to 10,000 spectators. The upper levels of the galleries have been reconstructed with the same greenish stone used to create the original building. Today it's used as a venue for rock concerts and the city's two annual Spanish-style *corridas* (bullfights). Ask the tourist office for dates and details. It's open November to April, Tuesday to Sunday 9:30am to 12:30pm and 2 to 5pm; and May to October, Tuesday to Sunday 9:30am to 12:30pm and 2 to 6pm. Admission is 2€ for all ages.

A half-kilometer (⅓ mile) north of town on rue du Théâtre-Romain, the **Théâtre Romain** (𝄡 **04-94-53-58-75**), not to be confused with the amphitheater, is largely in ruins. However, one wall and a few of the lower sections remain and are used as a backdrop for occasional summer concerts. The site is open 24 hours, and visits, which aren't monitored, are free. Northwest of the theater, you can see a few soaring arches as they follow the road leading to Cannes. These are the remaining pieces of the 40km (25-mile) aqueduct that once brought fresh water to Fréjus's water tower.

Cité Episcopale ★★   The town's most frequently visited site is its fortified cathedral in the heart of the Vieille Ville. At its center is the **Cathédrale St-Léonce,** completed in the 16th century after many generations of laborers had worked on it. It was begun in the 10th century, and parts of it date from the 12th and 13th centuries. Its most striking features are Renaissance—ornately carved walnut doors depicting scenes from the Virgin's life and tableaux inspired by Saracen invasions. The 5th-century **baptistery ★★** is one of the oldest in France. Octagonal like many paleo-Christian baptisteries, it features eight black granite columns with white capitals. Most interesting are the two doors, which are different sizes. Catechumens would enter by the smaller of the two; inside, a bishop would wash their feet and baptize them in the center outdoor pool. The baptized would then leave through the larger door; this signified their enlarged spiritual stature.

The most beautiful of all the structures in the Episcopal quarter is the 12th-century **cloister ★★**. The colonnade's two slender marble pillars are typical of the Provençal style. Inside, the wooden ceiling is divided into 1,200 small panels decorated with animals, portraits, and grotesques by 15th-century artists. A bell tower rises above the cloister, its steeple covered with colored tiles.

Place Formigé. (𝄡 **04-94-51-26-30**. Admission includes entrance to all sites, the museum, and (optional) guided tour of cloister and baptistery: 5€ adults, 3.50€ students 24 and under and children. June–Sept daily 9am–6:30pm; Oct–May Tues–Sun 9am–noon and 2–5pm.

More Sights

The small, round **Chapelle Cocteau,** avenue Nicola (𝄡 **04-94-53-27-06**), was designed by the artist, film director, social gadfly, and *prince des poètes* Jean Cocteau. It was built between 1961 and 1965, and was decorated by Cocteau himself. Its octagonal shape, low-slung with small windows, might remind you of an African thatch-covered hut. It's open Wednesday to Monday April to September from 2 to 6pm, and October to March from 2 to 5pm. Admission is free.

Just outside Fréjus are two curiosities that reflect the cultural mixture of France's early-20th-century empire. The **Pagode Hong-Hien** (𝄡 **04-94-53-25-29**), still used as a Buddhist temple, is about 2km (1¼ miles) northeast on R.N. 7. It was built in 1919 by soldiers conscripted from Indochina as a shrine to their fallen comrades. It's open daily from 9am to 7pm; winter hours are daily 9am to 5pm. Admission is 2€ for all ages. Off D4, leading to Bagnols, you can see the purple-red exterior of the **Mosquée Soudanaise** (no phone), built by Muslim soldiers conscripted from the French colony of Mali. Controlled by the French Ministry of Defense, it is off-limits to casual visitors.

The grand neoclassical **Villa Aurélienne,** avenue du Général-d'Armée Calliès (© **04-** **94-52-90-49**), was originally a holiday home for an English industrialist in the 1880s. It's the venue of a widely varied series of temporary art exhibitions. Admission prices vary according to the venue. Call for information. The park surrounding the villa hosts occasional festivals (see "Special Events" on p. 237).

Parc Zoologique, Le Capitou (© **04-98-11-37-37;** www.zoo-frejus.com), is off A8 about 5.5km (3½ miles) north of the center of Fréjus. The zoo is home to more than 250 species of animals and is open daily June to August 10am to 6pm; March, April, May, September, and October daily 10am to 5pm; and November to February daily 10:30am to 4:30pm. Admission is 14€ for adults, 9.50€ for children 3 to 9.

WHERE TO STAY

Hôtel L'Aréna ★★ This hotel in the center of the Vieille Ville was created from a former bank. Beautifully restored in bright Provençal colors, L'Aréna is an appropriately informal beach-town retreat. Each of the small but comfortable rooms opens onto a garden area where tropical plants give the air a sweet smell. Furnishings and mattresses are comfortable and simple, but not at all plush. The staff is friendly, and the hotel is a good value for the area.

145 rue du Général-de-Gaulle, 83600 Fréjus. © **04-94-17-09-40.** Fax 04-94-52-01-52. www.arena-hotel. com. 39 units. 85€–170€ double. AE, DC, MC, V. Parking 12€. Closed Dec 15–Jan 16. **Amenities:** Restaurant; bar; babysitting; pool (outdoor); room service. In room: A/C, TV, hair dryer, Wi-Fi (5€).

WHERE TO DINE

Les Potiers ★ (Finds) FRENCH/PROVENÇALE The town's smallest and most charming restaurant lies midway between the town hall and the ancient arena. Spearheaded by Richard François and his wife Marilou Fortunato (who supervises the dining room), it occupies a century-old stone house and has only 15 seats. The menu changes with the seasons but usually includes fried slabs of duckling foie gras; crayfish ravioli with ricotta cheese and hazelnut oil; crisp-roasted rack of lamb cooked in a salt crust; and cannelloni stuffed with strips of rabbit served with a saffron-flavored medley of vegetables. A dessert with undeniable charm is a platter with five small portions of crème brûlée, each with a different flavor.

135 rue des Potiers. © **04-94-51-33-74.** Reservations required. Main courses 16€–22€; fixed-price menus 25€–36€. MC, V. Mon–Sat noon–2pm and 7:30–9:30pm.

4 ST-RAPHAEL

3km (2 miles) E of Fréjus; 43km (27 miles) SW of Cannes

Between the red lava peaks of the Massif de l'Estérel and the densely forested hills of the Massif des Maures, St-Raphaël was first popular during Roman times, when rich families came to the resort here. Barbaric hordes and Saracen invasions characterized the Middle Ages incarnation. Not until 1799, when a proud Napoleon landed at the small harbor beach on his return from Egypt, did the city once again draw attention.

Fifteen years later, that same spot in the harbor was the point of embarkation for the fallen emperor's journey to exile on Elba. In 1864, Alphonse Karr, a journalist and ex-editor of *Le Figaro,* helped reintroduce St-Raphaël as a resort. Dumas, Maupassant, and Berlioz came here from Paris on his recommendation. Gounod also arrived; he composed

Romeo et Juliet here in 1866. Unfortunately, most of the Belle Epoque villas and grand hotels were destroyed during World War II when St-Raphaël served as a key landing point for Allied soldiers.

Today some of the mansions have been rebuilt and others have been replaced by modern resorts and buildings. However, the city still offers the wide beaches, good restaurants and hotels, and coastal ambience of other Côte d'Azur resorts—at a fraction of the price. This is why St-Raphaël, one of the richest towns on the coast, draws more families than couture-clad Parisians.

ESSENTIALS

GETTING THERE   St-Raphaël sits directly on the rail lines running parallel to the coast between Marseille in the west and the Italian border town of Ventimiglia in the east. Within some 3 hours you can take a fast **TGV train** from Paris to Marseille. For rail information and schedules, call ✆ **36-35,** or visit **www.voyages-sncf.com**. Once at Marseille, it is another 1¾ hours by train to St-Raphaël. Trains leave Marseille every hour during the day, costing 24€one-way. Trains from Cannes head east to St-Raphaël every 30 minutes during the day (25-min. trip); one-way fare costs 6.10€.

The **bus** station behind the train station provides local and regional service alike. **Aglobus** (✆ **04-94-95-16-71**) links directly with Fréjus, charging around 2.25€ each way for buses that run at 30-minute intervals, and around 6.50€ for service from Nice, a 60-minute transit. **Sodetrav** (✆ **04-94-95-24-82**) links St-Raphaël with St-Tropez (trip time: 70–90 min.); fares are around 9€ each way. Buses from Nice arrive every hour until 1am. Another option for local bus service into nearby hills and hamlets is provided by **Beltrame** (✆ **04-94-95-95-16**).

Between April and October, **Les Bateaux Bleus** (✆ **04-94-95-17-46**) provides waterborne transit—about a half-dozen boats per day—between a point near the railway station of St-Raphaël and St-Tropez for around 12€ each way.

By **car** from St-Tropez in the west, take D98A northwest to N98, at which point you drive east toward St-Raphaël. From Cannes, head west along N98.

GETTING AROUND   Normally, taxis line up at the bus station; if you can't find one, call ✆ **04-94-95-04-25.** You can rent bikes and scooters from **Patrick Moto,** 260 av. du Général-Leclerc (✆ **04-94-53-65-99**). Bikes rent for 12€, with a 130€ deposit; mountain bikes rent for 17€, with a 300€ deposit; and scooters go for 25€, with a 400€ deposit. MasterCard and Visa can be used for the deposit.

VISITOR INFORMATION   The **Office de Tourisme** faces the train station on rue Waldeck-Rousseau (✆ **04-94-19-52-52;** www.saint-raphael.com).

SPECIAL EVENTS   The **Competition Internationale de Jazz de New Orleans** is held during 3 days in early July, when Dixieland-style musicians from around the world congregate to display their talent. Call ✆ **04-98-11-89-00,** or contact the tourist office, for exact dates and musical venues. In mid-August, the **Festival St-Pierre des Pêcheurs** is conducted in and around the town center. Honoring the fishers who helped feed the town throughout most of its existence, it features a night of fireworks, a brief medieval-style procession to and from the village church, music, dancing on platforms built beside the port, and a series of jutes (mock naval battles btw. competing boat teams) where everyone gets soaking wet.

Of course, most visitors come here to have fun on the beaches. The best ones (some rock, some sand) are between the Vieux Port and Santa Lucia; stands rent watersports equipment on each beach.

The closest to the town center is the **Plage du Veillat,** a long stretch of sand that's crowded and family friendly. Within a 5-minute walk east of the town center is **Plage Beau Rivage,** whose name is misleading because it's covered with a smooth and even coating of light-gray pebbles that might be uncomfortable to lie on without a towel. History buffs will enjoy a 7km (4½-mile) excursion east of town to the **Plage du Débarquement,** a partly pebble-and-sand stretch that was hurled into world headlines on August 15, 1944, when Allied forces overran the southern tier of occupied France, bringing World War II to a more rapid conclusion. Today expect relatively uncrowded conditions, except during the midsummer crush.

St-Raphaël's answer to the decadence of nearby St-Tropez is most visible in the municipality's official nude beach, the **Plage de St-Ayguls,** 10km (6 miles) west of the town center. Surrounded by thick screens of reeds that thrive along the marshy seafront, it's a short, clearly signposted walk from the heart of the simple fishing village of St-Ayguls.

SEEING THE SIGHTS

St-Raphaël is divided in half by railroad tracks. The historical **Vieille Ville** (old city) lies inland from the tracks. Here you'll find St-Raphaël's only intact ancient structure, the **Eglise des Templiers,** place de la Vieille Eglise, Quartier des Templiers (© **04-94-19-25-75**). The 12th-century church is the third to stand on this site; two Carolingian churches underneath the current structure have been revealed during digs. A Templar watchtower sits atop one of the chapels, and at one time, watchers were posted to look out over the sea for ships that might pose a threat. The church served as a fortress and refuge in case of pirate attack. In the courtyard are fragments of a Roman aqueduct that once brought water from Fréjus. You can visit the church June to September every Tuesday to Saturday from 10am to noon and 2 to 5:30pm. Ironically, no Masses are conducted in this church on Sunday—it's a consecrated church, but one that's been relegated to something akin to an archaeological rather than religious monument.

St-Raphaël's other major church, **Notre-Dame-de-la-Victoire,** boulevard Félix-Martin (© **04-94-19-81-29**), was completed in 1887, an ostentatious monument to the gilded age of commerce that helped finance its construction. May to September, it's open daily from 7:30am to 10pm; October to April, it's open daily from 7am to 8pm. Entrance is free.

Near the Eglise des Templiers, the **Musée d'Archéologie Sous-Marine (Museum of Underwater Archaeology),** rue des Templiers (© **04-94-19-25-75**), displays amphorae, ships' anchors, ancient diving equipment, and other interesting items recovered from the ocean's depths. At one time, rumors circulated about a "lost city" off the coast of St-Raphaël. Jacques Cousteau came to investigate; instead of a sunken city, he discovered a Roman ship that had sunk while carrying a full load of building supplies. October to May, the museum is open Tuesday to Saturday from 9am to noon and 2 to 5:30pm. June to September, it's open Tuesday to Saturday 9am to noon and 2 to 6:30pm. Admission is free.

You'll also find **flower and fruit markets** in the old city. Stall owners open every morning. Every Tuesday from 9am to 6pm, vendors sell a variety of odds and ends. Also check out the **Marché Alimentaire de St-Raphaël,** where carloads of produce, fish, meat, wines, and cheeses are sold Tuesday to Sunday from 8am to 1pm at two sites—place Victor-Hugo and place de la République—a 5-minute walk apart.

The seafront's broad **promenades,** dotted with statues dedicated to Félix Martin (a 19th-c. mayor and tireless promoter of the resort) and Alphonse Karr (a 19th-c. artist and local luminary), wind between the beaches and hotels. Near the old port, a **pyramid** commemorating Napoleon's return to France from Egypt stands on avenue du Commandant-Guilbaud.

WHERE TO STAY

St-Raphaël has plenty of accommodations, but during summer even the less-than-desirable places fill up fast. Reserve well in advance.

Best Western Hôtel La Marina Overlooking the yacht-basin harbor at Santa Lucia, this hotel provides comfortable accommodations in a setting a bit removed from the crowded beaches. Most of the well-furnished rooms, each renovated and upgraded in 2005, have private balconies. The restaurant serves well-prepared regional food on a sunny terrace overlooking sailboats and yachts.

Nouveau Port Santa Lucia, 83700 St-Raphaël. (©) **800/528-1234** in the U.S. and Canada, or 04-94-95-31-31. Fax 04-94-82-21-46. www.lamarinasr-fr. 100 units. 105€–170€ double; 350€ suite. AE, DC, V. Parking 9€. **Amenities:** Restaurant; bar; babysitting; concierge; pool (outdoor); room service. *In room:* A/C, TV, hair dryer, minibar, Wi-Fi (free).

Hôtel Continental (Value) The Continental is a good choice for a cost-conscious beach vacation. Rooms come in a wide variety, ranging from compact (relatively cramped) to spacious, with rates charged according to view (seascape or urban). All have well-maintained tiled bathrooms. No meals are served other than breakfast, but two well-recommended restaurants lie within a short walk.

100 promenade du Président-René-Coty, 83700 St-Raphaël. (©) **04-94-83-87-87.** Fax 04-94-19-20-24. www.hotelcontinental.fr. 44 units. 75€–230€ double. AE, DC, MC, V. Parking 13€. **Amenities:** Lounge; babysitting. *In room:* A/C, TV, hair dryer, minibar, Wi-Fi (free).

Hôtel Excelsior This hotel, on the beachfront promenade, is a charming family-run place—the best address at St-Raphaël. The small to medium-size guest rooms are comfortably appointed, with tidy bathrooms; most have views of the ocean. A sand beach is directly across the street.

193 promenade du Président-René-Coty, 83700 St-Raphaël. (©) **04-94-95-02-42.** Fax 04-94-95-33-82. www.excelsior-hotel.com. 40 units. 160€–200€ double. AE, DC, MC, V. **Amenities:** Restaurant; pub; room service. *In room:* A/C, TV, hair dryer, minibar, Wi-Fi (free).

Villa Mauresque ★★ (Finds) This posh address lies 30 minutes from either Cannes or St-Tropez, and the little village of Boulouris itself is only a 5-minute drive from St-Raphaël. One of the richest authors of the 20th century, W. Somerset Maugham, lived in splendor in this villa, inviting famous movie stars, writers, and artists of his time as his houseguests. Today, the two neo-Moorish castles that make up the villa have been converted into the most elegant B&B along the Western Riviera framed by lush century-old palms and umbrella pines. The rooms are beautifully furnished and individually decorated. You might be sleeping where Noel Coward or even Marlene Dietrich slept long ago.

WHERE TO DINE

L'Arbousier ★ FRENCH/PROVENÇALE Thanks to the charm and humor of Christien Troncy, director of the dining room, and the cuisine of her husband, Philippe, this restaurant is a success story. Although the cozy restaurant can't boast gorgeous archi- tecture, something innately stylish and even fun keeps clients coming back to L'Arbousier. Flavors are rich, sunny, and sometimes earthy. Typical dishes are green asparagus and lobster served with lemon-flavored butter; cannelloni-shaped filets of red snapper and squid served with hearts of artichokes, chopped onions and peppers, and white wine; and a sophisti- cated version of roasted pigeon in a stewpot, accompanied by pigeon-stuffed ravioli, served with sherry sauce and pepper. Dessert might be a delectable crystallized version of local strawberries served with a pepper-flavored mint sauce.

6 av. de Valescure. ℂ **04-94-95-25-00.** www.arbousier.net. Reservations recommended. Main courses 25€–48€; fixed-price lunches 30€–59€; fixed-price dinners 44€–59€. AE, DC, MC, V. Tues–Sun noon– 2:30pm; Tues–Sat 7:30–10:30pm.

ST-RAPHAEL AFTER DARK

As this is a family vacation spot, the after-dark scene is a little sparse. Nights at the **Grand Casino,** square de Grand (ℂ **04-98-11-17-77**), feature slot machines and gambling, plus a nightly dance party in summer with an upbeat orchestra. The slot machines are open daily from 10am to 4am; gambling begins at 9pm, and the dance club opens at 10pm.

One of our favorite bars is **Le Coco Club,** Port Santa Lucia (ℂ **04-98-12-62-13**); open daily, where live music and stiff drinks contribute to a kind of gregarious, often flirtatious conviviality. Alternative choices include **La Réserve** (ℂ **04-94-95-02-02**), a popular disco with a punk-rock crowd between 16 and 25. Gay men and women tend to congregate at **Le Ganesh Pub,** 16 rue Charabois (ℂ **06-10-21-08-89**), where disco music and a long-standing reputation as a dance palace can be animated and fun for everyone. For more information, contact the town's tourist office.

5 MASSIF DE L'ESTEREL ★★★

3km (2 miles) NE of Fréjus; 8km (5 miles) SE of Cannes

Stretching for 39km (24 miles) of coast from La Napoule to St-Raphaël, this mass of twisted red volcanic rock is a surreal landscape of dramatic panoramas. Forest fires have devastated all but a small section of cork oak, adding barrenness to an already other- worldly place. This was once the stamping ground of a colorful 19th-century highway- man, Gaspard de Besse, who hid in the region's many caves and terrorized local travelers until, at age 25, he was hanged and decapitated by military authorities in the main square at Aix-en-Provence.

Following the path of the ancient Roman Aurelian Way, N7 traces the area's northern edge, running through the Estérel Gap between Fréjus and Cannes. This route offers the massif's most stunning vistas.

GETTING THERE Both of the area's twisted boundary roads run from Cannes to Fréjus, with N7 tracing the northern boundary and the southerly N98 following a route along the coast.

GETTING AROUND To get to the massif's summit, **Mont Vinaigre** (elevation 589m/ 1,962 ft.), turn right at the Testannier crossroads 11km (7 miles) northeast of Fréjus. A parking area allows you to leave your car and make the final 15 minutes of the ascent on foot, climbing to the observation deck of a watchtower for a view stretching from the Alps to the Massif des Maures. At La Napoule, turn around to follow the southwesterly trail of N98 back to Fréjus.

Turning inland just beyond Le Trayas at **Pointe de l'Observatoire,** you can ascend to the **Grotte de la Ste-Baume** for the views that inspired the medieval hermit St. Honorat, who once dwelt in the cave. Farther along N98, at **Pointe de Baumette,** is a memorial to the French writer and aviator Antoine de St-Exupéry. At Agay, turn inland again to reach the rocky **Gorge du Mal-Infernet,** a twisted rut in the earth, offering a contrast to the surrounding peaks with their overview of the region. Continuing along this inland route leads you to **Pic du Cap-Roux,** at 431m (1,438 ft.), and **Pic de l'Ours,** at 488m (1,627 ft.), both offering sweeping views of land and sea. Technically, the park is administered by the **Office National des Forêts** (© 04-94-44-16-45), from an office that's open 24 hours a day, and which is located at the northeastern entrance to the park, in the Maison Forestière, on the Route des Colles/Route du Pic de l'Ours. As the above-noted organization is more deeply concerned with maintenance and safety issues within the park, it's usually wiser to get touring and tourist information from the tourist offices of any of the towns and villages nearby.

VISITOR INFORMATION You can get additional information on sights, routes, and accommodations at the **Offices de Tourisme** in St-Raphaël, rue Waldeck-Rousseau (© 04-94-19-52-52); Fréjus, 325 rue Jean-Jaurès (© 04-94-51-83-83); Les-Adrets-de-l'Estérel, place de la Mairie (© 04-94-40-93-57); and Agay, boulevard de la Plage (© 04-94-82-01-85).

WHERE TO STAY

Note that the **Auberge des Adrets** (see below) also rents rooms.

L'Estirado des Andrets & Auberge Panoramique ★ (Finds In the heart of Estérel lies a combined hotel and restaurant that's worth a detour. The village of Les Andrets is between Cannes and St. Raphaël, between sea and hills. A stay, or even a stopover for lunch, is like a journey back to old-time Provence. Everything is traditional in style, with cozy, well-furnished bedrooms with a private bathroom. On a hot summer day, guests congregate at the outdoor swimming pool or else lounge in the sun against a scenic backdrop of forested hills. The food at Auberge Panoramique is among the best in the area, highlighting a *provençale* and French cuisine that changes with the seasons. Dining can be in the shade of a straw hut in summer or close to a roaring fireplace in winter.

83600 Les Andrets de l'Estérel. © **04-94-40-90-64.** Fax 04-94-40-98-52. www.estirado.com. 21 units. 75€–98€ double; 130€–150€ suite. MC, V. Free parking. **Amenities:** Restaurant; babysitting; pool (outdoor). *In room:* TV, hair dryer, Wi-Fi (free).

WHERE TO DINE

Auberge des Adrets ★★ PROVENÇALE/FRENCH Despite an official mailing address that places this medieval inn in Fréjus, it lies only 2km (1¼ miles) east of

Les-Adrets-de-l'Estérel. Records of its existence go back to A.D. 824, when troubadours sang and horses rested here after treks across a landscape even rougher and more arid than other points nearby. In 1653, the site was designated a Relais de Poste, where travelers and their horses could find lodging. Today it focuses on upscale versions of Provence's rural dishes, as interpreted by noted chef Christian Née. He presides over an antiques-filled dining room that spills out onto a large terrace overlooking arid landscapes and the faraway Baie de Cannes. Menu items are likely to include warm foie gras sautéed with roughly textured bread, magret of duckling roasted with a honey-flavored sesame sauce, a sophisticated roster of risottos (including one with lobster), and aromatic rack of lamb with an olive tapenade. Dessert might be a hot soufflé with black chocolate.

The hotel also offers 10 carefully decorated rooms, each with air-conditioning, some kind of ornate (usually baldachin) bed, and views over a garden. Doubles cost 181€ to 256€.

R.N. 7, 83600 Fréjus. ✆ **04-94-82-11-82.** www.auberge-adrets.com. Fax 04-94-82-11-80. Main courses 20€–78€; fixed-price menu 38€. AE, DC, MC, V. May to late Sept daily noon–2:30pm and 7:30–10:30pm. Closed off season.

6 LA NAPOULE-PLAGE ★

901km (560 miles) S of Paris; 8km (5 miles) W of Cannes

This secluded resort is on the sandy beaches of the Golfe de la Napoule. In 1919, the once-obscure fishing village was a paradise for the eccentric sculptor Henry Clews, son of a New York banker, and his wife, Marie, an architect. Clews fled America's "charlatans," whom he believed had profited from World War I. His house is now a museum.

ESSENTIALS

GETTING THERE The waterside community of La Napoule–Plage is part of La Mandelieu–La Napoule, which lies on the **bus** and **train** routes between Cannes and St-Raphaël. The one-way fare, for the bus or train, from Cannes to La Mandelieu–La Napoule is 2€. For information and schedules, call ✆ **36-35,** or visit **www.voyages-sncf. com**. If you're **driving,** take A8 west from Cannes.

VISITOR INFORMATION The **Office de Tourisme** is on avenue Henry-Clews (✆ **04-92-97-99-27;** fax 04-93-93-64-66; www.ot-mandelieu.fr).

THE MAIN ATTRACTION

Château de la Napoule/Musée Henry-Clews ★★ An inscription over the entrance to this fairy tale–like château reads: ONCE UPON A TIME. The château, a brooding, medieval-looking fortress whose foundations begin at the edge of the sea, was rebuilt from the ruins of a real medieval château. Clews covered the capitals and lintels with his own grotesque menagerie—scorpions, pelicans, gnomes, monkeys, lizards—the revelations of a tortured mind. Women and feminism are recurring themes in the sculptor's work; an example is the distorted suffragette depicted in his *Cat Woman.* The artist was preoccupied with old age in men and women alike, and admired chivalry and dignity in the man represented by Don Quixote—to whom he likened himself. Clews died in Switzerland in 1937, and his body was returned to La Napoule for burial. Marie Clews later opened the château to the public as a testimonial to the inspiration of her husband.

Bd. Henry-Clews. ✆ **04-93-49-95-05.** www.chateau-lanapoule.com. Admission 6€ adults, 4€ children 6 and under. Feb 7–Nov 7 daily 10am–6pm; Nov 8–Feb 6 daily 10am–5pm.

La Calanque (Value)   The foundations of this charming hotel date from the Roman Empire. The present hotel, run by the same family since 1942, looks like a hacienda, with salmon-colored stucco walls and shutters. Register in the bar in the rear (through the dining room). Bedrooms range from small to medium, each with a comfortable mattress. Those who take the bathroomless units will find the corridor bathrooms adequate and well maintained. Aside from a phone, in-room amenities in all units are a bit scarce. The hotel's restaurant spills onto a terrace and offers some of the cheapest meals in La Napoule.

Av. Henry-Clews, 06210 La Napoule. ℓ **04-93-49-95-11.** Fax 04-93-49-67-44. 17 units. 46€–61€ double. MC, V. Closed mid-Oct to Feb. **Amenities:** Restaurant; bar. *In room:* A/C (in some), TV.

L'Ermitage du Riou ★★ (Finds)   This old Provençal house, the most tranquil choice at the resort, is a seaside government-rated four-star hotel bordering the Riou River and the Cannes-Mandelieu golf club. The rooms are furnished in regional style, with authentic furniture and ancient paintings. Rooms range in size from medium to spacious, and each has an elegant bed and fine linens. The most expensive rooms have safes. Views are of the sea or the golf course.

Av. Henry-Clews, 06210 La Napoule. ℓ **04-93-49-95-56.** Fax 04-92-97-69-05. www.ermitage-du-riou.fr. 41 units. 126€–301€ double; 341€–529€ suite. AE, DC, MC, V. **Amenities:** Restaurant; bar; pool (outdoor); sauna. *In room:* A/C, TV, hair dryer, minibar, Wi-Fi (free).

Pullman Cannes Mandelieu Royal Casino ★★   A member of the Accor group, this Las Vegas–style hotel is on the beach near a man-made harbor, about 8km (5 miles) from Cannes. It was the first French hotel with a casino and the last (before building codes changed) to have a casino directly on the beach. The hotel has one of the most contemporary designs on the Côte d'Azur. Most of the good-size rooms angle toward a sea view; those facing the street are likely to be noisy, despite soundproofing. The restaurant **Le Féréol** (below) serves modern French cuisine and impressive lunchtime buffets.

605 av. du Général-de-Gaulle, 06212 La Mandelieu–La Napoule. ℓ **800/221-4542** in the U.S. and Canada, or 04-92-97-70-00. Fax 04-93-49-51-50. www.pullmanhotels.com. 213 units. 250€–520€ double; from 650€ suite. AE, DC, MC, V. Parking 12€. **Amenities:** 2 restaurants; 2 bars; babysitting; casino; concierge; health club; 2 tennis courts (lit). *In room:* A/C, TV, hair dryer, minibar, Wi-Fi (10€ per hr.).

WHERE TO DINE

Note that the restaurant in **La Calanque** (above) is open to nonguests.

Brocherie II SEAFOOD   The way this restaurant curves along the shoreline gives the impression that you're riding out to sea on a floating houseboat. You'll enter its precincts by crossing a gangplank lined with flaming torches. Specialties include virtually every fish that can be found in local waters—the freshest and best are grilled and served as simply as possible. Your choices of sauce include a rich hollandaise or béarnaise, or an herb-flavored version of white wine, butter, or vinaigrette. The heady version of bouillabaisse is priced at 42€ per person, and a selection of (very expensive) lobsters is chosen from the establishment's bubbling holding tank. Meat dishes include succulent brochettes of Provençal lamb with rosemary and red wine.

Au Port. ℓ **04-93-49-80-73.** Reservations recommended. Main courses 23€–31€; fixed-price menu 38€. MC, V. Daily 9am–10pm. Closed Jan.

Le Féréol ★ TRADITIONAL/MODERN FRENCH   This well-designed restaurant serves most of the culinary needs of the largest hotel (and only casino) in town. Outfitted

Following La Route Napoleon

On March 1, 1815, having escaped from a Senate-imposed exile on Elba that began in April 1814, Napoleon, accompanied by a small band of followers, landed at Golfe-Juan. The deposed emperor was intent on marching northward to re-claim his throne as emperor.

Though the details of his journey have been obscured by time, two versions of a local legend about one of his first mainland encounters exist. The first version claims that shortly after landing at Golfe-Juan, Napoleon and his military escort were waylaid by highwaymen unimpressed by his credentials. The other turns the story around, claiming that Napoleon's men, attempting to build a supply of money and arms, waylaid the coach of the prince de Monaco, whose principality, stripped of independence during the Revolution, had just been restored by Louis XVIII. When the prince told Napoleon that he was on his way to re-claim his throne, the exiled emperor stated that they were in the same business and bid his men to let the coach pass unhindered.

In the 1930s, the French government recognized Napoleon's positive influence on internal affairs by building Route 85, **La Route Napoleon,** to roughly trace the steps of the exiled emperor in search of a throne. It stretches from Golfe-Juan to Grenoble, but the most scenic stretch is in Provence, between Grasse and Digne-les-Bains. The route is well marked with commemorative plaques sporting an eagle in flight, though the "action" documented south of Grenoble revolves around simple stops made for food and sleep along the way.

After embarking from Cannes on the morning of March 2, the group passed through Grasse and halted just beyond St-Vallier-de-Thiey, spending the night. From this point to the end destination at Digne-les-Bains, the route touches only a handful of small settlements; the most notable is Castellane and the village of Barrème, where an encampment was set up on the night of March 3. The next day, the group stopped for lunch in Digne-les-Bains before leaving the region to continue north toward the showdown at Grenoble. Although the relais where he dined is long gone, you can stop at **Hostellerie de Préjoly,** avenue Gaston de Fontmichel, in St-Vallier-de-Thiey (© **04-93-42-60-86**). Cozy and historic, with a staff that's consciously tied into the travails and tribulations of Napoleon during his transit through their town, it serves tasty set-price menus for between 19€ and 37€. During July and August, it's open daily for lunch and dinner; but the rest of the year, it's closed Sunday and Tuesday night, and all day on Wednesday.

The **Office de Tourisme** at place du Tour, St-Vallier-de-Thiey (© **04-93-42-78-00**), can provide you with a detailed account of the trek, a map of the three campsites where Napoleon and his men slept, and a map indicating where the road deviates from Napoleon's actual route, now maintained as a hiking trail where you can follow in his footsteps. The office is open Monday to Saturday 9am to noon and 3 to 6pm.

in nautical style, it offers impressive lunch buffets. At night the room is candlelit and more elegant, and the view through bay windows is soothing. Menu items include Breton artichokes with a "surprise" stuffing composed of minced cured ham, cheese, and herbs; a "frivolity" of two kinds of exotic mushrooms plus a confit of quail all served atop a warm brioche; filet of John Dory with artichoke hearts, lavender, and scampi; and a succulent roasted veal with baby Provençal vegetables and herbs.

In the Pullman Cannes Mandelieu Royal Casino (p. 246), 605 av. du Général-de-Gaulle. (℗ **04-92-97-70-20.** Reservations recommended. Main courses 16€–30€; fixed-price buffet lunch 29€; fixed-price dinner 39€. AE, DC, MC, V. Sept–June Wed–Sun 12:30–2:30pm and 7–10:30pm; July–Aug daily 12:30–3:30pm and 7–11pm.

L'Oasis ★★★ MODERN FRENCH There's no more wonderful cuisine on the Western Riviera than at L'Oasis. At the entrance to the harbor of La Napoule, in a mid-20th-century house with a lovely garden and a re-creation of a medieval cloister, this restaurant became world famous under now-retired Louis Outhier. Today, his protégé, Stéphane Raimbault, prepares sophisticated cuisine. Because Raimbault cooked in Japan for 9 years, many of his dishes are of the "East meets West" variety. The cuisine falls roughly into traditional French or traditional *provençale,* with a touch of Japanese. The latter cuisine is evoked by crayfish cooked "in the fires of hell" and served with wok-fried baby vegetables. Traditional dishes include perfectly grilled Mediterranean fish or a masterful saddle of venison with hazelnuts, pepper sauce, and caramelized pears. The cellar houses one of the finest collections of Provençal wines anywhere. In summer, meals are served under the plane trees in the garden.

Rue Honoré-Carle. (℗ **04-93-49-95-52.** www.oasis-raimbault.com. Reservations required. Main courses 24€–115€; fixed-price lunch 58€–89€; fixed-price dinner 130€–190€. AE, DC, MC, V. Daily noon–2pm and 7:30–10pm. Closed Sun dinner and Mon Nov–Mar; closed mid-Dec to mid-Jan.

---

7 CANNES ★★★

905km (562 miles) S of Paris; 164km (102 miles) E of Marseille; 26km (16 miles) SW of Nice

When Coco Chanel came here, got a suntan, and returned to Paris bronzed, she startled the milk-white ladies of society. Today the golden bodies—in nearly nonexistent swimsuits—that line the sandy beaches of this chic resort continue the trend started by the late fashion designer.

Cannes is at its most frenzied during the International Film Festival at the Palais des Festivals on promenade de la Croisette. On the seafront boulevards, flashbulbs pop as the stars and wannabes emerge and pose and pose and pose. The festival's stellar activities are closed to most visitors, who are forced to line up in front of the Palais des Festivals. Known as "the bunker," this concrete structure is the venue for premiers that draw some 5,000 spectators. With international regattas, galas, *concours d'élégance,* and even a Mimosa Festival in February, something's always happening at Cannes—except in November, traditionally a dead month.

ESSENTIALS

GETTING THERE The Nice **international airport** (℗ **08-20-42-33-33; www.rca. tm.fr**) is a 30-minute drive northeast. Buses pick up passengers at the airport every 40 minutes during the day and drop them at the Gare Routière, place de l'Hôtel de Ville (℗ **04-93-45-20-08**). The fare is 6€.

Trains from the other Mediterranean resorts, Paris, and the rest of France arrive frequently throughout the day. By train, Cannes is 15 minutes from Antibes and 35 minutes from Nice. The TGV from Paris via Marseille reaches Cannes in about 5½ to 6 breathless hours. The one-way fare from Paris is about 50€ to 95€. For rail information and schedules, call ⑦ **36-35,** or visit **www.voyages-sncf.com.**

Rapide Côte d'Azur, place de l'Hôtel de Ville, Cannes (⑦ **04-93-39-70-30**), offers **bus** service to Nice and back every 20 minutes during the day (trip time: 1½ hr.). The one-way fare is 6€. Bus service from Antibes operates every half-hour.

By **car** from Marseille, take A51 north to Aix-en-Provence, continuing along A8 east to Cannes. From Nice, follow A8 southwest to Cannes.

VISITOR INFORMATION   The **Office de Tourisme** is at 1 bd. De La Croisette (⑦ **04-93-39-24-53;** fax 04-92-99-84-23; www.cannes.fr).

SPECIAL EVENTS   The **International Film Festival** at the Palais des Festivals on promenade de la Croisette is in the end of May. It attracts not only film stars but also seemingly every photographer in the world. You have a better chance of being named prime minister of France than you do of attending one of the major screenings. (Hotel rooms and tables at restaurants are equally scarce during the festival.) But the people-watching is fabulous. If you find yourself here at the right time, you can join the thousands who line up in front of the Palais des Festivals, where the premieres are held. With paparazzi shouting and gendarmes holding back fans, the guests parade along the red carpet, stopping for a moment to strike a pose. *C'est Cannes!*

You may be able to get tickets for some of the lesser films, which play 24 hours. For information, see "Provence Calendar of Events," in chapter 3, or visit **www.festival-cannes.org.**

SEEING THE SIGHTS

For many, Cannes consists of only one street, **promenade de la Croisette** ★★ (or just La Croisette), curving along the coast and split by islands of palms and flowers. It's said

---

Seeing Cannes from a Petit Train

One of the best ways to get your bearings in Cannes (and to get an idea of the difference between the city's new and old neighborhoods) is to board a white-sided *Petit Train touristique de Cannes.* The diesel-powered vehicles roll through the streets on rubber tires. They operate every day from 10am to between 7 and 11:30pm, depending on the season (there's no service in Nov). Choose from two itineraries: For views of glittery modern Cannes, board the train at a designated spot in front of either of the town's two casinos for a ride along La Croisette and its side streets. For a ride through the narrow streets of Vieux Cannes (Le Suquet), board the train at a clearly designated site on the seaward side of La Croisette, opposite the Hôtel Majestic. Both tours depart every hour. They last around 45 minutes, depending on traffic, and cost 7€ for adults, 3€ for children 9 and under, depending on the tour. (The tour of the old town is the less expensive.) A combination ticket to both tours (good on separate days, if you prefer) costs 10€ for adults, 5€ for children 9 and under. For details, call ⑦ **04-93-38-39-18; www.cannes-petit-train.com.**

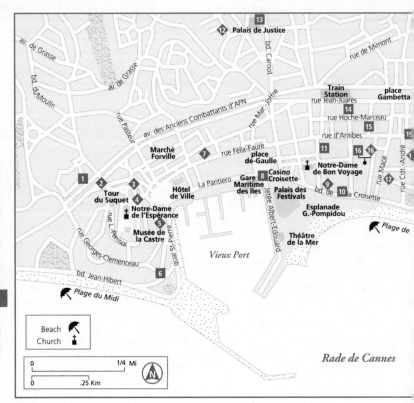

Vieux Port

Beach 🏖
Church ✝

0   1/4 Mi
0   .25 Km

Rade de Cannes

that Edward, Prince of Wales (before he became Edward VII), contributed to its original cost. But he was a Johnny-come-lately to Cannes. In 1834, Lord Brougham, a lord chancellor of England, set out for Nice and was turned away because of an outbreak of cholera. He landed at Cannes and liked it so much that he built a villa here. Returning every winter until his death in 1868, he proselytized it in London, drawing a long line of British visitors. In the 1890s, Cannes became popular with Russian grand dukes (it's said that more caviar was consumed here than in all of Moscow).

A port of call for cruise liners, the seafront of Cannes is lined with hotels, apartment houses, and chic boutiques. Many of the bigger hotels, some dating from the 19th century, claim part of the beach for the private use of their guests, but public areas do exist. Above the harbor, the old town of Cannes sits on Suquet Hill, with its 14th-century tower, the **Tour du Suquet,** which the English dubbed "the Lord's Tower."

Nearby is the **Musée de la Castre** ★, in the Château de la Castre, Le Suquet (© **04-93-38-55-26**). It contains paintings, sculpture, and works of decorative art. The ethnography section includes Peruvian and Maya pottery; one gallery is devoted to relics of Mediterranean civilizations, from the Greeks to the Romans, the Cypriots to the Egyptians. Five rooms hold 19th-century paintings. The museum is open daily in July and

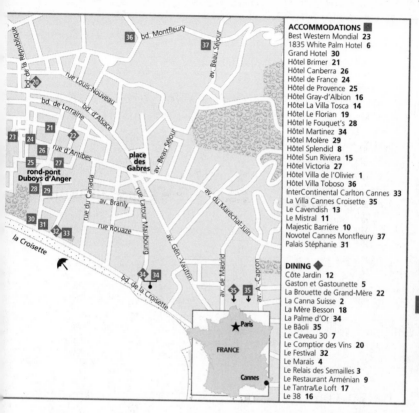

ACCOMMODATIONS
Best Western Mondial **23**
1835 White Palm Hotel **6**
Grand Hotel **30**
Hôtel Brimer **21**
Hôtel Canberra **26**
Hôtel de France **24**
Hôtel de Provence **25**
Hôtel Gray-d'Albion **16**
Hôtel La Villa Tosca **14**
Hôtel Le Florian **19**
Hôtel le Fouquet's **28**
Hôtel Martinez **34**
Hôtel Molère **29**
Hôtel Splendid **8**
Hôtel Sun Riviera **15**
Hôtel Victoria **27**
Hôtel Villa de l'Olivier **1**
Hôtel Villa Toboso **36**
InterContinental Carlton Cannes **33**
La Villa Cannes Croisette **35**
Le Cavendish **13**
Le Mistral **11**
Majestic Barriére **10**
Novotel Cannes Montfleury **37**
Palais Stéphanie **31**

DINING
Côte Jardin **12**
Gaston et Gastounette **5**
La Brouette de Grand-Mère **22**
La Canna Suisse **2**
La Mère Besson **18**
La Palme d'Or **34**
Le Bâoli **35**
Le Caveau 30 **7**
Le Comptior des Vins **20**
Le Festival **32**
Le Marais **4**
Le Relais des Semailles **3**
Le Restaurant Arménian **9**
Le Tantra/Le Loft **17**
Le 38 **16**

August 10am to 7pm; September to March Tuesday to Sunday 10am to 1pm and 2 to 5pm; April to June Tuesday to Sunday 10am to 1pm and 2 to 6pm. Admission is 4€ adults, 2.50€ ages 18 to 25, and free for ages 17 and under.

Though nobody plans a trip to Cannes to see churches, the city does contain some worthy examples. The largest and most prominent is **Notre-Dame de Bon Voyage,** square Mérimée, near the Palais des Festivals; it was built in a faux Gothic style in the late 19th century. The most historic church, **Notre-Dame de l'Espérance,** place de la Castre (© **04-93-99-55-07**), was built between 1521 and 1627 and combines both Gothic and Renaissance elements. The town's most unusual church is the **Eglise Orthodoxe Russe St-Michel Archange,** 36–40 bd. Alexandre-III (© **04-93-43-00-28**), built in 1894 through the efforts of Alexandra Skripytzine, a Russian in exile; it's capped with a cerulean-blue onion dome and a gilded triple cross. It is usually locked, except for services on Saturday at 5pm and Sunday between 9:30am and noon.

A DAY AT THE BEACH

Beachgoing in Cannes has more to do with exhibitionism and voyeurism than with actual swimming.

Ferrying to the Iles de Lérins

Across the bay from Cannes, the Lérins Islands are the major excursion from the port. Ferries depart every half-hour from 7:30am to 30 minutes before sundown. The largest of the ferry companies in Cannes is **Compagnies Estérel-Chanteclair,** 1 Port de Cannes (© **04-93-39-11-82**). Competitors include **Cie Horizon IV,** CQ (© **04-92-98-71-36**); **Compagnie Maritime Cannoise,** quai St. Pierre (© **04-93-38-29-92**); and **Trans-Côte d'Azur,** quai St-Pierre (© **04-92-98-71-30**; www.trans-cote-azur.com). Departures are from the Gare Maritime des Iles in Cannes. Round-trip fare is 11€ for adults, 5.50€ for children 5 to 10, and free for children 4 and under.

Ile Ste-Marguerite The first island is named after St. Honorat's sister, Ste. Marguerite, who lived here with a group of nuns in the 5th century. Today it is a youth center whose members (when they aren't sailing and diving) are dedicated to the restoration of the fort. From the dock where the boat lands, you can stroll along the island (signs point the way) to the **Fort de l'Ile,** built by Spanish troops from 1635 to 1637. Below the hill is the 1st-century-B.C. Roman town where the unlucky man immortalized in *The Man in the Iron Mask* was imprisoned.

One of French history's most perplexing mysteries is the identity of the man who allegedly wore the *masque du fer,* a prisoner of Louis XIV who arrived at Ste-Marguerite in 1698. Dumas popularized the legend that he was a brother of Louis XIV, and it has even been suggested that the prisoner and a mysterious woman had a son who went to Corsica and "founded" the Bonaparte family. However, the most common theory is that the prisoner was a servant of the

Plage de la Croisette extends between the Vieux Port and the Port Canto. Though the beaches along this billion-dollar stretch of sand aren't in the strictest sense private, they're *payante,* meaning entrance costs 15€ to 22€. You don't need to be a guest of the Noga Hilton, Martinez, Carlton, or Majestic to use the beaches associated with those hotels, though if you are you'll usually get a 50% discount. A wooden barricade that stops close to the sea separates each beach from its neighbors, making it easy for you to stroll from one to another.

Why should you pay a fee at all? Well, it includes a full day's use of a mattress, a chaise longue (the seafront isn't sandy or even soft, but covered with pebbles and dark-gray shingles), and a parasol, as well as easy access to freshwater showers and kiosks selling beverages. You can also dine at outdoor restaurants where no one minds if you appear in your swimsuit.

For nostalgia's sake, our favorite beach is the one associated with the **Carlton** (see "Where to Stay," below)—it was the first beach we went to, as teenagers, in Cannes. The merits of each of the 20 or so beaches vary daily depending on the crowd. And because every beach allows topless bathing (keep your bottom covered), you're likely to find the same forms of décolletage along the entire strip.

Looking for a free public beach where you'll have to survive without renting chaises or parasols? Head for **Plage du Midi,** sometimes called Midi Plage, just west of the Vieux Port (no phone), or **Plage Gazagnaire,** just east of the Port Canto (no phone). Here you'll find families with children and lots of caravan-type vehicles parked nearby.

superintendent, Fouquet, named Eustache Dauger. He might have earned his fate by aiding Fouquet in embezzling the king's treasury. At any rate, he died in the Bastille in Paris in 1703.

You can visit his cell at Ste-Marguerite, where it seems that every visitor has written his or her name. As you stand listening to the sound of the sea, you realize what a forlorn outpost this was.

Musée de la Mer, Fort Royal (© **04-93-43-18-17**), traces the history of the island, displaying artifacts of Ligurian, Roman, and Arab civilizations, plus the remains discovered by excavations, including paintings, mosaics, and ceramics. The museum is open April to June Wednesday to Monday 10am to noon and 2 to 6pm; July to September Wednesday to Monday 10am to noon and 3 to 7pm; October to March Wednesday to Monday 10am to noon and 2 to 5pm. Admission is 3€ for adults, free for students and children 17 and under.

Ile St-Honorat Less than 2km (only a mile) long, but richer in history than any of its sibling islands, the Ile St-Honorat is the site of a working monastery whose origins go back to the 5th century. Today the **Abbaye de St-Honorat,** les Iles de Lérins, 06400 Cannes (© **04-92-99-54-00**), maintains a combination of medieval ruins and early-20th-century ecclesiastical buildings, inhabited by a permanent community of about 30 Cistercian monks. If space is available, outsiders can visit, for prayer and meditation only, and spend the night. However, most visitors come to wander through the pine forests on the island's western side and sun themselves on its beaches.

OUTDOOR PURSUITS

BICYCLING & MOTOR SCOOTERING   Despite the roaring traffic, the flat landscapes between Cannes and satellite resorts such as La Napoule are well suited for riding a bike or motor scooter. At **Cycles Daniel,** 2 rue du Pont Romain (© **04-93-99-90-30**), *vélos tout terrain* (mountain bikes) cost 16€ a day. Motorized bikes and scooters cost 36€ per day; renters must be at least 14 years old. For larger scooters, you must present a valid driver's license. Another purveyor of bikes is **Mistral Location,** 4 rue Georges Clemenceau (© **04-93-39-08-53;** www.mistral-location.com), which charges 14€ per day.

BOATING   Several companies rent boats of any size, with or without a crew, for a day, a week, or a month. An outfit known for short-term rentals of small craft, including motorboats, sailboats, and canoes, is **Elco Marine,** 110 bd. du Midi (© **04-93-47-12-62**). For larger boats, including motor-driven and sailing yachts and craft suitable for deep-sea fishing, try **International Yacht Charter,** 45 La Croisette (© **04-93-34-27-77;** www.elcomarine.re.fr**).

GOLF   One of the region's most challenging courses, **Country-Club de Cannes-Mougins,** 175 av. du Golf, route d'Antibes, Mougins (© **04-93-75-79-13;** www.golf-cannes-mougins.com), 6.5km (4 miles) north of Cannes, is a 1976 reconfiguration by Dye & Ellis of a 1920s-era course. Noted for the olive trees and cypresses that adorn the flat terrain, it has many water hazards and technical challenges. Since 1981, the par-72 course has played host to the Cannes-Mougins Open, a stop on the PGA European Tour. The course is open to anyone (with proof of handicap) willing to pay greens fees of 150€ per person. An electric golf cart rents for 45€, golf clubs for 35€. Reservations are recommended.

SWIMMING   Cannes probably has more privately owned swimming pools per capita than anywhere else in France. If your hotel doesn't have one, consider an excursion to the **Piscine Pierre de Coubertin,** avenue P. de Coubertin (© **04-93-47-12-94**). Its length of almost 23m (75 ft.) makes this outdoor pool ideal for swimming laps. Because it's used for a variety of civic functions, including practices for local swim teams, hours are limited, so call ahead. Entrance costs 3€ for adults, 1.50€ for children 3 to 15.

TENNIS   Some resorts have their own courts. The city of Cannes also maintains a half-dozen courts (one made from synthetic resins, five clay-topped); you'll pay 10€ to 15€ per hour, depending on the court and the time you want to play, plus 3.25€ per hour for lighting. They're at **ASLM Tennis Municipal de la Bastide,** 220 av. Francis Tonner, 06400 Cannes (© **04-93-47-29-33**). If those courts are already taken, **ASLM Tennis Municipal Aérodrome,** Aérodrome de Cannes Mandelieu, 06400 Cannes (© **04-93-47-29-33**), also maintained by the municipality, charges the same rates for its five clay-topped courts.

SHOPPING

Cannes competes more successfully than many of its neighbors in a highly commercial blend of resort-style leisure, luxury glamour, and media glitz. So you're likely to find branch outlets of virtually every stylish Paris retailer.

Every big-name designer you can think of (Saint Laurent, Rykiel, Hermès) as well as big-name designers you've never heard of (Claude Bonucci, Basile, and Durrani) are here—but, more important, real-people shops (shops for gently worn star-studded cast-offs, flea markets for fun junk, and a fruit, flower, and vegetable market) thrive.

ANTIQUES   In the Palais de Festivals on La Croisette, Cannes stages one of France's most prestigious **antiques salons** in mid-July and late December or early January. Its organizers refuse to include low- or even middle-bracket stock. This is serious, with lots of 18th- and early-19th-century merchandise. Admission is 10€. Shipping services are available. For dates and information, contact the **Salon des Antiquaires de Cannes,** 34 Rue de L'Eglise, 75015 Paris (© **01-45-61-05-35**).

Looking for top-notch antiques dealers whose merchandise will wow you? One of the city's most noteworthy is **Hubert Herpin,** 20 rue Macé (© **04-93-39-56-18**). This store carries a wide selection of marble statues, marquetry, and 18th- and 19th-century furniture.

BOOKS   A year-round bookstore, **Ciné-Folie,** 14 rue des Frères Pradignac (© **04-93-39-22-99**), is devoted entirely to films. It's called *La Boutique du Cinema.* The outlet is the finest film bookstore in the south of France and also sells vintage film stills and movie posters.

CHOCOLATE & CANDIES   Several famous chocolatiers keep chocolate lovers in Cannes happy. **Chez Bruno,** 13 rue Hoche (© **04-93-39-26-63**), opened in 1929 and is maintained by a descendant of its founder; the shop is famous for *fruits confits* chocolates, as well as its *marrons glacés* (glazed chestnuts), made fresh daily.

DEPARTMENT STORES   Near the train station in the heart of Cannes, **Galeries Lafayette** has a small branch at 6 rue du Maréchal-Foch (© **04-97-06-25-00**). It's noted for the upscale fashion in its carefully arranged interiors.

(Fun Facts)   A Mammillary Tribute to a Courtesan

The twin cupolas of the InterContinental Carlton were modeled on the breasts of the most fabled local courtesan, **La Belle Otéro.** The hotel's main restaurant also carries her name.

DESIGNER SHOPS   Most of the big names in fashion, for men and women alike, line **promenade de la Croisette,** known as **La Croisette,** the main drag facing the sea. Among the most prestigious is **Dior,** 38 promenade de la Croisette (© **04-92-98-98-00**). The stores are in a row, stretching from the Hôtel Carlton almost to the Palais des Festivals, with the best names closest to the **Gray-d'Albion,** 38 rue des Ferbes (© **04-92-99-79-79**), which is both a mall and a hotel (how convenient). The stores in the Gray-d'Albion mall include **Hermès.** The two-section mall serves as a cut-through from the primary expensive shopping street, La Croisette, to the less expensive shopping street, **rue d'Antibes.**

FLEA MARKETS   Cannes has two regular flea markets. Casual, dusty, and increasingly filled with castaways from estate sales, the **Marché Forville,** conducted in the neighborhood of the same name, near the Palais des Festivals, is a stucco structure with a roof and a few arches but no sides. From Tuesday to Sunday, it's the fruit, vegetable, and flower market that supplies dozens of grand restaurants. Monday is *brocante* day, when the market fills with dealers selling everything from *grandmère*'s dishes to bone-handled carving knives.

On Saturdays, from 8am to 12:30pm, a somewhat disorganized and busy **flea market** takes place outdoors along the edges of the allée de la Liberté, across from the Palais des Festivals. Hours depend on the whims of whatever dealer happens to haul in a cache of merchandise, but it usually begins around 8am and runs out of steam by around 4:30pm. *Note:* Vendors at the two flea markets may or may not be the same.

FOOD   The street with the greatest density of emporiums selling wine, olives, herbs, cheese, bread, and oils is the appealing **rue Meynadier.**

A charming old-fashioned shop, **Cannolive,** 16–20 rue Vénizelos (© **04-93-39-08-19**), is owned by members of the Raynaud family, which founded the place in 1880. It sells Provençal olives and their byproducts—tapenades that connoisseurs refer to as "Provençal caviar," black "olives de Nice," and green "olives de Provence," as well as three grades of olive oil from regional producers. Oils and food products are at no. 16; gift items (fabrics, porcelain, and Provençal souvenirs) are sold next door.

MARKETS   At the edge of the Quartier Suquet, the **Marché Forville** is the town's primary fruit, flower, and vegetable market. On Monday it's a *brocante* market. See "Flea Markets," above.

PERFUME   The best and most expensive shop is **Bouteille,** 59 rue d'Antibes (© **04-93-39-05-16**). Its prices are higher than its competitors' because it stocks more brands, has a wider selection, and gives away occasional samples. Other shops dot rue d'Antibes. For reasonably priced perfumes, head to the boutiques associated with the Hôtel Gray-d'Albion.

Very Expensive

Hôtel Martinez ★★   Although it's a bit less appealing than the Carlton, this popular convention hotel is a desirable destination for the individual traveler, too. When the Art Deco hotel was built in the 1930s, it rivaled any other lodging along the coast in sheer size. Over the years, however, it fell into disrepair. But in 1982, the Concorde chain returned the hotel and its restaurants to their former luster, and today it competes with the Noga Hilton. The aim of the decor was a Roaring '20s style, and all units have full marble bathrooms, wood furnishings, tasteful carpets, and pastel fabrics. Called a hotel within a hotel, the penthouse floor has become the most chic place to stay at the resort; it features 11 suites, the most sought-after in town following a massive restyling. The hotel has a private beach, one of the finest restaurants in Cannes (**La Palme d'Or,** p. 261), and a water-skiing school.

73 bd. de la Croisette, 06406 Cannes. © **04-92-98-73-00.** Fax 04-93-39-67-82. www.hotel-martinez.com. 412 units. 545€–1,000€ double; from 2,900€ suite. AE, DC, MC, V. Parking 35€. **Amenities:** 3 summer restaurants; 2 winter restaurants; bar; babysitting; concierge; health club & spa; pool (outdoor); room service; 7 tennis courts (lit) nearby. *In room:* A/C, TV, hair dryer, minibar, Wi-Fi (30€).

InterContinental Carlton Cannes ★★★   Cynics say that one of the most amusing sights in Cannes watching vehicles dropping off huge amounts of baggage and numbers of fashionable (and sometimes not-so-fashionable) guests at the Carlton's grand gate. Built in 1912, the Carlton once attracted the most prominent members of Europe's *haut monde.* Today the hotel is more democratic, booking lots of conventions and motorcoach tour groups; however, in summer (especially during the film festival) the public rooms still fill with all the voyeuristic and exhibitionistic fervor that seems so much a part of the Riviera. Guest rooms are plush and a bit airier than you may expect. The most spacious rooms are in the west wing, and many upper-floor rooms open onto waterfront balconies.

58 bd. de la Croisette, 06400 Cannes. © **04-93-06-40-06.** Fax 04-93-06-40-25. www.intercontinental. com. 343 units. 230€–1,080€ double; from 800€ suite. AE, DC, MC, V. Parking 35€. **Amenities:** 3 summer restaurants; 1 winter restaurant; 2 bars; concierge; health club; room service. *In room:* A/C, TV, hair dryer, minibar, Wi-Fi (free).

Majestic Barrière ★★★   At the west end of La Croisette, the Majestic stands for glamour and has done so since 1926. Like the InterContinental Carlton (see below), it is a favorite with celebs during the annual film festival. Constructed around an overscale front patio, the hotel opens directly onto the esplanade and the sea. Inside, the setting is one of marble, crystal chandeliers, Oriental carpets, Louis XV silk furniture, and potted palms. The guest rooms are furnished with more of the same. All rooms are fitted with bedside controls and luxury amenities; the most special of the lot are 16 sea-view units with private terraces. The spacious, bright corner accommodations offer the best value. Bathrooms are sumptuous, with deluxe toiletries.

14 bd. de la Croisette, 06407 Cannes. © **04-92-98-77-00.** Fax 04-92-98-77-60. www.lucienbarriere.com. 305 units. 270€–870€ double; 465€–3,800€ suite. AE, DC, MC, V. Parking 33€. **Amenities:** 2 restaurants; bar; babysitting; concierge; pool (outdoor); room service. *In room:* A/C, TV, hair dryer, minibar, Wi-Fi (30 eu).

Palais Stéphanie ★   Formerly the Cannes Noga Hilton, this gleaming six-story contemporary hotel is one Cannes' most visible luxury sites. Within its glass, steel, and marble exterior, a spacious marble atrium-style lobby is dotted with red leather sofas and chairs and illuminated by a skylight. Guest rooms are carefully soundproofed, each with a balcony, a fresh coat of paint, and angular, contemporary-looking furniture from the mid-1990s. The in-house restaurant, Le Grand Bleu, is stylish, glossy, and upscale.

50 bd. De la Croisette, Cannes 06414. ✆ **04-92-99-70-00.** www.hotel-palaise-stephanie-cannes.com. 232 units. 210€–1,100€ double; 450€–3,500€ suite. AE, DC, MC, V. **Amenities:** Restaurant; bar; room service. *In room:* A/C, TV, hair dryer, minibar, Wi-Fi (free).

Expensive

1835 White Palm Hotel ★★   This seven-story hotel on the harborfront of Cannes offers views that extend over some of the most expensive private yachts in the Mediterranean. It has surrounding balconies and an open-air lounge on its top floor. A remake of an older hotel, it has a well-designed, bright interior, offering a well-trained staff and contemporary-looking upscale bedrooms, some with views over the sea.

1 bd. Jean-Hibert, 06407 Cannes. ✆ **04-92-99-73-00.** Fax 04-92-99-73-29. www.sofitel.com. 134 units. 276€–796€ double; 704€–1,958€ suite. AE, DC, MC, V. **Amenities:** 2 restaurants; bar; babysitting; concierge; pool (outdoor); room service. *In room:* A/C, TV, DVD, CD player, hair dryer, minibar, Wi-Fi (15€).

Grand Hôtel ★   Tall date palms and a lawn sweeping down to the waterfront esplanade lend this hotel a gracious air. A renovated structure of glass and marble, it is part of a complex of adjoining apartment-house wings and encircling boutiques. Eleven floors of rooms (with wall-to-wall picture windows) open onto tile terraces. Vibrant colors are used throughout: sea blue, olive, sunburst red, and banana. Those rooms with sea views are the most expensive. The hotel's private beach is below.

45 bd. de la Croisette, 06140 Cannes. ✆ **04-93-38-15-45.** Fax 04-93-68-97-45. www.grand-hotel-cannes. com. 76 units. 200€–540€ double; 1,760€ suite. AE, MC, V. Parking 25€. Closed Nov–Dec 14. **Amenities:** Restaurant; 2 bars; babysitting; pool (outdoor); room service. *In room:* A/C, TV, hair dryer, minibar, Wi-Fi (free).

Hôtel Gray-d'Albion ★★   The smallest of the major hotels, this four-star rated hotel occupies a contemporary, not particularly historic building. Now part of the Lucien Barrière chain, it enjoys a respectable though somewhat staid image. Groups form a large part of its clientele, but it caters to individual travelers as well. The medium-size rooms blend contemporary and traditional furnishings. Each unit has a balcony, but the views aren't notable, except from the eighth and ninth floors, which overlook the Mediterranean. The hotel's restaurant, **Le 38** (p. 262), features the simple yet refined French cuisine of celebrity chef Alain Roy.

38 rue des Serbes, 06400 Cannes. ✆ **04-92-99-79-79.** Fax 04-93-99-26-10. www.lucienbarriere.com. 200 units. 199€–549€ double; 419€–2,009€ suite. AE, DC, MC, V. **Amenities:** Restaurant; bar; babysitting; concierge; room service. *In room:* A/C, TV, hair dryer, minibar, Wi-Fi (15€).

Novotel Cannes Montfleury ★★   This is a classical, contemporary hotel that has carved out a good market for itself among independent travelers, although it can't compete with the big guns reviewed above. Although it seems distant from the crush of Cannes, it's actually only a short but winding drive away. The modern palace shares a 4-hectare (10-acre) park with a sports complex. The open-air curved outdoor pool is surrounded by palms. The guest rooms are stylishly filled with all the modern conveniences, including bedside controls.

25 av. Beauséjour, 06400 Cannes. ✆ **04-93-68-86-86.** Fax 04-93-68-87-87. www.novotel.com. 182 units. 115€–215€ double. AE, DC, MC, V. From Cannes, follow the signs to Montfleury or the blue-and-white signs to the Novotel Montfleury. **Amenities:** Restaurant; bar; babysitting; concierge; health club; pool (outdoor); room service. *In room:* A/C, TV, hair dryer, minibar, Wi-Fi (24€).

Best Western Mondial Just a 3-minute walk from the beach, this modern hotel sits above stores on a commercial street. Three-quarters of its rooms have views of the water, and the others overlook the mountains and a street. The soft Devonshire-cream facade has a few small balconies. The attractive rooms are the draw here, with matching fabrics for the comfortable beds and draperies, and sliding mirror doors on wardrobes.

77 rue d'Antibes and 1 rue Teïsseire, 06407 Cannes. ✆ 800/43-HOTELS [468357] or 04-93-68-70-00. Fax 04-93-99-39-11. www.bestwestern.com. 49 units. 110€–310€ double; 175€–410€ suite. AE, DC, MC, V. **Amenities:** Babysitting. *In room:* A/C, TV, hair dryer, Jacuzzi (in some), minibar, Wi-Fi (free).

Hôtel Brimer On a quiet street about 4 blocks from the seafront, this small hotel occupies the second floor of a four-story building constructed in the 1970s. It has since been renovated and upgraded by owner Brice Guëlle, who runs a tight ship. Bedrooms are well maintained, are unpretentiously but comfortably furnished, and are relatively affordable in high-priced Cannes. Breakfast is the only meal served, although the neighborhood has many bistros.

9 rue Jean Daumas, 06400 Cannes. ✆ 04-93-38-62-91. Fax 04-93-39-49-71. www.brimer.fr. 15 units. 61€–84€ double. AE, DC, MC, V. Parking free on street. **Amenities:** Breakfast room. *In room:* TV, hair dryer, minibar, Wi-Fi (free).

Hôtel Canberra This low-profile hotel occupies a marvelous location near the Palais des Festivals. It's often booked during the festival by independent producers hoping to hit the big time. The rooms are well maintained, a blend of traditional and modern; those with southern exposure are sunnier and cost more. Size ranges from small to medium, but each comes with a good mattress. Limited parking is available by the hotel's small garden.

120 rue d'Antibes, 06400 Cannes. ✆ 04-97-06-95-00. Fax 04-92-98-03-47. www.hotels-ocre-azur.com. 35 units. 145€–310€ double; 245€–450€ suite. AE, DC, MC, V. Parking 25€. **Amenities:** Restaurant; bar; babysitting; pool (outdoor). *In room:* A/C, TV, minibar, Wi-Fi (free).

Hôtel Le Fouquet's ★ (Finds) This intimate lodging draws a discreet clientele, often from Paris, who'd never think of patronizing the grand hotels. Riviera French in design and decor, it lies several blocks from the beach. Each of the cozy guest rooms is outfitted in bold Provençal colors and has contemporary, vaguely regional furniture. The owner is often on-site, making the hotel feel like an intimate B&B.

2 rond-point Duboys-d'Angers, 06400 Cannes. ✆ 04-92-59-25-00. Fax 04-92-98-03-39. www.le-fouquets. com. 12 units. 140€–280€ double. AE, DC, MC, V. Closed Nov 1–Apr 12. Bus: 1. **Amenities:** Babysitting; room service. *In room:* A/C, TV, hair dryer, minibar.

Hôtel Splendid ★ (Value) Opened in 1871, this is a favorite haunt of scholars, politicians, actors, and musicians. The ornate white building with wrought-iron accents looks out onto the sea, the old port, and a park. The rooms are decorated with antique furniture and paintings, and about 15 have kitchenettes. The more expensive rooms have sea views.

4-6 Rue Félix-Faure, 06400 Cannes. ✆ 04-97-06-22-22. Fax 04-93-99-55-02. www.splendid-hotel-cannes.fr. 62 units. 126€–146€ double. Rates include breakfast. AE, MC, V. **Amenities:** Babysitting; room service. *In room:* A/C, TV, hair dryer.

Hôtel Sun Riviera ★ This genteel hotel is less well known than the blockbuster mega-hotels nearby, but its reasonable prices almost guarantee a healthy roster of bookings throughout the summer and during the film festival. It's set in the heart of Cannes, near most of the important shops and downtown bars and restaurants. Cheerful, stylish, and welcoming, with an image that's deliberately set a notch or two below what you might have expected at the Carlton or the Majestic, it offers a discreetly opulent decor in the public rooms and medium-size bedrooms that are comfortably outfitted with conservative good taste.

138 rue d'Antibes, 06400 Antibes. © **04-93-06-77-77.** Fax 04-93-38-31-10. www.sun-riviera.com. 42 units. 134€–267€ double; 240€–450€ suite. AE, DC, MC, V. **Amenities:** Bar; babysitting; pool (outdoor). *In room:* A/C, TV, hair dryer, minibar, Wi-Fi (free).

Hôtel Victoria ★   The Victoria, a stylish modern hotel, offers accommodations with period reproductions. Nearly half the rooms have balconies overlooking a small park and the hotel pool. The accommodations facing the park cost a little more but are worth it. In all units, silk bedspreads, padded headboards, and quality mattresses create a boudoir feel. After a day on the beach, guests congregate in the paneled bar and sink comfortably into couches and armchairs.

Rond-point Duboys-d'Angers, 06400 Cannes. © **04-92-59-40-00.** Fax 04-93-38-03-91. www.hotel-victoria-cannes.com. 25 units. 110€–305€ double; 250€–435€ suite. AE, DC, MC, V. Parking 17€. Closed 2 weeks Dec, 2 weeks Feb. **Amenities:** Bar; babysitting; pool (outdoor). *In room:* A/C, TV, hair dryer, minibar.

Hôtel Villa de l'Olivier ★ (Finds)   Charming and personal, this is a hideaway with a low-key management style. In the 1930s, it was a private villa; in the 1960s it became a hotel, with a wing extending deep into its garden. Today, you'll find buildings with lots of glass overlooking a kidney-shaped pool, and decor combining the French colonial tropics with the romantic late 19th century and Provence. Rooms have upholstered walls and lots of Provençal accessories.

5 rue des Tambourinaires, 06400 Cannes. © **04-93-39-53-28.** Fax 04-93-39-55-85. www.hotelolivier. com. 24 units. 110€–360€ double; 145€–360€ triple; 260€–472€ suite. AE, DC, MC, V. Parking 10€. Closed Nov 22–Dec 27. **Amenities:** Bar; pool (outdoor); room service. *In room:* A/C, TV, hair dryer, Wi-Fi (free).

La Villa Cannes Croisette ★★ (Finds)   You can come close to living the movie-star life at this boutique hotel, set in a garden with lemon and olive trees. An outdoor pool is available if you don't want to take the free shuttle to the beach. The hotel also offers boat tours of offshore islands, plus free van rides around town. Handmade furniture, paintings from a local artist, and the tasteful Pierre Frey fabrics evoke a lend to the charm. Breakfast is served; for other meals many restaurants are nearby.

8 Traverse Alexandre-III, 06400 Cannes. © **04-93-94-12-21.** Fax 04-93-43-55-17. www.hotel-villa-cannes. com. 33 units. 110€–310€ double. 35€ extra person. AE, DC, MC, V. Parking 15€. **Amenities:** Breakfast room; health club; pool (outdoor). *In room:* TV, Wi-Fi (free).

Le Cavendish   Originally an 1897 private residence, this self-proclaimed "boutique hotel" opened its doors in 2001 after an exhaustive renovation. The only parts of the hotel not subject to this renovation were the elevator, the marble stairways, and the facade (a historical monument), creating a feel of updated antiquity. Despite the old-fashioned decoration, this hotel feels like home, replete with a lounge that doubles as a breakfast room and a bar, a salon, and an accommodating reception desk. The rooms retain their traditional charm.

11 bd. Carnot, 06400 Cannes. © **04-97-06-26-00.** Fax 04-97-06-26-01. www.cavendish-cannes.com. 34 units. 125€–240€ double. Rates include continental breakfast. AE, DC, MC, V. Parking 20€. **Amenities:** Lounge/bar. *In room:* A/C, TV, minibar, Wi-Fi (free).

Inexpensive

Hôtel de France ★ (Value)   This centrally located Art Deco hotel is 2 blocks from the sea and is one of the best of the affordable hotels. Rooms are functional, well maintained, and reasonably comfortable, with good beds. You can sunbathe on the rooftop.

85 rue d'Antibes, 06400 Cannes. © **04-93-06-54-54.** Fax 04-93-68-53-43. www.hotel-de-france.cote. azur.fr. 33 units. 87€–174€ double; 121€–217€ suite. AE, DC, MC, V. **Amenities:** Bar; babysitting. *In room:* A/C, TV, hair dryer, minibar (in some), Wi-Fi (3€ per hr.).

Hôtel de Provence (Value

Built in the 1930s, this hotel is small and unpretentious— a contrast to the intensely stylish, larger hotels of the competition. Most of the rooms have private balconies, and many overlook the shrubs and palms of the hotel's walled garden. Guest rooms are showing their age but are still comfortable. For Cannes this is a remarkable bargain. In warm weather, breakfast is served under the flowers of an arbor.

9 rue Molière, 06400 Cannes. © **04-93-38-44-35.** Fax 04-93-39-63-14. www.hotel-de-provence.com. 30 units. 79€–119€ double; 119€–149€ suite. AE, MC, V. **Amenities:** Bar; room service. *In room:* A/C, TV, hair dryer, minibar, Wi-Fi (9.90€).

Hôtel La Villa Tosca

This former Beaux Arts-style villa lies a minute's walk from the railway station and a 5-minute walk from the beach. Inside you'll find a wide assortment of rooms and room sizes, with the biggest having soaring ceilings and a sense of monumental spaciousness, and the smallest being cramped but with manageable beds. Simple and sparsely decorated, this is the type of hotel where you'll do little more than sleep. Seven of the rooms have tiny balconies overlooking the street. Expect a polite staff and a clientele that includes gay men and—to a lesser extent—women, many of whom are involved with aspects of the film industry.

11 rue Hoche, 06400 Cannes. © **04-93-38-34-40.** Fax 04-93-38-73-34. www.villa-tosca.com. 22 units. 82€–144€ double; 109€–161€ triple; 153€–220€ suite. AE, MC, V. **Amenities:** Room service. *In room:* TV, fridge, hair dryer, Wi-Fi (free).

Hôtel Le Florian

This hotel is on a busy but narrow, densely commercial street that leads directly into La Croisette, near the beach. Three generations of the Giordano family have maintained it since the 1950s. The hotel is basic but comfortable, and most rooms are rather small, with Provençal styling. Breakfast is the only meal available.

8 rue Commandant-André, 06400 Cannes. © **04-93-39-24-82.** Fax 04-92-99-18-30. www.hotel-leflorian. com. 35 units. 60€–80€ double. AE, MC, V. Parking 10€ nearby. Closed Dec to mid-Jan. Bus: 1. **Amenities:** Breakfast room. *In room:* A/C, TV, hair dryer, Wi-Fi (free).

Hôtel Molière ★ (Finds

Although it dates from around 1990, this hotel gives the distinct impression that it's one of the solidly established old-timers. The hotel lies just 100m (328 ft.) from the Croisette; you approach through a long garden studded with cypresses and flowering shrubs, in which tables and chairs are set out for gossip and contemplation. The neighborhood is quieter than you expect, just behind both the Noga Hilton and the Carlton. Bedrooms are outfitted with lots of fabric giving an overall impression of well-upholstered comfort without a lot of decorative flair. The staff works hard and is generally polite and cooperative.

5–7 rue Molière, 06400 Cannes. © **04-93-38-16-16.** Fax 04-93-68-29-57. www.hotel-moliere.com. 24 units. 112€–170€ double; 145€–190€ suite. Rates include breakfast. AE, MC, V. Closed Nov. **Amenities:** Room service. *In room:* A/C, TV, hair dryer, Wi-Fi (free).

Hôtel Villa Toboso

Adjacent to the largest sports center in Cannes, this former private villa is now a small, homey hotel. (In a romantic outburst, the former owner named it after the city in Spain where Cervantes's Don Quixote is said to have met Dulcinea.) The main lounge has a concert piano, and dancers from the neighboring Rosella Hightower School often frequent the place. Most of the bedrooms have windows facing the garden, and some have terraces and kitchens.

70€–130€ double. AE, DC, MC, V. Free parking. **Amenities:** Babysitting; pool (outdoor); room service. *In room:* A/C, TV, hair dryer, Wi-Fi (free).

Le Mistral (Value) This hotel may be named for the harsh wind that blows across Provence, but inside the renovated premises is a cool oasis. The location is just a minute's walk from le Palais des Festivals and La Croisette, and only a 3-minute walk from the train and bus stations. Rooms are soundproof, spacious, and well furnished, each with a private bathroom with shower. The rooms are spread across four floors, and there is no elevator. Only breakfast is served, but many restaurants and cafes are nearby.

13 rue des Belges, 06400 Cannes. ℂ **04-93-39-91-46.** Fax 04-93-38-35-17. www.mistral-hotel.com. 10 units. 77€–117€ double. AE, MC, V. **Amenities:** Breakfast room. *In room:* A/C, TV, hair dryer, Wi-Fi (free).

WHERE TO DINE
Very Expensive
La Palme d'Or ★★★ MODERN FRENCH
Movie stars on the see-and-be-seen circuit head here to enjoy some of the Riviera's finest hotel cuisine. The Taittinger family (of champagne fame) set out to establish a restaurant that could rival the competition—and succeeded. The result is this tawny-colored Art Deco marvel with bay windows, a winter-garden theme, and outdoor and enclosed terraces overlooking the pool, the sea, and La Croisette. The menu changes seasonally but is likely to include warm foie gras with fondue of rhubarb; filets of fried red mullet with a beignet of potatoes, zucchini, and olive-cream sauce; or crayfish, clams, and squid marinated in peppered citrus sauce. A modernized version of a Niçoise staple includes three parts of a rabbit with rosemary sauce, fresh vegetables, and chickpea rosettes. The most appealing dessert is wild strawberries from Carros with Grand Marnier–flavored *nage* and "cream sauce of frozen milk." The service is worldly without being stiff.

In the Hôtel Martinez (p. 256), 73 bd. de la Croisette. ℂ **04-92-98-74-14.** www.hotelmartinez.com. Reservations required. Main courses 65€–180€; fixed-price lunch 61€–180€; fixed-price dinner 79€–180€. AE, DC, MC, V. Tues–Sat 12:30–2pm and 8–10pm. Closed Jan–Feb.

Expensive
Gaston et Gastounette ★ TRADITIONAL FRENCH
For views of the marina, this is your best bet. Located in the old port, it has a stucco exterior with oak moldings and big windows, and a sidewalk terrace surrounded by flowers. It serves two different bouillabaisses—a full-blown authentic stewpot prepared only for two diners at a time and a less daunting individualized version designed as an appetizer. Other choices include baby turbot with hollandaise sauce; John Dory filets with wild mushrooms; and an unusual Japanese-style broth flavored with monkfish, saltwater salmon, and chives. Profiteroles with hot chocolate sauce make a memorable dessert.

7 quai St-Pierre. ℂ **04-93-39-49-44.** Reservations required. Main courses 25€–50€; fixed-price menus 40€–73€. AE, DC, MC, V. Daily noon–2pm and 7–10:30pm. Closed Dec 15–24 and Jan 3–20.

Le Bâoli ★ FRENCH/JAPANESE
One of the hip joints in Cannes occupies a waterfront site outfitted like a temple garden in Thailand, complete with lavishly carved doorways, potted and in-ground palms, and hints of the Spice Trade scattered artfully in the out-of-the way corners. Up to 350 diners at a time enjoy their meal either indoors or on a terrace overlooking the twinkling lights of La Croisette. After the dinner service, the place morphs into a dance venue where at least some of the clients might be dancing on

the tables. Menu items include Japanese-inspired *teppanyaki* dishes prepared tableside by a samurai-style chef, as well as French dishes that feature tartare of tuna spread on toasts, filet of sea wolf with fennel, and a particularly elegant version of macaroni that's "perfumed" with an essence of lobster. Vegetarians appreciate the availability of such dishes as risotto with green asparagus, broccoli, and fava beans. The name of the restaurant, incidentally, derives from a well in Indonesia with reputed mystical powers.

Port Canto, bd. de la Croisette. ✆ **04-93-43-03-43.** www.lebaoli.com. Reservations recommended. Main courses 24€–40€. AE, MC, V. Daily 8pm–midnight. Disco (no cover) nightly midnight–5am. Closed 1 month in winter.

Le Festival ★ TRADITIONAL FRENCH   Screen idols and sex symbols flood the front terrace of this restaurant during the film festival. Almost every chair is emblazoned with the names of movie stars (who may or may not have occupied it), and tables are among the most sought after in town. You can choose from the restaurant or the less formal grill room. Meals in the restaurant may include rack of lamb, *soupe des poissons* (fish soup) with rouille, simply grilled fresh fish, bouillabaisse with lobster, pepper steak, and sea bass flambéed with fennel. Items in the grill are more in the style of an elegant brasserie, served a bit more rapidly and without as much fuss but at more or less the same prices. An appropriate finish in either section may be smooth peach melba.

52 bd. de la Croisette. ✆ **04-93-38-04-81.** Reservations required. Main courses 22€–37€; fixed-price menu 43€. AE, DC, MC, V. July–Aug daily 9am–midnight; Sept–June daily 9am–11pm (until midnight during film festival). Closed Nov 18–Dec 28.

Le Tantra/Le Loft ★ FRENCH/ASIAN   An enduring favorite on the city's dine-then-dance circuit is this duplex-designed restaurant and disco on a side street that runs directly into La Croisette. On the street level, you'll find a Tao-inspired dining room. The menu focuses on a French adaptation of Asian cuisine, with lots of sushi; tempura that includes a succulent combination of deep-fried banana slices, zucchini flowers, shrimp, and lobster; a Japanese-style steak of Kobe beef marinated in teriyaki, soy, and garlic; and deep-fried noodles dotted with chunks of shrimp and lobster. Be warned in advance that the 9pm seating is relatively calm; the 11pm seating is more linked to the disco madness going on upstairs. There, in a venue lined with plush sofas and exposed stone, you'll witness all the gyrations and mating games of a scantily clad crowd of hipsters from across the wide, wide range of social types inhabiting Cannes.

13 rue du Dr. Monod. ✆ **04-93-39-40-39.** www.tantra-cannes.com. Reservations recommended. Main courses 25€–45€. AE, DC, MC, V. Daily 8–11pm. Dance club (no cover) nightly 11pm–5am.

Le 38 ★★ MODERN FRENCH   This restaurant manages to be cozy and grand at the same time, replete with leather chairs, warm colors, and intimate lighting. Antoine Durano's cuisine is subtle and sometimes surprisingly simple, not aiming for the cutting-edge cerebrality of the Cannes' more innovative restaurants. Examples are terrines of foie gras, roasted filets of John Dory with olives and baby mushrooms, grilled filet of beef with béarnaise sauce, and roasted lobster with truffle-studded risotto. Dishes developed specifically by Mr. Durand for this restaurant include marinated strips of swordfish grilled with sesame oil, and freshwater *sander* cooked in a sheath of pulverized olives. Dessert might be an old-fashioned and delicious version of crêpes Suzette.

In the Hôtel Gray-d'Albion (p. 257), 38 rue des Serbes. ✆ **04-92-99-79-79.** Reservations required. Main courses 20€–32€; fixed-price menus 38€–42€. AE, DC, MC, V. Tues–Sat 12:30–2pm and 7:30–10pm.

Côté Jardin ★ (Value) FRENCH/PROVENÇALE   Set near the courthouse (Palais de Justice) in the heart of commercial Cannes, this restaurant attracts loyal locals because of its unpretentious ambience and its reasonably priced and generous portions. You're offered three different choices as seating options: the glassed-in veranda on the street level, at a table amid the flowering shrubs of the garden terrace, or upstairs within the cozy Provençal dining room. The best menu options include open-faced ravioli filled with minced beef jowls, filets of red mullet with butter-flavored parsley sauce, a range of grilled and roasted meats and fish, and a dessert of praline and pineapple tart with vanilla-flavored cream sauce.

12 av. St-Louis. (✆ **04-93-38-60-28.** www.restaurant-cotejardin.com. Reservations required, especially in summer. Fixed-price menus 24€–38€. AE, DC, MC, V. Tues–Sat noon–2pm and 7:30–10pm. Closed 1 week in Oct.

La Brouette de Grand-Mère ★ (Finds) TRADITIONAL FRENCH   Few other restaurants in Cannes work so successfully at establishing a testimonial to the culinary skills of old-fashioned French cooking. Owner Christian Bruno has revitalized the recipes that many of the chic and trendy residents of Cannes remember from their childhoods, such as a savory meat-and-potato stew known as *pot-au-feu,* roasted quail served with cream sauce, and chicken casserole cooked with beer. Traditional starters may include sausage links, terrines, and baked potatoes stuffed with smoked fish roe and served with a small glass of vodka. Set in the heart of town just behind the Noga Hilton and the InterContinental Carlton, the place offers two dining rooms, each outfitted in Art Deco style, and an outdoor terrace.

9 bis rue d'Oran. (✆ **04-93-39-12-10.** Reservations recommended. Fixed-price menu, including aperitif and half bottle of wine, 35€. MC, V. Daily 7:30–10pm. Closed June 11–July 3 and Nov to mid-Dec.

La Canna Suisse ★ (Finds) SWISS   Decked out like a Swiss chalet, this small restaurant in Vieux Cannes specializes in the cheese-based cuisine of Switzerland's high Alps. The menu features two kinds of fondue—a traditional version concocted from six kinds of cheese and served in a bubbling pot with chunks of bread on skewers, and another that adds mushrooms (morels or cèpes) to the blend. The only other dining options here include raclette and equally savory *tartiflette* (an age-old recipe that combines boiled potatoes with fatback, onions, cream, herbs, and reblochon cheese). The long list of (mostly white) French and Swiss wines pairs wonderfully with these ultra-traditional dishes. Because its cuisine is so suitable to cold weather dining, the restaurant wisely opts to close during the crush of Cannes's midsummer tourist season.

23 rue Forville, Le Suquet. (✆ **04-93-99-01-27.** www.cannasuisse.com. Main courses 17€–26€; set-price menu 27€. AE, MC, V. Mon–Sat 7:30–10:30pm. Closed May 20 to late Aug.

La Mère Besson ★ TRADITIONAL FRENCH   The culinary traditions of the late Mère Besson, who opened her restaurant in the 1930s, endure in one of Cannes's favorite dining spots. The specialties are prepared with respect for Provençal traditions. Most delectable is *estouffade provençale* (beef braised with red wine and rich stock flavored with garlic, onions, herbs, and mushrooms). Every Friday, you can sample a platter with codfish, fresh vegetables, and dollops of the famous garlic mayonnaise (aioli) of Provence. Other specialties are fish soup, *bourride provençale* (thick fish-and-vegetable stew), and roasted rack of lamb with mint.

13 rue des Frères-Pradignac. (✆ **04-93-39-59-24.** Reservations required. Main courses 25€–29€; fixed-price dinner 28€–33€. AE, MC, V. Mon–Sat 7–10:30pm. Bus: 1.

Le Caveau 30 FRENCH/SEAFOOD This fine restaurant emphasizes fresh seafood. Begin with a seafood platter and follow with one of the chef's classic dishes, *pot-au-feu* "from the sea" or shellfish paella. Bouillabaisse is the most popular dish, of course, but you might prefer a *filet au poivre* (pepper steak) or even fresh pasta. The 1930s decor, air-conditioning, and terrace all make dining a pleasant experience.

45 rue Félix-Faure. ✆ **04-93-39-06-33.** www.lecaveau30.com. Reservations required. Main courses 16€–38€; fixed-price menus 25€–35€. AE, DC, MC, V. Daily noon–2:15pm and 7–11pm.

Le Comptoir des Vins TRADITIONAL FRENCH The owners first established this wine shop with bottles from 450 to 500 wine producers, some of them very obscure, from throughout France. Today the restaurant in the back of the store charms diners with white marble tables, bistro-style chairs, and sunlight flooding in from an overhead sky-light. You can order any of 10 kinds of wine by the glass, but if you're intrigued by something in the store, they will uncork it for you for the retail price and a surcharge of 10€. Menu items include an extensive selection of charcuteries and cheeses, piled high upon olive-wood planks, as well as a savory collection of meats, fish, and vegetarian dishes. All of these are designed to go well with wines; and with a vast inventory of vintages to choose from, the composition of a savory meal here is ripe with gastronomic possibilities.

13 bd. de la République. ✆ **04-93-68-13-26.** Reservations recommended. Main courses 13€–17€; fixed-price lunch 13€–15€. MC, V. Mon–Fri 10am–3pm; Mon–Sat 5:30pm–midnight. Closed 2 weeks in Feb and Sept.

Le Marais FRENCH This is the most successful gay restaurant in Cannes, with a crowd of mostly gay men from the worlds of fashion and entertainment, sometimes with their entourages. The setting is a warm and appealing mix of Parisian and Provençal, with paneled walls and a bustling terrace that is one of the most sought-after outdoor venues in town. Menu items include sea bream filet with olive-based tapenade sauce, and a "triptych" of meats that includes magret of duck, beef filet, and shoulder of lamb with mint sauce. Know in advance that this is primarily a restaurant and doesn't cater to a crowd of folks coming in just to drink.

9 rue du Suquet. ✆ **04-93-38-39-19.** www.restaurantlemarais.fr. Reservations recommended. Main courses 17€–23€; fixed-price menu 24€–27€. MC, V. Daily 7–11pm. Closed Sun Sept–May.

Le Relais des Semailles TRADITIONAL FRENCH This long-enduring favorite is reason enough to visit Le Suquet, Cannes's old town. The casual atmosphere is comple-mented by the food, based on available local ingredients. Zucchini flowers stuffed with crab, and breast of duck pan-fried with herbs and spices are always beautifully prepared. Try, if featured, the salad of wild greens *(mâche)* with truffles—sublime. The grilled sea bass is perfectly fresh and aromatically seasoned with herbs. Depending on what looked good at the market that day, the chef might be inspired to, say, whip up a rabbit salad with tarragon jus. The setting is intimate, offering casual dining out on the terrace or in air-conditioned comfort.

9 rue St-Antoine. ✆ **04-93-39-22-32.** Reservations required. Main courses 19€–43€; fixed price lunch 22€; fixed-price dinner 34€. AE, DC, MC, V. Tues–Fri noon–2pm; Mon–Sat 7:30–10:30pm.

Le Restaurant Arménien ★ (Finds) ARMENIAN/TURKISH/GREEK Cannes has always been one of the most cosmopolitan cities along the Riviera, and the success of this Armenian culinary outpost seems to prove it. It has no menu; for a set price, a medley of dishes is brought to your table in quantities you might find staggering. Expect about 20 cold plates, a dozen warm plates, enough vegetables to warm the heart of the most fanatical vegetarian, and at least five different desserts. There are lots of braised eggplants, tomatoes (stewed and raw alike), cracked wheat in the form of such dishes as *kechgeg* (stewed beef served on a bed of cracked wheat), cabbage stuffed with mint, grilled meatballs with fresh herbs, and many others. According to owners Christian and Lucie Panossian, about 80% of the dishes served here are steamed rather than fried, establishing this as one of the most health-conscious eateries in town. You'll find this place directly on the coastal boulevard, a short walk from the Hôtel Martinez.

82 La Croisette. (📞 **04-93-94-00-58.** www.lerestaurantarmenien.com. Reservations recommended. Fixed-price menu 42€. DC, MC, V. Sun noon–2:30pm (reservations required); daily 7:30–10:30pm. Closed Mon in winter.

CANNES AFTER DARK

Cannes is invariably associated with permissiveness, filmmakers celebrating filmmaking, and gambling. If gambling is your thing, Cannes has some world-class casinos, each loaded with addicts, voyeurs, and everyone in between. The better established is the **Casino Croisette,** in the Palais des Festivals, 1 jetée Albert-Edouard (📞 **04-92-98-78-00**). Run by the Lucien Barrière group and a well-respected fixture in town since the 1950s, it's a competitor of the newer **Palm Beach Casino,** place F-D-Roosevelt, Pointe de la Croisette (📞 **04-97-06-36-90;** www.lepalmbeach.com), on the southeast edge of La Croisette. Inaugurated in 1933 and rebuilt in 2002, it features three restaurants and Art Deco decor. The Palm Beach Casino is glossier, newer, and a bit hungrier for new business. Both casinos maintain slot machines that operate daily from 10am to 5am. Suites of rooms devoted to *les grands jeux* (blackjack, roulette, and chemin de fer) open nightly from 8pm to 4am.

7

Yet a third gambling den, **Casino des Princes,** is more intimate than either of its more flamboyant competitors, occupying the subterranean levels of the Noga Hilton Cannes, 50 bd. de la Croisette (📞 **04-97-06-18-50**). It is open nightly 8pm to 3am. A government-issued photo ID is necessary, and jackets for men are requested. Adjoining the casino is the hotel's most upscale restaurant, Restaurant/Bar des Princes, open for dinner nightly from 8pm to 2:45am.

The aptly named **Bar des Stars,** in the Restaurant Fouquet's in the Hôtel Majestic Barrière, 14 La Croisette (📞 **04-92-98-77-00**), is where deals go down during the film festival. Directors, producers, stars, press agents, and screenwriters crowd in here at festival time. Even without the festival, it's a lively place for a drink.

The popular nightclub **Whatnut's Bal-Room,** 7 rue Marceau (📞 **04-93-68-60-58**), in the commercial center of Cannes has two dance floors that feature radically different music: One is for 1980s-style disco; the other for house, garage, and modern forms of electronic sounds. Patrons are on the young side (ages 18–35), admission is free, and drinks cost 7€ to 12€. Open July to August daily 10:30pm to 5am; September to June Friday to Sunday 10:30pm to 5am.

Gays and lesbians will feel comfortable at **Le Vogue,** 20 rue du Suquet (📞 **04-93-39-99-18**), a mixed bar open Tuesday to Sunday from 7:30pm until 2:30am. Another gay option is **Disco Le Sept,** 7 rue Rouguière (📞 **04-93-39-10-36**), where drag shows appear nightly at 1:30am. Entrance is free, except on weekends, when its 16€ cover includes one drink. Straight nightclub goers favor Disco Le Sept as well. The most visible gay clientele in Cannes tend to gravitate toward **Le Nightlife,** 52 bd. Jean-Jaurès (📞 **04-93-39-20-50**), which was reoutfitted as a 1950s-retro venue that includes red vinyl banquettes, white walls, a busy bar, occasional drag shows, and lots of randomly scheduled and somewhat flippant theme parties. Open for drinks and dining daily 6pm to 2:30am, with fixed-price meals priced at 32€, it's a popular and convivial spot for same-sex socializing. A lot rougher, darker, and more shadowy is the gay male disco, **Le Divan,** 3 rue Rouguière (© **04-93-68-73-70**), located within a vaulted cellar that's designed to look a lot older than it really is. This place is not for the timid: If you opt for a visit here, leave your valuables in your hotel safe and remain alert. It's open Tuesday to Sunday 6pm until around 4am, depending on the crowds.

A discreet ambience prevails at **Zanzibar,** 85 rue Félix-Faure (© **04-93-39-30-75;** www.lezanzibar.com). A bartender confided to us, "If a gay man wants to meet a French version of Brad Pitt, especially at festival time, this is the place." The bar is open all night and caters to people of all sexual persuasions. At dawn the doors open and the last of the drag queens stagger out.

8 GRASSE ★★

906km (563 miles) S of Paris; 18km (11 miles) N of Cannes; 10km (6 miles) NW of Mougins

Grasse, a 20-minute drive from Cannes, is the most fragrant town on the Riviera, though it *looks* tacky modern. Surrounded by jasmine and roses, it has been the capital of the perfume industry since the days of the Renaissance. It was once a famous resort, attracting such royalty as Queen Victoria and Princess Pauline Borghese, Napoleon's promiscuous sister. Today some three-quarters of the world's essences are produced here from foliage that includes violets, daffodils, wild lavender, and jasmine.

ESSENTIALS

GETTING THERE **Trains** now run to Grasse from Nice, Cannes, or Antibes. One-way tickets cost 5.80€ from Cannes, 5.40€ from Antibes, and 8.40€ from Nice. For train schedules and more information, call © **36-35,** or visit **www.voyages-sncf.com. Buses** pull into town every 30 to 60 minutes daily from Cannes (trip time: 50 min.). The one-way fare is 1€. About 14 buses run every day from Nice (1 hr.). The one-way fare is around 1€. They arrive at the Gare Routière, place Notre Dame des Fleurs (© **04-93-36-08-44**), a 10-minute walk north of the town center. Visitors arriving by **car** take A8, which funnels in traffic from Monaco, Aix-en-Provence, and Marseille.

Visitor Information The **Office de Tourisme** is at Place du cours Honoré Cresp (© **04-93-36-03-56;** fax 04-93-36-86-36; www.grasse-riviera.com).

SEEING THE SIGHTS

A market for fruits and vegetables from the surrounding hills, **Marché aux Aires,** is conducted in the place aux Aires every Tuesday to Sunday 8am to noon.

Fun Facts **Pricey Petals**

It takes 10,000 flowers to produce 2.2 pounds of jasmine petals; almost a ton of petals is needed to distill 1½ quarts of essence. Keep these figures in mind when looking at that high price tag on a bottle of perfume.

Perfume Factories

Parfumerie Fragonard ★   One of the best-known perfume factories is named after an 18th-century French painter. This factory has the best villa, the best museum, and the best tour. An English-speaking guide will show you how "the soul of the flower" is extracted. After the tour, you can explore the museum, which displays bottles and vases that trace the industry back to ancient times. You can also skip the tour and just shop for perfume.

20 bd. Fragonard. (📞 **04-93-36-44-65.** www.fragonard.com. Mar–Oct daily 9am–6:30pm; Nov–Jan daily 9am–12:30pm and 2–6pm.

Parfumerie Molinard   This firm is well-known in the United States, where its products are sold at Saks, Neiman Marcus, and Bloomingdale's. In the factory you can witness the extraction of the essence of the flowers. You can also admire a collection of antique perfume-bottle labels and see a rare collection of perfume *flacons* by Baccarat and Lalique.

60 bd. Victor-Hugo. (📞 **04-93-36-01-62.** www.molinard.com. Free admission. Apr–Sept daily 9am–6:30pm; Oct–Apr Mon–Sat 9am–12:30pm and 2–6:30pm.

Museums

Additional information on the following museums can be found online at **www.musees degrasse.com**.

Musée d'Art et d'Histoire de Provence ★   This museum is in the Hôtel de Clapiers-Cabris, built in 1771 by Louise de Mirabeau, the marquise de Cabris and sister of Mirabeau. Its collections include paintings, four-poster beds, marquetry, ceramics, brasses, kitchenware, pottery, urns, and archaeological finds.

2 rue Mirabeau. (📞 **04-93-36-80-20.** Admission 3€ adults, 1.50€ children 10–16, free for children 9 and under. June–Sept daily 10am–12:30pm and 1:30–6:30pm; Oct–May Wed–Mon 10am–12:30pm and 2–5:30pm. Closed Nov 6–Dec 5.

Musée International de la Parfumerie   This museum houses interesting, often bizarre exhibits relating to the perfume industry. One of the most fascinating is a 3,000-year-old mummy's perfumed hand and foot, which owe their preservation to the perfuming process. In the fourth-floor greenery, you can smell the base elements that go into the creation of celebrated perfumes. Was that Elizabeth Taylor we saw whiffing and sniffing, perhaps trying to come up with some new exotic fragrance?

8 place de Cours. (📞 **04-93-36-80-20.** www.museedegrasse.com. Admission 3€ adults, 1.50€ children. Oct–May Wed–Mon 11am–6pm; June–Sept daily 10am–7pm.

Villa Musée Fragonard   The setting is an 18th-century aristocrat's town house with a magnificent garden in back. The collection displayed here includes the paintings of Jean-Honoré Fragonard, who was born in Grasse in 1732; his sister-in-law, Marguerite Gérard; his son, Alexandre; and his grandson, Théophile. Alexandre decorated the grand staircase.

23 bd. Fragonard. (📞 **04-93-36-52-98.** Admission 3€ adults, 1.50€ children 10–16, free for children 9 and under. June–Sept daily 10am–6:30pm; Oct–May Wed–Mon 10am–12:30pm and 2–5:30pm.

WHERE TO STAY

Bastide Saint-Mathieu ★★   This exclusive country house is the best place to stay in the Grasse area. Lying just to the southeast of Grasse, this beautifully restored 18th-century house provides beautiful suites and personal service. Each of the spacious suites is individually decorated and furnished to a high standard, with luxurious bathrooms with tub and shower. Thoughtful touches abound, including such extras as cashmere blankets and Ralph Lauren bathrobes. The staff will guide you to the area's finest restaurants.

3 chemin de Blumenthal, 06130 St. Mathieu (Grasse). ✆ **04-97-01-10-00.** Fax 04-97-01-10-99. 8 units. 270€–330€ double; 360€–380€ suite. Rates include breakfast. AE, MC, V. **Amenities:** Pool (outdoor). *In room:* A/C, TV, Wi-Fi (free).

Hôtel La Bellaudière Value   Part of the respected Logis de France chain, this unpretentious family-run hotel is 3km (1¾ miles) east of the town center in the hills above Grasse. The stone-sided farmhouse was built in stages beginning 400 years ago, with most of what you see today built in the 1700s. Guest rooms are simple but dignified, outfitted with Provençal motifs, and many have views of the sea. The hotel also features a garden terrace lined with flowering shrubs, and the friendly hosts offer a warm welcome. Fixed-price meals in the dining room cost 20€ to 25€ each.

78 rte. de Nice, 06130 Grasse. ✆ **04-93-36-02-57.** Fax 04-93-36-40-03. 17 units. 50€–71€ double. AE, DC, MC, V. Free parking. **Amenities:** Restaurant; room service. *In room:* TV, Wi-Fi (free).

Hôtel Panorama   Built in 1984 in the commercial center, this hotel lies behind a facade in a sienna hue that its owners call "Garibaldi red." The more expensive rooms have balconies, southern exposures, and views of the sea. Furnishings are basic and simple, although all the mattresses are reasonably comfortable. The hotel lacks a bar or restaurant, but the staff is cooperative and hardworking.

2 place du Cours, 06130 Grasse. ✆ **04-93-36-80-80.** Fax 04-93-36-92-04. www.hotelpanorama-grasse. com. 36 units. 60€–100€ double; 90€–110€ triple. Children stay free in parent's room. AE, MC, V. Parking 5€. **Amenities:** Room service. *In room:* A/C, TV, Wi-Fi, nonalcoholic minibar, Wi-Fi (free).

WHERE TO DINE

For inexpensive dining, you can head for **Hôtel La Bellaudière** (see above).

La Bastide St-Antoine (Restaurant Chibois) ★★★ FRENCH/PROVEN-ÇALE   La Bastide St-Antoine offers one of the grandest culinary experiences along the Riviera. In a 200-year-old Provençal farmhouse surrounded by 2.8 hectares (7 acres) of trees and shrubbery, chef Jacques Chibois serves a sophisticated array of dishes. The best examples are oysters flavored with yucca leaves, a terrine of foie gras with celery, roasted suckling lamb with a fricassee of fresh vegetables and basil, and fresh crayfish with sautéed flap mushrooms. Desserts may include strawberry soup with spice wine or ice cream made with olives and a hint of olive oil. The chef also does wonders with wild duck.

You can stay in one of nine rooms or seven suites, all decorated in Provençal style with upscale furnishings and comfortable beds. They have air-conditioning, safes, hair dryers, minibars, and TVs. Doubles cost 230€ to 395€; suites, 410€ to 910€.

48 av. Henri-Dunant. ✆ **04-93-70-94-94.** Fax 04-93-70-94-95. www.jacques-chibois.com. Reservations required. Main courses 39€–89€; fixed-price lunch Mon–Sat 59€–190€; fixed-price dinner 145€–190€. AE, DC, MC, V. Daily noon–2pm and 8–9:30pm.

9 MOUGINS ★

903km (561 miles) S of Paris; 11km (7 miles) S of Grasse; 8km (5 miles) N of Cannes

This once-fortified town on the crest of a hill provides an alternative for those who want to be near the excitement of Cannes but not in the midst of it. Picasso and other artists appreciated these rugged, sun-drenched hills covered with gnarled olive trees. Picasso arrived in 1936 and, in time, was followed by Jean Cocteau, Paul Eluard, and Man Ray. Picasso decided to move here permanently, choosing as his refuge an ideal site overlooking the Bay of Cannes near the Chapelle Notre-Dame de Vie. Here he continued to work and spent the latter part of his life with his wife, Jacqueline. Fernand Léger, René Clair, Isadora Duncan, and even Christian Dior have lived at Mougins.

Mougins is the perfect haven for those who feel that the Riviera is overrun, spoiled, and overbuilt. It preserves the quiet life very close to the international resorts. The wealthy come from Cannes to golf here. Though Mougins looks serene and tranquil, it's actually part of the industrial park of Sophia Antipolis, a technological center where more than 1,000 national and international companies have offices.

ESSENTIALS

GETTING THERE   In 2005, the French railways, **SNCF**, reactivated an antique rail line stretching between Grasse (the perfume capital) and Cannes, linking the hamlet of Mouans-Sartoux en route. The village of Mouans-Sartoux lies only 457m (1,500 ft.) from the center of Mougins. Rail service costs 2.60€ one-way from either Cannes or Grasse to Mouans-Sartoux. There are several trains per day. For more information call *©* **36-35,** or visit **www.voyages-sncf.com**. **Société Tam** (*©* **08-00-06-01-06**) runs buses between Cannes and Grasse. Bus no. 600 stops in Val-de-Mougins, a 10-minute walk from the center of Mougins. One-way fares from either Cannes or Grasse cost 1.25€. Given the complexities of a bus transfer from Cannes, it's a lot easier just to pay 22€ to 30€ for a **taxi** to haul you and your luggage north from Cannes.

However, the best way to get to Mougins is to **drive.** From Nice, follow E80/A8 west, then cut north on Route 85 into Mougins. From Cannes, head north of the city along N85. From La Napoule–Plage, head east toward Cannes on N7, then north at the turn-off to Mougins up in the hills.

VISITOR INFORMATION   The **Office de Tourisme** is at 15 av. Jean-Charles-Mallet (*©* **04-93-75-87-67;** fax 04-92-92-04-03; www.mougins-coteazur.org).

SEEING THE SIGHTS

For a look at the history of the area, visit the **Espace Culturel,** place du Commandant-Lamy (*©* **04-92-92-50-42**), in the St. Bernardin Chapel. It was built in 1618 and traces area history from 1553 to the 1950s. It's open December to October, Monday to Friday 9am to 5pm, Saturday and Sunday from 11am to 6pm (closed Nov). Admission is free.

You can also visit the **Chapelle Notre-Dame de Vie,** chemin de la Chapelle, 1.5km (1 mile) southeast of Mougins. The chapel, once painted by Winston Churchill, is best known for the priory next door, where Picasso spent his last 12 years. It was built in the 12th century and reconstructed in 1646; it was an old custom to bring stillborn babies to the chapel to have them baptized. The priory is still a private home occupied intermittently by the Picasso heirs. Alas, because of a series of break-ins and ongoing renovations, the chapel is open only during Sunday Mass from 9 to 10am.

Musée de l'Automobiliste ★★ **Kids**   This is one of the top attractions on the Riviera. Founded in 1984 by Adrien Maeght, this modern concrete-and-glass structure houses exhibitions and one of Europe's most magnificent collections of prestigious automobiles, which includes more than 100 vehicles dating from 1908 to the present. Within two steps of the sea, the museum explores the use of the automobile in civil and military contexts alike. Individual cars are on display for historic, aesthetic, technical, or sentimental reasons. Children appreciate the antique toys and antique model cars collected over many generations, and any teenager who has seen pimpmobiles on TV will appreciate the cool quotient of such rare luxury rides as the 1925 Hispano-Suiza H6B and its even more opulent J12 counterpart from 1933.

Aire des Bréguières or 772 Chemin de Font de Currault. (**C**) **04-93-69-27-80.** Admission 7€ adults, 5€ children 12–18, free for children 12 and under. Apr–Sept daily 10am–7pm; Oct–Mar Tues–Sun 10am–6pm.

WHERE TO STAY

Note that **Le Moulin de Mougins** (below) offers charming rooms and suites.

Le Manoir de l'Etang ★★ You'll get a strong sense of life in rural Provence within the thick, ivy-covered stone walls of this artfully renovated 19th-century manor house within a verdant 4-hectare (10-acre) park a short drive east from the center of Mougins. A mass of nearby olive trees and cypresses frames a small pond covered with lotuses and waterlilies. The owners have undertaken a stylish, urban-flavored renovation, some of it very contemporary-looking. The interior, including the airy bedrooms, is bright and modern, the perfect place for a hideaway, off-the-record weekend. The in-house restaurant serves artfully conceived food, some platters arranged in nearly sculptural forms. Despite its modern decorative style, the place still captures the romance of the old, romantic Riviera of long ago.

Aux Bois de Font-Merle, 66 allée du Manoir, 06250 Mougins. (**C**) **04-92-28-36-00.** Fax 04-92-28-36-10. www.manoir-de-letang.com. 20 units. 125€–275€ double; 300€–500€ suite; from 400€ apt for 4. AE, MC, V. Closed late Oct to Apr. **Amenities:** Restaurant; bar; pool (outdoor); room service. *In room:* A/C, TV, minibar.

Le Mas Candille ★★ This 200-year-old Provençal *mas* was recently renovated. The public rooms contain many 19th-century furnishings, and some open onto the gardens. Rooms are individually decorated in different styles, including Japanese, medieval, French colonial (Indochina), and Provençal regional. The dining room, with stone detailing and a massive fireplace with a timbered mantel, serves exceptional food. Fresh salads and light meals are available throughout the day. In clement weather, lunch is served on the terrace; dinner is served on the terrace in summer only. The staff at times might be just a bit too easygoing.

Bd. Clément Rebuffel, 06250 Mougins. (**C**) **04-92-28-43-43.** Fax 04-92-28-43-40. www.lemascandille. com. 46 units. 300€–365€ double; 695€–920€ suite. AE, DC, MC, V. **Amenities:** 2 restaurants; bar; gym; health club; 3 pools (outdoor); room service; spa. *In room:* A/C, TV, hair dryer, minibar, Wi-Fi (free).

WHERE TO DINE

Alain Llorca Le Moulin de Mougins ★★★ FRENCH   Chef Alain Lorca employs market-fresh ingredients in his "cuisine of the sun," a reference to Provence's light-drenched countryside. Food here is earthy but upscale, often with modern twists on old culinary traditions both from Provence and other parts of the French-speaking world. Examples include hearts of artichoke stuffed with marinated seafood; an *accras de morue* (codfish fritters) that one would expect in Martinique; spaghetti with shellfish; roasted Provençal goat with herbs; sweetbreads with mushrooms fried in grease; and a succulent version of magret of duckling with honey sauce, lemons, and polenta.

The inn also rents 11 accommodations with air-conditioning, minibars, and TVs. Rooms cost 160€ to 290€ double, suites 390€.

Notre-Dame de Vie, 06250 Mougins. (**C**) **04-93-75-78-24.** Fax 04-93-90-18-55. www.moulin-mougins. com. Reservations required. Main courses 59€–95€; fixed-price menu 59€–120€ lunch, 98€–180€ dinner. AE, DC, MC, V. Daily noon–2pm and 7:30–10pm.

Brasserie de la Méditerranée FRENCH/PROVENÇALE This outfit adds a much-needed informality to dining scene in Cannes. Set within a modern building overlooking the village's main square, it specializes in the kind of cuisine you'd expect in a bustling brasserie with a Provençal accent. Menu items include scallops with a balsamic vinaigrette; superb lobster served with a *barigoule* of artichoke hearts; sliced turbot in a white-butter sauce; and veal saltimbocca (with ham).

Place de la Mairie. ✆ **04-93-90-03-47.** Reservations recommended. Main courses 10€–37€; set menus 26€–50€ lunch, 38€–50€ dinner. AE, DC, MC, V. Daily noon–2:30pm and 6:30pm–midnight. Closed 2 weeks in Nov and 3 weeks in Jan.

L'Amandier de Mougins Café-Restaurant ★ NIÇOISE/PROVENÇALE This relatively inexpensive bistro was founded about a decade ago by the world-famous chef Roger Vergé. Today the restaurant carries on admirably under new owners. This restaurant serves simple platters in an airy stone house. The specialties, based on traditional recipes, may include terrine of Mediterranean hogfish with lemon; tartare of fresh salmon and seviche of tuna with hot spices; or magret of duckling with honey sauce and lemons, served with deliberately undercooked polenta.

Place du Commandant-Lamy. ✆ **04-93-90-00-91.** Reservations recommended. Main courses 30€–45€; fixed-price lunch 25€–44€; fixed-price dinner 34€–44€. AE, DC, MC, V. Daily noon–2pm and 7–9:30pm.

Le Feu Follet (Value) FRENCH/PROVENÇALE Although the two roughly plastered rooms that make up this restaurant always seem cramped, the quality (and affordability) of the cuisine make for a real draw. Only top-quality ingredients, the best in the market, go into the cooking at this restaurant beside the square in the old village. One longtime habitué described the Provençal vegetables here as being "filled with the sun." Typical dishes are baked filet of beef in red wine and butter, crayfish in lemon juice, and snails in garlic cream.

Place de la Mairie. ✆ **04-93-90-15-78.** Reservations required. Main courses 32€–38€; fixed-price menu 26€–55€. AE, MC, V. Tues–Sat noon–2pm and 7–10pm; Sun noon–3pm.

10 GOLFE-JUAN ★ & VALLAURIS

913km (567 miles) S of Paris; 6km (4 miles) E of Cannes

Napoleon and 800 men landed at Golfe-Juan in 1815 to begin his Hundred Days. Protected by hills, Golfe-Juan was also the favored port for the American navy, though today it's primarily a family resort known for its beaches. It contains one notable restaurant: Chez Tétou.

The 2km (1¼-mile) R.N. 135 leads inland from Golfe-Juan to Vallauris. Once merely a stopover along the Riviera, Vallauris (now noted for its pottery) owes its reputation to Picasso, who "discovered" it. The master came to Vallauris after World War II and occupied a villa known as "The Woman from Wales."

ESSENTIALS

GETTING THERE The sleepy-looking rail station in Golfe-Juan is on avenue de la Gare. To get here, you'll have to transfer from a **train** in Cannes. The train from Cannes costs 1.80€ each way. For railway information, call ✆ **36-35,** or visit **www.voyages-sncf.com**. **Buses** operated by Envibus (✆ **04-93-64-18-37**) make frequent trips from Cannes; the 20-minute trip costs 1€ each way; from Nice, the 90-minute trip costs 1.30€ each way.

You can **drive** to Golfe-Juan or Vallauris on any of the Riviera's three east-west highways. Although route numbers are not always indicated, city names are clear once you're on the highway. From Cannes or Antibes, N7 east is the fastest route. From Nice or Biot, take A8/E80 west.

VISITOR INFORMATION   The **Office de Tourisme** (www.vallauris-golfe-juan.fr) is on boulevard des Frères-Roustan, Golfe-Juan (© **04-93-63-73-12;** fax 04-93-63-21-07), and another on square du 8-Mai, 1945 Vallauris (© **04-93-63-82-58;** fax 04-93-63-13-66).

SEEING THE SIGHTS

Landlocked Vallauris depends on the sale of tourist items and ceramics. Merchants selling the colorful wares line both sides of **avenue Georges-Clemenceau,** which begins at a point adjacent to the Musée Picasso and slopes downhill and southward to the edge of town. Some of the pieces displayed in these shops are in poor taste. In recent years, the almost-universal emphasis on the traditional rich burgundy color has been replaced with a wider variety geared to modern tastes.

On the place du Marché in Vallauris, near the site where Aly Khan and Rita Hayworth were married, you'll see Picasso's **Homme et Mouton (Man and Sheep).** The town council of Vallauris had intended to ensconce this statue in a museum, but Picasso insisted that it remain on the square "where the children could climb over it and the dogs water it unhindered."

Bordering place de la Libération is a chapel shaped like a Quonset hut, containing the **Musée Picasso La Guerre et La Paix** ★ (© **04-93-64-71-83;** www.musee-picasso-vallauris.fr), and also the entrance to the 16th-century **Château de Vallauris** (same phone). Inside the château is a two-in-one museum, **Musée Alberto Magnelli** and the **Musée de la Céramique Moderne.** This trio of museums developed after Picasso decorated the chapel with two paintings: *La Paix* (Peace) and *La Guerre* (War), offering contrasting images of love and peace on the one hand, and violence and conflict on the other. In 1970, a house painter gained illegal entrance to the museum one night and, after whitewashing a portion of the original, substituted one of his own designs. When the aging master inspected the damage, he said, "Not bad at all." In July 1996, the site was enhanced with a permanent exposition devoted to the works of the Florentine-born Alberto Magnelli, a pioneer of abstract art. The third section showcases ceramics, traditional and innovative alike, from regional potters. All three museums are open June to August Wednesday to Monday 10am to 6pm, September to May Wednesday to Monday 10am to 12:15 and 2 to 5pm.

Admission costs 3.25€ for adults and 1.70€ for students and children 16 and under.

WHERE TO STAY

Hôtel Beau-Soleil   Built in 1973, this pink-and-white, boxy-looking hotel is set on a quiet cul-de-sac, within a 5-minute walk from the center of the town or the beach. The angles of the architecture might remind you of a modern-day adaptation by a 1920s-era cubist painter. Bedrooms are outfitted in Provence-inspired colors, with small-scale crystal chandeliers and big windows overlooking either the hotel's shaded terrace or the far-away hills. The social center is the shaded terrace, dotted with potted plants.

Impasse Beau-Soleil, 06220 Golfe-San-Juan (Vallauris). © **04-93-63-63-63.** Fax 04-93-63-02-89. www.hotel-beau-soleil.com. 30 units. 70€–136€ double. MC, V. Free parking. **Amenities:** Restaurant; bar; pool (outdoor). *In room:* A/C, TV, hair dryer, minibar, Wi-Fi (free).

Because of its position beside the sea, Golfe-Juan long ago developed into a warm-weather resort. The town's twin strips of beach are **Plage du Soleil** (east of the Vieux Port and the newer Port Camille-Rayon) and **Plage du Midi** (west of those two). Each stretches 1km (⅔ mile) and charges no entry fee, with the exception of small areas administered by concessions that rent mattresses and chaises and have snack kiosks. Regardless of which concession you select (on Plage du Midi they sport names such as Au Vieux Rocher, Palma Beach, and Corail Plage; on Plage du Soleil, Plage Nounou and Plage Tétou), you'll pay 12€ to 38€ for a day's use of a mattress. Plage Tétou is associated with the upscale **Chez Tétou** (below). If you don't want to rent a mattress, you can cavort unhindered anywhere along the sands, moving freely from one area to another. Golfe-Juan indulges bathers who remove their bikini tops, but in theory it forbids nude sun-bathing.

SHOPPING IN VALLAURIS

Galerie Madoura, avenue de Georges et Suzanne Ramié, Vallauris (© **04-93-64-66-39;** www.madoura.com), is the only shop licensed to sell Picasso reproductions. It's open Monday through Friday 10am to 12:30pm and 3 to 6pm. Some of the reproductions are limited to 25 to 500 copies. Another gallery to seek out is the **Galerie Sassi-Milici,** 65 bis av. Georges-Clemenceau (© **04-93-64-65-71;** www.sassi-milici.com), which displays works by contemporary artists.

Market days in Vallauris are Tuesday to Sunday 7am to 12:30pm at **place de l'Homme au Mouton,** with its flower stalls and local produce. For a souvenir, you may want to visit a farming cooperative, the **Cooperative Nérolium,** 12 av. Georges-Clemenceau (© **04-93-64-27-54**). It produces such foods as bitter-orange marmalade and quince jam, olive oils, and scented products such as orange-flower water. Another unusual outlet for local products is the **Parfumerie Bouis,** 50 av. Georges-Clemenceau (© **04-93-64-38-27**).

La Boutique de l'Olivier, 46 av. Georges-Clemenceau (© **04-93-64-16-63**), specializes in olive-wood objects. They include pepper mills, salad servers, cheese boards, free-form bowls, and bread-slicing boxes. **Terres à Terre,** 58 av. Georges-Clemenceau (© **04-93-63-16-80**), is known for its culinary pottery, made of local clay. Gratin dishes and casseroles have long been big sellers at this excellent terra-cotta pottery outlet.

WHERE TO DINE

Chez Tétou ★★★ SEAFOOD   In its own amusing way, this is one of the Côte d'Azur's most famous restaurants, capitalizing on the beau monde that came here in the 1950s and 1960s. Retaining its Provençal earthiness despite its high prices, it has thrived in a white-sided beach cottage for more than 65 years. Appetizers are limited to platters of charcuterie or several almost-perfect slices of fresh melon. Most diners order the house specialty, bouillabaisse. Also on the limited menu are grilled sea bass with tomatoes *provençale*, sole meunière, and several preparations of lobster—the most famous is grilled and served with lemon-butter sauce, fresh parsley, and basmati rice. Dessert may be a powdered croissant with grandmother's jams (winter) or raspberry-and-strawberry tart (summer).

Av. des Frères-Roustan, sur la Plage, Golfe-Juan. © **04-93-63-71-16.** Reservations required. Main courses 77€; bouillabaisse 96€–122€. No credit cards. Thurs–Sun and Tues noon–2:30pm; Thurs–Tues 8–10:30pm. Closed Nov to early Mar.

This Antibes suburb was developed in the 1920s by Frank Jay Gould as a resort. At that time, people flocked to "John of the Pines" to escape the "crassness" of Cannes. In the 1930s, Juan-les-Pins drew a chic crowd during winter. Today it attracts young Europeans in pursuit of sex, sun, and sea, in that order.

Juan-les-Pins is often called the "Coney Island of the Riviera" (although anyone who calls it that hasn't seen Coney Island in a long time). One newspaper writer called it "a pop-art Monte Carlo, with burlesque shows and nude beaches"—a description much too provocative for such a middle-class resort. Another newspaper said that Juan-les-Pins is "for the young and noisy." Even F. Scott Fitzgerald decried it as a "constant carnival." If he could see it now, he'd know that he was a prophet.

ESSENTIALS

GETTING THERE   Juan-les-Pins is connected by **rail** to most other Mediterranean coastal resorts, especially Nice (trip time: 30 min.; one-way fare: 4.80€). For rail information and schedules, call ⓒ **36-35,** or visit **www.voyages-sncf.com**. **Buses** arrive from Nice and its airport at 40-minute intervals throughout the day. A bus leaves for Juan-les-Pins from Antibes at place Guynemer (ⓒ **04-93-34-37-60**) daily every 20 minutes and costs 1.45€ one-way (trip time: 10–15 min.). To **drive** to Juan-les-Pins from Nice, travel along N7 south; from Cannes, follow the signposted roads. Juan-les-Pins is just outside of Cannes.

VISITOR INFORMATION   The **Office de Tourisme** is at 51 bd. Charles-Guillaumont (ⓒ **04-92-90-53-05;** fax 04-93-61-55-13; www.antibesjuanlespins.com).

SPECIAL EVENTS   The town offers some of the best nightlife on the Riviera, and the action reaches its height during the annual jazz festival. The 10- to 12-day **Festival International de Jazz,** in mid-July, attracts jazz masters and their fans. Concerts are in a temporary stadium, custom-built for the event in Le Parc de la Pinède. Tickets cost 20€ to 65€ and can be purchased at the Office de Tourisme in Antibes and Juan-les-Pins alike.

A DAY AT THE BEACH

Part of the reason people flock here is that the town's beaches have sand, unlike the pebble beaches at many of the other resorts along this coast. **Plage de Juan-les-Pins** is the most central beach. Its subdivisions, all public, include **Plage de la Salis** and **Plage de la Garoupe.** If you don't have a beach chair, go to the concessions operated by each of the major beachfront hotels. Even if you're not a guest, you can rent a chaise and mattress for around 17€ to 21€. The most chic is the area maintained by the Hôtel des Belles-Rives. Competitors more or less in the same category are La Jetée and La Voile Blanche, both opposite the tourist information office. Topless sunbathing is permitted, but total nudity isn't.

WATERSPORTS

If you're interested in scuba diving, check with your hotel staff, **Easy Dive,** Port Gallice (ⓒ **04-93-61-41-49;** www.easydive.fr), or **EPAJ,** embarcadère Courbet (ⓒ **04-93-67-52-59**). A one-tank dive costs 45€, including all equipment. **Water-skiing** is available at virtually every beach in Juan-les-Pins. Concessionaires include one outfit that's more or less permanently located on the beach of the Hôtel des Belles-Rives. Ask any beach attendant or bartender, and he or she will guide you to the water-skiing representatives who station themselves on the sands. A 1-hour session costs 30€ to 110€.

WHERE TO STAY
Expensive
Hôtel des Belles-Rives ★★★   This is one of the Riviera's fabled addresses, on a par with the equally famous Juana (see below), though the Juana claims superior cuisine. Once it was a holiday villa occupied by Zelda and F. Scott Fitzgerald, and the scene of many a drunken brawl. It later played host to such luminaries as the duke and duchess of Windsor, Josephine Baker, and Edith Piaf. A 1930s aura lingers through recent renovations, although the double-glazing and air-conditioning bring a welcome touch of modern amenities. As befits a hotel of this age, rooms come in a variety of shapes and sizes, from small to spacious. The lower terraces hold garden dining rooms, a waterside aquatic club with a snack bar and lounge, and a jetty. The whole complex has its own private beach and dock.

33 bd. Edouard Baudoin, 06160 Juan-les-Pins. ✆ **04-93-61-02-79.** Fax 04-93-67-43-51. www.bellesrives. com. 43 units. 175€–740€ double. AE, DC, MC, V. Free parking. Closed Jan–Mar 11. **Amenities:** 2 summer restaurants; 1 winter restaurant; 2 bars; babysitting; room service. *In room:* A/C, TV, hair dryer, minibar, Wi-Fi (27€).

Hôtel Juana ★★★   This balconied Art Deco hotel, beloved by F. Scott Fitzgerald, is separated from the sea by the park of pines that gave Juan-les-Pins its name. The hotel is constantly being refurbished, as reflected in the attractive rooms with mahogany pieces, well-chosen fabrics, tasteful carpets, and large bathrooms in marble or tile. The rooms often have such extras as balconies. The hotel has a private swimming club where you can rent a "parasol and pad" on the sandy beach at reduced rates. Nearby is a park with umbrella-shaded tables and palms.

La Pinède, av. Gallice, 06160 Juan-les-Pins. ✆ **04-93-61-08-70.** Fax 04-93-61-76-60. www.hotel-juana. com. 40 units. 220€–335€ double; 515€–1,250€ suite. AE, MC, V. Parking 18€. Closed early Nov to Feb 26. **Amenities:** Restaurant; 2 bars; babysitting; bike rentals; exercise room w/sauna; pool (outdoor). *In room:* A/C, TV, hair dryer, minibar, Wi-Fi (18€).

Moderate
Hôtel des Mimosas   This elegant 1870s-style villa sprawls through a tropical garden on a hilltop, a 10-minute walk to a good beach. The decor is a mix of high-tech and Italian-style comfort, with antique and modern furniture. Guest rooms come in a variety of shapes and sizes—some quite small. Try for one of the four rooms with a balcony or the nine rooms with a terrace. A pool sits amid huge palm trees. The hotel is usually fully booked in summer, so reserve far in advance.

Rue Pauline, 06160 Juan-les-Pins. ✆ **04-93-61-04-16.** Fax 04-92-93-06-46. www.hotelmimosas.com. 34 units. 95€–140€ double. AE, MC, V. Free parking. Closed Oct–Apr. From the town center, drive .4km (¼ mile) west, following N7 toward Cannes. **Amenities:** Bar; pool (outdoor); room service. *In room:* A/C, TV, hair dryer, minibar, Wi-Fi (in some; free).

Hôtel Le Pré Catelan   In a residential area near the town park, 200m (656 ft.) from a sandy beach, this year-round Provençal villa (built ca. 1900) features a garden with rock terraces, towering palms, lemon and orange trees, large pots of pink geraniums, and outdoor furniture. The atmosphere is casual, the setting uncomplicated and unstuffy.

Furnishings are durable and basic. As is typical of such old villas, guest rooms come in a variety of shapes and sizes. Some have kitchenettes, and more expensive units have terraces. Despite its setting in the heart of town, the garden lends a sense of isolation. Breakfast is the only meal served.

27 av. des Palmiers, 06160 Juan-les-Pins. ✆ **04-93-61-05-11.** Fax 04-93-67-83-11. www.precatelan.com. 24 units. 88€–154€ double; 158€–244€ suite. AE, MC, V. Parking 8€–10€. **Amenities:** Bar; babysitting; pool (outdoor). *In room:* TV, hair dryer, minibar, Wi-Fi (free).

Inexpensive

Hôtel Cecil (Value) A stone's throw from the beach, this well-kept small hotel is one of the best bargains in Juan-les-Pins. The expanded 19th-century villa hosts traditionally furnished, worn but well-kept rooms that range from small to midsize. The owners provide a courteous welcome and a good meal.

Rue Jonnard, 06160 Juan-les-Pins. ✆ **04-93-61-05-12.** Fax 04-93-67-09-14. www.hotelcecilfrance.com. 21 units. 55€–92€ double. AE, DC, MC, V. Parking 15€. Closed Nov 7–Jan 14. **Amenities:** Restaurant; babysitting; room service. *In room:* A/C, TV (in some), hair dryer.

Hôtel Le Passy Centrally located and blandly modern, Le Passy opens onto a wide flagstone terrace. The other side faces the sea and coastal boulevard. The furnishings are Nordic modern, and the newer rooms have little balconies. Those that overlook the sea carry the higher price tag. Most rooms are small but have comfortable beds. In high-priced Juan-les-Pins, this is considered one of the more affordable choices, even though it's a bit sterile.

15 av. Louis-Gallet, 06160 Juan-les-Pins. ✆ **04-93-61-11-09.** Fax 04-93-67-91-78. www.hotels-lepassy-cyrano.com. 35 units. 58€–105€ double. AE, DC, MC, V. Parking 8€–13€. **Amenities:** Lounge; babysitting; room service. *In room:* A/C, TV.

WHERE TO DINE

Expensive

Le Bijou Plage (Value) FRENCH/PROVENÇALE This upscale brasserie has flourished beside the seafront promenade since 1923. The marine-style decor includes lots of varnished wood and bouquets of blue and white flowers in a mostly blue-and-white interior. Windows overlook a private beach that's much less crowded than the public beaches nearby. The menu is sophisticated and less expensive than you'd expect. Examples include excellent bouillabaisse, grilled sardines, risotto with John Dory and truffled butter, steamed mussels with *sauce poulette* (frothy cream sauce with herbs and butter), grilled John Dory with a vinaigrette enriched by tapenade of olives and fresh basil, and a super-size *plateau des coquillages et fruits de mer* (shellfish and seafood). Don't confuse this informally elegant place with its beachfront terrace, open April 15 to September 15 daily noon to 4pm.

Bd. du Littoral. ✆ **04-93-61-39-07.** Reservations recommended. Main courses 19€–40€; fixed-price menu 22€–51€. AE, DC, MC, V. Daily noon–2:30pm and 7:30–10:30pm.

Moderate

Le Perroquet PROVENÇALE The cuisine is well presented and prepared, and the restaurant's ambience is in synch with the resort's carnival-like summer aura. Located across from the Parc de la Pinède, it's decorated with depictions of every imaginable form of the restaurant's namesake parakeet. Look for savory versions of fish, at its best when grilled simply with olive oil and basil, and served with lemons. A worthwhile appetizer is

the *assortiment provençale,* which includes tapenade of olives, marinated peppers, grilled 277
sardines, and stuffed and grilled vegetables. Steaks may be served with green peppercorns
or béarnaise sauce, and desserts include three types of pastries on the same platter.

Av. Georges-Gallice. (℗ **04-93-61-02-20.** Reservations recommended. Main courses 20€–30€; fixed-price
menu 29€–35€. MC, V. Daily noon–2pm and 7–11pm. Closed early Nov to Dec 26.

JUAN-LES-PINS AFTER DARK

For starters, visit the **Eden Casino,** boulevard Baudoin in the heart of Juan-les-Pins
(℗ **04-92-93-71-71**), and try your luck at the roulette wheel or at one of the slot
machines. The area with slot machines is open every day 10am to 5pm. *Les grands jeux*
are open daily 10pm to 5am. A photo ID is required, preferably a passport.

For a faux-tropical experience, head to **Le Pam Pam,** route Wilson (℗ **04-93-61-11-05**), where you can sip rum drinks in an atmosphere that celebrates reggae, Brazilian, and
African music and dance.

If you prefer high-energy reveling, check out the town's many discos. **Whisky à Gogo,**
boulevard de la Pinède (℗ **04-93-61-26-40**), attracts young trendsetters with its rock
beat. In summer it fills up with the young and restless. Between October and Easter, it's
closed. **Le Village,** 1 bd. de la Pinède (℗ **04-92-93-90-00**), parties with an action-packed dance floor and DJs spinning the latest sounds from the international music
scene. The cover charge is a stiff 20€, although it's free for women before 1am on Friday.

12 ANTIBES ★★ & CAP D'ANTIBES ★★

913km (567 miles) S of Paris; 21km (13 miles) SW of Nice; 11km (7 miles) NE of Cannes

On the other side of the Baie des Anges (Bay of Angels), across from Nice, is the port of
Antibes. This old Mediterranean town has a quiet charm unique on the Côte d'Azur. Its
little harbor is filled with fishing boats and pleasure yachts, and in recent years it has
emerged as a new hot spot. The marketplaces are full of flowers, mostly roses and carna-tions. If you're in Antibes in the evening, you can watch fishermen playing the traditional
Riviera game of boules.

Spiritually, Antibes is totally divorced from Cap d'Antibes, which is a peninsula stud-ded with the villas and outdoor pools of the super-rich. In *Tender Is the Night,* F. Scott
Fitzgerald described it as a place where "old villas rotted like water lilies among the
massed pines." Photos of film and rock stars lounging at the Eden Roc have appeared in
countless magazines.

ESSENTIALS

GETTING THERE   **Trains** from Cannes arrive at the rail station, place Pierre-Semard,
every 20 minutes (trip time: 15 min.); the one-way fare is 2.50€. Trains from Nice arrive
at the rate of 25 per day (trip time: 18 min.); the one-way fare is around 4.40€. For rail
information, call (℗ **36-35,** or visit **www.voyages-sncf.com.** The **bus** station, La Gare
Routière, place Guynemer (℗ **04-93-34-37-60**), receives buses from throughout
Provence.

If you're **driving,** follow E1 east from Cannes and take the turnoff to the south for
Antibes, which will lead to the historic core of the old city. From Nice, take E1 west until
you come to the turnoff for Antibes. From the center of Antibes, follow the coastal road,
boulevard Leclerc, south to Cap d'Antibes.

The **Office de Tourisme** is at 11 place du Général-de-Gaulle (© **04-92-90-53-00;** fax 04-92-90-53-01; www.antibesjuanlespins.com).

SEEING THE SIGHTS

Hans Hartung & Anna-Eva Bergman Foundation ★ (Finds)
Devotees of modern art can now visit the former home of this German abstract painter and his wife, also an artist. You must reserve space, as only 30 visitors are allowed on the weekly tour because of security reasons. The stark-white villa was designed by Hartung himself, who lived here until his death in 1989. The couple left 16,000 paintings, photographs, and engravings, and you get to see only a fraction on one visit. Exhibitions are rotated throughout the year.

173 chemin du Valbosquet. © **04-93-33-45-92.** www.fondationhartungbergman.fr. Admission 5€ adults, 3€ students, free for ages 15 and under. Guided tours Fri at 2pm. Bus: Line 7 to chemin du Valbosquet.

Musée Naval et Napoléonien (Kids)
In this stone-sided fort and tower, built in stages in the 17th and 18th centuries, resides a collection of Napoleonic memorabilia, naval models, and paintings. A toy-soldier collection depicts various uniforms, including one used by Napoleon in the Marengo campaign. A wall painting on wood shows Napoleon's entrance into Grenoble; another shows him disembarking at Golfe-Juan on March 1, 1815. In contrast to Canova's Greek-god image of Napoleon, a miniature pendant by Barrault reveals the general as he really looked, with pudgy cheeks and a receding hairline. In the rear rotunda is one of the many hats worn by the emperor. You can climb to the top of the tower for a view of the coast that's worth the admission price.

Batterie du Grillon, bd. J.-F.-Kennedy. © **04-93-61-45-32.** Admission 3€ adults; 1.50€ seniors, students, and ages 12–25; free for children 11 and under. June–Oct Tues–Sat 10am–6pm; Nov–May Tues–Sat 10am–4:40pm.

Musée Picasso ★★
On the ramparts above the port is the Château Grimaldi, once the home of the princes of Antibes of the Grimaldi family, who ruled the city from 1385 to 1608. Today it houses one of the world's great Picasso collections. Picasso came to town after the war and stayed in a small hotel at Golfe-Juan until the museum director at Antibes invited him to work and live at the museum. Picasso spent 1946 painting here. When he departed, he gave the museum all the work he'd done: 24 paintings, 80 pieces of ceramics, 44 drawings, 32 lithographs, 11 oils on paper, 2 sculptures, and 5 tapestries. In addition, a gallery of contemporary art exhibits Léger, Miró, Ernst, and Calder, among others.

Place du Mariejol. © **04-92-90-54-20.** Admission 6€, 3€ children 12–18, free for children 11 and under. July–Aug Wed and Fri 10am–8pm; Sept–June Tues–Sun 10am–6pm.

WHERE TO STAY

Very Expensive

Hôtel du Cap–Eden Roc ★★★ Legendary for the glamour of its setting and its clientele, this Second Empire hotel is like a country estate. Opened in 1870 and surrounded by masses of gardens, it boasts spacious public rooms, marble fireplaces, paneling, chandeliers, and upholstered armchairs. The guest rooms are among the Riviera's most sumptuous, with deluxe beds. Even though the guests snoozing by the pool—blasted out of the cliffside at enormous expense—appear artfully undraped during the day, evenings are upscale, with lots of emphasis on clothing and style. The world-famous Pavillon Eden Roc, near a rock garden apart from the hotel, has a panoramic sea view.

Venetian chandeliers, Louis XV chairs, and elegant draperies add to the Pavillon's drama. Lunch is served on a terrace, under umbrellas and an arbor.

Bd. J.-F.-Kennedy, 06600 Cap d'Antibes. (?) **04-93-61-39-01.** Fax 04-93-67-13-83. www.edenroc-hotel.fr. 130 units. 460€–880€ double; 970€–1,600€ suite. No credit cards. Closed mid-Oct to Apr. Bus: A2. **Amenities:** 2 restaurants; 2 bars; babysitting; concierge; exercise room w/sauna; pool (outdoor); room service. *In room:* A/C, TV (on request), hair dryer, Wi-Fi (18€).

Hôtel Impérial Garoupe ★★   Within steps of the beach, this hotel is the centerpiece of a small park with rows of pines that block some of the sea views. The heiress to the Moulinex housewares fortune built it in 1993; Gilbert Irondelle, son of the director of Antibes's Grand Hôtel du Cap-Ferrat, has transformed it into a posh hotel that's less intimidating than his father's more monumental vision. The plush rooms contain contemporary furnishings, luxury beds, and deluxe bathrooms. The restaurant serves French and international cuisine.

60–74 chemin de la Garoupe, 06600 Cap d'Antibes. (?) **800/525-4800** in the U.S., or 04-92-93-31-61. Fax 04-92-93-31-62. www.imperial-garoupe.com. 34 units. 285€–670€ double; 450€–890€ suite. AE, DC, MC, V. Bus: A2. **Amenities:** Restaurant; bar; babysitting; pool (outdoor); room service. *In room:* A/C, TV, hair dryer, minibar, Wi-Fi (free).

Expensive

La Baie Dorée   Set between the sea and the coastal road, this hotel appears to rise from the water like a series of boxy, interlocked rectangles, each capped with a terra-cotta roof and ringed with strategically positioned balconies and terraces. From its base, a pier jutting out to sea allows guests to swim and boat, despite the lack of a sandy beach nearby. Public areas are dignified modern spaces with high ceilings; rectilinear lines; simple, summery furnishings; and big windows that seem to flood the interior with views of the nearby sea, almost as if you were aboard a yacht. Each room has a private terrace and a neatly kept bathroom. The upper-tier rooms have Jacuzzis.

579 bd. de la Garoupe, 06160 Cap d'Antibes. (?) **04-93-67-30-67.** Fax 04-92-93-76-39. www.baiedoree. com. 17 units. 240€–520€ double; 345€–700€ suite or duplex. Extra bed 50€. AE, MC, V. Free parking. **Amenities:** Restaurant; 2 bars; babysitting; room service. *In room:* A/C, TV, hair dryer, minibar.

Moderate

Castel Garoupe (Value)   We highly recommend this Mediterranean villa, which was built in 1968 on a private lane in the center of the cape. It offers tastefully furnished, spacious rooms with fine beds. Many rooms have private balconies; some units have air-conditioning, and some have TVs. A tranquil garden is also on the premises.

959 bd. de la Garoupe, 06160 Cap d'Antibes. (?) **04-93-61-36-51.** Fax 04-93-67-74-88. www.castel-garoupe.com. 28 units. 125€–182€ double; 141€–267€ studio apt with kitchenette. AE, MC, V. Closed Nov to mid-Mar. Bus: A2. **Amenities:** 2 bars; babysitting; exercise room; room service; tennis court (lit). *In room:* Hair dryer, kitchenette, minibar, Wi-Fi (free).

Hôtel Beau Site   This white-stucco villa with a tile roof and heavy shutters is surrounded by eucalyptus trees, pines, and palms. Located off the main road, a 7-minute walk from the beach, it has a low wall of flowers and wrought-iron gates. The interior is like a country inn, with oak beams and antiques. The guest rooms are comfortable and well maintained.

141 bd. J.-F.-Kennedy, 06150 Cap d'Antibes. (?) **04-93-61-53-43.** Fax 04-93-67-78-16. www.hotel beausite.net. 27 units. 90€–155€ double; 140€–200€ suite. AE, DC, MC, V. Closed Oct 21–Mar 10. Bus: A2. **Amenities:** Bar; babysitting; bike rentals; pool (outdoor); room service. *In room:* A/C, TV, hair dryer, Wi-Fi (free).

Le Cameo   This 19th-century Provençal villa is in the center of town on a historic square. The rooms are old-fashioned and admittedly not for everyone. Mattresses are well-worn but still have comfort in them. Locals gather in the home-style dining room, with its bouquets of flowers and crowded tables. Look for a simple setting here and a friendly welcome from the accommodating staff.

Place Nationale, 06600 Antibes. (© **04-93-34-24-17.** Fax 04-93-34-35-80. 9 units, 5 with bathroom, 4 with shower only. 64€ double with shower; 69€ double with bathroom. AE, DC, MC, V. Parking 5.30€. Closed Jan–Feb. Bus: A2. **Amenities:** Restaurant; bar. *In room:* TV.

WHERE TO DINE

La Taverne du Saffranier (Value)   PROVENÇALE   Earthy and irreverent, this brasserie in a century-old building serves a changing roster of savory local specialties. Portions are generous. Examples are a platter of *petits farcis* (stuffed vegetables); a mini-bouillabaisse for single diners at a time; savory fish soup; and an assortment of grilled fish (including sardines) that's served only with a dash of fresh lemon.

Place du Saffranier. (© **04-93-34-80-50.** Reservations recommended. Main courses 16€–27€; fixed-price menu 25€. No credit cards. Feb–Mar Tues–Sun noon–2:30pm, Thurs–Sat 7–10:30pm; Apr–May and Oct–Dec Tues–Sun noon–2pm, Tues–Sat 7–10pm. Closed mid-Nov to early Feb.

Le Vieux Murs   FRENCH/SEAFOOD   This charming Provençal tavern is inside the 17th-century ramparts that used to fortify the old seaport, not far from the Musée Picasso. White paint complements soaring stone vaults, and a glassed-in front terrace overlooks the water. The owner, Philippe Bensimon, and his chef, Thierry Gratarolla, run a warm, welcoming place. They use market-fresh ingredients, especially seafood, which is prepared with flavor and served with style. Daily offerings depend on what was best at the market. Lusty *provençale* meat and poultry dishes are menu staples.

Promenade de l'Amiral-de-Grasse. (© **04-93-34-06-73.** www.lesvieuxmurs.com. Reservations recommended. Main courses 25€–33€; fixed-price menu 44€–60€. AE, DC, MC, V. Wed–Sun noon–2:30pm; Tues–Sun 7:30–10:30pm. Closed 3 weeks in Nov.

Restaurant de Bacon ★★★   SEAFOOD   The Eden Roc restaurant at the Hôtel du Cap is more elegant, but Bacon serves the best seafood around. Surrounded by ultraexpensive residences, this restaurant on a rocky peninsula offers a panoramic coast view. Bouillabaisse aficionados claim that Bacon offers the best in France. In its deluxe version, saltwater crayfish float atop the savory brew; we prefer the simple version—a waiter adds the finishing touches at your table. If bouillabaisse isn't to your liking, try fish soup with garlic-laden rouille sauce; fish terrine; sea bass; John Dory; or something from a collection of fish unknown in North America, for example, sar, pageot, or denti.

Bd. de Bacon. (© **04-93-61-50-02.** www.restaurantdebacon.com. Reservations required. Main courses 25€–145€; fixed-price lunch 49€–79€; fixed-price dinner 79€. AE, DC, MC, V. Wed–Sun noon–2pm; Tues–Sun 8–10pm. Closed Oct to mid-Feb.

8

The Eastern Riviera: From Biot to Monaco to Menton

At Biot, the Riviera continues east through a string of upscale resorts that embody the glamour of the Côte d'Azur. Several have been home to great writers and artists of the 20th century. Biot is no exception, with its museum dedicated to the art and life of longtime resident Fernand Léger. Nearby Villeneuve-Loubet pays tribute to another art: the haute cuisine of Auguste Escoffier, the greatest chef ever to run a kitchen in a nation with a rich culinary heritage.

Farther into the foothills, many artisans live, work, and sell their wares in Tourrettes-sur-Loup. Nearby Vence boasts Matisse's Chapelle du Rosaire, adorned by the painter in his twilight years. The great artist is represented side by side with his contemporaries in St-Paul-de-Vence's Fondation Maeght, a museum as modern as the art it houses. Along the coast, Cagnes-sur-Mer continues the region's list of who's who in the 20th century—it was once home to Simone de Beauvoir, and it contains Les Collettes, Renoir's final home.

Nice, the Riviera's capital, is one of the coast's few budget-oriented resorts, making it a good base for exploring the region. It features no less than five worthy museums and is filled with noteworthy architecture. Its residents have included Matisse, Stendhal, Nietzsche, George Sand, and Flaubert.

East of Nice is Villefranche-sur-Mer, a fishing village and naval port where small houses climb the hillside; these were once the residences of notables such as Aldous Huxley, Katherine Mansfield, and Jean Cocteau. If you can't afford to stay in ultrachic St-Jean-Cap-Ferrat, you can at least sample the lifestyle at the Musée Ile-de-France, former home of a Rothschild heir, Baronne Ephrussi. Beaulieu, another posh village, features a replica of an ancient Greek residence. Eze attracts with its garden of exotic plants, and the Roman ruins at La Turbie ensure a never-ending stream of visitors. Peillon is a scenic foothill village, seated 300m (1,000 ft.) above the nearby shore.

The tiny principality of Monaco is awash with royal romance, glamorous nightlife, and gambling. Just inland is the tranquil medieval mountain village of Roquebrune. Cap-Martin is another spot associated with the rich and famous—it has been ever since Empress Eugénie wintered here in the 19th century. And sleepy Menton, 8km (5 miles) east of Monaco, is more Italianate than French; it stands right at the border with Italy at the far eastern extremity of the Côte d'Azur.

The cornices of the Riviera stretch from Nice to Menton. The lower road, 32km (20 miles) long, is the **Corniche Inférieure.** Along this road are the ports of Villefranche, Cap-Ferrat, Beaulieu, and Cap-Martin. The 31km (19-mile) **Moyenne Corniche (Middle Road)** ★★, built between World War I and World War II, runs from Nice to Menton. Napoleon built the **Grande Corniche** ★★★—the most panoramic—in 1806. La Turbie and Le Vistaero are the principal towns along this stretch, which reaches more than 480km (1,600 ft.) high at Col d'Eze.

1 BIOT ★

917km (570 miles) S of Paris; 10km (6 miles) E of Cagnes-sur-Mer; 6km (4 miles) NW of Antibes

Biot has been famous for its pottery ever since merchants began to ship earthenware jars to Phoenicia and destinations throughout the Mediterranean. Biot was first settled by Gallo-Romans and has had a long, war-torn history. The potters and other artists still work at their ancient crafts today. Biot is also the place Fernand Léger chose to paint until the day he died.

ESSENTIALS

GETTING THERE Biot's **train** station is 3km (2 miles) east of the town center. Frequent service connects Nice and Antibes. For rail information and schedules, call ✆ **36-35,** or visit **www.voyages-sncf.com**. To **drive** to Biot from Nice, take N7 west. From Antibes, follow N7 east.

VISITOR INFORMATION The **Office de Tourisme** is at 46 rue St-Sébastien (✆ **04-93-65-78-00;** fax 04-93-65-78-04; www.biot.fr).

EXPLORING THE TOWN

To explore the village, begin at the much-photographed **place des Arcades,** where you can see the 16th-century gates and the remains of the town's former ramparts. The **Eglise de Biot,** place des Arcades (✆ **04-93-65-00-85**), dates from the 15th century, when it was built by Italian immigrants who arrived to resettle the town after its population was decimated by the Black Death. The church is known for two stunning 15th-century retables: the red-and-gold *Retable du Rosaire* by Ludovico Bréa, and the restored *Christ aux Plaies* by Canavesio. The church is open daily from 8am to 7:30pm year-round. And usually, but not always, on Friday or Saturday at 9pm, it's the site of Les Heures Musicales, wherein a series of concerts makes the ceiling vaults resonate with the sounds of classical music.

Musée d'Histoire Locale et de Céramique Biotoise This museum displays the historical and contemporary work of local glass-blowing artists, potters, ceramists, painters, and goldsmiths of the area. The museum, which can be visited in less than an hour, is mainly of interest to the serious collector, although it does help the casual visitor understand why Biot is the capital of glass blowing on the Riviera. Local craftsmen revived the old methods of making oil lamps and carafes in 1956, and have been working that way since. Local soils provide the best sand for glass blowing. Look for the narrow-spouted *pontons* from which a jet of liquid, such as wine, can be poured straight into one's mouth.

Place de la Chapelle. ✆ **04-93-65-54-54.** Admission 2€ adults, 1€ children 6–16, free for children 5 and under. Apr–Nov Wed–Sun 11am–7pm; Dec–Mar Wed–Sun 2–6pm.

Musée National Fernand-Léger ★★ The artist's widow, Nadia Léger, assembled this collection and donated it to the French government after the artist's death, in 1955. Léger's mosaic-and-ceramic mural enhances the stone-and-marble facade. On the grounds is a polychrome ceramic sculpture, *Le Jardin d'enfant;* inside are two floors of geometrical forms in pure, flat colors. The collection includes paintings, ceramics, tapestries, and sculptures showing the artist's development from 1905 until his death. His paintings abound with cranes, acrobats, scaffolding, railroad signals, buxom nudes, casings,

and crankshafts. The most unusual work depicts a Léger Mona Lisa *(La Giaconde aux*
Clés) contemplating a set of keys, a wide-mouthed fish dangling over her head.

Chemin du Val-de-Pôme (on the eastern edge of town, beside the road to the rail station). Ⓒ **04-92-91-50-30.** www.musee-fernandleger.fr. Admission 4.50€, free for children 17 and under. Apr–Oct Wed–Mon 10am–6pm; Nov–Mar Wed–Mon 10am–5pm.

SHOPPING

Glass, pottery, and other crafts your best bet in Biot. In the late 1940s, glassmakers created a bubble-flecked glass known as *verre rustique.* It comes in brilliant colors such as cobalt and emerald and is displayed in many store windows on the main shopping street, **rue St-Sebastien.** Interesting stores are also found in the pedestrian zone in Biot's historic center. Stroll along some of the oldest streets, such as the **rue des Tines** and the **place des Arcades.** Most of the glassworks, and many shops selling glass, are at the lower (southern) side of town, beside the **Route de la Mer.**

The best place to watch the glass blowers and buy glass is **Verreries de Biot,** 5 chemin des Combes (Ⓒ **04-93-65-03-00;** www.verreriebiot.com), at the edge of town. Established in 1956, it was the first, and remains the largest, of the many glass-blowing establishments. Have a look at one-of-a-kind collector pieces at the Galerie International du Verre, where the beautifully displayed glass is for sale, often at exorbitant prices. In July and August hours are Monday to Saturday 9:30am to 8pm, Sunday 10:30am to 1:30pm and 2:30 to 7:30pm. From September to June, hours are Monday to Saturday 9:30am to 6pm, Sunday 10:30am to 1:30pm and 2:30 to 6:30pm.

The namesake of the **Galerie Jean-Claude Novaro** (also known as Galerie de la Patrimoine), place des Arcades (Ⓒ **04-93-65-60-23**), is known as the "Picasso of glass artists." His works are pretty and colorful, though sometimes lacking the diversity and intellectual flair of the artists displayed at the Galerie International du Verre.

La Poterie Provençale, 1689 rte. de la Mer (Ⓒ **04-93-65-63-30;** www.poterie-provencale.com), is almost adjacent to the Musée Fernand-Léger, about 3km (3 miles) southeast of town. It is one of the last potteries in Provence to specialize in the tall, amphora-like containers known as *jarres.* The place refers to itself as *une jarrière* because of its emphasis on the containers.

WHERE TO STAY

Domaine du Jas Set at the base of the hill on which sits medieval Biot, this well-managed and intimate inn was built in the early 1990s in the form of three villa-inspired low-rise buildings clustered within a palm-studded garden around a rectangular swimming pool. Each unit has its own terrace or balcony, views of the pool or garden, and, in some cases, panoramas of medieval Biot rising dramatically on the slopes above. Color schemes, around the pool and within the bedrooms alike, reflect the ochers, strong yellows, and verdant greens of Provence; throughout, floors are sheathed with slabs of flagstones. The Mascella-Torgoman family (Patrick and Christine) maintain this place much like a private home where friends of the family happen to drop in for extended stays. The hotel does not have a reception desk, per se, but rather an informal ambience that might remind you of a private house party.

No formalized restaurant or bar is on the premises, but drinks and light luncheon platters and salads are served informally around the pool from May to September.

625 rte. de la Mer, 06410 Biot. Ⓒ **04-93-65-50-50.** Fax 04-93-65-02-01. www.domainedujas.com. 19 units. 120€–245€ double. Rates include continental breakfast. AE, MC, V. Free parking. Closed Jan 5–Mar 5. **Amenities:** Babysitting; pool (outdoor); room service; Wi-Fi (free). *In room:* A/C, TV, hair dryer.

Les Terraillers ★★★ MEDITERRANEAN   This stone-sided restaurant is .8km (about ½ mile) south of Biot, in a 16th-century ceramics studio. The cuisine of chef Claude Jacques, Michael Fulci, and their staff changes with the seasons and is more sophisticated and appetizing than that at many competitors. Examples are a platter containing two preparations of pigeon (thigh and breast cooked in different ways), served with a corn galette and the pigeon's own drippings; fish of the day in saffron sauce; roasted scallops with saffron and mussel-flavored cream sauce and leek confit; a tart with artichoke hearts and tomatoes en confit with lobster salad; braised John Dory *provençale* style, with olive oil and a fricassee of zucchini, artichokes, tomatoes, and olives; and ravioli filled with pan-fried foie gras and served with essence of morels and mushroom duxelles.

11 rte. du Chemin-Neuf. ✆ **04-93-65-01-59.** www.lesterraillers.com. Reservations required as far in advance as possible. Main courses 33€–48€; fixed-price lunch 39€–55€; fixed-price dinner 65€–110€. AE, MC, V. June–Sept Fri–Tues noon–2pm and 7–10pm. Closed Oct 25–Dec 2. Take rte. du Chemin-Neuf, following signs to Antibes.

---

2 TOURRETTES-SUR-LOUP ★

929km (577 miles) SE of Paris; 29km (18 miles) W of Nice; 6km (4 miles) W of Vence; 21km (13 miles) NE of Grasse

Often called the "City of Violets" because of the small purple flowers that abound beneath the olive trees, Tourrettes-sur-Loup sits atop a sheer cliff overlooking the Loup valley. Though violets are big business for the town (they're sent to the perfume factories in Grasse, made into candy, and celebrated during a festival held each Mar), you'll probably find the many shops lining the streets much more interesting. These small businesses are often owned by artisans who sell their own art—most notably hand-woven fabrics and unique pottery. Even if you're not interested in buying, walking through the Old Town is worth the trip up the hill.

The unusual city was built so that the walls of the outermost buildings form a rampart; three towers rising above the village give it its name. Access to these monuments is erratic and whimsical, depending on a local representative of the nearby **town hall** (✆ **04-93-59-30-11;** www.tourrettessurloup.com). In theory, the sites can be visited Monday through Friday from 9am to 6pm, but to make sure, consult the town hall.

ESSENTIALS

GETTING THERE   The nearest rail junction is at Cagnes-sur-Mer; buses run about every 45 minutes from Cagnes to Vence, where you must change to another bus to arrive in Tourettes (about six a day; trip time: 10 min.). The town has no bus station; the bus disembarks in the place du Village, in front of the Café des Sports. For **bus schedules** and information, call ✆ **04-93-42-40-79.** To go from Cagnes to Tourrettes takes about an hour—it's more convenient to take a taxi from Cagnes. **R.A.I.S.** taxis (✆ **04-93-59-32-87** or 06-07-10-65-38) line up at the train station and cost around 30€ to 35€ each way.

VISITOR INFORMATION   The **Office de Tourisme** is at 2 place de la Libération (✆ **04-93-24-18-93**).

SHOPPING

Tourrettes-sur-Loup is home to more crafts studios than any other town its size in Provence. Nearly 30 artisans, including a handful of noted ones from as far away as Paris, have set up their studios and outlets, often in stone-sided buildings facing the town's main street, **Grand'Rue.** The best way to sample their offerings is to wander and window-shop.

You'll find jewelry, in designs ranging from old-fashioned to contemporary, at **La Paësine,** 14 Grand'Rue (© **04-93-24-14-55**). Original clothing—sometimes in silk—for men and women, as well as draperies, bed linens, and tablecloths, usually in creative patterns, is available at the **Atelier Arachnée,** 8 Grand'Rue (© **04-93-24-11-42**). Ceramics crafted from local clay in patterns inspired by the many civilizations that have pillaged or prospered in Provence are sold at **Poterie Tournesol,** 7 Grand'Rue (© **04-93-59-35-62**). **Yvette Lamoureux Galerie,** 73 Grand'Rue (© **04-93-24-11-74;** www.yvette.lamoureux.fr), sells unusual bronzes, some authorized by well-known masters of the modernist movement. For a view of canvases by painters inspired by the colors and traditions of Provence, head for **Galerie Eponyme,** 65 Grand'Rue (© **04-93-24-39-72;** http://galerieeponyme.free.fr).

Looking for a pick-me-up after a day of shopping? Head for one of the region's best candy shops, **Confiserie des Gorges du Loup,** rue Pont St. Loup (© **04-93-59-32-91**), where age-old techniques are used to layer fresh fruit with sugar. The result is an ultra-chewy, ultrasweet confection that gradually melts as it explodes flavor—the taste has been called "angelic." Sample chocolate-covered orange peel, rose-petal jam, and sugar-permeated sliced apricots, tangerines, plums, cherries, and grapes. Even the local violets are transformed into edible, sugary treats.

WHERE TO STAY

Auberge Belles Terrasses   This hotel offers views of the faraway peninsula of Antibes and the sea beyond. Its boxy shape and terra-cotta roof were inspired by an architect's fantasy of an old Provençal manor house, and it was named after the terraces that are angled for maximum exposure to the view. The rooms are simple, traditional, and comfortable. Much of the allure of the *auberge* is its restaurant. Menu items include civet of roast suckling pig, young hen with freshwater crayfish, roast wild hare with mustard sauce, *provençale* frogs' legs with garlic-and-butter sauce, and assorted game dishes. Fixed-price menus range from 17€ to 27€.

1315 rte. de Vence, 06140 Tourrettes-sur-Loup. © **04-93-59-30-03.** Fax 04-93-59-31-27. 18 units. 56€–79€ double. AE, MC, V. Closed mid-Nov to mid-Dec. From town, drive about a kilometer (¹/₂ mile), following the signs toward Vence. **Amenities:** Restaurant. *In room:* TV, Wi-Fi (free).

Four Seasons Provence at Terre Blanche ★★★ (Kids)   Set almost directly atop the dividing line between Provence and the Côte d'Azur, this is one of the newest and plushest resorts to open in southern France. The location is 32km (20 miles) north of the Cannes-Mandelieu airport. It's also the only resort in the region with two 18-hole golf courses, each designed by Wales-born Dave Thomas, a big name in course design. Its look emulates one of the "perched villages" of medieval Provence.

The hotel's layout evokes an isolated cluster of masonry-sided villas, each painted ocher, capped with a terra-cotta roof, and connected by undulating brick walkways that snake across manicured lawns and gardens. Villas are artfully decorated with airy post-modern furnishings vaguely influenced by the traditions of Provence. Even the smallest of the accommodations here is a suite suitable for up to four occupants. The largest is a full-blown private villa for up to eight guests.

Domaine de Terre Blance, 83440 Tourrettes. ✆ **04-94-39-90-00.** Fax 04-94-39-90-01. www.fourseasons. com/provence. 110 suites. 375€–1,075€ suite for 2; 795€–13,500€ villas for 4–6. AE, DC, MC, V. **Amenities:** 2 restaurants; 2 bars; babysitting; children's programs; concierge; 2 golf courses; health club & spa; 2 pools (indoor & outdoor); room service. *In room:* A/C, TV, kitchenettes (in some), minibar, Wi-Fi (22€).

La Demeure de Jeanne ★ ⟨**Value**⟩   This is gem of a B&B is a large Provençal *mas* with an outdoor swimming pool and terraces overlooking the sea. Set on landscaped grounds, the rooms, including the suites, come in a variety of sizes and decor. Each of the accommodations is named after cats; the Green Cat Suite and the Master White Cat Suite are particularly luxurious. The public rooms, including the living room lounge and the library, are furnished in an inviting, traditional Provençal style that evokes a private home in the south of France. Standing next to the pool house is a 650-year-old olive tree.

907 rte. de Vence, 06140 Tourrettes-sur-Loup. ✆ **04-93-59-37-24.** Fax 04-93-24-39-95. www.demeure dejeanne.com. 4 units. 150€ double; 175€–250€ suite. Rates include a continental breakfast. No credit cards. Closed Oct–Apr. **Amenities:** Restaurant; pool (outdoor). *In room:* TV, no phone.

WHERE TO DINE

Auberge Belles Terrasses (see above) is also recommended for its cuisine, except on Monday, when it's closed to nonguests.

If you're looking for a head-on view of everyday Provençal life, consider either a *plat du jour,* a glass of pastis, or *un petit café* at the most colorful and animated pub in town, **le Café des Sports,** 1 rte. de Vence/place de la Libération (✆ **04-93-59-30-26**). Its paneled interior is representative of old-fashioned Provence. It's open for drinks and coffee every day from 6:30am to 8pm, although the generous *plats du jour,* priced at 10€ (credit cards not accepted), are trotted out only between noon and 2:30pm. Recorded music, gossip, chit-chat, and the sounds of local scandal-mongering permeate the place every day after around 7pm, when it's everybody's favorite hangout. Closed Monday and Tuesday in winter.

Faventia ★★★ PROVENÇALE/MEDITERRANEAN   If you're driving up from the coast into the hills of Provence, stop to enjoy Faventia's great charm and sublime cuisine made with the best of market-fresh ingredients. In an elegantly modern setting, the restaurant showcases a contemporary Mediterranean cuisine with a heavy *provençale* influence. Dishes are relatively simple and filled with flavor, backed up by a regional wine list. From the restaurant's hilltop perch, panoramic views open onto the nearby villages. In summer guests dine alfresco on a shaded terrace. The menu is forever changing and seasonally adjusted.

In the Four Seasons Resort Provence at Terre Blanche. ✆ **04-94-39-90-00.** Reservations required. Main courses 31€–45€; fixed-price menus 95€; Sun brunch 45€. AE, DC, MC, V. Sept–June Tues–Sat 7am–10pm; July–Aug Tues–Sat 7am–10:30pm; all year open for Sun brunch only.

---

3 ST-PAUL-DE-VENCE ★★

925km (575 miles) S of Paris; 23km (14 miles) E of Grasse; 27km (17 miles) E of Cannes; 31km (19 miles) N of Nice

ESSENTIALS

Getting There   The nearest **rail** station is in Cagnes-sur-Mer. Some 20 **buses** per day leave from Nice's Gare Routière, dropping passengers off in St-Paul-de-Vence (one-way fare: 1€), then in Vence. For information, call the **Compagnie SAP** (✆ **04-93-58-37-60**).

If you **drive** from Nice, take coastal A8 east, turn inland at Cagnes-sur-Mer, and follow signs north to St-Paul-de-Vence.

VISITOR INFORMATION   The **Office de Tourisme** is at 2 rue Grande (© **04-93-32-86-95;** fax 04-93-32-60-27; www.saint-pauldevence.com).

EXPLORING THE TOWN

Except for local residents and service-related deliveries (such as dropping your luggage off at your hotel), driving a car within the center of St-Paul's Old Town is prohibited. The pedestrians-only **rue Grande** is the most interesting street, running the entire length of St-Paul. Most of the stone houses along it are from the 16th and 17th centuries, many still bearing the coats of arms placed here by the original builders. Today most of them are antiques shops, arts-and-crafts galleries, and souvenir and gift shops—some are still artists' studios.

Near the church is the **Musée d'Histoire de St-Paul,** place de l'Eglise (© **04-93-32-41-13**), a museum in a village house that dates to the 1500s. It was restored and refurnished in 16th-century style, with artifacts illustrating the history of the village. It's open daily 10am to 12:30pm and 1:30 to 5:30pm. Admission is 3€ adults, 2€ students and children 5 to 18, free for children 4 and under.

Fondation Maeght ★★★   This avant-garde building houses one of the most modern art museums in Europe. Nature and the creations of men and women blend harmoniously in this unique achievement of the architect José Luis Sert. Its white concrete arcs give the impression of a giant pagoda rising from a hill in a pine forest.

A stark Calder rises like some futuristic monster on the lawn. In a courtyard, the bronze works of Giacometti and marble statues by Miró and mosaics by Chagall form a surrealistic garden. Built on several levels, the museum creates links between indoors and out with glass walls and terraces. The foundation, a gift "to the people" from Aimé and Marguerite Maeght, also provides a showcase for new talent. Enjoy the works of 20th-century artists: mosaics by Chagall and Braque, Miró ceramics in the "labyrinth," and Ubac and Braque stained glass in the chapel. On the property are a library, a cinema, and a cafeteria. In one showroom, you can buy original lithographs by artists such as Chagall and Giacometti, and limited-edition prints.

Outside the town walls. © **04-93-32-81-63.** www.maeght.com. Admission 11€ adults, 9€ students and ages 10–18, free for children 9 and under. July–Sept daily 10am–7pm; Oct–June daily 10am–12:30pm and 2:30–6pm.

La Collégiale de la Conversion de St-Paul   This church was constructed in the 12th and 13th centuries, though it was much altered over the years. The Romanesque choir is the oldest part, containing remarkable stalls carved in walnut in the 17th century. The bell tower was built in 1740, but the vaulting was reconstructed in the 1800s. Although the facade today isn't alluring, the church is filled with art, notably a painting of Ste-Cathérine d'Alexandrie attributed to Tintoretto; it hangs to the left as you enter. The Trésor de l'Eglise is one of the most beautiful in the Alpes-Maritimes, with a spectacular ciborium. Look also for a low relief of the Martyrdom of St-Clément on the last altar on the right. In the baptismal chapter is a 15th-century alabaster Madonna.

Place de l'Eglise. No phone. Free admission. Daily 9am–6pm (until 7pm July–Aug).

SHOPPING

Climb down some steep steps to a 14th-century wine cellar to visit **La Petite Cave de St-Paul,** 7 rue de l'Etoile (© **04-93-32-59-54**), which stocks an excellent selection of

8

regional wine. Among the shop's most prized wines are bottles from Le Mas Bernard, the winery owned by the Fondation Maeght, which owns only 3 hectares (7 acres) of vineyards west of St-Paul. The wine from Le Mas Bernard is very good and unavailable in the United States because of the small production. Other inventories within this shop include upscale and often esoteric wines from Provence, Les Alpes-Maritimes, and even the vineyards of the Ile St-Honorat, off the coast of Cannes, where a local monastery creates an extremely limited production of wine.

The village streets are chock-full of expensive boutiques and galleries. The top gallery is the **Atelier/Boutique Christian Choisy,** 5 rue de la Tour/Ramparts Ouest (© **04-93-32-19-06;** www.christianchoisy.com). Open daily 9:30am to 7pm.

WHERE TO STAY

La Colombe d'Or (p. 290) also rents deluxe rooms.

Expensive

Hôtel Le St-Paul ★★★ Converted from a 16th-century Renaissance residence and retaining many original features, this member of Relais & Châteaux is in the heart of the village. The guest rooms are decorated in sophisticated Provençal style with sumptuous beds One woman wrote us that while sitting on the balcony of room no. 30 she understood why Renoir, Léger, Matisse, and Picasso were inspired by Provence. Many rooms enjoy a view of the valley with the Mediterranean in the distance. The restaurant has a flower-bedecked terrace sheltered by the 16th-century ramparts and a superb dining room with vaulted ceilings.

86 rue Grande, 06570 St-Paul-de-Vence. © **04-93-32-65-25.** Fax 04-93-32-52-94. www.lesaintpaul.com. 16 units. 250€–400€ double; 320€–820€ suite. AE, DC, MC, V. Free parking. Closed mid-Dec to mid-Feb. **Amenities:** Restaurant; bar; babysitting; room service; 3 tennis courts (lit); Wi-Fi (free). *In room:* A/C, TV, hair dryer, minibar.

Hôtel Les Vergers de Saint-Paul ★ (Finds) This is a small *hôtel de charme,* as the French say, lying only 900m (2,952 ft.) from the center of the village in an idyllic setting surrounded by greenery. Near the famous Fondation Maeght, the hotel is beautifully modern. Bedrooms are tasteful, comfortable, and elegantly refined. All the accommodations come with a balcony or a terrace overlooking the large pool.

940 rte. de la Colle, 06570 St-Paul-de-Vence. © **04-93-32-94-24.** Fax 04-93-32-91-07. www.hotel-vergers-saint-paul-cote.azur.fr. 17 units. 110€–195€ double; 195€–245€ suite. AE, MC, V. **Amenities:** Bar; babysitting; pool (outdoor); room service. *In room:* A/C, TV, hair dryer, Wi-Fi (free).

La Grande Bastide ★★ (Finds) This 18th-century country home has been lovingly turned into a *hotel de charme,* and many famous guests who can afford more expensive digs prefer the homelike appeal of this place. The midsize bedrooms are artfully decorated in a Provençal style of soft pastel shades. All of the rooms open onto views of St-Paul (many also have a view of the sea). More panoramic views are visible from the terrace, where breakfast and snacks are served. Guests gather for their sundowner in the pool house, where sofas are placed in front of a blazing fire on chilly nights.

1350 rte. de la Colle, 06570 St-Paul-de-Vence. © **04-93-32-50-30.** Fax 04-93-32-50-59. www.la-grande-bastide.com. 14 units. 145€–240€ double; 300€ suite. AE, DC, MC, V. **Amenities:** Bar; pool (outside); room service. *In room:* A/C, TV, minibar, Wi-Fi (30€).

Villa St. Maxime ★★ (Finds) An elegant discovery, this is one of the most charming of the small boutique hotels along the Riviera. Set on beautifully landscaped grounds, the hotel features a large panoramic terrace, beautiful garden, and Olympic-size pool, all located beneath the ramparts of this old fortified town. While the town is ancient, the villa is like a work of contemporary art, built with Provençal stone sculpted in bold lines, with a retractable and glass-enclosed reception atrium. Vaulted and pillared halls are architectural grace notes, as is the sleek marble flooring. Views extend from almost every window, even of the faraway Mediterranean. The best room is the largest suite with additional separate rooms; it contains the most luxurious bathroom in the hills of Nice. Other rooms are also a delight. Accommodations open onto private balconies or terraces.

390 rte. de la Colle, 06570 St-Paul-de-Vence. ✆ **04-93-32-76-00.** Fax 04-93-32-93-00. www.villa-st-maxime.com. 6 units. 155€–240€ double; 190€–380€ suite. AE, MC, V. **Amenities:** Bar; babysitting; pool (outdoor). *In room:* A/C, TV, hair dryer, minibar, Wi-Fi (free).

Moderate

Auberge Le Hameau ★ (Value)   This romantic Mediterranean villa is on a hilltop on the outskirts of St-Paul-de-Vence, on the road to Colle at Hauts-de-St-Paul. Built as a farmhouse in the 1920s and enlarged and transformed into a hotel in 1967, it contains high-ceilinged rooms. You'll have a remarkable view of the surrounding hills and valleys. A vineyard and sunny terrace with fruit trees, flowers, and pool grace the hotel grounds.

528 rte. de la Colle (D107), 06570 St-Paul-de-Vence. ✆ **04-93-32-80-24.** Fax 04-93-32-55-75. www.le-hameau.com. 17 units. 120€–170€ double; 220€–270€ suite. MC, V. Closed Nov 15–Feb 15. From the town, take D107 about 1km (^{2}/₃ mile), following the signs south of town toward Colle. **Amenities:** Bar; pool (outdoor). *In room:* A/C, TV, hair dryer.

Auberge Les Orangers ★ (Finds)   M. Franklin has created a "living oasis" in his villa, which is configured like a highly personalized bed-and-breakfast. The scents of roses, oranges, and lemons waft through the air. The main lounge is decorated with original oils and furnished in Provençal style. Expect to be treated like a guest in a private home. The rooms, with antiques and Oriental carpets, have panoramic views. Banana trees and climbing geraniums surround the sun terrace.

Quartier les Fumerates, rte. de la Colle (D107), 06570 St-Paul-de-Vence. ✆ **04-93-32-80-95.** Fax 04-93-32-00-32. www.stpaulweb.com/hlo. 5 units. 130€–150€ double; 170€ suite. Rates include breakfast. MC, V. Free parking. From the town center, follow the signs to Cagnes-sur-Mer for 1km (^{2}/₃ mile) south. **Amenities:** Babysitting; room service. *In room:* Hair dryer.

Les Messugues ★ (Finds)   Those wishing to escape the tourist hordes of this hill town prefer this small inn close to the Maeght Foundation. The hotel lies only 1km from the center of the village. In fair weather, its attractively furnished bedrooms, each comfortably furnished, open onto a terrace. The doors of the rooms come from an 1800s prison. Activities center around a garden, whose centerpiece is a pool.

Domaine des Gardettes, 06570 St-Paul-de-Vence. ✆ **04-93-32-53-32.** 15 units. 95€–170€ double. AE, DC, MC, V. Closed Nov–Mar. **Amenities:** Pool (outdoor); Wi-Fi (free). *In room:* A/C, TV, hair dryer, Wi-Fi (in some; free).

Inexpensive

Hôtel Marc Hély   Provence-born Michel Ricard welcomes you to his family-managed *hotel de charme.* Off the main road into St. Paul, it commands a panoramic view of the village. Each of the tasteful and well-equipped bedrooms contains a balcony or a private patio. The garden helps ensure serenity even in this touristy part of France. Breakfast is served on the patio in the garden or on a veranda with a view of St. Paul, which is only 3 minutes away by car. Families can rent a suite that accommodates up to three guests.

535 rte. de Cagnes, 06480 La Colle sur Loup. ✆ **04-93-22-64-10.** Fax 04-93-22-93-84. www.hotel-marc-hely. com. 12 units. 75€–120€ double; 110€–190€ family suite. AE, DC, MC, V. Free parking. **Amenities:** Pool (outdoor); room service; Wi-Fi (free). *In room:* A/C, TV, hair dryer, minibar.

Les Bastides St-Paul This hotel is in the hills outside town, 1.5km (1 mile) south of St-Paul and 4km (2½ miles) south of Vence. Spread over two buildings, it offers comfortable carpeted rooms, each accented with regional artifacts and opening onto a terrace and garden. On the premises is a pool shaped like a cloverleaf. Longtime hoteliers Marie José and Maurice Giraudet head the responsive staff. Breakfast is served anytime.

880 rte. des Blaquières (rte. Cagnes-Vence), 06570 St-Paul-de-Vence. ✆ **04-92-02-08-07.** Fax 04-93-20-50-41. 20 units. 85€–140€ double. AE, DC, MC, V. From the town center, follow signs toward Cagnes-sur-Mer for 1.5km (1 mile) south. **Amenities:** Babysitting; pool (outdoor); room service; Wi-Fi (free). *In room:* A/C, TV, minibar, Wi-Fi (in some; free).

WHERE TO DINE

La Colombe d'Or ★ PROVENÇALE For over a decade, the "Golden Dove" has been St-Paul's most celebrated restaurant—not for cutting-edge cuisine or exotic experiments, but for its remarkable art collection. You can dine amid Mirós, Picassos, Klees, Dufys, Utrillos, and Calders. In fair weather everyone tries for a seat on the terrace. You may begin with smoked salmon or foie gras from Landes if you've recently won at the casino. If not, you can count on a soup made with fresh seasonal vegetables. The best fish dishes are poached sea bass with mousseline sauce, and sea wolf baked with fennel. Tender beef comes with *gratin dauphinois* (potatoes). A classic finish to any meal is a *soufflé flambé au Grand-Marnier.*

La Colombe also runs several guest rooms (16 doubles, 10 suites) in an original 16th-century stone house; two wings were added in the 1950s, one of which stretches into the garden next to the pool. Some units have exposed stone and ceiling beams; all are comfortable, with air-conditioning, minibars, and TVs. Prices are 285€ for a double, 380€ for a suite.

1 place du Général-de-Gaulle, 06570 St-Paul-de-Vence. ✆ **04-93-32-80-02.** Fax 04-93-32-77-78. www. la-colombe-dor.com. Reservations required. Main courses 17€–35€. AE, DC, MC, V. Daily noon–2pm and 7:30–10pm. Closed Nov–Dec and Jan 10–20.

4 VENCE ★

925km (575 miles) S of Paris; 31km (19 miles) N of Cannes; 24km (15 miles) NW of Nice

Travel up into the hills northwest of Nice, across country studded with cypresses, olive trees, pines, and banks of roses and oleanders to Vence. Outside the town, along boulevard Paul-André, two olive presses carry on with their age-old duties. But the charm lies in the Vieille Ville. Visitors invariably have themselves photographed on place du Peyra in front of the urn-shape Vieille Fontaine, a background shot in several motion pictures. The 15th-century square tower is also a curiosity.

ESSENTIALS

GETTING THERE The nearest **rail** station is in Cagnes-sur-Mer, about 10km (6¼ miles) southwest from Vence. From there, about 20 buses per day priced at 1.50€ go to Vence. For train information, call ✆ **36-35,** or visit **www.voyages-sncf.com.** Frequent **buses** (no. 400 or 94) originating in Nice take 45 minutes to reach Vence; the one-way

Exploring the Gorges du Loup

After paying your respects to Matisse at the Chapelle du Rosaire in Vence, you can take D2210 through some of the Riviera's most luxuriant countryside. The **Gorges du Loup** isn't as dramatic as the Grand Canyon du Verdon (p. 217) but still features a scenic 13km (8-mile) drive that loops along the gorge's eastern and western edges. This drive showcases waterfalls, most notably the **Cascades des Demoiselles,** with its partially fossilized plant life, and the 39m (130-ft.) **Cascade de Courmes.** Jagged glacial holes, best exemplified by the **Saut du Loup,** can also be found at the valley's northeastern end.

Gourdon, the only village along the gorge's western rim, has a year-round population of only 60 (100 if you include the population of the region immediately nearby), but in summer, its population swells into something approaching a honky-tonk tourist trap. If you stop here, ignore the dozens of souvenir shops and visit the immense and foreboding 13th-century **Château de Gourdon** (© 04-93-09-68-02; www.chateau-gourdon.com). The château houses two completely separate museums: **Musée Historique** features a collection of arms, furniture, sculpture (including *The Martyrdom of San Sebastian* by El Greco), and paintings (including *Descent from the Cross* by Rubens). Entrance costs 4€ for adults, 3€ for students and youth ages 10 to 18.

On the southeastern edge of the gorge, at Pont-du-Loup, go to **La Confiserie des Gorges du Loup,** rue Principale (© 04-93-59-32-91), where you can sample sweets while watching the confectioners sugarcoat tangerines or chocolate-dip orange peels. Less than a kilometer farther south, the 15th-century Gothic church at Le Bar-sur-Loup features a morbid *Danse Macabre,* a 15th-century painting of fallen and dancing humans whose souls are being wrested away by black demons and then weighed by St. Michael before being tossed into the pits of hell. Speculation links the anonymous work of art to the plague.

After taking in this sober vision, backtrack to Pont-du-Loup and travel 8km (5 miles) east to **Tourrettes-sur-Loup,** where you can find accommodations in an unspoiled medieval village on a rocky bluff high above a violet-filled valley.

If you're coming from Cannes, take A85 for 21km (13 miles) northwest to Grasse, and then travel east for 6km (3³/₄ miles) on Route 2085, where you'll turn north at Magagnosc, following D3 for 8km (5 miles) north to Gourdon, at the edge of the gorge. From Nice, take E80 for 3km (2 miles) west to Route 2085, and then drive 26km (16 miles) west to Magagnosc, to follow the same path north to Gourdon. Once in Gourdon, continue north on D3 along the western rim of the gorge; after 6km (4 miles), turn right onto D6 to return south along its eastern lip. Turn east on D2210 at Pont-du-Loup for a 8km (5-mile) drive to Tourrettes-sur-Loup, or continue on to Vence, another 3km (2 miles), where you can turn south on Route 36 for a 9km (5¹/₂-mile) drive back to the coast.

For more information, contact the **Office de Tourisme,** 22 cours Henri-Cresp, 06130 Grasse (© 04-93-36-66-66); place Grand-Jardin, 06140 Vence (© 04-93-58-06-38); or 5 rte. de Vence, 06140 Tourrettes-sur-Loup (© 04-93-24-18-93).

fare is 1.30€. For information, contact the **Compagnie SAP** (© **04-93-80-09-38**). To **drive** to Vence from Nice, take N7 west to Cagnes-sur-Mer, then D236 north to Vence.

VISITOR INFORMATION   The **Office de Tourisme** is on place Grand-Jardin (© **04-93-58-06-38;** fax 04-93-58-91-81; www.ville-vence.fr).

EXPLORING THE TOWN

If you're wearing the right kind of shoes, the narrow, steep streets of the Old Town are worth exploring. Dating from the 10th century, the cathedral on place Godeau is unremarkable except for some 15th-century Gothic choir stalls. Most visitors quickly pass through the narrow gates of this once-fortified walled town to where the sun shines more brightly.

Chapelle du Rosaire ★★   When the great Henri Matisse was 77, he set out to design and decorate his masterpiece—"the culmination of a whole life dedicated to the search for truth," he said. Matisse created the Chapelle du Rosaire for the Dominican nuns of Monteils. (Sister Jacques-Marie, a member of the order, had nursed him back to health after a serious illness.) From the front you might find it unremarkable and pass it by—until you spot a 12m (39-ft.) crescent-adorned cross rising from a blue-tile roof.

Matisse wrote: "What I have done in the chapel is to create a religious space . . . in an enclosed area of very reduced proportions and to give it, solely by the play of colors and lines, the dimensions of infinity." The light picks up the subtle coloring in the simply rendered leaf forms and abstract patterns: sapphire blue, aquamarine, and lemon yellow. In black-and-white ceramics, St. Dominic is depicted in only a few lines. The most remarkable design is in the black-and-white-tile Stations of the Cross, with Matisse's self-styled "tormented and passionate" figures.

The price of admission includes entrance to **L'Espace Matisse,** a gallery devoted to the documentation of the chapel's design and construction from 1949 to 1951. It also contains lithographs and religious artifacts that concerned Matisse.

Av. Henri-Matisse. © **04-93-58-03-26.** Admission 3€ adults, free for children 11 and under; contributions to maintain the chapel are welcome. Mon, Wed, and Sat 2–5:30pm; Tues and Thurs 10–11:30am and 2–5:30pm.

WHERE TO STAY
Very Expensive
Le Château du Domaine St-Martin ★★★   If you're heading into the hills above Nice and you seek luxury and refinement, this is your address. The château, in a 14-hectare (36-acre) park with terraced gardens, was built in 1936. The main building holds the standard units, while suites are housed in the tile-roofed villas. You can walk through the gardens on winding paths lined with tall cypresses and olive trees, and past the ruins of a chapel. The luxurious restaurant has a view of the coast and offers superb French cuisine. In summer, many guests prefer the poolside grill.

Av. des Templiers B.P. 102, 06142 Vence. © **04-93-58-02-02.** Fax 04-93-24-08-91. www.chateau-st-martin. com. 40 units, 6 villas. 290€–760€ double; 600€–1,500€ suite. AE, DC, MC, V. Closed Dec–Feb. From the town center, follow signs toward Coursegoules and Col-de-Vence for 1.5km (1 mile) north. **Amenities:** Restaurant; bar; babysitting; pool (outdoor); room service; spa; 2 tennis courts (lit). *In room:* A/C, TV, hair dryer, Wi-Fi (free).

Expensive
Hôtel Cantemerle ★   One of the most appealing places in Vence is cluster of Provençal buildings designed to resemble an old-fashioned compound. Capped with

rounded terra-cotta roof tiles, they stand on a lawn dotted with old trees, surrounding a
pool. Public areas, stylishly outfitted with Art Deco furniture and accessories, include a
paneled bar and a sun-flooded flagstone terrace where meals are served. Rooms aren't
overly large but contain unusual reproductions of overscale Art Deco armchairs, louvered
wooden closet doors, and balcony-style sleeping lofts with comfortable beds. The restaurant serves worthwhile regional and mainstream French cuisine.

258 chemin Cantemerle, 06140 Vence. ℂ **04-93-58-08-18.** Fax 04-93-58-32-89. www.cantemerle-hotel-
vence.com. 27 units. 190€–235€ double; 450€–500€ suite. AE, MC, V. Closed late Oct to mid-Mar. **Amenities:** Restaurant; bar; babysitting; exercise room; 2 pools (indoor & outdoor); room service. In room: A/C,
TV, hair dryer, minibar, Wi-Fi (free).

Maison du Frêne ★★ (Finds)   Charm and serenity greet you in this grandly restored
18th-century building that stands next to a famous ash tree from the 5th century. It is
decorated with fine pieces of art, attracting devotees of art and design to its central location. The lounge library's wonderful collection of original art books is at your disposal.
The comfortable bedrooms with wonderful views are spacious, well maintained, and
beautifully furnished. In the Pop Art Suite, you return to the '60s with Marilyn Monroe
and Andy Warhol as your "hosts." The main floor is the social area. A good French
breakfast is served in the large pink kitchen.

1 place du Frêne, 06140 Vence. ℂ **04-93-24-37-83.** www.lamainsondufrene.com. 4 units. 140€–180€
double. Rates include breakfast. MC, V. **Amenities:** Lounge. In room: A/C, TV, hair dryer, Wi-Fi (free).

Inexpensive
Auberge des Seigneurs ★   This 400-year-old stone hotel gives you a taste of old
Provence. The guest rooms are well maintained, but the management dedicates its energy
to the restaurant. Nevertheless, the Provençal-style rooms are comfortable, with lots of
exposed paneling and beams. Two have nonworking fireplaces. The restaurant is in a
stone building that used to be the kitchen of the Château de Villeneuve, where François
I spent part of his youth. The house specializes in grills prepared on an open spit in view
of the dining room, which holds a long wooden table and an open fireplace with a row
of hanging copper pots and pans.

1 rue du Docteur Biret, 06140 Vence. ℂ **04-93-58-04-01.** Fax 04-93-24-08-01. 5 units. 83€–95€ double.
DC, MC, V. Closed mid-Dec to mid-Jan. **Amenities:** Restaurant; bar; room service. In room: Hair dryer.

Le Floréal   On the road to Grasse, this pleasant, comfortable hotel offers a view of the
mountains and a refreshing lack of pretension. Many of the well-furnished rooms look
out into the garden, where orange trees and mimosa add fragrance to the breezes. Most
accommodations are medium-size, and each is comfortable, with quality mattresses and
fine linens.

440 av. Rhin-et-Danube, 06140 Vence. ℂ **04-93-58-64-40.** Fax 04-93-58-79-69. www.bestwestern.fr. 41
units. 78€–137€ double. AE, DC, MC, V. Free parking. **Amenities:** Restaurant; bar; pool (outdoor); room
service; sauna. In room: A/C, TV, hair dryer, Wi-Fi (free).

WHERE TO DINE
Auberge des Seigneurs (see above) is an excellent place to dine at reasonable prices.

La Farigoule PROVENÇALE   In a century-old house that opens onto a rose garden,
this restaurant specializes in *provençale* cuisine. Menu items are conservative but flavorful:
They include *bourride provençale* (bouillabaisse with a dollop of cream and lots of garlic);
shoulder of roasted lamb with a ragout of fresh vegetables, served with fresh thyme; and

such fish dishes as dorado with confit of lemons and fresh, aromatic coriander. In the summer, you can dine in the rose garden.

15 rue Henri-Isnard. ✆ **04-93-58-01-27.** Reservations recommended. Main courses 17€–32€. MC, V. Thurs–Mon noon–2pm and 7:30–10pm. Closed Dec 7–Jan 7.

Les Bacchanales ★ TRADITIONAL FRENCH   In a villa close to the Chapelle Matisse, chef Christophe Dufau attracts diners with his take on a traditional French cuisine. On the ground level is a contemporary art gallery, with the restaurant upstairs. Choose from several fixed-price menus that change throughout the year. Try such dishes as a platter of cured ham or a bowl of leek and potato soup, or perhaps foie gras of duckling with acacia-scented honey. A main course of roasted lamb with fresh rosemary and thyme is always reliable.

247 av. De Provence. ✆ **04-93-24-19-19.** Reservations recommended. Weekday lunch 34€–60€; Sun lunch 40€–60€; fixed-price dinners 50€, 60€, and 70€. MC, V. Thurs–Mon noon–2pm and 7–10pm. Closed last week of June and Nov 1–Dec 15.

5 CAGNES-SUR-MER ★ & LE HAUT-DE-CAGNES ★

917km (570 miles) S of Paris; 21km (13 miles) NE of Cannes

Cagnes-sur-Mer, like the Roman god Janus, has two faces. Perched on a hill in the "hinterlands" of Nice, **Le Haut-de-Cagnes** is one of the most charming spots on the Riviera. Naomi Barry of the *New York Times* wrote that it "crowns the top of a blue-cypressed hill like a village in an Italian Renaissance painting." At the foot of the hill is an old fishing port and rapidly developing beach resort called **Cros-de-Cagnes,** between Nice and Antibes.

For years, Le Haut-de-Cagnes attracted the French literati, including Simone de Beauvoir, who wrote *Les Mandarins* here. A colony of painters also settled in—Renoir stated that the village was "the place where I want to paint until the last day of my life."

ESSENTIALS

GETTING THERE   The **train** depot, Gare SNCF, lies in Cagnes-Ville (the more commercial part of town) at avenue de la Gare. It serves trains that run along the Mediterranean coast, with arrivals every hour from both Nice (trip time: 13 min.; one-way fare 3€) and Cannes (trip time: 23 min.; 3.90€). For rail information, call ✆ **36-35,** or visit **www.voyages-sncf.com.** Buses costing 2€ leave from Nice and Cannes and stop at Cagnes-Ville and at Béal/Les Collettes, within walking distance of Cros-de-Cagnes. For information, call the **Société de Transports de Cagnes** (✆ 04-93-20-45-05). The climb from Cagnes-Ville to Haut-de-Cagnes is strenuous; a free minibus runs daily about every 30 minutes year-round from place du Général-de-Gaulle in the center of Cagnes-Ville to Haut-de-Cagnes. By **car** from any of the coastal cities of Provence, follow the A8 coastal highway, exiting at CAGNES-SUR-MER/CROS-DE-CAGNES.

VISITOR INFORMATION   The **Office de Tourisme** is at 6 bd. Maréchal-Juin, Cagnes-Ville (✆ **04-93-20-61-64;** fax 04-93-20-52-63; www.cagnes-tourisme.com).

SPECIAL EVENTS   For 2 days every August a **Medieval Festival (La Fête Médiévale de Cagnes)** dominates the medieval core of Hauts de Cagnes. Highlights include equestrian tournaments, jousting exhibitions, and knights, knaves, and damsels in medieval

SEEING THE SIGHTS

The orange groves and fields of carnations of the upper village provide a beautiful setting for the narrow cobblestone streets and 17th- and 18th-century homes. Drive your car to the top, where you can enjoy the view from place du Château and have lunch or a drink at a sidewalk cafe.

While in Le Haut-de-Cagnes, visit the **fortress** on place Grimaldi. It was built in 1301 by Rainier Grimaldi I, a lord of Monaco and a French admiral (see the portrait inside). Charts reveal how the defenses were organized. In the early 17th century, the dank castle was converted into a more gracious Louis XIII–style château.

The château contains two interconnected museums, the **Musée de l'Olivier (Museum of the Olive Tree)** and the **Musée d'Art Moderne Méditerranéen (Museum of Modern Mediterranean Art),** 7 place Grimaldi (© **04-92-02-47-30**). The modern art gallery displays works by Kisling, Carzou, Dufy, Cocteau, and Seyssaud, among others, with temporary exhibitions. In one salon is an interesting *trompe l'oeil* fresco, *La Chute de Phaeton.* From the tower, you get a panoramic view of the Côte d'Azur. The museums are open Wednesday to Monday: May to September 10am to noon and 2 to 6pm, and October to April 10am to noon and 2 to 5pm. Admission to both museums is 3€ for adults and 1.50€ for students and children 17 and under.

A DAY AT THE BEACH

Cros-de-Cagnes, a part of Cagnes-Sur-Mer, is known for its 4km (2½ miles) of seafront, covered with light-gray pebbles smoothed by centuries of waves. These beaches are **Plages de Cros-de-Cagnes.** As usual, toplessness is accepted but full nudity is not.

At least five concessions along this expanse rent beach mattresses and chaises for 8€ to 15€.The most centrally located are **Tiercé Plage** (© **04-93-20-13-89**), **Le Cigalon** (© **04-93-07-74-82**), **La Gougouline** (© **04-93-31-08-72**), and **Le Neptune** (© **04-93-22-02-85**).

A NEARBY ATTRACTION

Musée Renoir & Les Collettes ★   Les Collettes has been restored to appear as it did when Renoir lived here, from 1908 until his death in 1919. Although crippled by arthritis, he continue to sculpt here; in order to paint, he used assistants and tied the brush to his hands.

The house was built in 1907 in an olive and orange grove. A bust of Mme Renoir graces the entrance room. You can explore the drawing room and dining room on your own before going up to the artist's bedroom. In his atelier are his wheelchair, easel, and brushes. The terrace of Mme Renoir's bedroom has a stunning view of Cap d'Antibes and Haut-de-Cagnes. On a wall hangs a photograph of one of Renoir's sons, Pierre, as he appeared in the 1932 film *Madame Bovary.* Although Renoir is best remembered for his paintings, in Cagnes he began experimenting with sculpture. The museum has 20 portrait busts and portrait medallions, most of which depict his wife and children. The curators say they represent the largest collection of Renoir sculpture in the world.

19 chemin des Collettes. © **04-93-20-61-07.** Admission 3€ adults, 1.50€ children 12–18, free for children 11 and under. May–Sept Wed–Mon 10am–noon and 2–6pm; Oct–Apr Wed–Mon 10am–noon and 2–5pm. Ticket sales end 30 min. before lunch and evening closing hours.

In Cagnes-sur-Mer

Domaine Cocagne ★   This is the finest hotel in Cagnes-sur-Mer. An inviting and modern building, it sits on a hilltop overlooking the Mediterranean and 4.8 hectares (12 acres) of park and forest. Many of the medium-size and well-furnished bedrooms open onto a view of the château. The restaurant serves a savory Mediterranean cuisine and has an excellent regional wine cellar. You can rent standard double rooms, or, if you're willing to pay more, a fully furnished apartment.

30 Chemin du Pain de Sucre, Colline de la rte. de Vence, 06800 Cagnes-sur-Mer. ✆ 04-92-**13-57-77.** Fax 04-92-13-57-89. www.domainecocagne.com. 29 suites. 150€–280€ double; 550€–850€ apt; 180€–400€ suite. AE, MC, V. **Amenities:** Restaurant; bar; babysitting; room service. *In room:* A/C, TV, hair dryer, minibar, Wi-Fi (free).

Hôtel Le Chantilly (Value)   This is the best bargain for those who prefer to stay near the beach. Built in a boxy and angular style in 1960, it won't win any architectural awards; but the owners have landscaped the property and made the interior as homey and inviting as possible, with Oriental rugs and potted plants. Most rooms are small but cozily furnished and well kept, often opening onto balconies. In fair weather you can enjoy breakfast, the only meal served, on an outdoor terrace.

31 chemin de la Minoterie, 06800 Cagnes-sur-Mer. ✆ 04-93-20-25-50. Fax 04-92-02-82-63. www.ch-demeures.com/chantilly. 17 units. 76€ double; 91€–104€ triple. AE, DC, MC, V. Free parking. **Amenities:** Babysitting; room service. *In room:* TV, minibar, Wi-Fi (free).

Villa Estelle ★★ (Finds)   Jean Cocteau, Renoir, and even Modigliani used to pass by the front door of this authentic Provençal mansion. The restored 14th-century villa opens onto a large terrace with Florentine-inspired columns set in a Mediterranean garden with terraces. The bougainvillea lends extra color to palm and orange trees, while white laurel blooms 8 months a year. All of the small to midsize bedrooms and suites are furnished with a personal touch and decorated with antiques and modern works of art alike. Many of the rooms open onto sea views, and old-fashioned charm is found around every corner. It's almost like staying in a private Provençal home. Guests convene in the living room with its old paintings, fine linen curtains, and rich velvet draperies.

5 montée de la Bourgade, 06800 Cagnes-sur-Mer. ✆ 04-92-02-89-83. Fax 04-92-02-88-28. www.villa-estelle.com. 5 units. 100€–150€ double; 125€–180€ junior suite; 155€–260€ suite. Rates include breakfast. AE, DC, MC, V. Free parking. **Amenities:** Wi-Fi (free). *In room:* A/C, TV, minibar.

In Le Haut-de-Cagnes

Le Cagnard ★★★   Several 13th-century houses were joined in the 1960s to form this glamorous Relais & Châteaux property. Enjoy dinner in the frescoed dining room or on the vine-draped terrace. The rooms and salons are furnished with such antiques as provincial chests, armoires, and Louis XV chairs. Each room has its own style: Some are duplexes, while others have terraces and views of the countryside.

The cuisine of chef Jean-Yves Johany is reason enough to make the trip. Fixed-price menus cost 50€ to 85€ at lunch and 72€ to 110€ at dinner. The hotel is open year-round; the restaurant closes from November to December 15 and on Monday, Tuesday, and Thursday at lunch.

Rue du Pontis-Long, Le Haut-de-Cagnes, 06800 Cagnes-sur-Mer. ✆ 04-93-20-73-21. Fax 04-93-22-06-39. www.le-cagnard.com. 25 units. 100€–255€ double; 130€–385€ suite. AE, DC, MC, V. Parking 10€. **Amenities:** Restaurant; bar; babysitting; room service. *In room:* A/C, TV, hair dryer, minibar.

In Le Haut-de-Cagnes

Fleur de Sel FRENCH/PROVENÇALE   Energetic owners Philippe and Pascale Loose run this charming restaurant in a 200-year-old stone-sided house in the center of the village. In two ocher-toned dining rooms outfitted with Provençal furniture and oil paintings, you'll enjoy the kind of cuisine that Philippe learned during stints at some of the grandest restaurants of France, including a brief time with Marc Meneau at L'Espérance in Vézelay. Tasty recommendations include foie gras with artichoke hearts in puff pastry; cappuccino of crayfish with paprika and pistachios; scallops braised with spinach; and filet of beef braised in a hearty local red wine, Bellet.

85 Montée de la Bourgade. ✆ **04-93-20-33-33.** www.restaurant-fleurdesel.com. Reservations recommended. Main courses 18€–36€; fixed-price menu 32€–55€. MC, V. Fri–Tues noon–2pm; Thurs–Tues 7:30–10pm. Closed 10 days in Nov.

Josy-Jo ★★ TRADITIONAL FRENCH   **Le Cagnard** (p. 296) has a more elegant setting, but the food at Josy-Jo is comparable. Behind a 200-year-old facade covered with vines and flowers, this restaurant was the home and studio of Modigliani and Soutine during their hungriest years. Paintings cover the walls, and the Bandecchi family runs everything smoothly. The menu features grilled meats and a variety of fish. You can enjoy brochette of gigot of lamb with kidneys; calves' liver; homemade terrine of foie gras of duckling; stuffed *provençale* vegetables "in the style of Grandmother"; and an array of salads.

8 place du Planastel. ✆ **04-93-20-68-76.** Reservations required. Main courses 25€–32€; fixed-price lunch 29€–40€. AE, MC, V. Mon–Fri 12:30–2pm; Mon–Sat 7:30–9:30pm. Closed Nov 19–Dec 22.

In Cros-de-Cagnes

Loulou (La Réserve) ★★ FRENCH   This restaurant, which like Josy-Jo and Cagnard has a Michelin star, makes the Cagnes area a gourmet enclave. It's across the boulevard from the sea and named for a famous long-departed chef. Brothers Eric and Joseph Campo prepare spectacular versions of fish soup; shrimp steamed and served with fresh ginger and cinnamon; and grilled versions of the catch of the day. These dishes are served as simply as possible, usually with just a drizzling of olive oil and balsamic vinegar. Meat dishes include flavorful veal kidneys with port sauce, and delectable grilled steaks, chops, and cutlets. Dessert may include a caramelized apple tart. The glassed-in veranda in front is a prime people-watching spot.

91 bd. de la Plage. ✆ **04-93-31-00-17.** www.louloureserve.com. Reservations recommended. Main courses 30€–103€; fixed-price menu 42€–49€. AE, MC, V. Mon–Fri noon–1:30pm and 7:30–9:30pm; Sat 7–9:30pm.

6 NICE ★★★

929km (577 miles) S of Paris; 32km (20 miles) NE of Cannes

The Victorian upper classes and Russian aristocrats loved Nice in the 19th century, but it's solidly middle class today and far less glamorous and expensive than Cannes. It's also the best excursion center on the Riviera, especially if you're dependent on public transportation. For example, you can go to San Remo, "the queen of the Italian Riviera," and return to Nice by nightfall. From the Nice airport, the second largest in France, you can travel by bus along the entire coast.

Nice is the capital of the Riviera, the largest city between Genoa and Marseille. It's also one of the most ancient, having been founded by the Greeks, who called it "Nike," or Victory. Because of its brilliant sunshine and relaxed living, it has attracted artists and writers. Among them were Dumas, Nietzsche, Apollinaire, Flaubert, Victor Hugo, George Sand, Stendhal, Chateaubriand, and Mistral. Henri Matisse, who made his home in Nice, said, "Though the light is intense, it's also soft and tender." The city has, on the average, 300 days of sunshine a year.

ESSENTIALS

GETTING THERE   Transatlantic and intercontinental flights land at **Aéroport Nice–Côte d'Azur** (© 08-20-42-33-33). From there, municipal bus no. 98 departs at 20-minute intervals for the Gare Routière (see below); the one-way fare is 1.50€. Bus nos. 23 and 99 go to Gare SNCF. More luxurious is a yellow-sided shuttle bus (*la navette de l'aéroport*) that charges 4€ for a ride between the airport and the bus station. A **taxi** from the airport into the city center will cost at least 30€ to 40€ each way. Trip time is about 30 minutes.

Trains arrive at Gare Nice-Ville, avenue Thiers (© 36-35; www.voyages-sncf.com). From there you can take trains to Cannes (5.80€), Monaco (2.80€), and Antibes (3.90€), with easy connections to anywhere else along the Mediterranean coast. The train station has a small tourist center, open Monday to Saturday 8am to 7pm and Sunday 9am to 6pm. If you face a long delay, you can eat at the cafeteria and even shower at the station.

Buses to and from Monaco, Cannes, St-Tropez, and elsewhere in France and Europe serve the main bus station, **Gare Routière**, 5 bd. Jean-Jaurès (© 08-92-70-12-06).

VISITOR INFORMATION   Nice maintains three tourist offices, the largest and most central of which is at 5 promenade des Anglais, near place Masséna (© 08-92-70-74-07; fax 04-92-14-46-49; www.nicetourisme.com). Additional offices are in the arrivals hall of the Aéroport Nice–Côte d'Azur and the railway station on avenue Thiers. Any office can make a hotel reservation (but only for the night of the day you show up) for a modest fee that varies according to the classification of the hotel.

GETTING AROUND   Most local buses serve the **Station Central SNCF,** 10 av. Félix-Faure (© 04-93-13-53-13; www.voyages-sncf.com), a very short walk from the place Masséna. Municipal buses charge 1€ for a ride within Greater Nice. To save money, consider buying a *carnet* entitling you to 10 rides for 8€. Bus nos. 2 and 12 make frequent trips to the beach.

No point within downtown Nice is more than about a 10-minute walk from the seafronting promenade, site of such well-known quais as the promenade des Anglais and the promenade des Etats-Unis. Bus nos. 2 and 12 run along its length, dropping passengers off at any of the beaches and concessions that front the edge of the sea.

Nice Tramway, with 21 stations, runs from Comte de Falican in north Nice south to the city center, including Place Massena and Pont Michel. All tickets cost 1€ and are available at ticket-dispensing machines located in all tram stations. For more information, call (© 08-11-00-20-06) or click on www.tramway-nice.org.

The best place to rent bikes and mopeds is **Energy Scoot,** promenade des Anglais (© 04-97-07-12-64), just behind the place Grimaldi. Open Monday to Friday 9am to noon and 2 to 7pm, it charges 15€ per day for a bike or moped, and requires a deposit of at least 55€, depending on the value of the machine you rent. Somewhat less appealing, but useful when Energy Scoot is closed, is **Nicea Rent,** 12 rue de Belgique (© 04-93-82-42-71). It charges about the same rates, but the staff isn't always on the premises.

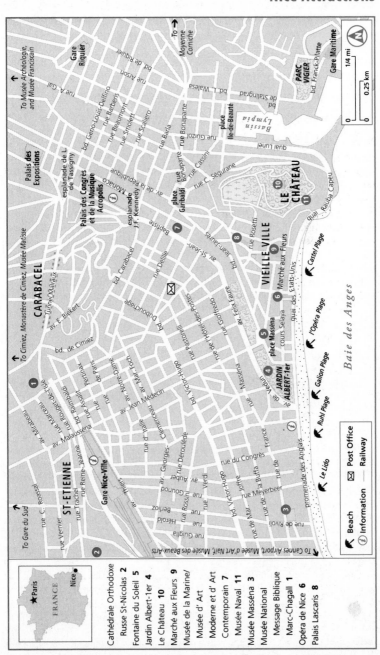

THE EASTERN RIVIERA

8

NICE

Map Legend

- Cathédrale Orthodoxe Russe St-Nicolas 2
- Fontaine du Soleil 5
- Jardin Albert-1er 4
- Le Château 10
- Marché aux Fleurs 9
- Musée de la Marine/ Musée d' Art Moderne et d' Art Contemporain 7
- Musée Naval 11
- Musée Masséna 3
- Musée National Message Biblique Marc-Chagall 1
- Opéra de Nice 6
- Palais Lascaris 8

★ Beach   ⊠ Post Office
ⓘ Information   — Railway

The **Nice Carnaval** draws visitors from all over Europe and North America. The "Mardi Gras of the Riviera" begins sometime in February, usually 12 days before Shrove Tuesday, celebrating the return of spring with 3 weeks of parades, *corsi* (floats), *veglioni* (masked balls), confetti, and battles in which young women toss flowers. Only the most wicked throw rotten eggs instead of carnations. The climax, a fireworks display on Shrove Tuesday, lights up the Baie des Anges (Bay of Angels). King Carnival goes up in flames on his pyre but rises from the ashes the following spring. For information, contact the tourist office (see above).

The **Nice Festival du Jazz** (☎ **01-47-23-07-58;** www.nicejazzfest.com) runs for a week in mid-July, when jazz artists perform in the ancient Arène de Cimiez.

EXPLORING THE CITY

In 1822, the orange crop at Nice was bad and the workers faced a lean time, so the English residents put them to work building the **promenade des Anglais** ★★, a wide boulevard fronting the bay. Split by "islands" of palms and flowers, it stretches for about 6km (4 miles). Fronting the beach are rows of grand cafes, the **Musée Masséna,** villas, and hotels—some good, others decaying.

In the east, the promenade becomes **quai des Etats-Unis,** the original boulevard, lined with some of the best restaurants in Nice, all specializing in bouillabaisse. Rising sharply on a rock is the site known as **Le Château,** the spot where the ducs de Savoie built their castle, which was torn down in 1706. All that remains are two or three stones—even the foundations have disappeared in the wake of Louis XIV's deliberate destruction of what was viewed at the time as a bulwark of Provençal resistance to his regime. The hill has been turned into a garden of pines and exotic flowers. To reach the panoramic site, you can take an elevator. The park is open daily from 8am to dusk.

At the north end of Le Château is the famous old **graveyard** of Nice, visited primarily for its lavishly sculpted monuments that make their own enduring art statement. It's the largest in France and the fourth largest in Europe.

Continuing east from Le Château and "the Rock," you reach the harbor, where the restaurants are even cheaper and the bouillabaisse is just as good. While sitting here lingering over an aperitif at a sidewalk cafe, you can watch the boats depart for Corsica (or perhaps take one yourself). The port was excavated between 1750 and 1830. Since then, an outer harbor—protected by two jetties—has also been created.

The "authentic" Niçoise live in **Vieille Ville** ★, the old town, beginning at the foot of "the Rock" and stretching out from place Masséna. Sheltered by sienna-tiled roofs, many of the Italianate facades suggest 17th-century Genoese palaces. The Old Town is a maze of narrow streets, many of them teeming with local life. Some, including the rue Masséna, the rue Droite, and the rue Pairolière, are reserved exclusively for pedestrians. On these narrow streets, you'll find some of the least expensive restaurants in Nice. Buy *la pissaladière* (an onion pizza), or *socca,* a crepe made with chickpea flour, from one of the local vendors. Many of the old buildings are painted a faded Roman gold, and banners of multicolored laundry flaps in the sea breezes.

While here, try to visit the **Marché aux Fleurs,** the flower market at cours Saleya. The vendors set up their stalls Tuesday to Sunday 8am to 6pm in summer, and from 8am until between 2 and 4pm in winter. A flamboyant array of carnations, violets, jonquils, roses, and birds of paradise is hauled in by vans or trucks and then displayed in the most fragrant market in town.

Nice's commercial centerpiece is **place Masséna,** with pink buildings in the 17th-century Genoese style and the **Fontaine du Soleil (Fountain of the Sun)** by Janoit, from

1956. Stretching from the main square to the promenade is the **Jardin Albert-1er,** with an open-air terrace and a Triton Fountain. With palms and exotic flowers, it's the most relaxing oasis at the resort.

MUSEUMS

Musée d'Art Moderne et d'Art Contemporain ★★

French and American avant-garde art from the 1960s until the 21st century is displayed in this quartet of square towers with rooftop terraces. Each section is linked by a glass passageway. We know of no other museum that so dramatically reveals the growth of parallel art movements in two countries. In the '60s, it was called American pop art, whereas on the Riviera it was known as Nouveau Réalisme, but the results are very similar. All the big names in pop art, including Andy Warhol, Roy Lichtenstein, and Robert Rauschenberg, are featured. One entire section of the museum is devoted to the French artist Yves Klein (1928–92). His two major works, *Garden of Eden* and *Wall of Fire,* can be seen on the rooftop terraces. Some of the outstanding works displayed are by artists of the Nice School, including Sacha Sosno, Robert Malavaal, Ben Vautier, and Jean-Claude Fahri.

Promenade des Arts. ℂ **04-97-13-42-01.** www.mamac-nice.org. Free admission. Tues–Sun 10am–6pm. Bus: 1, 2, 3, 5, 6, 16, or 25.

Musée des Beaux-Arts ★★

The collection is in the former residence of the Ukrainian Princess Kotchubey. It has an important gallery devoted to the masters of the Second Empire and the Belle Epoque, with an extensive collection of 19th-century French experts. The gallery of sculptures includes works by J. B. Carpeaux, Rude, and Rodin. Note the important collection by the Dutch Vanloo family, a dynasty of painters. One of its best-known members, Carle Vanloo, born in Nice in 1705, was Louis XV's premier *peintre.* A fine collection of 19th- and 20th-century art includes works by Ziem, Raffaelli, Boudin, Monet, Guillaumin, and Sisley.

33 av. des Baumettes. ℂ **04-92-15-28-28.** www.musee-beaux-arts-nice.org. Free admission. Tues–Sun 10am–6pm. Bus: 3, 9, 12, 22, 24, 38, 60, or 62.

Musée International d'Art Naïf Anatole-Jakovsky (Museum of Naive Art) ★

This museum is in the beautifully restored Château Ste-Hélène in the Fabron district. The museum's namesake, for years one of the world's leading art critics, once owned the collection. His 600 drawings and canvases were turned over to the institution and opened to the public. Artists from more than two dozen countries are represented in everything from primitive painting to 20th-century works.

Château St-Hélène, av. de Fabron. ℂ **04-93-71-78-33.** Free admission. Wed–Mon 10am–6pm. Bus: 9, 10, 12, or 23; 10-min. walk. Closed Dec 25, Jan 1, and May 1.

Villa Arson Nice ★

This complex—which includes a restored 18th-century building, and a concrete-and-stone structure from 1970—houses both the Art School of Nice and the National Center for Contemporary Art (Centre National d'Art Contemporain). The museum section stages special exhibitions of young, emerging French artists. The exhibitions are always changing. Chances are that all the art will be daringly avant-garde.

20 av. Stephen Liégeard. ℂ **04-92-07-73-73.** Free admission. Wed–Mon 2–6pm (until 7pm July–Aug). Bus: Ligne 7 (stop at Deux Avenues).

MORE SIGHTS

Cathédrale Orthodoxe Russe St-Nicolas à Nice ★

Ordered and built by none other than Tsar Nicholas II, this is the most beautiful religious edifice of the Orthodoxy outside Russia, and a perfect expression of Russian religious art abroad. It dates from the Belle Epoque, when a few of the Romanovs and their entourage turned the Riviera into a stamping ground (everyone from grand dukes to ballerinas walked the promenade). The cathedral is richly ornamented and decorated with icons. You'll spot the building from afar because of its collection of ornate onion-shaped domes. During church services on Sunday morning, the building closes to tourist visits.

Av. Nicolas-II (off bd. du Tzaréwitch). ℂ **04-93-96-88-02.** Admission 3€ adults, 2€ students, free for children 11 and under. May–Sept daily 9am–noon and 2:30–6pm; Oct–Apr daily 9:30am–noon and 2:30–5pm. From the central rail station, head west along av. Thiers to bd. Gambetta, then go north to av. Nicolas-II.

Palais Lascaris (Kids)   The baroque Palais Lascaris in the city's historic core is associated with the Lascaris-Vintimille family, whose recorded history predates the year 1261. Built in the 17th century, it contains elaborately detailed ornaments. An intensive restoration by the city of Nice in 1946 brought back its original beauty, and the palace is now classified as a historic monument. The most elaborate floor, the *étage noble,* retains many of its 18th-century panels and plaster embellishments. A pharmacy, built around 1738 and complete with many of the original delftware accessories, is on the premises.

15 rue Droite. ℂ **04-93-62-72-40.** Free admission. Wed–Mon 10am–6pm. Bus: 1, 2, 3, 5, 6, 14, 16, or 17.

NEARBY SIGHTS IN CIMIEZ

In the once-aristocratic hilltop quarter of **Cimiez** ★, Queen Victoria wintered at the Hôtel Excelsior and brought half the English court with her. Founded by the Romans, who called it Cemenelum, Cimiez was the capital of the Maritime Alps province. Recent excavations have uncovered the ruins of a Roman town, and you can wander among the diggings. The arena was big enough to hold at least 5,000 spectators, who watched contests between gladiators and wild beasts shipped in from Africa. To reach this suburb, take bus no. 15 or 17 from place Masséna.

Monastère de Cimiez (Cimiez Convent) ★   The convent embraces a church that owns three of the most important works by the locally prominent Bréa brothers, who painted in the late 15th century. See the carved and gilded wooden main altarpiece. In a restored part of the convent where some Franciscan friars still live, the Musée Franciscain is decorated with 17th-century frescoes. Some 350 documents and works of art from the 15th to the 18th centuries are on display, and a monk's cell has been re-created in all its severe simplicity. Also visit the 17th-century chapel. From the magnificent gardens, you'll have a panoramic view of Nice and the Baie des Anges. Matisse and Dufy are buried in the cemetery.

Place du Monastère. ℂ **04-93-81-00-04.** Free admission. Museum Mon–Sat 10am–noon and 3–6pm. Church daily 9am–6pm.

Musée Matisse ★   This museum honors the artist, who died in Nice in 1954. Seeing his nude sketches today, you'll wonder how early critics could have denounced them as "the female animal in all her shame and horror." Most of the pieces in the museum's permanent collection were painted in Nice, and many were donated by Matisse and his heirs. These include *Nude in an Armchair with a Green Plant* (1937), *Nymph in the Forest* (1935–42), and a chronologically arranged series of paintings from 1890 to 1919. The most famous of these is *Portrait of Madame Matisse* (1905), usually displayed near a portrait of the artist's wife by Marquet, painted in 1900. An assemblage of designs prepared as practice sketches for the Matisse Chapel at Vence are on display along with *The Créole Dancer* (1951), *Blue*

Nude IV (1952), and around 50 dance-related sketches drawn between 1930 and 1931.
The artist's last work, *Flowers and Fruit* (1953), is made of cut-out gouache.

In the Villa des Arènes-de-Cimiez, 164 av. des Arènes-de-Cimiez. ✆ **04-93-53-40-53**. www.musee-matisse-nice.org. Free admission. Wed–Mon 10am–6pm. Closed Jan 1, May 1, and Dec 25.

Musée National Message Biblique Marc Chagall ★★   In the hills of Cimiez, this handsome museum, surrounded by pools and a garden, is devoted to Marc Chagall's treatment of biblical themes. Born in Russia in 1887, Chagall became a French citizen in 1937. The artist and his wife donated the works—the most important Chagall collection ever assembled—to France in 1966 and 1972. On display are 450 of his oils, gouaches, drawings, pastels, lithographs, sculptures, and ceramics; a mosaic; three stained-glass windows; and a tapestry. Chagall decorated a concert room with brilliantly hued stained-glass windows. Temporary exhibits each summer feature great periods and artists of all times.

Av. du Dr.-Ménard. ✆ **04-93-53-87-20**. www.musee-chagall.fr. Admission 6.50€ adults, 4€ students, free for children 17 and under. May–Oct Wed–Mon 10am–6pm; Nov–Apr Wed–Mon 10am–5pm.

OUTDOOR PURSUITS

BEACHES   Along Nice's seafront, beaches extend uninterrupted for more than 7km (4⅓ miles), from the edge of Vieux Port (the old port) to the international airport, with most of the best bathing spots subdivided into public beaches and private concessionaires. None has sand; they're all covered with gravel (often the size of golf balls). The rocks are smooth but can be mettlesome to people with poor balance or tender feet. Tucked between the public beaches are the private beaches of such hotels as the Beau Rivage. Most of the public beaches consist of two sections: a free area and one where you can rent chaise longues, mattresses, and parasols, use changing rooms, and take freshwater showers. For that, you'll pay 10€ to 12€ for a half-day, 12€ to 20€ for a full day. Nude sunbathing is prohibited, but toplessness is common. Take bus no. 9, 10, 12, or 23.

GOLF   The oldest golf course on the Riviera is about 16km (10 miles) from Nice: **Golf Bastide du Roi** (also known as the Golf de Biot), route d'Antibes, Biot (✆ **04-93-65-08-48**). Open daily, this is a flat, not particularly challenging seafronting course. (Golfers must cross a highway twice before completing the full 18 holes.) Tee times are 8am to 6pm; you can play until the sun sets. Reservations aren't necessary, though on weekends you should probably expect to wait. Greens fees are 45€.

HORSEBACK RIDING   **Club Hippique de Nice,** 368 rte. de Grenoble (✆ **04-93-83-13-04;** www.nicecheval.com), rents about a dozen of its horses. About 5km (3 miles) from Nice, near the airport, it's hemmed in on virtually every side by busy roads and highways, and conducts all activities in a series of riding rings. Riding sessions should be reserved in advance; they last about an hour and cost 17€.

SCUBA DIVING   The best outfit is the **Centre International de Plongée (CIP) de Nice,** 2 ruelle des Moulins (✆ **06-09-52-55-57** or 04-93-55-59-50; www.cip-nice.com), adjacent to the city's old port, between quai des Docks and boulevard Stalingrad. A *baptême* (dive for first-timers) costs 30€. A one-tank dive for experienced divers, equipment included, is 35€; appropriate diver's certification is required.

TENNIS   The oldest tennis club in Nice is the **Nice Lawn Tennis Club,** Parc Impérial, 5 av. Suzanne-Lenglen (✆ **04-92-15-58-00;** French-only website www.nicelc.com). It's open daily 9am to 8pm from mid-October to mid-April (closed winter) and charges 15€

to 32€ per person for 2 hours of court time. The club has a cooperative staff, a loyal clientele, 13 outdoor clay courts, and 6 outdoor hard-surface courts. Reserve the night before.

SHOPPING

You may want to begin with a stroll through the streets and alleys of Nice's historic core. The densest concentrations of boutiques are along **rue Masséna, place Magenta, avenue Jean-Médecin, rue de Verdun,** and **rue Paradis,** and on the streets around them. A shop of note is **Gigi,** 10 rue de la Liberté (© **04-93-87-81-78**), which sells sophisticated clothing for women.

Opened in 1949 by Joseph Fuchs, the grandfather of the present English-speaking owners, the **Confiserie Florian du Vieux-Nice,** 14 quai Papacino (© **04-93-55-43-50**), is near the Old Port. Their specialty is glazed fruit crystallized in sugar or artfully arranged into chocolates. Look for exotic jams (rose-petal preserves, mandarin marmalade), candied violets, verbena leaves, and rosebuds, as well as a free recipe leaflet. One of the oldest chocolatiers in Nice, **Confiserie Auer,** 7 rue St-François-de-Paule, near the opera house (© **04-93-85-77-98**; www.maison-auer.com), was established in 1820. Since then, few of the original decorative accessories have changed. The shop specializes in chocolates, candies, and *fruits confits,* the signature Provençal goodies.

Façonnable, 7–9 rue Paradis (© **04-93-87-88-80**; www.faconnable.com), is the original site of a chain with several hundred branches around the world. This is one of the largest, with a wide range of men's suits, raincoats, overcoats, sportswear, and jeans. The look is youthful and conservatively stylish, and cut for French bodies. An outlet for women's clothing and sportswear (Façonnable Sport) and the main line of Façonnable women's wear (Façonnable Femmes) is across the street at 10 rue Paradis (© **04-93-88-06-97**).

If you're thinking of indulging in a *provençale pique-nique,* **Nicola Alziari,** 318 bd. Madeleine (© **04-93-44-45-12**), will provide everything from olives, anchovies, and pistous to aiolis and tapenades. It's one of Nice's oldest purveyors of olive oil, with a house brand that comes in two strengths: a light version that aficionados claim is vaguely perfumed with Provence, and a stronger version suited to the earthy flavors and robust ingredients of a Provençal winter. Also for sale are objects crafted from olive wood.

For arts and crafts, head to the **Atelier Contre-Jour,** 3 rue du Pont Vieux (© **04-93-80-20-50**). It carries painted-wood handicrafts, including picture frames; painted furniture; and silk lampshades, as well as decorative posters. **Plat Jérôme,** 34 rue Centrale (© **04-93-97-53-54**), stocks varnished pottery. Many artists' studios and galleries are on side streets near the cathedral in the Old Town.

La Couqueto, 8 rue St-François-de-Paule (© **04-93-80-90-30**), sells *santons,* the traditional Provençal figurines. The best selection of Provençal fabrics is at **Le Chandelier,** 7 rue de la Boucherie (© **04-93-85-85-19**), where you'll see designs by two of the region's best-known producers of cloth, Les Olivades and Valdrôme.

In addition to the flower market, **Marché aux Fleurs** (see "Exploring the City," above), the main flea market, **Marché à la Brocante,** also at cours Saleya, takes place Monday 8am to 5pm. Another flea market on the port, **Les Puces de Nice,** place Robilante, is open Tuesday to Saturday 9am to 6pm.

WHERE TO STAY

Very Expensive

Hôtel Negresco ★★★ The Negresco, on the seafront in the heart of Nice, is one of the Riviera's superglamorous hotels. The Victorian wedding-cake hotel is named after its founder, Henry Negresco, a Romanian who died a pauper in Paris in 1920. The

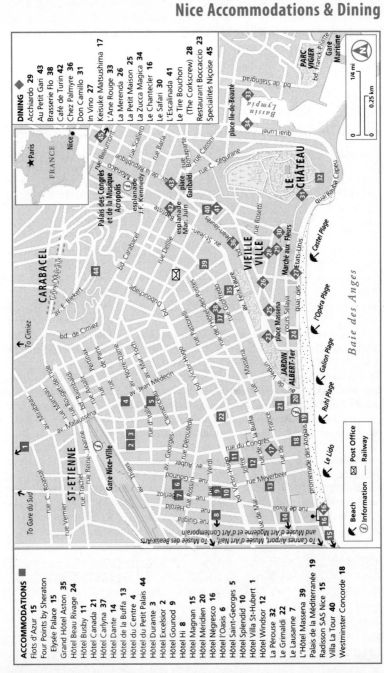

ACCOMMODATIONS
Flots d'Azur 15
Four Points by Sheraton
Elysée Palace 15
Grand Hôtel Aston 35
Hôtel Beau Rivage 24
Hôtel Busby 11
Hôtel Canada 21
Hôtel Carlyna 37
Hôtel Dante 14
Hôtel de la Buffa 13
Hôtel du Centre 4
Hôtel du Petit Palais 44
Hôtel Durante 3
Hôtel Excelsior 2
Hôtel Gounod 9
Hôtel Hi 8
Hôtel Magnan 15
Hôtel Meridien 20
Hôtel Négresco 16
Hôtel l'Oasis 6
Hôtel Saint-Georges 5
Hôtel Splendid 10
Hôtel Villa St-Hubert 1
Hôtel Windsor 12
La Pérouse 32
Le Grimaldi 22
Le Lausanne 7
L'Hôtel Massena 39
Palais de la Méditerranée 19
Radisson SAS Nice 15
Villa La Tour 40
Westminster Concorde 18

DINING ◆
Acchiardo 29
Au Petit Gari 43
Brasserie Flo 38
Café de Turin 42
Chez Palmyre 36
Don Camillo 31
In Vino 27
Keisuke Matsushima 17
L'Ane Rouge 33
La Merenda 26
La Petit Maison 25
La Zucca Magica 34
Le Chantecler 16
Le Safari 30
L'Escalinada 41
Le Tire Bouchon
(The Corkscrew) 28
Restaurant Boccaccio 23
Specialités Nicoise 45

country's châteaux inspired the interior and the exterior alike, with its mansard roof and domed tower. The hotel's decorators scoured Europe to gather antiques, tapestries, and art. Some of the accommodations, such as the Coco Chanel room, are outfitted in homage to the personalities who stayed here. Suites and public areas are even grander; they include the Louis XIV salon, reminiscent of the Sun King, and the Napoleon III suite, where swagged walls, a leopard-skin carpet, and a half-crowned pink canopy create a sense of majesty. The most expensive rooms with balconies face the Mediterranean and the private beach. The staff wears 18th-century costumes. One of the two restaurants, **Le Chantecler** (p. 313), is one of the Riviera's greatest.

37 promenade des Anglais, 06007 Nice Cedex. ⓒ **04-93-16-64-00.** Fax 04-93-88-35-68. www.hotel-negresco-nice.com. 146 units. 285€–570€ double; from 665€–1,840€ suite. AE, DC, MC, V. Free parking. **Amenities:** 2 restaurants; bar; babysitting; concierge; health club; room service. *In room:* A/C, TV, hair dryer, minibar, Wi-Fi (free).

La Pérouse ★★ (Finds)   Once a prison, La Pérouse has been reconstructed and is now a unique Riviera hotel. Set on a cliff, it's built right in the gardens of an ancient château-fort. No hotel affords a better view over the old city and the Baie des Anges alike. In fact, many people stay here just for the view. The hotel resembles an old Provençal home, with low ceilings, white walls, and antique furnishings. The lovely, spacious rooms are beautifully furnished, often with Provençal fabrics. Most have loggias overlooking the bay.

11 quai Rauba-Capéu, 06300 Nice. ⓒ **04-93-62-34-63.** Fax 04-93-62-59-41. www.hotel-la-perouse.com. 65 units. 175€–540€ double; 650€–1,500€ suite. AE, DC, MC, V. Parking 15€. **Amenities:** Restaurant (mid-May to mid-Sept); bar; babysitting; health club w/Jacuzzi; room service. *In room:* A/C, TV, hair dryer, minibar, Wi-Fi (free).

Palais de la Méditerranée ★★★   She's back! Long hailed as a Queen of the Nice Riviera, this glittering seaside palace on the promenade des Anglais reigned from 1929 to 1978 and then was shuttered. During its heyday, the hotel theater hosted everybody from Maurice Chevalier to American chanteuse Josephine Baker, who performed wearing high heels, a skirt of bananas, and nothing else. Its Art Deco facade was left intact after a restoration, but the interior was gutted. Monumental chandeliers and stained-glass windows, among other architectural features, were spared in the renovations. Bedrooms, midsize to grandly spacious, are outfitted in a tasteful modern decor, with luxurious bathrooms. Ninety of the bedrooms also open onto sea views. Behind the facade, the hotel's casino has been restored to its Art Deco glamour.

13–15 promenade des Anglais, 06011 Nice. ⓒ **04-92-14-77-00.** Fax 04-92-14-77-14. www.lepalaisdela mediterranee.com. 188 units. 285€–570€ double; 665€–1,840€ suite. AE, DC, MC, V. **Amenities:** Restaurant; bar; casino; concierge; exercise room w/Turkish bath; Internet (free); pool (outdoor); room service. *In room:* A/C, TV, hair dryer, minibar.

Expensive

Four Points by Sheraton Elysée Palace ★★

Views sweep out over the sea from most of the rooms of this hotel. Decor is conservative and contemporary, and the in-room amenities are typical. The seafront rooms, of course, are the more desirable. Rooms on the fifth, sixth, and seventh floors overlook the Mediterranean. Bathrooms are clad in marble with bidets, but you have to request robes and hair dryers from reception. The hotel has its own private beach a short walk from its premises.

59 promenade des Anglais, 06005 Nice. ⓒ **04-93-97-90-90.** Fax 04-93-44-50-40. www.elyseepalace. com. 143 units. 125€–285€ double; 265€–405€ suite. AE, DC, MC, V. Parking 17€. Bus: 9, 10, or 12. **Amenities:** Restaurant; bar; babysitting; pool; room service. *In room:* A/C, TV, hair dryer, minibar, Wi-Fi (free).

Grand Hôtel Aston ★   This elegantly detailed 19th-century hotel is one of the most alluring in its price bracket. After radical renovations, the rooms are now outfitted with comfortable furnishings and restored bathrooms. Room prices vary according to the view: over the street, the splashing fountains of place Masséna, or the coastline panorama from the uppermost floor. On summer evenings, a garden-style bar on the top floor sometimes schedules dance music.

12 av. Félix-Faure, 06000 Nice. © **04-92-17-53-00.** Fax 04-93-80-40-02. www.hotel-aston.com. 155 units. 180€–280€ double; 310€–560€ suite. AE, DC, MC, V. Parking 20€. Bus: 12 or 98. **Amenities:** 2 restaurants; bar; concierge; pool (outdoor); room service. *In room:* A/C, TV, hair dryer, minibar, Wi-Fi (free).

Hôtel Beau Rivage ★   This hotel across from the beach is famous for having housed both Matisse and Chekhov during its heyday around the turn of the 20th century. The interior has a bland but tasteful modern decor and a staff that seems to make a point of appearing overworked regardless of how few guests there might be. The soundproof rooms are vaguely Art Deco and small. For dining, Le Bistrot du Rivage is relatively formal and very appealing. Its specialties are meats and fish prepared on a large grill. Between May and September, tables are set on a terrace.

24 rue St-François-de-Paule, 06300 Nice. © **04-92-47-82-82.** Fax 04-93-80-55-77. www.nicebeaurivage. com. 118 units. 210€–400€ double; 350€–700€ suite. Children 11 and under stay free in parent's room. AE, DC, MC, V. Bus: 1, 2, 5, or 12. **Amenities:** Restaurant; bar; babysitting; concierge; room service. *In room:* A/C, TV, hair dryer, Internet (free), minibar.

Hôtel Hi ★ (Finds)   An architectural and decorative statement, this hotel occupies a former boardinghouse that dates to the 1930s. Spearheaded by Matali Crasset, a one-time colleague of Philippe Starck, a team of architects and engineers created one of the most aggressively avant-garde hotels in the south of France. Each of the nine high-tech room "concepts" is different. They range from hospital white-on-white to birch-wood veneer and acid green to cool violet and gray. The unconventional layouts may include a bathtub tucked behind a screen of potted plants or elevated to a position of theatrical prominence. Electronic gizmos include state-of-the-art CD systems. The Japanese word *hi* describes the black mottling on the back of an ornamental carp, which has traditionally been associated with good luck.

3 av. des Fleurs, 06000 Nice. © **04-97-07-26-26.** Fax 04-97-07-26-27. www.hi-hotel.net. 38 units. 239€–440€ double; from 440€ suite. AE, DC, MC, V. Parking 24€. Bus: 23. **Amenities:** Restaurant; bar; pool (outdoor); Turkish bath. *In room:* A/C, TV, Wi-Fi (free).

Hôtel Méridien ★   One of Nice's largest hotels, this one rises five floors above the junction of the promenade des Anglais and a small formal park, the Jardin Albert-1er. Built in the 1960s by Air France in an angular design with lots of shiny metal and glass, it was later acquired by Britain's Forte group and hosts many organized tours from Britain and northern Europe. Two escalators carry you up through a soaring, impersonal atrium to the reception area. The recently renovated guest rooms are modern and standard. The seafront rooms, though desirable for the view over the hotel's private beach, are actually the smallest in the hotel; space has been sacrificed to make way for terraces or balconies. The zesty restaurant, Le Colonia Café, celebrates the late-19th-century overseas conquests of France and England—the emphasis is on spicy, sometimes curried international cuisine.

1 promenade des Anglais, 06046 Nice. © **04-97-03-44-44.** Fax 04-97-03-44-45. www.lemeridien.com. 318 units. 195€–385€ double; 680€–1,575€ suite. Discounts of around 15% during selected dates Oct–Apr. AE, DC, MC, V. Bus: 8, 9, 10, or 3. **Amenities:** Restaurant; bar; concierge; health club & spa; pool (outdoor); room service. *In room:* A/C, TV, hair dryer, Internet (23€), minibar.

Hôtel Splendid ★   This is one of Nice's best modern hotels, on the corner of a wide boulevard lined with shade trees, 4 blocks from its private beach. Built on the site of the original Hôtel Splendid (ca. 1881), it was heralded as a new era in French hotels. Frequent renovations have kept the place fresh. The rooms usually have terraces or balconies, and several floors are reserved for nonsmokers. Accommodations come in various shapes and sizes, but all have private safes, electronic locks, and soundproofing. Beds are a bit narrow, but the mattresses are first class.

50 bd. Victor-Hugo, 06048 Nice. © **04-93-14-42-70.** Fax 04-93-87-02-46. www.splendid-nice.com. 127 units. 175€–270€ double; 265€–395€ suite. AE, DC, MC, V. Parking 22€. Bus: 9 or 10. **Amenities:** Restaurant; bar; pool; babysitting; health club w/sauna; room service. *In room:* A/C, TV, hair dryer, minibar, Wi-Fi (14€).

Radisson SAS Nice ★   Set alongside the major beachside thoroughfare of Nice, this streamlined and tastefully contemporary hotel has undergone more name and ownership changes than any other major hotel in town. In 1998, it was acquired by the Radisson chain, which inaugurated renovations to the public areas and bedrooms. Many business travelers come here. Standardized accommodations come with built-in furniture, double-glazing, and comfortable beds. Overall, one finds a sense of bustle, with an alert staff that's hip to the goings-on in Nice and along the Côte d'Azur—a feel of Paris-on-the-beach. Visitors enjoy soft piano music in the sophisticated lobby.

223 promenade des Anglais, 06200 Nice. © **04-93-37-17-17.** Fax 04-93-71-21-71. www.radissonsas. com. 331 units. 155€–330€ double; 290€–665€ suite. AE, DC, MC, V. Parking 22€. Bus: 8. Pets allowed. **Amenities:** Restaurant; bar; babysitting; concierge; health club w/sauna; pool (outdoor); room service. *In room:* A/C, TV, hair dryer, minibar, Wi-Fi (free).

Westminster Concorde ★   This 1860 hotel occupies a prominent position on the famous promenade. Among many renovations, its elaborate Belle Epoque facade has been restored to its former grandeur. The contemporary rooms are comfortable and have soundproof windows; a few open onto balconies. Most rooms have high ceilings, antique mirrors, French windows, and brass beds.

27 promenade des Anglais, 06000 Nice. © **04-92-14-86-86.** Fax 04-93-82-45-35. www.westminster-nice. com. 100 units. 180€–290€ double; from 350€ junior suite. AE, DC, MC, V. Parking 25€ in public lot next door. Bus: 9, 10, or 11. **Amenities:** Restaurant; bar; babysitting; concierge; room service. *In room:* A/C, TV, hair dryer, minibar, Wi-Fi (27€).

Moderate

Hôtel Busby   This nostalgic hotel has a faded early-20th-century grandeur. The Busby family, who were the original owners, refer to its ornate facade as "style Garibaldi" and have retained the balconies and the shutters on the tall windows. Renovated at regular intervals, yet looking a bit tired, the guest rooms are dignified; some contain mahogany twin beds and white-and-gold wardrobes. Mattresses are a bit worn, but are still comfortable.

36–38 rue du Maréchal-Joffre, 06000 Nice. © **04-93-88-19-41.** Fax 04-93-87-73-53. www.busby-hotel. com. 80 units. 130€–150€ double; 190€–210€ triple. AE, DC, MC, V. Closed Nov 15–Dec 20. Bus: 9, 10, 12, or 22. **Amenities:** Bar; babysitting. *In room:* A/C, TV, hair dryer, Wi-Fi (16€).

Hôtel du Petit Palais   This whimsical hotel occupies a mansion built around 1890; in the 1970s it was the home of the actor and writer Sacha Guitry (a name that's instantly recognized in millions of French households). It lies about a 10-minute drive from the city center in the Carabacel district near the Musée Chagall. Many of the Art Deco and

Italianate furnishings and Florentine moldings and friezes remain intact. The preferred rooms, and the most expensive, have balconies that afford sea views during the day and sunset views at dusk. Breakfast is served in a small but pretty salon.

17 av. Emile-Bieckert, 06000 Nice. ✆ **04-93-62-19-11.** Fax 04-93-62-53-60. www.guide-gerard.com. 25 units. 95€–170€ double. AE, DC, MC, V. Parking 12€. **Amenities:** Bar; babysitting; room service. *In room:* A/C, TV, hair dryer, minibar, Wi-Fi (free).

Hôtel Excelsior The Excelsior's ornate corbels and stone pediments rise grandly a few steps from the railway station. This much-renovated 19th-century hotel has modern decor, most of it from the mid-1990s, and rooms outfitted in Provençal tones have seen a lot of wear but are still comfortable. Furnishings are functional and conservative. A garden and the beach are a 20-minute walk through the residential and commercial heart of Nice.

19 av. Durante, 06000 Nice. ✆ **04-93-88-18-05.** Fax 04-93-88-38-69. www.excelsiornice.com. 42 units. 100€–140€ double. AE, DC, MC, V. Bus: 99. **Amenities:** Smoke-free rooms. *In room:* A/C, TV, hair dryer, Wi-Fi (21€).

Hôtel Gounod ★ A winning choice in the city center, this hotel is a mere 5-minute walk from the sea. Built around 1910 in a neighborhood where the street names honor composers, the Gounod boasts ornate balconies, a domed roof, and an elaborate canopy of wrought iron and glass. The attractive lobby and adjoining lounge are festive and stylish, with old prints, copper flowerpots, and antiques. The high-ceilinged guest rooms are quiet, and most overlook the gardens of private homes. Suites have safes. Guests have free unlimited use of the pool, cafe-bar, and Jacuzzi at the Hôtel Splendid, next door.

3 rue Gounod, 06000 Nice. ✆ **04-93-16-42-00.** Fax 04-93-88-23-84. www.gounod-nice.com. 45 units. 105€–150€ double; 140€–250€ suite. AE, DC, MC, V. Parking 15€. Closed Nov 20–Dec 20. Bus: 8. **Amenities:** Restaurant; bar; babysitting; health club & spa; Internet (free); room service. *In room:* A/C, TV, hair dryer, minibar.

Hôtel Windsor Ⓥ Value One of the most arts-conscious hotels in Provence is in a *maison bourgeoise* built by disciples of Gustav Eiffel in 1895. It's near the Negresco and the promenade des Anglais. Each unit is a unique decorative statement by a different artist. The heir and scion of the longtime owners, the Redolfi family, commissioned manifestations of his mystical visions after years of traveling through Asia, Africa, and South America. In the "Ben" room, for example, a Provençal artist of the same name painted verses of his own poetry. You can take your chances or select a room based on the photos on the hotel website. The fifth-floor superstructure holds the health club, steam room, and sauna. The garden contains scores of tropical and exotic plants, and the recorded sounds of birds singing in the jungles of the Amazon.

11 rue Dalpozzo, 06000 Nice. ✆ **04-93-88-59-35.** Fax 04-93-88-94-57. www.hotelwindsornice.com. 54 units. 90€–175€ double. MC, V. Parking 10€. Bus: 9, 10, or 22. **Amenities:** Restaurant; bar; babysitting; health club w/sauna; pool (outdoor). *In room:* A/C, TV, hair dryer, minibar.

L'Hôtel Masséna ★ Few other hotels evoke the Belle Epoque as gracefully or as authentically as this stone-and-wrought-iron monument to early-20th-century architecture. The owners have upgraded the bedrooms, transforming the hotel into a well-orchestrated bastion of calm and comfort. Many of the rooms are upholstered in fabrics depicting olive trees or olive branches. The most expensive rooms are airy, spacious, and outfitted in tones inspired by the colors of Provence. Less expensive rooms are altogether comfortable, albeit somewhat smaller. Although all units have soundproofing, the ones that are the quietest are those overlooking the hotel's back side or its interior courtyard.

58 rue Gioffredo, 06000 Nice. ✆ **04-92-47-88-88.** Fax 04-92-47-88-89. www.hotel-massena-nice.com. 110 units. 149€–269€ double; 520€ suite. Extra bed 30€. AE, DC, MC, V. Parking 25€. Bus: 15. **Amenities:** Bar; babysitting; room service. *In room:* A/C, TV, hair dryer, minibar, Wi-Fi (free).

Le Grimaldi Two gorgeous Belle Epoque buildings sharing an inner courtyard comprise this hotel set in the center of Nice. Inside, however, the decor of the rooms has been modernized, using glass, wrought iron, and fabrics to convey a sophisticated charm. The rooms contain contemporary amenities, and those on the upper floors overlook the rooftops of Nice. Among the best features of the place are its generous breakfast offerings: homemade Provençal jams, fresh fruit, and crusty pastries made by one of the town's best bakers.

15 rue Grimaldi, 06000 Nice. ✆ **04-93-16-00-24.** Fax 04-93-87-00-24. www.le-grimaldi.com. 46 units. 95€–205€ double; 200€–240€ junior suite. AE, DC, MC, V. **Amenities:** Bar. *In room:* A/C, TV, minibar, Wi-Fi (free).

Inexpensive

Flots d'Azur This three-story 19th-century villa is next to the sea and a short walk from the more elaborate and costlier promenade hotels. The rooms vary in size and decor; all have good views and sea breezes. Twelve units have TVs and minibars, and all units come with a tiled bathroom. Double-glazed windows cut down on noise. A small sitting room and sun terrace grace the front, where a continental breakfast is served.

101 promenade des Anglais, 06000 Nice. ✆ **04-93-86-51-25.** Fax 04-93-97-22-07. www.flotsdazur.com. 20 units. 55€–115€ double. MC, V. Free parking. Closed 10 days in Dec. Bus: 23. **Amenities:** Internet (free). *In room:* A/C, TV, hair dryer, minibar.

Hôtel Canada (Value) Lying 50m (164 ft.) from the sea, and just west of the landmark place Masséna, this is one of the bargains of Nice. Some two dozen marble steps lead up to the lobby, which is decorated with mirrors and paintings. Stairs, no elevator, take you to the bedrooms that range from small to spacious. Bedrooms are clean and comfortable, if a bit frayed here and there. The best room is no. 5, adjoining a terrace garden where breakfast is served. The best units are on the third floor with private balconies or terraces, some opening onto distant views of the water.

8 rue Halevy, 06000 Nice. ✆ **04-93-87-98-94.** Fax 04-93-87-17-12. www.hotel-canada-nice.cote.azur.fr. 15 units. 52€–95€ double. AE, DC, MC, V. **Amenities:** Room service. *In room:* A/C, TV, kitchenette (in some), minifridge (in some), Wi-Fi (free).

Hôtel Carlyna Built "sometime before 1940," and positioned in the commercial heart of Nice between two popular restaurants, this hotel offers simple, well-scrubbed functionality at relatively reasonable rates. The Bouvet family has owned the place since 1998 and has made many improvements since then. Each of the bedrooms is outfitted in soft tones of either red or blue and accessorized with cheerful fabrics.

8 rue Sacha-Guitry, 06000 Nice. ✆ **04-93-80-77-21.** Fax 04-93-80-08-80. www.carlyna-hotel-nice.com. 24 units. 63€–75€ double; 87€ triple. AE, MC, V. Bus: 1, 4, or 7. **Amenities:** Room service; Wi-Fi (4€). *In room:* A/C, TV.

Hotel Dante (Value) Bargain hunters in Nice head for this restored hotel, which lies only a stone's throw from the promenade des Anglais, in between the Sheraton and Negresco hotels, and about a 10-minute walk from the flower market and train station. The government grants it only two stars, but it is definitely recommendable for its well-maintained, comfortable, and attractively furnished bedrooms. Furnishings are very modern, almost evoking a Caribbean resort, and the English-speaking personnel is most helpful in guiding you through the intricacies of Nice. The most desirable rooms are those with a small kitchen, opening onto a private terrace.

12 rue Andrioli, 06000 Nice. © **04-93-86-81-00.** Fax 94-93-97-27-17. www.med-hotel.dr/hoteldanet-nice. com. 30 units. 56€–79€ double; 85€–95€ triple. AE, MC, V. **Amenities:** Room service. *In room:* TV, fridge, kitchen (in some; 5€ extra), minibar.

Hôtel de la Buffa ★ (Value)

Lying only a few steps from the promenade des Anglais and the pebbly beaches, this centrally located hotel combines charm with value. Decorated with flair, it offers a family atmosphere. Rooms are tastefully and comfortably furnished, with the larger accommodations suitable for a family of up to four. If you wish, a safe and a refrigerator can be installed in your room. Those units facing the streets have double-glazing on their windows. If you wish to partake of discounted meals, an arrangement can be made for you to take half or full board at the adjoining restaurant (which is under different management).

56 rue de la Buffa, 06000 Nice. © **04-93-88-77-35.** Fax 04-93-88-83-39. www.hotel-buffa.com. 13 units. 54€–74€ double; 95€ quad. AE, DC, V. Closed 3 weeks in Nov. Bus: 23. *In room:* A/C, TV, fridge (in some), hair dryer.

Hôtel du Centre

Near the train station, this simple, restored hotel dates from 1947. The rooms are very close to the attractions and bars of downtown Nice. The accommodations are rather basic, but tidily kept and adequate for an overnight stay. The staff is well versed in the many diversions of the city.

2 rue de Suisse, 06000 Nice. © **04-93-88-83-85.** Fax 04-93-82-29-80. www.nice-hotel-centre.com. 26 units. 50€–70€ double; 65€–100€ triple; 130€–180€ quad. MC, V. Parking 12€. Bus: 23 or 99. **Amenities:** Restaurant; Internet (free). *In room:* A/C, TV, hair dryer, minibar.

Hôtel Durante

A comfortable and much-modified building dating from around the turn of the 20th century, this hotel is very popular with producers, actors, and directors during the nearby Cannes Film Festival. Many rooms face a quiet courtyard. The furnishings have known better days, but the beds are still quite comfortable. The owner dispenses both charm and information about local cinematic events.

16 av. Durante, 06000 Nice. © **04-93-88-84-40.** Fax 04-93-87-77-76. www.nice-hotel-durante.com. 24 units. 70€–200€ double. AE, MC, V. **Amenities:** Bar; babysitting. *In room:* A/C, TV, hair dryer, fridge, kitchenette (in some), Wi-Fi (free).

Hôtel l'Oasis ★ (Finds)

In the semitropical garden here, you can imagine the ghosts of the influential people who stayed here during the first half of the 20th century when the place was a boardinghouse with good number of Russians. They included Anton Chekhov, who composed part of *Three Sisters* here, and Lenin, who spent a holiday here in 1911. Although an air of old-fashioned manners remains intact, bedrooms have been modernized many times since, most recently in a contemporary, vaguely Provençal motif, and they are well maintained. The location, about a 12-minute walk from the railway station, is convenient to virtually everything in Nice.

23 rue Gounod, 06000 Nice. © **04-93-88-12-29.** Fax 04-93-16-14-40. www.hoteloasis-nice.com. 38 units. 79€–180€ double. Rates include continental breakfast. AE, MC, V. Parking 8€. **Amenities:** Bar service in garden; babysitting; room service. *In room:* A/C, TV, hair dryer, Wi-Fi (free).

Hôtel Magnan

This well-run modern hotel was built around 1945 and has been repeatedly renovated. While a 10-minute bus ride from the heart of town, it's only a minute or so from the promenade des Anglais and the bay. Many of the simply furnished rooms have balconies facing the sea. The look is functional, but for Nice this is a good price, especially considering the comfortable beds. Owner Daniel Thérouin occupies the apartment on the top floor, guaranteeing close supervision. Breakfast can be served in your room.

Square du Général-Ferrié, 06200 Nice. ✆ **04-93-86-76-00.** Fax 04-93-44-48-31. www.hotelmagnan-nice. com. 25 units. 60€–85€ double. AE, MC, V. Bus: 23. *In room:* TV, Wi-Fi (free).

Hôtel Saint-Georges   Originally built during the grand days of Niçoise tourism, this hotel dates from around 1900 and still retains a few of its original architectural grace notes. A verdant patio and garden are set with clusters of iron chairs and tables, a perfect spot to enjoy breakfast or an afternoon read. Inside the motif is less nostalgic: It's angular and contemporary, and has mirrored, sometimes stark walls and efficient modern furnishings. Most bedrooms have high ceilings and casement doors that open onto tiny porches hemmed in with wrought-iron railings. The rooms are fairly small.

7 av. Georges Clemenceau, 06000 Nice. ✆ **04-93-88-79-21.** Fax 04-93-16-22-85. www.hotelsaint georges.fr. 30 units. 79€–99€ double; 100€–120€ triple. AE, DC, MC, V. Bus: 1 or 4. **Amenities:** Lounge; garden. *In room:* A/C, TV, hair dryer, Wi-Fi (free).

Hôtel Villa St-Hubert ★ (**Value**)   Set 5 blocks inland from the seacoast and the beach, this hotel consists of an interconnected pair of early-20th-century town houses. They're the property of the Chevalier family, who maintain clean, well-appointed bedrooms, each with a different color scheme. Bedrooms are medium in size, with firm mattresses. One of the hotel's most appealing corners is the ivy-covered, geranium-filled courtyard, the site of morning breakfast and afternoon teas. No meals are served other than breakfast, but in light of the many nearby restaurants, no one seems to mind.

26 rue Michel-Ange, 06100 Nice. ✆ **04-93-84-66-51.** Fax 04-93-84-70-96. www.villasainthubert.com. 13 units. 60€ double. AE, MC, V. Parking 7€. **Amenities:** Room service. *In room:* A/C (in some), TV, kitchenette (in some), hair dryer, minibar, Wi-Fi (free).

Le Lausanne   This is a solid, middle-bracket hotel with a central location in a commercial neighborhood in the heart of Nice. It was radically renovated in the mid-1990s and retains very few of its original architectural embellishments. Views from the windows look out over the street, and its efficient bedroom furnishings are standard for the well-respected Clarine chain. Overall, this is a reliable, although not particularly exciting, hotel choice.

36 rue Rossini, 06000 Nice. ✆ **04-93-88-85-94.** Fax 04-93-88-15-88. 35 units. 79€–99€ double. MC, V. Parking 11€. Bus: 8. **Amenities:** Babysitting. *In room:* A/C, TV, hair dryer, Wi-Fi (free 1st hr., then 1€ per hr.).

Villa La Tour ★ (**Finds**)   The owner of Villa La Tour once worked at the legendary Hotel Negresco, and she has brought her savvy to restoring this 18th-century convent. She runs one of the most atmospheric little hotels in the ancient city, and she also offers good value. Outside the door are many authentic old Provençal bistros and bars, and you are only a 10-minute walk from the beach. All of the comfortable rooms are tastefully furnished, with designer fabrics on the walls and chic lighting, but some are a bit cramped. If you need more space, ask for one of the *supérieure* units. The hallways are rather narrow, but the rooms themselves open onto views of the Old Town, a few containing small balconies. The little roof garden is a grace note.

4 rue de la Tour, 06300 Nice. ✆ **04-93-80-08-15.** Fax 04-93-85-10-58. www.villa-la-tour.com. 14 units. 48€–139€ double; 118€–150€ triple. AE, MC, V. **Amenities:** Room service. *In room:* A/C, TV, hair dryer, Internet (free).

Villa Saint-Exupéry (Value)   This former Carmelite monastery in Cimiez has been
completely renovated and turned into a first-rate hostel that is the most attractively
priced in the area. In winter it is a student residence, but in the busy summer months it
turns into a hotel catering to backpackers, seasoned travelers on a budget, artists, musicians, and, of course, students. The restored and comfort-filled villa offers good though
very standard hotel rooms (some with a kitchenette) as well as dormitory accommodations at youth hostel-level tariffs. Furnishings are modern and selected more for comfort
than style. Echoing its past life, the former chapel preserved its open stage and stained-
glass windows. The public lounge, where guests mingle, has five computers with free
Internet access. Guests are also welcome to use a fully equipped kitchen. Wine, beer, and
some other supplies are sold on the premises, while a supermarket lies just down the hill.

22 av. Gravier, 06100 Nice. ℂ **04-93-84-42-83.** Fax 04-93-52-44-31. www.vsaint.com. 60 units. 32€–80€
per person in a single or twin-bedded room; 16€ per person for dormitory bed. Rates include continental
breakfast. MC, V. Parking 18€–30€. **Amenities:** Bar; cooking facilities; Internet (free) *In room:* Kitchenettes
(in some).

WHERE TO DINE
Very Expensive
Le Chantecler ★★★ TRADITIONAL/MODERN FRENCH   This is Nice's most
prestigious and best restaurant. The walls are sheathed with panels removed from a château in Pouilly-Fuissé; a Regency-style salon is available for before- or after-dinner drinks;
and a collection of 16th-century paintings decorates the premises. A much-respected
chef, Bruno Turbot, revised the menu to include the most sophisticated and creative
dishes in Nice. They change almost weekly but may include turbot filet served with purée
of broad beans, sun-dried tomatoes, and asparagus; roasted suckling lamb served with
beignets of fresh vegetables and ricotta-stuffed ravioli; and a melt-in-your-mouth fantasy
of marbled hot chocolate drenched in almond-flavored cream sauce.

In the Hôtel Negresco (p. 304), 37 promenade des Anglais. ℂ **04-93-16-64-00.** Reservations required.
Main courses 36€–112€; fixed-price lunch 45€–90€; fixed-price dinner 90€–130€. AE, MC, V. Wed–Sun
12:30–2pm and 8–10pm. Closed Jan to mid-Feb. Bus: 8, 9, 10, or 11.

Expensive
Don Camillo ★★ ITALIAN/PROVENÇALE   Named in the 1950s after its founder,
Camille, a Niçoise patriot (who preferred the Italian version of his name), this nine-table
restaurant delivers some of Nice's most authentic Provençal food. Just off cours Saleya,
the dining room is adorned with pleasant, light colors and modern paintings, many of
which are for sale. The menu changes with the seasons, as supervised by owner Stéphane
Viano, but can include jumbo shrimp flambéed with pastis and served with deliberately
undercooked vegetables; risottos with vegetables from the vendors of the nearby cours
Saleya; filet of John Dory served with a confit of tomatoes and artichokes; and standing
roasted rack of lamb served with Provençal herbs and Parmesan-dusted zucchini.

5 rue des Ponchettes. ℂ **04-93-85-67-95.** www.doncamillo-creation.fr. Reservations recommended.
Fixed-price lunch 26€; fixed-price dinner 60€–80€. MC, V. Mon 8–9:30pm; Tues–Sat noon–1:30pm and
8–10pm. Bus: 8.

Keisuke Matsushima ★★★   The Japanese chef Keisuke Matsushima became the
second Japanese chef in France to be awarded the Michelin star. Against a backdrop of a
beige-and-black minimalist decor, he serves his imaginative creations. His inventive and
intensely flavored concoctions include Mediterranean sea bream with roasted, spiky

artichokes and mussels in a vegetable broth with carrot foam, or pigeon breasts caramelized and served with a wasabi emulsion. Other temptations include Sisteron lamb roasted and served with a Parma ham foam and a lamb jus flavored with mint. Brittany scallops appear with turnip carpaccio with a sweet-and-sour vinaigrette.

22 Ter rue de France. ☎ **04-93-82-26-06.** Reservations required. Fixed-price lunch 35€–45€; fixed-price dinner 65€–140€. AE, MC, V. Tues–Fri noon–2:30pm; Mon–Sat 7:30–10pm.

Specialités Niçoise ★ NIÇOISE   For several generations, this cozy restaurant was directed by a domineering matriarch, Mme. Barale, whose autocratic behavior with her guests and staff was almost legendary. Today, much liberated from the demands of its founder (Mme. Barale retired from the scene late in 2003), the venue now revolves less around her personality cult, but it can still be a lot of fun. The setting includes several interconnected dining rooms, each outfitted with gleaming copper pots, patterned fabrics, comfortable banquettes, and lots of ceramics. In a separate room, presented like objects in a museum, is a trio of Citroëns from the 1920s, each restored to its original glossiness. Menu items reflect the old-fashioned culinary traditions of Nice: *pissaladière*, salad Niçoise, house-made ravioli, and savory slices of spinach tart.

39 rue Beaumont. ☎ **04-93-89-17-94.** Reservations recommended. Main courses 12€–16€; fixed-price menu 28€, includes aperitif, wine, coffee, and after-dinner drinks. No credit cards. Sept–June Tues–Sun 8–11pm; July–Aug Wed–Sun 8pm–midnight.

Moderate

La Merenda ★★ (Finds) NIÇOISE   Because they don't have a phone, you have to go by this place twice: once to make a reservation and once to dine. It's worth the effort. Forsaking his chef's crown at Le Chantecler (above), Dominique Le Stanc opened this tiny bistro serving sublime cuisine. His food is a lullaby of gastronomic unity, with texture, crunch, richness, and balance. Le Stanc never knows what he's going to serve until he goes to the market. Look for specials on a chalkboard. Perhaps you'll find stuffed cabbage, fried zucchini flowers, or oxtail flavored with fresh oranges. Lamb from the Sisteron is cooked until it practically falls from the bone. Raw artichokes are paired with a salad of mâche. Service is discreet and personable. We wish we could dine here every day.

4 rue Terrasse. No phone. Reservations required. Main courses 36€–52€. No credit cards. Mon–Fri seatings at 7:15 and 9:15pm. Closed Feb 5–13 and Aug 1–15. Bus: 8.

L'Ane Rouge ★★ PROVENÇALE   Facing the old port and occupying an antique building whose owners have carefully retained its ceiling beams and stone walls, this is one of the city's best-known seafood restaurants. In the two modern yet cozy dining rooms, you can enjoy traditional specialties such as bouillabaisse, *bourride* (stew), filet of John Dory with roulades of stuffed lettuce leaves, mussels stuffed with bread crumbs and herbs, and salmon in wine sauce with spinach.

7 quai des Deux-Emmanuels. ☎ **04-93-89-49-63.** www.anerougenice.com. Reservations required. Main courses 26€–75€; fixed-price dinner 26€–95€. AE, DC, MC, V. Fri–Tues noon–2pm; Thurs–Tues 7–10:30pm. Closed Feb. Bus: 30.

Restaurant Boccaccio MEDITERRANEAN   Adjacent to place Masséna in a pedestrian zone that enhances the desirability of its streetfront terrace, this restaurant boasts worthy cuisine and a devoted local following. Bouillabaisse is reasonably priced here, and the range of fresh fish (grilled with lemon butter or baked in a salt crust) is broad and well prepared. The paella might remind you of Spain, and desserts such as cappuccino

tiramisu and crêpes suzette round out meals nicely. If the terrace doesn't appeal to you, a
large dining room upstairs was inspired by the interior of a yacht.

7 rue Masséna. (**04-93-87-71-76.** www.boccaccio-nice.com. Reservations recommended. Main courses 20€–40€. AE, DC, MC, V. Daily noon–2:30pm and 7–11pm. Bus: 4, 5, or 22.

Inexpensive

Acciardo ★ (Finds) PROVENÇALE   Ignored by guidebooks except ours, this local dive has been run by the Acciardo family since the end of World War II. Tourists rarely find their way to this little bastion of traditional family cooking. Drinking is pursued as avidly as eating here. The recipes are time twisted and include a classic Niçoise version of gnocchi, which is prepared with Swiss chard and served with a choice of three different sauces, including pistou, Gorgonzola, and tomato. Many locals also begin their meal with soupe au pistou. For a main dish, opt for the swordfish with confit of lemon, calves' liver with parsley and raw garlic, or spaghetti with Gorgonzola.

38 rue Droite. (**04-93-85-51-16.** Reservations 2 days in advance. Main courses 18€–25€. No credit cards. Mon–Fri noon–1pm and 7-10pm. Closed weekends in Aug.

Au Petit Gari TRADITIONAL FRENCH   Set beneath the arcades of the place Garibaldi, this restaurant features a hip and friendly staff and a distinctly and deliberately old-fashioned decor and menu. The setting evokes an early-20th-century bistro, replete with banquettes, etched glass, and a fast pace that keeps clients well fed and briskly moving in and out of available seats. The menu is written on blackboards and can include a gratin of scallops and shrimp served on braised leeks; a terrine of rabbit with prunes; deliberately undercooked tuna steak served with a tapenade of olives and mashed potatoes; and an old-fashioned magret (grilled breast) of duck.

2 Place Garibaldi. (**04-93-26-89-09.** www.aupetitgari.com. Reservations recommended. Main courses 15€–30€; set lunch 13€. MC, V. Mon–Fri noon–2pm and 7-10pm. Closed weekends and 2 weeks in Jan.

Brasserie Flo (Kids) TRADITIONAL FRENCH   This is the town's most bustling brasserie. In 1991, the Jean-Paul Bucher group, a French chain noted for its skill at restoring historic brasseries, bought the premises of a faded early-1900s restaurant near place Masséna and injected it with new life. The original frescoes cover the high ceilings. The place (which is affiliated with Brasserie Flo in Paris) is brisk, stylish, reasonably priced, and fun. The menu includes an array of grilled fish, *choucroute* Alsatian style, steak with brandied pepper sauce, and fresh oysters and shellfish.

2–4 rue Sacha-Guitry. (**04-93-13-38-38.** www.flonice.com. Reservations recommended. Main courses 16€–35€; fixed-price lunch 19€–34€; children's menu 14€; fixed-price dinner 24€–34€. AE, DC, MC, V. Daily noon–2:30pm and 7pm–midnight. Bus: 1, 2, or 5.

Café de Turin ★★ CONTINENTAL/SEAFOOD   The origins of this place began in 1900, when it served glasses and carafes of wine to local office workers and laborers. In the 1950s, it added a kitchen to its premises, and ever since, it's churned out the kinds of hearty, bistro-style platters that go well with wine and beer. Much of the energy is expressed outside, under the arcades of the central plaza (place Garibaldi), where local hipsters strut their stuff, people jump to their feet to table-hop, and harassed but well-intentioned waiters do their best to keep the food and beverages flowing. The place is celebrated for its *coquillage* (raw shellfish), attracting the likes of Princess Caroline, who drives over from Monaco. Other items include whatever species of grilled fish is available that day, pâtés, terrines, salads, pastas, and a satisfying selection of ice creams and pastries.

5 place Garibaldi. ✆ **04-93-62-29-52.** Reservations recommended weekends at night; otherwise, not necessary. Main courses 10€–34€. MC, V. Daily 9am–11pm. Bus: 9 or 10.

Chez Palmyre (Value) NIÇOISE/PROVENÇALE   "We don't care about food fashions or decoration, only local home cooking like my grandmother's," the owner with her coke-bottle glasses informs us. "All my food is local." She shops daily and changes her menu, depending on her inspiration that morning. In Vieux Nice, she caters to her regulars, feeding them some of the best fried sardines in old town. Try her rolled veal scallops filled with cheese and ham and served with a sauce of fresh tomatoes laced with wine. Many patrons come here to order her tripes á la niçoise, although this is an acquired taste for some. This place has been a virtual institution in Nice since 1925, and we expect it'll be around at least until the dawn of the next century.

5 rue Droite. ✆ **04-93-85-72-32.** Reservations recommended. Fixed-price menu (the only choice) 12€. MC, V. Mon–Sat noon–2pm and 7–10pm.

In Vino PROVENÇALE   The chef, who comes from the southeast of France, is justifiably proud of his wine list, with more than 70 vintages from throughout all of France's major wine regions, with a particular focus of bottles from the Rhône Valley. Throughout the week, the service is accompanied by low-volume jazz music. Once a month it's jazz night here with a live band. The decor is typical of a bistro in Lyon. You can order such tasty dishes as foie gras (many versions), or a magret of duckling. The chef also makes a cassoulet worthy of any served in Toulouse. Other dishes include the grilled fish of the day.

2 rue de l'Hôtel-de-Ville. ✆ **04-93-80-21-64.** Reservations recommended. Main courses 13€–22€. MC, V. Mon–Sat noon–3pm and 6pm–midnight. Closed first 2 weeks in Jan. Bus: 1, 2, or 5.

L'Escalinada ★ NIÇOISE   For more than half a century, locals have flocked to this favorite nest on a side street in Vieux Nice. You can dine inside under old beams or out on a sunny terrace. The moment you sit down, the waiter arrives with a bowl of chickpeas (garbanzos to some), and you help yourself, enjoying a glass of kir and a square of *pissaladière,* the Niçoise, onion-enriched version of pizza. For an appetizer, the *encornets* (squid stuffed with Swiss chard and rice) is a winner, as are the sautéed zucchini flowers or the roast red peppers. For the main course, we recommend *porchetta, cochon de lait farci,* or suckling pig rolled around various cuts of meats. You can try other classics such as beef carpaccio, veal kidneys, or even the stuffed sardines of the house (a particular favorite of ours).

22 rue Pairolière. ✆ **04-93-62-11-71.** Reservations recommended. Main courses 12€–23€. No credit cards. Daily noon–2:30pm and 7–11pm.

La Petite Maison ★★ (Finds) FRENCH/PROVENÇALE   This bustling and noisy tavern in the heart of the Old Town resides in a 19th-century grocery store. Locals guard the address, hoping it won't be mobbed by tourists. Those regulars include Elton John and his longtime companion, who live in a villa nearby. It's usually packed with diners wanting to taste this array of Niçoise cuisine, the authenticity of which is virtually unequaled in the city. Try the town's finest zucchini-blossom fritters, and finish with a dessert that will send you rushing to the phone to call *Gourmet* magazine—homemade ice cream flavored with pine nuts and candied orange blossoms. In between, you may enjoy a succulent array of grilled fish, pastas, and steaks, all prepared with the right Mediterranean touches and just enough garlic.

11 rue St-Francoise de Paule. ✆ **04-93-85-71-53.** www.lapetitemaison-nice.com. Reservations recommended. Main courses 12€–35€. AE, V. Mon–Sat noon–2:30pm and 7:30pm–midnight.

La Zucca Magica ★ (Finds) VEGETARIAN/ITALIAN   The chef at this popular harborside restaurant has been named the best Italian chef in Nice. That this honor should go to a vegetarian restaurant was the most startling part of the news. Chef Marco, who opened his restaurant in 1997 after cooking for many years in Rome, certainly has a fine pedigree—he's a relative of the late Luciano Pavarotti. He serves refined cuisine at reasonable prices, using recipes from Italy's Piedmont region and updating them with no meat or fish. The red-and-green decor (the colors of Italy) will put you in the mood for the creative cuisine. You'll have to trust Marco, though, because everyone is served the same meal. You can count on savory cuisine using lots of herbs, Italian cheeses, beans, and pasta. Lasagna is a specialty.

4 bis quai Papacino. (✆ **04-93-56-25-27.** www.lazuccamagica.com. Reservations recommended. Fixed-price lunch 17€; fixed-price dinner 29€. No credit cards. Tues–Sat 12:30–2pm and 7pm–midnight.

Le Safari ★ PROVENÇALE/NIÇOISE   The decor couldn't be simpler: a black ceiling, white walls, and an old-fashioned terra-cotta floor. The youthful staff is fashionable and relaxed, sometimes in jeans. Many diners prefer the outdoor terrace overlooking the Marché aux Fleurs, but all appreciate the reasonably priced meals that appear in generous portions. Menu items include a pungent *bagna cauda,* which calls for diners to immerse vegetables in a sizzling brew of hot oil and anchovy paste; grilled peppers bathed in olive oil; *daube* (stew) of beef; fresh pasta with basil; and an omelet with *blettes* (tough but flavorful greens). The unfortunately named *merda de can* (dog poop) is gnocchi stuffed with spinach and is a lot more appetizing than it sounds.

1 cours Saleya. (✆ **04-93-80-18-44.** Reservations recommended. Main courses 12€–25€; fixed-price menu 29€. AE, DC, MC, V. Daily noon–midnight. Bus: 1.

Le Tire Bouchon ("The Corkscrew") SOUTHWESTERN FRENCH   Set in the heart of the old city, this is a cozy restaurant with a bordeaux-tinged color scheme, two dining rooms, an old-fashioned decor, and an allegiance to the rich and hearty cuisine of France's southwest. The menu reflects the kind of conservative cuisine that hasn't changed very much since the days when its clients were children. The best examples include onion soup with a crusty top, cassoulet (the earthy pork-and-bean stew of Toulouse—but only in winter), confit of duckling, curried crayfish and monkfish, foie gras and pâté of duck with figs and hazelnuts, and various forms of fish. Many local residents have been dining here regularly since the place was established in 1991.

19 rue de la Préfecture. (✆ **04-93-92-63-64.** www.le-tire-bouchon.com. Reservations recommended. Main courses 20€–27€; set menu 28€–34€. AE, MC, V. Daily 7am–10:30pm. Bus: 9 or 10.

Beyond Nice
Restaurant Parcours Live ★ MEDITERRANEAN   This is the kind of place that Niçois gastronomes and foodies talk about in one-upmanship conversations with other locals. Its appeal derives from a combination of sweeping views, fabulous food, and the three monitors that provide real-time views of the food preparation rituals going on within the kitchens. Expect a century-old *mas* (farmhouse) Provençal, radically upgraded into a glossy, high-tech interior with seats for 85 diners at a time. Menu items, as supervised by two generations of the Galland family (son Fréderic capably handles the kitchens, *mamam* Danielle choreographs the dining rooms) vary with the seasons, but are likely to include Mediterranean tuna crusted with sesame seeds on a soy-soaked potato purée, fried slices of foie gras with fresh asparagus and morels, "filet mignon" of pork with hot sauce and truffled potatoes, and roasted scallops on a crispy bed of Jerusalem artichokes and mushrooms.

1 place Marcel Eusebi, 06950 Falicon. ℂ **04-93-84-94-57.** www.restaurant-parcours.com. Reservations recommended. Main courses 21€; fixed-price lunches (Mon–Fri only) 24€–28€; fixed-price dinners 39€–55€. AE, MC, V. July to mid-Sept Mon 8am–9:30pm; Tues–Sat 8am–9:30pm. From downtown Nice, drive north along the av. De Cimiez, then turn right onto the bd. Aire St-Michel, following the signs to the hamlet (pop. 2,000) of Falicon. In Falicon, signs clearly indicate the location.

NICE AFTER DARK

Nice has some of the most active nightlife along the Riviera. Evenings usually begin at a cafe. At kiosks around town, pick up a copy of *La Semaine des Spectacles,* which outlines the week's diversions.

The major cultural center on the Riviera is the **Opéra de Nice,** 4 rue St-François-de-Paule (ℂ **04-92-17-40-00;** www.opera-nice.org), built in 1885 by Charles Garnier, fabled architect of the Paris Opéra. It presents a full repertoire, with emphasis on serious, often large-scale operas. In one season you might see *Tosca, Les Contes de Hoffmann,* Verdi's *Macbeth,* Beethoven's *Fidelio,* and *Carmen,* as well as a *saison symphonique,* dominated by the Orchestre Philharmonique de Nice. The opera hall is also the major venue for concerts and recitals. Tickets are available (to concerts, recitals, and full-blown operas) a day or two prior to any performance. You can show up at the box office (Mon–Sat 10am–5:30pm, Sun 10am–6pm) or buy tickets in advance with a major credit card by phoning ℂ **04-92-17-40-17.** Tickets run 8€ for nosebleed (and we mean it) seats to 120€ for front-and-center seats on opening night.

Near the Hôtel Ambassador, **Le Before,** 18 rue des Congrès (ℂ **04-93-87-85-59**), is an aperitif bar—called *apero-bar*—where a stylish all-ages crowd goes before heading off to more dance-oriented places. The decor is "New York inspired," with lots of brick like you'd find in a Gotham cellar. Open daily from 6pm to midnight, with cold platters served until 10pm.

Cabaret du Casino Ruhl, in the Casino Ruhl, 1 promenade des Anglais (ℂ **04-97-03-12-22**), is Nice's answer to the more ostentatious glitter of Monte Carlo and Las Vegas. It includes just enough flesh to titillate; lots of spangles, feathers, and sequins; a medley of cross-cultural jokes and nostalgia for the old days of French *chanson;* and an acrobat or juggler. The 22€ cover includes one drink; dinner and the show, complete with a bottle of wine per person, costs 65€. Shows begin Friday and Saturday at 10pm. No jeans or sneakers.

The casino contains an area exclusively for slot machines, open daily from noon to 4am, with no admission fee. A more formal gaming room (jacket required, but not a tie), offers blackjack, baccarat, and chemin de fer. Presentation of a government-issued photo ID, preferably a passport, is required. It's open Sunday to Thursday 8pm to 4am, Friday and Saturday 5pm to 5am.

Le Relais, in the Hôtel Negresco, 37 promenade des Anglais (ℂ **04-93-16-64-00;** p. 304), is the most beautiful museum-quality bar in Nice, with an oxblood-red ceiling, Oriental carpets, English paneling, Italianate chairs, and tapestries. It was once a haunt of the actress Lillie Langtry. With its piano music and white-jacketed waiters, the bar still attracts a chic crowd.

Many bars in the Old Town cater to tourists and expats. They include the **Scarlett O'Hara Irish Pub,** at the corner of rue Rossetti and rue Droite (ℂ **04-93-80-42-22**); **Chez Wayne's,** 15 rue de la Préfecture (ℂ **04-93-13-46-99;** www.waynes.fr); and **William's Pub,** 4 rue Centrale (ℂ **04-93-62-99-63**), which has live music.

If you'd rather hang out with French people, try **La Civette,** 29 rue de la Préfecture (ℂ **04-93-62-35-51**), a popular spot for aperitifs. Two nearly adjacent sports bars with roughly equivalent decors, clienteles, and sports priorities are **Chez Wayne** (sharing space with Wayne's), 15 rue de la Prefecture, off place Rossetti in Vieux Nice (© **04-93-13-46-99**), and **Le Master Home Bar,** 11 rue de la Prefecture (© **04-85-95-51-64**). Both occasionally sponsor live bands, have more widescreens TVs for sporting events than you could possibly take in during one sitting, and offer the option of a rollicking and sometimes raucous good time. At Chez Wayne, Thursday is karaoke night. When live music is presented at either of these bars, it tends to begin around 9pm. **La Bodeguita,** 14 rue Chavin (© **04-93-92-67-24**) serves tapas, wine by the glass, and lots of beer, and both re-create some of the sun-and-salsa motifs of nightlife at its best in the Caribbean and South America.

By the port some of the best late-night action is at **White Lab,** 26 quai Lunel (© **04-93-26-54-79**), attracting a 20-plus crowd to its elegant confines. Everybody looks pink at night, helped in no small part by the bubble-gum decor. On most nights a cover of 15€ is imposed, with cocktails starting from 12€.

Also attracting the see-and-be-seen crowd is **Guest,** 5 quai des Deux Emmanual (© **04-93-56-83-83**). Along the waterfront, this club is chic, trendy, and romantic for dancing sweethearts of all persuasions. With its soft lighting, it's also a great pickup bar. A cover of 15€ is sometimes imposed, with cocktails costing from 12€.

A trend-conscious gay bar in Nice is **Le Klub,** 6 rue Halevy (© **04-95-16-27-56;** www.leklub.net), near the Casino Ruhl. Entrance costs 10€ and includes one drink. Expect a hard-dancing, high-energy crowd of mostly gay men, many of them under 35, as well as lots of straight people who come for the nonstop barrage of house music and the focus on dance, dance, dance.

7 VILLEFRANCHE-SUR-MER ★

935km (581 miles) S of Paris; 6km (4 miles) E of Nice

According to legend, Hercules opened his arms and Villefranche was born. It sits on a big blue bay that looks like a gigantic bowl, large enough to accommodate U.S. Sixth Fleet cruisers and destroyers. Quietly slumbering otherwise, Villefranche takes on the appearance of an exciting Mediterranean port when the fleet is in.

Once popular with such writers as Katherine Mansfield and Aldous Huxley, it's still a haven for artists, many of whom take over the little houses—reached by narrow alleyways—that climb the hillside. Two of the more recent arrivals who have bought homes in the area are Tina Turner and Bono.

ESSENTIALS

GETTING THERE **Trains** arrive from most towns on the Côte d'Azur, especially Nice (every 30 min.), but most visitors **drive** via the Corniche Inférieure (Lower Corniche). For more rail information and schedules, call © **36-35,** or visit **www.voyages-sncf.com.** Villefranche does not have a formal **bus** station. Ligne d'Azur company (© **08-10-06-10-06**) maintains service at 15-minute intervals aboard line no. 100 from Nice and from Monte Carlo. One-way bus transit from Nice costs 2€; one-way bus transit from Monaco is 3€. Buses deposit their passengers in the heart of town, directly opposite the tourist information office.

VISITOR INFORMATION The **Office de Tourisme** is on Jardin François-Binon (© **04-93-01-73-68;** www.villefranche-sur-mer.com).

The vaulted **rue Obscure** is one of the strangest streets in France. In spirit it belongs more to a North African casbah than to a European port. People live in tiny houses, and occasionally there's space enough for a courtyard. To get there, take rue de l'Eglise.

Jean Cocteau, the painter, writer, filmmaker, and well-respected dilettante, spent a year (1956–57) painting frescoes on the 14th-century walls of the Romanesque **Chapelle St-Pierre,** quai de la Douane/rue des Marinières (© **04-93-76-90-70**). He presented it to "the fishermen of Villefranche in homage to the Prince of Apostles, the patron of fishermen." One panel pays tribute to the Gypsies of the Stes-Maries-de-la-Mer. In the apse is a depiction of the miracle of St. Peter walking on the water, not knowing that an angel supports him. Villefranche's women, in their regional costumes, are honored on the left side of the narthex. The chapel charges 2€ admission for everyone (adults and children). It is open December 15 to November 15 Tuesday to Sunday 10am to noon and 4 to 8pm. (It's closed Nov 16–Dec 14)

WHERE TO STAY

Hôtel Versailles   Several blocks from the harbor and outside the main part of town, this three-story hotel gives you a perspective of the entire coast. The hotel offers comfortably furnished rooms and suites (suitable for up to three) with big windows and panoramas. Guests can order breakfast or lunch on the roof terrace. Rooms are clean and bright with comfortable beds.

7 av. Princesse-Grace-de-Monaco, 06230 Villefranche-sur-Mer. © **04-93-76-52-52.** Fax 04-93-01-97-48. www.hotelversailles.com. 46 units. 130€–260€ double; 250€–350€ suite. AE, DC, MC, V. Free parking. Closed Nov–Mar. **Amenities:** Restaurant; pool (outdoor); room service. *In room:* A/C, TV, Wi-Fi (10€ for 3 hr.).

Hôtel Welcome ★   This is as good as it gets in Villefranche. The Welcome was a favorite of author and filmmaker Jean Cocteau. In this six-story villa hotel outfitted with shutters and balconies, everything has been modernized and extensively renovated. Try for a fifth-floor room overlooking the water. All the midsize to spacious rooms are comfortably furnished. The sidewalk cafe is the focal point of town life. The on-site wine bar and the restaurant, St-Pierre, have open fireplaces and fruitwood furniture.

1 quai Amiral-Courbet, 06231 Villefranche-sur-Mer. © **04-93-76-27-62.** Fax 04-93-76-27-66. www.welcomehotel.com. 36 units. 98€–228€ double; 214€–380€ suite. AE, DC, MC, V. Closed Nov 10–Dec 20. **Amenities:** Bar; babysitting; Internet (free); room service. *In room:* A/C, TV, hair dryer, minibar.

Villa Vauban (Value   Your hosts, Alan and Brenda, are an English couple who have invested a lot of time and money in restoring this once-neglected property, turning it into a cozy nest for today's visitors. The location is adjacent to the old citadel, and the hotel opens onto a secluded garden. Five of the units are in the older main building with the remaining rooms in a wing with direct access to the garden, where breakfast can be taken. Guests meet and mingle in the elegant guest lounge.

11 av. Général de Gaulle, 06230 Villefranche-sur-Mer. ©/fax **04-93-55-94-51.** www.hotelvillavauban.com. 9 units. 95€–165€ double; 115€–190€ suite. MC, V. Free parking. **Amenities:** Breakfast room; Wi-Fi (free). *In room:* A/C, TV.

WHERE TO DINE

Chez Michel's FRENCH/PROVENÇALE   This bustling and animated brasserie is owned and managed by the husband-and-wife team Michel and Michelle. The setting is a cozily unpretentious dining room lined with Provençal landscapes. Well-prepared dishes of fresh ingredients include a filet of beef Rossini (layered with foie gras), wok-fried calamari, grilled sea bass with a tapenade of olives, rack of lamb with Provençal herbs, roasted veal with mustard sauce, and a roster of fresh chargrilled fish of the day that is usually served either with a basil-flavored vinaigrette or with lemon-flavored butter sauce. Salads, including versions with shrimp, are excellent.

Place Amélie Pollonnais. (© **04-93-76-73-24.** Reservations recommended. Main courses 16€–24€; fixed-price menus 22€–27€. AE, MC, V. Wed–Mon noon–3pm and 7–11pm.

La Mère Germaine ★ SEAFOOD   This is the best of the string of restaurants on the port. Plan to relax over lunch while watching fishermen repair their nets. Mère Germaine opened the place in the 1930s. These days a descendant, Remy Blouin, handles the cuisine, producing bouillabaisse celebrated across the Riviera. We recommend grilled sea bass with fennel, sole Tante Marie (stuffed with mushroom purée), lobster ravioli with shellfish sauce, and beef filet with garlic and seasonal vegetables. Perfectly roasted *carré d'agneau* (lamb) is prepared for two.

Quai Courbet. (© **04-93-01-71-39.** www.meregermaine.com. Reservations recommended. Main courses 25€–48€; fixed-price menu 41€; bouillabaisse 58€. AE, DC, MC, V. Daily noon–2:30pm and 7–10pm. Closed mid-Nov to Christmas.

8   ST-JEAN-CAP-FERRAT ★

938km (583 miles) S of Paris; 10km (6 miles) E of Nice

This place has been called "Paradise Found"—of all the oases along the Côte d'Azur, none has quite the snob appeal of Cap-Ferrat. It's a 15km (9-mile) promontory sprinkled with luxurious villas, outlined by sheltered bays, beaches, and coves. The vegetation is lush. The harbor of St-Jean accommodates yachts and fishing boats.

ESSENTIALS
GETTING THERE   Most visitors drive or take a **bus** or **taxi** from the rail station at nearby Beaulieu. Buses from the station at Beaulieu depart hourly for Cap-Ferrat; the one-way fare is 1€. There's also bus service from Nice. For bus information and schedules, call (© **04-93-85-64-44.** By **car** from Nice, take N7 east.

VISITOR INFORMATION   The **Office de Tourisme** is on 59 av. Denis-Séméria (© **04-93-76-08-90;** fax 04-93-76-16-67; www.ville-saint-jean-cap-ferrat.fr).

SEEING THE SIGHTS
One way to enjoy the scenery here is to wander on some of the public paths. The most scenic goes from **Plage de Paloma** to **Pointe St-Hospice,** where a panoramic view of the Riviera landscape unfolds.

You can also wander around the hamlet **St-Jean,** a colorful fishing village with bars, bistros, and inns.

Everyone tries to visit the **Villa Mauresque,** avenue Somerset-Maugham, but it's closed to the public. Near the cape, it's where Maugham spent his final years. When tourists tried to visit him, he proclaimed that he wasn't one of the local sights. One man did manage to crash through the gate, and when he encountered the author, Maugham snarled, "What do you think I am, a monkey in a cage?"

Once the property of King Leopold II of Belgium, the **Villa Les Cèdres** lies west of the port of St-Jean. Although you can't visit the villa, you can go to the nearby **Parc Zoologique,** boulevard du Général-de-Gaulle, northwest of the peninsula (© **04-93-76-04-98;** www.zoocapferrat.com). It's open May to September daily 9:30am to 7pm; March, April, and October daily 9:30am to 6pm (closed Nov–Feb). Admission is 15€ for adults, 11€ for students and children 3 to 10. This private zoo is in the basin of a drained lake. It houses a wide variety of reptiles, birds, and animals in outdoor cages.

Musée Ile-de-France (aka Villa Ephrussi de Rothschild) ★★   Built by Baronne Ephrussi de Rothschild, this is one of the Côte d'Azur's legendary villas. Born a Rothschild, the baronne married a Hungarian banker and friend of her father, about whom even the museum's curator knows little. She died in 1934, leaving the Italianate building and its gardens to the Institut de France on behalf of the Académie des Beaux-Arts. The museum preserves the wealth of her collection: 18th-century furniture; Tiepolo ceilings; Savonnerie carpets; screens and panels from the Far East; tapestries from Gobelin, Aubusson, and Beauvais; Fragonard drawings; Boucher canvases; Sèvres porcelain; and more. The gardens contain fragments of statuary from churches, monasteries, and palaces. An entire section is planted with cacti.

Av. Denis-Séméria. © **04-93-01-45-90.** www.villa-ephrussi.com. Admission 10€ adults, 7.50€ students and children 7–18. Feb–Oct daily 10am–6pm (until 7pm July–Aug); Nov–Jan Mon–Fri 2–6pm, Sat–Sun 10am–6pm.

WHERE TO STAY
Very Expensive
Grand Hôtel du Cap-Ferrat ★★★   One of the best features of this early-1900s palace is its location: at the tip of the peninsula in the midst of a 5.6-hectare (14-acre) garden of semitropical trees and manicured lawns. It has been the retreat of the international elite since 1908 and occupies the same celestial status as the Réserve and Métropole in Beaulieu (see "Beaulieu," below). Its cuisine even equals the Métropole's. Parts of the exterior have open loggias and big arched windows; you can also enjoy the views from the elaborately flowering terrace over the sea. Accommodations look as if the late Princess Grace might settle in comfortably: They're generally spacious and open to sea views. The beach is accessible by funicular from the main building. The hotel is open year-round.

71 bd. du Général-de-Gaulle, 06230 St-Jean-Cap-Ferrat. © **04-93-76-50-52.** Fax 04-93-76-04-52. www. grand-hotel-cap-ferrat.com. 72 units. 250€–1,600€ double; 850€–4,200€ suite. AE, DC, MC, V. Indoor parking 90€; outdoor parking free. Closed Dec–Apr. **Amenities:** 2 restaurants; 2 bars; babysitting; bikes; concierge; health club & spa; pool (outdoor); room service. *In room:* A/C, TV, hair dryer, minibar, Wi-Fi (free).

La Voile d'Or ★★   Established in 1966, the "Golden Sail" is a tour de force. It offers intimate luxury in a converted 19th-century villa at the edge of the little fishing port and yacht harbor, with a panoramic coast view. It's equal to the Grand Hôtel in every feature except cuisine, which is just a notch lower. The guest rooms, lounges, and restaurant open onto terraces. Accommodations are individually decorated, with hand-painted reproductions, carved gilt headboards, baroque paneled doors, parquet floors, antique clocks, and paintings. Guests gather on the canopied outer terrace for lunch and in a stately room with Spanish armchairs and white wrought-iron chandeliers for dinner.

31 av. Jean-Mermoz, 06230 St-Jean-Cap-Ferrat. © **04-93-01-13-13.** Fax 04-93-76-11-17. www.lavoiledor. fr. 45 units. 270€–782€ double; 512€–890€ suite. Rates include continental breakfast. AE, MC, V. Parking 25€. Closed mid-Nov to mid-Apr. **Amenities:** 2 restaurants; bar; babysitting; health club; Internet (free); 2 pools (outdoor); room service. *In room:* A/C, TV, hair dryer, minibar.

Expensive

Hôtel Royal Riviera ★★   Rising five graceful stories above the thin line that separates the quietly prestigious towns of St.-Jean and Beaulieu, this 1904 hotel evokes the Riviera's Gilded Age. Fans of Zelda and F. Scott Fitzgerald know they frolicked here in the '30s, creating pages that might have been torn from *Tender Is the Night*. In 1988, an unfortunate modernization destroyed much of the Belle Epoque charm of the palace, but Grace Leo-Andrieu, one of France's most inventive hoteliers, arrived from Paris to help the hostelry regain its old reputation. She can't help the location near the train tracks, which makes some of the front rooms noisy, but she's done everything else in her power to make the hotel ever more chic. It occupies a .4-hectare (1-acre) tract with a beach of its own, to which tons of sand are added at regular intervals. Bedrooms are posh and plush, with big windows, private balconies, deep sofas, and fruitwood armoires. The largest and most appealing are the corner units (any room ending in "16"). Regardless, each is charming and elegant.

3 av. Jean Monnet, 06230 St-Jean-Cap-Ferrat. ✆ **04-93-76-31-00.** Fax 04-93-01-23-07. www.royal-riviera. com. 96 units. 250€–870€ double; 700€–2,800€ suite. Rates include half-board. AE, DC, MC, V. Free parking. Closed Dec to mid-Jan. **Amenities:** 2 restaurants; bar; babysitting; pool (outdoor); room service. *In room:* A/C, TV, hair dryer, minibar, Wi-Fi (free).

Moderate

Hôtel Brise Marine   Built around 1878, this villa with front and rear terraces sits on a hillside. A long rose arbor, beds of subtropical flowers, palms, and pines provide an attractive setting. The atmosphere is casual and informal, and the rooms are comfortably but simply furnished. You can have breakfast in the beamed lounge or under the rose trellis. The little corner bar serves afternoon drinks.

58 av. Jean-Mermoz, 06230 St-Jean-Cap-Ferrat. ✆ **04-93-76-04-36.** Fax 04-93-76-11-49. www.hotel-brisemarine.com. 18 units. 155€–178€ double. AE, DC, MC, V. Parking 13€. Closed Nov–Jan. **Amenities:** Bar; room service. *In room:* A/C, TV, hair dryer, minibar, Wi-Fi (free).

Hôtel Le Panoramic ⓥⓐⓛⓤⓔ   This hotel, built in 1958 with a red-tile roof and much style and glamour, is one of the more affordable choices here. You'll reach the hotel by passing over a raised bridge lined with colorful flowers. The well-furnished rooms have a sweeping view of the water and the forest leading down to it. Accommodations are a bit small, but each is fitted with fine linens. Breakfast is the only meal served.

3 av. Albert-1er, 06230 St-Jean-Cap-Ferrat. ✆ **04-93-76-00-37.** Fax 04-93-76-15-78. www.hotel-lepanoramic. com. 20 units. 145€–175€ double. AE, DC, MC, V. Free parking. Closed mid-Nov to Dec 26. **Amenities:** Room service. *In room:* TV, Wi-Fi (free).

WHERE TO DINE

Capitaine Cook ★ PROVENÇALE/SEAFOOD   Next door to the fancy La Voile d'Or hotel (see above), a few blocks uphill from the village center, this restaurant specializes in hearty portions of seafood. You'll have a panoramic view of the coast from the terrace; inside, the decor is maritime and rugged. Oysters are a specialty; they're served on the half shell or in several creative ways with sauces and herbs. Roasted catch of the day is the mainstay, but filet mignon is also popular. The staff speaks English.

11 av. Jean-Mermoz. ✆ **04-93-76-02-66.** Main courses 17€–30€; fixed-price menu 26€–31€. MC, V. Fri–Tues noon–2pm; Thurs–Tues 7:15–11pm. Closed mid-Nov to Dec.

La Luna Rossa ★ ITALIAN   With the Italian border so close at hand, it's only natural that an Italian restaurant would open at this resort. Many different types of savory pastas are offered, along with the catch of the day which can be grilled if you wish. A wide selection of meats, freshly made salads, and other regional dishes, such as pan-fried squid, are a regular feature.

2 av. Denis-Séméria. © **04-93-76-03-97.** Reservations required. Main courses 18€–26€. MC, V. Wed–Sun noon–3pm; Tues–Sun 7:30–10:30pm.

Le Sloop FRENCH/PROVENÇALE   Le Sloop is the most popular and most reasonably priced bistro in this expensive area. Outfitted in blue and white inside and out, it sits at the edge of the port, overlooking the harbor. A meal may begin with a salad of flap mushrooms steeped *en cappuccino* with liquefied foie gras, or perhaps tartare of salmon with aioli and lemon crepes. You may follow with a filet of sea bass served with red-wine sauce, or a mixed fish fry of three kinds of Mediterranean fish, bound together with olive oil and truffles. Dessert may include strawberry soup with sweet white wine and apricot ice cream or any of about seven other choices, each based on "the red fruits of the region." The regional wines are reasonably priced.

Au Nouveau Port. © **04-93-01-48-63.** www.restaurantsloop.com. Reservations recommended. Main courses 28€–45€; fixed-price menu 27€ July–Aug. AE, MC, V. Thurs–Tues noon–2pm; Thurs–Mon 7–10pm. Closed mid-Nov to mid-Dec.

9 BEAULIEU ★

938km (583 miles) S of Paris; 10km (6 miles) E of Nice; 11km (7 miles) W of Monte Carlo

Protected from the cold north winds blowing down from the Alps, Beaulieu-sur-Mer is often referred to as "La Petite Afrique" (Little Africa). Like Menton, it has the mildest climate along the Côte d'Azur and is especially popular with the wintering wealthy. Beaulieu is graced with lush vegetation, including oranges, lemons, and bananas, as well as palms.

ESSENTIALS

GETTING THERE   **Trains** connect Beaulieu with Nice, Monaco, and the rest of the Côte d'Azur. For rail information, call © **36-35,** or visit **www.voyages-sncf.com**. **Bus** no. 100 leaves Nice every 15 minutes during the day stopping at Beaulieu-sur-Mer (trip time: 20 min.). Tickets cost 1.30€. Most visitors **drive** from Nice on the Moyenne Corniche or the coastal highway.

VISITOR INFORMATION   The **Office de Tourisme** is on place Georges-Clemenceau (© **04-93-01-02-21;** fax 04-93-01-44-04; http://otbeaulieu.free.fr).

EXPLORING THE TOWN

Villa Kérylos ★★, rue Gustave-Eiffel (© **04-93-76-44-09**), is a replica of an ancient Greek residence, painstakingly designed and built by the archaeologist Théodore Reinach, who mimicked ancient Grecian life here for 20 years. Inside the cabinets are filled with a collection of Greek figurines and ceramics. But most interesting is the reconstructed Greek furniture, much of which would be fashionable today. One curious mosaic depicts the slaying of the Minotaur and provides its own labyrinth (if you try to trace the path, expect to stay for weeks). It is open February 15 to November 1 daily 10am to 6pm (until 7pm July–Aug); November 2 to February 14 Saturday and Sunday 10am to 6pm. Admission is 8.50€ adults, 6.20€ for seniors and children 7 to 18, and free for children 6 and under.

Casino de Beaulieu, avenue Fernand-Dunan (📞 **04-93-76-48-00**; www.casinobeaulieu. com), was built in the Art Nouveau style in 1903. The slot machines are open daily, without charge, from 11am to 4am. The *salles des grands jeux* are open daily 9am to 4am. Management strongly recommends that men wear jackets. Entrance to the *grands jeux* costs 11€, and patrons must present a photo ID.

Also in the casino is a deluxe restaurant, **La Coupole** (📞 **04-93-76-48-00**), which overlooks the Mediterranean. The upscale *brasserie de luxe* serves seasonal gourmet cuisine that might include snails in garlic butter, roast breast of duckling with citrus sauce or with figs, and a wide array of grilled fresh fish. It's open Wednesday to Sunday from noon to 2pm and 7pm to midnight.

The town boasts an important church, the late-19th-century **Eglise de Sacré-Coeur,** a quasi-Byzantine, quasi-Gothic mishmash at 13 bd. du Maréchal-Leclerc (📞 **04-93-35-70-45**). With the same address and phone is the 12th-century Romanesque chapel of **Santa Maria de Olivo,** used mostly for temporary exhibits of painting, sculpture, and civic lore. Both sites are open daily from 8am to 7pm.

As you walk along the **seafront promenade,** you can see many stately Belle Epoque villas that evoke the days when Beaulieu was the very height of fashion. Although you can't go inside, you'll see signs indicating Villa Namouna, which once belonged to Gordon Bennett, the owner of the *New York Herald,* who sent Stanley to Africa to find Livingstone; and Villa Léonine, former home of the marquess of Salisbury.

A DAY AT THE BEACH

Don't expect soft sands. Some seasons might have more sand than others, depending on tides and storms, but usually the shore surface is covered with light-gray gravel that has a finer texture than beaches at other resorts nearby. The longer of the town's two free public beaches is **Petite Afrique,** adjacent to the yacht basin; the shorter is **Baie des Fourmis,** beneath the casino. **Africa Plage** (📞 **04-93-01-11-00**) rents mattresses for 8€ per day and sells snacks and drinks.

WHERE TO STAY
Very Expensive

La Réserve de Beaulieu ★★★ A Relais & Châteaux member, this pink-and-white *fin de siècle* palace is one of the Riviera's most famous hotels. Here you can sit, have an aperitif, and watch the sunset while a pianist plays Mozart. A number of the lounges open onto a courtyard with bamboo chairs, grass borders, and urns of flowers. The social life revolves around the main drawing room. The individually decorated guest rooms range widely in size and design; most overlook the Mediterranean, and some have a view of the mountains. Some have private balconies. The dining room has a frescoed ceiling, parquet floors, chandeliers, and windows facing the Mediterranean.

5 bd. du Maréchal-Leclerc, 06310 Beaulieu-sur-Mer. 📞 **04-93-01-00-01.** Fax 04-93-01-28-99. www. reservebeaulieu.com. 39 units. 180€–1,240€ double; 620€–3,160€ suite. AE, DC, MC, V. Parking 36€. Closed mid-Oct to mid-Dec. **Amenities:** Restaurant; bar; babysitting; concierge; exercise room; room service. *In room:* A/C, TV, hair dryer, minibar, Wi-Fi (free).

Moderate

Inter-Hôtel Frisia Most of the Frisia's rooms, decorated in a modern style, open onto views of the harbor; units boasting that water view are the most expensive. Two spacious suites with kitchenettes are in free-standing villas near the hotel's main building. Public areas include a sunny garden and inviting lounges. English is widely spoken here, and the management makes foreign guests feel especially welcome. Breakfast is the only meal served, but many reasonably priced restaurants are nearby.

2 bd. Eugène-Gauthier, 06310 Beaulieu-sur-Mer. © **04-93-01-01-04.** Fax 04-93-01-31-92. www.frisia-beaulieu.com. 32 units. 88€–135€ double; 175€–195€ suite. AE, MC, V. Parking 9€. Closed Nov 13–Dec 17. **Amenities:** Bar; babysitting; Internet (free); room service. *In room:* A/C, TV, hair dryer, minibar.

Inexpensive

Hôtel Le Havre Bleu (Value)   This is a great little bargain if you don't need a lot of services and amenities. Le Havre Bleu has one of the prettiest facades of any inexpensive hotel in town. In a former Victorian villa, the hotel has arched ornate windows and a front garden dotted with flowering urns. The impeccable guest rooms are comfortable and functional. The in-room amenities are few, except for a phone; the compact bathrooms have showers. Breakfast is the only meal served.

29 bd. du Maréchal-Joffre, 06310 Beaulieu-sur-Mer. © **04-93-01-01-40.** Fax 04-93-01-29-92. www.lehavreblue.com. 20 units. 62€–77€ double; 92€–97€ triple or quad. AE, MC, V. Free parking. **Amenities:** Room service; babysitting; Wi-Fi (free). *In room:* A/C, TV, Wi-Fi (in some; free).

Hôtel Marcellin   The early-20th-century Marcellin is a good budget selection in an otherwise high-priced resort. Built around 1900 for a local family, the sprawling, much-altered villa was divided into two about 25 years ago, and half was converted into this pleasant, cost-conscious hotel, while the other half remains a private home. The restored rooms come with homelike amenities and southern exposure. They're small to midsize, but comfortably furnished. The location isn't bad, either: in the congested town, near its western periphery, only a 5-minute walk from the beach. Breakfast is the only meal served, but many restaurants are nearby.

18 av. Albert-1er, 06310 Beaulieu-sur-Mer. © **04-93-01-01-69.** Fax 04-93-01-37-43. www.hotel-marcellin.com. 21 units. 60€–83€ double. MC, V. **Amenities:** Bar; babysitting; room service. *In room:* A/C, TV, fridge, hair dryer, Wi-Fi (free).

WHERE TO DINE

The African Queen INTERNATIONAL   Named for the Hollywood classic by its movie-loving founders, this hip and popular restaurant is filled with posters of Hepburn and Bogie and has a jungle-inspired decor. Much influenced by the United States, it has welcomed stars such as Jack Nicholson, Raymond Burr, Robert Wagner, and Diana Ross during the Cannes Film Festival. Menu specialties are a *dégustation de bouillabaisse,* African curry of lamb or beef and served like a rijsttafel with about a dozen condiments, or any of an array of steaks, fish, or shellfish. Less expensive are the seven or eight kinds of pizza, which even visiting Italians claim are very good. The bouillabaisse is vastly more expensive than the other main courses and should be ordered a day in advance. No one will mind if you stop in for only a strawberry daiquiri or piña colada. The check is presented in a videocassette case labeled—what else?—*The African Queen.*

Port de Plaisance. © **04-93-01-10-85.** www.africanqueen.fr. Reservations recommended. Main courses 18€–32€; pizzas 10€–12€. MC, V. Daily noon–midnight.

La Pignatelle (Value) FRENCH/PROVENÇALE   Despite its relatively low prices, La Pignatelle prides itself on the fresh ingredients in its robust *provençale* cuisine. Specialties include mushroom-stuffed ravioli with truffled cream sauce, succulent *soupe de poissons* from which the kitchen has labored to remove the bones, cassoulet of mussels, monkfish steak garnished with olive oil and herbs, fricassee of sea bass with shrimp, and *petite friture du pays,* which incorporates small fish with old Provençal traditions.

10 rue de Quincenet. ✆ **04-93-01-03-37.** Reservations recommended. Main courses 9€–27€; fixed-price lunch 15€–32€; fixed-price dinner 22€–32€. MC, V. Thurs–Tues noon–2pm and 7–10pm. Closed Nov.

Le Catalan (Value) FRENCH/CATALAN/INTERNATIONAL   This place is endlessly popular, and endlessly busy, thanks to relatively low prices and succulent food. You'll dine within any of three separate dining rooms or on a terrace overlooking the sea. The pizza comes in at least a dozen varieties and is baked to bubbling perfection in a wood-burning beehive oven. More substantial fare includes paella and zarzuela, pasta with shellfish, and a full roster of grilled meats and fish. Everybody from dockworkers in grimy clothes to plump society matrons from Paris dines here virtually elbow to elbow in an establishment that's acclaimed for its *égalité.*

52 bd. Général Leclerc. ✆ **04-93-01-02-78.** Reservations recommended. Pizzas 7€–12€; main courses 8€–20€. MC, V. Mon–Sat noon–2:30pm and 7–11pm.

Les Agaves ★★MODERN FRENCH   One of the most stylish restaurants in Beaulieu is in an early-1900s villa across the street from the railway station. U.S.-based publications such as *Bon Appétit* have praised the cuisine. Of note are curry-enhanced scallops with garlic-flavored tomatoes and parsley, terrine of pork with confit of onions, lobster salad with mango, bouillabaisse, rockfish soup, chopped shrimp with Provençal herbs, and several preparations of foie gras. Filet of sea bass with truffles and champagne sauce is delectable.

4 av. Maréchal Foch. ✆ **04-93-01-13-12.** Reservations recommended. Main courses 26€–35€; fixed-price menu 38€. AE, MC, V. Daily 7:30–10pm. Closed Nov 15–30.

10   EZE & LA TURBIE ★

941km (585 miles) S of Paris; 11km (7 miles) NE of Nice

The hamlets of Eze and La Turbie, though 6.4km (4 miles) apart, have so many similarities that most of France's tourist officials speak of them as if they were one. Both boast fortified feudal centers high in the hills overlooking the Provençal coast built during the early Middle Ages to stave off raids from corsairs. Clinging to the rocky hillsides around these hamlets are upscale villas, many of which were built in the 1950s by retirees. Culturally and fiscally linked to nearby Monaco, both Eze and La Turbie have a full-time population of fewer than 3,000.

ESSENTIALS

GETTING THERE   Eze (also known as Eze-Village) is connected to Nice by train and bus. A Corniche **train** leaves Nice twice an hour during the day, stopping at Eze just 20 minutes later; a one-way fare is 2.20€. **Bus** no. 82 from Nice departs 14 times a day for Eze, Monday to Saturday (with six departures on Sun); the 20-minute trip costs 1.30€.

By **car,** Eze is accessible via the Moyenne (Middle) Corniche road; La Turbie is accessible via the Grande (Upper) Corniche. Signs are positioned along the coastal road indicating the direction motorists should take to reach either of the hamlets.

The walk from Eze to the promontory of La Turbie is a steep climb of 6km (4 miles). You can also take a taxi from Eze. Most visitors travel to La Turbie by car.

The **Office de Tourisme** is on place du Général-de-Gaulle, Eze-Village (© **04-93-41-26-00**; www.eze-riviera.com).

EXPLORING THE TOWNS

The medieval cores of both towns contain restored galleries, boutiques, and artisans' shops. Two art galleries of particular note within Eze are **Galerie Sevek,** rue du Barri (© **04-93-41-06-22**), and **Galerie Doussot,** rue Principale (© **04-93-41-01-62**).

The leading attraction in Eze is the **Jardin d'Eze** ★, boulevard du Jardin-Exotique (© **04-93-41-10-30**), a showcase of exotic plants in Eze-Village, at the pinnacle of the town's highest hill. Admission is 5€ for adults, 2.50€ for students and ages 12 to 25, free for children 11 and under. In July and August, it's open daily 9am to 8pm; the rest of the year, it opens daily at 9am and closes between 5 and 7:30pm, depending on the time of sunset.

La Turbie boasts a ruined monument erected by Roman emperor Augustus in 6 B.C., the **Trophée des Alps (Trophy of the Alps)** ★. It's near a rock formation known as La Tête de Chien, at the highest point along the Grand Corniche, 450m (1,476 ft.) above sea level. The Roman Senate ordered the creation of the monument, which many locals call La Trophée d'Auguste, to celebrate the subjugation of the people of the French Alps by the Roman armies.

A short distance from the monument is the **Musée du Trophée d'Auguste,** rue Albert-1er, La Turbie (© **04-93-41-20-84**), a mini-museum containing finds from digs nearby and information about the monument's restoration. It's open May to September daily 9:30am to 1:30pm and 2:30 to 6:30pm, October to April daily 10am to 1:30pm and 2:30 to 5pm. Admission is 5€ for adults, 3.50€ for students and ages 18 to 25, free for children 17 and under. It's closed January 1, May 1, November, and December 25.

WHERE TO STAY

Auberge Le Soleil   This pale-pink late-19th-century villa is a few steps from the Basse Corniche. It has a quiet rear terrace, and the decor features rattan chairs, exposed brick, and lots of brass. In 2004, it was bought and transformed by the congenial, Italian-born Ester Parodi, who manages to imbue everyday situations with a welcome humor. Simply furnished doubles draw mainly a summer crowd, though the inn is open all year. Bedrooms are small but decently furnished. Half-board is a good deal here—the Mediterranean meals are satisfying and wine is included.

44 av. de la Liberté, 06360 Eze-Bord-de-Mer. © **04-93-01-51-46.** Fax 04-93-01-58-40. www.auberge-lesoleil.com. 8 units. 80€ double. Half-board 80€ per person extra. AE, DC, MC, V. **Amenities:** Restaurant. *In room:* TV, hair dryer, minibar.

Château Eza ★★★   This château is the former Riviera home of Prince William of Sweden. It stands at the edge of a cliff at 396m (1,300 ft.) looking out over the resort of St-Jean-Cap-Ferrat. Entered on a narrow cobblestone street, it offers sumptuous bedrooms, a celebrated gourmet cuisine, and service fit for royalty. The elegant bedrooms are spread over a cluster of restored buildings dating from the Middle Ages. Each of the guest rooms is reached by walking under stone passageways past cavelike shops. Although the setting is ancient, the rooms are thoroughly modernized, with private bathrooms, charming fireplaces, and private balconies opening onto panoramic views. Canopied beds, art objects, beautiful carpets, and valuable tapestries set the tone. This is as close as the Riviera gets to fantasy living.

units. 220€–655€ double; 640€–1,120€ suite. AE, DC, MC, V. Closed Nov to mid-Dec. **Amenities:** Restaurant; bar; babysitting. *In room:* A/C, TV, hair dryer, minibar, Wi-Fi (27€).

Hostellerie du Château de la Chèvre d'Or ★★★ One of the Eastern Riviera's grandest resort hotels, this miniature-village retreat was built in the 1920s in neo-Gothic style. The Relais & Châteaux property is a complex of village houses, all with views of the coastline. But unlike most villages in the area, this one doesn't have a beach. The decor of the "Golden Goat" maintains its character while adding modern comfort. The spacious guest rooms are filled with quality furnishings. Even if you don't spend the night, try to visit for a drink in the lounge to take in the panoramic view.

Rue du Barri, 06360 Eze-Village. ℂ **04-92-10-66-66.** Fax 04-93-41-06-72. www.chevredor.com. 35 units. 280€–870€ double; 950€–2,900€ suite. AE, DC, MC, V. Closed mid-Nov to early Mar. **Amenities:** 3 restaurants; bar; babysitting; exercise room w/sauna; Internet (free); room service. *In room:* A/C, TV, hair dryer, minibar.

La Bastide aux Camelias ★★ ⓕ**Finds** As its name suggests, an air of romantic nostalgic hangs over this super B&B, one of the best hideaways along the Eastern Riviera. Set in the middle of the park of the Grande Corniche, the little inn lies close to Eze Village, opening onto panoramic views in all directions. After a lovely French breakfast on the veranda, the day is yours. The swimming pool, surrounded by greenery, is a magnet, and there are such luxuries as a Jacuzzi, sauna, and a little spa. You can even play a game of boules in the shade of sherry trees. Each bedroom is individually decorated with softly draped fabrics, making for a comfortable, intimate atmosphere.

Rte. De l'Adret, 06360 Eze. ℂ **04-93-41-13-68.** www.bastideauxcamelias.com. 5 units. 110€–150€ double; 200€ suite. Rates include continental breakfast. Credit cards not accepted. **Amenities:** Internet (free); Jacuzzi; pool (outdoor); spa. *In room:* Fridge, hair dryer, no phone.

La Vielle Bergerie ★ ⓕ**Finds** Those who'd like to go the B&B route along the coast between Nice and Monaco could do no better than this lodging near the village of Eze. Roselyne Carpentier is the gracious innkeeper; living here is like being a guest in an old-fashioned Provençal home where everything is immaculate and beautifully decorated with traditional styling. The one bedroom comes with a private bathroom. You approach the old house at the entrance to the forest park, De La Revère, at the bend of a small road. The house is surrounded by terraces and gardens, including olive trees, and umbrella-shaded tables and chairs are placed out next to an old stone-built bread oven.

La Vieille Bergerie, 585 rte. de la Revère, 06360 Eze-Village. ℂ/fax **04-93-41-10-22.** www.lavieille bergerie.com. 1 unit. 100€–120€ double. Rates include continental breakfast. No credit cards. **Amenities:** Breakfast room. *In room:* No phone.

WHERE TO DINE

Le Troubadour FRENCH/PROVENÇALE The stone-fronted medieval house that contains this well-known restaurant has received diners such as local athletes and drag-race drivers from nearby Monaco. Today, within three dining rooms, you can order succulent and flavorful dishes that include braised rabbit in aspic, served with warm hearts of artichoke, foie gras, and carrots; a delightful filet of John Dory with stuffed and deep-fried zucchini blossoms; roasted rack of lamb with parsley sauce; and other dishes that showcase some aspect of the Mediterranean diet. You'll find the place close to the village church in the upper heights of Eze Village.

4 rue du Brec, Eze Village. ℂ **04-93-41-19-03.** Reservations recommended. Main courses 22€–38€; fixed-price menus 39€–52€. MC, V. Tues–Sat 1–2:30pm and 7:30–10pm. Closed Nov 15–Dec 20.

11 PEILLON ★★

19km (12 miles) NW of Nice

This fortified medieval town is the most spectacular "perched village" along the Côte d'Azur. At 300m (1,000 ft.) above the sea, it's also unspoiled, unlike those others filled with day-trippers and souvenir shops. The main incentive to visit Peillon is the town itself; its semifortified architecture makes you feel that even today it could lock its doors, bar its windows, and keep any intruder at bay.

ESSENTIALS

GETTING THERE   Only two **trains** a day stop near Peillon at St-Thècle, an antiquated station connecting Nice with Coni, a town across the border in Italy. For rail information and schedules, call ✆ **36-35,** or visit **www.voyages-sncf.com**. While you will find lots of dilapidated local color at the railway station of St-Thècle, you won't find taxis waiting or a bus service to carry you on to Peillon. If you can find a phone in St-Thècle, the phone number of the best local **cab service** is ✆ **06-13-43-89-24.** Transit from the railway station at St-Thècle to Peillon costs about 12€ each way. Most backpackers continue into Peillon by hitchhiking.

The T.R.A.M. bus line operates four buses a day from Nice, with multiple stops en route (trip time: around 25 min.). Don't expect it to be convenient—you'll be dropped off about 3km (2 miles) from Peillon's center, at a tiny crossroads known as Le Moulin. Many hardy souls opt to continue on to the center by foot because there's no transport into Peillon. For **bus information,** call ✆ **08-00-06-01-06.**

Few other towns in Provence are as easy to reach by **car** and as inconvenient to reach by public transportation. Peillon is an easy 25-minute drive (depending on traffic) northeast from Nice; take D2204 to D21.

VISITOR INFORMATION   The Peillon tourist office is located on the very short rue Centrale in Peillon-Village (✆ **06-24-97-42-25**), and is open for limited hours throughout the year. If the staff happens to not be open at the time of your call, the tourist office in Nice (✆ **04-93-79-92-04**) is usually well informed about the attractions and allures of Pellion. Barring that, you can always contact the Town Hall (La Mairie) of Peillon (✆ **04-93-79-91-04**), where staff members have in the past been extraordinarily helpful. Additionally, the receptionists at the town's most colorful inn, Auberge de la Madone (see below), are usually informative about the layout and attractions within their town.

EXPLORING THE TOWN

Specific sites of interest include the town's severely dignified parish church, the **Eglise St-Sauveur,** open daily from 8am to around 6pm. Built in a simple country-baroque style, it's the site of many marriages, baptisms, and wedding ceremonies. Another site of interest is the 15th-century **Chapelle des Pénitents Blancs,** on place August-Arnuls. It's usually locked, so visits require that you first drop by the Tourist Office on la rue Centrale in Peillon-Village (✆ **06-24-97-42-25**)—if it's convenient and if he or she isn't busy, an employee will accompany you with a key and wait for you while you admire the interior. The service is free, but a gratuity is appreciated. If you plunk .20€ into a machine near the gate, lights will illuminate the interior's noteworthy frescoes. Painted in 1491 by Jean Cannavesio, they represent the eight stages of the Passion of Christ.

The narrow streets radiate outward from the town's "foyer," **place Auguste-Arnuls,** which is shaded by rows of plantain trees centered around a fountain that has splashed water from its basin since 1800. Some of the streets are enclosed with vaulting and accented with potted geraniums and strands of ivy.

If you're in the mood for walking, consider a 2-hour, 12km (7½-mile) northward hike across the dry and rocky landscape to Peillon's remote, smaller sister, Peille.

WHERE TO STAY & DINE

Auberge de la Madone ★★   This hotel, with its well-recommended restaurant, is the leading choice and has been since it opened back in the 1930s. The oldest section of the stone-sided complex of buildings dates from the 12th century. Evocative of a sprawling Provençal *mas,* it gives you a real glimpse of a Provence from long ago. It's capped with terra-cotta tiles and draped with a small version of the hanging gardens of Babylon. On the opposite side of place Auguste-Arnuls from the rest of the village, its wide terrace opens onto a great view of the town's vertical, angular architecture. The guest rooms are comfortable and rustic, outfitted with Provençal themes and fabrics. The annex's accommodations are much simpler than those in the main building; rates depend on the plumbing and views.

The hotel restaurant is by far the most formal in town, serving lunch and dinner every day except Wednesday and during the annual winter closing. The menu can include unusual dishes such as *tourton des pénitents,* a salty tart enriched with 17 herbs, almonds, eggs, and cream; suckling lamb with garlic mashed potatoes and a tapenade of olives; farm-raised guinea fowl with a confit of pears; and a *pot-au-feu,* a savory kettle of seafood served with aioli. Fixed-price menus cost 32€ to 62€.

2 place Auguste Arnulf, 06440 Peillon. (℡) **04-93-79-91-17.** Fax 04-93-79-99-36. 20 units. Main building 95€–210€ double; 230€–390€ suite. Annex 42€–69€ double. AE, MC, V. Free parking. Closed Jan 9–31 and Nov 5–Dec 24. **Amenities:** Restaurant (closed Wed and Nov-Jan); bar. *In room:* TV, hair dryer, minibar, Wi-Fi (free).

12   MONACO ★★★

954km (593 miles) S of Paris; 18km (11 miles) E of Nice

The outspoken Katharine Hepburn once called Monaco "a pimple on the chin of the south of France." She wasn't referring to the principality's lack of beauty, but rather to the preposterous idea of having a little country, a feudal anomaly, taking up some of the Riviera's best coastline. Hemmed in by France on three sides and facing the Mediterranean, tiny Monaco staunchly maintains its independence. Even Charles de Gaulle couldn't force the late Prince Rainier to do away with his tax-free policy. As almost everybody in an overburdened world knows by now, the Monégasques do not pay taxes. Nearly all their country's revenue comes from tourism and gambling.

Monaco—or rather, its capital of Monte Carlo—has for a century been a symbol of glamour. Its legend was further enhanced by the 1956 marriage of the man who was at that time the world's most eligible bachelor, Prince Rainier III, to the American actress Grace Kelly. Ms. Kelly met the prince when she was in Cannes for the film festival to promote *To Catch a Thief,* the Hitchcock movie she made with Cary Grant. A journalist friend arranged a *Paris Match* photo shoot with the prince—and the rest is history. The

Monégasques welcomed the birth of daughter Caroline in 1957 but went wild at the birth of Albert, a male heir, in 1958. According to a 1918 treaty, Monaco will become an autonomous state under French protection if the ruling dynasty becomes extinct. However, the fact that Albert is still a bachelor has the entire principality concerned. The third royal daughter, Stephanie, was born in 1965.

Though not always happy in her role, Princess Grace won the respect and adoration of her people. In 1982, a sports car she was driving, with her daughter Stephanie as a passenger (not as the driver, as was viciously rumored), plunged over a cliff, killing Grace but only injuring Stephanie. The Monégasques still mourn her death.

Monaco became a property of the Grimaldi clan, a Genoese family, as early as 1297. With shifting loyalties, it has maintained something resembling independence ever since. In a fit of impatience the French annexed it in 1793, but the ruling family recovered it in 1814; however, the prince at that time couldn't bear to tear himself away from the pleasures of Paris for "dreary old Monaco."

ESSENTIALS

GETTING THERE   Monaco has rail, bus, and highway connections from other coastal cities, especially Nice. **Trains** arrive every 30 minutes from Cannes, Nice, Menton, and Antibes. For rail information, call ✆ **36-35,** or visit www.voyages-sncf.com. Monaco's railway station (Gare SNCF) is on avenue Prince Pierre. It's a long walk uphill from the train station to Monte Carlo. If you'd rather take a **taxi** but can't find one at the station, call ✆ **377-93-15-01-01.** You will face no border formalities when entering Monaco from mainland France.

In late 1999, Monaco opened an enormous train station .4km (¼ mile) east of the old station. This station has three exits on three levels, and if you don't know which exit to use, you might have trouble finding your hotel. Monaco is a confusing place to navigate, so you might want to pick up a free map at the station's tourist office (daily June–Sept 8:30am–7:30pm). Arriving at the Monaco train station after 9pm is like arriving on Wall Street after 9pm—it's desolate, without a soul on the street. On the bright side, Monaco restaurants serve dinner late, so you can usually get a full meal at least until 11pm.

Frequent **bus service** (every 15 min.) runs to Nice, Beaulieu, and Menton on line no. 100 of the French bus company **Rapides Côte d'Azur** (✆ **04-93-85-64-44;** www.rca. tm.fr). The trip from Nice to Monaco by bus takes a half-hour and costs 2.60€ round-trip or 1.30€ one-way. The times and prices are the same to Menton. The easiest place to catch a bus is in front of the gardens that face the Casino, but it also stops in front of the port (on bd. Albert-1er at the Stade Nautique stop) and at several other spots around town.

If you're **driving** from Nice to Monaco, take N7 northeast. The 19km (12-mile) drive takes about 35 minutes because of heavy traffic; Cannes to Monaco requires about 55 minutes. If driving from Paris, follow A6 to Lyon. In Lyon, take A7 south to Aix-en-Provence and A6 to Monaco.

VISITOR INFORMATION   The **Direction du Tourisme et des Congrés** office is at 2A bd. des Moulins (✆ **377-92-16-61-66;** fax 377-92-16-61-16; www.monaco-tourisme.com).

GETTING AROUND   The best way to get around Monaco is by **bus** (www.cam.mc), and you can buy bus cards, which cost 1.80€ per ride, directly on the bus. Bus stops are set up every few blocks on the main streets in town, including boulevard Albert-1er, avenue St-Martin in Monaco-Ville, and boulevard des Moulins in Monte Carlo. Buses go to all the major tourist sights; just look at the front of the bus to see the destination.

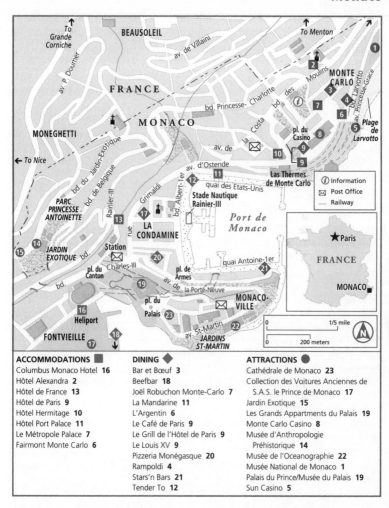

ACCOMMODATIONS ■
Columbus Monaco Hotel **16**
Hôtel Alexandra **2**
Hôtel de France **13**
Hôtel de Paris **9**
Hôtel Hermitage **10**
Hôtel Port Palace **11**
Le Métropole Palace **7**
Fairmont Monte Carlo **6**

DINING ◆
Bar et Bœuf **3**
Beefbar **18**
Joël Robuchon Monte-Carlo **7**
La Mandarine **11**
L'Argentin **6**
Le Café de Paris **9**
Le Grill de l'Hôtel de Paris **9**
Le Louis XV **9**
Pizzeria Monégasque **20**
Rampoldi **4**
Stars'n Bars **21**
Tender To **12**

ATTRACTIONS ●
Cathédrale de Monaco **23**
Collection des Voitures Anciennes de
  S.A.S. le Prince de Monaco **17**
Jardin Exotique **15**
Les Grands Appartments du Palais **19**
Monte Carlo Casino **8**
Musée d'Anthropologie
  Préhistorique **14**
Musée de l'Oceanographie **22**
Musée National de Monaco **1**
Palais du Prince/Musée du Palais **19**
Sun Casino **5**

For a **taxi,** call ☎ 377-93-15-01-01. Taxi stands are in front of the Casino on avenue de Monte-Carlo, at place des Moulins in Monte Carlo, at the Port de Monaco on avenue Président J. F. Kennedy, and in front of the Poste de Monte-Carlo on avenue Henry-Dunant. A **Hertz** car-rental office is at 27 bd. Albert-1er (☎ 377-93-50-79-60), and an **Avis** office is at 1 av. des Guelphs (☎ 377-97-97-18-55).

SPECIAL EVENTS   Two of the most-watched **car-racing events** in Europe are in January (Le Rallye) and May (the Grand Prix; www.monacograndprix.info). For more information, call ☎ 377-99-99-30-00. In June, Monte Carlo is home to a weeklong convention that attracts media moguls from virtually everywhere, **Le Festival International de la**

Number, Please: Monaco's Telephone System

Since 1996, Monaco's phone system has been independent of France.

To call Monaco from within France and the European Union, dial 00 (the access code for all international long-distance calls from France), followed by the **country code (377),** then the eight-digit local phone number. (Don't dial the 33 code; that's the country code for France.)

To call Monaco from North America, dial the international access code, 011, the country code, 377, then the eight-digit Monaco number.

To call any other country from within Monaco, dial 00 (the international access code), then the applicable country code, and the number. For example, to call Cannes, you would dial 00, 33 (France's country code), 4 (the city code, without the zero), and the eight-digit number.

Télévision, Grimaldi Forum, avenue Princesse-Grace (© **377-99-99-30-00**). Shows from all over the world are broadcast and judged on their merits.

EXPLORING THE PRINCIPALITY

The second-smallest state in Europe (Vatican City is the tiniest), Monaco comprises four parts. The Old Town, **Monaco-Ville,** on a promontory, "the Rock," 60m (200 ft.) high, is the seat of the royal palace and government building, as well as the Oceanographic Museum. To the west, **La Condamine,** the home of the Monégasques, is at the foot of the Old Town, forming its harbor and port sector. Up from the port (walking is steep in Monaco) is **Monte Carlo,** once the playground of European royalty and still the center for the wintering wealthy, the setting for the casino, gardens, and deluxe hotels. The fourth part, **Fontvieille,** is a neat industrial suburb.

Ironically, **Monte-Carlo Beach,** at the far frontier, is on French soil. It attracts a chic crowd, including movie stars in scanty bikinis and thongs. The resort has a freshwater pool, an artificial beach, and a sea-bathing establishment.

No one used to go to Monaco in summer, but now that has totally changed—in fact, July and August tend to be so crowded that it's hard to get a room. Furthermore, with the decline of royalty and multimillionaires, Monaco is developing a broader base of tourism (you can stay here moderately—but it's misleading to suggest that you can stay cheaply). The Monégasques very frankly court the affluent visitor. And at the casinos here, you can also lose your shirt. "Suicide Terrace" at the casino, though not used as frequently as in the old days, is still a real temptation to many who have foolishly gambled away family fortunes.

Life still focuses on the **Monte-Carlo Casino** ★, which has been the subject of countless legends and the setting for many films (remember poor Lucy Ricardo and the chip she found lying on the casino floor?). Depending on the era, you might have seen Mata Hari shooting a tsarist colonel with a jewel-encrusted revolver when he tried to slip his hand inside her bra to discover her secrets—military, not mammary. The late King Farouk, known as "the Swine," used to devour as many as eight roast guinea hens and 50 oysters before losing thousands at the table. Richard Burton presented Elizabeth Taylor with the obscenely huge Koh-i-noor diamond here. Surrounded by cultivated gardens, the casino stands on a **panoramic terrace** ★★, offering one of the grandest views along the entire Riviera.

SEEING THE SIGHTS

Cathédrale de Monaco   This is one of the most visited attractions in the principality, primarily because it contains the tomb of the former princess of Monaco, Grace Kelly, who first gained fame as an American film actress, winning an Oscar for *The Country Girl*. Many of the ruling Grimaldis are also buried here, mostly recently Prince Rainier III.

Dedicated to Saint Nicholas, the cathedral was consecrated in 1875. It stands on the site of the first parish of Monaco dating from 1252. In addition to the Grimaldi tombs, seek out the Greek Altar and the Episcopal throne in white carrara marble. The altarpiece was painted in the early 16th century by Bréa.

Av. St-Martin. ⓒ 377-93-30-87-70. www.cathedrale.mc. Free admission. Apr–Oct daily 8am–7pm; off season daily 8am–6pm.

Collection des Voitures Anciennes de S.A.S. le Prince de Monaco (Kids) Prince Rainier III opened a showcase of his private collection of more than 100 vintage autos, including the 1956 Rolls-Royce Silver Cloud that carried the prince and princess on their wedding day. Monaco shopkeepers gave it to the royal couple as a wedding present. A 1952 Austin Taxi on display was once used as the royal "family car." Other exhibits are a "woodie" (a 1937 Ford station wagon Prince Louis II used on hunting trips); a 1925 Bugatti 35B, winner of the Monaco Grand Prix in 1929; a 1903 De Dion Bouton; and a 1986 Lamborghini Countach.

Les Terrasses de Fontvieille. ⓒ 377-92-05-28-56. www.palais.mc. Admission 6€ adults, 3€ students and children 8–14, free for children 7 and under. Daily 10am–6pm. Closed Dec 25.

Jardin Exotique ★★   Built on the side of a rock, these gardens are known for their cactus collection. They were begun by Prince Albert I, who was a naturalist and scientist. He spotted some succulents growing in the palace gardens and created this garden from them. You can also explore the grottoes here, as well as the **Musée d'Anthropologie Préhistorique** (ⓒ 377-93-15-29-80). The view of the principality is splendid.

Bd. du Jardin-Exotique. ⓒ 377-93-15-29-80. www.jardin-exotique.mc. Admission (includes museum) 6.90€ adults, 3.60€ children 6–18, free for children 5 and under. Mid-May to mid-Sept daily 9am–7pm; mid-Sept to Nov 14 and Dec 26 to mid-May daily 9am–6pm. Closed Nov 15–Dec 25.

Les Grands Appartements du Palais ★   Most summer day-trippers from Nice want to see the home of Monaco's royal family, the Palais du Prince, which dominates the principality from "the Rock." A tour of the Grands Appartements allows you a glimpse of the Throne Room and some of the art (including works by Bruegel and Holbein) as well as Princess Grace's state portrait. The palace was built in the 13th century, and portions date from the Renaissance. The ideal time to arrive is 11:55am to watch the 10-minute **Relève de la Garde** (changing of the guard).

In a wing of the palace, the **Musée du Palais du Prince (Souvenirs Napoléoniens et Collection d'Archives)** holds a collection of mementos of Napoleon and Monaco. When the royal residence is closed, this museum is the only part of the palace the public can visit.

Place du Palais. ⓒ 377-93-25-18-31. www.palais.mc. Combination ticket 7€ adults, 3.50€ children 8–14, free for children 7 and under. Palace and museum June–Sept daily 9:30am–6pm; Oct daily 10am–5pm. Museum also open Nov 1–11 daily 10am–5pm; Dec 17–May Tues–Sun 10:30am–noon and 2–4:30pm. Palace closed Nov–May; museum closed Nov 12–Dec 16.

The Shaky House of Grimaldi

Monaco, according to Somerset Maugham, is 149 sunny hectares (370 acres) peopled with shady characters. The tax-free principality is the oddest fiscal and social anomaly in Europe, a blend of Las Vegas hype and aristocratic glitter whose luster has been sorely tarnished since the demise of Princess Grace ("a snow-covered volcano," said Alfred Hitchcock).

The marriage of the world's most eligible bachelor and the Hollywood golden goddess dominated headlines in April 1956. However, like Grace and Rainier themselves, the marriage did not age gracefully. Rainier's snide public assessments of his celebrity wife's accomplishments showed an unpleasant rivalry. In turn, Grace, beneath her cool veneer, was a lonely and frustrated woman who sought solace in a string of affairs.

The children of this ill-fated union have rebelled against the strictures imposed on them by their less-than-noble parents. More at home in the watering holes of big-city Paris than in the claustrophobic and judgmental homeland, they take turns being the one most likely to shock the multinational residents of their tax-free domain.

The most obviously disaffected is Stephanie, whose tantrums as a 13-year-old were duly noted by scads of journalists and whose sexual insouciance contributed, according to local wits, to the ill health of her late father. Her affairs have included the sons of Jean-Paul Belmondo and Alain Delon alike, also children of second-generation fame. For a time, she moved to Los Angeles, where she tried to build a show-business career. Promising beginnings in Stephanie's fertile roster of career options were stymied by maneuvering from the Grimaldi fortress. Her ambitions have mostly collapsed, as have her attempts to become a model or pop singer. In 1995, Stephanie married a former palace guard, Alain Ducruet, by whom she bore two children; however, a year later she divorced him because he had been caught cavorting naked with Miss Bare Breasts of Belgium. In 1998, Stephanie continued to make headlines by staying mum about her new baby's dad—Camille Marie Kelly was Stephanie's third child born out of wedlock. One palace guard summed up Stephanie's affairs and babies: "In these times, it's not a question of morals. A princess can do what she likes."

Everyone in his prospective kingdom constantly urges Albert, now the ruler, to take a bride and produce a male heir. He has publicly denied rumors of homosexuality and has cavorted with an assortment of famous faces, from Brooke Shields to Donna Rice to Claudia Schiffer. As a local commentator has said, "It's one thing for him to marry a bimbo; it's another to marry someone like his mother." At the moment (subject to change at any minute), Albert continues to play the field, finding no replacement to fill the shoes of Princess Grace. The ruler of Monaco can often be counted upon for a tabloid headline, as he's known to punch out a journalist or urinate in public.

In the summer of 2005, Prince Albert shocked his subjects when he acknowledged that he had fathered a child with an African-born Air France flight attendant. Little Alexandre, Albert's son with Nicole Coste, will never be eligible for the throne, however. The constitution of Monaco excludes illegitimate children from the line of succession. In another surprise on the night before assuming the throne, Albert also admitted that there may be others with paternity claims. He offered no further details.

Caroline, mother of three, has done her royal part. She would if she could, according to observers, force a power struggle with Albert for the right of succession. Her first husband, the much older businessman/boulevardier Philippe Junot, was the sort of man every mother hopes her daughter will not marry—which is probably why Caroline did. After she announced that she was divorcing womanizing Junot, the Vatican was called in to annul the marriage (which it finally did in 1992). Within a year of her mother's death, Caroline met and fell deeply in love with 27-year-old Stefano Casiraghi, son of an Italian industrialist. She was 4 months pregnant when they married in 1984, and she and Stefano had two more children (who remained "illegitimate" until 3 years after their father's death). In 1989, Stefano died in a speedboating accident and Caroline went into severe mourning, chopping off her hair and withdrawing from her duties. Eventually, she and her children moved to France and she returned to her position as "First Lady of Monaco." On January 23, 1999, her 42nd birthday, Caroline took a new husband, Prince Ernst of Hanover, who had been married to her best friend. Oddly, by marrying Ernst, she fulfilled the wishes of her late mother, who always wanted her to marry him. The couple will not be poor: Ernst is reportedly worth $800 million.

On May 31, 1997, Prince Rainier and his family marked the 700th anniversary of Grimaldi rule—6,600 Monégasques showed up for an open-air ceremony at place du Palais. With all their troubles and scandals, the clan has come a long way since January 8, 1297, when a political refugee from Genoa, Francesco Grimaldi, accompanied by some cronies in monks' clothing, persuaded the defenders of the local castle to give him shelter. Once he and his men penetrated the defenses, they ripped off their hoods and took the castle by force. The Principality of Monaco was born, and it's been in Grimaldi hands ever since.

After suffering from health problems with his heart and kidneys, Prince Rainier III died in 2005 at the age of 81. He had been Europe's longest-reigning monarch, having assumed the throne on May 9, 1949. Upon his death, the throne was assumed by Prince Albert, a shy, passionate sportsman often seen as a reluctant heir. Albert turned 51 on March 14, 2009. Should Albert die or fail to rule, Princess Caroline would assume the throne, according to a revised constitution in 2002 that sought to ensure the Grimaldi dynasty.

One Monégasque summed up the Grimaldi situation well: "I go to church every morning to pray for the prince and his family. I pray God will keep them safe and sane. Because that is my security. Without the Grimaldis, we would be merely hors d'oeuvres for France."

Musée National de Monaco ★ (Kids)   In a villa designed in a style similar to that of Charles Garnier (architect of Paris's Opéra Garnier), this museum houses a magnificent collection of antique mechanical toys and dolls. See the 18th-century Neapolitan crib, which contains some 200 figures. This collection, assembled by Mme de Galea, was presented to the principality in 1972; it originated with the 18th- and 19th-century practice of displaying new fashions on doll models.

17 av. Princesse-Grace. (℃ 377-93-30-91-26. www.monte-carlo.mc/musee-national. Admission 6€ adults, 3.50€ students and children 6–14, free for children 5 and under. Daily 10am–6pm.

Musée Océanographique de Monaco ★★ (Kids)   Albert I, great-grandfather of the present prince, founded this museum in 1910. In the main rotunda is a statue of Albert in his favorite costume: that of a sea captain. Displayed are specimens he collected during 30 years of expeditions; some were unknown before he captured them. The aquarium, one of the finest in Europe, contains more than 90 tanks, and even has a shark lagoon.

The collection is exhibited in the zoology room. You'll see models of the ships of his scientific cruises from 1885 to 1914. The most important part of the laboratory has been preserved and re-created as closely as possible. Skeletons of specimens, including a whale that drifted ashore at Pietra Ligure in 1896, are on the main floor. An exhibition devoted to the discovery of the ocean is in the physical-oceanography room on the first floor, and underwater movies are shown in the lecture room.

Av. St-Martin. (℃ 377-93-15-36-00. www.oceano.mc. Admission 13€ adults, 6€ children 6–18, free for children 5 and under. Apr–Sept daily 9:30am–7pm (until 7:30pm July–Aug); Oct–Mar daily 10am–6pm.

OUTDOOR PURSUITS
A Day at the Beach

Just outside the border, on French soil, the **Monte-Carlo Beach Club** adjoins the Monte-Carlo Beach Hôtel, 22 av. Princesse-Grace (℃ 04-93-28-66-66). The beach club has thrived for years; it's an integral part of Monaco's social life. Princess Grace used to come here in flowery swimsuits, greeting her friends and subjects with humor and style. The sand is replenished at regular intervals. You'll find two large pools (one for children), cabanas, a restaurant, a cafe, and a bar. As the temperature drops in late August, the beach closes for the winter. The admission charge of 90€, depending on the season, grants you access to the changing rooms, toilets, restaurants, and bar, and use of a mattress for sunbathing. A fee of 150€ to 200€ will get you a day's use of a private cabana. Most socializing occurs around the pool's edges. As usual, topless is de rigueur but bottomless isn't.

Monaco, the quintessential kingdom by the sea, offers swimming and sunbathing at the **Plage du Larvotto,** off avenue Princesse-Grace (℃ 377-93-30-63-84). This strip of beach is free, and the surface is frequently replenished with sand hauled in by barge. Part of it is open; other sections are private.

Other Outdoor Activities

GOLF   The prestigious **Monte Carlo Golf Club,** Route N7, La Turbie (℃ 04-92-41-50-70), on French soil, is a par-72 course with scenic panoramas. Certain perks (including use of electric carts) are reserved for members. In order to play, nonmembers are asked to show proof of membership in another club and provide evidence of their handicap. Greens fees for 18 holes are 120€ Monday to Friday, 150€ Saturday and Sunday. Clubs rent for 20€. The course is open daily 8am to sunset.

SPA TREATMENTS   In 1908, the Société des Bains de Mer launched a seawater (thalassotherapy) spa in Monte Carlo, inaugurated by Prince Albert I. It was bombed during World War II and didn't reopen until 1996. **Les Thermes Marins de Monte-Carlo,** 2 av. de Monte-Carlo (© 377-98-06-69-00; www.montecarlospa.com), is one of the largest spas in Europe. Spread over four floors are a pool, Turkish *hammam* (steam bath), diet restaurant, juice bar, two tanning booths, fitness center, beauty center, and private treatment rooms. A day pass, giving access to the sauna, steam rooms, fitness facilities, and pools, costs 85€. Massages cost 65€ for a 30-minute session, 125€ for a 60-minute session.

SWIMMING   Overlooking the yacht-clogged harbor, the **Stade Nautique Rainier-III,** quai Albert-1er, at La Condamine (© 377-93-30-64-83), a pool frequented by the Monégasques, was a gift from Prince Rainier to his subjects. It's open May to October daily 9am to 6pm (until midnight July–Aug). Admission for a one-time visit costs 4.70€ per person; discounts are available if you plan to visit 10 times or more. Between November and April, it's an ice-skating rink. If you want to swim in winter, try the indoor **Piscine du Prince Héréditaire Albert,** in the Stade Louis II, 7 av. de Castellane (© 377-92-05-42-13). It's open Monday, Tuesday, Thursday, and Friday 7:30am to 2:30pm; Saturday 1 to 6pm; and Sunday 8am to 1pm. Admission is 2.30€.

TENNIS & SQUASH   The **Monte Carlo Country Club,** 155 av. Princesse-Grace, Roquebrune-St-Roman, France (© 04-93-41-30-15; www.mccc.mc), has 21 clay and 2 concrete tennis courts. The 36€ fee provides access to a restaurant, health club with Jacuzzi and sauna, putting green, beach, squash courts, and the well-maintained tennis courts. Guests of the hotels administered by the Société des Bains de Mer (Hôtel de Paris, Hermitage, Mirabeau, and Monte Carlo Beach Club) pay half-price. Plan to spend at least half a day, ending a round of tennis with use of any of the other facilities. It's open daily 8am to 8 or 9pm, depending on the season.

SHOPPING

Bijoux Marlene, Les Galeries du Métropole, 207 av. des Spélugues (© 377-93-50-17-57), sells only imitation gemstones. They're shamelessly copied from the real McCoys sold by Cartier and Van Cleef & Arpels. Made in Italy of gold-plated silver, the jewelry (the staff refers to it as Les Bijoux Fantaisies) costs 10€ to 1,000€ per piece.

Boutique du Rocher, 1 av. de la Madone (© 377-93-30-91-17), is the larger of two boutiques Princess Grace opened in 1966 as the official retail outlets of her charitable foundation. The organization merchandises Monégasque and Provençal handicrafts. A short walk from place du Casino, the shop sells carved frames for pictures or mirrors; housewares; gift items crafted from porcelain, textiles, and wood; and toys and dolls. On the premises are workshops where artisans produce the goods. The second branch is at 25 rue Emile de Loth, Monaco-Ville (© 377-93-30-33-99).

If you insist on ultrafancy stores, you'll find them cheek by jowl with the Hôtel de Paris and the casino, lining the streets leading to the Hôtel Hermitage, and across from the gardens at the minimall Park Palace. **Allée Serge-Diaghilev** is just that, an alley, but a very tiny one filled with designer shops.

You don't have to be Princess Caroline to shop in Monaco, especially now with **FNAC** (© 377-93-10-81-81) in the heart of town. A branch of the big French chain that sells CDs, tapes, and books, it's at the **Galeries du Métropole,** 17 av. des Spélugues, in the Jardins du Casino, next to the Hôtel Métropole and across from the casino.

The Galeries du Métropole also has a few specialty shops worth visiting. Check out **Geneviève Lethu** (© 377-93-50-09-41) for colorful and country tabletop accessories; or **Manufacture de Monaco** (© 377-93-50-64-63; www.mdpm.com) for glorious bone china and elegant tabletop items. If the prices make you want to take to your bed, two doors away is a branch of the chic but often affordable French linen house **Yves Delorme** (© 377-93-50-08-70). **Royal Food** (© 377-93-15-05-04) is a gourmet grocery store down a set of curving stairs hidden in the side entrance of the mall; here you can buy food from France, Lebanon, and the United States, or stock up for *le pique-nique* or for day trips. This market is open Monday to Saturday 10am to 7:30pm.

For real-people shopping, stroll **rue Grimaldi,** the principality's most commercial street, near the fruit, flower, and food market (see below); and **boulevard des Moulins,** closer to the casino, where you'll see glamorous boutiques. **Rue Princesse-Caroline** is a pedestrian thoroughfare with shops less forbiddingly chic than those along boulevard des Moulins, and it's loaded with bakeries, flower shops, and the closest thing you'll find to funkiness in Monaco. Also check out the **Formule 1** shop, 15 rue Grimaldi (© 377-93-15-92-44), where everything from racing helmets to specialty key chains and T-shirts celebrates the roaring, high-octane racing machines.

No one comes to the Riviera for bargain shopping but, even in chic Monte Carlo, try **Stock Griffe,** 5 bis av. St-Michel (© 377-93-50-86-06). It slashes prices on Prada, Pucci, Escada, and the like. A tremendous amount of merchandise is packed into these tiny precincts. The place may be small, but not the discounts, some of which add up to an astonishing 90%. Greater reductions are for older garments that didn't move, but you can also snap up some newer fashions.

For a look at the heart and soul of the real Monaco, head to place des Armes for the **fruit, flower, and food market,** which starts daily at 7:30am. The indoor and outdoor market has a fountain, cafes, and hand-painted vegetable tiles beneath your feet. The outdoor market packs up at noon, and some dealers at the indoor market stay open to 2pm. If you prefer bric-a-brac, a small but funky (especially for Monaco) flea market, **Les Puces de Fontvieille,** is open on Saturdays 9:30am to 5:30pm on the Quai Jean-Charles Rey, immediately adjacent to Port de Fontvieille.

WHERE TO STAY

Very Expensive

Hôtel de Paris ★★★   On the resort's main plaza, opposite the casino, this is one of the world's most famous hotels. The ornate facade has marble pillars, and the lounge has an Art Nouveau rose window at the peak of the dome. The decor includes marble pillars, statues, crystal chandeliers, sumptuous carpets, Louis XVI chairs, and a wall-size mural. Elegant fabrics, rich carpeting, classic accessories, and an excellent restaurant make this hotel a favorite of the world's most discerning travelers. The guest rooms come in a variety of styles, with period or contemporary furnishings. Some units are enormous. Bathrooms are large, with marble and elegant brass fittings. *Note:* The rooms opening onto the sea aren't as spacious as those in the rear. Of the hotel's three restaurants, **Le Grill de l'Hôtel de Paris** and **Le Louis XV** (p. 343) are two of Monaco's most highly respected establishments.

Place du Casino, 98007 Monaco. © **377-92-16-30-00.** Fax 377-92-16-26-26. www.montecarloresort. com. 182 units. 420€–960€ double; from 760€ suite. AE, DC, MC, V. Valet parking 32€. **Amenities:** 3 restaurants; bar; babysitting; concierge; health club & spa; pool (indoor); room service. *In room:* A/C, TV, hair dryer, minibar, Wi-Fi (25€).

Hôtel Hermitage ★★   Picture yourself sitting in a wicker armchair, enjoying a drink under an ornate stained-glass dome with an encircling wrought-iron balcony. You can have all this at the cliff-top Hôtel Hermitage. The "palace," with its wedding-cake facade, was the creation of Jean Marquet (who also created marquetry). Most rooms have large brass beds and decoratively framed doors that open onto balconies. Even the smallest rooms are medium-size, and the largest one is fit for the biggest movie star with the most luggage. Large mirrors, elegant fabrics and upholstery, deluxe bathrooms and sumptuous beds make living here idyllic. Two floors were recently added to its century-old main building. Guest rooms are modern and sleek in the styling. High-season rates apply during Christmas, New Year's, Easter, and July and August.

Square Beaumarchais, 98005 Monaco Cedex. ☏ **377-98-06-40-00.** Fax 377-92-16-38-52. www.montecarlo resort.com. 280 units. 370€–940€ double; from 650€ junior suite; from 1,520€ suite. AE, DISC, MC, V. Parking 32€. **Amenities:** Restaurant; 2 bars; babysitting; concierge; health club w/sauna; pool (indoor); room service. *In room:* A/C, TV, hair dryer, minibar, Wi-Fi (20€).

Monte Carlo Bay Hotel & Resort ★★★   Occupying a 4-hectare (10-acre) Mediterranean garden, this is a plush Garden of Eden for the principality. It doesn't have the age or tradition of other Société des Bains de Mer properties, such as the Paris and the Hermitage, but it seemingly offers everything else—and is the most stunningly modern resort Monaco has ever seen.

Built right on the seashore, this is the first time in 75 years the society has launched a new hotel. Its aim is to recapture some of the splendor of the 1920s. Its neoclassical architecture, with arcades and colonnades, has created a new landmark in Monaco. The sumptuous nature of the resort is reflected in its waterfalls, terraces, spacious bedrooms, exotic woods, lavish marble, and even an indoor pool covered with a monumental glass dome, along with a luxurious spa and fitness club. Of the beautifully furnished bedrooms, more than three-fourths of them open onto sea views. Rooms are decorated with white oak furnishings, often sandstone floors, and soft Mediterranean pastels. The casino and the famous Jimmy'z Disco have made the hotel one of the hot addresses for after-dark diversions.

40 av. Princesse Grace, 98000 Monaco. ☏ **377-98-06-02-00.** Fax 377-98-06-00-03. www.montecarlobay. com. 334 units. 270€–800€ double; 750€–2,300€ suite. AE, DC, MC, V. Parking 15€. **Amenities:** 4 restaurants; 2 bars; babysitting; casino; concierge; health club & spa; nightclub & disco; 3 pools (indoor, outdoor & children's); room service. *In room:* A/C, TV, hair dryer, minibar, Wi-Fi (20€).

Expensive

Columbus Monaco Hotel ★★ (Value)   In the modern Fontvieille section of Monaco, this stylish, contemporary hotel faces Princess Grace's rose garden and the sea. Guest rooms are done in what owner Ken McCulloch calls "hybrid hip," a style that evokes Miami and London alike. Elegant touches include Lartigue photos of the Riviera, high-tech cabinets filled with video games, and chocolate leather furnishings. Guest rooms have deluxe linens and Frette bathrobes. The main disadvantage is that the hotel is in a condo complex whose residents share the pool. But a boat carries guests to a tranquil sandy beach nearby.

23 av. des Papalins, 98000 Monaco. ☏ **377-92-05-90-00.** Fax 377-92-05-23-86. www.columbushotels. com. 181 units. 310€–345€ double; 610€–920€ suite. AE, MC, V. Parking 28€. **Amenities:** Brasserie; bar; babysitting; concierge; exercise room; pool (outdoor); room service. *In room:* A/C, TV, hair dryer, minibar.

Fairmont Monte Carlo ★   Although a bit down the scale from the two previous choices, this is also a deluxe modern palace. It hugs the coast below the terraces that support the famous casino, on one of the most valuable pieces of real estate along the Côte d'Azur. Architecturally daring when built (some of its foundations were sunk into the seabed, and some of the principality's busiest highways roar beneath it), the resort is viewed as an integral enhancement of Monégasque life. It contains Monaco's highest concentration of restaurants, bars, and nightclubs—think of it as Las Vegas with a Gallic accent. The guest rooms are conservatively furnished with a pastel decor and flooded with light from big windows with views over the town or the sea. The restaurant **L'Argentin** (p. 345) serves grilled steaks, Argentine style.

12 av. des Spélugues, 98007 Monaco. ✆ **377-93-50-65-00.** Fax 377-93-30-01-57. www.fairmont.com/Montecarlo. 616 units. 365€–530€ double; 1,500€ suite. AE, DC, MC, V. Parking 34€. **Amenities:** 2 restaurants; 2 bars; babysitting; concierge; health club w/sauna; room service. *In room:* A/C, TV, hair dryer, Internet (20€), minibar.

Hôtel Port Palace ★★★   Although not quite as grand as the Paris or the Hermitage, this—the first boutique hotel in Monaco—also helps define luxury in the principality. Overlooking the yacht-clogged Monte Carlo Marina, it is excessively opulent; and each of the accommodations is a suite. All units are spacious and elegantly furnished, with state-of-the-art private bathrooms, some of which contain a private steam room. Only first-class materials went into the suites, including rare woods, refined silks, Carrara marble, and premium leather, along with all the modern amenities such as 42-inch plasma TV screens. The hotel's restaurant, Grand Large, is one of the finest in Monaco, without offering too serious a challenge to the gourmet citadels at the Hôtel de Paris.

7 av. John F. Kennedy, 98000 Monte-Carlo. ✆ **377-97-97-90-00.** Fax 377-97-97-90-01. www.portpalace. com. 50 suites. 175€–300€ junior suite; 235€–400€ deluxe junior suite; 375€–800€ corner suite; 525€–1,090€ executive suite. AE, DC, MC, V. **Amenities:** Restaurant; bar; concierge; health club & spa; room service. *In room:* A/C, TV, hair dryer, Jacuzzi, minibar, Wi-Fi (free).

Le Métropole Palace ★   In the heart of Monaco, this hotel is built on the site of the original Métropole, on Monte Carlo's "golden square." The hotel is superb in every way and has an array of handsomely furnished and beautifully decorated rooms. Each includes a radio, hypoallergenic pillows, and a full line of toiletries. Spaces are generous and furnishings are classical, including occasional antiques; all come with double-glazing and soothing pastel color schemes. Marble bathrooms have robes and often a whirlpool tub. The upscale Le Jardin serves splendid French and international cuisine, and Le Yoshi features Monaco's finest Japanese cuisine.

B.P. 19, 4 av. de la Madone, 98007 Monaco. ✆ **377-93-15-15-15.** Fax 377-93-25-24-44. www.metropole. mc. 146 units. 390€–760€ double; 720€–2,600€ suite. AE, DC, MC, V. Parking 35€. **Amenities:** 2 restaurants; bar; babysitting; concierge; pool (outdoor); room service; spa; Wi-Fi (free). *In room:* A/C, TV, hair dryer, Internet (20€), minibar.

Moderate

Hôtel Alexandra   This hotel is on a busy, often-noisy street corner in the center of the business district above the Casino Gardens. Its comfortably furnished guest rooms don't generate much excitement, but they're reliable and respectable. The Alexandra knows it can't compete with the giants of Monaco and doesn't even try, so it attracts those who'd like to visit the principality without spending a fortune.

35 bd. Princesse-Charlotte, 98000 Monaco. ✆ **377-93-50-63-13.** Fax 377-92-16-06-48. www.monaco-hotel.com/montecarlo/alexandra. 56 units. 120€–190€ double. AE, DC, MC, V. Parking 7€. **Amenities:** Room service; babysitting. *In room:* A/C, TV, hair dryer, minibar, Wi-Fi (17€).

Hôtel de France   Not all Monégasques are rich, as a stroll along rue de la Turbie will convince you. Here you'll find some of the cheapest accommodations and eateries in the high-priced principality. This 19th-century hotel, 3 minutes from the rail station, has modest furnishings but is well kept and comfortable. The guest rooms are small.

6 rue de la Turbie, 98000 Monaco. (℃) **377-93-30-24-64.** Fax 377-92-16-13-34. www.monte-carlo.mc/france. 24 units. 85€–108€ double. Rates include continental breakfast. MC, V. Parking 7.50€. **Amenities:** Bar; room service. *In room:* TV, hair dryer, Wi-Fi (free).

WHERE TO DINE
Very Expensive

Joël Robuchon Monte-Carlo ★★★MODERN FRENCH   One of the premier culinary mega-stars of France, Monsieur Robuchon now tickles the palate of the gastronomically jaded clientele of southern France from within this conservatively contemporary dining room in the landmark Hotel Metropole. The dining room is decorated in a color scheme of subtle green and brown, with a view that sweeps out over the nearby sea. It seats only 60 diners at a time.

The menu changes regularly, but dishes likely to remain long-term include grilled filets of John Dory seasoned with "perfumes of the Mediterranean," some of the best lamb chops in France (from the Sisteron region) served with a creamy and buttery version of mashed potatoes, caramelized quail with mashed potatoes and truffles sauce, and crayfish served with crisp-cooked pasta and basil sauce. If you're in the mood for dessert, the "chocolate temptation" is an alluring choice. If you're cutting costs, choose the fixed-price lunch rather than dinner. It includes two glasses of wine per person as part of the all-inclusive price.

In Le Metropole Palace, 4 av. Madone. (℃) **377-93-25-24-44.** Reservations required. Main courses 39€–70€; fixed-price 3-course lunch with wine and coffee 75€; fixed-price 7-course dinner without wine 180€. AE, DC, MC, V. Daily 12:30–2:30pm and 7:30–10:30pm.

Le Grill de l'Hôtel de Paris ★★★MODERN FRENCH   In the flood of publicity awarded to this hotel's street-level restaurant, Le Louis XV (see below), it's been easy to overlook the equally elegant contender on the rooftop. The view alone is worth the expense, with the turrets of the fabled casino on one side and the yacht-clogged harbor of Old Monaco on the other. The decor is gracefully modern, with an ambience somewhat less intense than that in the self-consciously cutting-edge Ducasse citadel downstairs. Despite that, the place is undeniably elegant, with a two-fisted approach to cuisine that includes every imaginable sort of grilled fish (sea wolf, monkfish, sole, salmon, mullet, cod, or turbot) and meat such as Charolais beef and roasted lamb from the foothills of the nearby Alps. In summer and fair weather, the ceiling opens to reveal the starry sky. The cuisine is backed up by one of the Riviera's finest wine lists, with some 600,000 bottles; the wine cellar is carved out of the rock below. Service is faultless but never intimidating or off-putting.

In the Hôtel de Paris (p. 340), place du Casino. (℃) **377-98-06-88-88.** Reservations required. Main courses 45€–65€; fixed-price menus 76€–150€. AE, DC, MC, V. Daily noon–2:15pm and 8–10:15pm. Closed Jan 6–31.

Le Louis XV ★★★FRENCH/ITALIAN   In the Hôtel de Paris, the Louis XV offers what one critic called "down-home Riviera cooking within a Fabergé egg." Star chef Alain Ducasse creates refined but not overly adorned cuisine, served by the finest staff in

Monaco. Everything is light and attuned to the seasons, with intelligent, modern interpretations of *provençale* and northern Italian dishes. You'll find chargrilled breast of baby pigeon with sautéed duck liver, an ongoing specialty known as "Provençal vegetables with crushed truffles," and everything from truffles and caviar to the best stewed salt cod on the coast. Ducasse divides his time between this enclave and his restaurants in Paris and New York. The hotel keeps its collection of rare fine wines in a dungeon chiseled out of the rocks.

In the Hôtel de Paris (p. 340), place du Casino. ✆ **377-98-06-88-64.** Reservations recommended. Jacket and tie required for men. Main courses 80€–120€; fixed-price dinner 130€–250€; fixed-price lunch 130€. AE, MC, V. Thurs–Mon 12:15–1:45pm and 8–9:45pm; also June–Sept Wed 12:15–1:45pm. Closed Feb 14–Mar 1 and Nov 28–Dec 28.

Expensive

Bar et Bœuf ★★ INTERNATIONAL   This restaurant is one of the many jewels in the crown of superchef Alain Ducasse, who is, according to many critics, both a culinary genius and the orchestrator of an upscale international assembly line. Gael Greene has referred to him as "Robo-Chef," and a small number of increasingly vocal critics complain about "franchise sprawl." You can still get a genuinely good meal here, even if none of it is prepared or even supervised by Ducasse. Bar et Boeuf is an upscale Gallic reinvention of a surf-and-turf restaurant. The only fish here is sea bass *(bar),* and the beef is perhaps the most cosseted and fussed-over meat in France. Examples include filets of sea bass with citrus marmalade and an assortment of species of braised celery; filet steak with Sicilian herbs; beef Wellington; and beef with a sauté of *taggiasche* (Italian) olives and wine glaze, served with fried spiny artichokes. The most lavish dish is *tournedos rossini* layered with foie gras and truffles, served with a tartare of truffled foie gras and pan-fried exotic mushrooms.

In the Sporting d'Eté Monte Carlo, av. Princesse-Grace. ✆ **377-98-06-71-71.** Reservations recommended. Main courses 32€–68€. AE, DC, MC, V. Late May to mid-Sept daily 8pm–1am. Closed rest of year.

Beefbar ★ STEAKS/FRENCH   One patron said that this restaurant buzzes with a "polyglot crowd of dealmakers, socialites, and preclub beauties," and so it does. A chic crowd comes to this elegant salon overlooking the Mediterranean to feast on everything from Argentine steaks to raw fish specials. The chef claims he selects only "the most noble pieces" from the slaughterhouses of the world, mostly from the United States, Argentina, and the Netherlands. The chef's Black Angus beef from Kansas is some of the best you are likely to find in the south of France. For the non-carnivore, there are many other choices such as tagliolini with flap mushrooms. You can also order lighter fare such as chicken Caesar salad. The menu is backed up by the best collection of bordeaux in Monaco.

42 quai Jean-Charles Rey. ✆ **377-97-77-09-29.** www.beefbar.com. Reservations required. Main courses 18€–69€; fixed-price menu 39€–90€. AE, MC, V. Daily 11:30am–3pm and 7–9:30pm.

La Mandarine ★★ FRENCH/MEDITERRANEAN   In the chic Port Palace Hotel, this restaurant lies on the sixth floor, opening onto a glittering vista of Monte Carlo's harbor and sea. A gourmet restaurant, it serves cuisine that specializes in fresh, natural ingredients, mostly fashioned into familiar Mediterranean dishes. You can feast on such expensive produce as lobster, tender veal, or a risotto studded with truffles. Two other superbly crafted specialties include sautées foie gras in a chutney-mango-coriander reduction and lacquered duck flavored with green curry. The ever-changing menu is backed up by one of the best wine cellars in Monaco, with some 20,000 bottles awaiting your selection.

7 av. President J. F. Kennedy. ✆ **377-97-97-90-00.** Main courses 30€–40€; fixed-price lunch 35€–43€. AE, MC, V. Daily noon–2pm and 7:30–10:30pm.

L'Argentin ★ STEAKS/GRILLS Decorated like a very upscale version of what you **345**
might have found on the Argentine plains, this stylish restaurant is on the lobby level of
the Fairmont Hotel. Within an environment loaded with autumn colors, polished copper, leather banquettes, and big windows overlooking the sea, diners enjoy some of the
best grilled-meat dishes in town. (A limited array of fish is served, but because the same
hotel also maintains a separate seafood restaurant, Le Pistou, on its seventh floor, most
clients are here for the meat.) One of the specialties on which this place has built its name
is a *tampiqueña*, a much-marinated spicy filet of beef served with guacamole, salsa, tor-
tillas, and a purée of string beans. An equally succulent choice is a standing hunk of roast
beef presented on a wheeled trolley and carved at tableside.

In the Fairmont Monte Carlo (p. 341), 12 av. des Splugues. ☎ **377-93-50-65-00.** Reservations recommended. Main courses 17€–98€. AE, DC, MC, V. Daily noon–3pm and 7:30–11:30pm.

Le Café de Paris (Overrated) TRADITIONAL FRENCH Its *plats du jour* are standard
fare, and its location, the plaza adjacent to the casino and the Hôtel de Paris, allows a
front-row view of the comings and goings of the nerve center of Monte Carlo. Tables are
crowded too closely together, and the waiters seem intent on rushing you through dinner.
We find this 1985 re-creation of old-time Monaco a bit too enraptured with the devil-
may-care glamour of early-1900s Monte Carlo. Despite that, the Café de Paris continues
to draw patrons who appreciate the razzmatazz and all the glass and chrome. Menu items
change frequently. Local office workers appreciate the platters, especially at lunchtime,
because they can be served and consumed quickly. They range from fresh grilled sea bass
to steak tartare with matchstick frites. Adjacent to the restaurant, you'll find (and hear)
a jangling collection of slot machines and a predictable cluster of boutiques.

Place du Casino. ☎ **377-92-16-20-20.** Reservations recommended. Main courses 15€–58€. AE, DC, MC,
V. Daily 8am–3am.

Rampoldi ★ FRENCH/ITALIAN More than any other restaurant in Monte Carlo,
Rampoldi is linked to the charming but somewhat dated interpretation of *La Dolce Vita.*
Opened in the 1950s at the edge of the Casino Gardens and staffed with a mix of old
and new, it's more Italian than French in spirit. It also serves some of the best cuisine in
Monte Carlo. Menu items include an array of pastas, such as tortellini with cream and
white-truffle sauce, sea bass roasted in a salt crust, ravioli stuffed with crayfish, and veal
kidneys in Madeira sauce. Crêpes Suzette make a spectacular finish.

3 av. des Spélugues. ☎ **04-93-30-70-65.** www.rampoldi.restaurants-monte-carlo.com. Reservations
required. Main courses 20€–55€. AE, MC, V. Daily 12:15–2:30pm and 7:30–11:30pm.

Tender To ★ ITALIAN/FRENCH Set with big windows, directly overlooking the
old port, this restaurant is also a wine bar. The Italian wine carte contains three times the
listings for French wines, the focus mainly on the region of Tuscany. The venue is very
much macho Italian. Menu items might include a selection of elegant pastas (tagliatelle
with smoked salmon and spaghetti with lobster), antipasti, and meat dishes such as filet
of beef *aux délices,* mignon of veal in orange sauce, or rack of lamb with Mediterranean
herbs. Other excellent courses include spaghetti with seafood and a superb filet of veal
with porcini mushrooms. The very fresh fish of the day is grilled to perfection. Dessert?
Why not a *cassata siciliana,* a Sicilian dessert made with ricotta cheese, lots of candied
fruit, sponge cake, almond paste, and liqueur? In summer, the restaurant expands onto
an outdoor terrace overlooking the yachts of the harbor.

quai Albert-1er. ☎ **377-93-50-77-21.** Reservations recommended. Main courses 13€–23€; fixed-price
menus 25€–55€. DISC, MC, V. Mon–Sat noon–2pm and 7–11pm. Closed Nov 1–15.

Pizzeria Monégasque FRENCH/ITALIAN   This *pizzeria de luxe* offers four dining rooms and an outdoor terrace. Almost anyone might arrive in a limousine or on a bicycle. Observing the local patrons will quickly convince you that Monaco is actually a rather small and gossipy town. The owner has grown accustomed to seeing all the follies and vanities of this town pass through his door; he serves pizzas, fish, and grilled meats to whomever shows up. Specialties are *magret du canard* (duckling), steaks, carpaccio, and beef tartare. Of the 10 kinds of pizza, the most popular are pizza Terrazzini (it includes cheese and pistou) and the "special" version that's served with Tunisian-style *merguez*.

4 rue Terrazzani. (℃ **377-93-30-16-38.** Pizzas 10€–12€; main courses 10€–22€. AE, MC, V. Mon–Fri noon–1:45pm; Mon–Sat 7:30–11pm (until midnight Fri–Sat). Closed Dec 25–Jan 1.

Stars 'n' Bars (Kids) AMERICAN/PACIFIC RIM   Modeled on the sports bars popular in the U.S., this place features two dining and drinking areas devoted to American-style food, as well as a bar decorated with memorabilia of notable athletes. No one will mind if you drop in just for a drink, but if you're hungry, the menu reads like an homage to the American experience. Try an Indy 500, a Triathlon salad, or the Breakfast of Champions (eggs and bacon and all the fixings). For kids under 12, order the Little Leaguer's Platter or pizza.

The owners also operate **Fusion Cuisine** (same address, phone, hours, and owners) in a space upstairs from the main dining room. Here, platters inspired by the cuisines of the Pacific Rim are featured, each within the same price range as the food served on the restaurant's street level. Examples include sushi, tempura, rice-based dishes, and fast-wok-fried dishes of meats and seafood.

6 quai Antoine-1er. (℃ **377-97-97-95-95.** www.starsnbars.com. Reservations recommended. Dinner salads and platters 10€–28€; sandwiches 11€–15€; pizzas 10€–15€. AE, DC, MC, V. June–Sept daily 11am–midnight; Oct–May Tues–Sun 11am–midnight. Bar until 3am.

MONACO AFTER DARK

CASINOS   **Sun Casino,** in the Monte Carlo Grand Hôtel, 12 av. des Spélugues (℃ **377-93-50-65-00**), is a huge room filled with one-armed bandits. It also features blackjack, craps, and American roulette. Additional slot machines are on the roof, with a wide view of the sea. Slot machines operate daily 10am to 4am, and gaming tables are open daily 5pm to 4am. Admission is free.

François Blanc developed the **Monte-Carlo Casino,** place du Casino (℃ **377-98-06-20-00**), into the most famous in the world, attracting the exiled aristocracy of Russia, Sarah Bernhardt, Mata Hari, King Farouk, and Aly Khan. The architect of Paris's Opéra Garnier, Charles Garnier, built the oldest part of the casino, and it remains an example of the 19th century's most opulent architecture. The building encompasses the casino and other areas for different kinds of entertainment, including a theater (Opéra de Monte-Carlo; see below) presenting opera and ballet. Baccarat, roulette, and chemin de fer are the most popular games, though you can play *le craps* and blackjack as well.

The casino's **Salle Américaine,** containing only slot machines, opens at 2pm Monday to Friday, noon on weekends. Doors for roulette and *trente et quarante* open at the same time. A section for roulette and chemin de fer opens at 3pm. Additional rooms open at 4pm with more roulette, craps, and blackjack. The gambling continues until very late or early, depending on the crowd. The casino classifies its "private rooms" as the more or other photo ID, and be at least 18. After 9pm, the staff will insist that men wear jackets and neckties for entrance to the private rooms.

The **Opéra de Monte-Carlo** is headquartered in the lavish, recently renovated Belle Epoque **Salle Garnier** of the casino. Tickets to the operas and other events scheduled inside range from 35€ to 120€. Tickets to events within the Salle Garnier are available from a kiosk in the Atrium du Casino (© **377-98-06-28-28;** www.opera.mc), located within the casino; tickets can be purchased Tuesday to Saturday 10am to 5:30pm.

Salle du Canton, Les Terrasses, avenue de Fontvieille (© **377-92-16-22-99** for tickets and information), which filled in for the Salle Garnier during renovations, now hosts smaller concerts, chamber music concerts, and some ballet. At the **Grimaldi Forum,** 10 av. Princesse-Grace (© **377-99-99-30-00** for tickets and information; www.grimaldi forum.com), chamber music and smaller orchestral pieces are usually performed. At both the Salle du Canton and the Grimaldi Forum, ballet tickets cost 8€ to 26€, concert tickets cost 15€ to 30€, and opera tickets cost 40€ to 150€.

If tickets are hard to come by, ask your hotel concierge for assistance.

DANCING & DRINKING The **Legend,** 3 av. des Spélugues (© **377-93-50-53-13**), is a favorite of the 25- to 30-year-old crowd who like a glamorous modern setting. It's open Thursday to Sunday 11:30pm to dawn. Entrance is free. The wildest night is Saturday, when it's mobbed. At **Le Living Room** (© **377-93-50-80-31**), 7 av. des Spélugues, crowds are international and dance oriented. It's open every night from 10:30pm until dawn. Cozy and comfortable, it's a bit more formal and sedate than the Legend, attracting patrons over 35. There's no cover. Two nearly neighboring piano bars are **Le Sass-Café,** 5 av. des Spélugues (© **377-93-25-52-00**), and the **Zebra Square Café,** 10 av. des Spélugues (© **377-99-99-25-50**). Drink prices start at around 8€. Toniest of all, and under the same management as the Hôtel de Paris, is **Jimmy's,** in the Sporting d'Eté, avenue Princesse-Grace (© **377-92-16-22-77**), open nightly 11pm to 5am.

Le Karement, in the Grimaldi Forum (© **377-99-99-20-20;** www.karement.mc) is sprawling, ultracontemporary, and bigger than any nightlife venue ever before seen in Monte Carlo. It boasts two bars inside, a third bar on an outdoor terrace, a sprawling bay window that encompasses a view of the sea, and the kind of house and garage music that the young and young-at-heart clientele can really dance to. Open Thursday to Saturday year-round 10pm to 4am (often later, if business allows), its cover is 20€ and includes your first drink.

Monaco has a large gay and lesbian population and attracts many gay visitors, but does not have any specific gay or lesbian bars. If you want to sample exclusive gay life, take the fast train to Nice for the night.

13 ROQUEBRUNE ★★ & CAP-MARTIN ★★

953km (592 miles) S of Paris; 5km (3 miles) W of Menton

Roquebrune, along the Grande Corniche, is a charming mountain village with vaulted streets. It has been restored, though some critics have found the restoration "artificial." Today its rue Moncollet is lined with artists' workshops and boutiques with inflatedly priced merchandise.

Two kilometers (1½ miles) west of Roquebrune, Cap-Martin is a satellite of the larger resort, associated with the rich and famous since Empress Eugénie wintered here in the 19th century. In time the resort was honored by the presence of Sir Winston Churchill, who came here often in his final years. Two famous men died here—William Butler Yeats in 1939 and Le Corbusier, who drowned while swimming off the cape in 1965. Don't look for a wide sandy beach—you'll encounter plenty of rocks against a backdrop of pine and olive trees.

ESSENTIALS

GETTING THERE Cap-Martin has **train** and bus connections from the other cities on the coast, including Nice and Menton. For railway information and schedules, call ℂ **36-35**, or visit **www.voyages-sncf.com**. To reach Roquebrune, you'll have to take a **taxi**. Roquebrune has no bus station: you get off on the side of the highway. For **bus** information, contact the Gare Routière in Menton (ℂ **04-93-35-93-60**). To **drive** to Roquebrune and Cap-Martin from Nice, follow N7 east for 26km (16 miles).

VISITOR INFORMATION The **Office de Tourisme** is at 218 av. Aristide-Briand, Roquebrune (ℂ **04-93-35-62-87**; fax 04-93-28-57-00; www.roquebrune-cap-martin. com). Two-hour walking tours of Roquebrune and St-Martin, each arranged with advance notice by the tourist office, cost 8€ for adults and 5€ for students and children 17 and under. Each departs from the tourist office and encompasses a running commentary in French and English alike on the visual and historical attractions of Roquebrune and Cap-Martin.

EXPLORING ROQUEBRUNE

Exploring Roquebrune will take about an hour. You can stroll through its colorful covered streets, which retain their authentic look even though the buildings are now devoted to handicrafts, gift and souvenir shops, and art galleries. From the parking lot at place de la République, head for place des Deux-Frères, turning left into rue Grimaldi. Then head left to **rue Moncollet.** This long, narrow street is covered with stepped passageways and filled with houses that date from the Middle Ages, most often with barred windows. Rue Moncollet leads into **rue du Château,** where you may want to explore the château.

Château de Roquebrune (ℂ **04-93-35-07-22**) was originally a 10th-century Carolingian castle; the present structure dates in part from the 13th century. Dominated by two square towers affording a panoramic view of the coast, today the Château houses a museum. The interior is open in July and August daily 10am to 12:30pm and 3 to 7:30pm; April to June and September daily 10am to 12:30pm and 2 to 6:30pm; February, March, and October daily 10am to 12:30pm and 2 to 6pm; November to January daily 10am to 12:30pm and 2 to 5pm. Admission is 3.50€ for adults, 2.50€ for seniors, 1.60€ students and children 7 to 11, free for children 6 and under.

Rue du Château leads to place William-Ingram. Cross this square to rue de la Fontaine and take a left. This leads you to the **Olivier millénaire (Millenary Olive Tree),** one of the oldest in the world—it's at least 1,000 years old.

On rue du Grimaldi is **Eglise Ste-Marguerite,** which hides behind a relatively common baroque facade that masks the 12th-century church. It's not entirely from that time, however, having undergone many alterations over the years. The interior is of polychrome plaster. Look for two paintings by a 17th-century local artist, Marc-Antoine Otto, who painted a Crucifixion (in the second altar) and a Pietà (above the entrance door). It's open Monday to Saturday 3 to 5pm, Sunday 10am to 5pm.

Cap-Martin is a rich town. At the center of the cape is a feudal tower that's now a tele-communications relay station. At its base you can see the ruins of the **Basilique St-Martin,** a priory constructed by the monks of the Lérins Islands in the 11th century. Privately owned, it is not open to visitors. After pirate raids in later centuries, notably around the 15th century, it was destroyed and abandoned. If you follow the road (by car) along the eastern shoreline of the cape, you'll be rewarded with a view of Menton against a backdrop of mountains. In the far distance looms the Italian Riviera, and you can see as far as the resort of Bordighera.

You can take one of the most interesting walks along the Riviera here. It lasts about 3 hours. The coastal path, **Sentier Touristique** ★, leads from Cap-Martin to Monte Carlo Beach. If you have a car, you can park in the lot at avenue Winston-Churchill and begin your stroll. A sign labeled PROMENADE LE CORBUSIER marks the path. As you go along, you'll take in a view of Monaco set in a natural amphitheater. In the distance, you'll see Cap-Ferrat and even Roquebrune. The path ends at Monte Carlo Beach.

If you have a car, you can take a **scenic 9.5km (6-mile) drive** ★. Leave the town on D23, following signs to Gorbio, a village on a hill reached by this winding road. Along the way you'll pass homes of the wealthy and view a verdant setting with pines and silvery olives. The site is wild and rocky, and the buildings were constructed to withstand pirate attacks. The most interesting street is rue Garibaldi, which leads past an old church to a panoramic belvedere.

WHERE TO STAY

Hôtel Victoria   This rectangular low-rise building is behind a garden in front of the Cap-Martin beach. Built in the 1970s, it was renovated in the mid-1990s in a neoclassical style that weds tradition and modernity. It's the second choice in town for those who can't afford the Vista Palace (below). Opening onto balconies fronting the sea, each of the midsize rooms is well furnished with contemporary furniture. The casual bar and lounge sets a stylishly relaxed tone. Breakfast is the only meal served.

7 promenade du Cap, 06190 Roquebrune–Cap-Martin. (℡ **04-93-35-65-90.** Fax 04-93-28-27-02. www. hotelmenton.com/hotel-victoria. 32 units. 84€–124€ double. AE, DC, V. Free parking outdoors; 10€ indoors. **Amenities:** Bar; room service. *In room:* A/C, TV, minibar.

Hôtel Vista Palace ★★★   This extraordinary hotel and restaurant stands above Cap-Martin on the outer ridge of the mountains running parallel to the coast, giving it a spectacular "airplane view" of Monaco. The design of the Vista Palace is just as fantastic: Three levels are cantilevered out into space so every unit seems to float. Nearly all the rooms have balconies facing the Mediterranean. You stay in luxe comfort here in grandly furnished guest rooms.

Grande Corniche, 06190 Roquebrune–Cap-Martin. (℡ **04-92-10-40-00.** Fax 04-93-35-18-94. www. vistapalace.com. 70 units. 300€–440€ double; 440€–870€ suite. Rates include continental breakfast. AE, DC, V. Parking 20€. **Amenities:** 3 restaurants; bar; babysitting; health club w/Jacuzzi; pool (outdoor); room service. *In room:* A/C, TV, hair dryer, minibar, Wi-Fi (8€ per 12 hr.).

Les Deux Frères ★ (Finds)   "The Two Brothers" (its English name) hangs over the Mediterranean with Monaco in the distance. This is a *restaurant avec chambres* and offers some of the best room deals in this pricey resort area. The hotel/restaurant was created from an 1854 schoolhouse, and each of the beautifully decorated bedrooms has a different theme, opening onto the square, the sea, or a mountain view. A mahogany bar takes up much of the lobby, and a narrow staircase leads up to the bathrooms. In addition to the restaurant, a cafe named Fraise et Chocolat (Strawberry and Chocolate), stands next to the hotel and serves a choice of sandwiches and drinks.

1 place Deux Frères, 06190 Roquebrune–Cap-Martin. ✆ **04-93-28-99-00.** Fax 04-93-28-99-10. www.les deuxfreres.com. 10 units. 75€–110€ double. MC, V. **Amenities:** Restaurant; bar. *In room:* A/C, TV, Wi-Fi (free).

WHERE TO DINE

Au Grand Inquisiteur ★ ⓕⓘⓝⓓⓢ TRADITIONAL FRENCH This 28-seat restaurant occupies a two-room vaulted cellar near the top of the medieval mountaintop village of Roquebrune. On the steep, winding road to the château, the building is made of rough-cut stone, with large oak beams. The cuisine, though not the area's most distinguished, is good, including the chef's duck special and scallops meunière. Most diners opt for the fresh fish. The wine list is exceptional—some 150 selections, most at reasonable prices.

18 rue du Château. ✆ **04-93-35-05-37.** Reservations required. Main courses 18€–24€; fixed-price menu 28€–38€. AE, MC, V. Daily 7:30–10:30pm. Closed Jan.

Hippocampe TRADITIONAL FRENCH Opened in 1963, this fine restaurant along the seafront offers a full view of the bay and even the Italian coastline. Made safe by a thick stone wall, its terrace is shaded by five crooked pines. The "Sea Horse" is a stone-and-glass garden house with a tile roof and scarlet-and-pink potted geraniums. Specialties include *filets de sole en brioche* with hollandaise sauce, coq au vin (chicken cooked in wine), terrine of hogfish and salmon in basil sauce, and galantine duck.

44 av. Winston-Churchill. ✆ **04-93-35-81-91.** Reservations required. Main courses 10€–60€; fixed-price menus 34€. AE, DC, MC, V. Tues–Sun noon–2:30pm and 7:30–10:30pm.

---

14 MENTON ★★

959km (596 miles) S of Paris; 63km (39 miles) NE of Cannes; 8km (5 miles) E of Monaco

Menton is more Italianate than French. Right at the border of Italy, Menton marks the eastern frontier of the Côte d'Azur. Its climate is the warmest on the Mediterranean coast, and in winter it attracts a large crowd of British seniors. The impact of these seniors on the population of 130,000 has earned Menton the sobriquet "the Fort Lauderdale of France."

According to a local legend, Eve was the first to experience Menton's glorious climate. When she and Adam were expelled from the Garden of Eden, she tucked a lemon in her bosom, planting it at Menton because it reminded her of her former stamping grounds. Lemons still grow in profusion here, and the fruit is given a position of honor at the Lemon Festival held over a 2-week period in February. Actually, the oldest Menton visitor might have arrived 30,000 years ago. He's still around—or, at least, his skull is—in the Musée de Préhistoire Régionale (see below).

Don't be misled by all those "palace-hotels" studding the hills. They are no longer hotels—they've been divided up and sold as private apartments. Many of these turn-of-the-20th-century structures were erected to accommodate elderly Europeans, English and German, who arrived carrying a book written by one Dr. Bennett in which he extolled the joys of living at Menton.

ESSENTIALS

GETTING THERE Menton has good **rail** and **bus** connections. Two trains per hour pull in from Nice (trip time: 35 min.; one-way fare: 4.40€), and two trains per hour arrive from Monte Carlo (trip time: 10 min.; 2€ one-way). For rail information and

schedules, call ✆ **36-35,** or visit **www.voyages-sncf.com**. RCA (✆ **04-93-85-64-44**)
runs buses between Nice, Monte Carlo, and Menton, usually around two per hour; the
round-trip fare from Nice is 4€.

Many visitors arrive by **car** on one of the corniche roads. The drive on N7 east from
Nice takes 45 minutes.

VISITOR INFORMATION   The **Office de Tourisme** is in the Palais de l'Europe, 8 av.
Boyer (✆ **04-92-41-76-76;** www.villedementon.com).

SEEING THE SIGHTS

Menton is situated on the Golfe de la Paix (Gulf of Peace) on a rocky promontory that
divides the bay in two. The fishing town, the older part with its narrow streets, is in the
east; the tourist zone and residential belt are in the west.

The filmmaker, writer, and artist Jean Cocteau liked this resort, and in the **Musée
Jean-Cocteau,** Bastion du Port, quai Napoléon-III (✆ **04-93-57-72-30**), you can see his
death portrait, sketched by MacAvoy. Some of the artist's memorabilia is here—stunning
charcoals and watercolors, brightly colored pastels, ceramics, and signed letters. The
museum is open Wednesday through Monday from 10am to noon and 2 to 6pm. Admission is 3€.

At **La Salle des Mariages,** in the Hôtel de Ville (town hall), rue de la République
(✆ **04-92-10-50-00**), Cocteau painted frescoes depicting the legend of Orpheus and
Eurydice, also the subject of his film *Orphée*. A tape in English helps explain them. The
room, with its red-leather seats and leopard-skin rugs, is used for civil marriage ceremonies. It's open Monday to Friday 8:30am to 12:30pm and 2 to 5pm. Admission is 1.50€.
Advance reservations are necessary.

Musée de Préhistoire Régionale, rue Lorédan-Larchey (✆ **33-93-35-84-64**), presents human evolution on the Côte d'Azur for the past million years. It contains the
25,000-year-old head of the *Nouvel Homme de Menton* (sometimes known as "Grimaldi
Man"), found in 1884 in the Baousse-Rousse caves. Audiovisual aids, dioramas, and
videocassettes enhance the exhibition. The museum is open Wednesday to Monday
10am to noon and 2 to 6pm. Admission is free.

Musée des Beaux-Arts, Palais Carnolès, 3 av. de la Madone (✆ **04-93-35-49-71**),
contains 14th-, 16th-, and 17th-century paintings from Italy, Flanders, Holland, and the
French schools, as well as modern paintings by Dufy, Valadon, Derain, and Leprin—all
acquired by a British subject, Wakefield-Mori. The museum is open Wednesday to Monday 10am to noon and 2 to 6pm. Admission is free.

A DAY AT THE BEACH

Menton's beaches stretch for 3.2km (2 miles) between the Italian border and the city
limits of Roquebrune and are interrupted only by the town's old and new ports. Col-
lectively, they're known as **La Plage de la Promenade du Soleil** and, with rare exceptions, are public and free. Don't expect soft sands or even any sand at all: The beaches are
narrow, are covered with gravel (or, more charitably, big pebbles), and are notoriously
uncomfortable to lie on. Don't expect big waves or tides, either. Who goes there? In the
words of one nonswimming resident, mostly Parisians or residents of northern France,
who are grateful for any escape from their urban milieux. Topless bathing is widespread,
but complete nudity is forbidden.

Unlike Cannes, where tens of thousands of chaises pepper the beaches, Menton has few
options for renting mattresses and parasols; most people bring their own. Two exceptions are

Le Splendid Plage (✆ 04-93-35-60-97) and **Les Sablettes** (✆ 04-93-35-44-77); both charge around 14€ for use of a mattress. They're immediately to the east of the Vieux Port.

WHERE TO STAY

Hôtel Aiglon   In a large park filled with Mediterranean vegetation, the converted villa offers a more intimate environment than any competing hotel in Menton. The rooms come in various shapes and sizes, each well upholstered and containing elegant beds. The magnet of the hotel is a heated pool surrounded by a veranda. The garden setting is beautifully maintained. An excellent *provençale* and international cuisine is offered in a dining room with windows opening onto the pool and garden.

7 av. de la Madone, 06500 Menton. ✆ **04-93-57-55-55.** Fax 04-93-35-92-39. www.hotelaiglon.net. 29 units. 90€–172€ double; 160€–212€ suite. Rates include continental breakfast. AE, DC, MC, V. Parking 8€. **Amenities:** Restaurant; bar; babysitting; pool (outdoor); room service; Wi-Fi (8€ per hr.). *In room:* A/C, TV, hair dryer, minibar, Wi-Fi (free).

Hôtel Chambord   This hotel is located on the main square next to the **Casino de Menton,** 1 av. Félix Faure (✆ 04-92-10-16-16). Built in 1977, with frequent renovations, it is well maintained, with rows of balconies and awnings. The comfortable guest rooms have generous space and are neatly organized, with modern furniture. Breakfast is the only meal served.

6 av. Boyer, 06500 Menton. ✆ **04-93-35-94-19.** Fax 04-93-41-30-55. www.hotel-chambord.com. 40 units. 100€–125€ double. AE, MC, V. Parking 10€. **Amenities:** Lounge. *In room:* A/C, TV, hair dryer, minibar, Wi-Fi (8€ per hr.).

Hôtel Le Dauphin   This affable three-star hotel lies just off the beach. The double-insulated rooms are bright and uncluttered, each with a balcony opening onto the mountain range or the sea. Small to medium in size, they are tidily maintained with modern safari-inspired (mahogany) furnishings. The attentive staff is welcoming. Three meals per day are served, featuring many specialties of Provence.

28 av. du Général-de-Gaulle, 06500 Menton. ✆ **04-93-35-76-37.** Fax 04-93-35-31-74. www.hotel-ledauphin.com. 28 units. 63€–109€ double; 80€–109€ triple. AE, MC, V. Parking 4€. Closed Nov 12–Dec 23. **Amenities:** Restaurant; bar; Wi-Fi (free). *In room:* A/C, TV, hair dryer, minibar.

Hôtel Méditerranée   This white-and-salmon hotel is 3 short blocks from the sea. A raised terrace with a view of the water, chaise longues, and potted plants are on the premises. The rooms are attractively decorated and include private balconies opening onto the sea. Most rooms are spacious, with comfortable beds (usually twins). The hotel also has a restaurant, which offers a veranda for dining in fair weather.

5 rue de la République, 06500 Menton. ✆ **04-92-41-81-81.** Fax 04-92-41-81-82. www.hotel-med-menton.com. 89 units. 76€–112€ double. Children 4 and under stay free in parent's room. AE, DC, MC, V. Parking 15€. **Amenities:** Restaurant; bar. *In room:* A/C, TV, hair dryer, minibar, Wi-Fi (free).

Hôtel Napoléon   This government-rated hotel benefited from one of the most radical renovations in Menton. In the process, the hotel added three theme suites, one of which is dedicated to Jean Cocteau, with many framed representations of his paintings. It sits on a palm-shaded avenue, just across from a beach, where it maintains a seasonal restaurant, open from May to September, and a scattering of parasols and chaise longues. Some of the public areas might remind you of a large living room. Guest rooms, each with contemporary furniture and vivid colors, have comfortable beds and balconies that overlook either the sea or the old town.

29 Porte de France, 06503 Menton. © **04-93-35-89-50.** Fax 04-93-35-49-22. www.napoleon-menton. com. 44 units. 94€–149€ double; 189€–259€ suite. AE, DC, MC, V. Free parking. **Amenities:** Bar; exercise room; pool (outdoor). *In room:* A/C, TV, hair dryer, minibar, Wi-Fi (10€).

Hôtel Princesse et Richmond   At the edge of the sea, this hotel boasts a facade of Mediterranean colors and a garden terrace. The building is a 1970s-style boxy structure with an angular design. The comfortable, soundproof, midsize rooms have modern and French traditional furnishings and balconies. Drinks are served on the roof terrace, where you can enjoy a view of the curving shoreline.

617 promenade du Soleil, 06500 Menton. © **04-93-35-80-20.** Fax 04-93-57-40-20. www.princess-richmond. com. 46 units. 88€–135€ double; 179€–226€ suite. AE, DC, MC, V. Parking 6€–9€. Closed Nov 3–Dec 16. **Amenities:** Restaurant; bar; exercise room; Jacuzzi; room service. *In room:* A/C, TV, hair dryer, minibar, Wi-Fi (13€).

Hotel Riva   A few steps across the seafront boulevard from the beach, this hotel feels like those found along the coast of southern Florida. Its angular design is punctuated with balconies and multileveled terraces. Bedrooms are small to medium in size but are elegantly furnished with quality mattresses and fine linens. High-quality materials such as marble and granite are used throughout, complementing dignified beechwood furniture. Other than breakfast and brunch, no meals are served, but considering the proximity of many restaurants, no one seems to mind.

600 promenade du Soleil, 06500 Menton. © **04-92-10-92-10.** Fax 04-93-28-87-87. www.rivahotel.com. 40 units. 95€–133€ double. AE, DC, MC, V. Parking 9€. **Amenities:** Bar; babysitting; Jacuzzi; sauna; Wi-Fi (free). *In room:* A/C, TV, minibar, hair dryer, Wi-Fi (13€).

WHERE TO DINE

Le Bruit Qui Court   FRENCH/MEDITERRANEAN   It's been on-site only since 2004, but already rumors *(les bruits qui court)* about the worthiness of this place have spread throughout Menton and its suburbs. The setting is a century-old building adjacent to the sea, with two dining rooms (one on an upstairs floor with a panorama of the sea) and a seafront terrace. Amid a color scheme inspired by the soft pumpkin and ocher tones of Provence, diners can choose from fresh menu items, some of which reflect the traditions of the coastal Mediterranean. The best examples include fried slabs of foie gras served with caramelized apples; grilled scallops served on a bed of braised leeks garnished with pink peppercorns; a *marmite des pêcheurs* (seafood stew) with saffron-flavored tomato sauce; and a very unusual version of Rossini-style tuna steak, cut down the middle and garnished with a slab of foie gras.

31 quai Bonaparte. © **04-93-35-94-64.** www.lebruitquicourt.fr. Reservations recommended. Main courses 17€–25€; set-price menus 23€–37€. AE, MC, V. Wed–Sun noon–2:30pm and 7–11pm. Closed Jan 10–Feb 10.

Petit Port   SEAFOOD   Small and charming, with enough Italian overtones to make you believe that you've finally crossed the border, this restaurant occupies a cozy, partially paneled dining room in a century-old house near the medieval port of Menton. Surrounded by nautical accents and oil paintings of the wide, blue sea, you'll enjoy a menu that focuses almost exclusively on seafood. Tasty specialties include grilled sardines, fish soup, and many different kinds of grilled fish. The kitchen will prepare the day's catch in whatever way your taste dictates.

4 rue Jonquier, at place Fontana. © **04-93-35-82-62.** Reservations recommended. Main courses 22€–30€; some shellfish platters 45€; fixed-price menu 20€–30€. AE, MC, V. Thurs–Tues noon–2:30pm; Thurs–Mon 7–11pm.

9

Fast Facts

1 FAST FACTS: THE SOUTH OF FRANCE

AREA CODE All French telephone numbers consist of 10 digits, the first two of which are like an area code. If you're calling anywhere in France from within France, just dial all 10 digits—no additional codes are needed. If you're calling from the United States, drop the initial 0 (zero).

ATM NETWORKS & CASH POINTS See "Money & Costs," p. 50.

AUTO CLUB An organization designed to help motorists navigate their way through breakdowns and motoring problems is **Club Automobile de Provence,** 149 bd. Rabatau, 13010 Marseille (© **04-91-78-83-00;** www. automobileclubprovence.com).

BUSINESS HOURS Business hours here are erratic, as befits a nation of individualists. Most banks are open Monday to Friday from 9:30am to 4:30pm. Many, particularly in smaller towns or villages, take a lunch break at varying times. Hours are usually posted on the door. Most museums close 1 day a week (often Tues), and they're generally closed on national holidays. Usual hours are from 9:30am to 5pm. Some museums, particularly the smaller and less-staffed ones, close for lunch from noon to 2pm. Most French museums are open on Saturday; many are closed Sunday morning but open Sunday afternoon. Again, refer to the individual museum listings.

Generally, offices are open Monday to Friday from 9am to 5pm, but always call first. In larger cities, stores are open from 9 or 9:30am (often 10am) to 6 or 7pm without a break for lunch. Some shops, particularly those operated by foreigners, open at 8am and close at 8 or 9pm. In some small stores, the lunch break can last 3 hours, beginning at 1pm.

CAR RENTALS See "Car Rentals" in section 3 of chapter 3. Also see "Airline, Hotel & Car Rental Websites," below.

CURRENCY See "Money & Costs," p. 50.

DRINKING LAWS The legal age for the purchase and consumption of alcohol is 16. But you'll rarely be carded. Still, it's smart to carry an ID (your own!). The police are very strict about driving while intoxicated. If convicted, you face a high fine and possibly jail time.

DRIVING RULES See "Getting There & Getting Around," p. 43.

ELECTRICITY In general, expect 200 volts, 50 cycles, though you'll encounter 110 and 115 volts in some older hotels. Adapters are needed to fit sockets.

EMBASSIES & CONSULATES All embassies are in Paris. The Embassy of the **United States,** 2 av. Gabriel, 8e (© **01-43-12-22-22;** http://france.usembassy. gov; Métro: Concorde), is open Monday to Friday 8:30am to 5pm. The Embassy of **Canada** is at 35 av. Montaigne, 8e (© **01-44-43-29-00;** www.international.gc.ca/canada-europa/france/menu-en.asp; Métro: F-D-Roosevelt or Alma-Marceau), open Monday to Friday 9am to noon and 2 to 5pm. The Embassy of the **United Kingdom** is at 35 rue du Faubourg St-Honoré,

8e (© **01-44-51-31-00;** http://ukinfrance. fco.gov.uk; Métro: Concorde or Madeleine), open Monday to Friday 9:30am to 1pm and 2:30 to 5pm. The Embassy of **Ireland** is at 4 rue Rude, Paris 75116 (© **01-44-17-67-00;** www.embassyof ireland.fr; Métro: Etoile), open Monday to Friday 9:30am to 1pm and 2:30 to 5:30pm. The Embassy of **Australia** is at 4 rue Jean-Rey, 15e (© **01-40-59-33-00;** www.france.embassy.gov.au; Métro: Bir Hakeim), open Monday to Friday 9:15am to noon and 2:30 to 4:30pm. The embassy of **New Zealand** is at 7 ter rue Léonard-de-Vinci, Paris 75116 (© **01-45-01-43-43;** www.nzembassy.com; Métro: Victor Hugo), open Monday to Friday 9am to 1pm and 2:30 to 6pm. The embassy of **South Africa,** 59 quai d'Orsay, 7e (© **01-53-59-23-23;** www.afriquesud.net; Métro: Invalides), is open Monday to Friday 9am to noon.

EMERGENCIES In an emergency while at a hotel, contact the front desk. Most staffs are trained in dealing with a crisis and will do whatever is necessary. If the emergency involves something like a stolen wallet, go to the police station in person. Otherwise, you can get help anywhere by calling © **17** for the police, © **18** for the fire department *(pompiers),* or © **15** for medical emergencies.

ETIQUETTE & CUSTOMS **Gestures:** If invited to someone's home, bring flowers, but never in the number of 13, which is said to bring bad luck. Don't bring any white flowers (for weddings), red carnations (bad will), or white lilies or chrysanthemums (for funerals). You can also bring wine, but make sure it's an expensive bottle; anything else is considered insulting.

Avoiding offense: Always try to arrive exactly on time if invited to a French house for dinner. Also, dress well.

Eating & drinking: Don't begin eating until the host or hostess has said, *"Bon appétit."*

Business etiquette: Say *"bonjour"* or *"bonsoir"* (good morning or good evening), with either a monsieur or madame, when meeting someone, even a shopkeeper. Upon leaving, say *"au revoir"* (goodbye), even if leaving a shop where you didn't buy anything. Business cards are exchanged after the initial intro.

GASOLINE (PETROL) See "Getting There & Getting Around," p. 43.

HOLIDAYS In France, holidays are *jours fériés.* Shops and many businesses (banks and some museums and restaurants) close on holidays, but hotels and emergency services remain open.

The main holidays include New Year's Day (Jan 1), Easter Sunday and Monday, Labor Day (May 1), V-E Day (May 8), Whitmonday (May 19), Ascension Thursday (40 days after Easter), Bastille Day (July 14), Assumption of the Blessed Virgin (Aug 15), All Saints' Day (Nov 1), Armistice Day (Nov 11), and Christmas (Dec 25).

HOSPITALS In **Nice** there is the Hôpital St-Roch, 5 rue Pierre Dévoluy (© 04-92-03-33-75); in **Monaco,** Centre Hospitalier Princesse Grace, av. Pastuer (© 377-97-98-99-00); in **Antibes,** Chemin des Quatres Chemins (© 04-92-91-77-77); in **Cannes,** Hôpital des Broussailles, 13 av. Des Broussailles (© 04-93-69-70-00).

INSURANCE For travel overseas, most U.S. health plans (including Medicare and Medicaid) do not provide coverage, and the ones that do often require you to pay for services upfront and reimburse you only after you return home.

As a safety net, you may want to buy travel medical insurance, particularly if you're traveling to a remote or high-risk area where emergency evacuation might be necessary. If you require additional medical insurance, try **MEDEX Assistance** (© **410/453-6300;** www.medexassist.com) or **Travel Assistance International** (© **800/821-2828;** www.travelassistance.com; for general information on services, call the company's **Worldwide Assistance Services, Inc.,** at ⓒ **800/777-8710**).

Canadians should check with their provincial health plan offices or call **Health Canada** (ⓒ **866/225-0709;** www.hc-sc.gc.ca) to find out the extent of their coverage and what documentation and receipts they must take home in case they are treated overseas.

Travelers from the U.K. should carry their European Health Insurance Card (EHIC), which replaced the E111 form as proof of entitlement to free/reduced cost medical treatment abroad (ⓒ **0845/606-2030;** www.ehic.org.uk). Note, however, that the EHIC covers only "necessary medical treatment," and coverage for repatriation costs, lost money, baggage, or cancellation, travel insurance from a reputable company should always be sought (www.travelinsuranceweb.com).

INTERNET ACCESS See "Internet/E-Mail" under "Staying Connected," in chapter 3.

LANGUAGE English is increasingly understood in France, especially among young people who have studied it in school. People are more likely to understand English in such centers as Paris and the Riviera than in the more remote provinces. Service personnel in hotels tend to speak English, at least at the front desk. A staff member at most restaurants will speak a bit of English. However, many people you encounter in France do not speak English, and you may want to carry a Berlitz handbook. For some basic vocabulary, see chapter 10.

LEGAL AID The French government advises foreigners to consult their embassy or consulate (see above) in case of an arrest or similar problem. The staff can generally offer advice on how you can obtain help locally and can furnish you with a list of local attorneys. If you are arrested for illegal possession of drugs, the U.S. Embassy

and consular officials cannot interfere with the French judicial system. A consulate can advise you only of your rights.

LOST & FOUND To speed the process of replacing your personal documents if they're lost or stolen, make a photocopy of the first few pages of your passport and write down your credit card numbers (and the serial numbers of your traveler's checks, if you're using them) before leaving your home country. Leave this information with someone at home—to be faxed to you in an emergency—and swap it with your traveling companion. Be sure to tell all of your credit card companies the minute you discover your wallet has been lost or stolen, and file a report at the nearest police precinct. Your credit card company or insurer may require a police report number or record of the loss.

Use the following numbers in France to report your lost or stolen credit card: for **American Express,** ⓒ **336/393-1111** (call collect; www.americanexpress.com); for **MasterCard,** ⓒ **08-00-90-13-87** (www.mastercard.com); and for **Visa,** ⓒ **08-00-90-11-79** (www.visaeurope.com). Your credit card company may be able to wire you a cash advance immediately or deliver an emergency card in a day or two.

MAIL Most post offices in France are open Monday through Friday from 8am to 7pm, and Saturday from 8am to noon. Allow 5 to 8 days to send or receive mail from your home. Airmail letters to North America cost .90€ for 20 grams. Letters to the U.K. cost .85€ for up to 20 grams. An airmail postcard to North America or Europe (outside France) costs .85€.

You can exchange money at post offices. Many hotels sell stamps, as do local post offices and cafes displaying a red TABAC sign outside.

PASSPORTS For Residents of the United States: Whether you're applying in person or by mail, you can download passport applications from the U.S. Department of State website at http://travel.state.gov. To find your regional passport office, either check the U.S. Department of State website or call the toll-free number of the **National Passport Information Center** (© 877/487-2778) for automated information.

For Residents of Canada: Passport applications are available at travel agencies throughout Canada or from the central **Passport Office,** Department of Foreign Affairs and International Trade, Ottawa, ON K1A 0G3 (© 800/567-6868; www.ppt.gc.ca). *Note:* Canadian children who travel must have their own passport. However, if you hold a valid Canadian passport issued before December 11, 2001, that bears the name of your child, the passport remains valid for you and your child until it expires.

For Residents of Ireland: You can apply for a 10-year passport at the **Passport Office,** Setanta Centre, Molesworth Street, Dublin 2 (© 01/671-1633; www.irlgov.ie/iveagh). Those under age 18 and over 65 must apply for a 3-year passport. You can also apply at 1A South Mall, Cork (© 021/494-4700), or at most main post offices.

For Residents of Australia: You can pick up an application from your local post office or any branch of Passports Australia, but you must schedule an interview at the passport office to present your application materials. Call the **Australian Passport Information Service** at © 131-232 or visit the government website at **www.smarttraveler.gov.au**.

For Residents of New Zealand: You can pick up a passport application at any New Zealand Passports Office or download it from the website. Contact the **Passports Office** at © 0800/225-050 in New Zealand or 04/474-8100, or log on to www.passports.govt.nz.

MAPS The best and most detailed maps are provided by Michelin, the tire people.

You can search their website at **www.viamichelin.com**. These maps are sold in good bookstores all over the world, and in nearly all bookstores in Languedoc, Provence, and the resorts strung along the Riviera.

If you're driving around France, the best road atlas to travel with is *Michelin's Atlas Routièr France,* which can be purchased with a spiral binding for greater convenience. *Plans,* or street maps, are distributed free by tourist offices, including Nice, Cannes, Monaco, and St-Tropez. Abbreviations in common use on these city maps are R for rue (street), AV for avenue, and Q for quay.

PHARMACIES If you need a *pharmacie* during off hours, have the front-desk staff at your hotel get in touch with the nearest Commissariat de Police. An agent there will have the address of a nearby pharmacy open 24 hours a day. French law requires that the pharmacies in any given neighborhood display the name and location of the one that remains open all night. In Paris, one of the most central all-nighters is **Pharmacy Les Champs "Derhy,"** 84 av. des Champs-Elysées, 8e (© 01-45-62-02-41; Métro: George V).

POLICE Call © 17 anywhere in France.

USEFUL PHONE NUMBERS U.S. Dept. of State Travel Advisory (© 202/647-5225, staffed 24 hr.); U.S. Passport Agency (© 202/647-0518); U.S. Centers for Disease Control International Traveler's Hotline (© 800/232-4636).

VISITOR INFORMATION Your best source of information before you go is the **French Government Tourist Office;** visit its website at www.franceguide.com. In the United States, call © 514/288-1904 to request information. In Canada, © 514/288-2026; in the United Kingdom, © 09068/244-123 (60p per minute), fax 020/7493-6594; in Ireland, call © 015/60-235-235; and in Australia, call © 02/9231-5244. There's no representative in

New Zealand—you will have to call the Australian office.

WATER Drinking water is generally safe, though it's occasionally been known to cause diarrhea. If you ask for water in a restaurant, it'll be served bottled (for which you'll pay) unless you specifically request *l'eau du robinet* (tap water). Your waiter may ask if you'd like your water *avec gas* (carbonated) or *sans gas* (without bubbles).

2 AIRLINE, HOTEL & CAR RENTAL WEBSITES

MAJOR AIRLINES

Aer Lingus
www.aerlingus.com

Aigle Azur
www.aigle-azur.fr

Air France
www.airfrance.com

Air Transat
www.airtransat.com

Alitalia
www.alitalia.com

British Airways
www.british-airways.com

CCM
www.aircorsica.com

Delta Air Lines
www.delta.com

El Al Airlines
www.el.co.il

Emirates Airlines
www.emirates.com

Germanwings Airlines
www.germanwings.com

Iberia Airlines
www.iberia.com

Lufthansa
www.lufthansa.com

Lufttransport
www.lufttransport.no

North American Airlines
www.flynaa.com

OLT Ostfriesische
www.olt.de

Royal Air Maroc
www.royalairmaroc.com

Royal Dutch Airlines
www.klm.com

Syrian Arab Airlines
www.syrianair.com

Tunisair
www.tunisair.com

BUDGET AIRLINES

Air Algèrie
www.airalgerie.dz

Air Austral
www.air-austral.com

Air Ivoire
www.airivoire.com

Air Madagascar
www.airmadagascar.com

Air Malta
www.airmalta.com

Air Méditerranée
www.air-mediterranee.fr

Air Sénégal International
www.airsenegal-international.com

Atlas Blue
www.atlas-blue.com

Baboo Airlines
www.flybaboo.com

BMI Baby
www.bmibaby.com

Brussels Airlines
www.brusselsairlines.com

Corsairfly
www.corsairfly.com

CSA Czech Airlines
www.csa.cz

easyJet
www.easyjet.com

Flybe Flights
www.flybe.com

New Axis Airways
www.fly-axis.com

Ryanair
www.ryanair.com

Tap Airlines
www.flytap.com

Transavia
www.transavia.com

Tuifly Airlines
www.tuifly.com

Twin Jet
www.twinjet.net

Yemenia
www.yemenia.com

MAJOR HOTEL & MOTEL CHAINS

Accor Hotels
www.accorhotels.com

Club Med
www.clubmed.fr

Concorde Hotels & Resorts
www.concorde-hotels.com

Châteaux & Hôtels Collection
www.historichotelsofeurope.com

Epoque Hotels
www.epoquehotels.com

InterContinental Hotels Group
www.ichotelsgroup.com

Le Meridien Hotels & Resorts
www.lemeridien.com

Luxury Retreats
www.luxuryretreats.com

Marriott Hotels
www.marriott.com

Relais & Châteaux
www.relaischateaux.com

Small Luxury Hotels of the World
www.slh.com

CAR RENTAL AGENCIES

ADA Car Rentals
www.ada.fr

Auto Europe
www.autoeurope.com

Avis
www.avis.com

Budget
www.budget.com

Hertz
www.hertz.com

Libertans
www.libertans.com

National
www.nationalcar.com

Sixt
www.sixt.com

10

Glossary of Useful Terms

If nothing else, learn basic greet-ings, and—above all—the life-raft phrase, *Parlez-vous anglais?* ("Do you speak English?"). Many people speak passable English and will use it liberally, if you show the basic courtesy of greeting them in their language.

1 USEFUL FRENCH WORDS & PHRASES

English	French	Pronunciation
Yes/No	**Oui/Non**	wee/noh
Okay	**D'accord**	*dah*-core
Please	**S'il vous plaît**	seel voo *play*
Thank you	**Merci**	*mair*-see
You're welcome	**De rien**	duh ree-*ehn*
Hello (during daylight)	**Bonjour**	bohn-*jhoor*
Good evening	**Bonsoir**	bohn-*swahr*
Goodbye	**Au revoir**	o ruh-*vwahr*
What's your name?	**Comment vous appellez-vous?**	kuh-*mahn* voo za-pell-ay-voo?
My name is	**Je m'appelle**	*jhuh* ma-pell
How are you?	**Comment allez-vous?**	kuh-*mahn* tahl-ay-voo?
I'm sorry/excuse me	**Pardon**	pahr-*dohn*

GETTING AROUND & STREET SMARTS

English	French	Pronunciation
Do you speak English?	**Parlez-vous anglais?**	par-lay-voo zahn-glay?
I don't speak French	**Je ne parle pas français**	jhuh ne parl pah frahn-*say*
I don't understand	**Je ne comprends pas**	jhuh ne kohm-*prahn* pas
Could you speak more loudly/ more slowly?	**Pouvez-vous parler plus fort/plus lentement?**	Poo-*vay* voo par-lay ploo for/ploo lan-te-*ment?*
What is it?	**Qu'est-ce que c'est?**	kess kuh *say?*
What time is it?	**Qu'elle heure est-il?**	kel uhr eh-*teel?*
What?	**Quoi?**	kwah?

English	French	Pronunciation
How? *or* What did you say?	**Comment?**	ko-*mahn?*
When?	**Quand?**	kahn?
Who?	**Qui?**	kee?
Why?	**Pourquoi?**	poor-*kwah?*
Where is?	**Où est?**	ooh eh?
here/there	**ici/là**	ee-*see*/lah
left/right	**à gauche/à droite**	a goash/a drwaht
straight ahead	**tout droit**	too drwah
Fill the tank (of a car), please	**Le plein, s'il vous plaît**	luh plan, seel-voo-*play*
I want to get off at	**Je voudrais descendre à**	jhe voo-*dray* day-son drah-ah
the airport	**l'aéroport**	lair-o-*por*
the bank	**la banque**	lah bahnk
the bridge	**le pont**	luh pohn
the bus station	**la gare routière**	lah gar roo-tee-*air*
the bus stop	**l'arrêt de bus**	lah-*ray* duh boohss
the cathedral	**la cathedral**	lah ka-tay-*dral*
the church	**l'église**	lay-*gleez*
exit (from a building or a freeway)	**une sortie**	ewn sor-*tee*
gasoline	**du pétrol/de l'essence**	duh pay-*troll*/de lay-*sahns*
hospital	**l'hôpital**	low-pee-*tahl*
museum	**le musée**	luh mew-*zay*
no smoking	**défense de fumer**	day-*fahns* de fu-may
one-way ticket	**aller simple**	ah-*lay* sam-pluh
round-trip ticket	**aller-retour**	ah-*lay* re-*toor*
second floor	**premier étage**	prem-ee-*ehr* ay-*taj*
slow down	**ralentir**	rah-lahn-*teer*
street	**rue**	roo
subway	**le métro**	le *máy*-tro
telephone	**le téléphone**	luh tay-lay-*phone*
ticket	**un billet**	uh *bee*-yay
toilets	**les toilettes/les WC**	lay twa-*lets*/les vay-*say*

NECESSITIES

English	French	Pronunciation
I'd like	**Je voudrais**	jhe voo-*dray*
a room	**une chambre**	ewn *shahm*-bruh
the key	**la clé (la clef)**	la clay

English	French	Pronunciation
How much does it cost?	C'est combien?/ Ça coûte combien?	say comb-bee-*ehn?*/sah coot comb-bee-*ehn?*
Do you take credit cards?	Est-ce que vous acceptez les cartes de credit?	es-kuh voo zaksep-*tay* lay kart duh creh-*dee?*
I'd like to buy	Je voudrais acheter	jhe voo-dray ahsh-*tay*
aspirin	des aspirines	deyz ahs-peer-*een*
condoms	des préservatifs	day pray-ser-va-*teef*
gift	un cadeau	uh kah-*doe*
map of the city	un plan de ville	uh plahn de *veel*
newspaper	un journal	uh zhoor-*nahl*
phone card	une carte téléphonique	ewn cart tay-lay-fone-*eek*
postcard	une carte postale	ewn carte pos-*tahl*
road map	une carte routière	ewn cart roo-tee-*air*
stamp	un timbre	uh *tam*-bruh

IN YOUR HOTEL

English	French	Pronunciation
Are taxes included?	Est-ce que les taxes sont comprises?	ess-keh lay taks son com-*preez?*
balcony	un balcon	uh bahl-cohn
bathtub	une baignoire	ewn bayn-*nwar*
hot and cold water	l'eau chaude et froide	low showed ay fwad
Is breakfast included?	Petit déjeuner inclus?	peh-*tee* day-jheun-*ay* ehn-*klu?*
room	une chambre	ewn *shawm*-bruh
shower	une douche	ewn dooch
sink	un lavabo	uh la-va-*bow*

2 FOOD, MENU & COOKING TERMS

English	French	Pronunciation
I would like to eat	Je voudrais manger	jhe voo-*dray* mahn-*jhay*
Please give me	Donnez-moi, s'il vous plaît	doe-nay-*mwah*, seel voo play
a bottle of	une bouteille de	ewn boo-*tay* duh
a cup of	une tasse de	ewn tass duh
a glass of	un verre de	uh vair duh
a cocktail	un apéritif	uh ah-pay-ree-*teef*
the check/bill	l'addition/la note	la-dee-see-*ohn*/la noat
a napkin	une serviette	ewn sair-vee-*et*

English	French	Pronunciation
Cheers!	**A votre santé!**	ah vo-truh sahn-*tay!*
fixed-price menu	**un menu**	uh may-*new*
Is the tip/service included?	**Est-ce que le service est compris?**	ess-ke luh ser-*vees* eh com-*pree?*
Waiter!/Waitress!	**Monsieur!/ Mademoiselle!**	mun-*syuh*/mad-mwa-*zel*
appetizer	**une entrée**	ewn en-*tray*
tip included	**service compris**	sehr-*vees* cohm-*pree*

MEATS

English	French	Pronunciation
beef stew	**du pot-au-feu**	dew poht o *fhe*
marinated beef braised with red wine and served with vegetables	**du boeuf à la mode**	dew bewf ah lah *mhowd*
chicken	**du poulet**	*dew poo*-lay
chicken, stewed with mushrooms and wine	**du coq au vin**	dew cock o vhin
ham	**du jambon**	dew jahm-*bohn*
lamb	**de l'agneau**	duh lahn-*nyo*
rabbit	**du lapin**	dew lah-pan
sirloin	**de l'aloyau**	duh lahl-why-*yo*
steak	**du bifteck**	dew beef-*tek*
veal	**du veau**	dew *voh*

FISH

English	French	Pronunciation
Mediterranean fish soup or stew	**de la bouillabaisse**	duh lah booh-ya-*besse*
lobster	**du homard**	dew oh-*mahr*
mussels	**des moules**	day *moohl*
mussels in herb-flavored white wine with shallots	**des moules marinières**	day moohl mar-ee-nee-*air*
oysters	**des huîtres**	dayz hoo-*ee*-truhs
shrimp	**des crevettes**	day kreh-*vette*
tuna	**du thon**	dew tohn
trout	**de la truite**	duh lah tru-*eet*

English	French	Pronunciation
eggplant	**de l'aubergine**	duh loh-ber-*jheen*
grapes	**du raisin**	dew ray-*zhan*
green beans	**des haricots verts**	day ahr-ee-coh *vaire*
lemon/lime	**du citron/du citron vert**	dew cee-tron/dew cee-tron *vaire*
potatoes	**des pommes de terre**	day puhm duh *tehr*
potatoes au gratin	**des pommes de terre dauphinois**	day puhm duh tehr doh-feen-wah
french-fried potatoes	**des pommes frites**	day puhm *freet*
spinach	**des épinards**	dayz ay-pin-*ards*
strawberries	**des fraises**	day *frez*

SOUPS & SALADS

English	French	Pronunciation
fruit salad	**une salade de fruit/ une macédoine de fruits**	ewn sah-lahd duh *fwee*/ewn mah-say-doine duh fwee
green salad	**une salade verte**	ewn sah-lahd *vairt*
lettuce salad	**une salade de laitue**	ewn sah-lahd duh lay-tew
onion soup	**de la soupe à l'oignon**	duh lah soop ah low-*nyon*

BEVERAGES

English	French	Pronunciation
beer	**de la bière**	duh lah bee-*aire*
milk	**du lait**	dew *lay*
orange juice	**du jus d'orange**	dew joo d'or-*ahn*-jhe
water	**de l'eau**	duh lo
red wine	**du vin rouge**	dew vhin *rooj*
white wine	**du vin blanc**	dew vhin *blahn*
coffee (black)	**un café noir**	uh ka-fay *nwahr*
coffee (with cream)	**un café crème**	uh ka-fay *krem*
coffee (with milk)	**un café au lait**	uh ka-fay o *lay*
coffee (decaf)	**un café décaféiné** (slang: **un déca**)	un ka-fay day-kah-fay-*nay* (uh *day*-kah)
coffee (espresso)	**un café espresso** (**un express**)	uh ka-fay e-*sprehss-o* (un ek-*sprehss*)
tea	**du thé**	dew *tay*

INDEX

AARP, 56

Abbaye de St-Honorat, 253

Abbaye Notre-Dame de Sénanque (near Gordes), 173

Above and Beyond Tours, 54

Academic and language trips, 57

Académie des Jeux-Floraux (Toulouse), 80

Access-Able Travel Source, 55

Accessibility, 54–55

Accessible Journeys, 55

Accommodations, 61–62. *See also* Accommodations Index
best, 11–12

Acti Raft (Castellane), 218

Adventure and wellness trips, 57–59

Adventure Center, 58

Aer Lingus, 46

Africa Plage (Beaulieu), 325

Agde, 112

Aigues-Mortes, 114–118

AirAmbulanceCard.com, 55

Air Canada, 44

Air France, 43, 44, 46, 49
senior discounts, 56

Air travel, 43–44, 46, 49

Aix en Musique, 187

Aix-en-Provence, 187–194
accommodations, 190–192
nightlife, 194
restaurants, 192–194
shopping, 189–190
sights and attractions, 188–189
special events, 187
traveling to, 187
visitor information, 187

Albi, 92–95

Allée Serge-Diaghilev (Monaco), 339

Amandine (Marseille), 200

American Airlines, 43

American Foundation for the Blind (AFB), 55

Amphithéâtre (Les Arènes)
Arles, 157–158
Fréjus, 237–238

Amphithéâtre Romain (Nîmes), 126

Antibes, 277–280

Antiques
Cannes, 254
Carcassonne, 99
Collioure, 107
Marseille, 200
Toulouse, 81

Antiquités François-Décamp (Marseille), 200

Antiquités Safi (Carcassonne), 99

Anti-Semitism, 55

Apartment rentals, 61–62

Apt, 181–184

Aqua Club (St-Tropez), 222

Aqua Viva Est (Castellane), 218

Arc de Triomphe (Orange), 134

Archaeological museums
Apt, 182
Narbonne, 111
Nîmes, 127

Archbishop's Palace (Narbonne), 111

Architecture, 24–29

Arles, 155–162
accommodations, 158–160
getting around, 155
nightlife, 162
restaurants, 161–162
sights and attractions, 155–158
traveling to, 155
visitor information, 155

Art, 24–29

Art galleries
Eze, 328
St-Paul-de-Vence, 288
Tourrettes-sur-Loup, 285
Vallauris, 273

Art museums, best, 7–8

Association des Paralysés de France, 54

Atelier Arachnée (Tourrettes-sur-Loup), 285

Atelier/Boutique Christian Choisy (St-Paul-de-Vence), 288

Atelier Contre-Jour (Nice), 304

Atelier de Cézanne (Aix-en-Provence), 188

Ateliers Marcel Carbonel (Marseille), 200

At Home Abroad, 62

ATMs (automated-teller machines), 51

Auch, 88–89

Au Gourmets (Montpellier), 120

Auto Europe, 48

Autour des Oliviers (St-Tropez), 226

Avignon, 140–152
special events, 142
traveling to, 141–142
visitor information, 142

Avis car rentals, 48
for disabled travelers, 55

Backroads, 57

Baie des Fourmis (Beaulieu), 325

Banquet Hall (Avignon), 142

Baptistery, Fréjus, 238

Bar à Thym (Toulon), 211–212

Barclay International Group, 62

Bar des Stars (Cannes), 265

Bar La Bodega (Toulouse), 88

Bar La Lampa (Toulon), 212

Basilique Notre-Dame-de-la-Garde (Marseille), 198, 199

Basilique St-Martin (Cap-Martin), 349

Basilique St-Nazaire (Carcassonne), 98–99
Basilique St-Paul-Serge (Narbonne), 112–113
Basilique St-Sernin (Toulouse), 78, 80
Basilique St-Victor (Marseille), 198
Bastide St-Louis (Carcassonne), 98
Bastille Day, 39
    Carcassonne, 98
Beaches. See also specific destinations and entries starting with "Plage"
    Beaulieu, 325
    best, 3–4
    Cannes, 251–252
    Cros-de-Cagnes, 295
    Golfe-Juan, 273
    Juan-les-Pins, 274
    Marseille, 201
    Menton, 351–352
    near Narbonne, 110
    Nice, 303
    nude, 215
    Ste-Maxime, 234
    St-Raphaël, 241
    St-Tropez, 222, 224
Beaulieu, 324–327
Bechard (Aix), 189
Bed & breakfasts (B&Bs), 61
Bijoux Marlene (Monaco), 339
Biking, 57
    Aix-en-Provence, 187
    the Camargue, 118
    Cannes, 253
    Ste-Maxime, 234
    St-Tropez, 224
Biot, 282–284
Bleu Provence (Nyons), 137
Boating and sailing
    Cannes, 253
    Grand Canyon du Verdon, 218
    St-Tropez, 224
Boat tours and cruises, Château d'If, 199–200
Bokao's Café (Avignon), 151
Bonnieux, 177–181
Books, recommended, 29
Bouteille (Cannes), 255
Boutique de l'Olivier (Vallauris), 273
Boutique du Rocher (Monaco), 339
Boutique Provençale (Nîmes), 128

Boy's Paradise (Toulon), 212
British Airways, 46
British Midland, 46, 47
Budget, 48
Buis-les-Baronnies (Rosans), 137
Bullfights
    Arles, 116
        Féria des Prémices du Riz, 40
        Féria Pascale (Easter Bullfighting Festival), 36
    the Camargue, 116
    Nîmes, 124
    Nuit Taurine (Nocturnal Bull Festival; St-Rémy), 39
Bureau de Location des Arènes (Nîmes), 130
Bus travel, 47

Cabaret du Casino Ruhl (Nice), 318
Café de Paris (St-Tropez), 233
Café Le Napoléon (Nîmes), 131
Café Sénéquier (St-Tropez), 233
Café van Gogh (Arles), 162
The Camargue, 63, 76
    gardiens (cowboys) of, 116–118
    suggested itinerary, 74–75
Canet-Plage (Perpignan), 106
Cannes, 248–266
    accommodations, 256–261
    beaches, 251–252
    nightlife, 265–266
    outdoor pursuits, 253–254
    restaurants, 261–265
    shopping, 254–255
    sights and attractions, 249–251
    special events, 249
    traveling to, 248–249
    visitor information, 249
Cannes Film Festival, 38, 249
Cannolive (Cannes), 255
Canoeing, Grand Canyon du Verdon, 218
Cap d'Antibes, 277
Cap-Martin, 348–350
Cap Morgiou, 197
Car breakdowns/assistance, 49
Carcassonne, 97–102
Carnival, Nice, 36

Carrée d'Art/Musée d'Art Contemporain (Nîmes), 126
Car rentals, 47–48
Car travel, 47–49
Cascade de Courmes, 291
Cascades des Demoiselles, 291
Casino Croisette (Cannes), 265
Casino de Beaulieu, 325
Casino des Princes (Cannes), 265
Casinos. See also specific casinos
    Beaulieu, 325
    Cannes, 265
    Juan-les-Pins, 277
    Monaco, 334–335, 346–347
    St-Raphaël, 243
Castillet/Musée des Arts et Traditions Populaires Catalans (Perpignan), 103
Castres, 95–97
Castrum (Roussillon), 176
Cathédrale de la Major (Marseille), 198
Cathédrale de Monaco, 335
Cathédrale d'Images (near Les Baux), 164
Cathédrale Notre-Dame des Doms (Avignon), 144
Cathédrale Orthodoxe Russe St-Nicolas à Nice, 301–302
Cathédrale Ste-Anne (Apt), 181–182
Cathédrale Ste-Cécile (Albi), 93
Cathédrale Ste-Marie (Auch), 88
Cathédrale Ste-Marie-Majeure (Toulon), 209
Cathédrale St-Etienne (Toulouse), 80
Cathédrale St-Jean (Perpignan), 104
Cathédrale St-Just (Narbonne), 111
Cathédrale St-Léonce (Fréjus), 238
Cathédrale St-Pierre (Montpellier), 119
Cathédrale St-Sauveur (Aix-en-Provence), 188
Cathédrale St-Théodorit (Uzes), 153
Cellphones, 60
Centers for Disease Control and Prevention, 52

Central Complex (Narbonne), 111

Centre International de Plongée (CIP) de Nice, 303

Centre National et Musée Jean-Jaurès (Castres), 96

Centre Sant-Vicens (Perpignan), 104

Céret, 103

Cézanne, Paul, 27, 187, 188–189
Atelier de Cézanne (Aix-en-Provence), 188

Chagall, Marc, 28
Musée National Message Biblique Marc Chagall (Cimiez), 303

Chapelle Cocteau (Fréjus), 238

Chapelle de la Miséricorde (St-Tropez), 224

Chapelle des Bourras (Chapelle Penitents-gris; Aix), 188

Chapelle des Pénitents Blancs (Peillon), 330

Chapelle du Rosaire (Vence), 292

Chapelle Notre-Dame de Vie (Mougins), 269

Chapelle Penitents-gris (Chapelle des Bourras; Aix), 188

Chapelle St-Jean (Avignon), 142

Chapelle St-Martial (Avignon), 142

Chapelle St-Nicolas (Avignon), 144

Chapelle St-Pierre (Villefranche-sur-Mer), 320

Chartreuse du Val-de-Bénédiction (Villeneuve-lez-Avignon), 151

Château Comtal (Carcassonne), 98

Château d'Eau (Montpellier), 120

Château de Bosc (Camjac), 94

Château de Flaugergues, 121

Château de Gordes, 172

Château de Gourdon, 291

Château de la Napoule, 6

Château de la Napoule/Musée Henry-Clews, 245

Château de l'Empéri (Salon de Provence), 184–185

Château de Roquebrune, 348

Château de Salses (near Perpignan), 104

Château des Baux (Les Baux), 164

Château de Vallauris, 272

Château de Vauvenarges (Aix-en-Provence), 188

Château d'Hyères, 213

Château d'If, 6, 199–200

Château du Pharo (Marseille), 199

Châteauneuf-du-Pape, 134, 138–140

Château Royal (Collioure), 107

Château Suffren (St-Tropez), 224

Chaussée des Géants (Roussillon), 176

Chez Bruno (Cannes), 254

Chez Maggi (St-Tropez), 233

Chez Tonton (Toulouse), 87

Chez Wayne (Nice), 318–319

Chez Wayne's (Nice), 318

Children, families with, suggested itinerary, 71–73

Chocolate
Cannes, 254
Châteauneuf-du-Pape, 139
Marseille, 200

Chocolaterie Castelain (Châteauneuf-du-Pape), 139

Chorégies d'Orange, 39

Churches and cathedrals, best, 8–9

Cimiez, 302–303

Cimiez Convent, 302

Ciné-Folie (Cannes), 254

Cité de l'Espace (Toulouse), 80

Cité Episcopale (Fréjus), 238

Climate, 35

Cloister, Fréjus, 238

Clos des Papes (Châteauneuf-du-Pape), 139

Club 55 (St-Tropez), 222

Club Hippique de Nice, 303

Club Nautique (Esparron), 218

Cockpit (Toulouse), 88

Coco Beach (Ramatuelle), 224

Cocteau, Jean, 28
Chapelle Cocteau (Fréjus), 238
Chapelle St-Pierre (Villefranche-sur-Mer), 320
Musée Jean-Cocteau (Menton), 351

Collection des Voitures Anciennes de S.A.S. le Prince de Monaco, 335

Collégiale de la Conversion de St-Paul (St-Paul-de-Vence), 287

Collegiale St-Paul (Hyères), 213

Colline St-Eutrope (Orange), 134

Collioure, 107–110

Collision-damage waiver (CDW), 48

Competition Internationale de Jazz de New Orleans (St-Raphaël), 240

Comptoir des Vins (Carcassonne), 99

Condo rentals, 61–62

Confiserie Auer (Nice), 304

Confiserie des Gorges du Loup (Pont-du-Loup), 291

Confiserie des Gorges du Loup (Tourrettes-sur-Loup), 285

Confiserie Florian du Vieux-Nice, 304

Confiserie Marcel Richaud (Apt), 183

Confiseur Le Coulon/Jean Ceccon (Apt), 183

Continental Airlines, 44

Cooking classes, 59

Cooperative Nérolium (Vallauris), 273

Coquillages Philippe (Sanary-sur-Mer), 230

Cordes-sur-Ciel, 5, 90–92

Corniche Inférieure, 15, 281

Corniche Président-J.-F.-Kennedy (Marseille), 197

Côte d'Azur (the Riviera), 64
eastern, 281–353
suggested itinerary, 71–73
western, 221–280

Country-Club de Cannes-Mougins, 253–254

Cours Mirabeau (Aix-en-Provence), 188

Credit cards, 51–52

Crime, 53

Cros-de-Cagnes, 294–297

Currency and currency exchange, 50–51

Customs regulations, 41–43

Cycles Daniel (Cannes), 253

Dancing GM Palace (Narbonne), 114

Daudet Festival (Fontvieille), 40

Delta Airlines, 43
De Sade, marquis, 177
Dior (Cannes), 255
Disabilities, travelers with, 54–55
Disco Le Maximo (Toulouse), 88
Disco Le Sept (Cannes), 265
Domaine de Mont-Redon (near Châteaneuf-du-Pape), 139
Dominique Sarraute (Carcassonne), 99
Donjon Gilles-Aycelin (Narbonne), 111
Driving rules, 49

Earthwatch, 56
EasyJet, 47
Eating and drinking. See Food and cuisine
Eden Casino (Juan-les-Pins), 277
Eglise de Biot, 282
Eglise de Sacré-Coeur (Beaulieu), 325
Eglise des Jacobins (Toulouse), 81
Eglise des Templiers (St-Raphaël), 241
Eglise Neuve (Bonnieux), 179
Eglise Notre-Dame (Villenueve-lez-Avignon), 151
Eglise Notre-Dame des Sablons (Aigues-Mortes), 115
Eglise Orthodoxe Russe St-Michel Archange (Cannes), 251
Eglise St-Benoît (Castres), 96
Eglise Ste-Marguerite (Roquebrune), 348
Eglise Ste-Maxime (Ste-Maxime), 234
Eglise St-Michel (Cordes-sur-Ciel), 91
Eglise St-Sauveur (Peillon), 330
Eglise St-Trophime (Arles), 156
Eglise St-Vincent (Les Baux), 163
EHIC (European Health Insurance Card), 53
Elco Marine (Cannes), 253
Elderhostel, 56
ElderTreks, 56
Entry requirements, 41–43

Equitours, 58–59
Escalier Monumental (Auch), 88
Escorted tours, 59
Espace Culturel (Mougins), 269
Eurailpass, 45–46
The Euro, 50
Euro-Bike & Walking Tours, 57
European Health Insurance Card (EHIC), 53
European Rail Timetable, 44
Eze, 327–329

Façonnable (Nice), 304
Families with children, suggested itinerary, 71–73
Fashions (clothing)
    Cannes, 255
    Marseille, 200
Fédération Nationale des Agents Immobiliers, 62
Fédération Nationale des Logis de France, 62
Felio (Marseille), 200
Féria de St-Rémy, 40
Féria des Prémices du Riz (Arles), 40
Féria Pascale (Easter Bull-fighting Festival; Arles), 36
Ferries, from England, 46
Festival Aix en Musique, 38
Festival d'Avignon, 40, 142
Festival de Carcassonne, 98
Festival de la St-Eloi (Maussane-les-Alpilles), 38
Festival de Marseille Méditerranée, 39
Festival de Radio France et de Montpellier, 119
Festival des Musiques d'Aujourd'hui (Marseille), 38
Festival d'Expression Provençale (Tarascon), 38
Festival International d'Art Lyrique & de Musique (Aix-en-Provence), 187
Festival International de Jazz (Juan-les-Pins), 274
Festival International de la Télévision (Monte Carlo), 333–334
Festival International du Photojournalisme (Perpignan), 103

Festival International Montpellier Danse, 119
Festival St-Pierre des Pêcheurs (St-Raphaël), 240
Festivals and special events, 36–41
Fête de la Chandeleur (Marseille), 36
Fête de la St-Eloi (Gémenos), 40
Fête de la Tarasque (Tarascon), 38–39
Fête de la Transhumance (St-Rémy), 38
Fête de la Véraison (Châteaneuf-du-Pape), 139
Fête de St-Sylvestre, 41
Fête des Bergers (Istres), 40
Fête des Gardians (Camargue Cowboys' Festival; Arles), 36, 38
Fête des Olives (Mouriès), 40
Fête des Pècheurs (Fishermen's Festival; Cassis), 39
Fête des Plantes (Fréjus), 237
Fêtes Daudet (Fontvieille), 40
Feu de la St-Jean (Fontvieille), 39
Films, 29–30
Fishing, 57
Flaugergues, Château de, 121
Flea markets
    Cannes, 255
    Monaco, 340
    Nice, 304
    Nîmes, 127
    Toulouse, 81
Flower markets
    Avignon, 146
    Cannes, 255
    Monaco, 340
    Nice, 300
    St-Tropez, 226
Flying Wheels Travel, 55
Flying with Disability, 55
FNAC (Monaco), 339
Foire aux Santons (Marseille), 40
Foire de Noël (Mougins), 40
Fondation Angladon-Dubrujeaud (Avignon), 144
Fondation Bemberg (Toulouse), 80
Fondation Louis Jou (Les Baux), 163
Fondation Maeght (St-Paul-de-Vence), 287
Fontaine du Soleil (Nice), 300

Fontaine Moussue (Salon de Provence), 184
Fontvieille (Monaco), 334
Food and cuisine, 31–33
    shops and markets
        Apt, 183
        Avignon, 146
        Cannes, 255
        Grasse, 266
        Marseille, 200–201
        Monaco, 340
        Montpellier, 120
        Nice, 304
        St-Raphaël, 242
        St-Tropez, 226
        Toulon, 209
        Tourrettes-sur-Loup, 285
        Vallauris, 273
    trips, 59
Formule 1 hotels, 62
Formule 1 shop (Monaco), 340
Fort de l'Ile (Ile Ste-Marguerite), 252
Fortress (Le Haut-de-Cagnes), 295
Fort Ste-Agathe (Ile des Porquerolles), 216
France: Homestyle, 61
Fréjus, 237–239
French Experience, 61
The French Kitchen, 59
Friche la Belle de Mai (Marseille), 198
Frioul If Express (Marseille), 199
Fromagerie Marrou (Marseille), 201

Galerie Doussot (Eze), 328
Galerie Eponyme (Tourrettes-sur-Loup), 285
Galerie Jean-Claude Novaro (Biot), 283
Galerie Madoura (Vallauris), 273
Galerie Sassi-Milici (Vallauris), 273
Galeries du Métropole (Monaco), 339
Galerie Sevek (Eze), 328
Galeries Lafayette (Cannes), 254
Galeries Tropéziennes (St-Tropez), 226
Ganesh Pub (St-Raphaël), 243

Gardiens of the Camargue, 116–118
Gasoline, 48–49
Gay.com Travel, 54
Gay Provence, 54
Gays and lesbians
    Avignon, 151
    Cannes, 265–266
    information and resources, 53–54
    Marseille, 208
    Montpellier, 124
    Nice, 319
    St-Raphaël, 243
    St-Tropez, 222, 233
    Toulon, 212
Geneviève Lethu (Monaco), 340
Gérard Blache (St-Nazaire-le-Desert), 137
Get Bar-MP Bar (Marseille), 208
Globus + Cosmos Tours, 59
Golf, 57–58
    Cannes, 253–254
    Monaco, 338
    Nice, 303
    St-Tropez, 224
Golf Bastide du Roi (Biot), 303
Golf Club de Beauvallon (St-Tropez), 224
Golf de Marseille la Salette, 57
Golf de Ste-Maxime-Plaza (St-Tropez), 224
Golf de Valcros (La Londe-Les Maures), 57–58
Golfe-Juan, 271–273
Golf International, 58
Gordes, 5–6, 172–175
Gorge du Mal-Infernet (Agay), 244
Gorges du Loup, 291
Gourdon, 291
Grand Canyon du Verdon, 217–220
Grand Casino (St-Raphaël), 243
Grande Corniche, 15, 281
Grande Expo du Pont du Gard (Nîmes), 127
Grand Tinel (Avignon), 142
Grasse, 266–268
Graveyard (Nice), 300
Gray-d'Albion (Cannes), 255
Grimaldi dynasty, 336–337
Grimaldi Forum (Monaco), 347

Grotte de la Ste-Baume, 244
Gruisson, 110
Guest (Nice), 319

Haddock Cafe (Nîmes), 131
Halle aux Grains (Toulouse), 87
Hans Hartung & Anna-Eva Bergman Foundation (Antibes), 278
Héliopolis, 215
Hermès (Cannes), 255
Hertz car rentals, 48
Hervé Baume (Avignon), 146
Hiking, 58
    Grand Canyon du Verdon, 218
History of Provence and The Riviera, 17–24
Homme et Mouton (Picasso; Vallauris), 272
Horreum Romain (Narbonne), 112
Horseback riding, 58–59
    Nice, 303
Hostelling International USA, 62
Hôtel Bosc (Albi), 94
Hôtel Colin d'Albertas (Apt), 182
Hôtel de Manville (Les Baux), 163
Hôtel des Porcelles (Les Baux), 163
Hôtel de Ville (City Hall)
    Arles, 156
    Narbonne, 111
    Toulon, 210
    Toulouse, 81
House rentals, 61–62
Hubert Herpin (Cannes), 254
Hyères, 212–214
Hyères-Plage, 212

Ile de Port-Cros, 216–217
Ile des Porquerolles, 215–216
Ile du Levant, 215
Ile Ste-Marguerite, 252–253
Ile St-Honorat, 253
Iles de Lérins, 252–253
Iles d'Hyères, 214–217
International Association for Medical Assistance to Travelers (IAMAT), 52
International Film Festival (Cannes), 38, 249

International Gay & Lesbian Travel Association (IGLTA), 54

International Society of Travel Medicine, 52

International Yacht Charter (Cannes), 253

Internet access, 60

Itineraries, suggested, 64–75
Languedoc-Roussillon and the Camargue in 1 week, 74–75
Provence and the Riviera for families, 71–73
Provence in 1 week, 64–66
The Riviera in 2 weeks, 66–71

Jaffier-Parsi (Avignon), 146
JAM (Montpellier), 124
Jardin Albert-1er (Nice), 301
Jardin de la Fontaine (Nîmes), 127
Jardin des Arômes (Nyons), 137
Jardin des Plantes (Montpellier), 119
Jardin d'Eze, 328
Jardin Exotique (Monaco), 335
Jazz festivals, 39, 40
Juan-les-Pins, 274
Nice, 300
St-Raphaël, 240
Jean-Jaurès, Musée (Castres), 96
Jimmy's (Monaco), 347
Juan-les-Pins, 274–277

Kayaking, Grand Canyon du Verdon, 218
Kelly's Irish Pub (St-Tropez), 233
Kemwel Drive Group, 48

La Bodeguita (Nice), 319
La Boutique de l'Olivier (Vallauris), 273
La Bulle (Carcassonne), 102
La Canebière (Marseille), 197
La Cave à Jazz (Marseille), 208
La Cité de la Musique (Marseille), 208

La Cité de l'Espace (Toulouse), 80
La Civette (Nice), 318
La Collégiale de la Conversion de St-Paul (St-Paul-de-Vence), 287
La Comédie (Nîmes), 131
La Condamine (Monaco), 334
La Confiserie des Gorges du Loup (Pont-du-Loup), 291
La Couqueto (Nice), 304
La Fromagerie Marrou (Marseille), 201
La Grande Expo du Pont du Gard (Nîmes), 127
La Joia (Aix), 194
La Maison des Gîtes de France et du Tourisme Vert, 61
La Maison Quinta (Perpignan), 104
La Napoule-Plage, 245–248
Languedoc-Roussillon, 63, 76–131
suggested itinerary, 74–75
La Paësine (Tourrettes-sur-Loup), 285
La Pelouse interdite (Toulouse), 87
La Petite Cave de St-Paul (St-Paul-de-Vence), 287–288
La Poterie Provençale (Biot), 283
La Réserve (St-Raphaël), 243
La Route Napoleon, 247
La Tantina de Bourgos (Toulouse), 87
La Turbie, 327–329
Lavender, 136–137
La Villa Rouge (Montpellier), 124
La Vinothèque (Châteauneuf-du-Pape), 139
La Voile Rouge (St-Tropez), 222
Le Bar du Port (St-Tropez), 233
Le Bar 113 (Toulon), 211
Le Before (Nice), 318
Le Black Bottom (Carcassonne), 102
Le Boat, 57
Le Café (St-Tropez), 233
Le Café van Gogh (Arles), 162
Le Capitole (Toulouse), 81
Le Cargo de Nuit (Arles), 162
Le C-Cafe (Nîmes), 131
Le Chandelier (Nice), 304

Le Château (Nice), 300
Le Circus (Marseille), 208
Le Coco Club (St-Raphaël), 243
Le Collegiale St-Paul (Hyères), 213
Le Corum (Montpellier), 124
Le Deep Lounge (Nîmes), 131
Le Dépôt (St-Tropez), 226
Le Divan (Cannes), 266
Le Duché (Uzes), 153–154
Le Four des Navettes (Marseille), 200–201
Le Frog & Le Roast Beef (Toulouse), 87
Le Ganesh Pub (St-Raphaël), 243
Legend (Monaco), 347
Léger, Fernand, Musée National (Biot), 282–283
Le Grand Café (Avignon), 150
Le Habana Bodegita-Club (Perpignan), 106
Le Haut-de-Cagnes, 294–297
Le Karement (Monaco), 347
Le Klub (Nice), 319
Le Living Room (Monaco), 347
Le Lounge 233 (Toulouse), 87
Le Master Home Bar (Nice), 319
Le Mistral (Aix), 194
Le Napoli (Perpignan), 106
Le Nightlife (Cannes), 265–266
Le O'Shannon Bar (Perpignan), 106
Le Pacha (Montpellier), 124
Le Pam Pam (Juan-les-Pins), 277
Le Papagayo (St-Tropez), 232
Le Pharaon (Marseille), 208
Le Pigeonnier (St-Tropez), 233
Le Purple (Toulouse), 87
Le Relais (Nice), 318
Lérins Islands, 252–253
Les Alyscamps (Arles), 156
Les Ambassadeurs (Avignon), 150
Le Sass-Café (Monaco), 347
Les Baux, 162–166
L'Escale Borély (Marseille), 201, 208
Les Caves du Roy (St-Tropez), 232
Les Chorégies d'Orange (Orange), 134

L'Esclave (Avignon), 151
Les Estivales (Perpignan), 102
Les Gardiens of the Camargue, 116–118
Les Grands Appartements du Palais (Monaco), 6–7, 335
Les Halles (Avignon), 146
Les Olivades (Aix), 189
Les Olivades Factory Store (Arles), 158
L'Espace Matisse (Vence), 292
Le Splendid Plage (Menton), 352
Les Puces de Fontvieille (Monaco), 340
Les Puces de Nice (Nice), 304
Les Sablettes (Menton), 352
Les Thermes Marins de Monte-Carlo (Monaco), 339
Le Village (Juan-les-Pins), 277
Le VIP Room (St-Tropez), 232–233
Le Visa pour l'Image (Perpignan), 103
Le Vogue (Cannes), 265
Le Woolloomooloo (Avignon), 150–151
L'Exit (Marseille), 208
Lingua Service Worldwide, 57
L'Interdit (Marseille), 208
Lubéron National Park, 182
Lulu Club (Nîmes), 131

Maison Carrée (Nîmes), 25, 126
Maison du Grand-Fauconnier (Cordes-sur-Ciel), 90
Maisons Gothiques (Cordes-sur-Ciel), 90
Manufacture de Monaco, 340
Maps, 49
Marché à la Brocante (Nice), 304
Marché Alimentaire de St-Raphaël, 242
Marché aux Aires (Grasse), 266
Marché aux Fleurs (Nice), 300
Marché aux Santons (Tarascon), 40
Marché Forville (Cannes), 255
Marine Air Sport (St-Tropez), 224
Marius Fabre (Salon de Provence), 185

Markets
   crafts, Ste-Maxime, 234
   flea
      Cannes, 255
      Monaco, 340
      Nice, 304
      Nîmes, 127
      Toulouse, 81
   flower
      Avignon, 146
      Cannes, 255
      Monaco, 340
      Nice, 300
      St-Tropez, 226
   food
      Apt, 183
      Avignon, 146
      Cannes, 255
      Grasse, 266
      Marseille, 200–201
      Monaco, 340
      Montpellier, 120
      Nice, 304
      St-Raphaël, 242
      St-Tropez, 226
      Toulon, 209
      Tourrettes-sur-Loup, 285
      Vallauris, 273
Marseille, 194–208
   accommodations, 201–204
   beaches, 201
   getting around, 196–197
   nightlife, 208
   panoramic views, 199
   restaurants, 204–207
   shopping, 200–201
   sights and attractions, 197–200
   traveling to, 196
   visitor information, 196
Massif de l'Esterel, 243–245
Massif des Calanques, 5, 197
Matisse, Henri, 28
   Musée Matisse (Cimiez), 302–303
   Chapelle du Rosaire (Vence), 292
Memorial du Débarquement en Provence (Toulon), 210
Menton, 350–353
Mercure chain, 62
Metal Café (Marseille), 208
Middle Ages, 19–20
Midnight Mass (Fontvieille), 41
Mistral Les Indiens de Nîmes (Avignon), 145

Mistral Location (Cannes), 253
Mme Faye-Nunez (Carcassonne), 99
Monaco, 281, 331–347
   accommodations, 340–343
   border crossings to, 43
   getting around, 332–333
   Grimaldi dynasty, 336–337
   nightlife, 346–347
   outdoor pursuits, 338–339
   restaurants, 343–346
   shopping, 339–340
   sights and attractions, 334–338
   telephone system, 334
   traveling to, 332
   visitor information, 332
Monaco Grand Prix de Formule, 38
Monaco-Ville, 334
Monastère de Cimiez, 302
Monastère de St-Paul-de-Mausolée (St-Rémy-de-Provence), 168
Money and costs, 50–52
Monsieur Carnaval (Toulouse), 87
Mont Cavalier (Nîmes), 127
Monte Carlo (Monaco), 334
Monte-Carlo Beach (Monaco), 334
Monte-Carlo Beach Club, 338
Monte-Carlo Casino (Monaco), 334–335, 346–347
Monte Carlo Country Club, 339
Monte Carlo Golf Club, 338
Monte Carlo Motor Rally, 36
Montpellier, 118–124
Mont Vinaigre, 244
Morgiou, 197
Mosquée Soudanaise (Fréjus), 238
MossRehab, 55
Mougins, 268–271
Moulin des Bouillons (Gordes), 172–173
Moyenne Corniche (Middle Road), 15, 281
Multicultural travelers, 55
Musée Agathois (Agde), 112
Musée Alberto Magnelli (Vallauris), 272
Musée Archéologique
   Apt, 182
   Narbonne, 111
   Nîmes, 127

Musée Calvet (Avignon), 144–145
Musée Cantini (Marseille), 198
Musée Charles-Portal (Musée d'Art et d'Histoire le Portail-Peint; Cordes-sur-Ciel), 90
Musée d'Anthropologie Préhistorique (Monaco), 335
Musée d'Archéologie Sous-Marine (St-Raphaël), 241
Musée d'Art Contemporain (Nîmes), 126
Musée d'Art et d'Histoire de Narbonne, 111–112
Musée d'Art et d'Histoire de Provence (Grasse), 267
Musée d'Art et d'Histoire le Portail-Peint (Musée Charles-Portal; Cordes-sur-Ciel), 90
Musée d'Art Moderne (Céret), 103
Musée d'Art Moderne et Contemporain (Cordes-sur-Ciel), 90–91
Musée d'Art Moderne et d'Art Contemporain (Nice), 301
Musée d'Art Moderne Méditerranéen (Le Haut-de-Cagnes), 295
Musée de Art et d'Histoire Militaire (Salon de Provence), 185
Musée de la Boulangerie (Bonnieux), 178
Musée de la Castre (Cannes), 250–251
Musée de la Céramique Moderne (Vallauris), 272
Musée de la Faïence (Marseille), 198
Musée de la Marine (Toulon), 210
Musée de la Mer (Ile Ste-Marguerite), 253
Musée de l'Annonciade (Musée St-Tropez), 225–226
Musée de Lapérouse (Albi), 93
Musée de l'Arles et de la Provence Antiques, 156
Musée de l'Automobiliste (Mougins), 269–270

Musée de l'Olivier (Museum of the Olive Tree; Le Haut-de-Cagnes), 295
Musée de Préhistoire et d'Histoire Naturelle (Nîmes), 127
Musée de Préhistoire Régionale (Menton), 351
Musée des Augustins, 80
Musée des Beaux-Arts
    Aix, 188–189
    Menton, 351
    Nice, 301
    Nîmes, 126
Musée des Santons (Les Baux), 163
Musée des Tapisseries (Aix), 188
Musée des Traditions Locales (Ste-Maxime), 234
Musée des Vieux Outils de Vignerons of the Caves du Père-Anselme (Châteauneuf-du-Pape), 139
Musée de Toulon, 210
Musée d'Histoire de Marseille, 198–199
Musée d'Histoire de St-Paul, 287
Musée d'Histoire Locale et de Céramique Biotoise (Biot), 282
Musée d'Histoire Naturelle (Marseille), 199
Musée du Château de Gordes, 172
Musée du Palais du Prince (Monaco), 335
Musée du Petit-Palais (Avignon), 145
Musée du Phonographe et de la Musique Méchanique (near Ste-Maxime), 234–235
Musée du Trophée d'Auguste (La Turbie), 328
Musée du Vieux-Nîmes, 127
Musée Fabre (Montpellier), 119
Musée Goya (Castres), 96
Musée Granet (Musée des Beaux-Arts; Aix), 188–189
Musée Grevin de la Provence (Salon de Provence), 185
Musée Grobet-Labadié (Marseille), 199
Musée Henry-Clews (La Napoule-Plage), 245
Musée Historique (Gourdon), 291

Musée Ile-de-France (Villa Ephrussi de Rothschild; St-Jean-Cap-Ferrat), 322
Musée International d'Art Naïf Anatole-Jakovsky (Nice), 301
Musée International de la Parfumerie (Grasse), 267
Musée Jean-Cocteau (Menton), 351
Musée Jean-Peské (Collioure), 107
Musée Lapidaire
    Avignon, 145
    Narbonne, 113
Musée l'Ephébe (Cap d'Agde), 112
Musée Louis-Vouland (Avignon), 145
Musée Masséna (Nice), 300
Musée Matisse (Cimiez), 302–303
Musée Municipal (Hyères), 213
Musée Municipal d'Orange, 134
Musée National de Monaco, 338
Musée National Fernand-Léger (Biot), 282–283
Musée National Message Biblique Marc Chagall (Cimiez), 303
Musée Naval et Napoléonien (Antibes), 278
Musée Nostradamus (Salon de Provence), 185
Musée Océanographique de Monaco, 338
Musée Picasso (Antibes), 278
Musée Picasso La Guerre et La Paix (Vallauris), 272
Musée Réattu (Arles), 156
Musée Renoir & Les Collettes (Cagnes-Sur-Mer), 295
Musée Requien (Avignon), 145
Musée St-Tropez (Musée de l'Annonciade), 225–226
Musée Toulouse-Lautrec (Albi), 93
Museon Arlaten (Arles), 156–157
Museum of Naive Art (Nice), 301
Museum of Paleontology (Lubéron National Park), 182
Music, 30

Narbonne, 110–114
National car rentals, 48
New Can Can (Marseille), 208
New Year's Eve), 41
Nice, 297–319
   accommodations, 304–313
   getting around, 298
   nightlife, 318–319
   outdoor pursuits, 303–304
   restaurants, 313–318
   shopping, 304
   sights and attractions,
    300–303
   traveling to, 298
   visitor information, 298
Nice Carnaval, 300
Nice Festival du Jazz, 300
Nice Jazz Festival, 39
Nice Lawn Tennis Club,
   303–304
Nicola Alziari (Nice), 304
Nikki Beach (St-Tropez), 222
Nîmes, 124–131
Noël Provençal (Les Baux), 41
Nostradamus, 166, 170, 184
   Musée (Salon de
    Provence), 185
Notre-Dame de Bon Voyage
   (Cannes), 251
Notre-Dame-de-la-Garde,
   Basilique (Marseille), 198,
   199
Notre-Dame-de-la-Victoire
   (St-Raphaël), 241
Notre-Dame de l'Espérance
   (Cannes), 251
Notre-Dame des Doms,
   Cathédrale (Avignon), 144
Notre-Dame de Sénanque,
   Abbaye (near Gordes), 173
Notre-Dame des Sablons,
   Eglise (Aigues-Mortes), 115
Notre-Dame de Vie, Chapelle
   (Mougins), 269
Notre-Dame La Daurade
   (Toulouse), 81
Now, Voyager, 54
Nuits Musicales d'Uzès, 153
Nuit Taurine (Nocturnal Bull
   Festival; St-Rémy), 39
NWA/KLM, 46

Ocher quarries (Roussillon),
   176
Olivia Cruises & Resorts, 54
Olivier millénaire
   (Roquebrune), 348

Opéra Comédie
   (Montpellier), 124
Opéra de Monte-Carlo, 347
Opéra de Nice, 318
Orange, 132–138

Pagode Hong-Hien (Fréjus),
   238
Palace of the Kings of
   Majorca (Perpignan), 104
Palais des Archevêques
   (Narbonne), 111
Palais des Papes (Avignon),
   6, 142
Palais des Rois de Majorque
   (Perpignan), 104
Palais Lascaris (Nice), 302
Palet des Pâpes (Châteaneuf-
   du-Pape), 139
Palm Beach Casino (Cannes),
   265
P&O Ferries, 46
Parc du Pharo (Marseille),
   199
Parc Regional de Carmargue,
   114
Parc St-Bernard (Hyères), 213
Parc Zoologique
   Fréjus, 239
   near St-Jean-Cap-Ferrat,
    322
Parfumerie Bouis (Vallauris),
   273
Parfumerie Fragonard
   (Grasse), 267
Parfumerie Molinard
   (Grasse), 267
Pastis, 33
Pâtissier Schoeller
   (Montpellier), 120
Peillon, 330–331
Pélerinage des Gitans
   (Gypsies' Pilgrimage; Stes-
   Maries-de-la-Mer), 38
Péniche Maison de la Violette
   (Toulouse), 81
Perfumes
   Cannes, 255
   Grasse, 267
   Vallauris, 273
Perpignan, 102–106
Perpignan Jazz Festival, 40
Petite Afrique (Beaulieu), 325
Petit Train touristique de
   Cannes, 249
Piano Bar Le Blues (Avignon),
   150

Picasso, Pablo, 28
   Château de Vauvenarges
    (Aix-en-Provence), 188
   Musée Picasso (Antibes),
    278
   Musée Picasso La Guerre et
    La Paix (Vallauris), 272
Pic de l'Ours, 244
Pic du Cap-Roux, 244
Piscine du Prince Héréditaire
   Albert (Monaco), 339
Piscine Pierre de Coubertin
   (Cannes), 254
Place AuguSte-Arnuls
   (Peillon), 331
Place de la Bouquerie (Apt),
   181
Place de la Comédie
   (Montpellier), 119
Place de l'Homme au Mouton
   (Vallauris), 273
Place des Arcades (Biot), 282
Place du Forum (Arles),
   155–156
Plage Beau Rivage
   (St-Raphaël), 241
Plage de Juan-les-Pins, 274
Plage de la Bouillabaisse
   (St-Tropez), 222
Plage de la Corniche
   (Marseille), 201
Plage de la Corniches
   (Nîmes), 131
Plage de la Croisette
   Cannes, 252
   Ste-Maxime, 234
Plage de la Garoupe
   (Juan-les-Pins), 274
Plage de la Nartelle (Ste-
   Maxime), 234
Plage de la Promenade du
   Soleil (Menton), 331
Plage de la Salis (Juan-les-
   Pins), 274
Plage de Pampelonne
   (St-Tropez), 222
Plage de St-Ayguls
   (St-Raphaël), 241
Plage des Eléphants
   (Ste-Maxime), 234
Plage des Graniers
   (St-Tropez), 222
Plage des Jumeaux
   (St-Tropez), 224
Plage des Salins (St-Tropez),
   222
Plage de Tahiti (St-Tropez),
   224

Plage du Casino
    (Ste-Maxime), 234
Plage du Débarquement
    (St-Raphaël), 241
Plage du Larvotto (Monaco),
    338
Plage du Midi
    Cannes, 252
    Golfe-Juan, 273
Plage du Prado (Marseille),
    201
Plage du Soleil (Golfe-Juan),
    273
Plage du Veillat (St-Raphaël),
    241
Plage Gazagnaire (Cannes),
    252
Plages de Cros-de-Cagnes,
    295
Planning your trip to
    Provence and the Riviera,
    35–62
    calendar of events, 36–41
    entry requirements, 41–43
    escorted general-interest
        tours, 59
    getting around, 47–50
    health concerns, 52–53
    money and costs, 50–52
    safety, 53
    special interest trips, 56–59
    specialized travel
        resources, 53–56
    sustainable tourism, 56
    telephones and cell-
        phones, 59–60
    traveling to Provence and
        the Riviera, 43–47
    when to go, 35–36
Plat Jérôme (Nice), 304
Pointe de Baumette, 244
Pont du Gard (Nîmes), 127
Pont Julien (Roussillon), 176
Pont St-Bénézet (Avignon),
    144
Port-Cros, 216–217
Port d'Hyères, 212
Porte Baruc (Hyères), 213
Porte d'Auguste (Nîmes), 127
Porte-St-Paul (Hyères), 213
Port Grimaud, 225
Port Mage (Les Baux), 163
Port Moderne (Marseille), 197
Poterie Tournesol (Tour-
    rettes-sur-Loup), 285
Prescription medications, 53
Procession des Pénitents
    (Arles and Collioure), 36
Procession du Christ Mort, 36

Promenade des Anglais
    (Nice), 300
Promenade du Peyrou
    (Montpellier), 119–120
Provence, 132–220
    brief description of, 63–64
    1-week itinerary, 64–66
Provence West, 61
Puyricard (Marseille), 200

Quai des Etats-Unis (Nice),
    300
Quartier de La Balance
    (Avignon), 144
Quartier Naturiste Cap
    d'Agde, 112

Rail Europe, 44
Rail passes, 44–45
Rampal (Salon de Provence),
    185
Reconstitution Historique
    (Salon-de-Provence), 39
Red Zone (Avignon), 150
Regions in brief, 63–64
Relais & Châteaux, 61
Renoir, Auguste, 27–28
    Musée Renoir & Les
        Collettes (Cagnes-Sur-
        Mer), 295
Rent Bike (Ste-Maxime), 234
Restaurants, best, 13–14
The Riviera (Côte d'Azur), 64
    eastern, 281–353
    suggested itinerary, 71–73
    western, 221–280
Rockstore (Montpellier), 124
Romans, ancient (ruins and
    antiquities)
    Aix-en-Provence, 187
    Amphithéâtre (Les Arènes;
        Fréjus), 237–238
    Amphithéâtre Romain
        (Nîmes), 126
    Arc de Triomphe (Orange),
        134
    architecture, 25
    history of, 18–19
    Horreum Romain
        (Narbonne), 112
    Musée de l'Arles et de la
        Provence Antiques, 156
    Musée du Trophée
        d'Auguste (La Turbie),
        328
    Musée Lapidaire (Avignon),
        145

pont du Gard (Nîmes), 127
pont Julien (Roussillon),
    176
Porte d'Auguste (Nîmes),
    127
Ruines de Glanum
    (St-Rémy-de-Provence),
    168
Théâtre Antique/
    Amphithéâtre (Les
    Arènes; Arles), 157–158
Théâtre Romain (Fréjus),
    238
Thermes de Constantin
    (Arles), 158
Trophée des Alps
    (La Turbie), 328
Roquebrune, 6, 347–350
Rosans, 137
Roussillon, 6, 175–177. See
    Languedoc-Roussillon
Route Napoleon, 247
Routes de la Lavande,
    136–137
Royal Food (Monaco), 340
Rue Grande (St-Paul-de-
    Vence), 287
Rue Obscure (Villefranche-
    sur-Mer), 320
Ruines de Glanum (St-Rémy-
    de-Provence), 168

Sacré-Coeur, Eglise de
    (Beaulieu), 325
Sade, marquis de, 178–179
Safety, 53
Ste-Anne, Cathédrale (Apt),
    181
Ste-Marguerite, Eglise
    (Roquebrune), 348
Ste-Marie-Majeure,
    Cathédrale (Toulon), 209
Ste-Maxime, 233–236
Ste-Maxime, Eglise
    (Ste-Maxime), 234
St-Guilhem Music Season, 39
St-Jean, Cathédrale
    (Perpignan), 104
St-Jean-Cap-Ferrat, 321–324
St-Just, Cathédrale
    (Narbonne), 111
St-Léonce, Cathédrale
    (Fréjus), 238
St-Michel Archange, Eglise
    Orthodoxe Russe (Cannes),
    251
St-Nazaire, Basilique
    (Carcassonne), 98

St-Nicolas à Nice, Cathédrale Orthodoxe Russe, 301–302

St-Paul-de-Vence, 286–290

St-Paul-Serge, Basilique (Narbonne), 112–113

St-Pierre, Cathédrale (Montpellier), 119

St-Pierre la Mer, 110

St-Raphaël, 239–243

St-Rémy-de-Provence, 166–172
    accommodations, 168–170
    restaurants, 170–172
    sights and attractions, 168
    traveling to, 168
    visitor information, 168

St-Sauveur, Cathédrale (Aix-en-Provence), 188

St-Sernin Basilica (Toulouse), 78, 80

St-Théodorit, Cathédrale (Uzes), 153

St-Tropez, 221–233
    accommodations, 226–230
    nightlife, 232–233
    outdoor pursuits, 222, 224
    restaurants, 230–232
    shopping, 226
    sights and attractions, 224–226
    traveling to, 222
    visitor information, 222

St-Trophime, Eglise (Arles), 156

St-Victor, Basilique (Marseille), 198

St-Vincent, Eglise (Les Baux), 163

Salle des Mariages (Menton), 351

Salle du Canton (Monaco), 347

Salon de Provence, 184–186

Salon des Antiquaires (Collioure), 107

Salon des Antiquaires de Cannes, 254

Salses, Château de (near Perpignan), 104

Sanary-sur-Mer, 230

Santa Maria de Olivo (Beaulieu), 325

Santos
    Aix, 190
    Marché aux Santons (Tarascon), 40
    Marseille, 40, 200
    Musée des Santons (Les Baux), 163
    Nîmes, 128

Santons Fouque (Aix), 190

SATH (Society for Accessible Travel & Hospitality), 55

Saut du Loup, 291

Savonnerie du Sérail (Marseille), 200

Scarlett O'Hara Irish Pub (Nice), 318

Scat Club (Aix), 194

Scuba diving
    Juan-les-Pins, 274
    Nice, 303
    St-Tropez, 224

Sémaphore, 235

Senior travelers, 55–56

Sentier Touristique (Cap-Martin to Monte Carlo Beach), 349

Séte, 123

Shanghai Express (Toulouse), 88

Shopping. See also Markets
    best, 14

Signac, Paul, 27, 225

SNCF (French National Railroads), 44, 47

Sodetrav, 47

Sormiou, 197

Souleiado (Avignon), 145

Souvenirs Napoléoniens et Collection d'Archives (Monaco), 335

Special events and festivals, 36–41

Spectacles Medievaux (Carcassonne), 98

Stade des Costières (Nîmes), 127

Stade Nautique Rainier-III (Monaco), 339

Statue de Suffren (St-Tropez), 224

Stein, Gertrude, 166, 168

Stock Griffe (Monaco), 340

Suncap Company (St-Tropez), 224

Sun Casino (Monaco), 346

Sun Force (St-Tropez), 224

Sustainable tourism, 56

Swimming
    Cannes, 254
    Monaco, 339

Tauck World Discovery, 59

Téléphérique (Toulon), 210

Telephones, 59–60

Temple de Diane (Nîmes), 127

Templiers, Eglise des (St-Raphaël), 241

Tennis
    Cannes, 254
    Monaco, 339
    Nice, 303–304
    St-Tropez, 224

Tennis-Club de St-Tropez, 224

Terre è Provence (Avignon), 146

Terres à Terre (Vallauris), 273

Théâtre Antique (Orange), 134

Théâtre Antique/ Amphithéâtre (Les Arènes; Arles), 157–158

Théâtre de la Cité (Toulouse), 87

Théâtre de Lacoste, 179

Théâtre de la Digue (Toulouse), 87

Théâtre du Capitole (Toulouse), 87

Théâtre Garonne (Toulouse), 87

Théâtre Municipal (Théâtre de Nîmes), 130

Théâtre National du Capitole (Toulouse), 81

Théâtre Romain (Fréjus), 238

Théâtre Zenith (Toulouse), 87

Thermes de Constantin (Arles), 158

Toulon, 209–212

Toulouse, 76–88
    accommodations, 81–84
    accommodations near, 86–87
    nightlife, 87–88
    restaurants, 84–86
    shopping, 81
    sights and attractions, 78–81
    traveling to, 78
    visitor information, 78

Toulouse-Lautrec, Henri de, 94
    Musée (Albi), 93

Tour Carrée des Dames (Ste-Maxime), 234

Tour de Constance (Aigues-Mortes), 115

Tour du Suquet (Cannes), 250

Tour Fenestrelle (Uzes), 153

Tour Magne (Nîmes), 127

Tour Philippe le Bel (Villenueve-lez-Avignon), 151

Tourrettes-sur-Loup, 284–286, 291

Tour St-Blaise (Hyères), 213

Trafalgar, 59

Trailfinders, 46
Train travel, 44–47, 49–50
    for travelers with
        disabilities, 54
Travel Health Online, 52
Trolley Bus (Marseille), 208
Trophée des Alps (La Turbie),
    328

Uba-Club (Perpignan), 106
US Airways, 44
Uzes, 152–155
Uzès, 5

Val d'Enfer, 164
Vallauris, 271–273
Van Gogh, Vincent, 29, 168
VAT (value-added tax), 52
Vence, 290–294
Verreries de Biot, 283
Vieille Eglise (Bonnieux),
    177–178
Vieille Ville (Nice), 300
Vieux Port (Marseille), 197
Vieux Toulon, 209
Villa Arson Nice, 301
Villa Aurélienne (Fréjus), 239

Village des Bories (near
    Gordes), 173
Villa Kérylos (Beaulieu),
    7, 324
Villa Les Cèdres (near St-
    Jean-Cap-Ferrat), 322
Villa Mauresque (St-Jean-
    Cap-Ferrat), 321
Villa Musée Fragonard
    (Grasse), 267
Villa rentals, 61–62
Villefranche-sur-Mer,
    319–321
Villeneuve-lez-Avignon,
    151–152
Violettes & Pastels
    (Toulouse), 81

Water-skiing, Juan-les-
    Pins, 274–275
Weather, 35–36
Whatnut's Bal-Room
    (Cannes), 265
Wheelchair accessibility,
    54–55
Whisky à Gogo (Juan-les-
    Pins), 277
White Lab (Nice), 319

Wi-Fi access, 60
William's Pub (Nice), 318
Wineries and vineyards,
    33–34
    Apt, 181
    best, 9–11
    Châteauneuf-du-Pape,
        138–139
    Château de Flaugergues,
        121
    Perpignan area, 103
Wine shops
    Auch, 89
    Carcassonne, 99
    St-Paul-de-Vence, 287–288

Yves Brayer Museum
    (Les Baux), 163
Yves Delorme (Monaco), 340
Yvette Lamoureux Galerie
    (Tourrettes-sur-Loup), 285

Zanzibar (Cannes), 266
Zebra Square Café (Monaco),
    347
Zoos
    Fréjus, 239
    near St-Jean-Cap-Ferrat, 322